ESTATE PLANNING

Principles and Problems

Aspen Casebook Series

ESTATE PLANNING

Principles and Problems

Third Edition

Wayne M. Gazur
Professor of Law
University of Colorado School of Law

Robert M. Phillips
Member of the Colorado Bar

Published by Wolters Kluwer Law & Business in New York.

Wolters Kluwer Law & Business serves customers worldwide with CCH, Aspen Publishers, and Kluwer Law International products. (www.wolterskluwerlb.com)

To contact Customer Service, e-mail customer.service@wolterskluwer.com, call 1-800-234-1660, fax 1-800-901-9075, or mail correspondence to:

Wolters Kluwer Law & Business
Attn: Order Department
PO Box 990
Frederick, MD 21705

Printed in the United States of America.

1 2 3 4 5 6 7 8 9 0

ISBN 978-1-4548-0537-3

Library of Congress Cataloging-in-Publication Data

Gazur, Wayne M., 1954-
Estate planning : principles and problems/Wayne M. Gazur, Robert M. Phillips. — 3rd ed.
p. cm. — (Aspen casebook series)
Includes index.
ISBN 978-1-4548-0537-3
1. Estate planning — United States. 2. Tax planning — United States.
I. Phillips, Robert M., 1949- II. Title.

KF750.G39 2011
346.7305'2-dc23

2011038036

About Wolters Kluwer Law & Business

Wolters Kluwer Law & Business is a leading global provider of intelligent information and digital solutions for legal and business professionals in key specialty areas, and respected educational resources for professors and law students. Wolters Kluwer Law & Business connects legal and business professionals as well as those in the education market with timely, specialized authoritative content and information-enabled solutions to support success through productivity, accuracy and mobility.

Serving customers worldwide, Wolters Kluwer Law & Business products include those under the Aspen Publishers, CCH, Kluwer Law International, Loislaw, Best Case, ftwilliam.com and MediRegs family of products.

CCH products have been a trusted resource since 1913, and are highly regarded resources for legal, securities, antitrust and trade regulation, government contracting, banking, pension, payroll, employment and labor, and healthcare reimbursement and compliance professionals.

Aspen Publishers products provide essential information to attorneys, business professionals and law students. Written by preeminent authorities, the product line offers analytical and practical information in a range of specialty practice areas from securities law and intellectual property to mergers and acquisitions and pension/benefits. Aspen's trusted legal education resources provide professors and students with high-quality, up-to-date and effective resources for successful instruction and study in all areas of the law.

Kluwer Law International products provide the global business community with reliable international legal information in English. Legal practitioners, corporate counsel and business executives around the world rely on Kluwer Law journals, looseleafs, books, and electronic products for comprehensive information in many areas of international legal practice.

Loislaw is a comprehensive online legal research product providing legal content to law firm practitioners of various specializations. Loislaw provides attorneys with the ability to quickly and efficiently find the necessary legal information they need, when and where they need it, by facilitating access to primary law as well as state-specific law, records, forms and treatises.

Best Case Solutions is the leading bankruptcy software product to the bankruptcy industry. It provides software and workflow tools to flawlessly streamline petition preparation and the electronic filing process, while timely incorporating ever-changing court requirements.

ftwilliam.com offers employee benefits professionals the highest quality plan documents (retirement, welfare and non-qualified) and government forms (5500/PBGC, 1099 and IRS) software at highly competitive prices.

MediRegs products provide integrated health care compliance content and software solutions for professionals in healthcare, higher education and life sciences, including professionals in accounting, law and consulting.

Wolters Kluwer Law & Business, a division of Wolters Kluwer, is headquartered in New York. Wolters Kluwer is a market-leading global information services company focused on professionals.

To Maija, Joel, and Lija.

W.M.G.

To Kelly, Matthew, Lindsey,
Karolyn, and Mallory.

R.M.P.

Summary of Contents

Contents

CHAPTER 17: Probate and an Estate Tax Return 479

Important Information About This Book

I. A Warning About the Forms

The forms supplied with this publication are highly edited, simplified, and/or incomplete in certain respects for the purpose of instruction and are not intended (and should not be used) for any other purposes.

II. Fictitious People and Events

Unless expressly stated otherwise, the individuals, entities, organizations, and other facts of the examples, exercises, and case studies are strictly fictitious. Any resemblance, in whole or in part, to actual persons, facts, or events is absolutely coincidental and unintended.

III. No Professional Advice

This publication is designed to provide accurate and authoritative information in regard to the subject matter covered. It is sold with the understanding that the publisher is not engaged in rendering legal, accounting, or other professional service and that the authors are not offering such advice in this publication. If legal advice or other expert assistance is required, the services of a competent professional should be sought.

IV. Circular 230 Disclaimer

This book (including the forms supplement, updates, or other accompanying materials) (collectively "this book"), is not intended or written to be used, and it cannot be used, by any taxpayer for the purpose of avoiding penalties that may be imposed on any taxpayer by the Internal Revenue Service. In addition, this book is not intended or written to support the promotion or marketing of any of the transactions or matters it addresses.

V. Editing Conventions

The Internal Revenue Code requires annual Consumer Price Index adjustments to certain income tax rate brackets and wealth transfer tax computational amounts (e.g., the reductions/exclusions/exemptions, as the case may be, provided in sections 2032A, 2503, 2523 & 2631). This publication uses the 2011 information that was available when this book was published.

This publication uses an abbreviated format, "UPC," for the Uniform Probate Code, and unless stated otherwise the sections reflect all amendments through July 1, 2011. This publication also uses an abbreviated format, "IRC," for the Internal Revenue Code, and unless stated otherwise the sections reflect all amendments through July 1, 2011.

All footnotes are numbered consecutively from the beginning of each chapter.

Preface and Acknowledgments

This book was written to serve as a resource for law school or graduate school instruction in estate planning. While the materials include some introductory discussion of crucial principles, we have not attempted a complete exposition of all of the law or issues. It is our guiding assumption that students will have prior or concurrent exposure to basic courses in Wills & Trusts and Federal Estate and Gift Taxation.

This book is intended to facilitate learning through the use of case studies that demonstrate a diverse set of client circumstances and concerns. Case Studies 1-7, 10, and 15 present no difficult federal taxation issues; they are suitable for students with knowledge only of wills and trusts. The balance of the case studies involves issues that require some knowledge of federal wealth transfer taxation and federal income taxation. We believe that some of the case studies would be appropriate for courses dealing with wills and trusts, federal estate and gift taxation, or elder law.

The case studies present questions that demand student analysis, whether for class discussion or in memorandum format. While some of the case studies build on one another, many are independent, so that a "cafeteria approach" may be applied in assigning selected case studies, depending on the teacher's focus. Further, with the inclusion of a forms supplement in electronic format, it is our hope that students will gain some comfort and expertise in the estate planning attorney's primary task — the drafting of documents to achieve client objectives.

We thank the Uniform Law Commission (also known as the National Conference of Commissioners on Uniform State Laws) for permission to use the following materials in the accompanying Forms Supplement: Statutory Power of Attorney from Section 1 of the Uniform Statutory Form Power of Attorney Act; Advance Health-Care Directive found in Section 4 of the Uniform Health-Care Decisions Act, Copyright © Uniform Law Commission & National Conference of Commissioners on Uniform State Laws. All rights reserved. Reprinted with permission.

Wayne M. Gazur and Robert M. Phillips

Boulder, Colorado
September 2011

Table of Principal Cases and IRS Pronouncements

ESTATE PLANNING

Principles and Problems

CHAPTER 1 Dealing with Clients

A. The Faces of Estate Planning

"Estate planning" encompasses a broad sweep of potential client objectives and corresponding legal principles. Clients often have multiple planning objectives, which may include one or more of the following: (a) the provision for and protection of others, such as family members or other loved ones, whether current survivors or future generations; (b) the orderly and efficient transmission of wealth, inter vivos and at death; (c) facilitation of the transition of ownership, management, and activity in business and investing relationships; (d) minimization of tax burdens, primarily income taxes and wealth transfer taxes; (e) the protection of the client and/or beneficiaries or other loved ones in asset management contexts (e.g., upon accident, illness, or incompetence due to the aging process); (f) fulfillment of the client's wishes with respect to health concerns (e.g., "living wills" and health care directives); (g) the protection of the client and/or beneficiaries or other loved ones in lifestyle contexts (e.g., in connection with marriage, cohabitation, and dissolution of relationships); and (h) the protection of the client and/or beneficiaries or other loved ones in professional or investing contexts (e.g., asset protection). This list is not, of course, exhaustive of all the possibilities.

The legal principles that the planner is called upon to employ in addressing all of the above objectives are formidable in breadth and complexity. They include knowledge and experience in (a) the law and drafting of Wills and trusts; (b) the law of estate administration; (c) business law (e.g., the law of closely held corporations, partnerships, and limited liability companies); (d) real estate law; (e) tax law (including the taxation of retirement accounts); (f) conservatorships, guardianships, and Medicaid;

(g) family law; (h) international issues; and (i) creditors' remedies and debtors' protections. This list as well is not exhaustive.

Accordingly, many estate planners, being mindful of the ethical rule of competence[1] as well as concerns about professional malpractice[2] and efficient practice, will tend to tackle certain basic areas, such as drafting Wills and trusts with some knowledge of the tax implications, but will refer clients to other advisors for advice in more specialized areas of practice, such as complex wealth transfer tax planning, family law, Medicaid planning, or business continuation. On the other hand, an attorney must be equally mindful of ABA Model Rule of Professional Conduct 7.4, which permits statements that the attorney practices only in certain fields or will not accept matters outside such fields but generally forbids descriptions such as "specialist," subject to some important exceptions.[3] The case studies in this book attempt to reflect this practice by emphasizing recurring fundamental themes that the typical estate planner faces but with a more general introduction to selected specialty practice areas. Others who are involved in the planning process are not necessarily attorneys. Estate planning for more complex estates is typically a team effort led by an attorney but with input from other persons, such as the client's accountant, investment advisor, professional services agent (e.g., for athletes, writers, or performing artists), life insurance advisor, property manager, asset appraisers, or trust officer.[4]

B. The Stages of Life and Estate Planning

Estate planning measures usually reflect the client's current or reasonably anticipated situation, so those measures change with the inevitable shifts in

1. ABA Model Rule of Professional Conduct 1.1 requires the "legal knowledge, skill, thoroughness and preparation reasonably necessary for the representation." *See* Model Rules of Prof'l Conduct R. 1.1 (2002).

2. *See generally* John R. Price & Samuel A. Donaldson, Price on Contemporary Estate Planning §1.6.1 (2011) (discussing malpractice implications of estate planning practice, including degree of liability to beneficiaries and intended beneficiaries); Stephanie B. Casteel et al., *The Modern Estate Planning Lawyer: Avoiding the Maelstrom of Malpractice Claims*, 22 Prob. & Prop. 46 (Nov./Dec. 2008).

3. If the attorney practices in a state that provides a mechanism for certification or recognition of a specialty, the attorney may communicate the fact of such certification. *See* Model Rules of Prof'l Conduct R. 7.4(d) (2002). If there is no such state procedure, the rule still permits communication of the fact that the attorney is certified as a specialist in a field by a named organization. In that case, unless the American Bar Association has accredited the named organization, the communication must clearly state that there is no procedure in the jurisdiction for approving certifying organizations.

4. Although estate planning has often been a team effort led by an attorney, that model is increasingly changing due to the rise of other nontraditional legal services providers, such as accounting firms, insurance agencies, investment advisors, and trust departments that offer estate planning services. Advice is one matter, but the drafting of the actual documents, once the exclusive province of the attorney, raises the issue of the unauthorized practice of law as well as other complex issues where planning advice and execution of that plan have been sought from a single firm encompassing a multidisciplinary practice (that is, where full-time, licensed lawyers work for firms that are owned by nonlawyers). This controversial and evolving area is beyond the scope of this book. *See, e.g.*, Quintin Johnstone, *Unauthorized Practice of Law and the Power of State Courts: Difficult Problems and Their Resolution*, 39 Willamette L. Rev. 795 (2003); Corinne N. Lalli, *Multidisciplinary Practices: The Ultimate Department Store for Professionals*, 17 St. John's J. Legal Comment. 283 (2003).

the client's needs and objectives. A single young adult's concerns are typically quite different from those of a married young adult or a young adult with a partner, particularly one with children. Providing for survivors and descendants is a driving factor in most estate plans, and the status of those survivors and descendants (e.g., infants versus adult children, the birth of grandchildren) produces the life stage characteristics of estate planning.

A wealthy client's concerns will be different from those of clients with modest wealth because the federal wealth transfer tax is an obstacle to many estate plans for large estates, and minimization of taxes consequently becomes a driving factor in planning for very wealthy clients. Some clients become wealthy through inheritances or fortuitous events at an early age. However, many only become wealthy over time from their vocation and prudent investments, so there is a life cycle aspect to their estate planning.

The client's impetus for seeking estate planning services often reflects, and is in response to, the occurrence of certain life events. Typical events are marriage, birth of a child, death of a family member or close friend, dissolution of marriage, significant inheritance, terminal illness, an impending medical procedure, common disasters,[5] or the expectation of extended or international travel. Another important impetus for many clients is a significant change in the tax laws. In recent years sweeping changes to the federal wealth transfer taxes have created a shifting and unpredictable backdrop for estate planners and clients alike.

The case studies in this book accordingly follow a general life cycle progression, starting with young, childless clients, moving to clients with children, and then addressing clients with significant wealth. There are always exceptions to this tidy view of client life and wealth cycles, and some of the case studies reflect that (e.g., Case Study 4-1 deals with the impending marriage of a young adult who is already wealthy from inheritances).

C. Developing Clients

For some new attorneys, the traditional way to build an estate planning practice is to join a law firm with an established estate planning client base. This permits the new attorney to gain experience and refine his or her legal skills with the security of a regular paycheck. Although one might be fortunate enough to find employment in the estate planning department of a large firm that has seemingly unlimited clients and work, it would be a mistake to ignore the development of one's own clients. First, firms change and there is no guarantee that an attorney will remain at a particular firm. The attorney might wish to relocate to another part of the country,

5. Some attorneys noted an increase in client interest in estate planning in the aftermath of the September 11, 2001, attacks. *See* David J. McCabe, *There But for the Grace...*, 10 Tr. & Est. 8 (Sept. 2002); Roy M. Adams, *Terrorism or Its Prospect — The Impact on Estate Planning*, 37 Inst. on Est. Plan. ¶1700 (2003).

or other opportunities could arise. Second, a portable "book of business," as client accounts are sometimes called, is a base of power, status, and job security, as well as a factor in partnership, in almost any law firm, no matter how much work is currently available. Third, in most firms, an important role of the partner, as compared with that of associates, is to cultivate client relationships. The ability to do that is something that one develops over one's entire career.

Smaller law firms perform much estate planning, and the emphasis on building a practice can be even more pronounced. Furthermore, some recent law school graduates strike out on their own or affiliate with an experienced attorney who is planning to retire. Client development is obviously an immediate concern for the new attorney in those situations.

There are a number of specialized books and articles addressing practice development; we won't repeat that material here. In our experience, much of client development is a question of persistent efforts and the attorney's temperament. Some new attorneys enjoy the estate planning work but don't relish the practice development. For them the process takes more time, so that favorable news of their skills has time to percolate from existing clients to potential new clients. However, for all attorneys at any stage of practice development, there is no substitute for the efficient and timely production of a high-quality work product.

By way of example, some typical client development activities include (not in any particular order):

- establishing relationships with senior estate planners in the community (e.g., asking them for advice and leads);
- participating in local bar association estate planning groups;
- publishing articles in local newspapers;
- making estate planning presentations at churches, clubs, retirement homes, etc.;
- making advertised estate planning presentations at a public venue (such as in a hotel meeting room);
- networking with accountants, financial planners, life insurance salespersons, money managers, real estate brokers, stockbrokers, and trust company officers;
- participating in business leads groups;[6]
- getting referrals from family, friends, and business acquaintances;
- developing referrals from public service activities (e.g., membership on prominent charitable or church boards, civic organizations, etc.);
- obtaining referrals from current and past clients;
- assuming overflow referrals from other attorneys;
- participating in local bar association lawyer referral programs;
- participating in a commercial lawyer referral program;

6. The attorney must be mindful of professional conduct considerations, including prohibitions on giving anything of value for recommending the attorney and potential disclosure of confidential client information. *See, e.g.*, Va. State Bar Standing Comm. on Leg. Ethics Op. 1846 (Feb. 2, 2009).

- joining estate planning "franchise" or "network" arrangements;
- advertising in the yellow pages;
- advertising in newspapers and targeted legal services directories;
- sending newsletters to clients and other professionals;
- creating and maintaining a content-rich Internet website;
- teaching laypersons (e.g., students at law schools, universities, community colleges, or community life-long education programs); and
- teaching continuing legal education programs.

D. Identifying the Client

In the sections that follow, we focus on dealings with a specific client. However, in several situations the answer to the seemingly simple question, "Who is the client?" will shape the manner in which the attorney structures the representation. This is governed by the engagement letter, discussed next, as well as by the client interview.

In Part K we discuss three common and potentially troublesome client scenarios: (1) married couples represented by a single attorney; (2) elderly clients for whom adult children seek to play a role in the estate planning process; and (3) overlapping representation of family members and family businesses by a single attorney. While we defer a discussion of those issues until Part K, it is wise to keep in mind how the single client model can become more complicated with the addition of other concerned parties.

E. The Engagement Letter

When it appears that a client will retain an attorney for an estate planning task, it is essential that the attorney and client sign an engagement letter. In light of the evolving life cycle of the client, estate planning can be never-ending in a sense, so it is essential to define and limit the scope of the attorney's involvement and representation based upon mutually agreed-upon expectations between the client and the attorney. At a minimum, the letter should describe what documents the attorney will prepare, the fee for the services,[7] and the time of payment. The ABA Model Rules of Professional Conduct require that the basis or rate of the fee

7. Professional fees incurred "in connection with the determination, collection, or refund of any tax" are deductible by the client for federal income tax purposes. *See* IRC §212(3). Accordingly, an attorney may be asked to identify the charges that involved tax planning. Also, in some cases, planning costs beyond tax planning may be deductible as investment expenses. *See* Frederick K. Hoops et al., Family Estate Planning Guide §4:3 (4th ed. 1994 & Supp. 2010-2011); Frank S. Berall, *Deductibility of Legal Fees for Estate Planning and Administration*, 17 No. 3 Prac. Tax Law. 35 (Spring 2003). This chapter and all subsequent chapters use an abbreviated citation format, "IRC," for the Internal Revenue Code, and unless stated otherwise, the sections reflect all amendments through July 1, 2011.

be communicated to the client, preferably in writing, before or within a reasonable time after commencing the representation.[8] The ABA Model Rules also permit the attorney to limit the objectives or scope of the representation if the client consents. This will typically be accomplished in the engagement letter.[9]

Effective June 20, 2005, the Treasury Department and the Internal Revenue Service (IRS) amended the regulations governing practice before the IRS, known as Treasury Department Circular No. 230 (Circular 230) found at 31 C.F.R. §§10.0 et seq.[10] The amendments are of particular concern to attorneys who may be construed as providing tax advice—federal wealth transfer taxes are at least an issue for many estate planning clients, while federal income tax consequences are an issue for almost all clients. Most attorneys appreciate that they must follow a high standard of care in writing a tax opinion letter and that the strictures of Circular 230 must be heeded.[11] However, the boundaries of Circular 230 "covered opinions" remain unclear to many practitioners. In response, attorneys may, somewhat indiscriminately, insert language in almost any client communication (including engagement letters and e-mails[12]), disclaiming the existence of a tax opinion or tax advice. Indeed, a popular estate planning magazine includes a general disclaimer at the beginning of each issue: "Circular 230 Notice—None of the articles published by *Trusts & Estates* in any medium are intended to be used, nor can they be used, for the purpose of avoiding U.S. tax penalties." This book includes a similar disclaimer in the prefatory materials.

Most attorneys discuss the proposed engagement letter at the initial client interview, and some clients sign a final agreement at that point. However, many attorneys send the final engagement letter to the client shortly after the interview. Doing so allows a more unhurried preparation of the final agreement, especially for a complex estate, and also allows the client to review the agreement carefully. A sample engagement letter follows as Exhibit 1.1. The letter below assumes a single client. As discussed in Part K, an engagement letter for a married couple involves additional considerations.

8. *See* Model Rules of Prof'l Conduct R. 1.5(b) (2002). Some states, notably California, have statutes governing attorney fee agreements and disclosures.

9. *See* Model Rules of Prof'l Conduct R. 1.2(c) (2002).

10. Articles discussing the application of Circular 230 are collected in Part M at the end of this chapter. *See also* Price & Donaldson, *supra* note 2, at §1.2.2. The American Bar Association has attempted to also issue opinions dealing with tax practice, but "state ethics rules and Circular 230 are not entirely compatible." *Id.* at pp.1-9.

11. A "legal opinion" can be created in a relatively informal communication. One commentator has described e-mails as "the great blackhole of the future.... [T]heir import in lawsuits is anything but casual." Robert W. Wood, *Liability for Tax Opinions: What's an Opinion and Who Can Sue?*, 86 Taxes 53, 65 (2008).

12. Attorneys commonly include a Circular 230 disclaimer in their e-mail signature for all client recipients.

EXHIBIT 1.1 SAMPLE ENGAGEMENT LETTER

[date]

Dear Matthew:

It was a pleasure to meet with you Tuesday in my office. The purpose of this letter is to summarize the issues we discussed and to provide a framework to guide our relationship as attorney and client. It includes a discussion and review of the general nature of the legal services that I recommend you need. Next, legal fees are explained. Finally, I summarize what you need to do to next.

Based upon my review of notes from our discussion, the information you have provided to me, your objectives, and the relevant law, I will prepare two legal instruments for you:

1. Will. This includes disposition of generalized personal property, specific gift dispositions to named persons or charities, estate administrative provisions, tax allocations, and naming of personal representative(s) and successors. Your estate will be divided into two equal shares and left outright to your two children, free of trust, if they survive you; if a child does not survive you, that child's share will pass to that child's living descendants, if any, by representation, with each descendant's share being held in trust for so long as they are under the age of 21.
2. Memorandum Disposition of Tangible Personal Property. This document permits you to make gifts of your tangible personal property (other than real estate, money, stocks and other intangibles) to specific beneficiaries. You may change this instrument over time at your convenience without an attorney.

[Note: This is obviously a "bare bones" document package in the interest of brevity. One would often include durable powers of attorney for financial and health care purposes at a minimum.]

Fees for providing legal services are based upon my time expended, from and including the initial client contact through the completion of the matter. My fixed fee for preparing the instruments discussed in this letter is $ _________, which I request be paid one-half with your return of this engagement letter, and the remaining one-half at the time of signing your documents. This fee includes up to three hours of office conferences (including the conference for signing the documents), drafting of all of the instruments, and up to an additional hour of telephone or e-mail consultation for questions during this process. Should you require more time than this for office consultations or telephone/email discussion, or should you request that I assist you in other tasks, such as retitling your assets, accounts, or real property ownership, I will be happy to do so, with the understanding that these additional services will be billed at my standard hourly rate of $ _________. Tasks that can be performed by my legal assistant, Ms. April Jones, under my supervision, will be billed at her hourly rate of $ _________.

Out-of-pocket expenses and incidentals incurred or advanced by us on your behalf such as filing fees, trust registration costs, appraisal fees, overnight couriers, significant amounts of photocopying, etc., will be in addition to the fee noted above and will be charged to you separately at cost.

[Note: It is standard large firm practice to charge for photocopying expenses (particularly when there are a number of existing documents, such as in litigation matters), postage, and long-distance telephone charges. In an estate planning practice one can incur significant costs to copy existing Wills, trusts, partnership agreements, etc., and some postage and telephone costs. However, for simpler matters, many clients find a charge for these items to be offensive. Given the widespread adoption of the Adobe Acrobat® format, the authors routinely provide CD or DVD copies of executed client documents in lieu of paper copies.]

Under [Name of State] law, whether I have completed the tasks you have asked me to complete or not, either of us can end our relationship and terminate this engagement at any time. If this engagement ends before all of the tasks are completed, you will still be responsible for any fees and costs actually incurred on your behalf prior to such termination.

continued on next page

During the course of this engagement it may be necessary or advisable for me to meet or speak with your accountant, actuary, insurance agent, financial advisor, or other third party, or to provide them certain information concerning this engagement. I will do so, but only at your request and with your permission. I will maintain paper and/or electronic records relating to professional services that I provide so that I am better able to assist you with your professional needs and, in some cases, to comply with professional guidelines. These records and files belong to me and I may destroy them seven years after the completion of this engagement or after seven years of inactivity concerning this matter. Upon request, any original documents that you have provided to me will be returned.

In the course of providing clients with legal services, I may receive significant personal financial information from my clients. As a client, you should know that all information that I receive from you is held in confidence and is not released to anyone outside my firm except as agreed to by you or as required under applicable law. In order to guard your nonpublic personal information, I maintain physical, electronic and procedural safeguards that comply with professional standards.

If, after reviewing this letter and discussing any questions you have, this letter reflects your understanding of the scope and terms of our relationship for this engagement, please sign the enclosed copy of this letter and return it to me, along with one-half of the fixed fees of $ _________, payable to _________, in the enclosed self-addressed envelope.

[Note: Some engagement letters include harsher language about the payment of fees, including an agreement to pay interest on delinquent amounts, as well as providing for reasonable attorney fees and other costs of collection. Opinions differ on the desirability of such language because it can offend clients. Further, the efficacy of such language can be in doubt because an attorney's lawsuit for fees may generate a counterclaim asserting malpractice. This engagement letter omits such language.]

In closing, I want to thank you for giving me the opportunity to provide legal services to you. If you have any questions concerning this letter or our relationship, please let me know. Upon receipt of your payment, I will acknowledge your payment and provide additional information and instructions to you. I look forward to working with you.

Sincerely,

Attorney Name

AN:kj

By my signature below, I acknowledge that I have read and understand this letter, which explains the terms and conditions upon which Attorney Name, attorney, agrees to represent me and that I agree to the terms and conditions described herein.

____

Client Signature and Date

F. The Non-Engagement Letter

New attorneys are often eager to speak with potential clients for free, and these inquiries are often by telephone. The potential clients may be reluctant to offer names, phone numbers, or addresses, apparently hoping for an absolutely free consultation without any follow-up from the attorney. In many cases this is at best a waste of time (one rarely hears from these callers again) and, at worst, is a dangerous practice for an attorney because it involves quick oral advice with caveats that are probably misunderstood, forgotten, or ignored by the potential client. Also, as discussed below, this practice has the potential for creating misunderstandings as to whether the attorney is representing the caller. In any event, in speaking to any unknown caller, the attorney should obtain, at a minimum, the name, address, telephone number, and email address of the other party at the beginning of the conversation. If the caller refuses to provide that information, the attorney should politely inform the caller that the attorney cannot discuss the matter over the telephone and invite the caller to make an office appointment.

A better practice is to require action on the part of the potential client to eliminate those who have only a passing interest. To that end, even established attorneys may offer a brief initial office consultation at no charge. Due to anxiety about the cost of legal services, some clients are reluctant to take initial steps without this offer. Other potential clients may press for a firm quote on expected fees at an early stage, even before meeting with the attorney. Firm quotes should be avoided until such time as all of the relevant facts are known. However, some attorneys offer "flat rates" for certain services, such as for drafting a "simple Will" or power of attorney. While that is the attorney's prerogative, the attorney must be willing to live by the quoted fee even if complications surface later.

As a consequence of these early telephone conversations or free initial consultations, there is a risk that the potential client might prematurely view the relationship as a client relationship such that there is an expectation that the attorney is "handling matters." This expectation can become very focused if something unfortunate occurs in the interim (e.g., the potential client passes away or becomes incompetent). Accordingly, it is good practice to communicate the attorney's understanding of the relationship in these situations. A sample non-engagement letter follows as Exhibit 1.2.

EXHIBIT 1.2 SAMPLE NON-ENGAGEMENT LETTER

[date]

Dear Matthew and Lindsey:

It was my pleasure to [briefly meet with you] [talk with you over the telephone] today concerning your interest in undertaking a review of your estate planning needs. At this point, however, you have not decided whether or not to go forward with this planning.

If and when you decide to proceed with your estate planning, please let me know and I can advise you at that time of what is required to engage me as your attorney. Until such time, however, I will be taking no action on your behalf.[13]

Best regards to both of you, and I would look forward to hearing from you.

Sincerely,

Attorney Name

AN:kj

13. If the prospective client has discussed a time-sensitive matter (e.g., filing a claim against an estate or disclaiming a property interest), the letter should also include a specific note that timely action is required nevertheless. *See, e.g.*, PRICE & DONALDSON, *supra* note 2, at §1.6.2.

G. Preparing for the Client Interview

If one is conducting an initial free consultation, the interview often serves as a social function with no substance. The attorney may discuss his or her background, experience, qualifications, and general approach in dealing with client matters. It is generally unwise to dispense legal advice of any nature until both parties have agreed to the scope and terms of the relationship. New attorneys need to appreciate that this is a mutual endeavor, and some potential clients will clearly appear to offer trouble. They may bitterly complain about fees at the outset; they may miss appointments; they may be rude or defensive; they may misrepresent their situation or concoct almost unbelievable stories. Relying upon reasonable intuition, the attorney probably should not represent such persons. Often the person's concerns become, upon further discussion, matters outside the attorney's area of practice or comfort. The attorney should consider referring that person to other competent counsel.[14]

If one is conducting an interview that will apparently lead to representing the person, the meeting is more focused. An immediate issue is whether the potential client should bring documents or other information to the interview. Some attorneys believe, as a fundamental matter, the potential client should bring copies of any relevant Wills, trusts, medical directives, or other papers. Other attorneys do not want to possess even copies of the potential client's existing documents until such time as the attorney-client relationship is firmly, if not formally, established. Many attorneys send a questionnaire to the potential client in advance of the meeting, often with a cover letter that confirms the time of the initial meeting, provides directions to the attorney's office, and so forth. Some attorneys request that the questionnaire be returned to the attorney before the scheduled initial conference, while others, in an attempt to not discourage the potential client, downplay the importance of completing the entire questionnaire. However, that information will need to be collected in some manner ultimately, and the person's attention and promptness in completing the questionnaire is often a good indicator of his or her commitment to the matter and desirability as a client.

H. Conducting the Client Interview

The attorney should treat the client interview as the most important task at hand. While it might be appropriate to use a legal assistant to gather information in a "clinic" setting, this may offend many clients, particularly at the first interview. This is an opportunity to make a favorable impression

14. *See, e.g.*, George M. Turner, Revocable Trusts, ch. 67, *Working with Difficult Clients* (5th ed. 2003 & Supp. 2010).

and to establish a personal connection. Hold all telephone calls and keep other interruptions to an absolute minimum (remember to silence any cell phone ring tones or audible email alerts). This is an important meeting for any client. An awkward issue that frequently arises is the presence of other persons during the interview. While the presence of family members can be helpful, particularly with an elderly client, someone else's presence does raise issues of confidentiality and subtle coercion. If the attorney will be representing more than one person, the attorney needs to discuss at the outset the issue of dual representation (generally in connection with married couples or multigenerational family members) and confidentiality. Some attorneys may choose to conduct separate initial interviews of married couples to discuss the ramifications of joint representation, particularly if the discussion concerns a second marriage for either spouse. These issues are raised in Part K.

If the client has not already completed and delivered a written questionnaire, we recommend that the attorney use a data summary checklist or questionnaire in connection with the interview.[15] A sample questionnaire follows as Exhibit 1.3. The sample questionnaire does not exhaust all of the areas that might be explored by the attorney in light of the client's circumstances, particularly one who is married or wealthy. Other areas could include the details of assisted reproductive technology arrangements, dissolution of marriage decrees or settlement agreements, marital agreements, beneficiaries with special needs, pets, funeral arrangements, and details of family or other closely held business or investment interests. The questionnaire helps organize the interview, reduces further calls to the client for additional information, and documents the interview. To eliminate some of the drudgery, the interviewing attorney can skip over obviously irrelevant portions and need not subject the client to each and every question. If the attorney has sent a copy of the questionnaire to the client in advance of the interview and the person brings the questionnaire to the initial conference, the attorney should review the questionnaire at the interview. A busy attorney may be working on several dozen planning matters at the same time, and it is difficult to remember the details of every case. Take copious notes during the client interview, even if you think you will remember the points, but not to the extent of not paying attention to the client.[16]

15. Some attorneys prefer an absolutely open-ended interviewing style. As demonstrated in Exercise 1-1, an open-ended interviewing style can be useful in drawing out information from a hesitant client. Indeed, improperly used, a questionnaire can resemble an endless cross-examination, offering little in the way of developing attorney-client rapport.

16. One finds disagreement among attorneys as to what client notes (and document drafts) should be retained in the attorney's files after the instruments are executed. The information may impact subsequent litigation in connection with the instruments. *See, e.g.*, Simpson v. Calivas, 139 N.H. 1, 650 A.2d 318 (1994) (probate court did not admit the attorney's notes concerning an ambiguous term in a Will, producing a malpractice claim by the disappointed devisee). *Compare* UPC §2-805 (permitting reformation of the terms of a governing instrument upon proof of the transferor's intention by clear and convincing evidence). Exhibit 1.1 addresses these document retention issues.

EXHIBIT 1.3 SAMPLE ESTATE PLANNING QUESTIONNAIRE (BASIC: UNMARRIED INDIVIDUAL)

I. Personal Information

Full Legal Name ______________________
Citizenship ______________________
Social Security No. ______________________
Place of Birth ______________________
Date of Birth ______________________
Home Address ______________________
County ______________________
Home Telephone ______________________
Cell Phone Number ______________________
Home Email Address ______________________
Fax Phone Number ______________________
Occupation ______________________
Employer/Business ______________________
Employer Address ______________________
Business Telephone ______________________
Business Email Address ______________________
Status of Health ______________________
Insurable? ______________________
Previously Married? ______________________

II. Objectives and Goals

Please briefly discuss what you would like to accomplish as part of this process. You may want to include in your discussion thoughts about the following issues as well as other issues important to you:

- Asset protection for children and descendants
- Estate and gift tax planning
- Intergenerational planning
- Simplification of estate administration
- Charitable objectives

____
____
____
____

III. Children/Grandchildren (include stepchildren and adopted children)

	Full Legal Name	Address	Date of Birth (or Date of Death if deceased)	Marital Status
Children				
Grandchildren				

IV. Parents, Brothers, and Sisters

If any relative is deceased, please write "(D)" after his or her name.

A. Parents

Mother: Full Name ______________________
City, State ______________________
Father: Full Name ______________________
City, State ______________________

B. Brothers and Sisters

1. Full Name ______________________
City, State ______________________
2. Full Name ______________________
City, State ______________________
3. Full Name ______________________
City, State ______________________

C. Other Dependents. Are any persons other than your minor children dependent on you? If so, describe relationship and degree of dependency:

____

____

[Note: In the interest of brevity the questionnaire omits collateral kindred such as nieces and nephews. The attorney would need to add this information for clients interested in primary or contingent gifts to such persons.]

V. Assets and Liabilities

ASSETS

(List current full value, disregarding any debt or liabilities attached to asset, and state how the property is held.)

1. **Liquid Assets** (Savings & Checking, CDs, Stocks & Bonds, and other securities; do **not** include retirement assets, such as IRAs; note those later in Item 6, below)

Description	Value	How is the Asset Titled?
________	$ ________	☐ My Name Only ☐ Joint Tenancy ☐ Tenants in Common
________	$ ________	☐ My Name Only ☐ Joint Tenancy ☐ Tenants in Common
________	$ ________	☐ My Name Only ☐ Joint Tenancy ☐ Tenants in Common

2. **Real Property** (current fair market value of real property — ignore any mortgage; enter that in Liabilities, below)

Description	Value	How is the Asset Titled?
Residence	$ ________	☐ My Name Only ☐ Joint Tenancy ☐ Tenants in Common
Other	$ ________	☐ My Name Only ☐ Joint Tenancy ☐ Tenants in Common

☐ Check if any real property is not located in [my state].

continued on next page

3. **Tangible Personal Property** (total fair market value of jewelry, antiques, art objects, household furnishings, automobiles, boats, airplanes, hobby collections, etc.)

Value — $ ________

How are the Assets Titled? — ☐ My Name Only ☐ Joint Tenancy ☐ Tenants in Common

4. **Closely Held Business Interests** (approximate value of any business interests)

Description — ________

Value — $ ________

How is the Asset Titled? — ☐ My Name Only ☐ Joint Tenancy ☐ Tenants in Common

Describe, briefly, the Business Interests (name, how organized, etc.): ________________
____
____

5. **Life Insurance** (Enter the following information for each life insurance policy, including Group Plans)

Name of Insurance Company	Type: (T)erm, (W)hole Life, (O)ther	Insured's Name	Owner of Policy	$ Amount of Death Benefit	**Beneficiary Name(s)**

(Copy this section as necessary for additional insurance policies)

6. **Retirement Plans** (Current value of retirement / employee benefit plans, including IRAs, 401(k)s, pension, profit sharing, etc., and the primary and contingent beneficiaries of each. Attach additional pages as necessary)

IRA (Traditional) $ ________
Primary Beneficiary: ________________
Contingent Beneficiary: ________________

IRA (Roth) $ ________
Primary Beneficiary: ________________
Contingent Beneficiary: ________________

401(k) (Regular) $ ________
Primary Beneficiary: ________________
Contingent Beneficiary: ________________

401(k) (Roth) $ ________
Primary Beneficiary: ________________
Contingent Beneficiary: ________________

Other Plan $ ________
Primary Beneficiary: ________________
Contingent Beneficiary: ________________

7. **Other Assets** (Describe any other assets in which you may have an interest that has not otherwise been included in this Questionnaire. For example, intangible personal property (patents, licenses, copyrights, etc.), deferred compensation plans, transferable club memberships, royalty rights, etc.) ____

____

____

LIABILITIES

1. Credit Cards $ ____________________
2. Mortgage on:
   Residence $ ____________________
   Other Real Estate $ ____________________
3. Notes Payable $ ____________________
4. Other liabilities not shown above (please describe) $ ____________________

INCOME

1. Employment $ ____________________
2. Other $ ____________________

Special Situations. Please check if any of the following apply to you:

Party to a buy-sell agreement ☐
Party to a lawsuit ☐
Outstanding obligations under divorce decree ☐
Have a "special needs" dependent ☐
I am storing, or may store, frozen eggs, sperm, or embryos ☐

Existing Documents. Do you currently have any of the following instruments? (check all that apply)

Will ☐ (Year _____ State _____)
Power of Attorney for Property ☐ (Year _____ State _____)
Power of Attorney for Health Care ☐ (Year _____ State _____)
Final Arrangements Representative ☐ (Year _____ State _____)
Living Will ☐ (Year _____ State _____)
Living/Revocable Trust ☐ (Year _____ State _____)
Divorce/Separation Agreement ☐

If available, please provide a copy (only a copy!) of any of the above documents, as well as any Trust Agreements of any trusts in which you may have an interest (as beneficiary, trustee, power to appoint assets, etc.) to me.

Please Read and Sign Below Before Returning

The information you provide in this questionnaire will be relied upon by me in making recommendations concerning your estate planning. If the information given is either incorrect

continued on next page

or incomplete, those recommendations may be inappropriate, or worse, harmful. I, therefore, rely upon you to take the necessary time and diligence to provide me with data which can and will be used by me in helping you meet your objectives. I cannot be responsible for recommendations made or conclusions reached which later prove to be erroneous because of incorrect or incomplete data.

I have read the above statement and affirm that the information provided in this form is true and accurate to the best of my knowledge as of this _________ day of _________, 20_________.

____

Signature

Some clients may tell you what to *do* (e.g., "I am here for you to prepare a simple revocable trust. That is all that I need!"). You may want to deflect this and instead encourage the client to tell you what he or she wants to *accomplish*. The attorney's role is to evaluate the client's objectives and then to determine the best way to accomplish these objectives. The end result may be that you end up doing what the client initially told you to do, but more often this is not the case.

Although this discussion focuses on the preparation of estate planning documents for the living, some clients will be dealing with the death of a loved one. Other clients will themselves be *in extremis* or terminally ill. Before turning to the more comfortable routine of immersing oneself in substantive matters and the details of the client's situation, the attorney must appreciate and employ the communication skills that will be helpful in this difficult time for the client.[17]

EXERCISE 1-1

A SAMPLE CLIENT INTERVIEW

Part A:

This is a partial transcript of an estate planning interview conducted by Attorney (A) with Client (C), Mr. John Jay Brown, a widower, age 78. It is not necessarily an example of good interviewing technique. In terms of substance, the interview would be conducted much differently if the client's situation and planning aspirations were complicated, particularly with respect to family relationships and wealth.

A: Good morning. Thank you for coming in today.

[The time of day can affect a client's level of attentiveness. This appointment was scheduled for mid- to late-morning, which can be a good time of day for an elderly individual.]

17. *See, e.g.*, Gary Glober, *How to Effectively and Efficiently Interact with Grieving Clients*, 22 Prob. & Prop. 61 (July/Aug. 2008).

C: You're welcome. I had a tough time finding a parking place. It would help if you had some assigned parking.

[Many estate planning clients are busy and/or elderly. Convenient parking can be an important amenity.]

A: I agree. We have been working on that, but nothing has come up so far. [pause] So, you are here to talk about your estate plan.

C: Yep.

A: My assistant sent you our estate planning questionnaire. Did you have an opportunity to review it?

C: I didn't catch all of that. I am a little hard of hearing.

A: Oh, I am sorry. Have you tried a hearing aid?

[Some attorneys are accustomed to being answer persons, sometimes extending that to painfully obvious questions or to matters outside their expertise. While intended as helpful, a client could consider this as condescending or otherwise insulting.]

C: [bristling a bit] Of course I have tried one. The nerves are dead and hearing aids just don't work.

A: I am sorry. Let me repeat what I said. And, if at any time I am not clear, please ask me to repeat myself. I had asked you whether you had a chance to look at the questionnaire that my assistant sent you last week.

C: I glanced at it, but it was too much detail and legalese.

[This is a pitfall in sending a detailed questionnaire to a client, particularly an elderly or easily distracted client. This is a pivotal point in the interview. Many attorneys would not want to elicit the detailed information in this direct, painstaking, questioning manner. It is not an efficient use of anyone's time. This is better left for the questionnaire, particularly for a client with a hearing impairment. However, if the client is apparently unable or reluctant to tackle the questionnaire, the attorney can: (1) repeat the request for a complete questionnaire after tactfully explaining its importance and then salvage that part of the interview that can be accomplished under the circumstances; (2) conduct the interview with a focus on client objectives and general matters and then introduce the client to a legal assistant who can work with the client in completing the questionnaire (while this can offend a client who expects personal attention solely from the attorney, an experienced legal assistant can often overcome those objections; attorneys differ on the degree of direct client involvement they prefer from legal assistants); (3) decline representation of the client, particularly if the client appears to be showing an early indifference to the process (it is not uncommon for some clients not to finish even simple estate planning projects); or (4) as is the approach below, continue with the interview, completing the questionnaire in the process.]

continued on next page

A: That is okay. I will work through some of it with you now. First, your middle name is J-A-Y?
C: Yes.
A: And you are widowed?
C: Yes.
A: When did your wife pass away?

[Note the phrase "pass away": many attorneys will struggle to avoid using "die" or "death" in an interview. "If something were to happen to you" becomes a euphemism for death, and "time of probate" becomes a euphemism for time of death. Depending on the situation, however, after discussing the issue with their clients, other attorneys prefer from the outset to be direct in talking about such obviously sensitive subjects as death and incompetence. Their point of view is that there is no easy way to discuss or disguise these matters, so they might as well be straightforward and move through the issues. For many clients this candor is refreshing and relieves their anxieties in a more positive manner than the use of obvious euphemisms. For others, however, it is not. As an attorney gains experience, he or she will be better able to decide, on a client-by-client basis, which approach may be more appropriate.]

C: June 5, three years ago.
A: What was her full name?
C: Sarah Jane Brown.
A: Did she have a Will or trust?
C: Yes, a Will. It was only a couple of pages.
A: Do you have a copy of it?
C: Yes. [pause] But why do you need that? If I recall correctly, my lawyer said that we didn't need to probate it.
A: Well, that could have been the case, but I want to be sure that we don't overlook something.
C: I will try to find it, but I don't see why you need it. And I don't want you to spend a bunch of time on something that was settled years ago.
A: It is just a precaution. It shouldn't take much time for my review.

[1-1.1: What is the attorney concerned about in terms of the deceased spouse's Will?]

[1-1.2: What has the attorney already overlooked in this interview?]

A: We need to look at your property and debts so I can get an idea of how to proceed. What would you estimate to be the total value of your assets, and then what would you estimate to be the total value of your debts?

[1-1.3: What is the attorney interested in?]

C: Well, . . . I . . .
A: Let me assure you that everything you say I will hold in strict confidence; this is a private matter.

C: Well, I would guess that my house, bank accounts, and car are worth around $450,000.
A: Any debts?
C: Nope. I never even had a mortgage. Always saved first and then paid cash.

[C is obviously proud of the $450,000 estate that thrift built, but A overlooks an opportunity to comment positively. A, caught up in the details of dutifully making a list of assets, fails to see the opportunity to compliment Mr. Brown and make a little human connection with him.]

A: Any other assets, like life insurance, home furnishings, coin or gun collections?
C: None to speak of. Maybe $20,000 total.

[1-1.4: A quickly reviews the asset and debt aspects of the client questionnaire with C. At this point, from what you have seen, what aspect of C's assets has A potentially overlooked?]

A: Let's talk about your family. Over the telephone you indicated that you have a son and a daughter.
C: Yes. Jack Brown and Sarah Brown.
A: Could you give me their full names and ages?
C: Jack Edward Brown, 44; Sarah Edna Brown, 42.
A: Any grandchildren?
C: Jack has a daughter, Susie, who is about 27, and a son, Mike, who is about 22. Sarah didn't marry.
A: What are Susie's and Mike's full names?
C: Susan Jennifer Brown and Michael Jay Brown.
A: Do you recall their dates of birth?
C: Not offhand.
A: We will need that information, so could you please get that from Jack?
C: Okay.

[This alone is not necessarily an indication that C's competence is an issue. It is common for relatives (other than parents or siblings) to not know or remember exact dates of birth of other family members.]

A: How would you like to distribute your property in your Will?
C: Wait a minute. Do I need a Will? I have heard that probate is expensive and drags on. I received some literature in the mail describing a "living trust" that eliminates all of that.

[This type of sidetracking can occur, particularly if the attorney is not following a well-organized approach. A should have addressed probate, Wills, and Will substitutes near the beginning of the interview. Chapter 15 considers a discussion of the revocable trust versus a Will. That debate in part turns on whether applicable state law imposes statutory fiduciary fees

continued on next page

or attorney fees for probate. The revocable trust issue is symptomatic of fundamental problems with the attorney's overall approach to the interview. This attorney became immersed in the details without any appreciation of what the client wanted. The attorney should have asked about the questionnaire, and then, even if the questionnaire had been completed, engaged first in a much broader discussion with the client. The attorney could have begun by asking the client why he was there. What would the client like to accomplish? Why is that important to you? What can I do for you? This could then lead into a discussion of estate planning approaches in terms of Wills as opposed to trusts, planned dispositions to family or charity, and so forth. The client can sometimes lead new attorneys down this road of premature specificity, particularly if the client comes to the interview with the disposition of a certain asset that is occupying his or her thoughts. Assume that A and C discuss this point and arrive at a Will as the dispositive instrument.]

A: So, how would you like to distribute your property?

C: Everything equally, half and half. I have always treated my kids equally, and I don't want to stop now.

[Even with a simple Will, contingent beneficiaries and the division of the estate in case Jack or Sarah predeceases the testator can complicate the discussion. While an attorney usually points out the various combinations of events, it can frighten the client (or trigger grandiose plans for disposition) to the point that the discussion produces almost endless layers of beneficiaries.]

> *[1-1.5: C obviously does not yet appreciate how his simple "half and half" rule would operate under unexpected situations. How would you lead the discussion with C?]*

[Assume that the other details of the interview are completed.]

A: I will mail a draft of your Will to you in about three weeks. Please review it and call me if you see any errors, have any questions, or have decided to make any changes to your plan.

> *[1-1.6: Any concerns about the three weeks' period or this approach?]*

[Some attorneys will use a larger type font in documents for elderly clients, although broaching this issue can be delicate in some cases.]

C: I really don't understand a lot of this stuff.

A: I would also be happy to discuss it with you in my office or by telephone. We can then arrange a convenient time for you to sign your Will. We need to do that here, since we have a notary public and witnesses available in the building.

C: Thank you. I need to meet my daughter for lunch.

Part B:

This is a partial transcript of an estate planning interview conducted by Attorney (A) with Client (C), from Part A. A will use the more open-ended interviewing style that we recommend.

A: Good morning. I am glad that we can meet. What can I do for you?
C: As I told you on the phone, I suppose that I ought to get my legal affairs in order.
A: Good. What specifically do you have in mind?
C: Well, I have a grown son and daughter, and I want them to inherit my property when I die . . . but I want that with the least amount of fuss, including attorney fees.

[One might ask about grandchildren at this point, but there probably isn't a need to go to that level of detail yet. Moreover, A doesn't know if C completed the part of the estate planning questionnaire providing that information.]

A: Let's talk a little more about that. Did you have an opportunity to complete the questionnaire that my assistant sent you last week?

[If C completed the questionnaire beforehand, A can review that and avoid repeating a lot of the same questions.]

C: No. It was a lot of detail. It seemed too complicated.
A: That's okay. I will need some of that information eventually, but we can work on that. [pause] You told me earlier that you are a widower?
C: Yes. I lost my wife about three years ago.
A: I am sorry. [pause] Could you describe for me, in general, what types of property you own, any debts, and so forth.
C: Well, I really don't have those numbers with me.
A: I just need very rough numbers at this time, so I have an idea of what approach would work best for you.
C: I really don't want a Will and any probate. I have heard about some kind of living trust that can avoid all of that.

[Elderly clients in particular can receive a lot of direct mail offers for revocable trust kits and assorted other materials on estate planning. Some of these materials can portray probate as a horrible thing to be avoided. Even a client otherwise unsophisticated in legal matters may come to the office with a firm preconception about probate. Depending on the laws of the state, A may want to discuss alternatives to probate. However, A first needs to know if A is dealing with a complex, tax-driven estate, on the one hand, or a very simple estate, on the other hand, that might present even Medicaid planning issues.]

A: It may. We can discuss that, but first I need to know a little more about your overall situation. Okay? [pause] Do you own a home?

[For this client, it is probably better to break the valuation task into discrete smaller bits, but not overly detailed, by using examples of general asset classes that C can think about, rather than asking what C's abstract "net worth" is.]

continued on next page

C: Yes.
A: What would be your estimate of its value?
C: Well, the county assessor seems to think it is worth a lot.
A: Taxes certainly keep rising in this area. What is your sense of your home's value?
C: I would say around $250,000.
A: Do you have a mortgage?
C: No. Never had one.
A: Good. Not many clients can say that.
C: I don't like debt.
A: Now, let's go through some of your other assets. Do you own . . .

[Here the attorney could walk the client through a list of likely assets that an elderly client might own (such as checking accounts, savings accounts, CDs, stocks, bonds, retirement accounts, collections, cars, and so forth). It is easier to discuss and have the client focus on the value of one asset at a time rather than expect any reliable answer to the question "What would be your estimate of the value of your other assets?" The attorney can add up the values quickly on a notepad and ask for general confirmation or agreement from the client.]

A: [After going through the basic list . . .] Well, it looks like you own about $470,000 in property. Do you think there is anything we missed? Do you have any life insurance, annuities, or other investments that we didn't include?
C: No.
A: Do you currently have a Will, power of attorney, or other estate planning documents?
C: None that I can recall.
A: Let's talk about probate, because you have voiced concern about that. In this state, I would estimate that probate costs would be approximately $________ for you. If we used a living trust instead, the direct costs of probate would be less, but there are some other considerations. For example, . . .

[A and C discuss the pros and cons of a Will as the primary dispositive device, as compared with a living trust. A then gives his assessment of C's situation and his advice for what C should do.]

C: That sounds like a good plan. All of this seems to be a lot simpler than I thought it would be. I want you to take care of this for me.

[This is the end of the transcript. A has already elicited crucial information from C, but without unnecessary detail. Fortunately, C's estate does not appear to be very complicated. More important, as compared with the approach in Part A, A has attempted to establish rapport with C and a listening relationship at the outset.]

EXERCISE 1-2

A CLIENT INTERVIEW SIMULATION

Case Study 2-1 in Chapter 2 is a copy of the existing Will of an elderly widow, Alice Goodwin Smith. In Chapter 2 you will be asked to review and comment on that Will. Assume that the client is still alive and wishes to update her Will. Breaking into groups designated by the teacher, the teacher will furnish one half of the class with a list of the client's significant information, and those students will act as the client. The other half of the class will act as the attorney drafting the revised Will. The two subgroups will then participate in a simulated client interview using the client questionnaire at Exhibit 1.3.

I. The Client Balance Sheet and Document Summary

The client questionnaire and interview will capture a lot of client family information. However, there are two distinct areas that need be addressed concerning assets and other financial information. First, the attorney needs to determine the nature of the client's assets and obligations. With married couples particularly, it is important to ascertain the character of the assets (e.g., common law property, community property, separate property), as well as the manner of ownership (e.g., sole ownership, joint tenancy, tenancy in common, life insurance ownership and beneficiaries, registration of financial accounts). Second, it is important to estimate the values of assets for tax implications, on the one hand, for larger estates or, on the other hand, for the potential use of small estate administration procedures. For very wealthy clients, the attorney will need to deal with other professionals such as accountants, money managers, appraisers, and trustees. A sample client balance sheet follows as Exhibit 1.4.[18]

In a simple client situation, the planning documents might consist of a Will, a durable power of attorney for property, and a durable power of attorney for healthcare. For wealthier clients, the planning documents may include irrevocable life insurance trusts, charitable trusts, generation-skipping trusts, other inter vivos trusts, private foundations, family limited partnerships or limited liability companies, and closely held business interests. While the level of complexity will vary, it is good practice to summarize the proposed planning documents in writing and to have the client confirm that these are the relevant documents you have both agreed will be produced. Exhibit 1.5 shows a sample client document summary.

18. This balance sheet would need to be modified in community property jurisdictions to reflect separate property and community property. Those distinctions are further complicated by statutes in community property states, such as California, which permit community property with rights of survivorship.

EXHIBIT 1.4 SAMPLE CLIENT BALANCE SHEET

	Husband	Wife	Joint	Total
ASSETS				
1. Liquid Assets				
Savings Accounts				
Safe Savings Bank			5,000	5,000
Checking Accounts				
Daily Bank			86,650	86,650
Investments				
Stocks			500,000	500,000
Bonds			135,000	135,000
2. Real Property				
876 Elm Street (residence)			449,000	449,000
Oak Creek Property			375,000	375,000
3. Tangible Personal Property				
Jewelry & Furs			2,500	2,500
Antiques/Art Objects			8,000	8,000
Other Household Furnishings			10,000	10,000
Automobiles	22,000	12,000		34,000
4. Closely Held Businesses				
Fair Market Value		250,000		250,000
5. Other Businesses				
East Way Partnership	300,000			300,000
6. Life Insurance				
Face Amount	100,000	100,000		200,000
7. Retirement Plans				
IRAs (Traditional)	167,000	45,000		212,000
401(k) (Traditional)	585,000			585,000
8. Other Assets				
Total Current Assets	1,174,000	542,000	1,436,150	3,152,150
9. Expected Future Assets				
Gifts				
Inheritance		1,000,000		1,000,000
Total Expected Assets		1,000,000		1,000,000
TOTAL POTENTIAL ASSETS	1,174,000	1,542,000	1,436,150	4,152,150
LIABILITIES				
1. Current Accounts				
Charge Accounts, etc.			2,000	2,000
Taxes payable				
2. Unsecured Notes to Banks				
3. Notes Payable to Others				
4. Mortgages				
Residence			150,000	150,000
Oak Creek			225,000	225,000

5. Other Mortgages				
6. Other Debts				
401(k) Loan	38,000			38,000
Total Current Liabilities	38,000		377,000	415,000
7. Expected Future Liabilities				
Taxes				
Other				
Total Future Liabilities				
TOTAL POTENTIAL LIABILITIES	38,000		377,000	415,000
Net Assets Value	1,136,000	1,542,000	1,059,150	3,737,150
(+ one half joint property)	529,575	529,575		
NET ESTATE VALUE	1,665,575	2,071,575		

EXHIBIT 1.5 SAMPLE CLIENT DOCUMENT SUMMARY

Will (with Trusts for Children).

Your Will disposes of your generalized personal property, makes specific gifts to named persons and charities, names your personal representative (and successors), nominates a trustee (and successors), and addresses general administrative provisions.

It will also provide that on your death, your residuary probate estate is to be divided into equal shares and held, in separate trusts, for the benefit of your children. If either of your children should predecease you, then the share of the deceased child will instead be added to the trust of your surviving child. If both of your children were to predecease you, your entire estate will be distributed outright to your niece, Mallory Sonapear.

Each trust created for your children will operate as follows:

Until the child is twenty-one (21), the trustee may distribute income and principal for the child's health, education, support, and maintenance. If a child should die before that child's trust is completely distributed, then the remaining assets of the deceased child's trust will be distributed to your other child's trust. You requested that the descendants of the deceased child not be included in this situation, but instead that any remaining assets go to your other surviving child.

Once a child attains the age of twenty-one (or upon your death if the child is already twenty-one years of age or older), the assets of that child's trust will become available to that child, upon demand at any time during that child's lifetime. At any point during this period the trustee may also distribute income and principal to that child for that child's health, education, support, and maintenance at the discretion of the trustee. Each trust will terminate when all of the assets have been withdrawn or distributed.

Health Care Durable Power of Attorney.

This is a comprehensive instrument related to health care that combines advance directives (sometimes referred to as a "living will"), designation of your primary health care agent and

continued on next page

successors, and a complete expression of your preferences concerning anatomical gifts. It also designates your preference for guardian of your person if that should become necessary.

Durable Power of Attorney for Property.

This instrument includes authority for a designated person of your choice to act on your behalf in financial matters if you are unable to do so prior to your death. It also designates your preference of conservator of your estate if that should become necessary.

Designation of Contingent Guardian.

Unless directed otherwise by a court, the surviving legal parent of a minor child will be appointed guardian of the minor child. This instrument permits you to name a person to be the legal guardian of any minor or otherwise incapacitated children for whom such an appointment becomes necessary in the event that both legal parents are deceased.

J. Client Competence

An attorney is ethically bound to consider the client's competence to engage in estate planning activities.[19] Even if the attorney, through observation and experience, concludes that the client appears to be competent, as is the usual case, the close cases require more attention. Because possible incompetence raises the issue of a Will contest, the attorney must consider whether further evidence of competence is desirable.

On rare occasions, and only following the client's grant of permission and appropriate Health Insurance Portability and Accountability Act of 1996[20] (HIPAA) authorizations, the attorney might seek the opinion of the client's regular physician, who has, one hopes, observed the client over an extended period, or the opinion of a mental health specialist, a measure that clearly raises the issue of competence. The attorney might document his or her questioning of the client with respect to issues of competence ("Do you understand what we are doing here today?"; "Who are your children and grandchildren?"; "How did you decide to include or exclude potential devisees?," etc.) at the time the documents are executed, all within the presence of the witnesses or others who might be needed

19. *See* Model Rules of Prof'l Conduct R. 1.14 (2002); Bernard A. Poskus, *Rule of Professional Conduct 1.14 and the Diminished Capacity Client*, 39 Colo. Law. 67 (May 2010).

20. *See generally* Jacqueline Myles Crain, *HIPAA-A Shield for Health Information and a Snag for Estate Planning and Corporate Documents*, 40 Real Prop. Prob. & Tr. J. 357 (2005); Daniel B. Evans, *What Estate Lawyers Need to Know About HIPAA and "Protected Health Information,"* 18 Prob. & Prop. 20 (July/Aug. 2004); Michael L. Graham, *Important HIPAA Compliance Issues for the Estates and Trusts Lawyer*, 39 Inst. on Est. Plan. ¶800 (2005); Michael L. Graham & Jonathan G. Blattmachr, *Planning for the HIPAA Privacy Rule*, 29 ACTEC J. 307 (2004); Martin M. Shenkman, *Estate Planning Documents Need to Address HIPAA Issues*, 36 Est. Plan. 14 (Mar. 2009).

later to testify as to the client's demeanor, attitude, attention, and other observable details.[21] Some attorneys might videotape the document execution ceremony and include a number of witnesses to the client's demeanor at that time. Other attorneys, however, take the position that unless they regularly videotape the execution ceremonies of all clients, the act of singling out an occasional client to videotape raises, and may even add support to, the question of that particular client's competence. In Part M we refer you to other discussions of measures for dealing with possible client competence concerns.

K. Conflicts of Interest

Many clients see the estate planning process as a family matter. In many situations this presents no problems, but in other cases it can be particularly difficult.

1. Married Couples

Married couples often deal with the attorney on a joint basis as a couple. It is recommended that both sign a joint representation letter. The letter should explain the potential conflicts and the attorney's response to them, in compliance with ABA Model Rule of Professional Conduct 1.7. A sample joint representation letter, Exhibit 1.6, deserves your careful attention. The terms of the joint representation letter are usually included as part of the engagement letter rather than drafted as a separate document.

EXHIBIT 1.6 SAMPLE JOINT REPRESENTATION LETTER

[date]

Dear Matthew and Lindsey:

As an estate planning attorney, I am often asked to represent both husband and wife as they develop and implement their estate plans. However, there are ethical rules governing all lawyers that limit my ability to represent multiple clients, including husband and wife. I may not, for example, ethically represent both of you in this or any matter if your interests are, or become, directly adverse to each other. If you were to each engage your own lawyer, you would each have your own advocate for your position and any information that you disclosed to your separate lawyer would remain confidential and unavailable to your spouse.

continued on next page

21. Obtaining contemporaneously prepared written statements from the witnesses of their observations at the time of the execution ceremony may also be considered. A helpful resource that includes a "Capacity Worksheet for Lawyers" is a joint publication, the American Bar Association Commission on Aging and the American Psychological Association, Assessment of Older Adults with Diminished Capacity: A Handbook for Lawyers (2005).

However, most of my clients would prefer that I represent both of them, and fortunately there is an exception under the rules. Specifically, I can represent both of you if I reasonably believe that by providing legal services to both of you it will not adversely affect my representation of either of you. Based upon discussions that both of you have had with me, I believe that as to estate planning your interests are in common and not adverse and that I can represent you both at this time. Thus, I agree to represent both of you provided that you agree that the following three considerations will apply to our relationship:

a. Discussions that either of you have with me outside the presence of your spouse, or information in any form that either of you provide to me, will not be protected by the attorney-client privilege from disclosure to your spouse. I will not agree with either of you to withhold information from your spouse.

b. If during the course of my representation of both of you, differences of opinion arise between you about your proposed estate plan, I cannot advocate or promote one of your positions over the other. Should your differences of opinion rise to the level of conflict such that in my judgment I cannot continue to represent you both, I will withdraw as lawyer for both of you and advise both of you to obtain separate counsel.

c. These considerations and my representation of both of you will be limited to the legal services that you specifically engage me to perform.

Sincerely,

Attorney Name

AN:kj

By our signatures below, we each acknowledge that we have read and understand this letter that explains the conditions upon which Attorney Name, Attorney, agrees to represent both of us and that we consent to Attorney jointly representing both of us on the terms and conditions described herein. We also agree that as between ourselves, with respect to information either of us provides to Attorney, there shall be no confidential communications.

__________________________ __________________________

Client Signature and Date Client Signature and Date

[Note: This letter deals only with the joint representation issue. Along the lines of Exhibit 1.1, the parties would need to execute a general engagement letter speaking to the scope of the engagement and fees. The joint representation language could be included in that engagement letter, or it could be referenced as a separate letter.]

The sample joint representation letter describes the manner in which the joint representation will be conducted in the ordinary course, as well as the consequences if a conflict arises. The express waiver of client confidentiality in the letter is contrary to the general rule that a lawyer must maintain client confidences.[22] However, as demonstrated by Exercise 1-3

22. *See* Model Rules of Prof'l Conduct R. 1.6 (2002). However, note that the waiver of confidentiality is as to the other spouse only, not as to any other third party.

below, while the waiver is an imperfect measure if maintaining all confidences is a priority, preserving client confidences in a joint spousal representation can produce very difficult dilemmas for the spouses and the attorney. Indeed, because of the potential consequences attendant to the waiver of confidentiality, it may be desirable to discuss the consequences of the waiver of confidentiality separately with each spouse at the outset. This separate interview usually promotes candor and an informed waiver of confidentiality. On the other hand, the presence of deep, undisclosed confidences may suggest that the potential conflicts between the two spouses are too great for a joint representation, whether on a confidential basis or not. Nevertheless, it has been our experience that virtually all married couples, after consultation, do agree to a joint representation with a waiver of confidentiality.

EXERCISE 1-3

JOINT REPRESENTATION OF SPOUSES

Husband is a successful small business owner who has been a client of your firm for several years. You meet with Husband and Wife jointly on Wednesday morning to update their estate plan. The three of you work on an estate planning questionnaire resembling Exhibit 1.3. With the exception of some minor differences for modest legacies, the two proposed Wills are almost identical, providing for the survivor and ultimately their two adult children. You conclude the meeting, noting that you will mail drafts to them within two weeks.

(a) Husband calls you that afternoon. He states that he has a 20-year-old child by a former mistress. He directs that his Will be modified to split the remainder in thirds for each child. In his words: "I assume that my Will is my business. My Wife won't be reading the drafts, and this won't come up for years. She is taken care of in any event under the Will." How do you proceed? How could you have prevented finding yourself in this ethical dilemma?

(b) Assume the same facts as in (a), except that Husband and Wife execute the Wills as originally envisioned, and Husband then calls you 18 months later and wants to execute a codicil to effect the change in the above paragraph. How do you proceed? How could you have prevented finding yourself in this ethical dilemma?

(c) Assume that for federal wealth transfer planning, one of your proposed recommendations is the transfer of $400,000 of Husband's assets to Wife. (We defer until Chapter 11 a discussion of why this might be desirable.) Assume that neither (a) nor (b) occurs, but that Wife called you later that afternoon to ask you about the details of the transfer. She indicates that the transfer is important for "her sense of security." She tells you that while Husband and Wife are "relatively content now, we have had some rough spots during our marriage." How do you proceed?

2. Elderly Clients

With elderly clients, one often faces the issue of an adult child (often the primary caregiver) who wishes to participate in planning meetings. While the client might see this as an absolutely appropriate request, the presence of the child can suggest subtle coercion. Indeed, it may at least introduce the appearance of coercion or undue influence, *particularly if there are other children who are not present and who are treated differently.* Furthermore, the presence of third-party nonclients may introduce questions concerning the confidentiality of the discussion and issues regarding waiver of the attorney-client privilege.

EXERCISE 1-4

THE ELDERLY CLIENT AND THE ROLE OF RELATIVES

(a) Daughter telephones you, reportedly following a referral from an acquaintance. She indicates that she and Mother, age 75, wish to meet with you as soon as possible to discuss deeding Mother's house to Daughter to "avoid probate." (Mother reportedly does not like to drive her automobile to unfamiliar destinations.) Assume that Daughter is Mother's sole child and that Mother would consider Daughter to be the sole object of Mother's bounty. (We defer an examination of whether this is an advisable estate planning measure until Chapter 15.) How will you conduct the client interview?

(b) Assume that Daughter in (a) is one of two children. The other child is reportedly "estranged from Mother; he hasn't visited her or spoken with her for years." How will you conduct the client interview?

(c) Daughter states that Mother, although of moderate wealth, is so frugal that she is reluctant to pay for any professional advice. Daughter consequently wants to pay for the consultation and all costs of the implementation of any plan. What is your response?

3. Overlapping Representation

With wealthy clients particularly, the dealings of the parents and the children may become quite enmeshed over the years. The attorney may represent the parents to begin with, and then the representation blossoms to include the children, or vice versa. While this might be considered a reward for effective long-term representation of the family, it can also produce awkward, if not improper, situations in the estate planning process.

EXERCISE 1-5

REPRESENTATION OF MEMBERS OF A FAMILY BUSINESS

Your law firm has represented ABC, Inc., a closely held family business, and its principal shareholder, A. A has two children: B, who is working in the business as a vice president and owns a minority stake in the corporation; and C, who works as an educator and owns a minority stake in the corporation. A's estate plan has included a specific bequest of a controlling interest in ABC, Inc. to B, with some compensating legacies to C. You have worked with both A and B on ABC, Inc.'s business matters, and A has on occasion referred to B as "my successor in the business."

A recently contacted you and requested that you prepare a codicil that divides the stock in ABC, Inc. roughly equally between B and C such that B would no longer enjoy majority control. In A's words, "I question B's judgment, and I think that the company needs the active input of C in major decisions." A further instructs you to "keep this confidential. This is all found money to B and C, and none of their affair while I am still alive." How do you proceed?

[Consider Hotz v. Minyard, *304 S.C. 225, 403 S.E.2d 634 (S.C. 1991).]*

4. The Attorney as Beneficiary

Client gifts to an estate planning attorney present several possible concerns. The Model Rules of Professional Conduct provide that "A lawyer shall not prepare an instrument giving the lawyer or a person related to the lawyer as parent, child, sibling, or spouse any substantial gift from a client, including a testamentary gift, except where the client is related to the donee."[23] The attorney may consequently be subject to disciplinary action. In addition, the situation may raise a presumption of undue influence that could cause the gift to fail.[24]

In the following case the attorney halfheartedly attempted to avoid the conflict but compounded his problems with some evasive post-mortem behavior.

People v. Berge
620 P.2d 23 (Colo. 1980)

. . . The respondent was charged with violating [a state supreme court rule governing practice by lawyers] and the Code of Professional

23. Model Rules of Prof'l Conduct R. 1.8(c) (2002).
24. *See generally* Price & Donaldson, *supra* note 2, at §1.6.8.

Responsibility, including DR5-101, by reason of the following acts: (1) exerting undue influence upon a client in connection with preparation and execution of his will in which the respondent was named as a beneficiary, (2) failing to adopt appropriate safeguards to avoid undue influence and the appearance of impropriety with respect to the drafting and execution of that will, and (3) failing to deal candidly with heirs and potential beneficiaries while acting as attorney for the personal representative of his deceased client's estate. . . .

The respondent was licensed to practice law in Colorado on September 10, 1951. He represented Allen C. Stephenson in various matters from about 1958 until Stephenson's death on May 8, 1976. The services included preparing a will, serving as attorney for Stephenson's mother's estate, and representing Stephenson in various real property and business matters. Prior to 1958 the respondent had assisted one of his law partners in various matters on behalf of Stephenson, including a successful appeal challenging an order of distribution of property incident to Stephenson's divorce. . . .

The respondent prepared a will which Stephenson signed on February 3, 1967. That will contained bequests of $10 each to three aunts and an uncle, left art objects and travel mementos to the Denver Art Museum, and divided the residue two-thirds to the Denver Dumb Friends League (DFL) and one-third to Angel Memorial Animal Hospital. A bank was named as executor. The executor was directed to retain a member of the respondent's law firm to perform all legal services for probate of the estate as a condition to being appointed executor.[25]

In June 1968 Stephenson told the respondent that he wished to make a new will. Stephenson brought a copy of the 1967 will to the respondent's office. On that copy Stephenson had penciled comments relating to the changes which he wished to make. One such change was the inclusion of a bequest of part of the estate residue to the respondent.

The respondent declined to prepare the new will because he was to be a beneficiary. He recommended two prominent Denver attorneys to Stephenson, but these suggestions were rejected. Stephenson asked if there was "somebody here" who could draft the will. The respondent suggested another attorney, Mr. Smith (a fictitious name), whom he described as an independent practitioner, and Stephenson agreed that Smith should prepare the will.

Smith rented office space from the respondent's law firm. All office expenses, including telephone, rent, and secretarial salaries, but excluding

25. Many family fiduciaries will employ the drafting attorney anyway due to an assumption that the drafting attorney will already have familiarity with the case, to somewhat honor the decedent's choice of the attorney who drafted the instrument, or due to simple expediency in simplifying the selection of an attorney. Fiduciaries that are determined to not use the drafting attorney, such as a bank trust department, can probably refuse to be bound by the clause. Professors Price and Donaldson do not recommend this practice. *See* PRICE & DONALDSON, *supra* note 2, at §1.6.7.—EDS.

stationery, were shared on a proportional basis. The telephone system also was shared, and the access to Smith's office was through the front door of the offices of the respondent's firm. Smith had a close relationship with members of the respondent's firm; they drank coffee together in the office daily.

After Stephenson agreed that Smith should prepare the will, the respondent called Smith over the office intercommunications system. The two met, out of Stephenson's presence, and the respondent told Smith that he had just learned that Stephenson wanted to make the respondent a beneficiary in his new will. The respondent asked Smith to prepare the will and he agreed.

Immediately thereafter, Stephenson met with Smith in the latter's office and, utilizing the marked-up copy of the 1967 will, a new will was drafted substantially in accordance with the marked-up copy. If any changes were made, they were only clarifications. Smith and Stephenson did not discuss Stephenson's family situation, the possible tax consequences of the proposed will, or any of the other factors which could have affected that document materially. Smith gave Stephenson no substantive advice. The conference took only ten to fifteen minutes.

The new will increased the specific bequests to Stephenson's aunts and uncle from $10 each to $100 each. The DFL, which in the 1967 will had been named as recipient of two-thirds of the residuary estate, was to receive a specific bequest of $25,000 under the new will. The Angel Memorial Animal Hospital was to receive nothing. The residuary estate then was divided fifty-three percent to Leon DuCharme and forty-seven percent to the respondent. A requirement similar to that found in the 1967 will with respect to naming the respondent or his firm as attorneys for the estate was included in the 1968 will. In addition, a clause was added specifying that, if any beneficiary should challenge a provision of the will, the legacy to that beneficiary would lapse and fall into the residuary estate. This clause did not appear in the 1967 will but appeared in handwritten or typed form on the marked-up copy used to draft the 1968 will. All changes were based upon the notes appearing on the copy of the 1967 will.

On June 27, 1968, three to five days after the first meeting with respect to the new will, Stephenson returned to execute the will. Smith was unable to find a third witness nearby, so he requested the respondent to act as a witness. In the presence of Stephenson, the respondent, and another witness, Smith read the provisions of the will relating to the respondent, and Stephenson executed the will.[26]

Smith performed the work as a favor to the respondent. Although Smith considered Stephenson to be his client for the purpose of the will, Smith kept no client file on this matter and did not charge Stephenson

26. Colorado law provides that the signing of a Will by an interested witness does not invalidate the Will, although it is not a recommended practice in light of undue influence considerations — Eds.

for his services. The only times Smith saw Stephenson were in the two meetings during which the 1968 will was drafted and executed.

On May 8, 1976, Stephenson died in Hawaii, where he customarily spent the winter months during the later years of his life.[27] On May 11, 1976, a petition for appointment of a special administrator in the Stephenson estate, signed by DuCharme as petitioner and naming the respondent as his attorney, was filed in Denver probate court. An order appointing DuCharme as special administrator and an acceptance of that appointment were signed and filed in probate court that same day.

On May 20, 1976, DuCharme and the respondent went to Hawaii and took possession of the decedent's stock certificates, an inventory of stocks and other personal property, a copy of the 1967 will, and decedent's savings passbook reflecting a balance of approximately $197,000. . . . The handwritten inventory contained about 55 entries reflecting significant holdings in such corporations as Texaco, Inc., and Pepsi Cola. The value of such stocks, as later reported in the inventory filed with the probate court, was $280,794.68. Also found among Stephenson's effects was a handwritten note requesting that the respondent and another be notified in case of accident or serious illness. Stapled to the note was the respondent's business card with a handwritten notation, "My attorney. Please notify in case of accident or serious injury."

Upon returning to Denver, DuCharme and the respondent went through Stephenson's home. Although they were unable to find the original 1968 will, they did locate a copy of that will in a file cabinet in the home.

On June 18, 1976, a petition for formal probate of the will and formal appointment of a personal representative was filed in the Denver probate court by the respondent as attorney for the bank which had been named as personal representative in the will. A copy of the 1968 will was attached. As part of the petition for formal probate, a paragraph was attached explaining where and when the copy had been found and stating that a search had been made in an unsuccessful effort to locate the original will.[28]

The respondent sent a notice of hearing on the petition for formal probate to the devisees and heirs. The notice was accompanied by the petition for formal probate and by the respondent's letter dated June 22, 1976, containing the following underlined statement: "It is not necessary for you to be present at that time (the time of presentation of the will for probate) in order to receive the bequest which was left to you under the terms of the Will." The notice was not accompanied by a copy of the will or any information as to the size of the bequests.

27. The maintenance of multiple residences is very typical behavior for very wealthy or retired individuals, but the case suggests that the decedent's domicile remained in Colorado — Eds.

28. Colorado follows the majority rule that a presumption of revocation arises if the decedent had last possession of the Will, and it cannot be found. However, if that presumption is overcome, the contents of the lost Will can be established by a copy — Eds.

A representative of the DFL learned of Stephenson's death and had heard that Stephenson had named the DFL as the recipient of a substantial bequest. The DFL representative met with the respondent on June 24, 1976, to request information about the bequest. When told that it was $25,000, the representative expressed surprise, stating that it was her understanding that the DFL was to receive either one-third or two-thirds of an estate of approximately $400,000. The respondent told the DFL representative that the size of the estate was more like $250,000. The representative requested, and was shown, a copy of the will. She asked where the money was going and was told that Stephenson didn't have much and that the respondent and another man were getting some. As it developed, the gross estate was $593,786 as shown in the court records.

The DFL retained counsel to investigate the matter. Negotiations ensued, resulting in a stipulated settlement by which, after payment of $100 each to the three aunts and the uncle and distribution of pictures, art objects, and travel mementos to the Denver Art Museum, the residuary estate was to be divided one-third to the residuary devisees under the 1967 will (the DFL and Angel Memorial Animal Hospital) and two-thirds to the residuary devisees under the 1968 will (DuCharme and the respondent). The court approved the stipulation, and distribution was made on that basis. As a consequence of the settlement, the charities received $195,204 and DuCharme and the respondent received the gross amount of $390,409. After taxes and expenses the respondent received $113,681.

We agree with the conclusion of the Grievance Committee that the respondent's conduct in connection with the preparation and execution of Stephenson's 1968 will and in dealing with the heirs and beneficiaries in the administration of Stephenson's estate violated accepted rules or standards of legal ethics. . . . The respondent's lack of candor in dealing with the heirs and beneficiaries also violated the highest standards of honesty, justice, and morality. . . . Our review of the record satisfies us that the charge that the respondent exerted undue influence upon his client in connection with preparation and execution of his will has not been established by clear and convincing evidence.

I.

Although Ethical Consideration EC 5-5 had not been adopted when the relevant events took place, it simply makes explicit some long-accepted standards of legal ethics which are relevant here. It provides, in pertinent part:

"If a client voluntarily offers to make a gift to his lawyer, the lawyer may accept the gift, but before doing so, he should urge that his client secure disinterested advice from an independent, competent person who is cognizant of all the circumstances. Other than in exceptional circumstances, a lawyer should insist that an instrument in which his client desires to name him beneficially be prepared by another lawyer selected by the client."

The respondent's efforts to "urge" Stephenson to obtain disinterested advice were limited to suggesting two other attorneys. When Stephenson rejected those suggestions and asked whether "somebody here" could prepare the will, the respondent immediately suggested Smith.

The close relationship of the respondent and his firm with Smith is inconsistent with the appearance of independence. Much more importantly, the manner in which Smith handled this matter establishes that he was not independent in fact. His inquiry into the facts essential to proper representation was minimal. He did not inquire into Stephenson's family situation, the size of his estate, or any other facts essential to proper representation. He gave Stephenson no substantive advice, but acted only as a scrivener in making changes noted on a copy of an earlier will. One of these changes, which should have suggested discussion or advice, was the introduction of a new provision intended to nullify the bequest to any beneficiary who should challenge the will. He never billed Stephenson even though he had no expectation of becoming attorney for the estate. Smith candidly admitted that his services in the matter were performed as a favor to the respondent. From the record, Smith appears to be a competent, experienced attorney. The way he treated this matter testifies eloquently to the close relationship between the respondent and Smith and to Smith's lack of independence. We agree with the conclusion of the hearing committee that the respondent's conduct in referring Stephenson to Smith violated accepted rules or standards of legal ethics....

Although of lesser significance, we conclude that the respondent's election to act as a witness to the will also was inconsistent with his duty to dissociate himself from the preparation and execution of a will which named him as beneficiary of almost half of the residuary estate.

II.

We conclude that the respondent's conduct in dealing with Stephenson's heirs and with the DFL violated [a state supreme court rule governing practice by lawyers].

The respondent's financial interests as beneficiary of a very substantial bequest and as attorney for the personal representative greatly increased the importance of dealing with the beneficiaries candidly. Lack of candor under such circumstances does not comport with either accepted standards of legal ethics or the highest standards of honesty, justice, and morality.

A.

No original will had been found. The respondent was the beneficiary of a large bequest in the copy of the will submitted for probate. The estate was very substantial. The bequests to the heirs were minimal. The form of notice advised the beneficiaries that the original will had not been found. It did identify the beneficiaries, but not the amounts of the bequests. All of the heirs lived outside Colorado. The respondent chose to supplement the notice with a cover letter. In that letter he disclosed none of the facts which might have caused the heirs to realize that a large estate was at stake and that their own bequests were minimal. However, the respondent did include and underline a sentence which would have the logical effect of reducing the possibility that the heirs might inquire and question the probate of the will. That sentence, quoted earlier, told each heir that she need not appear in order to receive the bequest left to her under the terms of the will. Characterizing this conduct most favorably to the respondent, it lacks candor. Under the facts of the instant case, this conduct is at odds with accepted standards of legal ethics and with the highest standards of honesty, justice, and morality.

B.

The respondent also failed to satisfy his duty of candor with respect to the inquiry of the DFL about the bequest to that organization. He estimated the size of the estate to be less than half the amount it developed to be. Even though the size of the estate had not been definitely established when the respondent met with the representative of the DFL, he had seen a stock inventory and savings passbook in Hawaii which gave him a basis to make a more accurate estimate of the size of the estate. The conclusion of the hearing committee that the respondent failed to deal candidly with the DFL is supported by clear and convincing evidence. Under the circumstances of this case, that failure also was contrary to the respondent's obligations. . . .

III.

. . . Although the conduct of the respondent was seriously at variance with his ethical obligations as a lawyer and was of a type which tends to bring the legal profession into disrepute with the public, our review of the record discloses no evidence that the distribution of assets directed in the 1968 will did not reflect the testator's true testamentary intent. We also take into account that the record reflects no prior disciplinary action against the respondent in almost thirty years of practice of law in the state of Colorado.

After weighing the relevant considerations, we conclude that a ninety-day suspension from the practice of law is the appropriate discipline and now order such suspension, beginning on the date of issuance of this opinion. . . .

QUESTION

The Court found that it had not been established by clear and convincing evidence that the attorney had exerted undue influence upon his client. Did this finding have any impact on the disposition of the client's estate?

L. Execution and the Completion/Termination Letter

Following the initial client meeting, the attorney may need to make some follow-up telephone calls for additional information. In working with an estate of any complexity, most attorneys will send drafts of the documents to the client for comment. If necessary, multiple rounds of drafts will be circulated. With very wealthy clients, the client may request that other professionals, such as accountants and trust officers, review the drafts. With some transactions, such as the purchase of life insurance or the creation of an irrevocable trust, the review by representatives of the insurer and the trust company, if a professional trustee is used, will be the ordinary course.

Occasionally, with simpler estates, some attorneys will dispense with sending drafts to the client and will explain the documents to the client at the execution ceremony. Minor changes might be made at that time. In our experience, this process is not desirable. The review and modifications can take a lot of time; staff is not always available to make the document changes; and one might only then find that some information is still missing. In addition, if the Will is contested, cross-examination questions for the drafting attorney will likely include whether drafts were sent to the client for review before signing. We consequently recommend that the attorney always send drafts in advance, with "DRAFT" and a date, in case of multiple drafts, clearly marked across each page of each document. For computer-literate clients or for other advisors, one can send documents as email attachments (e.g., as ".pdf" or Adobe Acrobat® files, a format that can be made nonmodifiable but printable, if desired). If the client has reviewed the final drafts before the signing ceremony, it makes the process less rushed; permits the attorney to focus on other problems that may surface; and adds some support, if necessary later, to the assertion that the client has read, carefully considered, and understands the document he or she is about to sign.

Once the client has signed all of the documents, it might appear that the estate planning process has come to an end. However, estate planning is constantly evolving as outside factors (the client's situation, the economy, the law, etc.) continue to change. The client may continue to see you as his or her attorney, watching over the matter for him or her and keeping abreast of changes in the law and assessing their impact on the client. After all, that is what you do! Unfortunately, there is no realistic way that you can do this for every client you have ever represented. Plus, you have no way of knowing what changes may have occurred in the clients' personal situations (e.g., marriage, dissolution of marriage, death, births of children or grandchildren, receipt of inheritances, relocation to another state, etc.). Accordingly, it is good practice for the attorney to send a closing, or disengagement, letter to the client outlining the attorney's future responsibilities to the client. A sample completion/termination letter follows as Exhibit 1.7. It is common for the attorney to include in this letter instructions concerning the safekeeping of the Will and other documents. The letter may also encourage the client to prepare a so-called "letter of instruction" for the benefit of his or her family members. The letter of instruction should disclose information such as the location of the client's Will, the location of the safe deposit box (and key), the location of life insurance policies, stock certificates, certificates of deposit and the like, a list of current debts and other obligations, a list of current professional advisors, etc. Some clients provide this information to the person or institution that will serve as the personal representative of the estate; others give it to family members. A sample client letter of instruction is included as Form E-2 in the Forms Supplement.[29]

EXHIBIT 1.7 SAMPLE DISENGAGEMENT LETTER

[date]

Robert and Kelly Client
31461 Island Breeze Drive
Louisville, CO 80027

Re: Executed Estate Planning Documents

Dear Robert and Kelly:

Enclosed are the original instruments that you executed in my office on January 25, [current year], and a bound set for each of you containing one copy of each of the following instruments:

1. **Will**
2. **Statutory Power of Attorney for Property**
3. **Health Care Durable Power of Attorney**
4. **Designation of Guardian**

I will also keep an electronic copy of each executed instrument in my file. In addition, I am enclosing an original, unexecuted **Memorandum Disposition of Tangible Personal Property** with instructions on its use as we have discussed.

The original documents you signed should be kept in a safe deposit box or in another secure place. If you keep your Will in your residence and upon your death it cannot be found, there could be a strong presumption that you revoked your Will and you could die intestate (without a Will). Your personal representative and successor designees should be told where the original Will is kept. Indeed, you should take this occasion to review information with your personal representative and family members that they would require in the event of your unexpected death. Such matters would include the location of your safe deposit box, the identity of your accountant, stockbroker, and other advisors, the location of life insurance policies, a listing of your principal assets and debts, and so forth.

continued on next page

29. The letter is typically quite personal and may include information as to mundane details of everyday life such as where the home water shutoff valve is located. *See, e.g.*, THEODORE E. HUGHES & DAVID KLEIN, THE EXECUTOR'S HANDBOOK: A STEP-BY-STEP GUIDE TO SETTLING AN ESTATE FOR PERSONAL REPRESENTATIVES, ADMINISTRATORS, AND BENEFICIARIES 25-31 (2d ed. 2001) (discussing the contents of a letter of instruction); John J. Scroggin, *The Family Love Letter*, 13 No. 2 PRAC. TAX LAW. 5 (Winter 1999) (offering an example of a comprehensive letter of instruction, albeit by another name). T. Rowe Price, an investment services firm, offers its clients a complimentary Family Records Organizer CD-ROM "to provide one secure, interactive place to store your family's personal information regarding investments, insurance, wills, and more." T. Rowe Price, INVESTOR 25 (June 2007).

Under no circumstances should you attempt to change or mark upon any of the enclosed documents without consulting an attorney. Generally, in order to ensure that any changes are valid, they must be made by an amendment executed with the same formalities as were observed in the execution of the original instrument.

In closing, it has been a pleasure working with you in the preparation of these instruments. Unless you engage me to perform additional legal services for you in the future, I will be taking no further action on your behalf. As time passes, however, should you have any questions or should your goals or estate situation change, please let me know. Because it is almost certain that over time the tax laws will change, I recommend that periodically you contact me or another estate planning attorney to determine if and how any such changes in the law may or may not affect your situation.[30]

Best regards to you in the future.

Sincerely,

Attorney Name

AN:kj

EXERCISE 1-6

GETTING YOUR FEET WET

Part A: Using Forms B and C found in the Forms Supplement, prepare a very simple Will and a personal property memorandum (if the governing law selected by your teacher permits such a memorandum) for the client in Exercise 1-1. Do not prepare any other documents, such as health care durable powers of attorney, durable powers of attorney for property, etc.

Part B: Using Forms I and J found in the Forms Supplement, prepare a pourover Will and revocable trust for the client in Exercise 1-1. Do not prepare any other documents.

While the statutory requirements for a Will execution are relatively simple, good practice requires great care. One can refer to a number of comprehensive lists of steps for the Will execution ceremony, all of which differ in some respects with regard to the level of detail or points of style.[31] These checklists aim for an execution procedure that would be valid in all states. The Will execution procedures checklist should not be viewed as a shameful crib sheet for a seemingly inexperienced attorney. Although a checklist does serve the purpose of preventing oversights in procedure, it serves another purpose as well. It is an important evidentiary record to be completed and included in the client's Will file as a written record of what occurred at the ceremony. A sample execution checklist follows as Exhibit 1.8.

30. Some attorneys would resist this implied "clean break" by arguing that it discourages repeat business. It seems to us that this paragraph does not foreclose the mailing of carefully crafted general follow-up letters or newsletters.

31. *See, e.g.*, A. James Casner & Jeffrey N. Pennell, Estate Planning §3.1.1 (6th ed. 1995 & Supp. 2009-2010); Jesse Dukeminier et al., Wills, Trusts, and Estates 242-245 (8th ed. 2009); David K. Johns, *Will Execution Ceremonies: Securing a Client's Last Wishes*, 23 Colo. Law. 49 (Jan. 1994).

EXHIBIT 1.8 SAMPLE WILL EXECUTION CHECKLIST

ALICE GOODWIN SMITH [date]

EXECUTION OF WILL

Testator Specimen Signatures

[Note: The testator is a widow, and the specimen signatures capture her married and unmarried names.]

____________________________ ALICE GOODWIN SMITH
____________________________ ALICE GOODWIN JONES

Witnesses

1) ____________________________
Print Name

____

____
Print Home Address

____
Print Home Telephone Number

2) ____________________________
Print Name

____

____
Print Home Address

____
Print Home Telephone Number

Notary

<u>Mary A. Cooper, Commission Expires [date]</u>
Print Name

<u>Preparation</u>

Assemble participants in quiet room and close the door:

- ☐ Testator
- ☐ Witnesses
- ☐ Notary Public
- ☐ __________ Attorney

[Note: The attorney should keep interruptions to an absolute minimum once the door is closed and everyone is assembled. Note that the only participants are the testator, witnesses, a notary public, and the presiding attorney. Other family members would generally be excluded to avoid the appearance of undue influence or other complications.]

continued on next page

Make introductions as necessary and provide an overview of the execution ceremony that is to follow. Place testator under oath and ask (question and answer to be heard by all in room):

1. ☐ Is this your Will? (Should be YES)
2. ☐ Have you read it and do you understand it? (Should be YES)
3. ☐ Does it dispose of your property in accordance with your wishes? (Should be YES)
4. ☐ Do you request __________ and __________ to witness the signing of your Will? (Should be YES)

[Note: Some checklists include additional questions for the testator to establish competency, such as whether he/she is over age 18, married, name of any spouse, names and ages of any children, etc. Some checklists include questions to be completed by the attorney as to the physical appearance, demeanor, etc., of the testator. The David K. Johns article cited in note 31 provides a very comprehensive checklist of that nature.]

Place each witness under oath and ask (question and answer to be heard by all in room):

1. ☐ Are you each over age 18? (Should be YES)
2. ☐ Are either of you related to the testator? (Should be NO)
3. ☐ Do either of you presently have any interest in the testator's Will or estate? (Should be NO)

Execution

[Note: Some checklists insist on the use of blue ink for signatures. Using blue ink is good practice in light of digital reproduction technology that makes black ink copies almost indistinguishable from the originals. It will also help your staff in distinguishing copies from originals.]

Testator (in presence of notary and both witnesses)

[Note: This part of the checklist contemplates the use of a two-step Will in which the testator signs twice. See Form H in the Forms Supplement. This checklist requires that the testator and the witnesses initial each page. Other integration techniques such as a secure binding and running over sentences between pages will reinforce/support the integration of the Will.]

1. ☐ Initial each page at the bottom.
2. Locate the paragraph at the end that begins with "IN WITNESS WHEREOF..." and
   - ☐ Read the paragraph aloud to the witnesses and notary.
   - ☐ Enter date and sign your name as printed.
3. Locate the following paragraph, Attestation and Affidavit, and
   - ☐ Read the paragraph aloud to the witnesses and notary.
   - ☐ Enter date and sign your name as printed.

Witnesses (in presence of each other, the testator, and the notary)

1. ☐ Initial each page at the bottom.
2. ☐ Print your name in the paragraph (Attestation & Affidavit) to be read by the witnesses AND in the paragraph for the notary.
3. ☐ Read aloud the witnesses' statement to the notary.
4. ☐ Enter date and sign your name.

Notary

1. ☐ Enter date and signature.
2. ☐ Affix seal.
3. ☐ Enter document in Notary's journal book.

[Note: The notary laws of many states require that the notary maintain a log book in which the date of acknowledgment and a description of the document is entered.]

EXERCISE 1-7

A WILL EXECUTION CEREMONY SIMULATION

Hold an execution ceremony in class using the Will drafted in Exercise 1-6. Follow the execution formalities of your state (or other jurisdiction designated by your teacher). The signature section of Form B is in UPC format, so modify it for the law chosen by your teacher.

Following the Will execution, the issue arises as to where the original documents will be stored. As demonstrated by the following exercise, there is no simple answer to this question.

EXERCISE 1-8

CUSTODY OF THE WILL

The estate law department of the ABC Law Firm meets weekly to discuss current issues impacting the firm's practice. This week's topic was the disposition of client Wills. Partner A offered her assessment. "We should encourage our clients to leave the original executed Wills with us. We offer a secure place in our safe. The client and family know where to find the Will. We avoid the agonizing textbook cases about partial physical revocations and amendments, as well as third-party destruction of the Will." Partner B was less sanguine in his appraisal. "We should not adopt the role of being a safe deposit box company. I don't think we are equipped for that degree of responsibility. Moreover, when does our responsibility end?" Partner C offered an additional perspective. "We can't bill our hourly rates on most estate planning. I want the family to return to us for the administration work. In my experience, maintaining custody of the original Will is an important part of that."

Question: As the new associate in the department, you have been asked by the partners to write a memorandum evaluating the Will custody arguments and proposing a standard policy for the firm. How would your answer change, if at all, if you were considering this question as a sole practitioner?

M. Reference Materials

Treatises

Overview of the Planning Process

- Frederick K. Hoops et al., Family Estate Planning Guide, ch. 1, *Family Estate Planning* (4th ed. 1994 & Supp. 2010-2011).
- John R. Price & Samuel A. Donaldson, Price on Contemporary Estate Planning ¶1.1 (2011).
- George M. Turner, Revocable Trusts, ch. 1 (5th ed. 2003 & Supp. 2010).
- Harold Weinstock & Martin Neumann, Planning an Estate, ch. 1, *Introduction to Estate Planning* (4th ed. 2002 & Supp. 2010).

Practice Development

- Daniel B. Evans, How to Build and Manage an Estates Practice (1999) [hereinafter "Evans I"].
- Daniel B. Evans, Wills, Trusts, and Technology: An Estate and Trust Lawyer's Guide to Automation (2d ed. 2004).

Engagement Letters

- Price & Donaldson, *supra*, §1.6.2.
- Jeffrey A. Schoenblum, Page on the Law of Wills, vol. 7, ch. 20F (2d ed. 2010) (examples of joint and separate spousal representation engagement letters).

Non-Engagement Letters

- Price & Donaldson, *supra*, §1.6.2.

The Client Interview

- Hoops et al., *supra*, ch. 3, *Preparation for the Initial Interview*.
- L. Rush Hunt & Lara Rae Hunt, A Lawyer's Guide to Estate Planning—Fundamentals for the Legal Practitioner, ch. 1, *Beginning the Process* (3d ed. 2004).
- Robert M. Bastress & Joseph D. Harbaugh, Interviewing, Counseling and Negotiating: Skills for Effective Representation, ch. 4, *Anatomy of the Initial Client Interview* (1990).
- Turner, *supra*, ch. 9, *First Meeting with Clients.*

Client Competence

- American Bar Association Commission on Law and Aging & American Psychological Association, Assessment of Older Adults with Diminished Capacity: A Handbook for Lawyers (2005).

- Roger W. Andersen, Understanding Trusts and Estates 30-32 (4th ed. 2009).
- William M. McGovern et al., Wills, Trusts and Estates 315-326 (4th ed. 2010).

Will Execution

- Andersen, *supra*, 40-49 & 57.
- A. James Casner & Jeffrey N. Pennell, Estate Planning §3.1.1 (6th ed. 1995 & Supp. 2009-2010).
- Hoops et al., *supra*, §17.32.
- McGovern et al., *supra*, 197-212.
- Price & Donaldson, *supra*, §4.32.

Client Conflicts

- Price & Donaldson, *supra*, §§1.6.7, 1.6.8 & 1.6.9.

Custody of the Will

- Andersen, *supra*, 70.
- Price & Donaldson, *supra*, §1.4.1.
- Evans I, *supra*, 106-108; 114-117.

Will Contests

- Casner & Pennell, *supra*, §3.1.2.

Articles

Overview of the Planning Process

- J. Thomas Eubank, *The Estate Lawyer Must Be Competent to Do What?*, 11 Inst. on Est. Plan. ¶1700 (1977).
- Robert H. Feldman, *Reviewing Wills and Trusts: What Planners Should Look For*, 29 Est. Plan. 299 (2002).
- Robert H. Feldman, *What to Look for in Reviewing Estate Plans (with Forms)*, 17 No. 3 Prac. Tax Law. 53 (Spring 2003).
- Gary Glober, *How to Effectively and Efficiently Interact with Grieving Clients*, 22 Prob. & Prop. 61 (July/Aug. 2008).
- John R. Price, *Professional Responsibility in Estate Planning: Progress or Paralysis?*, 21 Inst. on Est. Plan. ¶1800 (1987).
- Dean P. Shearer, *Guidelines for Reviewing and Revising an Estate Plan*, 27 Est. Plan. 164 (2000).
- William H. Soskin, *The Client Interview: A Crucial Tool in Estate Planning*, 31 Est. Plan. 294 (2004).
- Lauren J. Wolven & Susan T. Bart, *Human Issues in Estate Planning for the Family Business Owner*, 14 ALI-ABA Est. Plan. Course Materials J. 5 (Aug. 2008).

Practice Development

- Roy M. Adams, *The Economics of Estate Planning Practice: Dollars and Sense*, 28 Inst. on Est. Plan. ¶1700 (1994).
- Jonathan G. Blattmachr, *Looking Back and Looking Ahead: Preparing Your Practice for the Future: Do Not Get Behind the Change Curve*, 36 ACTEC J. 1 (Summer 2010).
- William P. Cantwell, *Estate Planning Economics: Getting a Client, Doing the Work, and Getting Paid*, 14 Inst. on Est. Plan. ¶2000 (1980).
- Douglas K. Freeman, *Guidelines for Developing and Expanding a Successful Estate Planning Practice*, 17 Est. Plan. 8 (1990).
- Wendy S. Goffe & Rochelle L. Haller, *From Zoom to Doom? Risks of Do-It-Yourself Estate Planning*, 38 Est. Plan. 27 (Apr. 2011).
- Louis S. Harrison & Emily J. Kuo, *Fees: How to Charge, Collect and Defend Them*, 148 Tr. & Est. 50 (Mar. 2009).
- Stephan R. Leimberg, *Useful Suggestions for Building an Estate Planning Practice*, 25 Est. Plan. 395 (1998).
- Russ Alan Prince, *To the Entrepreneur Goes Financial Success*, 30 Tr. & Est. 27 (Nov. 2002).

Engagement Letters

- Frank S. Berall, *Engagement Letters Clarify a Lawyer's Representation*, 30 Est. Plan. 315 (2003).
- Bruce S. Ross, *I Do, I Don't & I Won't: The Ethics of Engagement Letters*, 31 Inst. on Est. Plan. ¶3100 (1997).

Non-Engagement and Disengagement Letters

- Pamela Blake, *The Nonengagement Letter and the Disengagement Letter*, 46 Wash. St. B. News 44 (1992).
- Malcolm A. Meyer, *Disengaging an Engagement*, 10 Prob. & Prop. 5 (Mar./Apr. 1996).

Legal Malpractice

- Martin D. Begleiter, *The Gambler Breaks Even: Legal Malpractice in Complicated Estate Planning Cases*, 20 Ga. St. U. L. Rev. 277 (2003).
- Matthew W. Breetz, *The Strict Privity Rule—A Limit on Estate Planner Liability*, 46 No. 2 for the Defense 36 (Feb. 2004).
- Melissa Hutchinson Brown, *Estate Planning Malpractice: A Guide for the Alabama Practitioner*, 45 Ala. L. Rev. 611 (1994).
- Stephanie B. Casteel et al., *The Modern Estate Planning Lawyer: Avoiding the Maelstrom of Malpractice Claims*, 22 Prob. & Prop. 46 (Nov./Dec. 2008).

- Jeffrey L. Crown, *Prophylaxis for Probate Practitioners: Malpractice Protection and Malpractice Prevention*, 26 INST. ON EST. PLAN. ¶1900 (1992).
- Martha Neil, *Texas Opens Door a Crack to Estate Planner Suits*, 5 No. 2 A.B.A. J.E.-RPT. 5 (May 19, 2006).
- John T. Rogers, Jr. & Sean K. Higgins, *Statutes of Limitations for Malpractice Claims in Estate Planning*, 31 EST. PLAN. 259 (2004).

Client Competence and Will Contests

- Donna R. Bashaw, *Are In Terrorem Clauses No Longer Terrifying? If So, Can You Avoid Post-Death Litigation with Pre-Death Procedures?*, 2 NAELA J. 349 (2006).
- Gerry W. Beyer, *Drafting in Contemplation of Will Contests*, 38 No. 1 PRAC. LAW. 61 (Jan. 1992).
- Jonathan G. Blattmachr, *Reducing Estate and Trust Litigation Through Disclosure, In Terrorem Clauses, Mediation and Arbitration*, 36 ACTEC L. J. 547 (2010).
- Jack Challis, *In Terrorem Clauses: Avoiding Will Contests and Disinheritance (With Sample Provisions)*, 17 ALI-ABA EST. PLAN. COURSE MATERIALS J. 35 (June 2011).
- Pamela Champine, *Expertise and Instinct in the Assessment of Testamentary Capacity*, 51 VILL. L. REV. 25 (2006).
- Dana G. Fitzsimons, Jr., *Guardianship Litigation and Pre-Death Will Contests Are on the Rise*, 36 EST. PLAN. 39 (Jan. 2009).
- Lawrence A. Frolik, *The Challenges of Estate Planning with a Very Old Client*, 34 EST. PLAN. 3 (2007).
- Lawrence A. Frolik & Mary F. Radford, *"Sufficient" Capacity: The Contrasting Capacity Requirements for Different Documents*, 2 NAELA J. 303 (2006).
- Sharon B. Gardner et al., *Dementia and Legal Capacity: What Lawyers Should Know When Dealing with Expert Witnesses*, 6 NAELA J. 131 (Fall 2010).
- Thomas G. Gutheil, *Common Pitfalls in the Evaluation of Testamentary Capacity*, 35 J. AM. ACAD. PSYCHIATRY & L. 514 (2007).
- Howard M. Helsinger, *Advising the Trust or Estate Litigant: When to Raise or Fold*, 37 EST. PLAN. 3 (July 2010).
- John B. Huffaker & Michael B. Novakovic, *How to Determine If a Client Has Testamentary Capacity*, 21 EST. PLAN. 323 (1994).
- A. Frank Johns, *Older Clients with Diminishing Capacity and Their Advance Directives*, 39 REAL PROP. PROB. & TR. J. 107 (2004).
- Michael A. Kirtland, *Dealing with Mental Capacity Issues in Estate Planning*, 30 EST. PLAN. 192 (2003).
- David K. Leitner, *How to Assure an Estate Plan Will Be Upheld after Death*, 33 EST. PLAN. 35 (2006).

- Lela P. Love & Stewart E. Sterk, *Leaving More Than Money: Mediation Clauses in Estate Planning Documents*, 65 WASH. & LEE L. REV. 539 (2008).
- Judith G. McMullen, *Keeping Peace in the Family While You Are Resting in Peace: Making Sense of and Preventing Will Contests*, 8 MARQ. ELDER'S ADVISOR 61 (2006).
- Jennifer Moye, *Evaluating the Capacity of Older Adults: Psychological Models and Tools*, NAELA Q. 3 (Summer 2004).
- Amy K. Rosenberg, *Being of Sound Mind: Standards for Testamentary (and Other) Capacity*, 40 COLO. LAW. 89 (July 2011).
- Stephen C. Simpson, *Avoiding a Will Contest: Estate Planning and a Legislative Solution*, 37 HOUS. LAW. 36 (July/Aug. 1999).
- Robert Solomon, *Helping Clients Deal with Some of the Emotional and Psychological Issues of Estate Planning*, 18 PROB. & PROP. 56 (Mar./Apr. 2004) (advising parents considering an unequal division of their estate).
- Thomas Spahn, *Dealing with Clients of Diminished Capacity*, EXPERIENCE 41 (Winter 2007).
- Richard F. Spiegle & Spencer J. Crona, *Legal Guidelines and Methods for Evaluating Capacity*, 32 COLO. LAW. 65 (June 2003).
- Lisa M. Stern & Leonard S. Baum, *Implement Strategies to Help Guard Against Will Contests*, 37 EST. PLAN. 21 (June 2010).

Will Execution

- David K. Johns, *Will Execution Ceremonies: Securing a Client's Last Wishes*, 23 COLO. LAW. 49 (Jan. 1994).

Client Conflicts (*See also* "Joint Representation of Married Couples" in Ch. 5 reference materials and "Conflicts of Interest in Estate Administration" in Ch. 17 reference materials).

- Thomas W. Abendroth et al., *Managing the Risk of Liability in an Estate Planning Practice*, 30 EST. PLAN. 373 (2003) (includes discussion of joint representation of spouses and representation of members of a family business).
- Michael V. Bourland & David P. Dunning, *Ethics and Professional Responsibility Issues in the Family Business Arena*, Estate Planning for the Family Business Owner, SF09 ALI-ABA 343 (ALI-ABA Continuing Legal Education, Aug. 10, 2000).
- Victoria Blachly, *Making Waivers Work: Joint Representation*, SL003 ALI-ABA 429 (ALI-ABA Continuing Legal Education, July 21-22, 2005).
- Naomi Cahn & Robert Tuttle, *Dependency and Delegation: The Ethics of Marital Representation*, 22 SEATTLE U. L. REV. 97 (1998).
- Teresa Stanton Collett, *Disclosure, Discretion or Deception: The Estate Planner's Ethical Dilemma from a Unilateral Confidence*, 28 REAL PROP. PROB. & TR. J. 683 (1994).

- Teresa Stanton Collett, *The Ethics of Intergenerational Representation*, 62 FORDHAM L. REV. 1453 (1994).
- Constance Tromble Eyster, *Engagement Letters and Common Conflicts of Interest in Joint Representation*, 38 COLO. LAW. 43 (Feb. 2009).
- April A. Fegyveresi, *Conflicts of Interests in Trust & Estate Practice*, 8 GEO. J. LEGAL ETHICS 987 (1995).
- Paul Fisher, *The Power Tools of Estate Conflict Management: Recharging the Culture of Estate Conflicts, Part 1*, 24 PROB. & PROP. 42 (May/June 2010).
- Paul Fisher, *The Power Tools of Estate Conflict Management: Recharging the Culture of Estate Conflicts, Part 2*, 24 PROB. & PROP. 42 (July/Aug. 2010).
- Charles C. Groppe, *Ethics and Professional Responsibility in Estate Planning*, 340 PLI/EST 553 (PLI Order No. 8802, Dec. 7-8, 2006) (discussing ethics in connection with estates and taxation).
- Joy M. Miyasaki, *Avoiding Ethics Dilemmas for Trust and Estate Counsel (With Forms for Practitioners)*, 22 No. 1 PRAC. TAX LAW. 35 (Fall 2007).
- *Report of Special Study Committee on Professional Responsibility: Comments and Recommendations on the Lawyer's Duties in Representing Husband and Wife*, 28 REAL PROP. PROB. & TR. J. 765 (1994).
- Mary F. Radford, *Ethical Challenges in Representing Families in Family Limited Partnerships*, 35 ACTEC J. 2 (Summer 2009).
- John T. Rogers, Jr., *Who's the Client? Ethics for Trust and Estate Counsel*, 339 PLI/EST 675 (PLI Order No. 8761, Sept./Oct. 2006) (discussing such issues as conflict of interest and fiduciary duties).
- Michael H. Rubin, *The Intersection of Conflicts of Interest and Imputation of Knowledge*, 22 PROB. & PROP. 46 (Nov./Dec. 2008).
- Hollis F. Russell & Peter A. Bicks, *Joint Representation of Spouses in Estate Planning: The Saga of Advisory Opinion* 95-4, 72 FLA. B.J. 39 (Mar. 1998).
- Jay A. Soled & Herbert L. Zuckerman, *Perils of Estate Planning*, EXPERIENCE 47 (Spring 2007).
- Thomas Spahn, *Creating and Defining Joint Representations*, EXPERIENCE 45 (Spring 2007).
- G. Warren Whitaker, *Classic Issues in Family Succession Planning*, 17 PROB. & PROP. 32 (Mar./Apr. 2003).

Custody of the Will

- Gerald P. Johnston, *An Ethical Analysis of Common Estate Planning Practices—Is Good Business Bad Ethics?*, 45 OHIO ST. L.J. 57, 126-133 (1984).

IRS Circular 230 Requirements

- Roy M. Adams, *Circular 230: A Nine Hundred-Pound Gorilla*, 40 INST. ON EST. PLAN. ¶1700 (2006).
- Ronald D. Aucutt, *Circular 230: Estate Planning Issues*, SM026 ALI-ABA 1181 (ALI-ABA Continuing Legal Education, Nov. 13-17, 2006).
- Jonathan Blattmachr et al., *Circular 230 Redux: Questions of Validity and Compliance Strategies*, SL023 ALI-ABA 107 (ALI-ABA Course of Studies Materials, Sept. 2005).

CHAPTER 2

A Review of the Fundamentals of Drafting Wills

The Will and the trust (separately or in various combinations) are the two principal instruments that estate planners employ for the transmission of wealth, although, as discussed in Part D of this chapter, non-trust Will substitutes may play a significant role. This discussion assumes that the reader has other training in the law of Wills and trusts. Accordingly, this discussion omits areas of general doctrine such as capacity, undue influence, alterations and revocation, mistake, and ambiguity. This chapter instead focuses on those concepts that directly affect the drafting of client Wills. Chapters 7, 8, 9, 11, 13, and 15 address selected issues in the drafting of trusts.

A list of the basic themes in the law of Wills is short. It is important that: (a) the Will describes the recipients of the property; (b) the Will describes the property to be disposed of; (c) the Will describes the manner in which the property is to be distributed among the recipients; (d) the Will applies to the property in question (e.g., Will substitutes such as joint tenancies with rights of survivorship do not control); and (e) the Will is written and executed in accordance with required legal formalities.

A. Describing the Recipients of Property

Describing the recipients of property under a Will can often be confusing. This confusion is produced by the existence of three sets of definitions—

from the law of intestate succession, the law of Wills, and the law of trusts. These definitions are often incorrectly used interchangeably, but they sometimes correctly overlap, particularly in Wills and trusts.

1. Basic Definitions

"Heirs." This term is defined by reference to state intestate succession statutes.[1] The use of "heirs" however, is not confined to intestate applications, as one frequently encounters Wills and trusts[2] that use this terminology and incorporate the intestate succession scheme.[3] "Heirs" may include a surviving spouse, ancestors, descendants, and collateral relatives. A person's heirs are not determined until the time of death, so the use of this term in an instrument that is effective prior to the person's death may create problems of interpretation.[4]

"Issue" or "Descendants." These terms are often used interchangeably.[5] While the Uniform Probate Code (UPC) defines both terms, "descendants" is the term used in the operative sections of the UPC. In this book we will follow that convention and use "descendants" to the exclusion of "issue." However, one will still encounter the common use of the term "issue" in estate planning documents. Under the UPC and the common law applicable in most other states, the terms bear the same interpretation for Wills and trusts.[6] These terms exclude ancestors, spouses, stepchildren and collateral relatives, so one must modify the language to include other beneficiaries.[7]

A drafting issue is whether one should (a) use the terms without elaboration; (b) use the terms but provide internal definitions in the instrument; (c) use the terms but incorporate by reference the definitions of the terms in the applicable probate code as of the date of the instrument's execution; or (d) use the terms but incorporate by reference the definitions of the terms in the applicable probate code as of the relevant date (e.g., the date of termination of a trust, the date of death, the date of distribution of assets, etc.). An attorney must be acutely aware of this issue whenever using a Will or trust form. Our preference is for approach (b) or (c) or a combination of both, but in drafting long-term instruments such

1. *See, e.g.*, UPC §1-201(20); CAL. PROB. CODE §44 (West 2002); FLA. STAT. ANN. §731.201 (West Supp. 2011); MASS. ANN. LAWS ch. 190B, §1-201(21) (LexisNexis Supp. 2010); N.Y. EST. POWERS & TRUSTS LAW §§1-2.5 & 2-1.1 (McKinney 1998); TEX. PROB. CODE ANN. §3(o) (Vernon Supp. 2010). This and all subsequent chapters use an abbreviated citation format, "UPC," for the Uniform Probate Code, and unless stated otherwise the sections reflect all amendments through July 1, 2011.

2. *See, e.g.*, UPC §2-711.

3. For example, it is common for Wills or trusts to include a contingent disposition to heirs as a default if other takers do not survive.

4. *See generally* WILLIAM M. MCGOVERN ET AL., WILLS, TRUSTS AND ESTATES 466-469 (4th ed. 2010); JOEL C. DOBRIS ET AL., ESTATES AND TRUSTS 846-860 (3d ed. 2007).

5. *See, e.g.*, UPC §§1-201(9) & 1-201(24).

6. *See, e.g.*, UPC §2-708; GEORGE GLEASON BOGERT ET AL., TRUSTS AND TRUSTEES §182, at 264-306 (rev. 2d ed. 1979 & Supp. 2010); JESSE DUKEMINIER ET AL., WILLS, TRUSTS, AND ESTATES 867-869 (8th ed. 2009).

7. *See, e.g.*, CAL. PROB. CODE §50 (West 2002) & CAL. PROB. CODE §6205 (West Supp. 2009); N.Y. EST. POWERS & TRUSTS LAW §1-2.10 (McKinney 1998).

as irrevocable trusts, this comes at some risk. Without moorings to the evolving law, there is a risk of not anticipating the impact of future developments (e.g., advances in reproductive technology).

"Children" or "Grandchildren." Some instruments will describe dispositions to "children,"[8] and some will also describe dispositions to "grandchildren." For many instruments, however, the term "descendants" will be used instead to provide flexibility for the possibility of the death of class members or the addition of others (e.g., birth of great-grandchildren). Note also that "children" usually does not include stepchildren (*see infra* note 11).

"Parents." Unmarried individuals often include testamentary gifts to their parents. Stepparents present interpretative difficulties in the use of this term. UPC §1-201(32), for example, defines "parent" as the person who would take under the intestate succession statutes and excludes stepparents, foster parents, and grandparents.

"Collateral Relatives." An attorney must be extremely careful in the use of language describing gifts to collateral relatives. Half-siblings and stepsiblings present interpretation issues. "Nieces" and "nephews" "by marriage" (i.e., related by blood to one's spouse) and "aunts" and "uncles" "by marriage" (i.e., the aunt or uncle of a spouse) present other interpretation issues. For example, does an "uncle" include the spouse of an aunt of one's spouse? The UPC excludes relatives by affinity (that is, nieces, nephews, aunts, and uncles described above "by marriage") but includes relationships by the half blood with those by the whole blood (the half-siblings described above). Stepsiblings, however, are excluded.[9]

2. Complications

a. Stepchildren and Foster Children. Unless expressly provided otherwise in the Will or trust, the UPC denies stepchildren and foster children the status of "child," which in turn precludes their status as descendants.[10] The UPC definition also precludes their status as a "child" for intestate succession purposes, which would affect instruments incorporating those definitional rules. The UPC definitions apply to both Wills and trusts. In a state not adopting the UPC, one must confirm the status of these individuals in both the Wills and trusts context.[11]

8. The Uniform Probate Code provides a definition of "child" at UPC §1-201(5).

9. *See* UPC §2-705(c) & (d).

10. *See* UPC §§1-201(5) & 1-201(9). However, a stepchild (or the stepchild's descendants) may take under intestate succession (but not as a relationship by blood) to prevent escheat to the state. *See* UPC §2-103(b).

11. *See, e.g.*, Cal. Prob. Code §26 (West 2002) ("child" generally does not include a stepchild or foster child); Fla. Stat. Ann. §731.201(3) (West Supp. 2011) (for intestate succession purposes "child" does not include a foster child or a stepchild); Mass. Ann. Laws ch. 190B, §1-201(5) (LexisNexis Supp. 2010) ("child" does not include a stepchild or a foster child); Tex. Prob. Code Ann. §41(b) (Vernon Supp. 2010) (half-bloods of an intestate receive half of what the whole blood heirs receive unless all collateral kindred are of half blood).

b. Adopted Children. Parting with the common law, the UPC, with exceptions, treats an adopted child as a child of the adopting parents.[12] Under the UPC, this rule is incorporated into the definitions of "child" and "descendant," so it percolates into the law of Wills and trusts.[13] Although many families treat adoptees on an equal footing with blood descendants, "adult adoptions" (i.e., the adoption of a person who is an adult) can create opportunities for chicanery and litigation and need to be addressed in the instrument with care.[14]

EXERCISE 2-1

STEPCHILDREN AND ADOPTED INDIVIDUALS

A. Draft language that includes a stepchild as a "child" of the decedent.
B. Does the following language adequately address possible concerns about the manipulative use of adult adoptions?

> *An adopted child, and the adopted child's descendants by blood or adoption, shall be considered descendants of the adopting person and the adopting person's ancestors only if the adoption is by a legal proceeding commenced while the adopted child is less than 25 years of age.*

c. Afterborn Takers. UPC §2-104 provides that an individual in gestation is treated as living at the relevant time if the individual lives 120 hours or more after birth. Under the UPC structure, this is confined to a rule of intestate succession unless the Will referred to the individual as a member of a class, such as "my children."[15] However, UPC §2-302 makes special provision for children omitted from a parent's Will, and that provision would address this issue. Nevertheless, a drafter of any Will should ensure that the instrument anticipates this event. The UPC omitted children provision does not apply to trusts, so the drafter would need to refer to the law of trusts for an answer or address the issue in the instrument. Our preference is for an express treatment in the instrument. Addressing afterborn takers (particularly those conceived after the death of a parent) has become a more complex issue due to the continued development of advanced medical procedures discussed in the next section.

12. *See* UPC §2-118(a).
13. *See* UPC §§1-201(5) & 1-201(9).
14. *See, e.g.*, UPC §2-705(f) (in construing the dispositive provisions of a Will or trust of a transferor who is not the adopting parent, an adopted individual is not considered the child of the adopting parent unless the adoption took place before the adoptee reached 18 years of age, the adoptive parent was the adoptee's stepparent or foster parent, or the adoptive parent functioned as a parent of the adoptee before the adoptee reached 18 years of age).
15. UPC §2-705(g)(1) provides that a "child in utero is treated as living at that time if the child lives 120 hours after birth."

EXERCISE 2-2

AFTERBORN INDIVIDUALS

A. Does the following language adequately address the status of afterborn takers?

> *A person who is conceived before, but born alive after, an event, shall be treated as if he or she had been born alive at the time of the event.*

B. Testator has two children, Cynthia A. Smith (born April 1, ten years ago) and John Q. Smith (born December 2, four years ago). Draft Will language that would include Cynthia and John, as well as any newborn children, as Testator's children.

C. Concerning Testator from Part B, draft Will language that would include Cynthia and John as Testator's only children.

d. Advanced Medical Procedures. Family law and trusts and estates law is still developing concerning the status of children who are the product of various fertility and conception techniques (commonly known as Assisted Reproductive Technology or Artificial Reproductive Technology or "ART"), such as artificial insemination, in vitro fertilization, the use of surrogates, and frozen semen or frozen embryos (including those contributed by a deceased individual while alive or extracted shortly after death).[16] Resources discussing these issues are collected in Part H.

The UPC grapples with these issues in the trusts and estates context principally in §§2-120 (assisted reproduction including placement of eggs, sperm, or embryos), 2-121 (children born to "gestational carriers," otherwise known as surrogates), and 2-705 (amended rules for class gifts).[17] The UPC rules do not necessarily coordinate with, or are broad enough to address, the family law implications of the ART measures, which are beyond our scope. The UPC rules are quite technical, and, if past experience with statutes of this type is any guide, the rules could be amended in the future to address unforeseen technical concerns or advances in ART.

16. The Uniform Parentage Act deals with the "Child of Assisted Reproduction" in Article 7 and the "Gestational Agreement" in Article 8. *See* UNIF. PARENTAGE ACT (amended 2002) Article 7, 9B U.L.A. 354 (2001 & Supp. 2010) & UNIF. PARENTAGE ACT (amended 2002) Article 8, 9B U.L.A. 360 (2001 & Supp. 2010). *See* Morgan Kirkland Wood, *It Takes a Village: Considering the Other Interests at Stake When Extending Inheritance Rights to Posthumously Conceived Children*, 44 GA. L. REV. 873, 889-893 (2010) (discussing statutes in California, Colorado, Delaware, Florida, Louisiana, North Dakota, Ohio, Texas, Utah, Virginia, and Washington, plus the UPC, dealing with posthumously conceived children).

17. *See, e.g.*, MCGOVERN ET AL., *supra* note 4, at 117-121 (discussing ART and the UPC provisions); Lee-ford Tritt, *Technical Correction or Tectonic Shift: Competing Default Rule Theories Under the New Uniform Probate Code*, 61 ALA. L. REV. 273 (2010) (discussing the UPC ART provisions); Susan N. Gary, *We Are Family: The Definition of Parent and Child for Succession Purposes*, 34 ACTEC J. 171 (2008) (discussing the UPC provisions).

The concerns of two groups dominate this area from an estate planning perspective: (a) the impact of ART on the parents' testamentary transfers; and (b) the impact of ART on the transfers of others, usually other family members.

Much of the trusts and estates litigation has concerned the first group, principally in terms of whether posthumously conceived children qualify for Social Security survivor benefits with reference to state intestate succession law.[18] Beyond Social Security, the Will or trust of the individual would require attention to matters such as clear disposition and use (including possible destruction) of the preserved genetic material.[19] The attorney should examine any agreements that the individual executed with an ART provider or a partner to the ART procedure, inasmuch as those agreements may conflict with (or, on the other hand, buttress) the Will or trust disposition of the material.[20] Beyond the scope of this book, the individual would also need to coordinate the inter vivos disposition of the genetic material and the family law consequences stemming from its use, particularly if the individual parts ways with another partner to the ART procedure.[21] If children are born from the ART procedure, careful attention must be given to the definition of "children" to effectuate the parents' intent that children already born through ART (or to be born by ART posthumously) are included or excluded.

With respect to the impact of ART on the transfers of other family members in defining their "descendants," the relevant jurisdiction may not have yet adopted a statutory solution, and a drafter may not be content to abide by evolving rules pronounced by courts.[22] In such a jurisdiction, a drafter could incorporate by reference the UPC rules or craft provisions

18. *See, e.g.*, Finley v. Astrue, 601 F. Supp. 2d 1092 (E.D. Ark. 2009) (Social Security benefits denied for child born through posthumous implantation of embryos following the father's death); Khabbaz v. Commissioner, Social Security Administration, 155 N.H. 798, 930 A.2d 1180 (2007) (Social Security benefits denied for child born through posthumous artificial insemination using deceased father's sperm); Gillett-Netting v. Barnhart, 371 F.3d 593 (9th Cir. 2004) (Social Security benefits granted for child born through posthumous in vitro fertilization using deceased father's sperm); Woodward v. Commissioner of Social Security, 435 Mass. 536, 760 N.E.2d 257 (2002) (Social Security benefits granted for children born through posthumous artificial insemination using deceased father's sperm).

19. *See, e.g.*, Hecht v. Superior Court, 16 Cal. App. 4th 836, 20 Cal. Rptr. 2d 275 (Cal. Ct. App. 1993) (devise of decedent's sperm bank deposits to his girlfriend). In *Hecht* the Will stated: "I bequeath all right, title, and interest that I may have in any specimens of my sperm stored with any sperm bank or similar facility to Deborah Ellen Hecht." *Id.* at 276. Although the decedent executed a "Specimen Storage Agreement," the release of the sperm to Ms. Hecht was unclearly stated.

20. *See, e.g.*, Estate of Kievernagel v. Kievernagel et al., 166 Cal. App. 4th 1024, 83 Cal. Rptr. 3d 311 (Cal. Ct. App. 2008) (The "IVF Back-Up Sperm Storage and Consent Agreement" stated that upon the decedent's death, the sperm was to be discarded; in the absence of any intent to the contrary, that language controlled in spite of the widow's request for the sperm.).

21. *See, e.g.*, Dominic J. Campisi et al., *Heirs in the Freezer: Bronze Age Biology Confronts Biotechnology*, 36 ACTEC J. 179, 234 (Summer 2010) (Sample "Model IVF Contract" providing for disposition of genetic material upon divorce, separation, death or incapacity of one or both parties, abandonment, and end of a set term of years.).

22. *See, e.g.*, Martin B., 17 Misc. 3d 198, 841 N.Y.S.2d 207 (N.Y. Sur. Ct. 2007) (status of posthumously conceived grandchildren as "issue" and "descendants" of the settlor grandparent).

drawn from their principles, particularly in providing evidence of intent and prescribing class closing deadlines. On the other hand, even in an adopting jurisdiction, a drafter (and client) may not be comfortable with the UPC rules.[23] Faced with these concerns, the drafter may be left with the challenging task of fashioning a comprehensive response in the instrument. [24]

3. Survival and Lapse of Gifts

a. General Rule. The common law provided that if a designated recipient of a gift did not survive the decedent, the gift to the designated recipient failed or "lapsed."

b. Survival Clauses. The common law rule, which looks to the moment of death, creates controversies in the case of simultaneous death and may fail to carry out the decedent's wishes of "property only for the living" or subject the property to "double probate" in the case of death of the recipient soon after the death of the decedent. For intestate succession purposes, the UPC generally requires that an individual who fails to survive the decedent by 120 hours be deemed to have predeceased the decedent.[25] The UPC extends the 120-hour survival rule to both Wills and trusts.[26] However, UPC §2-701 bows to the specific terms of the instrument, so it is common for instruments to require survival for a longer period, such as 30 days.[27] Some state statutes prescribe no statutory survival period, and some prescribe different periods.[28]

23. The UPC provisions can produce a child with no genetic link to either parent. If a third-party transferor of property (e.g., an ancestor) is uncomfortable with that fact (which would also manifest in most adoptions), instrument language could enforce the third-party's intent. *See, e.g.*, Bruce A. Fowler & Teresa C. Baird, *Frozen in Time: Planning for the Posthumously Conceived Child*, 37 COLO. LAW. 45, 53 (June 2008) (sample trust provision referring to assisted reproduction "whereby such descendant provided either the sperm or the egg"). Professor Tritt expresses only cautious acceptance of the UPC default rules and recommends that attorneys expressly define "parent," "child," "descendant," etc. for each testator. *See* Tritt, *supra* note 17, at 334-336. Professor Pennell recommends that attorneys ask their clients about the impact of ART, particularly the posthumous conception aspect of providing "a blank check to an in-law child to make more beneficiaries." Jeffrey N. Pennell, *Planning for the Next Generation(s) of Clients: It's Not Your Father's Buick, Anymore*, 34 ACTEC J. 2, 15 (Summer 2008).

24. *See, e.g.*, JEFFREY A. SCHOENBLUM, PAGE ON THE LAW OF WILLS, vol. 7 (Forms), ch. 26F, Forms 26.02 & 26.02A (2010) (one form addresses children born of artificial insemination or embryo transfer, regardless of source; the other form requires that a child or descendant contribute genetic material to the ART procedure).

25. *See* UPC §2-104.

26. *See* UPC §2-702.

27. *See, e.g.*, JOHN R. PRICE & SAMUEL A. DONALDSON, PRICE ON CONTEMPORARY ESTATE PLANNING, §4.15.4, Form 4-6 (providing example of a 60-day general survivorship requirement) (2011). In drafting marital deduction clauses for federal estate taxation purposes, one can encounter up to six-month survival clauses due to IRC §2056(b)(3). However, this can produce an adverse estate tax result if the plan requires that some assets flow to the "surviving" spouse in order to use the IRC §2010 applicable exclusion amount. The Deceased Spousal Unused Exclusion Amount can mitigate some of those consequences; see Chapter 11.

28. *See, e.g.*, MASS. ANN. LAWS ch. 191B, §11 (LexisNexis 1994) (prescribing a 30-day survival period for statutory Wills).

*c. **Antilapse Statutes.*** The language of an instrument may modify the impact of lapse on account of the beneficiary's death by specifying alternate beneficiaries. In addition, many state statutes, as a rule of construction, override the common law doctrine of lapse such that a substitute gift is created. These "antilapse statutes" generally require a limited familial relationship between the decedent and the devisee who fails to survive. UPC §2-603(b), for example, provides that if the devisee fails to survive the decedent and is a grandparent, a descendant of a grandparent, or a stepchild of the decedent, and the deceased devisee leaves surviving descendants, a "substitute gift" is created in the devisee's surviving descendants.

The UPC provision does not apply in the case of a contrary intention in the instrument, but that intention must be very strongly stated, because language such as "if he survives me" or "my surviving children" is *not*, in the absence of additional evidence, a sufficient indication of an intent to override the antilapse provisions.[29] Accordingly, under the UPC, if one wishes to preclude application of the antilapse provisions, one might state "to A if she survives me, and if she does not, to B's descendants" or "to A if she survives me, and if A does not survive me, this gift shall lapse." The official comments to UPC §2-603 are quite helpful in drafting language to preclude application of the antilapse provisions.

The application of antilapse statutes is complex at best, and an examination of statutes outside the UPC is beyond the scope of this book. Not all state statutes provide for substitute gifts. Express drafting will usually override the common law lapse doctrine as well as antilapse statutes producing a substitute gift. One must, however, be aware of peculiar statutes like the UPC that require very determined drafting in order to override the statutory scheme for substitute gifts.

EXERCISE 2-3

LAPSE PROVISIONS

Would the following Will language override the UPC antilapse provisions?

> *Antilapse. I direct that the antilapse statutes of MyState and other states shall not be applicable to this Will.*

In our experience, a failure to deal with lapse is often the hallmark of tentative and poor overall drafting that does not anticipate other outcomes, including the possibility of the death of the designated beneficiary before the testator. This would be the case even in a state that does not follow the strong antilapse presumption of the UPC. Our approach to

29. *See* UPC §2-603(b)(3).

drafting in general is to control the outcome through clear language, and this area is no different. In drafting any bequest, the drafter must determine (a) if the survival period needs to be extended (e.g., "if he survives me" versus "if he survives me for 30 days"); (b) the disposition of the gift if the primary taker fails to survive (e.g., "and if he does not survive me for 30 days, then the property shall pass to Jennifer Amber Jones, if she survives me for 30 days"); (c) the disposition of the property if the alternate taker fails to survive (e.g., "and if Jennifer Amber Jones does not survive me for 30 days, this gift shall lapse and pass as a part of my residuary estate"); and (d) whether to include an ultimate "catch-all disposition," which may direct the property to formula beneficiaries such as those persons who would take the property by intestate succession. These steps force the drafter to consider the "no takers" issue and, most important, to discuss it with the client.[30]

d. Class Gifts. Class gifts enjoyed different treatment under the common law because if a member of the class failed to survive the decedent, that member's share was divided among the other surviving members of the class rather than becoming part of the general residue of the decedent's estate (or in the case of a lapsed residuary bequest, passing by intestate succession). The interpretation of whether a class gift existed was often uncertain. The UPC antilapse statute overrides the common law rule by creating a substitute gift in the surviving descendants of any deceased class member devisee in certain close familial situations, rather than dividing the lapsed amount among the other surviving members of the class.[31] Gifts to "issue," "descendants," "heirs of the body," "heirs," "heirs at law," "next of kin," "relatives," or "family" are not subject to the antilapse provisions because the definitions themselves incorporate implicit intergenerational survival rules.[32]

B. Describing the Property

1. Plain Meaning, Mistakes, and Ambiguity

While the strict application of the plain meaning rule in Will construction is increasingly riddled by judicial exceptions and distinctions, which we

30. In describing survivors, the attorney must be careful to identify the time at which the determination is to be made. A residuary clause to "my grandchildren living at the time of my death" is not a problem. However, if the "survivors" are the remainderpersons following a life estate or term of years, incomplete drafting may raise the issue of whether "surviving" is determined at the time of the decedent's death or at a later termination or distribution date. *See* McGovern et al., *supra* note 4, at 458-459. *Compare* UPC §2-711 (the property passes to the persons under the intestate succession law as if the designated individual died when the disposition is to take effect in possession or enjoyment).

31. *See* UPC §§2-603(b)(2) & 2-604(b).

32. *See* UPC §§2-603(b)(2), 2-708 & 2-711.

will not attempt to restate, reading the cases is a reminder of how carefulness in drafting can avoid the uncertainty and expense of litigation. Litigation breeders include sloppy use of terms like "per stirpes"; incorrect or incomplete names of charities or persons; general versus specific references to spouses (e.g., Mrs. Brown or Elisabeth Meritt Brown — what happens if Mr. and Mrs. Brown divorce?); inconsistent references to one individual (e.g., "my wife" in one portion of the instrument and simply "Mary" in another portion); uncertain references to the role of an individual or to the individual himself or herself (e.g., "I give $5,000 to Jack, my trustee": is that a gift in trust or a gift to Jack individually?); erroneous relationships (e.g., "my son Elizabeth": is that a gift to the son or to Elizabeth?); incorrect real property descriptions; incorrect fractional or percentage allocations (e.g., "25 percent to each of my five children"); and so forth. Such mistakes are multiplied by the widespread use of computer-aided document drafting, which can replicate the same mistake in a host of kindred documents.

2. Ademption and Accessions

The common law provided that if bequeathed property did not exist at the time of the decedent's death, the gift was "adeemed" and void. While that has some practical appeal, it can defeat the intent of the decedent, if, for example, the decedent wanted a beneficiary to receive his or her principal residence rather than just the described piece of real estate that was the principal residence at the time the Will was executed. Some of these issues can be addressed through drafting. Interpretative doctrines and statutes address others.

States that strictly apply the "identity theory" will consider a gift adeemed if the decedent does not own it at the time of death. New York law, for example, generally follows an identity theory approach.[33]

Statutes such as UPC §2-606 apply the more flexible "intent theory," which attempts to carry out the decedent's intent. In its most limited application, the intent theory would pass to the beneficiary the identifiable proceeds from the disposition of the property, such as the balance of the unpaid purchase price, unpaid condemnation awards, unpaid casualty insurance proceeds, and property received in foreclosure of a gifted secured obligation.[34] California law, for example, generally follows the UPC in that respect.[35] More liberal applications of the intent theory would extend to property received in replacement for specifically gifted property or provide a cash bequest as a substitute for property previously disposed of if it can be shown that the ademption would be inconsistent

33. *See* N.Y. Est. Powers & Trusts Law §§1-2.17, 3-4.2, 3-4.3, 3-4.4 & 3-4.5 (McKinney 1998).

34. *See, e.g.*, UPC §2-606(a)(1)-(4).

35. *See* Cal. Prob. Code §§21131 & 21132 (West Supp. 2007).

with the decedent's plan of distribution.[36] An attorney must be keenly aware of these doctrines in dealing with specific bequests of property, particularly in light of the almost inevitable turnover in real estate assets, stocks and bonds, art, and automobiles.

A related issue is the doctrine of "accessions"—whether a gift of specific property includes additions to the property. Improvements to real estate are usually tied to property law doctrines of fixtures versus moveable items. The strongest application of the accessions doctrine is generally found in connection with securities and the products of stock dividends, stock splits, dividend reinvestment programs, and reorganizations.

C. The Division of Property

Gifts to "my descendants" are quite common in Wills and trusts, but more direction is generally required. For example, if a grandparent is gifting property to "descendants," what happens if some children predecease the grandparent but leave surviving grandchildren? The law developed answers to these questions, but not without some confusion. Much of the confusion stems from the scrivener's careless use of terms such as "per stirpes" without appreciating the conflicting interpretations of such expressions. Such varying interpretations may be further compounded due to the context in which the term is used. For example, if used in a Will or trust, the common law might supply the rules of construction, but if used in reference to intestate succession, the terms may be defined by statute.

1. Strict Per Stirpes or English Per Stirpes

Under this distribution scheme, the shares of an estate are determined at the highest level of descendants (that is, the first generation below the decedent/donor), irrespective of whether anyone is still surviving at that level. For example, assume that the decedent had two children, both of whom are dead. One child is survived by a child (decedent's grandchild #1) and the other child is survived by two children (decedent's grandchildren #2 and #3). The estate is divided into two equal "shares" so one-half is inherited by grandchild #1, and the other one-half is split between grandchildren #2 and #3. The distinction will become clearer with the next example.

36. *See, e.g.*, UPC §2-606(a)(5) & (6).

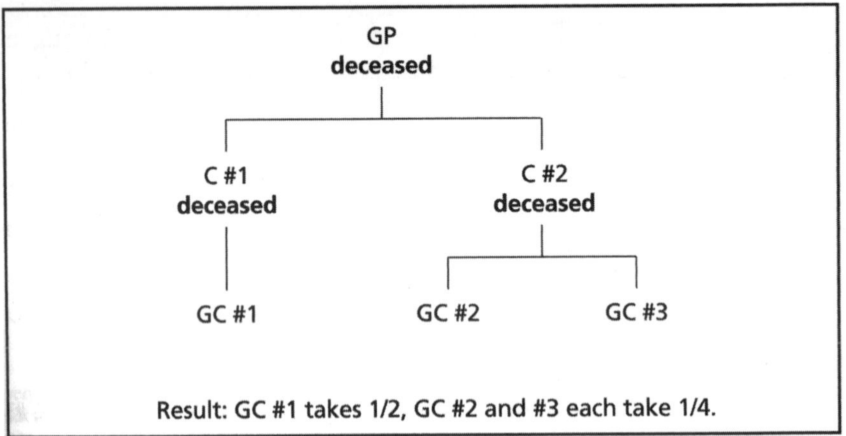

2. Modern Per Stirpes or American Per Stirpes or Per Capita with Representation

Under this system, the shares in the example above would be determined at the closest generation to the decedent with at least one descendant living at the time of the decedent's death. Grandchildren #1, #2, and #3 would each take a third.

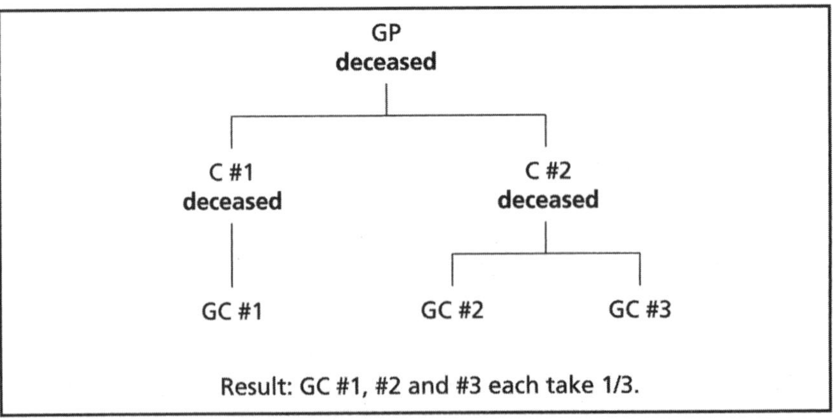

3. Uniform Probate Code Per Capita at Each Generation (Referred to as "By Representation" in the UPC)

As in modern per stirpes, the division is made at the first level below the decedent with any surviving descendants. However, the shares of all deceased persons at that level are combined in one pot and divided equally among members of the next generation who do not have parents surviving. In the example above, the same result as under modern per stirpes would be produced. However, assume that the grandparent had a third child (child #3) who survived. Under strict per stirpes, grandchild #1 would take one-third, grandchildren #2 and #3 would take one-sixth each, and child #3 would take one-third. Modern per stirpes would produce the same result. The UPC per capita at each generation rule would give one-third to child #3 and split two-thirds of the estate among grandchildren #1, #2, and #3, with each receiving two-ninths of the estate. The official comments to UPC §2-106 provide some helpful illustrations of the impact of the three systems.

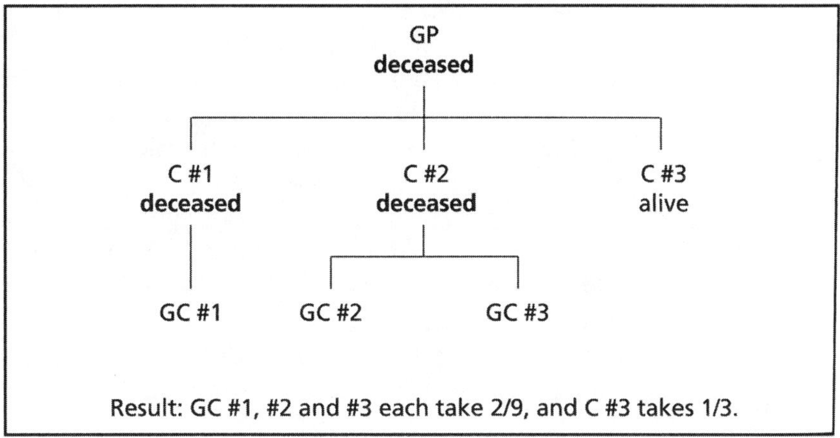

Result: GC #1, #2 and #3 each take 2/9, and C #3 takes 1/3.

4. Drafting

The majority rule provides that the use of phrases such as "per stirpes" in a Will invokes the interpretations from the applicable intestate succession provisions. As a drafting matter, however, one should not leave this to the uncertainties of "the majority rule." UPC §2-709 applies the UPC §2-106 per capita at each generation intestate rules to Wills and trusts calling for distribution either "by representation" or "per capita at each generation." Common usage often applied "by representation" and "per stirpes" interchangeably, so the UPC approach may produce some unexpected results. Under the UPC, distributions "per stirpes" are governed by strict or English per stirpes rules.

Empirical studies suggest that most clients prefer the modern per stirpes rule to the English per stirpes rule.[37] If the competing rules could produce different distributions in the client's situation, either at the time of signing the document or in the future, the attorney needs to explain the different options to the client.

5. Abatement and Apportionment

The doctrine of "abatement" provides that if there is insufficient property in the estate to satisfy all bequests, specific bequests are preserved, and

37. *See* Dukeminier et al., *supra* note 6, at 88.

residuary and then general bequests are reduced. The instrument may state an order of abatement; in the absence of such direction, a statute such as UPC §3-902 supplies an abatement order.

"Apportionment" deals with the issue of which beneficiaries bear the debts and obligations of the estate, including taxes, that are to be paid during administration of the estate.[38] The general common law rule provided that the residuary bequest, as a residue, bore the debts and expenses of the estate. Federal and state wealth transfer taxes are sometimes treated differently, however, because the taxes are imposed on the value of the property that each beneficiary receives, irrespective of whether it is a specific, general, or residuary bequest. Some states follow "equitable apportionment," in which even a specific bequest will be reduced by its proportionate amount of the overall estate tax burden. UPC §3-916, for example, offers such a rule, and it also applies to property passing outside of the Will by reason of the decedent's death. New York law, for example, generally follows an equitable apportionment scheme.[39] On the other hand, Florida law provides a default rule that taxes shall be paid by the residuary estate.[40] This is a critical issue in drafting instruments for estates subject to wealth transfer taxes.[41]

Our experience is that, generally, clients prefer that taxes be applied proportionately against all assets within the probate estate *except* specific gifts or general bequests of modest sums (that is, "I give $1,000 to Amanda" should mean Amanda gets $1,000, not possibly $957.42 after taxes). If the nonprobate transfers of an estate are large, clients are also likely to want apportionment to apply to these nonprobate assets.

PRACTICE POINTER: If a client instructs you to provide for a gift of specific property, you should consider and discuss with your client at least three issues: (a) what happens if the property is sold or exchanged (*ademption*)?; (b) if the property is or could become encumbered, is the beneficiary to receive it subject to or free of the encumbrance (*exoneration*)?;[42] (c) if the property is part of an estate subject to state or federal wealth transfer taxes, should the bequest or devise be reduced by its share of those taxes (*apportionment*)?

38. Not all estate obligations are necessarily retired. A related issue is whether specific bequests are to be received free of debt or subject to existing encumbrances. This invokes the doctrine of "exoneration." *See, e.g.*, UPC §2-607.

39. *See* N.Y. EST. POWERS & TRUSTS LAW §2-1.8(c)(1) (McKinney Supp. 2011).

40. *See* FLA. STAT. ANN. §733.817(5) (West Supp. 2011).

41. *See, e.g.*, A. JAMES CASNER & JEFFREY N. PENNELL, ESTATE PLANNING §3.3.21.2 (6th ed. 1995 & Supp. 2009-2010) (listing items to consider when drafting a tax clause); Daniel B. Evans, *Tax Clauses to Die for*, 20 PROB. & PROP. 38 (July/Aug. 2006).

42. It has been our experience that many retired individuals still have mortgages on their personal residences. In some cases the mortgages are so-called "reverse mortgages" created to withdraw a retirement cash stream from the home. Those obligations are typically extinguished in accordance with the terms of the mortgage upon the earlier to occur of the sale of the home or the death of the surviving joint tenant. In other cases the mortgages are "cash back" refinancing, raising issues of where the proceeds flow if there are multiple beneficiaries of the estate.

6. Spousal Protections

The testator's division of property among intended recipients is not unfettered. In a community property law jurisdiction, the testator will not own, nor be able to devise, the testator's spouse's share of community property. In common law property jurisdictions, absent a Marital Agreement the "elective share" must be respected. Planning in light of spousal protections is discussed in Chapters 4 and 9.

7. Trusts

Although this chapter is largely devoted to principles of Wills, the potential impact of trusts cannot be ignored. A preliminary question for any client is whether the property will pass to the beneficiary outright or in trust. If a trust is desirable, it can be created under the Will (a "testamentary trust"), or the client might transfer assets to a trust established prior to the decedent's death (an "inter vivos trust") by their Will (a so-called "pourover Will" or "pourover clause"). Trusts may be created in other contexts, such as the irrevocable trust (discussed in Chapters 8, 11, and 13) and the revocable trust (discussed in Chapter 15).

D. Will Substitutes

Experienced estate planners often review elaborate existing Wills that have little impact on the transmission of wealth. Particularly with married couples, the transfer of the bulk of the assets is often accomplished as a matter of law through joint tenancy survivorship, joint ownership of financial accounts, the use of "payable-on-death" or "transfer-on-death" designations, beneficiary deeds, and life insurance and retirement account beneficiary designations. These issues are addressed in Chapter 5. Because it is an interviewing, planning, and drafting issue, the attorney must be aware that this is often the case and must appreciate when it may be appropriate to advise the client to revise those arrangements so that the client's Will controls and directs their distribution (federal wealth transfer tax issues are often an issue in that regard; see Chapter 11).

E. Execution Formalities

Much of the estate planner's work will involve Wills generated and printed by computers to be executed in accordance with prescribed formalities. Holographic Wills are generally not a desired tool of the professional estate planner except in exigent circumstances, such as advising a client *in extremis* and removed from access to witnesses. While requirements vary from state to state, most states require at least the following: a written instrument (i.e., not audio or videotape), signed by the testator (or someone directed by the testator to sign on his or her behalf), and witnessed by at least two other individuals.[43] While not required, as a practical matter virtually all states permit by statute some form of a "self-proving" affidavit that the testator and witnesses sign under oath before a notary public to facilitate the probate of the Will without requiring the testimony of the witnesses in court concerning the execution of the Will.[44] However, in a Will contest, where issues of capacity and undue influence are often raised, the testimony of the witnesses may nonetheless be useful and be required.

In some states, an interested witness may void the Will, or at least the gift to that witness. Compare UPC §2-505, which does not invalidate the Will or any of its provision due to an interested witness. Under California law, by comparison, a Will that devises property to a witness is still valid, but it creates a presumption that the witness used duress, menace, fraud, or undue influence. If the witness cannot overcome that presumption, he or she may still take that portion of the devise that does not exceed the share he or she would have been entitled to if the decedent had died intestate.[45] Massachusetts law voids the gift to the witness.[46] Illinois, New York, and Texas law also voids the gift to the witness, but the witness may be entitled to an amount referring to his or her share of the intestate estate.[47]

While UPC §2-504, for example, contemplates a one-step self-proving affidavit, where the testator and the witnesses sign the instrument only once (*see, e.g.*, Case Study 2-1), some states and attorneys use two-step self-proving Wills. In one version of the two-step affidavit, the testator signs the Will and then the testator and the witnesses all sign a combined attestation and affidavit (*see, e.g.*, Form B in the Forms Supplement). In another, more elaborate version of the two-step procedure, each group signs twice: the Will as such is signed and witnessed by all and then the affidavit is signed by all. An attorney using either two-step approach must supervise the execution ceremony even more carefully, since oversights can easily occur. A sample Will execution checklist is included in Part L of Chapter 1.

43. *See, e.g.*, UPC §2-502 (two witnesses or, since the 2008 amendments to the UPC, acknowledged by the testator before a notary public or other individual authorized by law to take acknowledgments); CAL. PROB. CODE §6110 (West Supp. 2009); FLA. STAT. ANN. §732.502 (West 2010); 755 ILL. COMP. STAT. ANN. 5/4-3 (West 2007); MASS. ANN. LAWS ch. 190B, §2-502 (West Supp. 2010); N.Y. EST. POWERS & TRUSTS LAW §3-2.1 (McKinney 1998); TEX. PROB. CODE ANN. §59 (Vernon 2003). Vermont law required three witnesses until 2005, but now requires two witnesses. *See* VT. STAT. ANN. tit. 14 §5 (Supp. 2010). *Compare* Frank S. Berall, *Oral Trusts and Wills: Are They Valid?*, 33 EST. PLAN. 17 (2006); Gerry W. Beyer & Claire G. Hargrove, *Digital Wills: Has the Time Come for Wills to Join the Digital Revolution?* 33 Ohio N.U. L. Rev. 865 (2007).

44. *See, e.g.*, UPC §2-504, which provides for a self-proved Will, and Form B in the Forms Supplement, which uses a self-proving execution format.

45. *See* CAL. PROB. CODE §6112 (West 2009).

46. *See* MASS. ANN. LAWS ch. 190B, §2-505 (LexisNexis Supp. 2010) (voiding gift unless there are two other witnesses who aren't similarly benefited by the Will).

47. *See* 755 ILL. COMP. STAT. ANN. 5/4-6 (West 2007); N.Y. EST. POWERS & TRUSTS LAW §3-3.2 (McKinney 1998); TEX. PROB. CODE ANN. §61 (Vernon 2003).

F. Drafting Style

Much has been written about good legal drafting skills, and there are a number of potentially conflicting themes encompassed by "good drafting." Many drafters consider "plain language" and the absence of legalese as a goal. One can quickly read the first page or two of a Will and form a pretty accurate impression of the scrivener in that regard. On the other hand, there is some unavoidable technical language to the craft (for example, the interpretation of "per stirpes") that becomes lengthier and possibly technically inaccurate with simplification efforts. While that is not a defense of perpetuating "boilerplate," one must recognize that many laypersons do not care to read their entire estate planning instruments, so writing for that audience at the expense of technical accuracy can be counterproductive.[48]

Apart from a spare and efficient drafting style that eschews elaborate and lengthy exposition and impenetrable legalese, an attorney must draft clearly to anticipate ambiguities. At the next level, an attorney must draft technically and be cognizant of the issues that turn upon language, whether from a tax standpoint or through application of special doctrines such as the Rule Against Perpetuities.

We have included herein, in Part H, set out hereinbelow, certain citations to articles on good drafting. Pardon our attempt at humor in the preceding sentence, but one sign of possibly turgid drafting is the use of words with "here" as the root, such as "hereby," "herein," "hereinabove," "hereinbelow," and "hereinafter."

G. CASE STUDY 2-1

The Last Will and Testament of Alice Goodwin Smith

REVIEW OF A CLIENT'S CURRENT WILL

Alice Goodwin Smith is an elderly widow born January 15, [age 88]. A copy of her current Will, executed five years ago, follows. The Will is not a good piece of drafting; it suffers from various problems of structure and language. The exercises that follow it will address some of those issues.

48. It is for this reason that the authors prefer to structure documents so that most, if not all, of the variable, client-specific information (e.g., personal representative nominees, trustee nominees, guardians, etc.) is included in the beginning pages of a document. By doing so, the information is more quickly and easily located *and* it is more likely the client will read the text.

LAST WILL AND TESTAMENT OF ALICE GOODWIN SMITH

I, Alice Goodwin Smith, a resident of MyCounty, MyState, being of sound mind and memory, do hereby revoke any prior Wills and codicils made by me and do hereby make, publish, and declare this to be my last Will and testament.

I. Family

My spouse was Charles Gordon Smith, deceased as of February 18, [10 years ago]. My children now living are John Aston Smith, born June 24, [age 60], Elisabeth Barnes Smith, born January 15, [age 56], Alice Thayer Jones, born August 28, [age 54], and Rebecca Simpson Smith-Brown, born September 15, [age 52]. Any reference in my Will to my children is to such children, excluding John Aston Smith, as well as any children subsequently legally adopted by me. Any reference in my Will to my descendants is to my children and their descendants. I know that I have a son, John Aston Smith, of MyCity, MyState, but I intentionally make no provisions in this Will for him. Any reference to my children shall be deemed to exclude the said John Aston Smith.

II. Tangible Personal Property

I give all my household goods, personal effects, and other articles of tangible personal property not used in a trade or business, together with any insurance policies covering such property and claims under such policies, in accordance with a written statement that I may prepare describing the property and the persons who are to receive it. If for any reason no such written statement is in existence at my death, or to the extent such written statement fails to dispose of all of such property effectively, I give such property not disposed of, to my children, but not to their descendants, to be divided among them as they shall agree. In case my children do not agree upon the division of such property within three months after the appointment of my personal representative, my personal representative shall make the division. All expenses of storage, packing, shipping, delivery, and insurance or of sale shall be paid as expenses of administration.

III. Specific Bequests

A. I give to my daughter Elisabeth Barnes Smith, but not to her descendants, my 1981 Honda Accord Hatchback LX automobile.
B. I give to my daughter Rebecca Simpson Smith-Brown the sum of $25,000.00.
C. I give to my daughter Alice Thayer Jones the sum of $25,000.00, if she survives me. If she does not survive me this gift shall lapse.
D. I give to my daughter Alice Thayer Jones the sum of $10,000, to be held and applied by her as trustee, for the care and benefit of my beloved Labrador dog, Jacob. Such trustee shall apply the income, and invade corpus as necessary, of such trust as required for the reasonable and customary expenses of Jacob's care, including, by way of illustration and not limitation, pet food, collars and leashes, vaccinations, brushes, sleeping pads, veterinary charges, and temporary kennel fees (inasmuch as the trustee shall also in the normal course serve as custodian of Jacob in her home).
E. I give to my church, Saint Mary (1221 Cascade Avenue, MyCity, MyState 80000), the sum of $2,000.
F. I give the sum of $50,000, to be divided equally among my grandchildren surviving at the time of the distribution of my estate.

IV. Residuary Estate

I give all the rest and residue of my estate, including property referred to above that is not effectively disposed of, to my descendants by representation. I do not exercise any power of appointment by the provisions of this article.

V. Appointment of Fiduciaries

I nominate my daughter Elisabeth Barnes Smith as my personal representative. If she fails or ceases to act as my personal representative, I nominate my daughter Alice Thayer Jones as my personal representative.

VI. Fiduciaries' Powers

A. My fiduciaries may perform every act reasonably necessary to administer my estate and any trust established under my Will. They may partition, sell, exchange, grant, convey, deliver, assign, transfer, lease, option, mortgage, pledge, hypothecate, abandon, borrow, loan, contract, distribute in cash or kind or partly in each at fair market value on the date of distribution, without requiring pro rata distribution of specific assets and without requiring pro rata allocation of the tax bases of such assets. They may establish reserves, release powers, and abandon, settle or contest claims. They may employ attorneys, accountants, appraisers, custodians of the trust assets, and other agents or assistants as deemed advisable to act with or without discretionary powers and compensate them and pay their expenses from income or principal or both. In addition to all of the above powers, my fiduciaries may exercise those powers set forth in the MyState Fiduciaries' Powers Act, including amendments to the Act after the date of this instrument. I incorporate such Act as it exists today by reference and make it a part of this instrument.

B. Any trust established under this instrument shall be administered free of active judicial intervention. It shall be subject only to the jurisdiction of a court being invoked by the trustees or other interested parties or as otherwise provided by law. I direct that no fiduciary shall be required to give any bond in any jurisdiction. Any fiduciary under this instrument shall be entitled to reasonable compensation for services actually performed and to be reimbursed for expenses properly incurred.

VII. Spendthrift Provision

No beneficiary shall have any right to anticipate, sell, assign, mortgage, hypothecate, pledge or otherwise dispose of or encumber all or any part of any trust estate established for his or her benefit under this instrument. No part of such trust estate, including income, shall be liable for the debts or obligations of any beneficiary or be subject to attachment, garnishment, execution, creditor's bill or other legal or equitable process.

VIII. Perpetuities Savings[49] Clause

All trusts created hereunder shall in any event terminate no later than 21 years after the death of the last survivor of the group composed of myself and those of my descendants living at my

continued on next page

49. This clause is routinely referred to as a "saving" or "savings" clause. A leading casebook supports the use of "saving" clause, and although Ms. Smith's attorney used "savings" clause, this book follows the other convention. *See* DUKEMINIER ET AL., *supra* note 6, at 897-899. Although the inclusion of such clauses was once routine, an attorney may need to revise the language if the jurisdiction has modified the common law Rule Against Perpetuities; see Chapter 13.

death. The property held in trust shall be discharged of any trust and shall immediately vest in and be distributed to the persons then entitled to the income therefrom in the proportions in which they are beneficiaries of the income, and for this purpose only, any person then eligible to receive discretionary payments of income of a particular trust shall be treated as being entitled to receive the income (if more than one person are so treated, the group of such persons shall be treated as being entitled to receive such income as a class, to be distributed among them, by representation).

IX. Taxes

I direct that all estate, inheritance and succession taxes payable by reason of my death shall be paid from my residuary estate. Notwithstanding the prior language of this Article, in no event shall estate taxes be allocated to or paid from any gift to the extent it is deductible (under section 2055 of the Internal Revenue Code of 1986, as amended) from my estate for wealth transfer taxation purposes.

X. Miscellaneous

A. A child adopted by any person and the descendants by blood or adoption of such child shall be considered the descendants of such adopting person and of such person's ancestors. For purposes of this Will, any beneficiary shall be deemed to have predeceased me if such beneficiary dies within 30 days after the date of my death. Whenever a distribution to descendants by representation is called for by this instrument, the distributable assets are to be divided into as many shares as there are, at the time such assets are distributable, living descendants in the nearest degree of kinship and deceased descendants in the same degree who left then living descendants. Each then living descendant in the nearest degree shall receive one share and the share of each deceased descendant in the same degree shall be divided among the deceased descendant's descendants in the same manner.

B. The laws of MyState shall determine the validity and construction of my Will. If any part of this instrument shall be adjudicated to be void or invalid, the remaining provisions not specifically so adjudicated shall remain in full force and effect. Except as otherwise provided in this instrument, terms shall be as defined in MyState Probate Code as amended after the date of this instrument and after my death.

I, Alice Goodwin Smith, sign my name to this instrument consisting of four pages on October 25, [five years ago], and being first duly sworn, do hereby declare to the undersigned authority that I sign and execute this instrument as my last Will and that I sign it willingly (or willingly direct another to sign for me), that I execute it as my free and voluntary act for the purposes therein expressed, and that I am eighteen years of age or older, of sound mind, and under no constraint or undue influence.

____
Testatrix[50]

We, Elisabeth Barnes Smith and Jennifer I. Jones, the witnesses, sign our names to this instrument, being first duly sworn, and do hereby declare to the undersigned authority that Alice Goodwin Smith signs and executes this instrument as her last Will and that she signs it willingly

50. The UPC, for example, has adopted the gender-neutral term of "testator" to include an individual of either sex. *See* UPC §1-201(52). This simplifies the preparation of Wills.

(or willingly directs another to sign for her) and that she executes it as her free and voluntary act for the purposes therein expressed, and that each of us, in the presence and hearing of Alice Goodwin Smith, hereby sign this Will as witness to her signing, and that to the best of our knowledge Alice Goodwin Smith is eighteen years of age or older, of sound mind, and under no constraint or undue influence.

________________________	________________________
Witness 7745 East Brown Circle MyCity, MyState 80000	Witness 6132 Copper Way #327D MyCity, MyState 80000

STATE OF MYSTATE)
) ss.
COUNTY OF MYCOUNTY)

Subscribed, sworn to, and acknowledged before me by Alice Goodwin Smith, the testatrix and subscribed and sworn to before me by Elisabeth Barnes Smith and Jennifer I. Jones, witnesses, on October 25, [five years ago].

Witness my hand and official seal.

My commission expires __________________.

____
Notary Public

EXERCISE 2-4

A SIMULATED CLIENT INTERVIEW

Ms. Smith wishes to update her Will. Using the client questionnaire in Exhibit 1.3 in Chapter 1 and her existing Will above, conduct a simulated interview of Ms. Smith. One-half of the class will form groups acting as the interviewing attorney, with the other half acting as Ms. Smith. Your teacher will provide the "client" students with a summary of Ms. Smith's current information.

EXERCISE 2-5

REVIEW OF MS. SMITH'S WILL

Ms. Smith's Will is a typical instrument for an elderly person of moderate wealth with adult children. (a) Read the Will carefully and discuss any provisions that you find to be troubling, awkward, unclear, incomplete, or that otherwise require modification. (b) Please redraft the first sentence of the Will in a more concise way, eliminating unnecessary "legalese" flourishes.

EXERCISE 2-6

CODICIL PRACTICE

Assume that you are now ready to update Ms. Smith's Will. In view of the context of her overall situation and her existing Will, evaluate the appropriateness of using a codicil[51] versus a completely new Will.

EXERCISE 2-7

THE DISPOSITION OF MS. SMITH'S ESTATE

Assume that the value of Ms. Smith's estate, net of claims and administration expenses, is $400,000. Assume that Ms. Smith died at the scene of a car accident at 3:30 p.m. on January 8, [current year]. Her daughter, Rebecca Simpson Smith-Brown, was the driver of the car in which Ms. Smith was riding, and Rebecca passed away at 10 a.m. January 10, [current year]. Using your knowledge of Ms. Smith's family from Case Study 2-1 and these additional facts, discuss the disposition of Ms. Smith's estate under the terms of her existing Will. Assume that the UPC (or a different statute as directed by your teacher) applies.

EXERCISE 2-8

APPORTIONMENT OF ESTATE TAXES

Assume that the value of Ms. Smith's estate, net of claims and administration expenses (but not federal estate and generation-skipping transfer taxes), is $8,000,000. Assume for convenience that the amount of the federal estate taxes is $1,000,000 (MyState imposes no wealth transfer taxes). How much will Saint Mary's Church receive as a bequest under those facts? Is the Will's apportionment provision fair to the other devisees? Why do you suppose that the attorney chose this method of apportionment?

H. Reference Materials

Treatises

Fundamentals of Wills and Trusts Law

- ROGER W. ANDERSEN, UNDERSTANDING TRUSTS AND ESTATES (4th ed. 2009).
- FREDERICK K. HOOPS ET AL., FAMILY ESTATE PLANNING GUIDE (4th ed. 1994 & Supp. 2010-2011).

51. For an example of a well-drafted codicil, *see* DOBRIS ET AL., *supra* note 4, at 362-363.

- William M. McGovern et al., Wills, Trusts and Estates (4th ed. 2010).
- John R. Price & Samuel A. Donaldson, Price on Contemporary Estate Planning (2011).
- George M. Turner, Revocable Trusts (5th ed. 2003 & Supp. 2010).

Children Born from Advanced Medical Procedures

- A. James Casner & Jeffrey N. Pennell, Estate Planning §2.2.4.3 (6th ed. 1995 & Supp. 2009-2010).
- McGovern et al., *supra*, §2.11.
- Price & Donaldson, *supra*, §4.14.

Drafting Style

- Thomas R. Haggard & george w. kiney, legal drafting (2d ed. 2007).
- Hoops et al., *supra*, ch. 17, *Drafting Wills.*
- Kevin D. Millard, Drafting Wills, Trusts, and Other Estate Planning Documents—A Style Manual (2006).
- Price & Donaldson, *supra*, §§4.14 & 4.15, Forms 4-4 & 4-5 (providing examples of clauses describing family and specific bequests).
- Jeffrey A. Schoenblum, Page on the Law of Wills, v. 7 (Forms), ch. 26F (2010).

Drafting Ambiguities and Errors

- McGovern et al., *supra*, §6.1.

Articles

Adoption

- Donald E. Cohen, *Adoption Can Have Unexpected Effects on Inheritance and Overall Estate Plan*, 18 Est. Plan. 8 (1991).
- Donald E. Cohen, *Adult Adoption May Qualify One as a Beneficiary*, 19 Est. Plan. 88 (1992).
- Angela Chaput Foy, *Adult Adoption and the Elder Population*, 8 Marq. Elder's Advisor 109 (2006).
- Peter Wendel, *Inheritance Rights and the Step-Partner Adoption Paradigm: Shades of the Discrimination against Illegitimate Children*, 34 Hofstra L. Rev. 351 (2005).

Children Born from Advanced Medical Procedures

- James E. Bailey, *An Analytical Framework for Resolving the Issues Raised by the Interaction between Reproductive Technology and the Law of Inheritance*, 47 DePaul L. Rev. 743 (1998).

- Michelle L. Brenwald & Kay Redeker, Note, *A Primer on Posthumous Conception and Related Issues of Assisted Reproduction*, 38 WASHBURN L.J. 599 (1999).
- Nomi R. Cahn, *Parenthood, Genes, and Gametes: The Family Law and Trusts and Estates Perspectives*, 32 U. MEM. L. REV. 563 (2002).
- Dominic J. Campisi et al., *Heirs in the Freezer: Bronze Age Biology Confronts Biotechnology*, 36 ACTEC J. 179 (Summer 2010).
- Ronald Chester, *Freezing the Heir Apparent: A Dialogue on Postmortem Conception, Parental Responsibility, and Inheritance*, 33 HOUS. L. REV. 967 (1996).
- Michael K. Elliott, *Tales of Parenthood from the Crypt: The Predicament of the Posthumously Conceived Child*, 39 REAL PROP. PROB. & TR. J. 47 (2004).
- Bruce A. Fowler & Teresa C. Baird, *Frozen in Time: Planning for the Posthumously Conceived Child*, 37 COLO. LAW. 45 (June 2008).
- Susan N. Gary, *Posthumously Conceived Heirs: Where the Law Stands and What to Do About It Now*, 19 PROB. & PROP. 32 (Mar./Apr. 2005).
- Susan N. Gary, *We Are Family: The Definition of Parent and Child for Succession Purposes*, 34 ACTEC J. 171 (2008).
- Kathleen R. Guzman, *Property, Progeny, Body Part: Assisted Reproduction and the Transfer of Wealth*, 31 U.C. DAVIS L. REV. 193 (1997).
- Sharona Hoffman & Andrew P. Morriss, *Birth after Death: Perpetuities and the New Reproductive Technologies*, 38 GA. L. REV. 575 (2004).
- Charles P. Kindregan, Jr. & Maureen McBrien, *Posthumous Reproduction*, 39 FAM. L.Q. 579 (2005).
- Christie E. Kirk, *Assisted Reproduction: Children Conceived Posthumously Entitled to Inheritance Rights*, 30 J.L. MED. & ETHICS 109 (2002).
- Kristine S. Knaplund, *Legal Issues of Maternity and Inheritance for the Biotech Child of the 21st Century*, 43 REAL PROP. TR. & EST. L.J. 393 (2008).
- Kathryn Venturatos Lorio, *From Cradle to Tomb: Estate Planning Considerations of Procreation*, 57 LA. L. REV. 27 (1996).
- Kathryn Venturatos Lorio, *Conceiving the Inconceivable: Legal Recognition of the Posthumously Conceived Child*, 34 ACTEC J. 154 (2008).
- Lesa McCrimmoo, *Gametes, Embryos and the Life in Being: The Impact of Technology on the Rule Against Perpetuities*, 34 REAL PROP. PROB. & TR. J. 697 (2000).
- Joshua S. Rubenstein, *Planning for Life after Death: The Ability to Control the Disposition of One's Remains and the Posthumous Use of One's Genetic Material*, 44 INST. ON EST. PLAN. ¶700 (2010).

- Joshua S. Rubenstein, *Posthumous Control Over One's Remains and Use of Genetic Material*, 37 EST. PLAN. 24 (Feb. 2010).
- Lee-ford Tritt, *Technical Correction or Tectonic Shift: Competing Default Rule Theories Under the New Uniform Probate Code*, 61 ALA. L. REV. 273 (2010).
- Morgan Kirkland Wood, *It Takes a Village: Considering the Other Interests at Stake When Extending Inheritance Rights to Posthumously Conceived Children*, 44 GA. L. REV. 873 (2010).

Drafting Style (*See also* "Drafting Pointers" in Ch. 3 reference materials and "Drafting Technique" in Ch. 4 reference materials.)

- Albert S. Barr, III, *Ten (More or Less) Tried Tools to Temper the Tribulation Tethered to Traditional Tactics and Techniques: Making "Common" Planning and Drafting Errors Less Common*, 30 INST. ON EST. PLAN. ¶1800 (1996).
- Michael G. Ferguson, *Wills and Trusts: Meeting the Drafting Challenges (with Sample Clauses)*, 43 No. 6 PRAC. LAW. 31 (Sept. 1997).
- John L. Garvey, *Drafting Wills and Trusts*, 71 OR. L. REV. 47 (1992).
- Edward Halbach, *Drafting and Overdrafting: A Voyeur's View of Recurring Problems*, 19 INST. ON EST. PLAN. ¶1300 (1985).
- Helen W. Gunnarsson, *Anatomy of a Will: A Step-By-Step Guide*, 97 ILL. B.J. 506 (Oct. 2009).
- Sidney G. Saltz, *Drafting Made Easy*, 15 PROB. & PROP. 32 (May/June 2001).
- Joseph M. Scheuner & Olen M. Bailey, Jr., *A Legal and Practical Guide to the Disposition of Tangible Personal Property at Death*, 20 PROB. & PROP. 66 (May/June 2006).
- Edward S. Schlesinger, *English as a Second Language for Lawyers*, 12 INST. ON EST. PLAN. ¶700 (1978).
- William Schwartz, *Sins of Omission and Commission in the Drafting of Wills and Trusts*, 13 INST. ON EST. PLAN. ¶1100 (1979).
- Thomas S. Word, Jr., *A Brief for Plain English Wills and Trusts*, 14 U. RICH. L. REV. 471 (1980).

Drafting Ambiguities and Errors

- Pamela R. Champine, *My Will Be Done: Accommodating the Erring and the Atypical Testator*, 80 NEB. L. REV. 387 (2001).
- J. Henderson, *Mistake and Fraud in Wills*, 47 B.U. L. REV. 303 (1967).

Estate Planning for Pets

- Gerry W. Beyer, *Estate Planning for Pets*, 15 PROB. & PROP. 7 (July/Aug. 2001).

- Gerry W. Beyer, *Pet Animals: What Happens When Their Humans Die?*, 40 Santa Clara L. Rev. 617 (2000).
- Frances Carlisle & Paul Franken, *Drafting Trusts for Animals*, 218 N.Y.L.J. 1 (Nov. 13, 1997).
- Stephanie B. Casteel, *Estate Planning for Pets*, 21 No. 6 Prob. & Prop. 8 (Nov./Dec. 2007).
- Frances H. Foster, *Should Pets Inherit?*, 63 Fla. L. Rev. 801 (2011).
- Rachel Hirschfeld, *Estate Planning Strategies for People Who Have Pets*, 36 Est. Plan. 24 (July 2009).
- Rachel Hirschfeld, *Ensure Your Pet's Future: Estate Planning for Owners and Their Animal Companions*, 9 Marq. Elder's Advisor 155 (2007).
- Gabriela N. Sandoval, *The Basics of Pet Trusts for Estate Planning Attorneys*, 37 Colo. Law. 49 (May 2008).
- Jennifer R. Taylor, *A "Pet" Project for State Legislatures: The Movement Toward Enforceable Pet Trusts in the Twenty-First Century*, 13 Quinnipiac Prob. L.J. 419 (1999).

Other

- http://www.abanet.org/rppt/publications/magazine/home.html (last visited Mar. 2, 2011) (the ABA website for Probate & Property, which offers a number of useful articles not confined to those in this chapter).
- Alexander A. Bove, Jr., *What's It Like to Be Dead and What If You Come Back?*, 37 Est. Plan. 28 (Apr. 2010) (emerging issues in determining whether a person is dead).

CHAPTER 3 The Young Adult

A. Why Plan?

If one focuses only on the asset transmission role of estate planning in the context of the typical young, unmarried (and not otherwise in a significant cohabiting relationship) adult without children, there is some question as to whether any planning is necessary. Taking into account consumer debt and student loans, many young adults probably have little financial net worth. For example, recent median income for males and females ages 25-34 was $33,415 and $25,553, respectively.[1] Moreover, the laws of intestate succession and nonprobate transfer provisions, such as joint accounts or beneficiary designations, offer a default estate plan. As discussed below, an issue for planners is whether those other regimes should be relied upon. In that regard, the laws of intestate succession often pass assets of the unmarried adult to the parents rather than to siblings, and that may be an undesired result. In addition, if probate is required (e.g., because the decedent was the sole owner of a parcel of real property at his or her death[2]), a Will may permit the testator to make decisions about important matters such as the selection of the personal representative.

It would generally be untrue to claim that the young individual must prepare a Will or trust in order to accomplish other goals of estate planning (i.e., those not involving the distribution of assets). For example, one such objective would be the preparation of medical care directives and a so-called "living will." There is no shortage of opportunities to execute such

1. U.S. Census Bureau, Statistical Abstract of the United States 2011 No. 701 (130th ed. 2010).

2. But *see* Section C.6.b and note 24, *infra*.

instruments without the assistance of an attorney, and a number of Internet sites offer the forms. In addition, most health care facilities also make these forms available.[3] However, except for anticipated procedures, it is often too late for such action when the individual is ultimately admitted to a health care facility.

The challenge of estate planning for the young adult is produced by a combination of factors, including: (1) a practical view that the assets in question really don't matter that much and that other measures will adequately address those assets; (2) the fact that protection of spouses or offspring is not a concern; and (3) a conviction that the probability of debilitating injury, illness, or even death is quite remote.

B. Intestate Succession

Every state has a statutory scheme for intestate succession. The prescribed results vary. Under the Uniform Probate Code (UPC), the estate of an unmarried decedent without offspring would pass to the decedent's parents equally if both survive, or all to a single surviving parent.[4] The UPC requires that an heir survive the decedent by 120 hours, unless the result would be escheat to the state.[5] The UPC succession pattern is followed in several influential states.[6] Other states modify that result if only one parent survives.[7] Assuming the existence of probate assets, a Will is required if the decedent wishes to alter the intestate succession scheme to essentially disinherit some or all of the statutorily prescribed takers or to reallocate the portions that each heir would otherwise take.

C. Nonprobate Transfers

Even if the young adult does not own a residence, he or she will probably own bank accounts, an automobile, some clothing and home furnishings, and perhaps an Individual Retirement Account (IRA) or other retirement asset. The disposition of these assets upon death may be accomplished

3. This is in part due to federal law, which requires health care providers to furnish adult patients with information about their rights to make health care decisions. *See* Patient Self-Determination Act of 1990, 42 U.S.C. §1395cc(f)(1) (2006).

4. *See* UPC §2-103(a)(2).

5. *See* UPC §2-104.

6. *See, e.g.*, Cal. Prob. Code §6402 (West 2009) (if no surviving spouse or domestic partner); Fla. Stat. Ann. §732.103 (West 2010); Mass. Ann. Laws ch. 190B, §2-103 (LexisNexis Supp. 2010); N.Y. Est. Powers & Trusts Law §4-1.1 (McKinney 1998).

7. *See, e.g.*, 755 Ill. Comp. Stat. Ann. 5/2-1(d) (West 2007) (if only one parent survives, a double share passes to the parent and the remainder to siblings or their descendants); Tex. Prob. Code Ann. §38(a) (Vernon 2003) (if only one parent survives, then one-half goes to the parent and one-half to siblings and their descendants; however, if there are no siblings or descendants of siblings, then the sole surviving parent inherits the entire probate estate).

largely outside the probate system, assuming that the young adult has taken advantage of the nonprobate disposition alternatives. Those alternatives, however, are not without their pitfalls.

1. Bank Accounts

The disposition of bank accounts may be handled through the use of multiple-party accounts with family members or, alternatively, by using a payable-on-death (POD) designation. In either situation, the account owner needs to be familiar with the legal consequences stemming from the use of each. In that regard, the primary information source will often be the financial institution, which may offer advice that is rushed or perfunctory or otherwise of uneven quality.

There are three general nonexclusive themes under the UPC multiple-party account rules.

First, the owner of the account may designate another person (e.g., a family member) as an "agent" to make transactions on behalf of the owner of the account. This agency may be "durable" such that it survives the incapacity of the principal.[8] Unless the agent is also designated as a POD beneficiary, the agent has no beneficial rights to sums on deposit.[9] One generally would see this structure used as a lifetime planning measure for incapacity or illness, not as a testamentary disposition. For example, an elderly person who fears possible incapacity or who wishes to have a family member attend to banking matters for convenience might use an agency account. Because the principal retains legal rights to the account, the use of an agency account generally does not have any special federal gift tax consequences.[10]

Second, the owner of the account may designate another person as a "co-owner." Joint ownership of accounts generally requires the execution of signature cards by all owners. Although signature cards may be mailed to family members at a distance, this requires attention to detail and follow-up that some individuals lack. Some family members may object to being parties to checking accounts due to concerns about potential liability for overdrafts. The co-owners' rights to information concerning the accounts may raise privacy or autonomy concerns. During the lifetime of all parties, the account belongs to the parties in proportion to their net contributions to the sums on deposit unless there is clear and convincing evidence of a different intent.[11] This is a serious drawback to the use of joint accounts, because the "clear and convincing evidence" standard is not foolproof at best, or can invite litigation or attempts to dissipate the account at worst. Upon the death of a party to a multiple-party account, the sums on deposit belong to the surviving party.[12] Often this result

8. *See* UPC §6-205(b).
9. *See* UPC §6-211(d).
10. *See* Chapter 16 for an overview of the federal wealth transfer taxes.
11. *See* UPC §6-211(b).
12. *See* UPC §6-212(a).

produces litigation stemming from claims by other family members that the joint titling was simply for the decedent's convenience, and the intent was to create an agency relationship — not to make a testamentary gift to the surviving account holder.[13] The mere creation of a multiple-party account does not usually have any special federal gift tax implications.[14]

Third, the young adult could use a POD designation. This is often the best solution. The POD designee has absolutely no right to sums on deposit during the lifetime of any party,[15] nor any risk concerning liabilities associated with the account. Bank statements and other information are usually not available to the POD beneficiary. The designation of the POD beneficiary is generally unequivocal as a testamentary disposition. Because the account owner retains the right to change the POD designation up to the time of his or her death, this designation does not have any special federal gift tax implications.[16]

Although multiple-party accounts can pass as nonprobate assets, the recipient may be required to return a portion of the funds to an appointed personal representative if the other assets of the estate are insufficient to pay claims against the estate.[17]

2. Securities Accounts

The disposition of securities accounts may be achieved through the use of transfer-on-death (TOD) designations under state laws that operate in a fashion similar to POD bank accounts.[18]

3. Automobiles

While the laws of many states permit joint title registration with rights of survivorship, this can be unwieldy on the acquisition and disposition of the automobile and may raise concerns about the potential liability of the joint titleholder for accidents.[19]

4. Clothing, Personal Effects, and Home Furnishings

These assets are generally of modest value, and there are typically no title documents. They are considered "tangible personal property" and are often distributed to family members under separate provisions in a Will. If there is no Will, or if the Will is not probated, family members who gain possession of the articles generally can readily dispose of them to third parties, provided that other family members or potential claimants

13. *See, e.g.*, the official comment to UPC §6-212.

14. *See* Treas. Reg. §25.2511-1(h)(4) (as amended in 1997). *See* Chapter 16 for an overview of the federal wealth transfer taxes.

15. *See* UPC §6-211(c).

16. *See* Treas. Reg. §25.2511-1(h)(4) (as amended in 1997).

17. *See, e.g.*, UPC §6-102.

18. *See, e.g.*, UPC §§6-301 to 6-311.

19. *See, e.g.*, Victor E. Schwartz et al., Prosser, Wade & Schwartz's Torts, 673-678 (11th ed. 2005); Mich. Comp. Laws Ann. §257.401 (West 2010) ("The owner of a motor vehicle is liable for an injury caused by the negligent operation of the motor vehicle . . .").

acquiesce. If there are unpaid creditors, the family members would take the assets subject to those claims.[20]

5. Retirement Accounts and Life Insurance Policies

Retirement accounts and life insurance policies permit the owner to designate primary and secondary beneficiaries with few complications. Although the young adults discussed in this chapter usually see little need for the immediate purchase of life insurance, a modest amount of group term life insurance[21] is often an employer-provided benefit.

6. Real Estate

a. Joint Tenancies. The creation of a joint tenancy with another family member is generally not a good idea. The creation of a joint tenancy with rights of survivorship is an irrevocable gift of a one-half interest and will generally produce a gift under the federal gift tax.[22] While a gift tax may not be due in light of existing exclusions and credits (see Chapter 16), the filing of a gift tax return will be required, involving additional and unnecessary expense to the young adult. If the real estate is a personal residence, the young adult may not be eligible for the generous exemption from income tax on any gain with respect to the one-half owned by the non-occupant family member.[23] Transactions requiring the actions of the property's owners become more complicated, and the young adult has his or her financial affairs now enmeshed with the opinions, emotions, and credit concerns of another family member.

b. Transfer-on-Death Deeds. In light of the potential difficulties produced by joint tenancies of real estate, some states have enacted statutes that create a survivorship interest resembling a TOD securities interest through the use of a statutory "transfer-on-death deed" or "beneficiary deed." The beneficiary generally has no lifetime rights or responsibilities with respect to the property, the beneficiary designation may be changed during the owner's lifetime, and the property passes to the designated beneficiary upon the owner's death as a nonprobate transfer.[24]

20. That would not be true if the decedent had a spouse or dependent children because of typical exempt property and family allowance laws enacted for the protection of the surviving spouse and family. The young adult who is the focus of this chapter is assumed to lack such a spouse or children.

21. The amount is often limited to $50,000, the maximum that can be offered to the employee as a nontaxable fringe benefit. *See* IRC §79.

22. *See* Treas. Reg. §25.2511-1(h)(5) (as amended in 1997).

23. *See* IRC §121.

24. *See, e.g.*, UPC §§6-401-6-417 (Uniform Real Property Transfer on Death Act); Ariz. Rev. Stat. Ann. §33-405 (West 2007); Ark. Code Ann. §18-12-608 (Supp. 2009); Colo. Rev. Stat. §15-15-402 (2010); Kan. Stat. Ann. §59-3501 (2005); Minn. Stat. Ann. §507.071 (West Supp. 2010-2011); Mo. Ann. Stat. §461.025 (West 2007); Nev. Rev. Stat. Ann. §111.109 (LexisNexis 2010); N.M. Stat. §45-6-401 (2008); Ohio Rev. Code Ann. §§5302.22 & 5302.23 (West Supp. 2010); Wis. Stat. Ann. §705.15 (West Supp. 2010); *see also* John R. Price & Samuel A. Donaldson, Price on Contemporary Estate Planning §§3.40 to 3.44 (2011).

D. Small Estate Proceedings

If the young adult owns assets that are not transmitted by nonprobate measures, probate administration of the estate may still not be necessary. The UPC, for example, permits the successors of the decedent to collect the decedent's property by offering an affidavit to third parties who hold assets of the decedent.[25] The UPC provision applies only if the value of the entire probate estate does not exceed $5,000,[26] and it applies only to personal property. However, if the decedent owned real estate not titled in a survivorship form, some form of probate will generally be required to convey the real property.

Even if the estate is subject to administration, the UPC, for example, permits an abbreviated closing if the value of the estate does not exceed the amount of the homestead allowance, exempt property allowance, family allowance, and any administration, funeral, and medical expenses of the last illness of the decedent.[27]

E. Selection of Fiduciaries

Selection of fiduciaries is one of the reasons often given for executing a Will. A person nominated as personal representative in the Will is given first priority for appointment under the UPC.[28] In the absence of a surviving spouse and a nomination in a Will, the competition is otherwise generally among devisees or heirs. While most Wills routinely waive bonding of fiduciaries (another reason often given for executing a Will), the UPC already dispenses with bonding for the personal representative in most situations.[29] This, of course, assumes that administration will be required, which may not be accurate for the various reasons discussed above. Chapter 7 addresses considerations in the selection of the persons who will serve as fiduciaries.

While a Will (or under the UPC, a Will or other signed writing)[30] can serve as a parental appointment of a guardian for unmarried minors (a significant reason for executing a Will cited by most married couples with minor children), that is not a factor for the young adults with no children, as discussed in this chapter.

25. *See* UPC §3-1201.
26. The dollar limit may be higher in adopting states. Colorado, for example, imposes a limit of $50,000 of assets. *See* COLO. REV. STAT. §15-12-1201 (2010).
27. *See* UPC §§3-1203 & 3-1204.
28. *See* UPC §3-203(a)(1).
29. *See* UPC §3-603.
30. *See* UPC §5-202(a).

F. Planning for Youthful Incapacity

Chapter 15 addresses planning measures to be employed in dealing with incapacity. While many readily see the pertinence of this topic to the elderly, it is often ignored with younger clients. However, while incapacity can be a consequence of the aging process or illness, it can also be produced by injury or accident. Those injuries are more likely to occur to younger individuals engaged in a more active, perhaps reckless, lifestyle (e.g., due to automobile accidents, physical altercations, sports, and recreational activities).

Planning for incapacity generally focuses on two themes: management of the financial affairs of the individual and providing for the physical care of the individual.

1. Conservatorships

A conservatorship may be the default measure for dealing with a young individual's financial affairs. This function may be referred to as a "guardianship" or "guardianship of the property" in some states where the protective functions are not split to focus on either the health (guardianship) or property (conservatorship) of the protected person. This process is generally under court supervision, which introduces delay and costs, often without much real oversight protection if there are no opposing interests.

2. Revocable Trusts

A properly structured revocable trust (discussed in Chapter 15) may be an effective structure for the management of an incapacitated person's financial affairs. It can operate largely free of court supervision with flexibility in investments and distributions as provided in the trust instrument. Moreover, by establishing the trust while competent, an individual can select the trustees who may serve in the event of the individual's inability to do so. The revocable trust in the context of a single, young, healthy adult with relatively few assets, however, has drawbacks in terms of cost of formation and maintenance.

3. Durable Powers of Attorney

While practice and circumstances vary, many planners would not create a revocable trust for a young adult with few assets simply for asset management purposes unless incapacity was likely. They would, however, generally suggest the execution of a "durable" power of attorney for property that would survive the incapacity, but not the death, of the principal.[31]

31. *See, e.g.*, UPC §§5B-101 to 5B-302 (adopting the Uniform Power of Attorney Act (2006) as a replacement for the Uniform Durable Power of Attorney Act).

Drafting issues include: (1) deciding on an immediate grant of authority to the agent, with the expectation that the trusted agent would not use this unless the principal is incapacitated, versus a "springing" authority that is not effective until incapacity;[32] (2) selecting the agent and successors; and (3) drafting the language of the power such that it is broad enough to anticipate various transactions yet specific enough to convince third parties that they can rely on it in specific instances.[33] A sample general power of attorney, Form D-2, is in the Forms Supplement.[34] In states adopting the Uniform Statutory Form Power of Attorney Act or the Uniform Power of Attorney Act (2006), the drafter's task of trying to describe a broad range of powers is aided by the opportunity to "check off" powers from a statutorily prescribed list.[35] A sample statutory power of attorney, Form D-1, is in the Forms Supplement. However, if the period of incapacity is prolonged or the proposed transaction is unusual, a conservatorship may nonetheless be unavoidable.

4. Medical Care Directives and Living Wills

With respect to health care decisions, many individuals may have specific concerns (e.g., certain religious faiths do not permit blood transfusions,

32. Although a springing authority can appear attractive in terms of blending a measure of protection with the simplicity of durable powers of attorney, determining if the principal is incapacitated can introduce some complexity. Further, third parties may be more reluctant to accept the authority of the agent (that is, has the authority "sprung"?), often requiring a judicial approval process, the avoidance of which is a primary objective of preparing durable powers of attorney. While the instrument may try to address this issue by prescribing some procedure (typically introducing the opinions of the principal's physician), the privacy rules of the Health Insurance Portability and Accountability Act of 1996 (HIPAA) can frustrate that inquiry. The Uniform Power of Attorney Act (2006) §109 provides that the power is effective when executed unless the instrument provides otherwise. If the power becomes effective upon the occurrence of a future event or contingency, the Act provides rules as to how that determination is made, and it provides HIPAA authority to the agent for the purposes of obtaining access to health care information and communicating with the principal's health care provider. In Part I (Reference Materials) we refer you to discussions of the HIPAA considerations.

33. We don't generally recommend that the principal distribute copies of the power of attorney in advance of disability to various parties, such as investment advisors, who would rely on it in the event of disability. However, if the power of attorney is ultimately presented to persons who may rely on it, it is good practice to record who has received a copy or otherwise been presented with a power of attorney in case the power of attorney is subsequently revoked or modified. In that situation, the client would be advised to retrieve the document and/or send a letter to the recipient of the document stating that the power has been revoked. *See* FREDERICK K. HOOPS ET AL., FAMILY ESTATE PLANNING GUIDE §2:9 (4th ed. 1994 & Supp. 2010-2011).

34. Third parties at a minimum usually will request a copy of the power of attorney. Although it is probably implied by the fact of presentation, third parties may also request an express written representation from the agent that the power is valid and has not been revoked. Some forms include an addendum to this effect, which is executed by the agent. *See, e.g.*, A. JAMES CASNER & JEFFREY N. PENNELL, ESTATE PLANNING §3.10.4.5 (6th ed. 1995 & Supp. 2009-2010).

35. The Uniform Power of Attorney Act (2006) adopts the "initial-the-box" power selection approach of the Uniform Statutory Form Power of Attorney Act. However, as discussed in the General Comment to Part 2 of the Uniform Power of Attorney Act (2006), it imposes a general default rule precluding gift making authority and identifies specific acts that may be authorized only by an express grant in the instrument, to avoid the inference of authority from a selection of the general authority category. Concerning gifts, it should be noted that an express "general authority" to make gifts is intended by the Act to permit only gifts that qualify for the annual gift tax exclusion under IRC §2503(b). The document can provide "specific authority" to make gifts in excess of the annual gift tax exclusion; however, such language must clearly and expressly authorize gifts in excess of the annual gift tax exclusion amount.

others do not permit the withholding of nourishment under any circumstances, some people would refuse electric shock therapy, etc.). Most hospitals provide forms that permit an individual to give directions as to the manner of his or her care, but it is often too late if the care is the result of an emergency. Law and practice vary from state to state, and all of these decisions are subject to the concerns of the client. In some cases the client will be focusing on avoiding protracted care while incapacitated where there is little or no hope for recovery and will desire a so-called "living will" that specifies when care will be terminated (e.g., where assisted breathing or feeding is required) with little discretion to be exercised by third parties. A sample living will is part of Form F in the Forms Supplement.[36] In other cases, the law will permit the use of durable powers of attorney that include health care issues and guide the discretion of the agent in dealing with unforeseeable events. A sample health care power of attorney is part of Form F in the Forms Supplement.[37]

State statutes usually address this area; thus an attorney must draft the documents in light of applicable statutory constraints. For example, the Uniform Health-Care Decisions Act[38] (adopted in at least nine states: Alabama, Alaska, California, Delaware, Hawaii, Maine, Mississippi, New Mexico, and Wyoming) incorporates three structures. Section 2 of the Act provides for a health care power of attorney and also permits advance decisions by the individual such as those provided in a living will. Section 5 provides for a surrogate for health care decisions, which surrogate would usually operate in the absence of a health care power of attorney. Section 5 also establishes a list of persons, primarily family members, who could be designated after the onset of incapacity to make health care decisions affecting the incapacitated individual.

5. Organ and Tissue Donations

The related issue of organ and tissue donations should be considered.[39] This can be a sensitive topic that raises client concerns about premature termination of medical care, possible disrespectful use of the body for medical training, disfigurement of the corpse, objections based on religious beliefs, and delays in funeral services. The attorney needs to be

36. A popular living will form intended for direct client use is the Five Wishes® booklet, available online for a nominal fee from www.agingwithdignity.org (last visited Feb. 20, 2011).

37. The documents in the Forms Supplement are intentionally simplified. For a collection of complex and detailed living wills, health care proxies, and medical directives, including a living will for a person of the Orthodox Jewish faith, *see* Jeffrey A. Schoenblum, Page on the Law of Wills, vol. 7 (Forms), ch. 54F (2010). *See also* Hoops et al., *supra* note 33, App. 9 (general power of attorney form).

38. Unif. Health-Care Decisions Act (1993), 9 U.L.A. (Part IB) 83 (2005).

39. As of February 20, 2011, the national patient waiting list had 110,428 people in need of one or more transplants. From January 2010 through November 2010, 26,218 transplants were performed, and there were 13,252 donors during that same period. *See Organ Procurement and Transplantation Network*, http://www.optn.org/data (last visited Feb. 20, 2011).

aware of these types of concerns and be prepared to discuss the scope of the donation as well as typical procedures.[40] Sample anatomical gift preference language is included in Forms E-1 and F of the Forms Supplement.

6. Final Arrangements Instructions and Client Letter of Instruction

We have deferred until Chapter 7 a discussion of two documents that are not often executed by the young, unmarried adult who is the subject of this chapter. The so-called "Final Arrangements Instructions" document is drafted by the attorney (see Form E-1 in the Forms Supplement) and primarily addresses disposition of the body, anatomical gifts, and service arrangements. The "Client Letter of Instruction" (see Form E-2 in the Forms Supplement) is written by the client to his or her personal representative or family members to alert them to the location of important documents, financial accounts, and so forth. Ironically, it could be that the single unmarried individual is one of the best candidates for these types of documents, inasmuch as he or she probably doesn't live with someone who would otherwise know or have ready access to that information. However, the preparation of both of these documents may take a lot more commitment to the estate planning process than a young, unmarried adult without children or significant assets would typically be concerned about.

G. Using Form Documents (Part I)[41]

New attorneys, as well as experienced attorneys to a lesser degree, are able to gain valuable ideas through reviewing forms prepared by other attorneys. There are recurring patterns one finds in Wills and trusts, from the inclusion of fundamental clauses to alternative ways of expressing the standards for trust distributions. The new attorney needs to develop a sense of what provisions are commonly found in particular legal forms and the function of those provisions. Below is a brief discussion of the fundamental clauses that one often finds in Will forms. Chapter 8 includes a discussion of drafting issues for trusts. This is intended only as a brief introduction to these concepts; most are discussed in more detail in other parts of the book. Some drafting checklists are collected in the materials at Part I. Form B in the Forms Supplement is a "simple Will" that would be appropriate for an unmarried, childless,

40. *See generally* Gloria S. Neuwirth, *Guidelines for Clients Contemplating Organ Donation*, 23 EST. PLAN. 345 (1996).

41. Part II of "Using Form Documents" appears in Chapter 4, Part F. Part III appears in Chapter 5, Part F. Part IV appears in Chapter 8, Part E.

young adult. That form addresses many of the core provisions described below.[42]

1. Description of the Testator

This is usually the opening line of the Will. It is suggested that the attorney list other names used by the testator (e.g., "I, Margaret Jane Smith, also known as Margaret J. Smith, also known as Maggie Smith, formerly known as Margaret Jane Thompson") whenever there is the possibility that any of the client's assets may be titled under different names or variations of the same name.

2. Revocation of Prior Wills

Unless the instrument is a codicil, the Will should include language that expressly revokes all prior Wills and codicils.

3. Statement Concerning Family

This section provides information about the current spouse, if any, and the testator's children. If the testator is a widower or widow, one might name the deceased spouse and note that the marriage was ended by reason of his or her death on a certain date. If the testator has stepchildren, it is also usually good practice to list them here and expressly describe how they and their descendants are to be treated; that is, whether they are to be considered as "children" of the testator or are excluded. Generally, more remote descendants, such as grandchildren, are not described because they are covered under the definition of "descendants" or other applicable term used by the instrument. This is also a good section in which to set forth any limitations or exclusions the testator may want concerning any potential heir who is to be excluded from taking under the Will or by intestacy.

4. Payment of Debts and Expenses

Sometimes a Will directs the personal representative to pay the "just debts and expenses" of the decedent, including funeral expenses, plus taxes imposed on the estate. Form B in the Forms Supplement does not include this clause, except for a provision concerning taxes, because the estate is usually required by law to pay the decedent's debts if not otherwise barred. If the issue is included in the Will, careful drafting is demanded, because, for example, sloppy language may raise an argument that the personal

42. Several states have adopted "statutory Will" forms that provide basic "check-the-box" and "complete-the-box" alternatives for simple estates. *See, e.g.*, CAL. PROB. CODE §6240 (West Supp. 2011); ME. REV. STAT. ANN. tit. 18-A, §2-514 (West 1998); MICH. COMP. LAWS ANN. §700.2519 (West Supp. 2010); N.M. STAT. §45-2A-17 (2008).

representative is required to exonerate all bequests (e.g., pay off a mortgage encumbering real property owned by the decedent).[43]

5. Tangible Personal Property Disposition

This section deals with household goods, personal effects, automobiles, pets, and other personal property that the testator may want to direct to specific individuals, rather than be included in the residuary clause. If specific gifts of tangible personal property are to be made, a married client may prefer that they be made only upon the death of the surviving spouse. One would normally see these items bequeathed to the surviving spouse or, failing that, to the surviving children. One might also encounter specific bequests to grandchildren from a grandparent of special books, furniture, or jewelry. If permitted by applicable state law, a personal property memorandum will often be referenced in this section.[44] Form C in the Forms Supplement provides a sample tangible personal property memorandum.

The "tangible personal property" referred to in Form C is defined in the Will. Section 2.1 of Form B (Simple Will), for example, includes an expansive listing of examples of such property. Some attorneys include additional language to the effect that any questions as to whether an item is applicable tangible personal property is to be determined by the personal representative, whose decisions are conclusive and binding.[45]

6. Specific Bequests and Residuary Bequests

This is the operative focus of the entire Will. In some cases (e.g., if minor beneficiaries or federal wealth transfer tax planning are considerations) the bequest will be held in trust, whether by pourover to an existing trust or held under the terms of a testamentary trust expressly defined in the Will. In crafting the bequests the attorney must consider potential disclaimers and the doctrines of lapse and ademption. The Will should also address whether interest is payable on cash gifts.[46]

43. *See, e.g.*, CASNER & PENNELL, *supra* note 34, §3.2.3. The UPC, however, provides that a general directive to pay debts does not create a right of exoneration for specific devises. *See* UPC §2-607.

44. *See, e.g.*, UPC §2-513. An amendable memorandum in the style of the UPC format is not permitted by many states. However, if the writing is executed prior to the Will, it might be capable of being included within the incorporation by reference doctrine. New York law, however, does not permit a UPC-style memorandum, nor does New York generally recognize incorporation by reference. *See* WILLIAM M. MCGOVERN ET AL., WILLS, TRUSTS AND ESTATES §6.2 n.4 (4th ed. 2010).

45. *See, e.g.*, THOMAS M. FEATHERSTON, JR. ET AL., DRAFTING FOR TAX AND ADMINISTRATION ISSUES 138-139 (2000). *Compare* David Altshuler, *The Sentimental Auction* 145 TR. & EST. 54 (Dec. 2006) (describing a method by which devisees are given "points" to "bid" on items of personal property).

46. *See, e.g.*, UPC §3-904, which provides for payment of interest on general pecuniary devises beginning one year after the personal representative's appointment.

7. Designation of Fiduciaries

The Will nominates the personal representative and successor nominees and designates the trustees and successor trustees of any trusts created under the instrument. If the testator has minor children, the Will nominates guardian(s) and conservator(s), as well as successor nominees, for the children.

8. Waiver of Fiduciary Bonding

Although the requirement for bonding is relaxed by some statutes, such as the UPC, a Will may waive any bond required for fiduciaries. The language of Section 1.3 of Form B in the Forms Supplement discusses the bonding requirement and refers to the requirement as separate from "sureties." This reflects a technical view that a bond is simply an individual's written agreement acknowledging personal liability for certain obligations. A "surety" is another party who agrees to be financially responsible to the extent the fiduciary fails to meet its stated obligations under the bond.[47] However, statutes such as the UPC combine both aspects in the use of the term "bond."[48] Modern discussions also tend to combine both concepts.[49]

9. Fiduciary Powers and Responsibilities

Although state statutes often grant broad powers to fiduciaries, Wills typically include a list of additional powers. For example, if an estate owns a significant illiquid asset such as a family business, the attorney should pay particular attention to whether the fiduciaries should be permitted to manage such assets without regard to fiduciary principles encouraging diversification and the disposal of nonproductive assets. The compensation of fiduciaries and their removal or replacement are also critical issues.

10. Spendthrift Clauses

Many Wills include the potential creation of a trust, and most clients wish to include a spendthrift clause for the protection of the beneficiary. As discussed in Chapter 13, the spendthrift clause must be drafted with care, because, in some states it could otherwise prevent a beneficiary from disclaiming[50] or giving away assets, which may be desired for other planning purposes such as federal wealth transfer tax planning.

47. *See* Charles E. Rounds, Jr. & Charles E. Rounds, III, Loring and Rounds: A Trustee's Handbook §3.5.4.3 (2010).

48. *See, e.g.*, UPC §§3-601 to -606. *Compare* Tex. Prob. Code Ann. §233 (West 2003) ("he and the sureties on his bond . . .").

49. *See generally* The Law of Probate Bonds (William A. Downing & Jeffrey M. Frank eds., 2001).

50. Like the predecessor act, the Uniform Disclaimer of Property Interests Act provision found at UPC §2-1105(a) permits a person to disclaim an interest or power even if its creator imposed a spendthrift provision or similar restriction on transfer or a restriction or limitation on the right to disclaim.

11. Saving Clauses

The Rule Against Perpetuities (RAP) lurks in the background of trusts created under the Will but can also apply to outright bequests under certain circumstances. In jurisdictions in which the rule applies, a saving clause is generally included in the Will. As discussed in Chapter 13, the traditional saving clause often requires modifications to reflect the emergence of legislation that has limited or eliminated the RAP.

12. Apportionment of Estate Taxes

This clause addresses whether the residuary beneficiaries, all beneficiaries, or some other combination bear the burden of estate taxes imposed on the estate, as introduced in Chapter 2. The attorney has a number of options in structuring the apportionment clause. Some would use equitable apportionment, where all beneficiaries bear their proportionate share of estate taxes, for all estate assets, including nonprobate transfers (if state law or the form of the nonprobate transfer—for example, a revocable trust—permits the recovery or offset of the apportioned taxes). As an alternative, some would exclude specific gifts from apportionment, particularly if they are of less than a certain value, in which case the residue will bear most, if not all, of the tax burden.

13. Survivorship

This clause generally addresses two issues. First, if the testator wishes to modify the survival period under applicable law, that can be accomplished under this clause. It may be desirable for the survival period for a surviving spouse to be a longer period than that established for other beneficiaries, largely to avoid "double probate" of assets upon the close sequential deaths of the spouses. That said, if federal wealth transfer taxation is a consideration, the survival contingency for the surviving spouse must be handled very carefully lest the survivor not receive any marital assets. Second, primarily for federal wealth transfer tax planning, it is often advantageous to establish the order of deaths by specifying who is deemed the survivor when both spouses die under simultaneous or effectively simultaneous circumstances. These issues are impacted by the Deceased Spousal Unused Exclusion Amount discussed in Chapter 11.

14. Applicable Law

Generally the decedent's estate is administered in the decedent's state of domicile at his or her death, with ancillary administration in other states where real property is located. The decedent's state of domicile may be different from the state of domicile at the time the Will was executed. Wills often provide that the laws of the state of domicile at the time of execution govern the validity and construction of the Will. However, the laws of the state of domicile at the time of death usually control the application of the Will, particularly with respect to spousal rights.[51]

15. Definitions

Many Wills do not rely solely on state statutes or common law; the document will define important terms such as "descendants" or "by representation." This is discussed in Chapter 2.

16. Self-Proving Affidavit

A Will generally needs only to be witnessed;[52] it does not require acknowledgment before a notary public. However, the addition of such an acknowledgment may obviate the need for locating the witnesses, the witnesses' appearance in court, or the proffer of affidavits for the admission of the Will to probate.[53] This is discussed in Chapter 2.

EXERCISE 3-1

ASSESSING THE NOTARIZED WILL

You are a sole practitioner, and it is usually inconvenient to find witnesses who will observe the execution of Wills. Further assume that your clients are domiciled in a state that has adopted the UPC notarized Will provisions. What are the considerations in using a notarized Will as compared with an attested (as well as self-proved) Will?

H. CASE STUDY 3-1

Sarah Martin

THE UNMARRIED PROFESSIONAL

Sarah Madeline Martin is age 25, unmarried, a college graduate (B.S. in Computer Science), and works as a system consultant for a publicly traded software company. Her annual salary is approximately $65,000.

51. *See, e.g.*, UPC §2-401. A valid Will executed in one state will be recognized and valid in all states. Thus, a change of domicile should not affect the validity of the Will. However, because of the change in applicable state law that may apply at the client's death following such a relocation, the attorney should advise the client to have the Will promptly reviewed by local counsel after such a relocation.

52. UPC §2-502(a)(3)(B) dispenses with the witness requirement if the testator's signature is acknowledged by the testator before a notary public or other individual authorized by law to take acknowledgments. Some states recognize the validity of "holographic" Wills where the material portions of the document are in the testator's handwriting and the document is signed by the testator (with or without witnesses). *See* UPC §2-502(b).

53. *See, e.g.*, UPC §§2-504 & 3-406(b). While the underlying themes of self-proving affidavits are relatively comparable from state to state, the formalities of expression do vary. Because this is a formalistic matter, one should take care in following the statutorily prescribed format for the particular state in which the Will is executed.

She participates in an employer-sponsored 401(k) plan to which the employer contributes 10 percent of her salary. She holds 1,000 nonqualified stock options on her employer's stock with an exercise price that is still significantly above the market price of the stock. Sarah regularly contributes the maximum permissible amount to a Roth IRA.

Sarah currently rents a townhouse but is considering a home purchase. She leases an automobile for $399 per month. She owes $22,000 in student loans and $3,000 in credit card balances.

In addition to enjoying travel, Sarah is an avid bicyclist and skier.

Sarah's mother (Janet Smothers Martin) and father (Edward James Martin) dissolved their marriage almost six years ago. Her father remarried, but her mother has not. Sarah's younger sister (her only sibling), Ellen Allison Martin, age 16, lives with Sarah's mother. Sarah and her mother currently reside in a state that has adopted the most recent version of the Uniform Probate Code.

EXHIBIT 3.1 DESIGNATION OF BENEFICIARY

1. Personal Information

Sarah	M.	Martin
First Name	MI	Last Name
333-44-2823	08-25-[25 years ago]	
Social Security Number	Date of Birth (mm-dd-yyyy)	

2. Plan Account Number

43244456B

3. Your Primary Beneficiaries

Janet Smothers Martin	06-25-[55 years ago]	
Name	Date of Birth (mm-dd-yyyy)	
Mother	333-38-0004	100%
Relationship	Social Security Number or Taxpayer ID Number	Allocation%

4. Your Contingent Beneficiaries

Ellen Allison Martin	03-25-[16 years ago]	
Name	Date of Birth (mm-dd-yyyy)	
Sister	333-48-1000	100%
Relationship	Social Security Number or Taxpayer ID Number	Allocation%

5. Spousal Rights Declaration

I am exempt from federal spousal rights to survivor benefits requirements.
X I am not married.

6. I, the undersigned, agree that:

Any prior beneficiary designations for this retirement plan account will be revoked and any benefits due by reason of my death will be payable to the beneficiary(ies) named on this form.

I understand that this designation is subject to all of the terms and conditions of the retirement plan account agreement.

I understand that the laws of the State of New York shall govern the interpretation and application of this designation.

Sarah M. Martin	July 15, [three years ago]
Your Signature	Today's Date (mm-dd-yyyy).

While Sarah is not estranged from her father, she does not visit him often, and she telephones him only infrequently. She is much closer to her mother and joins her mother and sister for at least one international travel adventure each year.

Part A: When Sarah enrolled in her employer's 401(k) plan, she designated her mother as the primary beneficiary and her sister as the secondary beneficiary. A copy of the beneficiary designation form is reproduced as Exhibit 3.1. Sarah followed this pattern in establishing her Roth IRA. Discuss any planning concerns presented by this arrangement.

Part B: Sarah is considering a transfer in connection with her employment that would require her to move to another state, Illinois. Discuss any planning concerns presented by this possible development.

Part C: If Sarah retained you as her estate planning attorney today, what steps would you take, what additional information, if any, would you request, and what specific documents would you prepare?

I. Reference Materials

Treatises

General References

- ROGER W. ANDERSEN, UNDERSTANDING TRUSTS AND ESTATES ch. 2, *Intestacy*; ch. 5, *Other Nonprobate Devices*; ch. 6, *Planning for Incapacity* (4th ed. 2009).

- A. James Casner & Jeffrey N. Pennell, Estate Planning ch. 8, *Nonprobate Transfers: Life Insurance*; ch. 9, *Nonprobate Transfers: Retirement Benefits* (6th ed. 1995 & Supp. 2009-2010).
- William M. McGovern et al., Wills, Trusts and Estates ch. 2, *Intestate Succession*; §4.7 (payable-on-death contracts); §4.8 (joint tenancy); §13.2 (necessity for administration); ch. 14, *Planning for Incapacity* (4th ed. 2010).
- John R. Price & Samuel A. Donaldson, Price on Contemporary Estate Planning (2011).
- George M. Turner, Revocable Trusts §13:8 (joint tenancy or tenancy by the entirety); §13:12 (combination of methods) (5th ed. 2003 & Supp. 2010).
- Harold Weinstock & Martin Neumann, Planning an Estate ch. 6, *Avoiding Probate*; ch. 10, *Life Insurance*; ch. 13, *Employee Benefits* (4th ed. 2002 & Supp. 2010).

Retirement Plan Beneficiary Designations

- Casner & Pennell, *supra*, §9.4.
- Natalie B. Choate, Life and Death Planning for Retirement Benefits (7th ed. 2011).
- Frederick K. Hoops et al., Family Estate Planning Guide §24:29 (4th ed. 1994 & Supp. 2010-2011).
- Price & Donaldson, *supra*, ch. 13, *Estate Planning for Retirement Plans and IRAs.*
- Weinstock & Neumann, *supra*, ch. 13, *Employee Benefits.*

Selection of Fiduciaries

- Price & Donaldson, *supra*, §§4.26 & 10.42.

Multistate Planning

- Hoops et al., *supra*, ch. 19, *Conflict of Laws and Multi-State Estates in Family Estate Planning.*

Planning with Stock Options

- Hoops et al., *supra*, §§24:2 to 24:6.
- Price & Donaldson, *supra*, §7.19.

Planning for Simultaneous Death

- McGovern et al., *supra*, 366-368.
- Price & Donaldson, *supra*, §4.15.3.

Medical Decision Making by Proxy

- Casner & Pennell, *supra*, §3.10.
- McGovern et al., *supra*, §14.5.
- Price & Donaldson, *supra*, §4.37.

Drafting Pointers

- HOOPS ET AL., *supra*, ch. 17, *Drafting Wills.*
- PRICE & DONALDSON, *supra*, ch. 4, *Wills and Related Documents*; ch. 10, *Trusts.*

HIPAA Issues

- CASNER & PENNELL, *supra*, §3.10.2.
- PRICE & DONALDSON, *supra*, §§4.35.8 & 4.36; Forms 4-34 (HIPAA provision in durable power of attorney) & 4-35 (authorization of disclosure of protected health information).

Articles

Nonprobate Transfers

- Michael J. Berger, *How Title to Assets Is Held Can Determine Whether Probate Is Avoided*, 18 EST. PLAN. 98 (1991).
- Susan N. Gary, *Transfer-on-Death Deeds: The Nonprobate Revolution Continues*, 41 REAL PROP. PROB. & TR. J. 529 (2006).
- Dennis M. Horn & Susan N. Gary, *TOD Deeds—The Latest Tool in the Toolbox*, 24 PROB. & PROP. 12 (Mar./Apr. 2010).
- John H. Langbein, *The Nonprobate Revolution and the Future of the Law of Succession*, 97 HARV. L. REV. 1108 (1984).
- Kara Peischl Marcus, *Totten Trusts: Pragmatic Pre-Death Planning or Post-Mortem Plunder*, 69 TEMP. L. REV. 861 (1996).
- William M. McGovern, Jr., *Nonprobate Transfers under the Revised Uniform Probate Code*, 55 ALB. L. REV. 1329 (1992).

Retirement Plan Beneficiary Designations (*See also* "Retirement Asset Tax Planning" in Ch. 12 reference materials.)

- Edward V. Atnally, *Estate Planning and Retirement Benefits—An Approach Toward Simplification*, Part 1, PROB. & PROP. 22 (July/Aug. 2009); Part 2, PROB. & PROP. 56 (Sept./Oct. 2009).
- John P. Dedon & Pamela M. Buskirk, *IRA Beneficiary Designations Stretch or Shorten Payout Period*, 38 EST. PLAN. 9 (Feb. 2011).
- Gayle Stutzman Evans, *Estate Planning with Qualified Plans and IRAs*, Basic Estate and Gift Taxation and Planning, SK026 ALI-ABA 229 (ALI-ABA Continuing Legal Education, June 1-3, 2005).
- Thomas E. Lund, *Coordinating Beneficiary Designations with the Estate Plan*, 36 EST. PLAN. 27 (Nov. 2009).
- Lee A. Snow, *Final IRA Distribution Rules Expand and Clarify Tax-Saving Opportunities*, 29 EST. PLAN. 395 (2002).
- Lee A. Snow, *The Pension Protection Act's Retirement Provisions Affecting Individuals*, 34 EST. PLAN. 3 (2007).
- John Strohmeyer, *Swimming Against the Stream: Advising Clients on Their IRA Options*, 25 PROB. & PROP. 24 (July/Aug. 2011).

- Kaja Whitehouse, *Beneficiary Designation Form Is Key to Passing on Your Interests*, WALL ST. J., at D3 (June 4, 2002).

Organ and Tissue Donations

- James F. Blumstein, *The Use of Financial Incentives in Medical Care: The Case of Commerce in Transplantable Organs*, 3 HEALTH MATRIX 1 (1993).
- David M. English, *Gift of Life: The Lawyer's Role in Organ and Tissue Donation*, 8 PROB. & PROP. 10 (Mar./Apr. 1994).
- Carol Sikov Gross, *2002 Legal Aspects of Organ, Tissue Donation*, 4 LAW. J. 5 (Feb. 22, 2002).
- Tanya K. Hernandez, *The Property of Death*, 60 U. PITT. L. REV. 971 (1999).
- Charles M. Jordan, Jr. & Casey J. Price, *First* Moore, *Then* Hecht: *Isn't It Time We Recognize a Property Interest in Tissues, Cells, and Gametes?*, 37 REAL PROP. PROB. & TR. J. 151 (2002).
- Sara Lind Nygren, Comment, *Organ Donation by Incompetent Patients: A Hybrid Approach*, 2006 U. CHI. LEGAL F. 471 (2006).
- Alex McDonald, *End of Life Issues: Organ and Tissue Donation*, 13 UTAH B.J. 20 (Feb. 2000).
- Jennifer L. Mesich-Brant & Lawrence J. Grossback, *Assisting Altruism: Evaluating Legally Binding Consent in Organ Donation Policy*, 30 J. HEALTH POL. POL'Y & L. 687 (2005).
- Gloria S. Neuwirth, *Guidelines for Clients Contemplating Organ Donation*, 23 EST. PLAN. 345 (1996).
- Joanna E. Scannell, *Funeral Arrangements and Organ Donations*, DRAFTING WILLS AND TRUSTS IN MASS. ch. 3 (MACLE 2002).
- *United Network for Organ Sharing*, www.unos.org (last visited Feb. 20, 2011).

Medical Decision Making by Proxy

- Rhonda H. Brink, *A Glimpse Through the Planning Window of the Young, Terminal Client*, 25 INST. ON EST. PLAN. ¶600 (1991).
- Donna A. Casey & David M. Walker, *The Clinical Realities of Advance Directives*, 17 WIDENER L. REV. 429 (2011).
- Casey Frank, *Surrogate Decision-Making for "Friendless" Patients*, 34 COLO. LAW. 71 (Apr. 2005).
- Ardath A. Hamann, *Family Surrogate Laws: A Necessary Supplement to Living Durable Powers of Attorney*, 38 VILL. L. REV. 103 (1993).
- Shari A. Levitan & Helen Adrian, *Brave New World: Ethical Issues Involving Surrogate Health Care Decisions*, 20 PROB. & PROP. 31 (Jan./Feb. 2006).
- Victor C. McCuaig, Jr. & Jed C. Albert, *Health Care Proxies: How Do We Inform Our Clients?*, 63 N.Y. ST. B.J. 24 (Nov. 1991).
- Charles P. Sabatino, *Effective Planning for Health Care Decision Making (with Sample Provisions)*, 13 ALI-ABA EST. PLAN. COURSE MATERIALS J. 33 (Feb. 2007).

- Marah Stith, *The Semblance of Autonomy: Treatment of Persons with Disabilities under the Uniform Health-Care Decisions Act*, 22 Issues L. & Med. 39 (2006).

Selection of Fiduciaries (*See also* same heading in Ch. 7 reference materials.)

- Steve R. Akers, *Selection of Trustees: A Detailed Review of Gift, Estate and Income Tax Effects and Non-tax Effects*, 38 Inst. on Est. Plan. ¶300 (2004).
- Alison Barnes, *The Virtues of Corporate and Professional Guardians*, 31 Stetson L. Rev. 941 (2002).
- Peter Ogden Brown, *So You Want to Be a Fiduciary? The Players and the Game in the 90's*, 25 Inst. on Est. Plan. ¶1400 (1991).
- Louis D. Laurino, *The Duties and Responsibilities of the Attorney/Fiduciary*, 19 Inst. on Est. Plan. ¶1600 (1985).
- Paula A. Monopoli, *Drafting Attorneys as Fiduciaries: Fashioning an Optimal Ethical Rule for Conflicts of Interest*, 66 U. Pitt. L. Rev. 411 (2005).
- Kimbrough Street, *Growls or Gratitude? Practical Guidelines for Selection of Individual Trustees and Design of Trustee Succession Plans*, 40 Inst. on Est. Plan. ¶300 (2006).

Drafting Pointers (*See also* "Drafting Style" in Ch. 2 reference materials and "Drafting Technique" in Ch. 4 reference materials.)

- Karin J. Barkhorn, *Basic Will Drafting*, (PLI N.Y. Practice Skills Handbook Series No. FO-OOGK, Aug. 2002) (includes drafting checklist).
- Dennis I. Belcher & Dana G. Fitzsimons Jr., *Beware of Patented Estate Planning Techniques!*, 20 Prob. & Prop. 24 (Nov./Dec. 2006).
- James G. Dickinson, *Avoiding Conflicts Among Beneficiaries Over Bequests of Personal Property*, 17 Est. Plan. 216 (1990).
- Daniel B. Evans, *Tax Clauses to Die For*, 20 Prob. & Prop. 38 (July/Aug. 2006).
- Helen W. Gunnarsson, *Anatomy of a Will: A Step-By-Step Guide*, 97 Ill. B.J. 506 (Oct. 2009).
- Edward S. Schlesinger, *English as a Second Language for Lawyers*, 12 Inst. on Est. Plan. ¶700 (1978).

Planning with Stock Options

- Natalie B. Choate, *Estate Planning for the Non-Insured, Non-Qualified Compensation: Selected Aspects*, 31 Inst. on Est. Plan. ¶1500 (1997).
- Daniel H. Markstein, *Giving Well Is the Best Revenge: Planning Opportunities with Stock Options*, 34 Inst. on Est. Plan. ¶1300 (2000).

- Jeff J. Saccacio, *Planning Issues and Impacting Opportunities for Entrepreneurs*, 35 INST. ON EST. PLAN. ¶700 (2001).

Planning for Simultaneous Death

- Keith A. Pagano, Note, *Simul et Semel: Estate Planning Principles and the Simultaneous Death Act's Corresponding Tax Consequences*, 14 QUINNIPIAC PROB. L.J. 449 (2000).
- Gerald Le Van, *Simultaneous Death after ERTA*, 17 INST. ON EST. PLAN. ¶1800 (1983).

HIPAA Issues

- Jacqueline Myles *Crain*, *HIPAA-A Shield for Health Information and a Snag for Estate Planning and Corporate Documents*, 40 REAL PROP. PROB. & TR. J. 357 (2005).
- Daniel B. Evans, *What Estate Lawyers Need to Know About HIPAA and "Protected Health Information"*, 18 PROB. & PROP. 20 (July/Aug. 2004).
- Michael L. Graham, *Important HIPAA Compliance Issues for the Estates and Trusts Lawyer*, 39 INST. ON EST. PLAN. ¶800 (2005).
- Michael L. Graham & Jonathan G. Blattmachr, *Planning for the HIPAA Privacy Rule*, 29 ACTEC J. 307 (2004).
- Thomas J. Murphy, *Drafting Health Care Proxies to Comply with the New HIPAA Regs.*, 30 EST. PLAN. 559 (2003).
- Thomas J. Murphy, *Dealing with HIPAA: Powers of Attorney, Record Releases, Court Orders, and Subpoenas*, 5 MARQ. ELDER'S ADVISOR 183 (2004).
- Martin M. Shenkman, *Estate Planning Documents Need to Address HIPAA Issues*, 36 EST. PLAN. 14 (Mar. 2009).

Intellectual Property Issues

- Peter R. Afrasiabi, *What Estate Planners Need to Know About Copyrights*, 37 EST. PLAN. 33 (Mar. 2010).
- Naomi Cahn, *Postmortem Life On-line*, 25 PROB. & PROP. 36 (July/Aug. 2011).
- Nathan J. Dosch & Joseph W. Boucher, *E-Legacy: Who Inherits Your Digital Assets?*, 83 WIS. LAW. 10 (Dec. 2010).

CHAPTER 4

The Wealthy Young Adult Contemplating Marriage

A. Preserving Family Wealth

1. Dissolution of Marriage

Roughly one-half of first marriages in the United States end in divorce.[1] After considering issues concerning any dependent children, financial matters take center stage in the proceedings. The principal financial concerns are the division of property and the determination of any continuing support obligations. The financial aspect of marriage, with an eye toward its potential dissolution, is a recurring theme in several case studies in this book. Wealthy families may be particularly concerned about the dissipation of inherited wealth stemming from the divorce(s) of their offspring. That is the focus of this chapter.[2]

1. *See* Rose M. Kreider, *Number, Timing, and Duration of Marriages and Divorces: 2001*, 9 (Feb. 2005), available at http://www.census.gov/prod/2005pubs/p70-97.pdf; *see also* http://www.divorcereform.org/rates.html and http://www.cdc.gov/nchs.

2. While this chapter focuses on the preservation of inherited wealth, a young adult who wins the lottery or signs a large sports or entertainment contract, or otherwise acquires significant wealth early in his or her life, will have similar issues to consider. For an article suggesting that a marital agreement may be appropriate for almost every married couple with property, *see* Erika L. Haupt, *For Better, For Worse, For Richer, For Poorer: Premarital Agreement Case Studies*, 37 Real Prop. Prob. & Tr. J. 29 (2002); *see also* Stephanie B. Casteel, *Planning and Drafting Premarital Agreements*, 20 No. 1 Prac. Tax. Law. 33 (Fall 2005).

2. Freedom of Disposition

Even if the marriage is preserved, it will ultimately end by death, and state laws may limit the disposition of assets at death. (*See, e.g.*, Chapter 5 for a discussion of the spousal elective share.) Although attitudes vary, some wealthy families view the core invested principal of multigenerational inherited wealth as held by the current generation in trust for future generations. Accordingly, legally imposed limits on disposition of wealth raise the concern of alternative dispositions to individuals outside the family, to charities, or for other uses.

3. Fundamental Principles

A full discussion of the property aspects of marriage is beyond the scope of this book and the expertise of many estate planners, but there are some general principles that should be understood by a planner.

a. Common Law Property States. In a common law property state, each spouse is considered to own, in his or her own name, property held at the beginning of the marriage, plus property inherited by or gifted to that spouse or acquired with the earnings of that spouse during the marriage. Joint titling or commingling of assets may raise issues of implied gifts or difficulty in tracing the source of those assets, thus creating, as a practical if not legal matter, joint assets. This is the pure property law aspect of common law property doctrine, which focuses on the manner in which legal title to assets is held. Upon the death of a spouse, the property rules are modified. While a deceased spouse can dispose of the assets owned by that spouse, that ability is limited by statutorily imposed spousal protections for the benefit of the survivor such as the elective share. In the case of divorce, the property rules are also modified, but not in a manner that neatly coordinates with the limitations on testamentary dispositions.

State law in this area varies widely. The majority of common law property states classify property as either "marital property" or "separate property" at the time of divorce. Property acquired prior to marriage and gifts and inheritances generally retain their separate property status. However, some states permit the equitable division of all property owned by either spouse regardless of its origin. Other states allow the division of separate property if a division of only marital property would be unfair.

b. Community Property States. Arizona, California, Idaho, Louisiana, Nevada, New Mexico, Texas, and Washington are considered community property states. (Puerto Rico is also a community property jurisdiction.) Wisconsin, through adoption of marital property legislation roughly following the Uniform Marital Property Act,[3] is often considered the

3. Unif. Marital Property Act (1983), 9A U.L.A. 110 (1998).

substantial equivalent of a community property state.[4] The Alaska Community Property Act[5] provides for an elective community property regime.

Within the community property system there is a great deal of difference among the states in the details of application, so this discussion is very general. The guiding presumption is that all property acquired during a marriage, other than gifts and inheritances, is community property in which each spouse owns a one-half interest regardless of the manner of titling. Appreciation and income with respect to separate property generally remain separate property unless the spouses' efforts have produced that increase, subject to the "Texas rule."[6] The community property states vary in the presumptions to be applied in determining whether acquired property is community property.[7] An individual in a community property state must be circumspect to avoid the transmutation of separate property into community property, or vice versa, through commingling or the manner of titling.[8]

A decedent can only dispose of his or her share of the community property but is free to dispose of his or her own separate property. In a divorce, community property is divided, but separate property generally is not. Alimony may be awarded in some community property jurisdictions to varying degrees.[9]

An important planning issue is the impact of movement by married couples to and from community property jurisdictions. That topic is addressed in Chapter 10.

4. The IRS ruled that the Wisconsin law creates community property for federal income tax purposes. *See* Rev. Rul. 87-13, 1987-1 C.B. 20. Although the Wisconsin statute creates equal ownership of marital property, the separate equitable distribution provisions govern property distribution in dissolution of marriage. *See, e.g.*, Howard S. Erlanger & June M. Weisberger, *From Common Law Property to Community Property: Wisconsin's Marital Property Act Four Years Later*, 1990 Wis. L. Rev. 769, 782-787.

5. Alaska Stat. §§34.77.010 through 34.77.995 (2010). *See generally* Jonathan G. Blattmachr et al., *Tax Planning with Consensual Community Property: Alaska's New Community Property Law*, 33 Real Prop. Prob. & Tr. J. 615 (1999).

6. Under the community property law of some states, notably Texas as well as Idaho and Louisiana, the income from separate property may be considered community property. Uniform Marital Property Act §4 similarly provides that income, but not the appreciation, from gifts or inheritances of a spouse (which would be separate property) is treated as marital property.

7. There are at least four competing presumptions of community property status: the so-called "acquisition," "long marriage," "possession," and "unlimited" approaches. *See, e.g.*, William A. Reppy Jr. & Cynthia A. Samuel, Community Property in the United States 54 (2d ed. 1982).

8. In creating joint tenancies in real estate, California law, for example, requires an express written declaration that the community property interest is being converted. *See* Cal. Fam. Code §852 (West 2004). *See generally* Grace Ganz Blumberg, Community Property in California, 113-135 (4th ed. 2003) (explaining California law of transmutation).

9. In Texas, for example, a spouse in a marriage of ten or more years' duration who lacks sufficient property and earning ability for self-support may be awarded alimony or spousal support but generally for not more than three years. *See* Tex. Fam. Code Ann. §§8.051 & 8.054 (Vernon 2006).

B. Marital Agreements

A couple contemplating marriage, as well as a couple already married, may execute a contract for the purpose of settling the marital rights and obligations of either or both of the parties. Among other things, the agreement usually defines the rights of each spouse to certain property, the right of a spouse to "take against the Will" in the event of the death of the other, and the respective rights and liabilities of the husband and wife to property and maintenance in the event of dissolution of marriage. Provided that certain statutory and other requirements are met, these agreements are enforceable in most states, although such agreements generally cannot limit child support obligations or fix spousal maintenance (alimony) at what may be "unconscionable" levels as determined at the time of divorce. Some may view these agreements as unromantic, pessimistic, and cynical, creating ill will that "sows the seeds of divorce." Indeed, it is often the parents of the bride or groom who are the instigators of such agreements, particularly as they relate to protecting multigenerational "family" property from dispersion in the event of divorce.

There are a number of local practice variations and details to marital agreements.[10] As general guidelines: (a) the agreement should be written and executed with formalities such as before a notary public; (b) the parties should provide an accurate and complete disclosure to one another of their financial status, including all assets, liabilities, and income; (c) each party should be represented by competent and independent legal counsel, who should also sign the agreement; (d) each party should be advised of and understand the implications of the document and the consequences that would result but for the agreement; (e) the negotiations should be free of coercive behavior (e.g., drafting and executing the document the night before the wedding, while not absolutely and necessarily fatal to the enforceability of the agreement, certainly raises concerns that are less likely to arise in an agreement discussed and negotiated over several months); and (f) waivers of spousal rights to retirement plan benefits must be handled with special care.[11]

The Uniform Probate Code (UPC) provides some direction for the drafting of agreements waiving the elective share and other probate-related rights, but the provisions do not directly address dissolution of

10. Some states, for example, require that the agreements be acknowledged before a notary. *See, e.g.*, N.Y. Dom. Rel. Law §236(B)(3) (McKinney 2010).

11. Individual Retirement Accounts (IRAs) are generally not subject to the Employee Retirement Income Security Act (ERISA) and the Retirement Equity Act of 1984. However, employer-sponsored retirement plans may be subject to ERISA. Generally, only a spouse may execute a waiver, meaning that *prospective* spouses cannot waive their spousal rights under ERISA in a prenuptial agreement. They can, however, in a prenuptial agreement contractually agree to deliver waivers of such rights *after* they are married. *See, e.g.*, Treas. Reg. §1.401(a)-20, Q-28. In addition, the spouse generally must be at least 35 years of age to be able to waive the benefits. See 29 U.S.C. §1055(c)(7). *See generally* Denise K. Mills, *Beware of the Trap—Marital Agreements and ERISA Benefits*, 23 Colo. Law. 577 (Mar. 1994).

marriage issues.[12] The Uniform Premarital Agreement Act,[13] which has been adopted by 25 states and the District of Columbia, more broadly addresses these issues. However, the Act does not apply to postnuptial agreements or cohabitation agreements.

In a common law property state, the marital agreement, by defining contractually what is or will be deemed separate property and marital property, can limit the surviving spouse's rights to the decedent's estate, thereby freeing the decedent to dispose of his or her property without additional limitation. With respect to dissolution of marriage, the agreement may limit spousal support or maintenance claims, but such limitations may be subject to claims of unconscionability. The agreement may also establish guidelines for the computation and division of marital property (e.g., the agreement may absolutely exclude as marital property all gifts, inheritances, and assets brought into the marriage, including appreciation of those assets).

In a community property state, the agreement may limit spousal support or maintenance claims, again often subject to claims of unconscionability. It may also establish guidelines for the possibly unequal division of otherwise community property upon divorce or its disposition by Will and may establish rules for dealing with separate property to avoid transmutation into community property.

C. Irrevocable Trusts

While a marital agreement can be a very flexible planning tool, it is a consensual agreement that requires the acquiescence of both parties to the marriage. This can be a divisive issue. Moreover, there is no control by other family members over the specific terms to be included in the agreement or the possibility of both spouses revoking or otherwise modifying the agreement at a later time. Even if the agreement is not revoked or otherwise modified, there is no assurance that the agreement will even be used or that the parties will keep their contractually defined separate assets separate—they are always free to commingle or gift the assets to each other. Consequently, an irrevocable multigenerational trust created and funded by the family of the prospective bride or groom may be employed as yet another tool to preserve family wealth.

The terms of the irrevocable multigenerational trust may provide for a discretionary sprinkling of income or corpus among the descendants of the creator of the trust, the settlor. The trust would also commonly include a spendthrift clause. While the possible consequences vary widely according

12. *See, e.g.*, UPC §2-213.
13. Unif. Premarital Agreement Act (1983), 9C U.L.A. 39 (2001).

to state law and the express terms of the trust, issues to be considered include: (a) in a common law property state that considers gifts and inheritances as marital property, and depending upon the express terms of the trust, a beneficiary/spouse may not be considered to own a property interest in the trust, or a property interest capable of being valued in terms of including the asset itself or its appreciation as a marital asset; (b) in a common law property state following an all-inclusive marital property rule, property distributions received during the marriage might be considered marital property; (c) in a common law or community property state, the beneficiary's interest in the trust, as well as in the income distributions, could be considered separate property (subject to exceptions such as the Texas rule, which might include the income) for purposes of property division, but the appreciation of such separate property interest during the marriage could be considered marital property; (d) in a common law or community property state, the discretionary distributions of income might be excluded from the recipient's resources in determining spousal support obligations; and (e) under the majority rule, the spendthrift clause would not defeat a judgment for spousal support or child support, assuming that in light of the discretionary nature of the beneficiary's interest, there is a property interest to attach.[14]

The undesirable gaps in the list of possible consequences suggest that an irrevocable trust alone cannot accomplish complete preservation of family wealth.

The following case demonstrates one court's approach to this issue, which ultimately relied on its application of common law future interest rules.

In re Marriage of Guinn
93 P.3d 568 (Colo. App. 2004)

Cheryl A. Guinn (wife) appeals from the property division entered as part of the trial court's permanent orders in this proceeding to dissolve her marriage to David L. Guinn (husband). She specifically challenges the trial court's determination that husband's income interest in an irrevocable trust created by his parents did not constitute a property interest. We affirm.

The parties married in 1987, and their marriage was dissolved in 2002. In 1990, husband's parents created an irrevocable generation-skipping trust. Under the terms of the trust, husband is to receive the net income in annual or more frequent distributions. The trust also allows discretionary payment of corpus to husband if such payments are reasonably necessary for husband's health, maintenance, support, and education. Upon husband's death, the corpus is to remain in trust for the benefit

14. *See, e.g.*, Unif. Trust Code §503 (spendthrift provision is unenforceable against a claims for child support or spousal support or maintenance).

of husband's descendants. Husband has no power of appointment or other right to direct the disposition of the trust. In short, husband is a lifetime income beneficiary, and his children hold the remainder.

The trial court found, and the parties do not dispute, that husband had no property interest in the corpus of the trust, although he had a right to so much of the income as the trustees elected to allocate during his life.

Husband's parents initially funded the trust with $400,000 worth of publicly traded stock. They made subsequent cash contributions of $16,000 in 1999 and $51,000 in 2000, for total contributions of $467,000. At the time of the permanent orders hearing, the trust corpus had appreciated to approximately $818,869.

The pertinent powers granted to the trustees include the power to invest in any kind of property, the power to determine in the exercise of reasonable discretion what is principal and what is income of the trust, and the power to apportion and allocate receipts and expenditures between those respective accounts.

The current trustees are husband's parents. According to the testimony of husband's father, the investment philosophy for the trust is to maximize the growth potential of the portfolio to take advantage of the estate tax laws for which the trust was formed. Consistent with that philosophy and the acknowledged customary practice for the management of similar trusts, the trust returns show that capital gains have been generally allocated to principal while the distributions of income to husband comprised the interest and dividend income earned.

On appeal, wife contends that the trial court erred in finding that husband's income interest was not property subject to division. She argues his interest constituted an enforceable right in the trust rather than an expectancy and is therefore property under [the marital property statute]. We disagree.

The trial court has great latitude to effect an equitable division of marital property based on the facts and circumstances of each case. The trial court, in exercising its discretion, must first determine whether an interest constitutes "property" and then must determine whether the property is marital or separate.... A reviewing court will not disturb a trial court's decision regarding division of property unless there has been a clear abuse of discretion....

In Colorado, income from a spouse's separate property, as well as appreciation in that separate property during the marriage, is deemed to be marital property and therefore subject to division.... Previously, we have not considered whether income received by a spouse that is generated from the property of a third party is marital property. We conclude that it is not.

In determining whether husband's right to income represents a property interest to be classified and valued for purposes of [the marital property statute], the trial court found that the obligation to distribute income to husband was mandatory, not discretionary. The court also found that husband could not require the trustees to invest with maximum income potential for his benefit and that the investment strategy was "solely in the hands of the trustees." Also, the trial court distinguished various decisions that have classified remainder interests as fixed interests constituting property, noting that under traditional property law, if husband possessed a life estate in real estate, his interest would arguably have some value. However, the court further observed that the parties cited no case holding that a beneficiary's interest in income from a trust is property and that unlike the general scenarios involving a right to future income, here, neither party contributed anything to the trust or to its postformation appreciation. The court concluded that husband's interest was not "property" subject to division under [the marital property statute]. The court, therefore, held that it was unnecessary to classify husband's interest as either marital or nonmarital or some combination thereof.

As for husband's right to discretionary payments of corpus if needed, the trial court determined that it had only a nominal value and apparently did not consider that interest at all in the determination of the property division. Nor did the court conclude that such payments amounted to an interest in the trust corpus such that husband's interest could be considered separate property. Wife does not dispute this ruling.

When a trust permits trustees to distribute to a beneficiary so much, if any, of income as they in their discretion see fit, a beneficiary has no property interest or rights in the undistributed funds. The rights held by the beneficiary are merely an expectancy. . . . Thus, the income beneficiary of a discretionary trust has no contractual or enforceable right to the corpus and cannot force any action by the trustee unless the trustee performs dishonestly or does not act at all. Because the beneficiary possesses no "property" interest, the income received from the trust is a gift under [the marital property statute] which is not divisible. . . .

Here, the trustees were required to pay income to husband although they had discretion to choose the investments and to allocate earnings to principal or income. Thus, husband had a right to income, assuming any income was declared by the trustees. However, this right could hardly be classified as a remainder interest.

In contrast, a remainder interest in an irrevocable trust represents a present fixed right to future enjoyment that gives rise to a vested property interest in the trust property even if that interest is subject to complete divestment or defeasance. . . . That remainder interest also qualifies as a gift of separate property to the beneficiary. However, any appreciation of the interest during the marriage constitutes marital property under [the marital property statute] to the extent its present value at the time of the decree exceeds its value at the time of acquisition. . . .

A division of this court determined that a spouse's remainder interest in a revocable trust is also a property interest rather than a mere expectancy and that the increase in the value of that interest during the marriage is marital property. . . . Following that decision, however, the General

Assembly enacted [legislation] which excludes from the definition of "property" any interest a party possesses under a third-party instrument that is alienable or revocable. . . .

Here, even though the obligation to distribute the income is mandatory, no amount is specified, and the income, if any, is not determined until it is declared by the trustees and distributed to husband. . . . In sharp contrast to the situation where a beneficiary has a vested property interest in the corpus or in a remainder, here, husband's trust income derives from property vested in third parties — the next generation remaindermen — not from property in which he holds an interest. The nature of this income interest is not disputed, making the facts of this case somewhat unusual.

At least one authority suggests that in circumstances such as these, "a special category of gift" is created "because of the beneficiary's inability to reach the corpus." Michael Diehl, *The Trust in Marital Law: Divisibility of a Beneficiary Spouse's Interests on Divorce*, 64 Tex. L. Rev. 1301, 1349-50 (1986). Thus, where a beneficiary owns no separate property interest in the corpus of a trust, the income is deemed to be his separate property, not subject to division as marital property. Diehl, *supra*. According to this view, where a beneficiary receives both an interest in the corpus and the right to draw down so much of it as he needs, he receives an equitable property interest in the trust, and the income derived therefrom is marital. . . . However, when the beneficiary has no interest in the corpus, and no right to control how the corpus is invested, we conclude that the income is a mere gratuity deriving from the beneficence of the settlors. . . .

. . . We are unable to conclude that undeclared and unrealized future income could be exchanged for value, pledged as a sum certain, or listed on a sworn financial statement as a definite asset. In the absence of some ownership interest in the corpus itself, we conclude that even a mandatory right to unrealized future discretionary allocations of income is an expectancy arising from the largess of the settlors and does not constitute property for purposes of [the marital property statute].

The judgment is affirmed.

QUESTION

Assume that the husband's parents instead funded the irrevocable trust with a very spacious home and the trust instrument permitted the husband, his descendants, and his current spouse or companion (if any) to occupy the premises (and any replacement property) at no expense to them. How do you think the Court would have handled that? Do you find the Court's treatment of the mandatory income interest convincing? If not, how would you value such an interest? How would you advise the settlors to structure the arrangement for use of the home?

D. Conditional Bequests

This topic is generally discussed at length in a Wills and Trusts course, so our discussion is very cursory. A family might attempt to influence a young adult concerning marriage decisions by threatening to disinherit him or her with respect to assets that the older generation has accumulated. Under the majority rule, a requirement that the beneficiary marry within a certain religious faith will be upheld if considered reasonable by the court.[15] On the other hand, a requirement that the beneficiary divorce a spouse in order to receive a bequest will generally not be upheld.[16] Both of these conditional bequests require some action on the part of the beneficiary or some state of affairs tied to the beneficiary—to marry someone, to divorce someone, or to be in some sort of marital arrangement at some specified time. It would seem that they can be largely circumvented if the Will or other governing instrument sets no requirements upon the beneficiary but also simply provides little or nothing to him or her with no further elaboration. This can provide leverage to the older generation in insisting on other measures such as a marital agreement, albeit at the risk of damaged family relationships.

Conditional bequests are increasingly found in irrevocable trusts, particularly those cast in terms of distributions tied to "incentives" for desired behavior.[17] See Chapter 13.

E. The Impact of Dissolution of Marriage on Estate Planning Documents

Upon a divorce or annulment of a marriage, statutes such as the UPC revoke any revocable disposition of property to the former spouse or certain relatives of the former spouse.[18] The UPC revokes dispositions made in a Will as well as revocable dispositions made in Will substitutes such as revocable inter vivos trusts and life insurance and retirement plan beneficiary designations.[19] The UPC also revokes provisions conferring a power of appointment on the former spouse or on a relative of the former

15. *See* Jesse Dukeminier et al., Wills, Trusts, and Estates 27-35 (8th ed. 2009).

16. *Id.* at 34-35.

17. *See, e.g.*, Judy Barber, *The Psychology of Conditional Giving: What's the Motivation?*, 21 Prob. & Prop. 57 (Nov./Dec. 2007).

18. *See, e.g.*, UPC §2-804. The UPC also revokes dispositions to certain relatives of the former spouse. A stepchild who was not adopted by the decedent will be considered a relative of the former spouse.

19. Joint bank accounts are troublesome, because the UPC definition of the pertinent "governing instrument" includes POD designations but does not mention joint accounts. *See* UPC §1-201(18). On the other hand, the UPC severs joint tenancies in "property" with rights of survivorship, and "property" includes personal property. *See* UPC §1-201(38).

spouse[20] and nominations of the former spouse or a relative of the former spouse to serve in any fiduciary or representative capacity such as personal representative, executor, trustee, conservator, agent, or guardian.[21]

Although the UPC converts joint tenancies with right of survivorship into tenancies in common,[22] the UPC in this context does not address irrevocable dispositions, such as irrevocable trusts, but the attorney can achieve a similar result through appropriate drafting in the trust instrument itself. In Chapter 8 we discuss irrevocable trust language that anticipates the possibility of dissolution of marriage.

What advice, if any, should an attorney provide to a client involved, or about to be involved, in a dissolution of marriage proceeding? If the divorcing couple lives in a state that has not adopted a statute as extensive as the UPC, the attorney may consider amending the client's Will, severing joint tenancies, and so forth, either prior to or while the dissolution of marriage proceeding is pending. If the divorcing couple lives in a state that has adopted a statute similar to the UPC, such amendments may seem less pressing, but there is always the risk that the concerned client could die before the divorce or annulment becomes final. All of this pre-dissolution planning is subject, however, to statutory provisions prohibiting such actions on grounds of public policy, as well as possible intervention of, or standstill restrictions imposed by, the family law court and the ultimate treatment of these issues in any final separation agreement.[23] Furthermore, the impact of the spousal election, omitted spouse, and other statutory provisions, as well as any existing prenuptial or postnuptial marital agreements must also be evaluated.

F. Using Form Documents (Part II)[24]

The case study in Part G involves using a simple marital agreement form (Form K) from the Forms Supplement. We will include other discussions of forms practice in later chapters in connection with more complex documents. Here are some preliminary points.

1. Know Your Source

Legal forms are everywhere. One can find them on Internet sites,[25] in self-help publications in bookstores, in stationery supply stores, at trust

20. *See* UPC §2-804(b)(1)(ii).
21. *See* UPC §2-804(b)(1)(iii).
22. *See* UPC §2-804(b)(2).
23. Unilateral amendments to retirement plan beneficiary designations may be impossible to a degree due to the required spousal benefit mandated by the Retirement Equity Act of 1984, discussed in Chapter 5.
24. Part I of "Using Form Documents" appeared in Chapter 3, Part G. Part III appears in Chapter 5, Part F. Part IV appears in Chapter 8, Part E.
25. Westlaw offers a number of general and state-specific databases for estate planning, many of which include sample forms. For a list of Westlaw estate planning databases, *see* WILLIAM M. MCGOVERN ET AL., WILLS, TRUSTS AND ESTATES 743-757 (4th ed. 2010).

companies or banks, and in law libraries.[26] While many of them are adequate for their purposes, many others are not. Like the forms in this book, which generally reflect a UPC structure, many of the forms do not reflect specifics of local practice. Bar associations and continuing legal education programs have developed forms in many states. While those forms can be very basic in approach, they often provide a sound footing. One of the valuable tools that a new attorney can acquire in practice is access to a forms file, or document drafting software, developed by a competent source.

2. Use the Right Form

An experienced estate planning attorney will tell you that one repeatedly encounters certain fact patterns in practice generally calling for similar planning measures. One objective of this book is to introduce the reader to a number of those recurring fact patterns. While all Will forms share some common provisions, there are a number of specialized provisions responding to specific fact patterns. One does not usually start with a single form and add the specialized provisions. Unless the attorney automates such a process using drafting software, adjusting and adding to a single form is an inefficient use of time and can produce oversights and serious omissions. Instead, one usually starts with a basic package of alternate forms (e.g., a simple Will, a Will with a contingent trust, a Will with a marital deduction formula clause and a testamentary trust, a Will with a marital deduction formula and two testamentary trusts, and so forth) and then directly tailors that form to the specific facts.

3. Understand the Form

Completing legal forms may appear to be deceptively simple, amounting to little more than filling in the blanks. One should *read every word* of a form *each time* one uses it because some new issue might be triggered on the specific facts at hand. One should understand the role of each clause and the impact of the language, and, particularly with tax-sensitive documents, one should be careful in modifying the language. While experienced attorneys might review a number of forms to glean new ideas, an inexperienced attorney might not appreciate the advantages and disadvantages of competing approaches.

26. American Law Institute, American Bar Association, and Practising Law Institute publications are excellent sources of forms that are not specific to a given state. A good comprehensive source for Wills language is JEFFREY A. SCHOENBLUM, PAGE ON THE LAW OF WILLS, vol. 7 (Forms) (2010). *See also* JEFFREY A. SCHOENBLUM, ANDERSON'S ESTATE PLANNING FORMS AND CLAUSES (2d ed. 2000 & Supp. 2005) (a freestanding reprint of Chapter 7 of PAGE ON THE LAW OF WILLS). Both of the Schoenblum publications include the forms on a pocket part CD-ROM.

4. Strive for Uniformity

One sometimes sees practitioner instruments that are a hodgepodge of provisions lifted from various unrelated forms by multiple authors. A good forms set will contain definitions, powers, and other provisions that are uniform.[27] This approach permits one to refine the language, perhaps across many different types of documents that all use the same clause. This approach also permits one to become very acquainted with the language and to keep the language up-to-date across multiple forms.

5. Automate

While it is well beyond the scope of this book to discuss the benefits and burdens of automated document drafting, it should be apparent that with the technological tools available today, all estate planning practices should use a computer in developing and producing documents.[28]

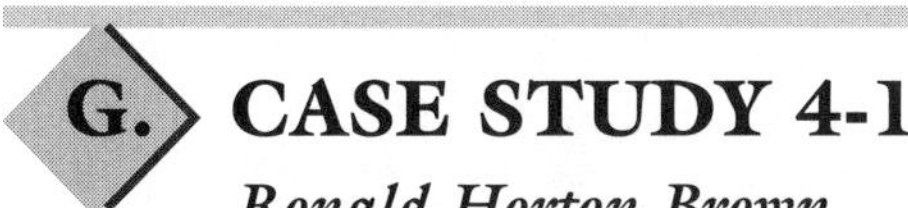

G. CASE STUDY 4-1

Ronald Horton Brown

THE HEIR CONTEMPLATING MARRIAGE

Ronald Horton Brown, age 28, is engaged to be married to Janet Elizabeth Scott, age 26. Ron, a graduate of an exclusive private university, is employed as a junior stock analyst. He earns approximately $200,000 annually in salary and bonuses. Janet, a graduate of the same private university, is employed as a bank economist. She earns approximately $85,000 annually in salary. Neither Ron nor Janet owns a personal residence at this time.

Ron's father is a retired partner in a private investment firm. Ron's mother has devoted much of her time to charitable service activities. Ron's parents' financial net worth is approximately $40,000,000. Ron has one older sister.

Janet's father is a recently retired surgeon, and her mother, while principally a homemaker, has worked as a substitute teacher. Janet's parents' financial net worth is approximately $5,000,000. Janet has two older siblings.

27. Law professors and some practicing attorneys are dismissive of standard terms and definitions as mere "boilerplate." While boilerplate is not a substitute for thinking, as well as responsive and creative drafting, the omission of well-conceived definitions and protections is a litigation breeder.

28. Indeed, much of the competition for estate planners, at least for less wealthy clients, is from widely available self-help drafting software and online document preparation services such as LegalZoom.com. *See generally* Jonathan G. Blattmachr, *Looking Back and Looking Ahead: Preparing Your Practice for the Future: Do Not Get Behind the Change Curve*, 36 ACTEC J. 1 (Summer 2010); Wendy S. Goffe & Rochelle L. Haller, *From Zoom to Doom? Risks of Do-It-Yourself Estate Planning*, 38 EST. PLAN. 27 (Apr. 2011).

Ron and Janet each like to live well. They spend significant sums on clothing, dining, memberships, automobiles, recreation, and travel. Ron and Janet each owe $15,000 and $8,000, respectively, on revolving credit charge cards. The value of Ron's investment portfolio (including self-directed retirement plan assets) is approximately $100,000. The value of Janet's is approximately $35,000.

Ron is a limited partner in several real estate investment limited partnerships created by his father. The partnerships own a community shopping center, two apartment complexes, and a professional arts office building. Ron's parents gifted interests in the partnerships to Ron, and the current value of Ron's interests is approximately $1,000,000.

Ron is one of several beneficiaries of a family trust created by his paternal grandparents in 1940. Ron has received discretionary distributions of income from time to time from the family trust. When Ron reaches the age of 30, he will receive quarterly income distributions totaling approximately $1,250,000 annually until he reaches age 65 (plus discretionary distributions of principal if necessary under the standard of the trust).

Ron's parents plan to give a unit in a cooperative, 1235 Roxbury, #21, MyCity, MyState 80000 (valued at approximately $1,500,000) to Ron and Janet as a wedding gift.

Part A: Acting on advice from his favorite uncle, Ron has requested an assessment of the wealth preservation implications of his pending marriage. Prepare that assessment, assuming that a common law property regime applies and a statute such as the UPC has been adopted.

Part B: Prepare the assessment in Part A but assume that community property law applies.

Part C: Based on your assessment in Part A, describe any planning measures that should be implemented.

Part D: Based on your assessment in Part B, describe any planning measures that should be implemented.

Part E: Assume that Ron and Janet agree to execute a marital agreement. Ron agrees to waive any rights (in dissolution of marriage or upon Janet's death) to amounts that Janet might receive as gifts and inheritances from her family. Janet agrees to waive any rights (in dissolution of marriage or upon Ron's death) to amounts that Ron might receive as gifts and inheritances from his family. Ron and Janet agree to deposit their salaries in a joint checking/savings account from which household expenses will be paid. Ron and Janet will be permitted to separately title and invest any proceeds from gifts, inheritances, or trust distributions. Ron agrees to waive any rights to spousal support or maintenance. Janet agrees to waive any rights to spousal support or maintenance. Notwithstanding the foregoing, upon dissolution of marriage or upon Ron's death while married to Janet, Janet shall be entitled to receive 50 percent of the marital property (after the exclusions described above). Further, if the marriage lasts at least five years, Janet shall receive (in addition to the 50 percent share of marital property), an additional amount necessary to bring the total sum (including the share of marital property) to $500,000. If the marriage lasts for at least ten years, the minimum shall be increased to $1,000,000. If the marriage lasts for at least fifteen years, the minimum shall be increased to $1,500,000. After the fifteenth year of marriage, the $1,500,000 minimum will be adjusted to allow for inflation as measured by the national Consumer Price Index, computed from the fifteenth year of the marriage until Janet reaches age 65. The marital agreement should address standard issues, such as who will bear the attorney fees incurred in its preparation, the degree of judicial review of the agreement, express waivers of possible defenses to its enforcement, the payment of attorney fees upon divorce or in litigation to enforce or contest the agreement, and covenants to preserve the confidentiality of the agreement and its exhibits.

Recognizing that in practice one would often consult with a matrimonial law specialist, draft the marital agreement for Ron and Janet, assuming a common law property state and using as a guide Form K (Sample Marital Agreement), found in the Forms Supplement. Unless your teacher provides other directions, assume that you are representing Ron.

Part F: Assume that Janet's attorney insists upon some payments to Janet in the nature of alimony or maintenance. The proposal is that if any children are born and the marriage ends in divorce, Janet would receive $10,000 per month in spousal support or maintenance until the youngest child reaches the age of 25. What are the state law and federal tax law implications of this change?

H. Reference Materials

Treatises

Dissolution of Marriage

- Frederick K. Hoops et al., Family Estate Planning Guide ch. 18 (4th ed. 1994 & Supp. 2010-2011).
- J. Thomas Oldham, Divorce, Separation and the Distribution of Property (1987 & Supp. 2010).
- John Tingley & Nicholas B. Svalina, Marital Property Law (rev. 2d ed. 1994 & Supp. 2010).
- Brett R. Turner, Equitable Distribution of Property (3d ed. 2005 & Supp. 2010-2011).

The Elective Share

- Roger W. Andersen, Understanding Trusts and Estates 147-166 (4th ed. 2009).
- A. James Casner & Jeffrey N. Pennell, Estate Planning §3.4 (6th ed. 1995 & Supp. 2009-2010).
- William M. McGovern et al., Wills, Trusts and Estates 160-171 (4th ed. 2010).

Community Property

- Andersen, *supra*, 145-146.
- McGovern et al., *supra*, 171-183.
- John R. Price & Samuel A. Donaldson, Price on Contemporary Estate Planning §§3.22 to 3.39 (2011).
- William A. Reppy, Jr. & Cynthia A. Samuel, Community Property in the United States (2d ed. 1982).

Marital Agreements

- Andersen, *supra*, 163-166.
- Edward A. Haman, How to Write Your Own Premarital Agreement (2d ed. 1998).
- Hoops et al., *supra*, §§18:5 & 18:8.
- Alexander Lindey & Louis I. Parley, Lindey and Parley on Separation Agreements and Antenuptial Contracts (2d ed. 1999 & Supp. 2010).
- McGovern et al., *supra*, 183-190.
- Laura W. Morgan & Brett R. Turner, Attacking and Defending Marital Agreements (2001).
- Katherine E. Stoner & Shae Irving, Prenuptial Agreements: How to Write a Fair and Lasting Contract (3rd ed. 2008).
- Tingley & Svalina, *supra*, ch. 25, *Waiver of Rights to Widow's Allowance*; ch. 26, *Antenuptial Agreements Affecting Property Rights on Separation or Divorce*; ch. 27, *Postnuptial and Separation Agreements*; ch. 30, *Nondisclosure of Property Interests When Making Antenuptial Agreements*; & ch. 31, *Form of Execution or Acknowledgment as Affecting Validity of Antenuptial Agreement.*

Will Contracts

- Andersen, *supra*, 70-73.
- McGovern et al., *supra*, 244-253.
- Price & Donaldson, *supra*, §§4.7 & 4.28.

Revocation by Operation of Law

- Andersen, *supra*, 64.
- Averill, *supra*, 225-226.
- Casner & Pennell, *supra*, §3.1.3.

- McGovern et al., *supra*, 266-268 (divorce).
- Price & Donaldson, *supra*, §4.20.5.

Conditional Bequests

- Andersen, *supra*, 171-174.
- Hoops et al., *supra*, §17:24.
- McGovern et al., *supra*, 192-195.

Drafting Pointers

- Hoops et al., *supra*, app. 17 (example of premarital agreement).
- Jeffrey A. Schoenblum, Page on the Law of Wills, vol. 7, Forms 30.01 (effect of divorce on will); 31.01 (elective share); 63.01 (premarital agreement) (2010).
- Stoner & Irving, *supra*, app. C, *Clauses for Building Your Prenup*.
- George M. Turner, Revocable Trusts app. 12 (example of premarital agreement) (5th ed. 2003 & Supp. 2010).

Articles

Overview of Wealth Preservation

- Richard A. Oshins & Stevens J. Oshins, *Protecting and Preserving Wealth in the Next Millennium* (Part 1), 137 Tr. & Est. 52 (Sept. 1998); (Part 2), 137 Tr. & Est. 68 (Oct. 1998).
- Gideon Rothschild, *Protecting the Estate from In-Laws and Other Predators*, 35 Inst. on Est. Plan. ¶1700 (2001).

Community Property Law (*See also* same heading in Ch. 5 reference materials.)

- Karen E. Boxx, *Community Property Across State Lines*, 19 Prob. & Prop. 9 (Jan./Feb. 2005).
- Jeffrey T. Drake, *Devolution Agreements: Non-Probate Dispositions of Community Property in Idaho and Washington*, 34 Idaho L. Rev. 591 (1998).
- Stanley Johanson, *The Migrating Client: Estate Planning for the Couple from a Community Property State*, 9 Inst. on Est. Plan. ¶800 (1975).
- Kenneth W. Kingma, *Property Division at Divorce or Death for Married Couples Migrating Between Common Law and Community Property States*, 35 ACTEC J. 74 (2009).
- Shelly D. Merritt, *Planning for Community Property in Colorado*, 31 Colo. Law. 79 (June 2002).
- Terrance J. Mullin, *Understanding the Testamentary Effects of Community Property Rules*, 79 Fla. B.J. 49 (Jan. 2005).
- Jeremy T. Ware, *Section 1014(b)(6) and the Boundaries of Community Property*, 5 Nev. L.J. 704 (2005).

Marital Agreements (*See also* same heading in Ch. 9 reference materials.)

- Cory Adams, *Part Three: Getting Married, Prenuptial Agreements*, 11 J. Contemp. Legal Issues 121 (2000).
- Suzanne D. Albert, *The Perils of Premarital Provisions*, 48 R.I. B.J. 5 (Mar. 2000).
- Jeffrey A. Baskies, *A Practical Guide to Preparing and Using Prenuptial Agreements*, 27 Est. Plan. 347 (2000).
- Dennis I. Belcher & Laura O. Pomeroy, *For Richer, For Poorer: Strategies for Premarital Agreements*, 12 Prob. & Prop. 54 (Nov./Dec. 1998).
- Dennis I. Belcher, *How to Tie a Tight Knot With a Marital Agreement*, 35 Inst. on Est. Plan. ¶400 (2001).
- Dennis I. Belcher & Laura O. Pomeroy, *A Practitioner's Guide for Negotiating, Drafting and Enforcing Premarital Agreements*, 37 Real Prop. Prob. & Tr. J. 1 (2002).
- Gail Frommer Brod, *Premarital Agreements and Gender Justice*, 6 Yale J.L. & Feminism 229 (1994).
- Stephanie B. Casteel, *Planning and Drafting Premarital Agreements*, 20 No. 1 Prac. Tax. Law. 33 (2005).
- Stephanie B. Casteel, *Planning and Drafting Premarital Agreements*, ALI-ABA Est. Plan. Course Materials J. 5 (Apr. 2010).
- Jana Aune Deach, Case Comment, *Premarital Settlements: Till Death Do Us Part—Defining the Enforceability of the Uniform Premarital Agreement Act in North Dakota*, In re Estate of Lutz, 74 N.D. L. Rev. 411 (1998).
- Erika L. Haupt, *For Better, For Worse, For Richer, For Poorer: Premarital Agreement Case Studies*, 37 Real Prop. Prob. & Tr. J. 29 (2002).
- Mary Kay Kisthardt & Nancy Levit, *High Income/High Asset Divorce: An Annotated Bibliography*, 17 J. Am. Acad. Matrim. Law. 441 (2001).
- Allison A. Marston, Note, *Planning for Love: The Politics of Prenuptial Agreements*, 49 Stan. L. Rev. 887 (1997).
- Christine C. Nierenz, *Marital Agreements and the Colorado Marital Agreement Act*, 32 Colo. Law. 59 (Aug. 2003).
- Jeffrey G. Sherman, *Prenuptial Agreements: A New Reason to Revive an Old Rule*, 53 Clev. St. L. Rev. 359 (2005-2006).
- Judith E. Siegel-Baum & Joshua W. Averill, *Postnuptial Agreements Can Resolve Personal and Estate Planning Issues*, 29 Est. Plan. 405 (2002).
- Sarah Ann Smith, *The Unique Agreements: Premarital and Marital Agreements, Their Impact Upon Estate Planning, and Proposed Solutions to Problems Arising at Death*, 28 Idaho L. Rev. 833 (1991/1992).

- Clare H. Springs & Jackson M. Bruce, Jr., *Marital Agreements: Uses, Techniques, and Tax Ramifications in the Estate Planning Context*, 21 INST. ON EST. PLAN. ¶700 (1987).
- Jeffery R. Thurrell, *Part Three: Getting Married, The Premarital Agreement: A "Warm-Hearted" Planning Device*, 11 J. CONTEMP. LEGAL ISSUES 126 (2000).
- Donna Beck Weaver, *The Collaborative Law Process for Prenuptial Agreements*, 4 PEPP. DISP. RESOL. L.J. 337 (2004).
- Susan Metzger Weiss, *Sign at Your Own Risk: The "RCA" Prenuptial May Prejudice the Fairness of Your Future Divorce Settlement*, 6 CARDOZO WOMEN'S L.J. 49 (1999) (critique of premarital agreements endorsed by the Rabbinical Council of America for partners of the Jewish faith).
- *Premarital Agreement Short Form—Anticipating the Needs of Two Financially Independent Parties*, 18 FAM. ADVOC. 16 (Summer 1995) (sample agreement).

Dissolution of Marriage

- Sarah C. Acker, Comment, *All's Fair in Love and Divorce: Why Divorce Attorney's Fees Should Constitute a Dissipation of Marital Assets in Order to Retain Equity in Marital Property Distributions*, 15 AM. U. J. GENDER SOC. POL'Y & L. 147 (2006).
- Donna G. Barwick, *Divorce: Right Up There with Death and Taxes, Estate Planning Techniques in the Context of Divorce*, 29 INST. ON EST. PLAN. ¶1700 (1995).
- Marc A. Chorney, *Interests in Trusts as Property in Dissolution of Marriage: Identification and Valuation*, 40 REAL PROP. PROB. & TR. J. 1 (2005).
- Marc A. Chorney, *Interests in Trust in Divorce: What the Settlor Giveth the Divorce Court May Taketh Away*, 40 INST. ON EST. PLAN. ¶1600 (2006).
- Julie S. Erikson, *Divorce and the Effects of CRS 15-11-804 on Estate Planning Documents*, 34 COLO. LAW. 93 (Jan. 2005).
- Pamela A. Gordon, *The Big, Bad D's: Debts and Death in Divorce Part II*, 25 COLO. LAW. 75 (Sept. 1996) (discussing the impact of divorce on the estate plan).
- Suzanne Griffiths & Melanie Jordan, *Determining When Trusts Are Property for the Purpose of Equitable Division*, 39 COLO. LAW. 39 (June 2010).
- Steve Lass & Matt Seidman, *Property or Expectancy: The Division of Trust Assets at Dissolution of Marriage*, 30 COLO. LAW. 63 (Feb. 2001).
- Carolyn S. McCaffrey, *The Use of Trusts in Planning for the Dissolution of Marriage*, 20 INST. ON EST. PLAN. ¶1800 (1986).
- http://www.divorcereform.org/rates.html (last visited Feb. 26, 2011).

- Rose M. Kreider, *Number, Timing, and Duration of Marriages and Divorces: 2001*, at 9 (Feb. 2005), available at http://www.census.gov/prod/2005pubs/p70-97.pdf (last visited Feb. 26, 2011).
- Jeffrey A. Zaluda, *Estate Planning with Respect to Divorce*, 22 EST. PLAN. 352 (1995).

Post-Mortem Spousal Rights

- Donna Litman, *The Interrelationship Between the Elective Share and the Marital Deduction*, 40 REAL PROP. PROB. & TR. J. 539 (2005).
- Malcolm A. Moore, *Focus on Estate Planning for the Surviving Spouse: Changing from Wide Angle to Zoom Lens*, 32 INST. ON EST. PLAN. ¶1000 (1998).
- Jeffrey N. Pennell, *Minimizing the Surviving Spouse's Elective Share*, 32 INST. ON EST. PLAN. ¶900 (1998).

Trusts as Protective Devices

- Ronald D. Aucutt, *Structuring Trust Arrangements for Flexibility*, 35 INST. ON EST. PLAN. ¶900 (2001).
- Robert T. Danforth, *Article Five of the UTC and the Future of Creditors' Rights in Trusts*, 27 CARDOZO L. REV. 2551 (2006).
- John K. Eason, *Policy, Logic, and Persuasion in the Evolving Realm of Trust Asset Protection*, 27 CARDOZO L. REV. 2621 (2006).
- Keith A. Herman, *How to Protect Trust Assets from a Beneficiary's Divorce*, 63 J. MO. B. 228 (Sept./Oct. 2007).
- A.W. King III, *Trusts Are Being Created with More Flexibility Resulting in Assets Remaining in Trust for Longer Periods of Time*, 138 TR. & EST. 28 (Jan. 1999).
- A. W. King III et al., *Dynasty Trusts: What the Future Holds for Today's Technique*, 135 TR. & EST. 28 (Apr. 1996).
- Steven J. Oshins, *Asset Protection Other Than Self-Settled Trusts: Beneficiary Controlled Trusts, FLPs, LLCs, Retirement Plans and Other Creditor Protection Strategies*, 39 INST. ON EST. PLAN. ¶300 (2005).
- Max M. Schanzenbach & Robert H. Sitkoff, *Perpetuities or Taxes? Explaining the Rise of the Perpetual Trust*, 27 CARDOZO L. REV. 2465 (2006).

Conditional Bequests

- Judy Barber, *The Psychology of Conditional Giving: What's the Motivation?*, 21 PROB. & PROP. 57 (Nov./Dec. 2007).
- Howard M. McCue III, *Planning and Drafting to Influence Behavior*, 34 INST. ON EST. PLAN. ¶¶ 600, 601.1 (2000).
- Jeffrey G. Sherman, *Posthumous Meddling: An Instrumentalist Theory of Testamentary Restraints on Conjugal and Religious Choices*, 99 U. ILL. L. REV. 1273, 1277-1278 (1999).

- Shelley Steiner, Note, *Incentive Conditions: The Validity of Innovative Financial Parenting by Passing Along Wealth and Values*, 40 VAL. U. L. REV. 897 (2006).
- Joshua C. Tate, *Conditional Love: Incentive Trusts and the Inflexibility Problem*, 41 REAL PROP. PROB. & TR. J. 445 (2006).
- Ellen Evans Whiting, *Controlling Behavior by Controlling the Inheritance: Considerations in Drafting Incentive Provisions*, 15 PROB. & PROP. 6 (Sept./Oct. 2001).
- Lauren J. Wolven & Shannon L. Hartzler, *Carefully Craft Conditions on Lifetime and Testamentary Gifts*, 38 EST. PLAN. 20 (Aug. 2011).

Drafting Technique (*See also* "Drafting Style" in Ch. 2 reference materials and "Drafting Pointers" in Ch. 3 reference materials.)

- Albert S. Barr, III, *Ten (More or Less) Tried Tools to Temper the Tribulation Tethered to Traditional Tactics and Techniques: Making "Common" Planning and Drafting Errors Less Common*, 30 INST. ON EST. PLAN. ¶1800 (1996).
- Edward S. Schlesinger, *English as a Second Language for Lawyers*, 12 INST. ON EST. PLAN. ¶700 (1978).

CHAPTER 5

The Young Married Couple (Without Children)

A. Why Plan?

Chapter 3 discusses planning for the young adult. For the young adult it was noted that much planning in terms of Will or trust drafting may be obviated as a practical matter due to the use of Will substitutes such as joint tenancy, joint ownership of financial accounts, life insurance and retirement account beneficiary designations, with a "backstop" of the intestate succession laws. The same could be said for much of the planning for a young married couple without children, assuming there are no federal wealth transfer tax considerations. Indeed, particularly when the planning involves joint ownership of assets, the congruent interests shared by most married couples make those measures less troubling compared to the titling of assets with other family members. On the other hand, marriage brings two families together, and difficulties may arise in planning for possible dispositions of wealth outside the marital relationship.

B. Intestate Succession

Upon the death of the husband or wife, in the absence of surviving children the Uniform Probate Code (UPC), for example, does not necessarily pass all of the probate estate to the surviving spouse if there is a surviving parent of the deceased. If a parent survives the decedent, the surviving spouse receives the first $300,000 (adjusted for inflation) of the probate estate, plus three-fourths of any balance of the intestate probate estate.[1] The parents of the decedent receive the balance of the probate estate.[2] If the intestate probate estate exceeds the $300,000 floor, execution of a Will is required to alter this result. Also, if either spouse has children not of this marriage, the decedent's intestate probate estate will be divided between the surviving spouse and the decedent's child/children.

Beyond the UPC there is no uniform rule of succession. Under Florida, Illinois and New York law, for example, the surviving spouse receives the entire intestate probate estate if there are no surviving lineal descendants.[3] By comparison, under Texas law the surviving spouse receives the entire intestate probate estate only if the decedent had no surviving father, mother, or siblings (or their descendants).[4] Likewise, under Massachusetts law, the decedent's parents and next of kin may be entitled to a share of the decedent's intestate probate estate to the partial exclusion of the surviving spouse.[5] Under California law, the parents of the decedent may share in the decedent's intestate probate estate to the partial exclusion of the surviving spouse.[6]

C. Nonprobate Transfers

The bulk of a young couple's assets may be the subject of nonprobate transfers. While some might conclude that a Will might be accordingly relegated to a backstop role, we believe that *everyone* should have a Will. Too many unexpected events can occur after the client leaves the attorney's office (e.g., receipt of an inheritance, divorce or death of a spouse, a lottery win). Moreover, many of the nonprobate transfer measures require updating and an attention to detail often not valued by many clients. How many clients can recall the identity of all of their primary and conditional[7]

1. *See* UPC §2-102(2). The dollar amounts in UPC §2-102 are subject to increase or decrease for changes in the Consumer Price Index. *See* UPC §1-109.

2. *See* UPC §2-103(a)(2); *see also* Ronald J. Scalise Jr., *Honor Thy Father and Mother? How Intestacy Law Goes Too Far in Protecting Parents*, 37 SETON HALL L. REV. 171 (2006).

3. *See* FLA. STAT. ANN. §732.102 (West 2010); 755 ILL. COMP. STAT. ANN. 5/2-1(c) (West 2007); N.Y. EST. POWERS & TRUSTS LAW §4-1.1(a)(2) (McKinney 1998).

4. *See* TEX. PROB. CODE ANN. §38(b)(2) (Vernon 2003).

5. *See* MASS. ANN. LAWS ch. 190B, §2-102 (LexisNexis Supp. 2010).

6. *See* CAL. PROB. CODE §§6401(c)(2)(B) & 6402(b) (West Supp. 2009) (surviving domestic partners receive the same treatment afforded surviving spouses).

7. A "conditional" beneficiary is also sometimes referred to as a "secondary" beneficiary, or a "contingent" beneficiary, or an "alternate" beneficiary. In each case, the meaning is the same: To whom is the asset to be distributed upon the death of the owner in the event the "primary" beneficiary predeceases the owner or otherwise cannot take the asset (e.g., if an individual disclaims the asset, or in the case of an entity, the entity is dissolved or non-existent)?

beneficiaries? It also has been our experience that clients often focus on identifying the primary beneficiaries (usually their spouse) of nonprobate assets but give little thought to the conditional beneficiaries. The impact of the untimely death of both spouses in a single event is usually not considered by the clients. While not every Will is probated, the preparation of a Will encourages the client to consider his or her estate plan, including a review of the beneficiary designations of the client's nonprobate assets, and to possibly carry through with that planning for life. Furthermore, the preparation of a Will often leads to the preparation of other highly pertinent instruments, such as durable powers of attorney and medical care directives.

1. Bank and Securities Accounts

It will generally not be objectionable for planning purposes, or to the married couple as a practical matter, that checking, savings, and investment accounts be held in joint ownership. However, there can be notable exceptions to this rule.

First, because separate property brought to the marriage is often excluded from marital property for dissolution of marriage purposes, a married individual with significant savings and investments before marriage may wish to keep those in an account titled solely in his or her name. Even without having entered into a marital agreement, the surviving spouse's receipt of these amounts upon death, if that is desired, can be handled with payable-on-death or transfer-on-death designations. Planners also commonly encounter this desire for separate accounts in connection with significant gifts or inheritances received during the marriage. Second, maintaining separate accounts may create a measure of protection from creditors if only one of the spouses is a party to the contract in question or is the tortfeasor. Third, maintaining separate accounts may create opportunities for the extension of credit and permit each spouse to establish his or her own credit history.

2. Automobiles

For convenience, many married couples title their automobiles in both spouses' names, while others leave it to whoever is at the dealership at the time the title documents are drawn. Even if the automobile is titled in only one spouse's name, one can often easily transfer title upon the death of a spouse by using small estate or affidavit procedures (see Chapter 3). A discussion of tort law and car insurance is beyond the scope of this book, but some planners prefer single ownership of automobiles, particularly if each spouse regularly drives a separate automobile, to minimize potential tort liability stemming from ownership of the vehicle.

3. Clothing, Personal Effects, and Home Furnishings

As noted in Chapter 3, these assets are generally of modest value and have no title documents.[8] These articles generally can be passed to family members or sold to third parties with few objections. However, many planners suggest that ownership of valuable items (art, fine furniture, rugs, jewelry, collections, etc.) be established upon acquisition. There are at least three reasons for this. First, if the survivor, rather than the deceased, owns the asset, probate of that item is not a concern. If, on the other hand, the decedent owned the asset, while it may be subjected to probate, there is no additional burden to probating all of an asset as compared with only probating one half of an asset. Thus, the reasoning is that there is a 50/50 chance that the asset will only need to be probated once (that is, the non-owner dies first), but even if it is probated twice, there is little additional burden. Second, if the item has appreciated and is owned solely by the decedent, while estate tax consequences might follow (we are assuming that is not the case), in almost all cases income tax benefits will be increased because the adjusted basis of the asset becomes the fair market value of the entire asset on the date of death.[9] Of course, this cuts both ways if the decedent owned assets that declined in value. Third, from a creditor protection standpoint, the asset might avoid the grasp of the non-owner spouse's creditors or bankruptcy estate.

4. Retirement Accounts and Life Insurance

The surviving spouse will generally be the designated beneficiary of retirement accounts. With respect to retirement accounts governed by the Retirement Equity Act of 1984 (REA),[10] the surviving spouse must be the designated primary beneficiary of at least 50 percent of the decedent's retirement benefit.[11] REA generally applies to "qualified" plans under income tax nomenclature; it does not apply, for example, to Individual Retirement Accounts (IRAs). Furthermore, a surviving spouse is entitled to special income tax elections in withdrawing retirement plan assets (see Chapter 12).

8. State statutes may provide simplifying presumptions of joint ownership. *See, e.g.*, Colo. Rev. Stat. §15-11-805 (2010) (tangible personal property in the joint possession and control of the decedent and his or her surviving spouse is generally presumed to be owned by the decedent and the surviving spouse in joint tenancy with right of survivorship if ownership is not otherwise evidenced by a certificate of title, bill of sale, or other writing).

9. *See* IRC §1014.

10. Pub. L. No. 98-397, 98 Stat. 1426 (1984), codified in scattered sections of Titles 26 and 29.

11. *See generally* IRC §417 as amended by REA; *see also* Egelhoff v. Egelhoff ex rel. Breiner, 532 U.S. 141 (2001) (holding that a state statute that automatically revoked, upon divorce, the designation of a spouse as beneficiary of a nonprobate asset was preempted, as it applied to ERISA benefit plans); Lawya Rangel, *'Til Designation Do Us Part:* Egelhoff v. Egelhoff, 14 J. Contemp. Legal Issues 163 (2004).

The surviving spouse will also generally be the designated beneficiary of life insurance. For young couples this is often employer-provided group term life insurance. However, as the couple accumulates wealth and federal wealth transfer taxes become a concern, the surviving spouse generally is *not* the direct beneficiary of life insurance proceeds owned by the decedent (see Chapter 11). Designation of the contingent beneficiary under retirement accounts and life insurance policies becomes a planning issue.

5. Real Estate

It is generally not objectionable that a married couple hold their principal residence in joint tenancy with rights of survivorship or in tenancy by the entirety if federal wealth transfer taxes are not an issue. In addition to the ease of administration upon the death of either (generally only a certified death certificate and an affidavit need be recorded in the real estate records), joint ownership of the couple's residence, often their most significant asset, seems to be a natural reflection of the marital partnership. There are some exceptions to this treatment.

First, as noted above in connection with bank and securities accounts, if one of the spouses is bringing a residence to the marriage or has received it as a gift or inheritance from his or her family, it might be prudent to maintain separate titling, whether in a common law property or community property jurisdiction.[12] Second, if one of the spouses has a poor credit history or may face creditor proceedings, single ownership might be advised. Third, for federal wealth transfer tax planning purposes, it is often the case that joint ownership is used so predominantly that the first spouse to die cannot use all of his or her available tax credits. Designating one spouse to own the residence is often employed by planners in order to increase the taxable estate of the "poorer" spouse so as to permit his or her estate to take maximum advantage of whatever tax credits might otherwise be unavailable. While federal wealth transfer taxes are largely beyond the scope of this chapter (there is a brief introduction below), the overuse of joint tenancies is such a recurring tax planning issue that we raise it here, albeit somewhat prematurely. However, as discussed in Part E of this chapter, this drawback to joint tenancies has been mitigated for many couples by the "Deceased Spousal Unused Exclusion Amount" introduced by the Tax Relief, Unemployment Insurance Reauthorization, and Job Creation Act of 2010.

The planner must appreciate that, unlike financial accounts that provide for a contingent beneficiary, joint tenancy real estate by its fundamental nature does not. The potential impact of simultaneous death must therefore be considered.

12. IRC §121 provides that a married couple can still qualify for the full $500,000 gain exclusion even if both are not owners.

D. Spousal Protections

The law has developed several measures for the protection of the surviving spouse, largely to protect either spouse from completely disinheriting the other without his or her permission (see Chapter 4, Part B). Dower and curtesy have largely been replaced by "forced" or "elective" share statutes. UPC §2-202 is an example of a comprehensive elective share statute. We will not discuss the elaborate mechanics of that provision or the various alternative state approaches.[13] In addition, in the estate administration process, the surviving spouse may be entitled to additional monetary benefits.[14] As demonstrated in Chapter 4, the elective share as well as the potential division of marital property upon dissolution of marriage must be considered in structuring any estate plan for a married individual lest much of it be undone by the survivor's election. REA's spousal beneficiary designation, discussed above in connection with retirement plans, is another protection that must be considered.

Statutes such as UPC §2-301 enforce a share for a surviving spouse omitted from the deceased spouse's Will if it was executed before their marriage. That section should serve to remind the attorney that a common reason for an estate planning "checkup" is to redraft existing Wills in light of a new marriage.

E. Federal Wealth Transfer Tax Considerations (Part I)[15]

Chapter 16 presents an overview of the federal wealth transfer tax.[16] Certain aspects of the tax will also be discussed in the context of later case studies that are more tax-driven in content. However, because the treatment of spouses is probably the most significant planning aspect of

13. *Compare* FLA. STAT. ANN. §732.2065 (West 2010) (elective share is 30 percent of elective estate); 755 ILL. COMP. STAT. ANN. 5/2-8 (West 2007) (surviving spouse entitled to one half of estate if decedent is not survived by a descendant, one third if survived by a descendant); MASS. ANN. LAWS ch. 191, §15 (LexisNexis 1994) (surviving spouse receives one third of estate if decedent was survived by issue; if the decedent was survived by kindred but no issue, the surviving spouse takes $25,000 and one half of the remaining property; elective share property in excess of $25,000 is taken as a life estate unless the decedent is not survived by issue or kindred); N.Y. EST. POWERS & TRUSTS LAW §5-1.1-A(a)(2) (McKinney Supp. 2011) (elective share is the greater of $50,000 (or the capital value of the net estate if less than $50,000), or one third of the net estate). Georgia does not provide for a spousal elective share; however, a surviving spouse may get 12 months of support upon the filing of a petition with the probate court. *See* GA. CODE ANN. §53-3-5 (LexisNexis Supp. 2010).

14. *See, e.g.*, UPC §2-402 (homestead allowance); UPC §2-403 (exempt property allowance); and UPC §2-404 (family allowance).

15. Part II of "Federal Wealth Transfer Tax Considerations" appears in Chapter 8, Part C.

16. Three coordinated taxes comprise the federal wealth transfer taxes: the gift tax, the estate tax, and the tax on generation-skipping transfers. In this discussion, we refer to the levies of the federal wealth transfer tax system as a single "tax" to simplify matters.

the federal wealth transfer taxes for many clients, these issues deserve a preview.[17]

Very broadly speaking, the federal gift tax is imposed on an individual's lifetime gifts in excess of certain exclusions such as the IRC §2503(b) annual gift exclusion and the IRC §2503(e) unlimited exclusion for certain transfers for educational or medical expenses. In addition to these gift exclusions, an individual is allowed a lifetime gift tax "applicable exclusion amount" in the aggregate amount of $5,000,000.[18] Thus, one may make lifetime gifts totaling $5,000,000 in addition to annual exclusion gifts and qualifying educational or medical expenses without payment of a gift tax.[19]

The estate tax is imposed on the amount of the individual's estate (after deducting funeral and administration expenses and other debts and obligations), including all probate and nonprobate property owned by the decedent, passing to other than a surviving spouse or a charitable donee to the extent such transfers exceed the "applicable exclusion amount" available to the decedent's estate. The applicable exclusion amount is $5,000,000[20] but is scheduled to increase after calendar year 2011 in multiples of $10,000 to account for cost-of-living adjustments.[21]

17. Chapter 11 provides an in-depth treatment of federal wealth transfer taxation planning for spouses.

18. *See* IRC §2505(a) (speaking to an "applicable credit amount" referring to the tax that would be due on the $5,000,000 applicable exclusion amount described in IRC §2010(c)).

19. Prior to the enactment of the Economic Growth and Tax Relief Reconciliation Act of 2001 (EGTRRA), the lifetime exclusion for gifts was equal in amount to the estate tax exclusion, as is again the case under the Tax Relief, Unemployment Insurance Reauthorization, and Job Creation Act of 2010. EGTRRA temporarily unlinked the applicable exclusion amount prescribed by IRC §2010 and pertaining to the estate tax from the lifetime gift applicable exclusion amount prescribed by IRC §2505. Accordingly, an individual dying in 2009 with a $3,500,000 taxable estate would pay no federal estate taxes, but an inter vivos gift of the same $3,500,000 would require the payment of a gift tax. For an explanation of the "de-unification" of the wealth transfer taxes under EGTRRA using numerical examples, *see* IRA MARK BLOOM ET AL., FEDERAL TAXATION OF ESTATES, TRUSTS AND GIFTS 39-40 (rev. 3d ed. 2003). There are other considerations in making an inter vivos gift. First, any payment of gift taxes involves the payment of money today, rather than in the future. That is generally not advantageous except for some individuals anticipating imminent death and wishing to exclude the gift taxes paid from the estate tax base (but *see* IRC §2035, which limits this strategy for gifts made within three years of death). Second, if the gifted asset is certain to appreciate greatly or if valuation discounts may be produced for the remainder of the taxable estate, the payment of a gift tax may still be advantageous, although that may not be attractive to many clients (or possible due to liquidity concerns) if the cash outlay is substantial. Furthermore, an inter vivos gift of appreciated property loses the IRC §1014 basis adjustment available under current law. Third, if it is determined that a married couple should maximize their lifetime gifts to third parties, then even ignoring the impact of additional gifts permitted by the annual gift exclusion provided by IRC §2503(b) or the educational and medical transfers permitted by IRC §2503(e), $10,000,000 in gifts can be made free of tax if each spouse gifts $5,000,000, or by the couple electing gift splitting. *See* IRC §2513.

20. Cumulative lifetime post-1976 taxable gifts (i.e., gifts exceeding the IRC §§2503(b) & 2503(e) exclusions) are added to the estate in computing a tentative estate tax (*see* IRC §2001(b)(1)). However, a credit is permitted for gift taxes actually paid (*see* IRC §2001(b)(2)), and the estate tax applicable exclusion amount is not diminished by prior uses of the gift tax applicable exclusion amount, so the result is a tax on the aggregate sum at potentially higher progressive tax rates, rather than a double tax being imposed on those gifts. For an explanation with numerical examples *see* BLOOM ET AL., *supra* note 19, at 35-38.

21. The Tax Relief, Unemployment Insurance Reauthorization, and Job Creation Act of 2010 will, however, expire December 31, 2012, unless extended; see Chapter 11.

There are two fundamental principles at work here. First, wealth transferred to a U.S. citizen spouse during lifetime or to a surviving U.S. citizen spouse at death is generally deductible from taxable transfers.[22] The transfer tax on the assets is not lost forever; it is simply deferred, with the tax being eventually imposed on the surviving spouse's disposition of the assets. Nontaxable gifts, charitable transfers, declines in value, and consumption of the assets by the surviving spouse will, of course, reduce the value of the assets taxable at the surviving spouse's death. Second, each spouse has at least $5,000,000 of transfer tax exclusion available (before inflation adjustment), so that if both spouses' exclusions are fully used, the couple may pass $10,000,000 to other family members during their lives,[23] or at their deaths, or partially during their lives and the remainder at their deaths, free of federal wealth transfer taxes.

The preceding two principles are reflected in various strategies. As discussed below and at greater length in Chapter 11, the Deceased Spousal Unused Exclusion Amount ("DSUEA") introduced by the Tax Relief, Unemployment Insurance Reauthorization, and Job Creation Act of 2010 has the potential to alter these measures.

1. Full Utilization of the Applicable Exclusion Amount

If one's objective is to pass the maximum amount to other family members free of federal wealth transfer taxes, then each spouse's full applicable exclusion amount must be used. Because transfers to the surviving spouse do not require or use any of the decedent's exclusion amount, a plan to maximize the wealth that passes to other family members could be that the first spouse to die transfers up to the then maximum available exclusion amount of assets to persons, including trusts, other than the surviving spouse, with the rest of the estate, if any, passing to the surviving spouse. As discussed in point 4, below, if federal estate taxes were the sole planning consideration, the DSUEA could permit some couples (with aggregate wealth of less than $10,000,000) to skip this nonspousal diversion of assets upon the first spouse's death.

2. The Formula Clause and Nonspousal Share

Simple estates often use the so-called "I love you Will," in which everything is bequeathed to the survivor. Apart from Wills and trusts, nonprobate devices such as joint tenancy with right of survivorship and account beneficiary designations can accomplish the same result.

However, estates requiring federal wealth transfer taxation planning will often express the bequest as a "formula clause" that separates the estate of the first to die into two general pots: (1) one pot, equal to the

22. *See* IRC §§2523 (inter vivos transfers) & 2056 (testamentary transfers).
23. *See supra* note 19.

applicable exclusion amount then available to the decedent, passes to the children or other family members or to a trust for the benefit of the family generally[24] — this is intended to use fully the maximum applicable exclusion available to the decedent as discussed in point 1, above; and (2) the balance passes to the surviving spouse outright or into a marital trust for the surviving spouse's exclusive benefit (certain technical requirements for such a trust must be followed). Again, the DSUEA may eliminate the use of formula clauses for some couples, as simplification was the intended aim in the adoption of the provision.

3. Titling of Property

If the maximum exclusion amount is to be fully utilized, it is preferable (1) that each spouse owns property valued in an amount at least equal to the maximum applicable exclusion available to that spouse and that such property will be included in his or her estate; and (2) that enough property passes to nonspousal beneficiaries to fully utilize this exclusion. Yet again, the availability of the DSUEA may mitigate this concern for some couples.[25]

While the formula clause in the Will is intended to produce these results, it only operates on probate assets, although it references nonprobate assets in its calculation. Accordingly, a common planning measure is to sever existing joint ownerships (e.g., joint tenancy with right of survivorship or tenancy by the entirety) in order to create separate property (e.g., assets held by both spouses as tenants in common or assets held solely in the name of one spouse) that will pass through the probate estate by the Will's formula clause, rather than passing directly to the surviving spouse under survivorship provisions.

We will revisit these issues in more detail in Chapters 11 and 16. At this point, it is important to know that a disposition of all of one's assets to one's surviving spouse becomes potentially undesirable from a federal wealth transfer taxation standpoint as the value of the combined estates (both probate and nonprobate, husband and wife) approaches and exceeds \$5,000,000 because that increases the probability that the aggregated pot of assets held by the survivor spouse will exceed the federal estate tax exclusion available to the surviving spouse upon his or her death.

24. A surviving spouse is generally a permitted beneficiary of this trust, referred to as a "bypass trust," "credit shelter trust," or "family trust." Some planners refer to one trust as the "A trust" and the other as the "B trust," so one may encounter references to "A/B trust" planning.

25. In the authors' viewpoint, because of the uncertainty surrounding future estate tax laws, and because of other potential limitations in the applicability of the DSUEA at the death of the second spouse, if a couple's combined estate exceeds \$5,000,000, it may be prudent to use or "shelter" the first spouse to die's applicable exclusion amount immediately upon the death of the first spouse rather than relying upon the DSUEA being available in the future at the second spouse's death. Uncertainty and other factors aside, the DSUEA can raise some complicated planning issues. *See, e.g.*, Marvin D. Hills, *Subsequent Remarriage Complicates Exclusion Amount Portability*, 38 Est. Plan. 3 (May 2011).

Conversely, for aggregate estates (total of husband and wife's assets) valued at less than the applicable exclusion amount, the impact of the federal wealth transfer taxation system is of virtually no concern.

4. The DSUEA's Impact on Planning Strategies

The DSUEA[26] modifies the foregoing principles and strategies by permitting a surviving spouse to use any of the applicable exclusion amount of the first spouse to die that was not used on the death of the first spouse. Assuming no prior taxable gifts and that all of the assets of the first spouse to die passed to the surviving spouse using the marital deduction,[27] the surviving spouse could be left with a potential $10,000,000 exclusion amount that could be used to shelter the collection of assets passed to, or for the benefit of, the survivor. An election to preserve the "unused" exclusion amount must be made in an estate tax return filed for the first spouse to die.

At first blush, it would seem that "I Love You" plans will become predominant and that formula clauses, bypass trusts, and attention to separate titling of assets are no longer necessary. While that may be true for some couples, there are other considerations at play.[28] We defer until Chapter 11 a more complete analysis of the role of the DSUEA and its impact on marital wealth transfer tax planning.

F. Using Form Documents (Part III)

Chapters 3 and 4 contain "Using Form Documents (Part I)" and "Using Form Documents (Part II)," respectively. You may wish to review that material.[29] This chapter introduces a married couple with a relatively simple estate. Chapter 7 adds children to the picture. Chapter 11 involves a married couple with significant assets that compel consideration of the federal wealth transfer tax considerations. While the forms that an attorney would use for each of these clients would share many common provisions (e.g., definitions of "descendants," saving clauses, and fiduciary powers), the forms for the latter two situations would typically involve the use of trusts.

In addition, comparing the trusts in Chapter 7 to those in Chapter 11 would disclose that the trusts discussed in Chapter 11, being tax-driven, differ significantly from those in Chapter 7. Our point is that the Will form for this chapter, Form B in the Forms Supplement, is about the simplest Will that one would use. However, that does not mean that the more

26. *See* IRC §2010(c).

27. *See* IRC §2056. Assets may also have passed to charities; if structured correctly, those gifts would be eligible for the estate tax charitable deduction. *See* IRC §2055. Certain claims against the estate, as well as administration expenses, would also be deductible from the estate. *See* IRC §2053.

28. *See supra* note 25.

29. Part IV appears in Chapter 8, Part E.

complex forms one would use for Chapter 7 or Chapter 11 Wills are better, more complete forms. They are simply addressing a *different* planning situation. The drafting of Wills and trusts is akin to building fine furniture: If one chooses the proper tools for the task, it will often compensate for deficiencies in skill, while the wrong tools in anyone's hands will almost never create the best final product. In estate planning, selection of the appropriate document is a skill in itself.

G. Planning for Pets

Although many of the persons described throughout this book are likely to own companion pets,[30] pets may be particularly important to the childless couples who are the focus of this chapter. The nature of planning for pets is not unlike estate planning for humans because the arrangements can range from the very informal to the highly structured. Too often, pets are overlooked in couple's estate planning documents (if any documents even exist), requiring family, friends, or neighbors (or animal control authorities) to deal with the surviving pets.

At the most basic level, pet owners may merely provide for an informal testamentary gift of the pets (perhaps in a UPC §2-513 memorandum of tangible personal property referenced in the governing instrument) and nothing more. In a more formal approach, the pets may be the object of a testamentary gift in a Will or other governing instrument, along with a sum of money, coupled with a precatory request that the money be used for the care of the animals.

The most formal arrangement would enlist a testamentary trust to provide funds for the care of the pet, designation of caretakers for the pets, instructions concerning the care of the pets, and provisions directing the disposition of any funds remaining in the trust upon the death of the pets.

Under the common law, pet trusts were unenforceable "honorary trusts" due to the lack of a human beneficiary who could enforce the trust.[31] The Uniform Probate Code and the Uniform Trust Code expressly permit enforceable trusts for the benefit of animals.[32] As demonstrated by the sample language below, the caretaker of the animals may not be the trustee, particularly if significant sums of money or multiple and unique animals are involved.

30. Pet ownership is positively correlated with household wealth and household size. Of the sampled households, 37.2 percent owned dogs (an average of 1.7 dogs per household) and 32.4 percent owned cats (an average 2.2 cats per household). *See* BUREAU OF STATISTICS, TREASURY DEPARTMENT, STATISTICAL ABSTRACT OF THE UNITED STATES: 2011 *Table 1240 Household Pet Ownership 2006* (130th ed. 2010).

31. *See* WILLIAM M. MCGOVERN ET AL., WILLS, TRUSTS AND ESTATES 441-442 (4th ed. 2010).

32. *See* UPC §2-907 & Unif. Trust Code §408.

PET TRUST

9.1. Authority for Pet Trust. My trustee[33] *shall administer the trust funds for the care of my domestic and pet animals that survive me, including any offspring in gestation at the time of my death (hereinafter "my pets"), as provided by [enabling statute] as amended after my death. Trustee shall register the trust if required by statute. Included among my pets are my dogs "__________," "__________," and "__________," if they survive me, and any other domestic and pet animals that I own and that survive me, including any offspring in gestation at the time of my death.*

9.2. Disposition of Income and Principal. Trustee shall apply the interest and, if necessary, the principal of the trust for the care of my pets to their caretakers[34] *in such amounts as my trustee deems necessary or advisable for the health, support and maintenance of my pets. Any undistributed income may be added to principal from time to time at the discretion of my trustee.*

9.3. Guidelines to Trustee. Without in any way limiting the absolute discretion of trustee over distributions of income and principal from this trust, or the placement of animals subject to this trust, trustee should consider that the primary purpose of this trust is to provide a warm, caring and loving environment for my pets in a fashion similar to that which I have provided for them during my lifetime. Among other things, their environment shall include good nutrition, exercise, grooming and veterinary care and my pets should be afforded any and all reasonable luxuries. Trustee shall compensate each caretaker of my pets, including any interim caretaker or caretakers, a reasonable amount for time spent walking and maintaining my pets. None of my pets should be kept alive by artificial means. Any of my pets may be humanely euthanized on the recommendation of that pet's caretaker after consultation with a veterinarian, whenever, in the judgment of the caretaker and veterinarian, the animal would suffer unduly if kept alive.

33. This provision envisions that the trustee of other testamentary trusts shall also serve as the trustee of the pet trust. If that were not the case, separate provisions addressing nomination, removal, and successor trustees of the pet trust would need to be added.

34. When a trustee and a caretaker both exist, the trustee typically occupies the traditional role of a trustee of a trust, including being responsible as a fiduciary for the management and care of the assets of the trust. On the other hand, a caretaker is responsible for the day-to-day nutrition, hygiene, medical care, exercise, shelter, etc. of a pet, and is not responsible for the management and care of the trust funds. The trustee and the caretaker need not be separate persons, however.

> *9.4. Caretaker.*
>
> *a. Primary. I nominate ______________________, of ________, MyState, to be caretaker of my pets.*
>
> *b. Successors. If for any reason a nominated or appointed caretaker is unable, unwilling or fails to serve, my trustee shall have the responsibility of appointing one or more successor caretakers. Any caretaker may resign upon notice to my trustee. Each caretaker must be an adult. My trustee shall have the power to remove or replace any caretaker at any time, and need not give the caretaker being removed or replaced any reason, cause or ground for such removal or replacement.*
>
> *9.5. Termination. This trust shall continue for so long as any of my pets, or their offspring in gestation at the time of my death, shall live. This trust shall terminate upon the death of the last of my pets and any principal and undistributed income then remaining in the trust shall be distributed to the beneficiaries who would have received my remaining residuary estate as provided in ARTICLE ________ had I died on the same date as, but immediately after, termination of the Pet Trust.*

H. CASE STUDY 5-1

Paul and Linda Davis (Part I)

THE YOUNG PROFESSIONAL COUPLE WITHOUT CHILDREN

Paul William Davis, age 30, and Linda Nottingham Davis, age 28, have been married for five years. Paul is a Certified Public Accountant employed by a small accounting firm. His annual salary is $60,000. Linda is an Assistant Professor of philosophy at a small private college. Linda has been employed in this capacity for two years, and she hopes to be awarded tenure in another four years. Linda's salary is $40,000. They currently have no children.

Paul and Linda own a home appraised at $200,000, subject to a $150,000 mortgage (245 Granite Drive, FirstCity, FirstState 80001). The home is titled in joint tenancy with rights of survivorship. They own two automobiles. Paul purchased the older car when he was single, and he has remained the sole owner. Their recently purchased sport utility vehicle is principally driven by Linda and is titled in both of their names.

Paul participates in his employer's 401(k) plan (current balance $35,000) and also contributes to a Roth IRA (current balance $7,500); Linda is the primary beneficiary under all of Paul's accounts. Linda participates in her employer's defined contribution pension plan (current balance $20,000) and also contributes $200 monthly to a supplemental annuity under IRC §403(b)(7) using pre-tax dollars (current balance $7,000); Paul is the primary beneficiary under all of Linda's accounts.

Paul and Linda maintain a joint checking account with an average balance of $1,000, and they have approximately $10,000 in money market accounts, also held in joint tenancy. They have no other investments outside of their retirement plans because Paul has convinced Linda of the benefits of the income tax deductibility of the contributions, as well as the tax-deferred growth of those investments, and, after funding their retirement plans, they have little in excess funds.

Paul and Linda own a dog, a two-year-old chocolate Labrador named Cookie. Paul's parents are both alive and in good health, and he has one sibling (married, with two children). Linda's parents are both alive and in good health. She is an only child, but she is very close to her cousin (daughter of her mother's sister) and her cousin's immediate family (the cousin has three children).

Paul and Linda do not have a Will.

Part A: Paul is by nature very frugal and skeptical of professional advice. He is of the opinion that with their modest assets and existing beneficiary designations, "planning would be a waste of effort and money. We should wait until Linda is awarded tenure so that we know we will be staying around here." Based on these facts, discuss whether Paul and Linda need any estate planning. Be specific in fully discussing any potential risks that you identify. Further, describe any instruments that you would propose. Assume that the UPC (or a different statute as directed by your teacher) applies.

Part B: What is the role of Sections 7.4 and 7.5 in the Form B Will in an estate like Paul and Linda's?

Part C: Using the applicable forms from the Forms Supplement as guides, draft any instruments that you have proposed for Paul and Linda.

The family tree: Jack Edward Davis & Susan Ebert Davis, 1213 Lodge Lane, MyCity, MyState 80000 (Paul's parents). Carter Simpson Nottingham & Carol Anna Nottingham, 3412 Shady Pines, Bigtown, State2, 80002 (Linda's parents). Cookie, a chocolate Labrador, doghouse in Paul and Linda's backyard. Erica Davis Jones (Paul's sister), Jennifer Sarah Davis and Thompson Edward Davis (Paul's niece and nephew, ages 5 and 2, respectively), 2444 Alpine, Smalltown, State3, 80003. Rachel Alice White (Linda's cousin), Jade Alice White, Crystal Jill White, and Thomas Rock White (Rachel's children, ages 8, 6, and 1, respectively), 1010 Woodstock, Quainttown, State4, 80004. Neither set of parents is currently in need of additional funds. Paul would prefer that their property pass to Paul's sister and family. Linda respects that, but would prefer that some of the property (say $15,000) go to her cousin and her children.

Part D: Paul and Linda's estate is composed largely of retirement plan assets. If you were counseling a potential beneficiary of their estate, would you advise the beneficiary to prefer retirement plan assets over other property, or vice versa, or express no preference?

I. Reference Materials

Treatises:

Joint Representation of Married Couples

- John R. Price & Samuel A. Donaldson, Price on Contemporary Estate Planning §1.6.7 (2011).
- Susan P. Shapiro, Tangled Loyalties: Conflict of Interest in the Legal Practice 81-96 (2002) (discussing issues that arise when representing more than one family member).
- George M. Turner, Revocable Trusts §§6:5 to 6:10; app. 11 (conflict of interest form) (5th ed. 2003 & Supp. 2010).

Joint Ownership of Assets

- Roger W. Andersen, Understanding Trusts and Estates 116-123 (4th ed. 2009) (joint interests, life insurance, and retirement funds).
- A. James Casner & Jeffrey N. Pennell, Estate Planning ch. 10, *Concurrent Interests* (6th ed. 1995 & Supp. 2009-2010).
- William M. McGovern et al., Wills, Trusts and Estates 655-658 (4th ed. 2010) (rights of creditors).
- Price & Donaldson, *supra*, §§2.21, 3.11 & 3.21.
- George M. Turner, *supra*, §13:8 (joint tenancy or tenancy by the entirety).

Community Property (*See also* same heading in Ch. 4 reference materials.)

- McGovern et al., *supra*, 171-183.
- Price & Donaldson, *supra*, §§3.22 to 3.39.
- William A. Reppy, Jr. & Cynthia A. Samuel, Community Property in the United States (2d ed. 1982).

Dissolution of Marriage (*See also* same heading in Ch. 4 reference materials.)

- Frederick K. Hoops et al., Family Estate Planning Guide ch. 18 (4th ed. 1994 & Supp. 2010-2011).
- John Tingley & Nicholas B. Svalina, Marital Property Law (rev. 2d ed. 1994 & Supp. 2010).

- Brett R. Turner, Equitable Distribution of Property (3d ed. 2005 & Supp. 2010-2011).

Retirement Plan Spousal Beneficiary Designations (*See also* same heading in Ch. 3 reference materials.)

- Natalie B. Choate, Life and Death Planning for Retirement Benefits (7th ed. 2011).
- L. Rush Hunt & Lara Rae Hunt, A Lawyer's Guide to Estate Planning ch. 11, *Retirement Plans and Benefits* (3d ed. 2004).
- Hoops et al., *supra*, §24:29.

Articles

Joint Representation of Married Couples (*See also* "Client Conflicts" in Ch. 1 reference materials.)

- Victoria Blachly, *Making Waivers Work: Joint Representation*, SL003 ALI-ABA 429 (ALI-ABA Continuing Legal Education, July 21-22, 2005).
- Teresa Stanton Collett, *And the Two Shall Become As One... Until the Lawyers Are Done*, 7 Notre Dame J.L. Ethics & Pub. Pol'y 101 (1993).
- Teresa Stanton Collett, *Love Among the Ruins: The Ethics of Counseling Happily Married Couples*, 22 Seattle U. L. Rev. 139 (1998).
- James R. Wade, *When Can a Lawyer Represent Both Husband and Wife in Estate Planning?*, 1 Prob. & Prop. 12 (Mar./Apr. 1987).

Overall Planning for Married Couples

- Malcolm A. Moore, *Focus on Estate Planning for the Surviving Spouse: Changing from Wide Angle to Zoom Lens*, 32 Inst. on Est. Plan. ¶1000 (1998).
- Malcolm A. Moore, *Estate Planning for the Surviving Spouse*, Estate Planning in Depth, SK093 ALI-ABA 1073 (ALI-ABA Continuing Legal Education, June 19-24, 2005).
- G. Warren Whitaker & Michael J. Parets, *My Client Married an Alien: Ten Things Everyone Should Know About International Estate Planning*, 18 Prob. & Prop. 25 (Mar./Apr. 2004).

Joint Ownership of Assets

- Jonathan S. Batten, Note, *No Estate Tax Fractional Interest or Lack of Marketability Discount Allowed for Jointly Owned Property Held by Married Couple:* Estate of Young v. Commissioner, 52 Tax Law. 391 (1999).
- Samuel M. Fetters, *An Invitation to Commit Fraud: Secret Destruction of Joint Tenant Survivorship Rights*, 55 Fordham L. Rev. 173 (1986).

- Fred Franke, *Asset Protection and Tenancy by the Entirety*, 34 ACTEC J. 210 (2009).
- Miriam A. Goodman, *Joint Tenancy with a Noncitizen Spouse: An Estate and Gift Tax Guide for the Perplexed*, 16 PROB. & PROP. 41 (Feb. 2002).
- Kathryn G. Henkel, *Asset Protection Techniques*, 29 INST. ON EST. PLAN. ¶600 (1995) (separate property as asset protection measure; *see also* Ch. 12 of this book).
- John H. Martin, *The Joint Trust: Estate Planning in a New Environment*, 39 REAL PROP. PROB. & TR. J. 275 (2004).
- Melinda S. Merk, *Joint Revocable Trusts for Married Couples Domiciled in Common-Law Property States*, 32 REAL PROP. PROB. & TR. J. 345 (1997).
- John V. Orth, *The Perils of Joint Tenancies*, 44 REAL PROP. TR. & EST. L.J. 427 (2009).
- Guerino J. Turano & Philip H. Ward, Feature, *Joint Tenancy and Tenancy by the Entirety: The Pros and Cons*, 83 ILL. B.J. 309 (June 1995).

Community Property Law (*See also* same heading in Ch. 4 reference materials.)

- Karen E. Boxx, *Community Property Across State Lines*, 19 PROB. & PROP. 9 (Jan./Feb. 2005).
- Stephen L. Harms, *Joint Tenancy, Transmutation and the Supremacy of the Community Property Presumption:* Swink v. Fingado, 30 IDAHO L. REV. 893 (1994).
- Shelly D. Merritt, *Planning for Community Property in Colorado*, 31 COLO. LAW. 79 (June 2002).
- Emily Osborn, *The Continuing Evolution of American Community Property Law: Comment: The Treatment of Unearned Separate Property at Divorce in Common Law Property Jurisdictions*, 1990 WIS. L. REV. 903.
- Jeremy T. Ware, *Section 1014(b)(6) and the Boundaries of Community Property*, 5 NEV. L.J. 704 (2005).

Dissolution of Marriage (*See also* same heading in Ch. 4 reference materials.)

- Dennis I. Belcher, *How to Tie the Knot with a Marital Agreement*, 35 INST. ON EST. PLAN. ¶400 (2001).
- Marc A. Chorney, *Interests in Trusts as Property in Dissolution of Marriage: Identification and Valuation*, 40 REAL PROP. PROB. & TR. J. 1 (2005).
- Marc A. Chorney, *Interests in Trust in Divorce: What the Settlor Giveth the Divorce Court May Taketh Away*, 40 INST. ON EST. PLAN. ¶1600 (2006).

- Julie S. Erikson, *Divorce and the Effects of CRS 15-11-804 on Estate Planning Documents*, 34 Colo. Law. 93 (Jan. 2005).
- J. Thomas Oldham, *ALI Principles of Family Dissolution: Some Comments*, 1997 U. Ill. L. Rev. 801 (1997).

The Elective Share

- William Forsberg, *Partners in Life and at Death: The New Minnesota Elective Share of a Surviving Spouse Statute*, 23 Wm. Mitchell L. Rev. 377 (1997).
- Susan N. Gary, *Share and Share Alike? The UPC's Elective Share*, 12 Prob. & Prop. 18 (Mar./Apr. 1998).
- Donna Litman, *The Interrelationship Between the Elective Share and the Marital Deduction*, 40 Real Prop. Prob. & Tr. J. 539 (2005).
- Jeffrey N. Pennell, *Minimizing the Surviving Spouse's Elective Share*, 32 Inst. on Est. Plan. ¶900 (1998).
- Howard M. Zaritsky, *Attack of the Surviving Spouse: The Evolving Problems of the Elective Share*, 23 Inst. on Est. Plan. ¶500 (1989).

Retirement Plan Spousal Beneficiary Designations (*See also* "Retirement Plan Beneficiary Designations" in Ch. 3 reference materials and "Retirement Asset Tax Planning" in Ch. 12 reference materials.)

- Albert Feuer, *When Are Releases of Claims for ERISA Benefits Effective?*, 38 J. Marshall L. Rev. 773 (2005).
- Jennifer Howard, *ERISA Preemption: Whether State Common Law Doctrines of Substantial Compliance Fall Under the Purview of ERISA*, 92 Ky. L.J. 551 (2003-2004).
- Leslie A. Klein & Frank P. VanderPloeg, *Retirement Equity Act (REA) Workshop: Spousal Consents and Other Issues*, Basic Law of Pensions, Welfare Plans, and Deferred Compensation, SK012 ALI-ABA 97 (ALI-ABA Continuing Legal Education, July 12-16, 2004).
- Thomas E. Lund, *Coordinating Beneficiary Designations with the Estate Plan*, 36 Est. Plan. 27 (Nov. 2009).
- Pamela D. Perdue, *Spousal Rights (Joint and Survivor Benefits, Pre-Retirement Survivor Benefits, and Qualified Domestic Relations Orders)*, Fundamentals of Employee Benefits Law, SL066 ALI-ABA 219 (ALI-ABA Continuing Legal Education, Mar. 2-4 2006).
- Keron A. Wright, Comment, *Stuck on You: The Inability of an Ex-Spouse to Waive Rights Under an ERISA Pension Plan*, 45 Washburn L.J. 687 (2006).

Estate Planning for Pets

- Gerry W. Beyer, *Estate Planning for Pets*, 15 Prob. & Prop. 7 (July/Aug. 2001).
- Gerry W. Beyer, *Pet Animals: What Happens When Their Humans Die?*, 40 Santa Clara L. Rev. 617 (2000).

- Frances Carlisle & Paul Franken, *Drafting Trusts for Animals*, 218 N.Y. L.J. 1 (Nov. 13, 1997).
- Stephanie B. Casteel, *Estate Planning for Pets*, 21 No. 6 PROB. & PROP. 8 (Nov./Dec. 2007).
- Rachel Hirschfeld, *Estate Planning Strategies for People Who Have Pets*, 36 EST. PLAN. 24 (July 2009).
- Rachel Hirschfeld, *Ensure Your Pet's Future: Estate Planning for Owners and Their Animal Companions*, 9 MARQ. ELDER'S ADVISOR 155 (2007).
- Gabriela N. Sandoval, *The Basics of Pet Trusts for Estate Planning Attorneys*, 37 COLO. LAW. 49 (May 2008).
- Jennifer R. Taylor, *A "Pet" Project for State Legislatures: The Movement Toward Enforceable Pet Trusts in the Twenty-First Century*, 13 QUINNIPIAC PROB. L.J. 419 (1999).

CHAPTER 6

Unmarried Couples

A. Lifestyle Considerations

Unmarried couples who cohabit comprise a significant segment of the U.S. population.[1] It appears that they make up a far from monolithic group in terms of the reasons for adopting this lifestyle. Some senior citizens who are widows or widowers do not remarry due to concerns about complicating the disposition of their separate property, the potential impact of remarriage on the level of Social Security or pension benefits, and financial responsibility for long-term care expenses.[2] Other couples of all ages may have been previously married and divorced and voice reluctance about ever being in a marital relationship again. Some couples wish to avoid the so-called "marriage penalty" under the federal income tax.[3] Some couples don't believe that marriage is necessary for their relationship, but they envision a lengthy period of commitment

1. According to the 2000 census, 5,230,703 persons lived with an unmarried partner, representing 1.9 percent of the population. *See* U.S. Census Bureau, Profile of General Demographic Characteristics, Census 2000 Summary File 2, http://factfinder.census.gov. Based on the same census data, another source claims that there were 9.7 million Americans living with an unmarried different-sex partner and 1.2 million living with a same-sex partner. *See* U.S. Census Bureau (2000) compiled at http://www.unmarried.org/statistics.html. According to the U.S. Census Bureau's 2005 American Community Survey, opposite-sex unmarried couples comprised 4.7 percent of 111,090,617 total U.S. households; same-sex couples comprise 0.7 percent of total U.S. households. As evidence that marriage itself appears to be declining, the same survey concluded that unmarried households became the majority of all U.S. households in 2005. *See* http://factfinder.census.gov.

2. *See, e.g.*, Marvin Rachlin, *What Is a Spouse's Liability for Medicaid Benefits Paid?*, 30 Est. Plan. 117 (2003); Andrew D. Wone, Note, *Don't Want to Pay for Your Institutionalized Spouse? The Role of Spousal Refusal and Medicaid in Long-Term Planning*, 14 Elder L.J. 485 (2006).

3. The Jobs and Growth Tax Relief Reconciliation Act of 2003 provided some partial marriage penalty relief by increasing the size of the 15 percent income tax rate bracket and increasing the income tax standard deduction for a married couple filing a joint return to be

(the potential for a "common law marriage" should be evaluated). Many young couples live in a very loosely committed relationship with no immediate expectations of a greater legal commitment. Other couples live together for a "trial period" with the expectation that it will culminate in marriage.

Gay and lesbian couples are an important, but fundamentally different, subset of these groups. While they share many of the same concerns with heterosexual couples, their situation is unique in that while heterosexual couples may "elect" a new legal status by marrying, that option is generally not recognized or widely available to same-sex couples.

Considering the numerous types of cohabiting relationships, some of which are akin to roommates simply sharing expenses, this chapter focuses on planning for those in more committed relationships. That commitment may be primarily financial, such as the joint ownership of a home. The commitment may be broader and extend to entrusting another to make health care decisions or treating the cohabitant as the object of bequests.

B. The State and Federal Law Implications of Marriage

The status of marriage invokes the state's statutes and judicial decisions dictating how the financial affairs of the relationship will be handled in the absence of the couple's explicit agreements to the contrary (e.g., through the use of marital agreements, as discussed in Chapter 4). For example, the dissolution of marriage laws provide an established set of default rules governing the division of property and the provision for spousal support or maintenance. The probate laws generally provide protection of the surviving spouse in the form of spousal allowances and exemptions during probate, some form of elective or "forced" share of the decedent's estate, and some formula share of an intestate estate. While these rules may be imperfect, unmarried couples generally do not benefit from even these "imperfect" protections.

Depending on varying state laws, the status of marriage may permit the couple to use the following specific legal tools:

- the spousal share of an intestate estate;[4]
- the spousal homestead, exempt property, and family allowances;[5]
- the spousal elective share;[6]
- marital property division in dissolution of marriage;

twice that for a single individual. The Working Families Tax Relief Act of 2004 extended these measures through 2010. The Tax Relief, Unemployment Insurance Reauthorization, and Job Creation Act of 2010 extended the measures through 2012.

4. *See, e.g.*, UPC §2-102.
5. *See, e.g.*, UPC §§2-402, 2-403 & 2-404.
6. *See, e.g.*, UPC §2-202.

- spousal support or maintenance in dissolution of marriage;
- community property or tenancy by the entirety;
- the joint federal income tax return;[7]
- the unlimited marital deduction for federal wealth transfer tax purposes (see Chapters 11 and 16);
- gift "splitting" for federal wealth transfer tax purposes (see Chapter 16);
- Social Security survivor benefits;[8]
- required spousal beneficiary designations under retirement plans governed by the Retirement Equity Act of 1984;[9]
- spousal benefits under employer benefit packages;
- and priority, in the absence of a designation, in nomination of a personal representative,[10] conservator,[11] and health care decision surrogate.[12]

C. Substitute Measures

Through planning, the attorney can address many of the issues facing the unmarried couple that would otherwise have uncertain or undesirable results. A primary focus of planning is the disposition of assets and the provision of support if the relationship is terminated during lifetime or by death. The federal wealth transfer aspects of inter vivos gifting can be mitigated to a small degree by the careful use of annual gifts that qualify for gift tax exclusion. However, these lifetime gifts are generally irrevocable, and in the event the relationship ends, they are not automatically reversible. In contrast, a married couple can, although they should not necessarily do so, entirely address the federal wealth transfer aspects of their relationship only at the death of a spouse. This is because of the

7. Even if a state permits same-sex marriage, the Defense of Marriage Act precludes the couple from claiming married status for federal income tax purposes, including the filing of a joint return and the use of the married filing jointly tax rates. *See infra* note 30 and accompanying text. However, if one of the partners in a nonmarital relationship earns little income and the other partner provides over one-half of his or her support, the supporting partner may be able to claim an income tax personal exemption for the supported partner. *See* IRC §152(d). However, an individual is not treated as a member of the supporting partner's household (precluding the exemption) if at any time during the taxable year the relationship between the partners is in violation of local law. *See* IRC §152(f)(3). Even if the personal exemption is available, the supporting partner will be unable to claim head of household status income tax rates solely on that basis. *See* IRC §2(b)(3)(B)(i).

8. A divorced spouse may be eligible for Social Security retirement benefits based on the former spouse's Social Security record if the divorced spouse was married to the former spouse for at least ten years.

9. Pub. L. No. 98-397, 98 Stat. 1426 (1984), codified in selected sections of Titles 26 and 29.

10. *See, e.g.*, UPC §3-203.

11. *See, e.g.*, UPC §5-413 ("an adult with whom the respondent has resided for more than six months before the filing of the petition" is seventh in priority).

12. *See, e.g.*, Unif. Health Care Decisions Act (1993) §5, 9 U.L.A. (Part I.B) 111 (2005).

favorable tax provisions, principally the marital deduction, provided to married couples (see Chapters 11 & 16). Because the marital deduction is so central to most estate planning related to married couples, lack of such a deduction for an unmarried couple makes planning alternatives for the unmarried couple only a second-best solution that requires creative and careful planning by the attorney.[13]

1. Ownership of Real Estate

As between an unmarried couple, if real estate is acquired or held as tenants in common, a taxable gift for federal gift tax purposes may be produced if the contributions to the purchase are not made consistent with the percentage of ownership. The same would be true of a joint tenancy. From a state law standpoint, the creation of the tenancies is a completed transfer that cannot be undone without the consent of all parties in title, although a joint tenancy can be converted to a tenancy in common if either of the parties engages in certain transactions inconsistent with the joint tenancy relationship. However, neither party is protected with respect to possible disposition of the other party's interest in the real estate. Moreover, in the situation of a tenancy in common, if one co-owner dies intestate, the surviving co-owner will not receive the decedent's interest in the property because the unmarried survivor is not an applicable family member under the intestate succession statute.[14] The responsibilities of the co-owners for ongoing costs and expenses, such as real property taxes, maintenance, and utilities, are, however, resolved by varying property law principles, which, if necessary, must be enforced by recourse to costly and slow judicial remedies.

To avoid these problems and the potential conflicts they raise, there should be an enforceable mechanism, usually a contract, in place that will set forth how the property is to be disposed of in the event the couple's relationship ends. In such an agreement, for example, the couple could agree that the property is to be sold and could provide as to how the proceeds are to be divided. Alternatively, the agreement might specify that one of them shall retain the property or exclusively enjoy the benefit of the property and provide how the other's interest, or his or her estate's interest, in such property is to be purchased. An important consideration will be the elimination (through a novation or refinancing) of the selling partner's liability for any existing secured indebtedness. Owners of undivided interests in real estate often execute such co-ownership agreements that spell out additional important issues such as (a) how repairs will be made and paid for, (b) how improvements will be decided upon and paid

13. One can find surprising state law variations. For example, Alaska does not recognize a joint tenancy in real property between unmarried individuals. *See* ALASKA STAT. §34.15.130 (LexisNexis 2010).

14. This statement and others in a similar vein may be qualified to varying degrees due to the emergence of domestic partnership, civil union, and designated beneficiary legislation and same-sex marriage, discussed in Part D.

for, (c) when the property will be sold, and (d) whether co-owners have a first right of refusal on the sale of the property. Unmarried couples who are co-owners of real property should consider entering into a similar agreement. In addition, while there is no divorce court to fall back on, partition is an option that will eventually force the sale of real property, but such action is costly and messy.[15]

2. Financial Accounts

For convenience, unmarried couples often create joint checking or savings accounts to which each makes contributions and to which each has access (a joint signature requirement for withdrawals in excess of $xxx might also be considered). Joint titling of more substantial savings or securities accounts as a Will substitute may present many of the standard concerns: (a) loss of privacy with respect to reporting statements and other affairs; (b) potential lifetime access to, or complete dissipation of, the accounts by the noncontributing party; and (c) potential access to the accounts by creditors of the noncontributing party.

A payable-on-death (POD) or transfer-on-death (TOD) designation often provides a better alternative without the lifetime concerns but still with limitations of its own. For example, with a simple POD or TOD designation, the designated beneficiary is not protected against changes or modifications of the POD or TOD designations by the owner. If the POD or TOD beneficiary is removed, resulting in no beneficiary designation on the account, then, as with real estate interests, the survivor will not receive the property if his or her partner dies intestate. Compare this to the situation of a surviving spouse who retains the protection of the elective share if the deceased spouse has removed the surviving spouse from the beneficiary designation on a POD or TOD account. Unfortunately for the unmarried surviving partner, that protection is not available.

3. Beneficiary Designations

The parties are free to designate one another as beneficiaries of life insurance policies (employer-provided group term life insurance is commonly encountered) and retirement plans, and they frequently do so. However, there are at least three caveats. First, there generally is no statute such as those that commonly exist for married couples that will revoke those designations upon the termination of the relationship.[16] Compare statutes such as Uniform Probate Code (UPC) §2-804, which are invoked

15. If one of the parties is to remain the owner of the property during his or her lifetime and the principal concern is the disposition of the property upon the owner's death, there are simpler options. The owner could simply devise the property to the survivor by Will. In states that recognize transfer-on-death deeds (discussed in Chapter 3), the survivor could be designated as the beneficiary.

16. The impact of dissolution of marriage on Wills and revocable transfers is discussed in Chapter 4, Part E. For a number of reasons, if the parties enter into a contractual agreement, it is wise to expressly and objectively define in the agreement what event or events constitute the

by divorce or annulment. Second, there is no requirement of a spousal beneficiary designation under employer retirement plans,[17] inasmuch as the parties are not spouses. And finally, as noted earlier, if there is no beneficiary designation and the decedent dies intestate or names another beneficiary, it is likely that the surviving partner will not receive any of the proceeds.

4. Wills and Will Contracts

If either party dies intestate, the survivor, unless otherwise a relative, will not take under the laws of intestate succession because he or she is not a spouse.[18] It is crucial that both of the unmarried partners execute Wills if one or the other individual is to be benefited. The parties are free to execute Wills in favor of one another, but the surviving individual will be unable to summon spousal protection measures such as the elective share, homestead exemption, exempt property allowance, or family allowance in the event the decedent did not adequately provide for the surviving partner.

Unmarried couples who wish to provide testamentary gifts to one another with more assurances could enter into a Will contract under which the parties would contractually agree to make certain testamentary dispositions to one another.[19] A Will contract should expressly address the murky issue of whether the contract can be rescinded by either party prior to the death of the first party,[20] although the attorney must appreciate that Will contracts between married couples are inherently more difficult to repudiate. If, for example, the Will contract can be and is repudiated prior to death, the survivor of a marital relationship may still have elective share rights. Further, if the marital relationship is severed, divorce procedures take time, and the divorce law provides protections such as property division and spousal support to the former spouse. Unmarried couples do not enjoy the benefits of those statutory safety nets.

5. Revocable Trusts

Unmarried couples who wish to provide for one another financially may use revocable trusts as a substitute for a Will. While the Will contract

"end" or "termination" of the relationship. By doing so, provisions in the agreement that are triggered by the end of the relationship (such as the division and distribution of property) can be resolved with less acrimony. Furthermore, doing so may also permit the parties to contractually create a limited amount of protection similar to that available under statutes such as UPC §§2-802 and 2-804.

17. *See* Retirement Equity Act of 1984, Pub. L. No. 98-397, 98 Stat. 1426 (1984), codified in scattered sections of Titles 26 and 29.

18. Again, this may be qualified by domestic partnership, civil union, and designated beneficiary legislation and same-sex marriage, discussed in Part D.

19. *See, e.g.*, UPC §2-514.

20. It is sometimes asserted that a Will contract is not binding until the death of the first party and thus can be rescinded by either party prior to that time. *See, e.g.*, William M. McGovern et al., Wills, Trusts and Estates 247-248 (4th ed. 2010). The genesis of this doctrine is explained in Eugene F. Scoles et al., Problems and Materials on Decedents' Estates and Trusts 255-256 (6th ed. 2000).

discussed in the prior section could be utilized, it is difficult to administer and offers less security because it could invite financial dissipation and concealment by either party. By way of comparison, the revocable trust offers benefits in preserving the joint assets, particularly if an independent trustee oversees the trust.[21] A more assured result may be achieved through the use of a joint revocable trust that becomes irrevocable upon the first death of a party to the relationship, although there are other consequences and considerations that must be reviewed before such a trust is used, a discussion that is beyond the scope of this book.[22] Revocable trusts are discussed in more detail in Chapter 15.

6. Palimony

The domestic partnership agreement discussed below is a contract between an unmarried couple that sets forth their respective expectations and obligations under the relationship. In the absence of a written agreement, one or both of the individuals may be able to allege the existence of an oral contract the terms of which are subject to the uncertainties of proof at trial. The path-breaking case was *Marvin v. Marvin*.[23]

7. Domestic Partnership or Cohabitation Agreements

These agreements may be referred to by other titles, but they are essentially marital agreements for unmarried couples. The agreement is a contract that sets forth the respective duties of the two parties, often including nonfinancial issues such as who will care for the home, do the grocery shopping, etc. Among other issues frequently dealt with in such an agreement are provisions establishing the organization of household finances (e.g., a joint checking account but separate accounts for other purposes); what assets will be pooled (all earnings or only a portion?; are inheritances free of the agreement?). How assets are to be titled (particularly the residence, although other assets, such as investments or rental properties, may also be of concern); how assets are to be managed during the term of the agreement (repairs, improvements, and sale); under what conditions and circumstances the relationship is to be deemed terminated for purposes of the agreement; how assets are to be divided if the relationship

21. *See* George M. Turner, Revocable Trusts, app. 104 (5th ed. 2003 & Supp. 2010), for an example of a "Contract Not to Revoke or Amend" to be executed in connection with a joint revocable trust, which can be used as a substitute for a Will. This weds the more transparent asset collection and management of a revocable trust with an agreement resembling a Will contract.

22. For example, if wealth transfer taxes are a concern of the gifting party, all of the various transfers present potential tax issues when the transfer is complete, irrespective of whether achieved by Will, survivorship, or POD provisions, or the completion of a revocable transfer.

23. 18 Cal. 3d 660 (1976), *judgment after trial modified*, 122 Cal. App. 3d 871 (1981). Although *Marvin* does not foreclose enforcement of such contractual rights as a matter of public policy, California courts have generally denied the status-based incidents of marriage to unmarried cohabitants, such as a claim for loss of consortium if a partner is injured. *See* Grace Ganz Blumberg, Community Property in California 466 n.6 (4th ed. 2003). However, some of those incidents of marriage may be extended to unmarried same-sex partners and certain partners of the opposite sex by domestic partnership legislation.

terminates during lifetime; if a support obligation will be payable to anyone if the relationship terminates during lifetime; the division and care of pets; and testamentary provisions for the survivor if the relationship terminates by death might also be considered in the agreement.

As is apparent from this brief sampling of potential contract terms, the domestic partnership/cohabitation agreement is an attempt to address lifetime asset management and lifestyle issues as well as asset distribution and support obligations upon termination of the relationship during lifetime or by death—all in a single agreement. This is a complex, broad, and comprehensive document that takes considerable planning and skill to draft correctly. The agreement will require other documents, such as Wills, durable powers of attorney, health care powers of attorney, and deeds, and will require coordination among the various instruments. Inasmuch as the agreement touches Wills, it should comply with the formalities of a Will contract. Because the agreement may also touch real estate, it must also comply with any recording requirements.

In addition, a thorough agreement will address all of these issues in the event the couple later marries or is deemed to be legally married (either as a result of common law marriage in those states that permit common law marriage or perhaps by future legislation permitting legal marriage between same-sex couples). More than likely, however, actual marriage will often cause the partners to focus on different issues, such as the elective share, so the agreement may need to be amended to operate in all respects as a traditional marital agreement. If children are born to, or adopted by, the couple, additional issues beyond the scope of this book are added to the already extensive list of possible considerations. The estate planning attorney should recognize at the outset and communicate to his or her clients that a complete agreement will be a formidable project if it is to be done correctly.[24]

D. Gay and Lesbian Couples

1. Same-Sex Marriage and Other Relationship Recognition

As noted above, the planning for gay and lesbian couples is largely the same as for heterosexual couples, except that the former cannot choose to change their status to "married." However, a growing list of states

24. For a sample form domestic partnership agreement, see FREDERICK K. HOOPS ET AL., FAMILY ESTATE PLANNING GUIDE, app. 35 (4th ed. 1994 & Supp. 2010-2011). *See also* Monica A. Seff, *Cohabitation and the Law*, *in* FAMILIES AND LAW 166-168 (Lisa J. McIntyre & Marvin B. Sussman eds., 1995) (example of nonmarital cohabitation agreement); TURNER, *supra* note 21, app. 195 (outline of marital equivalent agreement).

recognize the status of gay and lesbian couples in varying degrees. This area is quickly evolving, and additional change must be expected.

Connecticut, Iowa, Massachusetts, New Hampshire, New York, Vermont, and the District of Columbia issue marriage licenses to same-sex couples.[25] California, Delaware (effective January 1, 2012), Hawaii (effective January 1, 2012), Illinois, Nevada, New Jersey, Oregon, Rhode Island, and Washington recognize domestic partnerships or civil unions that provide the equivalent of spousal rights to same-sex couples.[26] Colorado, Maine, and Wisconsin recognize designated beneficiaries[27] or domestic partnerships that provide some spousal-equivalent rights to same-sex couples.[28]

Some jurisdictions have a registry for gay and lesbian relationships and unmarried couples of the opposite sex, which, while not the equivalent of marriage, is at least symbolic of the couple's level of commitment and may or may not be cited in any acrimonious litigation such as palimony suits. Major cities such as Atlanta, Boston, Denver, New York City, San Francisco, Washington, D.C., and over 40 others allow such registrations.[29] Employers are increasingly expanding benefits packages to include gay and lesbian partners as well as unmarried opposite-sex couples.

In 1996, Congress enacted the Defense of Marriage Act (DOMA),[30] which for federal purposes limits marriage to individuals of opposite genders. DOMA Section 2 seeks to preclude full faith and credit recognition of same-sex marriage licenses in other nonadopting states. DOMA Section 3 provides that "in determining the meaning of any Act of Congress, or of any ruling, regulation, or interpretation of the various administrative bureaus and agencies of the United States, the word 'marriage' means only a legal union between one man and one woman as husband and wife, and the word 'spouse' refers only to a person of the opposite sex who is a husband or a wife." Section 3 of DOMA would preclude husband and wife status under federal statutes, including the federal tax laws. It has been reported that the application of at least 1,138 federal statues involve husband and wife status.[31] DOMA has been declared unconstitutional by several lower courts, and, barring a legislative solution, a resolution by the U.S. Supreme Court would appear likely at some point.[32]

25. *See* "Marriage Equality & Other Relationship Laws" at http://www.hrc.org/documents/Relationship_Recognition_Laws_Map.pdf (last visited July 29, 2011).

26. *Id.*

27. *See, e.g.*, Note, Nicole C. Berg, *Designated Beneficiary Agreements: A Step in the Right Direction for Unmarried Couples*, 2011 U. Ill. L. Rev. 267 (2011).

28. *See supra* note 25.

29. *See* http://www.unmarriedamerica.org/dp-reg.html (last visited Mar. 5, 2011).

30. Pub. L. No. 104-99, 101 Stat. 2419, codified as 1 U.S.C. §7 and 28 U.S.C. §1738c (2000).

31. *See* Jerry Simon Chasen, *Is DOMA Doomed?*, 25 Prob. & Prop. 22 (Jan./Feb. 2011).

32. *See, e.g., id.*; Frank S. Berall, *Update on Evolving Legal Status of Same-Sex Marriages*, 37 Est. Plan. 21 (Dec. 2010). On February 23, 2011, President Obama instructed the Justice Department to no longer defend the constitutionality of DOMA Section 3. *See* http://www.nytimes.com/2011/02/24/us/24 marriage.html.

2. Special Planning Measures

There are some special concerns. Some commentators suggest that Wills executed by gay and lesbian individuals in favor of their partners may be more susceptible to attack on grounds such as undue influence, reflecting a community's view of these relationships.[33] That the same degree of undue influence potential would not be ascribed to an otherwise identical heterosexual relationship, a relationship that would seem to offer no fewer opportunities for undue influence or coercion, makes the underlying reasoning behind such views all the more clear. In fact, in some jurisdictions, the domestic partnership/cohabitation agreement might be construed as against public policy, particularly in those states that have enacted legislation or constitutional amendments prohibiting same-sex marriage or other similar arrangements pertinent to such unmarried couples.[34] The attorney must evaluate these concerns. A potential response may be to employ measures that are more self-effectuating, such as joint accounts, beneficiary designations, TOD deeds,[35] and revocable trusts,[36] as opposed to Wills or contractual provisions requiring explicit enforcement measures.[37]

QUESTION

If one or both sections of DOMA were held unconstitutional by the United States Supreme Court, how would estate planning for same-sex couples be impacted? Should estate planning documents (e.g., the design of trusts) account for such potential consequences?

E. Conflicts of Interest

There is no evidence that individuals in an unmarried committed relationship share confidences with and demonstrate trust toward their partner any

33. *See, e.g.*, JOEL C. DOBRIS ET AL., ESTATES AND TRUSTS 471-485 (3d ed. 2007); SCOLES ET AL., *supra* note 20, at 39.

34. *See* Joseph F. Morrisey, Lochner, Lawrence, *and Liberty*, 27 GA. ST. U. L. REV. 609, 668 nn.294 & 295 (2011) (listing states that have statutes or constitutional amendments against same-sex marriage); Chasen, *supra* note 31, at 27 (e.g., in jurisdictions prohibiting same-sex civil unions or partnership contracts, one might avoid references to spouses and "style the agreement more as a business agreement.").

35. Transfer-on-death deeds for real estate are discussed in Chapter 3. *See also* JOAN M. BURDA, ESTATE PLANNING FOR SAME-SEX COUPLES 61 (2004).

36. *See generally* DOBRIS ET AL., *supra* note 33, at 482-485 (planning strategies for gay, lesbian, and transgendered testators).

37. *See* Chapter 2, Section A.2.d (dealing with Wills and trusts identification of children created through Assisted Reproductive Technology, including surrogates and artificial insemination); Erica Bell, *Estate Planning for Domestic Partners, Same-Sex Spouses and Non-Traditional Families*, 356 PLI/Est 547 (PLI Tax Law & Est. Plan Series No. 23066, Sept. 13-14, 2010) (general estate planning measures).

less than if they were married. However, as discussed in Chapter 1, some planning situations do not permit representation of both spouses by the same attorney. That potential conflict is perhaps even more pronounced with unmarried partners because of the absence of protective measures such as the forced elective share. Accordingly, at a minimum, the attorney must discuss the potential conflicts with both partners and require the informed execution of a written consent to dual representation if the attorney chooses to represent both parties. We, however, do not encourage such dual representation; and we recommend that in the preparation and negotiation of any kind of contract (including marital agreements, cohabitation agreements, property agreements, etc.), it is always preferable that each party have his or her own independent legal representation.

F. CASE STUDY 6-1

Elizabeth Green and Cindy Jones

THE COHABITING COUPLE

Elizabeth Sarah Green and Cindy Eileen Jones have been living together as a couple for approximately five years. They rented several apartments during that time, and their anticipated purchase of their first home has prompted them to now review the legal implications of their relationship. After years of being renters, Elizabeth and Cindy are eager to be homeowners. In addition, home ownership in their community has been a good investment.

Elizabeth is age 49, and she divorced her first and only husband at age 32. Cindy, age 55, has never married. Both partners are in good health. Neither has any children.

Elizabeth works as an underwriter for a casualty insurer, and her annual salary is approximately $65,000. Elizabeth has worked for her current employer for approximately eight years. Her prior salary history was uneven, so she intends to work until she is 65 so that she can maximize her savings and the benefits under her employer's 401(k) plan.

Cindy earns approximately $38,000 as an elementary school teacher. While Cindy is near retirement age under the school district's retirement plan, she plans to teach until she is 62.

Elizabeth and Cindy make equal contributions to a joint checking account for household expenses, but they otherwise keep their financial accounts separate.

The home purchase would require a greater monthly outlay than their current $800 monthly rent. The monthly payment of principal, interest, and taxes on the proposed $225,000 mortgage would be $1,620. Elizabeth believes that she could pay the entire monthly payment, but it would be tight. Cindy believes that she can afford about one-half of that amount, but with her car loan payments and some credit card balances, her budget would also be tight. The down payment and closing costs will require $30,000. Elizabeth has little in savings, but Cindy could provide all of this amount.

Like marriage, the future of Elizabeth and Cindy's relationship cannot be predicted. However, their past five years together have been generally happy.

Elizabeth's mother is a widow, age 75, and Elizabeth has two siblings. Both siblings are married, and Elizabeth has four nephews and nieces. Elizabeth expects that she will inherit approximately $300,000 from her mother.

Cindy is an only child, and both of her parents are deceased.

Assume that Elizabeth and Cindy reside in a common law property state.

Part A: Elizabeth does not wish to benefit her siblings, but she would like to make a modest testamentary gift to one of her nieces, who is now a single parent of limited financial means. At this point, it appears to Elizabeth that Cindy will be her primary testamentary beneficiary. Cindy would like to make some modest testamentary gifts to charity, but it appears to her that Elizabeth will be her primary testamentary beneficiary.

Discuss the planning issues presented by the relationship of Elizabeth and Cindy, and the manner in which you would structure the acquisition and titling of the home. Identify particular instruments that should be prepared and any salient drafting issues.

Part B: Assume further that Elizabeth has a 25-year-old son from her marriage. He is currently unmarried and has no children. Elizabeth would like to make a modest testamentary gift to him immediately upon her death, but otherwise would devote the balance of her assets to provide for Cindy's well-being for the rest of her life.

Discuss the additional planning issues presented by this change in facts, including the impact on the titling of the home. Identify particular instruments that should be prepared and any salient drafting issues.

G. Reference Materials

Treatises

Unmarried Households

- MARGARET C. JASPER, LIVING TOGETHER: PRACTICAL LEGAL ISSUES (2003).
- Monica A. Seff, *Cohabitation and the Law*, *in* FAMILIES AND LAW 141-165 (Lisa J. McIntyre & Marvin B. Sussman eds., 1995).

- GEORGE M. TURNER, REVOCABLE TRUSTS ch. 61, *Nontraditional Family Relationships* (5th ed. 2003 & Supp. 2010).
- RALPH WARNER ET AL., LIVING TOGETHER: A LEGAL GUIDE FOR UNMARRIED COUPLES (14th ed. 2008).

Same-Sex Relationships

- JOAN M. BURDA, ESTATE PLANNING FOR SAME-SEX COUPLES (2004).
- FREDERICK K. HOOPS ET AL., FAMILY ESTATE PLANNING GUIDE §§33:4 to 33:8 (4th ed. 1994 & Supp. 2010-2011).
- JASPER, *supra*, ch. 2, *Same-Sex Relationships.*
- DANIEL R. PINELLO, AMERICA'S STRUGGLE FOR SAME-SEX MARRIAGE (2006).
- MARK STRASSER ET AL., DEFENDING SAME-SEX MARRIAGE (2007).

Domestic Partnerships and Cohabitation Agreements

- BURDA, *supra*, ch. 3, *Agreements and Contracts.*
- JASPER, *supra*, ch. 3, *The Living Together Agreement.*
- LINDEY AND PARLEY ON SEPARATION AGREEMENTS AND ANTENUPTIAL CONTRACTS, ch. 11, *Marriage, Registered Domestic Partnerships, Civil Unions, and Children* (2d ed. 1999 & Supp. 2010) (forms).
- Seff, *supra*, 166-168 (example of nonmarital cohabitation agreement).
- TURNER, *supra*, app. 195 (outline of marital equivalent agreement).
- WARNER ET AL., *supra*, ch. 3, *Living Together Agreements: Why and How.*

Conflicts of Interest and Nontraditional Couples

- HOOPS ET AL., *supra*, §§33:2 to 33:3.
- TURNER, *supra*, §6:10.

Articles

Unmarried Households

- Erica Bell, *Estate Planning for Domestic Partners, Same-Sex Spouses, and Non-Traditional Families*, 356 PLI/EST 547 (PLI Tax Law and Est. Plan. Series No. 23066, Sept. 13-14, 2010).
- Frank S. Berall, *Tax Consequences of Unmarried Cohabitation*, 18 No. 2 PRAC. TAX LAW. 55 (Winter 2004).
- Frank S. Berall, Estate *Planning Considerations for Unmarried Same or Opposite Sex Cohabitants*, 23 QUINNIPIAC L. REV. 361 (2004).
- Lynne M. Casper & Philip N. Cohen, *How Does POSSLQ Measure Up? National Estimates of Cohabitation*, DEMOGRAPHY 37:2, at 237 (May 2000).
- Gail E. Cohen, *Estate Planning for the Unique Needs of Unmarried Partners*, 30 EST. PLAN. 188 (2003).

- Thomas P. Gallanis, *Domestic Partners and Inheritance: Past, Present, Future*, 39 INST. ON EST. PLAN. ¶1700 (2005).
- Wendy S. Goffe, *Estate Planning for the Unmarried Couple/Non-Traditional Family*, Estate Planning in Depth, SK093 ALI-ABA 1285 (ALI-ABA Continuing Legal Education, June 19-24, 2005).
- Wendy S. Goffe, *Estate Planning for the Unmarried Adult*, Estate Planning in Depth, SR042 ALI-ABA 567 (ALI-ABA Continuing Legal Education, June 13-18, 2010).
- Jennifer Tulin McGrath, *The Ethical Responsibilities of Estate Planning Attorneys in the Representation of Non-Traditional Couples*, 27 SEATTLE U. L. REV. 75 (2003).
- Joshua S. Rubenstein, *Estate Planning for Unmarried Partners: Detriment or Opportunity?*, 149 TR. & EST. 21 (July 2010).
- E. Gary Spitko, *An Accrual/Multi-Factor Approach to Intestate Inheritance Rights for Unmarried Committed Partners*, 81 OR. L. REV. 255 (2002).

Unmarried Heterosexual Couples

- Liza M. Burby, *Why Couples Who Have Lived Together a Long Time Decide to Get Married*, N.Y. NEWSDAY at B13 (Nov. 3, 1998).
- Ann Laquer Estin, *Ordinary Cohabitation*, 76 NOTRE DAME L. REV. 1381 (2001).
- Randall J. Gingiss, *Second Marriage Considerations for the Elderly*, 45 S.D. L. REV. 469, 471 (2000).
- Joanna Lyn Grama, Note, *The "New" Newlyweds: Marriage Among the Elderly, Suggestions to the Elder Law Practitioner*, 7 ELDER L.J. 379 (1999).
- Amy K. Rosenberg, *The Common Law Spouse in Colorado Estate Administration*, 35 COLO. LAW. 85 (2006).

Same-Sex Relationships

- Dawn Allison, *The Importance of Estate Planning Within the Gay and Lesbian Community*, 23 J. MARSHALL L. REV. 445 (1998).
- Frank S. Berall, *Update on Evolving Legal Status of Same-Sex Marriages*, 37 EST. PLAN. 21 (Dec. 2010).
- Mary L. Bonauto, *Advising Non-Traditional Families: A General Introduction*, 40 B.B.J. 10 (Oct. 1996).
- Aimee Bouchard & Kim Zadworny, *Growing Old Together: Estate Planning Concerns for the Aging Same-Sex Couple*, 30 W. NEW ENG. L. REV. 713 (2008).
- Patricia A. Cain, *A Review Essay: Tax and Financial Planning for Same-Sex Couples: Recommended Reading*, 8 LAW & SEXUALITY 613 (1998).
- Patricia A. Cain, *Planning for Same-Sex Couples in 2011*, 17 ALI-ABA EST. PLAN. COURSE MATERIALS J. 5 (June 2011).

- David Chambers, *What If? The Legal Consequences of Marriage and the Legal Needs of Lesbians and Gay Male Couples*, 95 MICH. L. REV. 447 (1996).
- Adam Chase, *Tax Planning for Same-Sex Couples*, 72 DENV. U. L. REV. 359 (1995).
- Patience Crozier, *Nuts and Bolts: Estate Planning and Family Law Considerations for Same-Sex Families*, 30 W. NEW ENG. L. REV. 751 (2008).
- Matthew R. Dubois, Notes, *Legal Planning for Gay, Lesbian and Non-Traditional Elders*, 63 ALB. L. REV. 263 (1999).
- Leon Gabinet, *"Same-Sex Divorce" Update: The Impact of New IRS Guidance in ILM 201021050*, 28 J. TAX'N INV. 89 (2010).
- Sherif Girgis et al., *What Is Marriage?*, 34 HARV. J.L. & PUB. POL'Y 245 (2011).
- Stephen J. Hyland, *Civil Unions in New Jersey*, 146 TR. & EST. 26 (Feb. 2007).
- Peter Nicolas, *Common Law Same-Sex Marriage*, 43 CONN. L. REV. 931 (2011).
- Raymond Prather, *Considerations, Pitfalls, and Opportunities That Arise When Advising Same-Sex Couples*, 24 PROB. & PROP. 24 (May/June 2010).
- Camille M. Quinn & Shawna S. Baker, *Essential Estate Planning for Constitutionally Unrecognized Families in Oklahoma: Same-Sex Couples*, 40 TULSA L. REV. 479 (2005).
- Ralph Randazzo, *Elder Law and Estate Planning for Gay and Lesbian Individuals and Couples*, 6 MARQ. ELDER'S ADVISOR 1 (2004).
- E. Gary Spitko, *The Expressive Function of Succession Law and the Merits of Non-Marital Inclusion*, 41 ARIZ. L. REV. 1063 (1999).
- Sean R. Weissbart, *Strategies to Minimize Estate and Gift Tax for Same-Sex Couples*, 37 EST. PLAN. 33 (Feb. 2010).
- Jennifer Wriggins, *Marriage Law and Family Law: Autonomy, Interdependence, and Couples of the Same Gender*, 41 B.C. L. REV. 265 (2000).

Domestic Partnership and Cohabitation Agreements

- Paul J. Buser, *Domestic Partner and Non-Marital Claims Against Probate Estates:* Marvin *Theories Put to a Different Use*, 38 FAM. L.Q. 315 (2004).
- Wendy S. Goffe, *Preparing Effective Cohabitation Agreements for Unmarried Couples*, 34 EST. PLAN. 7 (2007).
- Katherine C. Gordon, Note, *The Necessity and Enforcement of Cohabitation Agreements: When Strings Will Attach and How to Prevent Them—A State Survey*, 37 BRANDEIS L.J. 245 (1989-1999).

- Max Gutierrez, Jr., *Estate Planning for the Unmarried Cohabitant*, 13 INST. ON EST. PLAN. ¶1600 (1979).
- S. Jeanne Hall, *Estate Planning for Domestic Partnerships*, Valuation, Taxation & Planning Techniques for Sophisticated Estates, 332 PLI/EST 389 (PLI, Mar. 21-22, 2005).
- Andrea P. Heinbach & Pierce J. Reed, Wilcox v. Trautz: *The Recognition of Relationship Contracts in Massachusetts*, 43 B.B.J. 6 (Nov./Dec. 1999).
- Marissa J. Holob, Note, *Respecting Commitment: A Proposal to Prevent Legal Barriers from Obstructing the Effectuation of Interstate Goals*, 85 CORNELL L. REV. 1492 (2000) (includes background information on status of domestic partnerships).
- Beth L. Kramer, *Domestic Partnership Agreements*, 330 PLI/EST 927 (PLI Tax Law and Est. Plan. Course Handbook Series No. 2902, Sept./Oct. 2004).

Other Resources (last visited Aug. 20, 2011)

- http://www.unmarried.org
- http://www.palimony.com
- http://www.lambdalegal.org
- http://www.unmarriedamerica.org

CHAPTER 7

The Married Couple (with Young Children)

A. Another Stage of Life

Individuals have shifting estate planning objectives and needs over the course of their lives. Cohabitation and marriage are both events that provide a great impetus for planning. The birth or adoption of children is another important stage of life, and for some people it eclipses marriage itself. (One may divorce a spouse, but one is always a parent.)

Estate planning for the parents of young children is best approached by considering a tragic "what if" assumption that both parents pass away while the children are still dependent on them. There are two principal planning objectives: (1) care, nurturing, direction, and education of the orphaned children; and (2) management and protection of the parents' wealth and application of that wealth for the benefit of the children.

B. The Selection and Nomination of Protectors

A significant component of estate planning is the individual's selection, or nomination where ultimate appointment is subject to court approval, of persons who will carry out the directions of the individual, generally after he or she has passed away, or who must fulfill some role that the individual was performing prior to his or her death. While the client will focus on the important question of who initially will serve in those capacities, it is almost equally important that multiple successor appointees/nominees also be designated in case the primary person is ultimately unwilling or unable to serve. While a client should refrain from designating or nominating a person for any such role without that person's prior approval, that approval is generally not well informed. For most people, the appointment will be the first time they serve in that capacity, and the appointment will take effect at a future date (or perhaps never). It is difficult to fully appreciate in advance the responsibility, inconvenience, and possible emotional toll that accompany the required duties.

1. Personal Representatives or Executors

If both spouses pass away, the collection and distribution of their probate estate will be the responsibility of a third party, commonly referred to as a "personal representative" or "executor." The terminology can be a bit more elaborate. A personal representative nominated in a Will is referred to as an "executor," while a personal representative appointed by the court for an intestate estate or if the decedent's Will did not make a valid designation of a person who is to serve, is often referred to as an "administrator." In some jurisdictions, an administrator "cum testamento annexo," or c.t.a., may be appointed when an executor is not nominated in the Will or fails to qualify, while an administrator "de bonis non," or d.b.n., is a personal representative who succeeds an administrator. An administrator who is both c.t.a. and d.b.n. is a successor acting under a Will.[1] The Uniform Probate Code (UPC) refers to all of these persons with one common term, "personal representative." We will use that terminology in the interest of simplicity.[2]

Under the UPC, for example, the highest priority for appointment as personal representative is given to the person nominated in the Will,[3] so the Will serves an important function. The period following the loss of both parents will be a time of distress for the children and other family members. Still, the administration of the parents' estates must be carried out in an able and conscientious manner lest the children's inheritance be dissipated. (The role of the personal representative in administration of the estate is discussed in Chapter 17.)

While many personal representatives are drawn from among family members[4] and have no experience in the role (the attorney counsels

1. *See generally* A. James Casner & Jeffrey N. Pennell, Estate Planning §2.7.1 (6th ed. 1995 & Supp. 2009-2010).

2. However, some aspects of these distinctions are reflected in other contexts. For example, the "letters" that are issued to the personal representative in the administration of the estate include "letters testamentary" for a testate estate as well as "letters of administration" for an intestate estate. *See* UPC §1-201(27).

3. *See* UPC §3-203.

4. Older clients often wish that one or more of their adult children act as the personal representative or co-personal representatives, as the case may be. The young dependent children who are the focus of this chapter would not be similarly situated. In any event, multiple fiduciaries present other problems, such as coordination of communications between fiduciaries, allocating voting power and the aggregate level of fiduciary compensation. *See generally* William M. McGovern et al., Wills, Trusts and Estates 581-582, 536-596-597 (4th ed. 2010).

them on procedures), the selection should not be based solely on who "has the time" or who "is close to the children." This is an important financial and legal task that requires attention to detail, conscientious hard work, good judgment, and absolute honesty. If no family members are appropriate nominees, the nomination of a professional should be considered, such as an attorney[5] or an institutional trust department. Even family personal representatives are entitled to a reasonable fee if they do not waive it,[6] based on their level of experience and hours of work in some states[7] or a permitted set percentage of the value of the estate in other states.[8] A floundering family personal representative who is too frequently calling upon an attorney for advice on commonsense issues (the attorney bills the estate for that advice) may turn out to be more expensive in the long run.

Another consideration may be the proximity of the personal representative to the domicile of the decedent. The estate will be administered in the local jurisdiction of the decedent's domicile, so it may be more convenient, efficient, and less costly to appoint a personal representative who lives in or near the decedent's place of domicile. Nonresident personal representatives will typically need to file papers with the probate court subjecting them to the jurisdiction of the local court. While this is a simple procedure, all other things being equal, one may prefer to choose a personal representative who is local.

2. Final Arrangements Representative and Client Letter of Instruction

The death of both parents may leave no adult with direction as to the decedents' wishes concerning funeral, memorial, and other arrangements.

5. The issue of the drafting attorney serving as a fiduciary must be handled with care. *See generally id.* at 595-596; Joel C. Dobris et al., Estates and Trusts 1029, 1034 (3d ed. 2007). Model Rule of Professional Conduct 1.8 may preclude the attorney from indirectly or directly suggesting that he or she serve in that capacity. *See, e.g.*, John R. Price & Samuel A. Donaldson, Price on Contemporary Estate Planning §4.26.1 (2011). In one older survey, 48 percent of the responding estate planners replied that they sometimes, often, or always accept fiduciary appointments. Malcolm A. Moore & Jeffrey N. Pennell, *Practicing What We Preach: Esoteric or Essential?*, 27 Inst. on Est. Plan. ¶¶ 1200, 1203 (1993).

6. *See* Rev. Rul. 66-167, 1966-1 C.B. 20 (providing guidance for renunciation of an executor's fee without income or gift tax consequences). The full text of the ruling is reproduced in Chapter 17.

7. UPC §3-719 provides that the personal representative is entitled to "reasonable compensation" for services. *See also* 755 Ill. Comp. Stat. Ann. 5/27-1 (West 2007) (representative entitled to reasonable compensation for services); Mass. Ann. Laws. ch. 190B §3-719 (LexisNexis Supp. 2010) (personal representative entitled to reasonable compensation for services). A "reasonable compensation" may not be limited to an hourly rate (in part because the rate or the number of hours might be unreasonable) and could be influenced by custom, the size and complexity of the estate, and so forth. *See generally* McGovern et al., *supra* note 4, at §12.7.

8. *See, e.g.*, Cal. Prob. Code §10800 (West Supp. 2011) (providing for a personal representative fee of 4 percent of the first $100,000 of value of the estate, declining as a percentage with increases in the size of the estate, culminating with "a reasonable amount" for all value above $25,000,000); Fla. Stat. Ann. §733.617 (West 2010) (scheduled fees starting at 3 percent for the first $1,000,000 of assets, declining as the size of the estate increases); Tex. Prob. Code Ann. §241(a) (Vernon 2003) (limit of 5 percent of the gross fair market value of the estate subject to administration, with certain exclusions for liquid accounts and life insurance proceeds).

While final arrangements instructions are appropriate for all clients, they are a particularly helpful planning tool in this situation, and the parents should prepare a written expression of their directions concerning these matters and designate an individual (the "final arrangements representative" (FAR)),[9] who will supervise the activities. Because there may be limited access to a safe deposit box, where Wills are often kept, the instructions should generally be expressed in a separate writing, and a copy should be given in advance to the FAR. Sample final arrangements instructions are included as Form E-1 in the Forms Supplement.

While the personal representative and final arrangements representative are often the same person(s), for practical reasons clients may prefer to designate a local person as the FAR when the personal representative resides in a distant locale. The FAR's responsibilities are immediate, and designating someone who is not immediately available and nearby may not be desirable.

The FAR will ordinarily incur substantial costs in carrying out these instructions. UPC §3-701, for example, permits the personal representative to carry out such written instructions prior to appointment, and in many cases the personal representative will also be the designated final arrangements representative. If the final arrangements representative is not also the nominee for personal representative, UPC §3-701 provides that the personal representative "may ratify and accept acts on behalf of the estate done by others where the acts would have been proper for a personal representative." The designation of the FAR should include an express direction by the decedent that the actions of the FAR within the scope of the designation shall be ratified and accepted as acts on behalf of the estate. This issue could also be addressed in the Will.

As discussed in Chapter 1, the parents may wish to compose a client letter of instruction that provides information about the location of the safe deposit box, location of financial assets and important documents, and so forth. A sample client letter of instruction is included as Form E-2 in the Forms Supplement.

9. To our knowledge, the "final arrangements representative" is our nomenclature. A Westlaw search of law review articles and state statute databases did not reveal the use of that term. The powers of the FAR are consequently derived from several sources. As also noted in the accompanying paragraphs of the text, if the FAR is also the personal representative, statutes such as UPC §3-701 permit a person named executor in a Will to carry out written instructions of the decedent relating to the decedent's body, and funeral and burial arrangements. If the FAR is not the personal representative, statutes such as UPC §3-701 permit the personal representative to ratify and accept acts performed by others on behalf of the estate where the acts would have been proper for a personal representative. Although the UPC mentions instructions concerning the body of the decedent, the Uniform Anatomical Gift Act (1968), originally adopted by all states, also provides for specific immunity from civil action or criminal proceedings for anatomical gifts made pursuant to the act or for good faith attempts to do so. *See* Uniform Anatomical Gift Act (1968), §7(c), 8A U.L.A. 69, 146 (2003); Uniform Anatomical Gift Act (1987), §11(c), 8A U.L.A. 3, 64 (2003); Revised Uniform Anatomical Gift Act (2006), §18, 8A U.L.A. 34, 108 (Supp. 2010). *See generally* Russell E. Haddleton, *What to Do with the Body? The Trouble with Postmortem Disposition,* 20 Prob. & Prop. 55 (Nov./Dec. 2006).

3. Guardians

In some states the term "guardian" encompasses protection of an individual's body and welfare (e.g., daily care and educational and medical decisions) as well as management of the individual's finances. In this discussion, we will use the modern bifurcated structure of the UPC in which the protector of the individual's body and welfare is a "guardian" and the manager of the individual's finances is a "conservator."

On the death of one parent, the other parent will almost always have priority as the continuing guardian of the child even if the parents have divorced, unless the court finds the surviving parent to be unfit or if the surviving parent's parental rights have been severed in a prior adjudication. Assuming the death of both parents, UPC §5-202, for example, permits parental appointment of a guardian for a minor by Will or by other writing signed by the parent. Because a minor will typically live with the guardian, the parents must choose the guardian wisely. Family members or close friends with children are often nominated. Hopefully, the nominated guardian will share the parents' values and will have an existing relationship with the child. Under the UPC a minor who is at least 14 years of age has a significant voice in the appointment of a guardian.[10] The guardian needs to appreciate the demands of the appointment (due to age or their own health concerns, grandparents can be less than optimal candidates), particularly when the wards are very young and the anticipated term of guardianship will be long.

4. Conservators

If the parents have left more than trivial amounts of property to their minor children, a conservator will often be required to manage the property and make payments to the guardian or others for the care and benefit of the children. Third parties such as life insurance companies often refuse to make disbursements to a minor unless a conservator has been appointed. Under the UPC there is a specified order in which the court must consider otherwise qualified persons to be a conservator. The court must first consider conservators, guardians, or other fiduciaries that may have been appointed by another court.[11] A child who is at least 14 years of age, however, may have a voice in the selection of the conservator.[12] Otherwise, the parents may nominate the conservator in their Wills.

The duties and powers of the conservator are prescribed by state statutes. These duties and powers may be inflexible or provide incomplete direction in some situations. Conservatorships are subject to court supervision, so there is continuing expense in meeting the reporting requirements. In the absence of an adverse party there is some question about the

10. *See* UPC §§5-203 & 5-206(a).
11. *See* UPC §5-413(a)(1).
12. *See* UPC §5-413(a)(2).

degree of protective scrutiny that this oversight produces. While the UPC is quite liberal in dispensing with bonding of personal representatives,[13] it generally requires that a conservator furnish bond.[14] A conservator is usually entitled to reasonable compensation for services rendered.[15]

Conservatorships are often criticized as expensive and cumbersome. If significant amounts of wealth are involved, a clear drawback is the termination of the conservatorship when the child reaches age 18 or 21 and receives all of the property without further direction or supervision. Another drawback is that if there are several children, the conservator generally cannot use the assets of one child for the possibly greater needs of another, assuming that such marshaling of assets was in fact desired by the parents.

While the guardian and the conservator may be separate persons, clients often designate the same individuals to serve in both capacities. This makes sense in some situations, but there are some drawbacks. First, the guardian is usually chosen for protective and nurturing characteristics and may not possess the money management and recordkeeping skills required of a conservator. Second, if the guardian's household is of much more modest wealth than the ward's, the ward's higher standard of living may create friction with the guardian, the guardian's children, and so forth. Granted, this friction cannot be avoided by using a separate conservator, but not doing so can invite abuses (e.g., the ward foots the bill for everyone on excursions) that might be avoided if the two functions are separated. That said, in some situations, not naming the guardian also as the conservator could be taken as an insult.

Much of this has a bleak, pessimistic tone that can feed on an attorney's fears about the unpredictable and generate even more imagined problems.[16] Nevertheless, the attorney needs to tactfully touch on these issues with the parents without raising their anxiety levels or impugning the character of others concerning the parents' choice of guardian or conservator. It has been our experience that clients frequently prefer to separate the functions of conservator and guardian where significant assets are held for the benefit of the children free of trust—it is a question of preserving some checks and balances. Also, where the client has several good candidates for the various positions, the client may spread the nominations among two different people in the interest of fairness.

Other issues need to be addressed with care and some foresight. For example, some clients might name "John and Sally Marshall as guardians

13. *See* UPC §3-603.
14. *See* UPC §5-415.
15. *See* UPC §5-417.
16. Spendthrift behavior is not the only concern. Having the same individual serve as both guardian and conservator may be to the beneficiary's detriment if that person is overly parsimonious in a good faith attempt to avoid the appearance of overreaching. It may be better that the guardian is given money to, for example, hire domestic help or add a bedroom or bathroom for the child. *See* Charles E. Rounds, Jr. & Charles E. Rounds, III, Loring and rounds: A Trustee's Handbook §3.2.6 (2010).

of ______" where John is the decedent's brother and Sally is his sister-in-law. What happens if John and Sally divorce? Would a designation of "John Marshall as guardian of ______" take care of that possibility more appropriately? What happens if John dies? Possible alternatives run from naming another sibling of the decedent as a successor guardian to leaving the child in the presumably comfortable atmosphere of the sister-in-law's home by naming Sally as successor guardian.

5. Trustees

Unlike the conservator, whose role is dictated by statute, the powers of the trustee are largely conferred by the terms of the trust instrument.[17] As an alternative to conservatorships and as a measure for the tailored management of wealth, the trust is an important estate planning tool, even for estates of modest wealth. If a trust is created by a Will—that is, it is a "testamentary trust"—the trustee will be appointed in the Will. If the trust is an established trust, whether already funded or to be fully funded as a pourover from the Will, the trustees will have already been appointed in the trust instruments. (We defer a discussion of irrevocable trusts until Chapters 8 and 11 and a discussion of revocable trusts until Chapter 15.) If forced to do so, a court will appoint a trustee. It is often said that a trust will not fail for the lack of a trustee,[18] but most clients would prefer input on that decision. It is important to designate successor nominees for various positions.

The selection of a trustee is an important decision because the position can create pitfalls and possible surcharges for the unschooled, careless, or inept individual. Some trust creators appoint cotrustees, one being a family member for oversight and family input, and one being an institution for professional management. In response to a client's questions concerning the differences between personal representatives and trustees, one might observe that the personal representative position is a "temporary job" for someone responsible for gathering and inventorying assets, paying bills, preparing final tax returns, and distributing the assets. Personal representatives are eventually discharged, typically within a year or so after the decedent's death. On the other hand, a trusteeship should be thought of as a "long-term job" that requires many of the same skills, but in addition (and this is probably the most important attribute) *the ability to exercise discretion and be fair*. If there is any indication of historical family conflict, often a neutral third-party individual or an institution is a better choice than a family member.

17. The Uniform Trust Code does prescribe a number of rules governing trusts, but most can be overridden by the terms of the trust instrument. *See* UNIF. TRUST CODE (2000), 7C U.L.A. 362 (2006 & Supp. 2007) §105(b). *See generally* Suzanne Brown Walsh, *Drafting Under the Uniform Trust Code (With Sample Provisions),* 21 PRAC. TAX LAW. 23 (Winter 2007).

18. AUSTIN WAKEMAN SCOTT ET AL., SCOTT AND ASCHER ON TRUSTS §11.4 (5th ed. 2006).

While many family member trustees serve very capably, problems may arise. Uncle Bill may be the family authority on financial investments, but those skills do not necessarily provide him with the prudence and diligence, not to mention the equitable fairness, required of a trustee. Uncle Bill also may lack the attention to keep records and report taxes (the trust may be required to file annual federal, state, or local income tax returns). At a minimum, most trusts require (by the express terms of the trust or by statute) the trustee to provide some level of accounting or other written reports to the beneficiaries at least annually.[19] However, due to cost considerations and concerns about long-term investment underperformance by some professional or institutional trustees, Uncle Bill may nevertheless be appointed. Although a bond may be required by the terms of the trust, many trust instruments excuse it when a family trustee is named.[20]

The client should be reminded, tactfully, of at least two points: (1) well-intentioned negligence or inattentiveness in investing and management can be devastating to the trust over the long term; this risk can be mitigated somewhat by assigning investment responsibility to someone other than Uncle Bill, including an institution or professional investment advisor; (2) Uncle Bill may have or may develop a hidden substance abuse, other debilitating addiction, or suffer personal financial reverses or simply become a thief if tempted. Uncle Bill's waiver of his trustee fee for the children's benefit may foster some resentment in him over the longer term, permitting self-justification of fiduciary breaches. Unlike an institutional trustee with other assets, even if mismanagement is discovered, Uncle Bill may have dissipated his own assets, leaving little practical recourse or recovery by the disappointed beneficiaries. Again, this risk can be reduced by requiring a bond or by the trust instrument's assignment of investment and management responsibility to professionals,[21] leaving the family member to assume more of an advisory position with respect to distributions and other matters.[22] However, those safeguards

19. *See e.g.*, Robert Whitman, *Providing Information to Beneficiaries (With Sample Forms)*, 15 ALI-ABA Est. Plan. Course Materials J. 5 (Feb. 2009).

20. *See, e.g.*, UPC §7-304 (first sentence); Unif. Trust Code (2000) §702(a), 7C U.L.A. 563 (2006).

21. For sample language placing investment authority in an investment advisor, *see* Jeffrey A. Schoenblum, Page on the Law of Wills, vol. 7 (Forms), ch. 85F (2000). A trustee may "delegate" some of its responsibilities to another person. *See* Uniform Prudent Investor Act (1994) §9 (delegation of investment and management functions). In a "directed" trust, the trust instrument assigns certain responsibilities to a trustee, while other responsibilities (and powers) may reside with another trustee. *See, e.g.*, Jesse Dukeminer et al., Wills, Trusts, and Estates 723-724 (8th ed. 2009) (discussing "Delegated Versus Directed Trusts"); Richard W. Nenno, *Directed Trusts: Can Directed Trustees Limit Their Liability?*, 21 Prob. & Prop. 45 (Nov./Dec. 2007).

22. If multiple fiduciaries are used, the instrument must carefully specify when unanimity is required and when a majority vote controls. Even if a majority vote rule is adopted, a dual-fiduciary structure has the potential for deadlock. *See generally* McGovern et al., *supra* note 4, at 581-582. In addition, state law varies as to whether multiple fiduciaries each collect a full fee or divide a single fee. *Id.* at 596-597.

may reduce or eliminate the desired cost savings that prompted the selection of a family member trustee in the first place.

C. Dealing with Life Insurance and Retirement Plans

We single out life insurance and retirement plans because, after a home, they are probably the most significant assets held by a young couple with children. There is a general reluctance by third-party payers to distribute insurance or retirement plan proceeds to minors unless a conservatorship has been established (the proceeds under the terms of the account documents are generally held, with interest, by the payer). However, if a trust for the benefit of the minors is named as a secondary beneficiary (after the other spouse) of the account in question, payment will generally be forthcoming upon proof of the trust's due formation.

Chapter 11 addresses the freestanding irrevocable life insurance trust (ILIT), a trust that is established during the client's lifetime to be the owner and beneficiary of life insurance policies on the client's life. The ILIT is often part of a federal wealth transfer tax planned structure, but the costs and complexities will generally be unnecessary, unattractive, or impractical for clients with modest estates and modest levels of life insurance. The traditional estate planning solution is the contingent testamentary trust for the benefit of minors, discussed below.

D. The Contingent Trust

Form G in the Forms Supplement is an example of a non-tax-driven Will that includes a contingent testamentary trust. The trust's formation is contingent upon neither spouse surviving (otherwise the estate passes outright to the survivor). Only then does the probate estate pass to the testamentary trust for the benefit of the children (*see* Section 3.2, Form G). It is standard practice to set forth the terms of the trust in the Will for use only if necessary (*see* Article 4, Form G). In that respect a testamentary trust as part of a public probate document may not enjoy the confidentiality of trusts often available to trusts formed outside of the Will. For that reason wealthier estates (or estates more concerned with privacy) may establish a number of trusts before the decedent's death, and the estate plan might use a simple pourover Will to transmit any remaining probate assets to selected trusts.[23] On the other hand, relatively modest estates that

23. A testamentary trust is created as part of the estate probate process. If the trust is thereafter subject to unduly cumbersome oversight by the probate court, an inter vivos trust

employ the contingent testamentary trust for minors probably do not require such confidentiality nor justify the added expense of multiple documents. For clients who otherwise wish to limit the probate of their estates, another alternative is to structure a contingent trust share within a revocable trust, discussed in Chapter 15, because the trust instrument is generally not a public document.

A standard provision of many well-drafted Wills is a clause that permits the personal representative to distribute assets to the custodian of accounts established under the Uniform Gifts to Minors Act or Uniform Transfers to Minors Act.[24] In our view, these custodianships are not appropriate for the protection of orphaned children if a significant amount of wealth is involved. Depending on state law, the accounts often terminate at the time the minor reaches age 21, and the child (and the child's creditors) will have unfettered access to the remaining funds at that point. For many children, this invites problems. Moreover, until the child attains such age, the terms of the statute, not the terms of a trust, dictate the application of the assets. Finally, a separate account must be established for each child, which does not permit the marshaling of family wealth.

The attorney's drafting for a testamentary trust involves standard trust drafting, but within the confines of the Will. The more difficult issues involve the distribution of trust proceeds. Does the client want the children to receive the balance of the trust proceeds in a lump sum upon reaching a certain age? Or does the client prefer staggered distributions such as at age 21, 25, 30, 35, and so forth? Should distributions be mandatory or only in the discretion of the trustee? Should distributions be mandatory or only upon demand of the beneficiary? If the distributions are discretionary, what guidelines should the trustee use?

Consider also the following:

1. Are "educational" expenses limited to tuition, required fees, books, and supplies, or do they also include room and board, transportation, and a reasonable allowance for living expenses? Should such expenses be included only if the beneficiary is a full-time student? Should only an attendance at an accredited institution qualify?
2. If distributions are to be permitted for the education of a beneficiary, should there be a limit as to how many years qualify, or should the instrument apply a more uncertain but flexible standard tied to identifiable progress toward a degree?[25] What

may be a better solution. *See, e.g.*, DOBRIS ET AL., *supra* note 5, at 542-543. For estates without significant federal wealth transfer taxation concerns, the inter vivos receptacle could be a revocable trust (see Chapter 15) rather than the ILIT (Chapter 11).

24. UNIF. TRANSFERS TO MINORS ACT §5 (1983), 8C U.L.A. 1, 27 (2001), expressly permits distributions from an estate to the custodian of a minor.

25. For example, one commentator suggests that the definition of "education" be limited to undergraduate education and be confined to four years so that minors are not tempted to prolong their education. John H. Martin, *The Draftsman Views Wills for a Young Family*, 54 N.C. L. REV. 277, 299 (1976).

types of education qualify (e.g., trade school versus a liberal arts education)? What levels of schools qualify (e.g., elementary, secondary, postsecondary, graduate, or professional, or all)? What types of schools qualify (e.g., public, private, or correspondence/ internet programs)?
3. Should distributions or loans to a beneficiary to start a business be permitted? Should they be encouraged? Must the "business" be a profit-making enterprise, or are not-for-profit activities acceptable (such as seed money to establish a nonprofit organization)?
4. Is assisting a child in the purchase of a first home a priority? Are outright distributions desired, or should the trust be permitted only to make loans, taking a security interest in the property?
5. Should the trustee be permitted, or directed, to "hold back" distributions, even those that would otherwise be mandatory, under certain circumstances? Should incentive clauses be included? ("Holdback" and "incentive" clauses are discussed in Chapter 13.)
6. If a single trust is for the benefit of more than one child and the children are of widely differing ages, when does the trust break (e.g., when the youngest is 21), and may the older children receive interim distributions before that time, even after completing all higher education?

The "pot" versus "separate" trust structures are two general solutions to the last question. One approach when there are multiple young children of relatively close ages, is to accumulate all of the trust assets in one "pot" for the benefit of all the children.[26] As an example, a typical pot trust might operate along the following lines: Until all the children graduate from high school, the trustee is instructed to pay the guardian the reasonable expenses of the children's care and education. During the high school years questions may arise concerning whether funds for automobiles, private schools, and trips abroad qualify under this standard. As each child enters the college years, the trustee is instructed to pay the educational expenses of the child, using guidelines established in the trust that respond to many of the questions raised above.

After a child completes his or her higher education, it is a common expectation that the child will seek gainful employment. Additional distributions may therefore be limited unless extraordinary circumstances arise, such as medical or health needs, so that assets are preserved for the care and education of younger siblings. Once the youngest child reaches a certain age, such as 25, before which time he or she will have had an opportunity to complete an undergraduate degree, the remaining assets of the trust are divided equally among all of the children and either

26. However, if one of the children has special needs, a separate trust share may be created for that child, and the trust would continue until the special need has passed, which could be for life. The special needs trust would typically include provisions tailored to coordinate with public assistance; see Chapter 15.

distributed outright to the children at that point or held in further trust under terms specified in the Will.

One drawback to the pot trust is that if older children are permitted to tap trust assets for graduate education and the distribution date is set at age 25 without modification, this can be a disadvantage for the youngest child, who would not have as much time as his or her elder siblings in which to pursue graduate studies. Another drawback to a pot trust arises if the children widely vary in age, as the older children will need to wait for the final distribution until the youngest sibling reaches the prescribed age of distribution. That drawback can be mitigated a bit, particularly if the trust assets are substantial, if the trustee can make discretionary distributions to the older children during the waiting period. For some issues, there is no perfect drafting solution, and the client is once again encouraged to select a trustee who will be fair and equitable.

Nonetheless, many clients with younger children, or of modest estates, prefer the pot trust approach because it is simpler to administer and it supports the primary goal of most parents—that their children receive an education so that they can become successful young adults. The pot trust supports this goal by marshaling assets toward that end such that the plan would be considered a success if all the decedents' children are as well educated as possible considering their intellectual gifts and motivation, and not a dime remains in the trust.

However, the pot trust approach has other drawbacks in terms of perceived fairness. Students with scholarships derive fewer benefits from the trust. Students who attend more expensive schools derive more benefits, and students who pursue graduate school may derive even more benefits (or fewer if they are the youngest). Children who do not pursue higher education derive fewer benefits from the trust, but this can be compensated somewhat by distributions to assist in starting businesses or to acquire housing.

A "share" or separate trust approach may answer these criticisms by the apportionment of a separate but equal share of a single trust, or by an actual division of the assets into separate, but equal, trusts, to each child upon the occurrence of a certain event. In our experience, most clients prefer this approach if their children are older. Under this approach, for example, the trust could be divided into equal shares of a single trust or, alternatively, into actual separate trusts immediately upon the death of the second spouse, with each share or separate trust being managed solely for the benefit of a single child. This would avoid the issues of fairness to all siblings, as it inherently provides for a greater responsiveness to the separate needs of each child. It also avoids the multiple problems inherent in a pot trust that can arise with children of widely varying ages. However, if the trust assets are modest or the children are very young, the administrative burden of maintaining separate trusts (or even separate trust shares in a single trust) for many years may make this approach less attractive.

In our experience, while most parents express providing security for their orphaned children as their primary objective in such planning, a close second is to make the plan, structure, and administration as simple and fair to all of their children as possible. Reflecting the endless flexibility of the trust, the combinations of distribution schemes are equally endless, and it is the attorney's job not merely to explain these options, but to rely upon his or her experience to cull from the endless possibilities those that will satisfy the client's objectives in the most elegant and simplest manner possible.[27]

E. CASE STUDY 7-1

***Paul and Linda Davis* (Part II)**

THE ARRIVAL OF CHILDREN

We are revisiting Paul and Linda Davis from Case Study 5-1 in Chapter 5. It is seven years later, and Paul is now 37 and Linda is 35. Linda was awarded tenure at her university and promoted to the rank of Associate Professor. Paul is a partner in his accounting firm. Paul and Linda now have two children, John Ashford Davis, age 5 (born January 5, five years ago), and Abigail Carol Davis, age 2 (born August 15, two years ago). They do not plan to have any more children.

Paul's annual earnings as a new partner average $90,000. Linda's annual salary is $50,000. With the births of the children they sold their former residence and purchased a new home (410 Ithaca Circle, FirstCity, FirstState 80001) appraised at $350,000, subject to a $300,000 mortgage, titled in joint tenancy with rights of survivorship. They lease two automobiles, one of which is driven by Paul and the other by Linda. Paul's balances in his 401(k) plan and his Roth IRA[28] are $175,000 and $30,000, respectively. Linda's balances in her pension plan and supplemental annuity are $75,000 and $30,000, respectively. Paul is the primary beneficiary under all of Linda's accounts, and Linda is the primary beneficiary under all of Paul's accounts.

Two years ago Paul purchased a $500,000 term life insurance policy on his life, designating Linda as the primary beneficiary.

While their joint checking account still has an average balance of $1,000, their money market account balances have grown to $40,000.

All of the relatives described in Case Study 5-1 are still living.

27. Examples of pot trust and sprinkle trust clauses are included in SCHOENBLUM, *supra* note 21, at ch. 77F.

28. Paul, a CPA, should be aware that his joint income with Linda is now approaching a level at which his eligibility for a Roth IRA contribution will be reduced or eliminated. *See* IRC §408A(c)(3)(A) & (C)(ii).

Part A: Paul and Linda wish to revise the Wills they executed in connection with Case Study 5-1 if that is necessary. Discuss the types of revisions you would suggest as well as any other estate plan modifications.

Part B: Assume that on July 5, Year 1, Paul and Linda each execute Wills that incorporate contingent testamentary trusts for their children. Assume further that on August 1, Year 1, Paul changes the secondary beneficiary designation on his life insurance policy to reflect the modifications to the estate plan. On January 3, Year 3, Paul, by codicil, makes some minor changes to his Will.

Below are six alternative ways of expressing the secondary life insurance beneficiary designation that is filed with the life insurance company. Linda has already been designated as the primary beneficiary. Discuss the desirability of each approach and identify the one that you would use. If none is correct, propose new language.

1. "The Estate of Paul William Davis."
2. "The Children's Trust Created Under the Will of Paul William Davis."
3. "The Children's Trust Created Under the Will of Paul William Davis, executed July 5, Year 1."
4. "The Trustee of the Children's Trust Created Under the Will of Paul William Davis."
5. "The Trustee of the Children's Trust Created Under the Will of Paul William Davis, executed July 5, Year 1."
6. "The Trustee of the Children's Trust (for the benefit of John Ashford Davis and Abigail Carol Davis) Created Under the Will of Paul William Davis, executed July 5, Year 1."

Part C: Draft a new Will for Linda or Paul, as your teacher directs, using Form G from the Forms Supplement. Linda and Paul believe that the assets of their estate would best be used for the higher education of their children, so the trust should reflect flexibility in providing for that. Linda finished her Ph.D. in philosophy at age 25, and she believes that her rush to complete the degree did not permit her to explore other interests. In addition, with two children, it appears that the life insurance and other assets would be adequate, and substantial trust principal would remain. Paul is concerned that the children would not be mature enough to handle that amount of money free of a trust.

After some discussion with you, Paul and Linda have requested that the Wills reflect the following plan: a pot trust approach with liberal discretionary distributions for higher education until age 30. Distributions would be permitted for the care and education of each child until age 18, at which time the higher education provisions would have priority, but not be exclusive. Discretionary distributions could be made at any age in the event of extraordinary circumstances affecting the health, education, or welfare of the children. When the younger child reaches age 30, one-third of the trust shall be further divided between and distributed to each child. When the younger child reaches age 35, one-half of the remaining principal of the trust shall be divided between and distributed to each child. When the younger child reaches age 40, the remaining principal of the trust shall be divided between and distributed to each child, and the trust shall terminate. Paul and Linda, in consultation with their family, have decided that Paul's sister should act as guardian and personal representative, with Linda's cousin as the secondary nominee for both positions. Paul's father, a retired executive, would be the initial trustee, and the alternate trustee would be Linda's mother, who is currently a financial planner.

Part D: Assume that instead of three years there are 12 years' difference in age between Paul and Linda's children. Draft an alternative distribution plan that you would recommend for the children's trust under these circumstances.

Part E: Some clients want to include personal messages to their family members in their Wills or other estate planning instruments. The client might wish to explain the reasons for his or her treatment of the devisees or share some of his or her core personal values. These types of instruments are sometimes referred to as "ethical Wills."[29] The client with young children in particular might consider this type of expression to be very important. Assume that Paul has spoken of the importance of thrift and independence, while Linda has spoken of the importance she places on family and education. Draft language for their Wills that would convey these messages.

Part F: Assume that Paul and Linda divorce, and neither has remarried. Paul and Linda share custody of the children. What are the pertinent considerations in drafting either Paul or Linda's Will under these circumstances?

F. Reference Materials

Treatises

Annual Exclusion Gifts to Children

- John R. Price & Samuel A. Donaldson, Price on Contemporary Estate Planning §§7.2.1, 7.2.2 (2011).

29. *See, e.g.*, Zoe M. Hicks, *Is Your (Ethical) Will in Order?*, 33 ACTEC J. 154 (2008); Steven Keeva, *A Legacy of Values*, 91 A.B.A. J. 88 (Oct. 2005); Constance D. Smith, *New and Improved Testaments for Estate Planning Documents*, 32 Colo. Law. 73 (Dec. 2003); Jim Stovall, The Ultimate Gift (2001).

- Richard B. Stephens et al., Federal Estate and Gift Taxation: Including the Generation-Skipping Transfer Tax ¶9.04(1) (8th ed. 2002 & Supp. 2011).
- Harold Weinstock & Martin Neumann, Planning an Estate: A Guidebook of Principles and Techniques §§8:18 to 8:20; §§8:35 to 8:37 (4th ed. 2002 & Supp. 2010).

Selection of Fiduciaries

- Theodore E. Hughes & David Klein, the Executor's Handbook: A Step-by-Step Guide to Settling an Estate for Personal Representatives, Administrators, and Beneficiaries (3d ed. 2007).
- L. Rush Hunt & Lara Rae Hunt, A Lawyer's Guide to Estate Planning: Fundamentals for the Legal Practitioner 125-128 (3d ed. 2004).
- Price & Donaldson, *supra*, §4.25 (appointment of guardian); Form 4-19 (appointment of guardian); §10.42 (selection of trustee).
- George M. Turner, Revocable Trusts ch. 15, *Choosing the Appropriate Trustee and Kinds of Trusteeship*; ch. 16, *Choosing a Corporate Trustee*; ch. 17, *Special Trustee or Independent Trustee* (5th ed. 2003 & Supp. 2010)).

Planning for Couples with Young Children

- Price & Donaldson, *supra*, §4.21.3 ("pot" trust vs. separate trusts).
- Weinstock & Neumann, *supra*, §§3:6 to 3:20.

Single Parents

- Frederick K. Hoops et al., Family Estate Planning Guide §§33:9 to 33:12 (4th ed. 1994 & Supp. 2010-2011).

Funeral Instructions

- James Casner & Jeffrey N. Pennell, Estate Planning §3.2.1 (6th ed. 1995 & Supp. 2009-2010).
- Price & Donaldson, *supra*, §4.11.
- Turner, *supra*, apps. 73 & 74 (burial directives); apps. 75 & 76 (cremation directives).

Ethical Wills

- Jim Stovall, The Ultimate Gift (2001).

Articles

Single Parents

- Richard M. Horwood, *Estate Planning Specifically for the Single Parent*, 25 Est. Plan. 77 (1998).

Planning for Couples with Young Children

- Kay W. Abramowitz, *Planning for the Less-Wealthy Client (With Forms)*, 22 PRAC. TAX LAW. 53 (2008).
- Mary Beth Beattie, *Top 10 Myths and Misconceptions in Estate Planning*, 36 MD. B.J. 3 (Mar./Apr. 2003) (avoiding probate).
- Martha Chadwick Holt, *Minors' Guardianship in an Age of Multiple Marriage*, 29 INST. ON EST. PLAN. ¶500 (1995).
- Kristine S. Knaplund, *Grandparents Raising Grandchildren and the Implications for Inheritance*, 48 ARIZ. L. REV. 1 (2006).
- John H. Martin, *The Draftsman Views Wills for a Young Family*, 54 N.C. L. REV. 277 (1976) (discussion at 299-304 concerning structuring trust shares).
- William M. McGovern, Jr., *Trusts, Custodianships, and Durable Powers of Attorney*, 27 REAL PROP. PROB. & TR. J. 1 (1992).
- Paul A. Meints, *A Trust and Estate Planning Questionnaire for Families with Minor Children*, 16 No. 1 PRAC. TAX LAW. 33 (Fall 2001).
- Judith L. Poller, *What Planning Strategies Should Be Used When Both Spouses Work?*, 25 EST. PLAN. 358 (1998).
- Thomas L. Popejoy, Jr., *The Family Legal Checkup: A Guide to Planning and Drafting Wills for Middle-Income Couples with Minor Children*, 8 N.M. L. REV. 171 (1978).
- Gail Levin Richmond, *Planning for Orphans, Quasi Orphans and Disabled Persons*, 18 INST. ON EST. PLAN. ¶1500 (1984).
- John R. Wiktor, *Reaching Potential: Planning for Families with Young Children*, 28 J. TAX'N INV. 73 (2011).

Selection of Fiduciaries (*See also* same heading in Ch. 3 reference materials.)

- Steve R. Akers, *Twenty-Five Things You Have to Know about Appointing Trustees*, 17 PROB. & PROP. 36 (July/Aug. 2003).
- Steve R. Akers, *Selection of Trustees: A Detailed Review of Gift, Estate and Income Tax Effects and Non-tax Effects*, 38 INST. ON EST. PLAN. ¶300 (2004).
- Susan P. Brachtl, *Problems of Fiduciaries as Powerholders*, 17 INST. ON EST. PLAN. ¶1700 (1983).
- Thomas C. Gaspard, *What Are the Implications When a Lawyer Serves as Trustee?*, 28 EST. PLAN. 542 (2001).
- J.E. Harker, *Choosing a Trustee: The Case for the Corporate Fiduciary*, 8 PROB. & PROP. 44 (May/June 1994).
- Frederick R. Keydel, *Trustee Selection, Succession, and Removal: Ways to Blend Expertise with Family Control*, 23 INST. ON EST. PLAN. ¶400 (1989).
- Louis D. Laurino, *The Duties and Responsibilities of the Attorney/Fiduciary*, 19 INST. ON EST. PLAN. ¶¶ 1600, 1601.2 (1985).

- Malcolm A. Moore & Jeffrey N. Pennell, *Practicing What We Preach: Esoteric or Essential?*, 27 Inst. on Est. Plan. ¶1200 (1993) (survey of practicing lawyers, including questions about selection of fiduciaries).
- Malcolm A. Moore & Jeffrey N. Pennell, *Survey of the Profession II*, 30 Inst. on Est. Plan. ¶1500 (1996).
- Charles W. Pieterse & Charles E. Coates III, *Exculpatory Clauses May Give Trustees Extra Protection from Liability*, 37 Est. Plan. 26 (Mar. 2010).
- Susan L. Repetti, *Lawyer As Trustee*, 14 ALI-ABA Est. Plan. Course Materials J. 5 (June 2008).
- Kimbrough Street, *Practical Guidelines for Selecting an Individual Trustee*, 20 Est. Plan. 268 (1993).
- Kimbrough Street, *Growls or Gratitude? Practical Guidelines for Selection of Individual Trustees and Design of Trustee Succession Plans*, 40 Inst. on Est. Plan. ¶300 (2006).

Trust Distributions Provisions

- Mark L. Ascher, *Recent Regulatory Developments Relation to Subchapter J*, 35 Inst. on Est. Plan. ¶1200 (2001).
- Christopher P. Cline, *Drafting and Administering Discretionary Trusts: Can Beneficiary Happiness and Trusts Coexist?*, 16 ALI-ABA Est. Plan. Course Materials J. 49 (Oct. 2010).
- E. James Gamble, *Fiduciary Principles of Trust Distribution, Investments, Adjustments, and Conversions*, Estate Planning in Depth, SK093 ALI-ABA 1 (ALI-ABA Continuing Legal Education, June 19-24, 2005).
- Seth Krasilovsky, *Exercising Discretion in Administering Discretionary Trusts*, 36 Est. Plan. 32 (June 2009).
- Gerald E. Lunn, Jr., *Promoting a Favorable Outcome for Children With Large Inheritances*, 35 Est. Plan. 15 (Aug. 2008).
- Paul A Meints, *Using Trusts to Provide Incentives, Rewards, Remembrances, and Other Benefits to Chosen Beneficiaries*, 15 No. 2 Prac. Tax Law. 25 (Winter 2001) (includes an excellent checklist suggesting different approaches and sample language).
- Howard M. McCue III, *Planning and Drafting to Influence Behavior*, 34 Inst. on Est. Plan. ¶600 (2000).
- Joshua C. Tate, *Conditional Love: Incentive Trusts and the Inflexibility Problem*, 41 Real Prop. Prob. & Tr. J. 445 (2006).

Funeral Instructions

- Michael Gilfix & Carolyn A. Chandler, *Burials—Going Green, Greener and Greenest*, 148 Tr. & Est. 58 (Feb. 2009).
- Ann M. Murphy, *Please Don't Bury Me Down in That Cold Cold Ground: The Need for Uniform Laws on the Disposition of Human Remains*, 15 Elder L.J. 381 (2007).

Ethical Wills

- Zoe M. Hicks, *Is Your (Ethical) Will in Order?*, 33 ACTEC J. 154 (2008).
- Steven Keeva, *A Legacy of Values*, 91 A.B.A. J. 88 (Oct. 2005).
- Martin M. Shenkman, *Integrating Religious Considerations into Estate and Real Estate Planning*, 25 Gpsolo 14 (Sept. 2008).
- Constance D. Smith, *New and Improved Testaments for Estate Planning Documents*, 32 Colo. Law. 73 (Dec. 2003).

CHAPTER 8

Gifts from Grandparents

A. The Transferor's Concerns in Intergenerational Wealth Transfers

Much of estate planning involves intergenerational wealth transfers. Even the simplest Will may involve testamentary gifts to children or grandchildren. The potential transferors are not limited to grandparents, nor are the concerns of grandparents particularly unique, except perhaps for the application of the federal generation-skipping transfer tax (GSTT). However, in estate planning one often sees a pattern of gift planning by grandparents, hence the title of this chapter.

There are a number of explanations for this pattern of gift planning. The grandparents are usually the oldest living generation in the family, so it may be an appropriate time for planning as a general matter. With a lifetime of accumulation, the grandparents are usually at the crest of their financial worth. The grandparents might be moved into action by some family event, such as the births of their grandchildren. Finally, potential tax savings can be a great motivator.

Transferors[1] of intergenerational wealth typically have two principal concerns: (1) the creation of structures to carry out their wishes during life and after death; and (2) the minimization of taxes. The first concern will

1. Interchangeably in this discussion, we may use the terms "transferor," "donor," "settlor," or "grantor" on the one hand, and "transferee," "donee," "recipient," or "beneficiary" on the other hand.

usually focus on the management and preservation of family wealth in light of the uncertainties of the changing investment climate, possibly requiring professional asset management, and the conduct of the beneficiaries (e.g., divorce, mental illness, substance abuse, criminal behavior, excessive hedonistic and spendthrift behavior). Focusing on wealth preservation may be balanced by genuine concern for the use of that wealth in supporting the success and happiness of younger generations. Donors often seek to encourage productive behavior and impart values[2] to the beneficiaries in the hope of helping them become successful individuals. These goals can be implemented through provisions that promote education and public service or provide investment capital. Additionally, the grandparent client may seek to ensure the security and, one hopes, the happiness of the beneficiaries by providing an income to maintain a lifestyle consistent with their station in life.

It is unquestioned that much of the focus of planning structures is on the tax minimization aspect. However, experienced estate planners will tell you that the first aspect, a desire to control the human elements, often is equally or even more important to the client.

B. Selecting the Form of the Gift

1. Outright Gifts

An outright gift, free of trust or other supervision, is a popular form of wealth transfer, largely because of its practical simplicity, particularly if made in cash, and the emotional value in witnessing the recipient's enjoyment and appreciation of the gift. The outright gift is not, of course, limited to a lifetime gift; it may take the form of a testamentary bequest. However, large outright gifts are not desirable for minors, because gifts of a significant amount may require the appointment of a conservator for the minor. It is also difficult to make outright gifts for the benefit of individuals who are unborn. Irrespective of the age of the beneficiary, the transferor loses control over the management and use of the gift. In that respect, while the types of property that could be subject to outright gifting are unlimited (e.g., closely held corporate stock, publicly traded corporate stock, real estate, collectibles, and limited partnership and limited liability company interests), the structure of the ownership is still relatively limited to the forms discussed in this section (outright gifts, custodianship, or trust).

2. *See, e.g.*, Howard M. McCue III, *Planning and Drafting to Influence Behavior*, 34 INST. ON EST. PLAN. ¶¶ 600, 601.2 (2000); Ellen Evans Whiting, *Controlling Behavior by Controlling the Inheritance: Considerations in Drafting Incentive Provisions*, 15 PROB. & PROP. 6 (Sept./Oct. 2001); Gerald E. Lunn, Jr., *Promoting a Favorable Outcome for Children with Large Inheritances*, 35 EST. PLAN. 15 (Aug. 2008).

In terms of the federal wealth transfer taxes, outright lifetime gifts are a relatively simple matter if valuation is not a significant issue. (Valuation discounts are discussed below and in Chapter 16.) They generally qualify for the IRC §2503(b) gift exclusion, which permits annual exclusion gifts to each donee, doubling the exclusion if spousal gift splitting is employed,[3] free of federal wealth transfer taxes, including the GSTT.[4]

2. Direct Educational and Medical Gifts

Transfers made directly to educational institutions for tuition and fees (but excluding other costs such as books, supplies, room and board, etc.[5]) and to medical care providers are unlimited in amount without the imposition of federal gift tax or the GSTT.[6] Such gifts may be *in addition to* the annual §2503(b) gift exclusion.

3. Custodial Accounts

All 50 states, plus Washington, D.C., and the U.S. Virgin Islands, have adopted a form of either the Uniform Gifts to Minors Act[7] (UGMA) or the Uniform Transfers to Minors Act[8] (UTMA). Because of the legal difficulties in dealing with ownership by a minor, financial institutions will often require the creation of an UGMA/UTMA custodial account. This is a low transaction cost alternative because it is dictated by statute and does not require a trust agreement. The minor reports the income directly on his or her income tax return; no separate trust income tax return is required. Gifts to an UGMA/UTMA custodian qualify for the annual gift exclusion. The Will of a decedent can permit or direct transfers to an UGMA/UTMA custodian. The range of investments permitted by the UTMA rules is broader than those under the UGMA.

As noted above, the minor reports the custodial account income directly on his or her income tax return. For children under the age of 24,[9] the "kiddie tax" imposed by IRC §1(g) presents a planning concern. However, the answer to the income tax rate problem will not be the formation of a trust that retains and accumulates its income because of the fiercely progressive income tax rates applied to trusts. Accordingly, for

3. *See* IRC §2513.

4. For outright gifts, the annual gift tax exclusion under IRC §2503(b) functions also as a GSTT exclusion under IRC §2642(c)(3).

5. *See* Treas. Reg. §25.2503-6(b)(2) (1984).

6. *See* IRC §§2503(e) & 2642(c)(3).

7. South Carolina and Vermont are the lone remaining adopters of the UGMA. *See* S.C. Code Ann. §§63-5-500 et seq. (2010); Vt. Stat. Ann. tit. 115 §§3201 et seq. (2010).

8. All states except for South Carolina and Vermont, plus Washington, D.C., and the U.S. Virgin Islands have adopted the UTMA. *See* Table of Jurisdictions Wherein Act Has Been Adopted, 8C U.L.A. 1 (2001 & Supp. 2010).

9. The Tax Increase Prevention and Reconciliation Act of 2005 increased the applicable age from 14 to 18 for tax years beginning after December 31, 2005. The Small Business and Work Opportunity Tax Act of 2007 amended the provision again, effective for taxable years after 2007. Under the latter legislation, this increasingly complex law could impact children until they reach age 24.

either accumulation trusts or nontrust alternatives such as UGMA/ UTMA custodial accounts, a low turnover, low current income, high growth investment or insurance product might be used. Nevertheless, due to the inhospitable trust income tax rates, which can subject the income to the highest marginal income tax rates in many cases, the UGMA/UTMA custodial account may be more desirable in any event, even if the kiddie tax applies.

The principal drawback of the UGMA/UTMA structure is that it usually requires that the assets be distributed by the time the child reaches age 18 or 21.[10] At this age the child may not have started or finished college, or even be interested in college. However, any property remaining in the UGMA/UTMA account at that time must be distributed outright to the child and be subject to the whims of a possibly unwise and immature young adult as well as to the claims of unforeseen creditors. From this standpoint, it is an inflexible structure not particularly desirable for large amounts of property.

There are some additional drawbacks to UGMA/UTMA accounts. If the transferor of the gift also serves as the custodian, as is frequently the case when parents establish such accounts for their children, it is fairly well settled that the custodial assets will be included in the transferor/custodian's taxable estate upon his or her death.[11] There are other tax concerns if the transferor is a grandparent and a parent is the designated custodian.[12] If the transferor is a parent and if the child is too young to execute a Will and then passes away, the child's assets will pass through intestate succession, usually back to the parents. This is because the UGMA/ UTMA statute permits only a single beneficiary—there is no provision in the statute permitting the designation of remainder beneficiaries. This is troublesome if the parents already have wealth transfer tax concerns or if they are divorced.

4. Section 529 Programs

The Small Business Job Protection Act of 1996 added section 529 to the Internal Revenue Code. This section was liberalized by the Taxpayer Relief Act of 1997 and again significantly liberalized by the Economic Growth and Tax Relief Reconciliation Act of 2001. In 2006, the benefits of section

10. Several states permit a delay in the transfer of property to a minor up to age 25 in certain circumstances. *See, e.g.*, ALASKA STAT. §13.46.195(e) (2010); CAL. PROB. CODE §3920.5 (West 2009); NEV. REV. STAT. ANN. §167.034 (LexisNexis 2009).

11. *See, e.g.*, Rev. Rul. 59-357, 1959-2 C.B. 212.

12. Rev. Rul. 59-357, *id.*, asserts that if the custodial property is used for the support of the minor, the parent will be taxed on the income of the account. If the parent is the grantor, IRC §677(b) would support this result. However, the ruling more broadly asserts that this would be the case even if the parent is neither grantor nor custodian. Further, some commentators assert that if the parent is the custodian, even if not the grantor, the property may still be included in the parent's estate under general power of appointment principles. *See, e.g.*, JEROME A. MANNING ET AL., MANNING ON ESTATE PLANNING §4:5 (5th ed. 1995 & Supp. 2009). Indeed, the official comment to UTMA §9 concludes that "it is generally still inadvisable for a donor to appoint himself custodian or for a parent of the minor to serve as custodian."

529 as expanded by the 2001 legislation were made permanent[13] by the Pension Protection Act of 2006. There are two basic types of section 529 plans—prepaid education arrangements (PEAs) and education savings accounts (ESAs). In a PEA, a person purchases tuition credits or certificates that entitle a beneficiary to payment of a specific amount of future tuition. The amount of future tuition is guaranteed by the plan and does not increase or decrease with the fund sponsor's actual investment performance. In contrast, with an ESA, a person makes contributions to an account established for the purpose of paying a beneficiary's "qualified education expenses," as discussed below, and the ultimate value of the account depends on the performance of the investments in the plan.

While the terms of the programs vary from state to state (some states permit a state income tax deduction for contributions) and from educational institution to educational institution (educational institutions may offer these programs), many of the provisions are similar because they are imposed to comply with the umbrella requirements of section 529. An account owner has some continuing flexibility in making new choices because, subject to plan limitations or penalties, section 529 permits rollovers from one plan to another without adverse tax consequences.[14] An appraisal of the desirability of specific plans is beyond the scope of this book.[15] Because ESAs are reportedly much more popular than PEAs, the balance of this discussion will focus on ESAs.

Contributions to a section 529 program may be made only in cash[16] and are gifts for federal wealth transfer taxation purposes, but they qualify for the IRC §2503(b) annual gift exclusion. A contribution in excess of the annual gift exclusion may, by election, be spread over a five-year period. Thus, one may effectively contribute five years of annual gift exclusions

13. The changes made by the Economic Growth and Tax Relief Reconciliation Act of 2001 were otherwise scheduled to sunset for tax years beginning after December 31, 2010. The 2006 legislation also authorizes the IRS to issue regulations that will clarify the tax treatment of section 529 plans and address potential abuses. For a critical analysis of the tax avoidance afforded by section 529 plans see Wayne M. Gazur, *Abandoning Principles: Qualified Tuition Programs and Wealth Transfer Taxation Doctrine*, 2 PITT. TAX REV. 1 (2004).

14. *See* IRC §529(c)(3)(C).

15. *See, e.g.*, Susan T. Bart, *No Taxpayer Left Behind: Tax-Wise Techniques for Funding Education*, Planning Techniques for Large Estates, SS010 ALI-ABA 63 (ALI-ABA Continuing Legal Education, Nov. 15-19, 2010); savingforcollege.com, comparing 529 Plans, http://www.savingforcollege.com/college_savings_201 (last visited Aug. 19, 2011) (providing detailed information on all plans); http://www.finaid.org/savings/529plans.phtml (last visited Aug. 19, 2011). The Independent 529 Plan (marketed as the Private College 529 Plan) is a prepaid tuition fund offered by a consortium of 270 private colleges. As a PEA, the investment in tuition certificates does not depend on investment returns, and an additional feature is that the participating institutions must offer a discount on their regular tuition rates. *See* http://www.independent529-plan.org (last visited Mar. 8, 2011).

16. *See* IRC §529(b)(2). Another tax-exempt investment with a longer term perspective not confined to educational expenses is the Roth IRA. If the child receives the earned income necessary for qualifying contributions to a Roth IRA, gifts to the child to enable his or her full funding of a Roth IRA might be attractive to some clients. Likewise, if a grandparent owns a Roth IRA, tax-free distributions from the account could be a source of funds that could be used to make educational gifts. However, the grandparent would need to weigh that immediate use against using beneficiary designations of the account later as part of an income tax-exempt testamentary gifting plan.

(double the gift with IRC §2513 gift splitting) in a lump sum without the imposition of a gift tax.[17] If the transferor dies within the five-year period, the amounts allocable to the periods after death are included in the transferor's estate for federal wealth transfer tax purposes as incomplete gifts.

Aside from the benign federal gift tax implications, the section 529 programs also offer a very significant federal income tax benefit that is the compelling aspect of these programs. Subject to a number of qualifications, neither the designated beneficiary nor the contributor ever report federal taxable income with respect to any distribution or earnings under such a program if the proceeds are used for "qualified higher education expenses."[18] The qualified expenses include tuition, fees, books, supplies, equipment, and room and board.[19] Distributions may be used for any form of higher education, from an associate's degree up through graduate and professional schooling. However, most section 529 plans impose a limit on contributions based on five years of undergraduate enrollment at the highest-cost school allowed by the program.[20]

Section 529 plans are an attractive gifting option for grandparents who have the grandchildren's education as a priority. The structure is largely dictated by the terms of the particular section 529 plan, so the fees, if any, for instrument drafting are minimal. The oversight of the account is simplified because the statute does not permit direct or indirect investment direction by any contributor or designated beneficiary.[21] A designated beneficiary may be changed to a new person who is a member of the family of the original designated beneficiary without adverse tax consequences,[22] although a GSTT may be imposed if the substitute designated beneficiary is a generation below the generation of the former beneficiary.[23] If the account proceeds are not completely exhausted by higher education expenses, a distribution of the remainder is subject to income tax plus a 10 percent penalty. The possible imposition of this penalty imposes some practical limits on overfunding the account in addition to any limits imposed by the fund sponsor.

17. *See* IRC §529(c)(2). This assumes that the GSTT exclusion under IRC §2642(c) applies in the same manner. Some states impose limits on state income tax deductions or credits allowable for section 529 plan contributions, so donors in such states may avoid lump sum contributions that would exceed those limits.

18. *See* IRC §§529(c)(1) & (3).

19. *See* IRC §529(e)(3).

20. This reflects a safe harbor limitation found in Prop. Treas. Reg. §1.529-2(i)(2), 63 Fed. Reg. 45019-01 (Aug. 24, 1998).

21. *See* IRC §529(b)(4). The IRS allows plan provisions that permit a shift in investment strategy once per calendar year or upon a change in the designated beneficiary. *See* IRS Notice 2001-55, 2001-2 C.B. 299.

22. *See* IRC §529(c)(3)(C).

23. *See* IRC §529(c)(5). Family members include the spouse of the beneficiary, a son or daughter (or his or her descendant) of the beneficiary, a stepson or stepdaughter of the beneficiary, a brother, sister, stepbrother, or stepsister of the beneficiary, a father or mother (or his or her ancestor) of the beneficiary, a stepfather or stepmother of the beneficiary, a son or daughter of a brother or sister of the beneficiary, a brother or sister of the beneficiary's mother or father, a son-in-law, daughter-in-law, father-in-law, mother-in-law, brother-in-law, or sister-in-law of the beneficiary, a spouse of any of the preceding individuals, and a first cousin of the beneficiary. *See* IRC §529(e)(2).

An attorney must carefully read the details of the 529 plan in question, as these details vary from plan to plan. For example, an examination should disclose who has the power to change the designated beneficiary. Often it is the account owner, who may or may not be the person making the significant contributions to the plan. Likewise, who is the recipient of any remaining balance of the plan? Again, this is often the account owner, who may not have been a major contributor to the plan.[24] How are these rights of the account owner exercised if the account owner passes away? For example, are the rights transmissible?[25] What happens for federal gift tax purposes if the parent account owner receives a refund of amounts contributed by others on behalf of a child?[26] It seems that the answers to these questions largely turn on the identity of the account owner. Although others may have gifted the funds for the purchase, the account owner designated in the contract could, hypothetically, demand a refund and leave the child without any funds. On the other hand, if the child is designated as the account owner, even under guardianship it would seem that the child has a right to all of the funds for college, plus the refund of any moneys not used for that purpose. Why would a child permit the designation of new family member beneficiaries as a substitute for a direct refund to the child?[27]

If a fund permits the purchase of tuition contracts by any person, including an entity, that introduces the use of an irrevocable trust to purchase such contracts. The implications of that structure are beyond the scope of this book, but they include providing a repository for (and redirection of) any unutilized funds and permitting continuity in ownership of the 529 account.[28] However, it is fair to say that much of the

24. Prop. Treas. Reg. §1.529-1(c), 63 Fed. Reg. 45019-01 (Aug. 24, 1998), defines the "account owner" as the person entitled to change beneficiaries, to designate others to whom funds may be paid out, or to receive distributions if no other person is so designated. *See generally* Adam Winger, *Pick on Someone Your Own Size: Exposing the Account Owner's Silent Assault on §529 Savings Accounts*, 35 ACTEC J. 277 (Winter 2009) (a critical review of control by section 529 account owners).

25. Some commentators have noted that there is no authority that a change in the account owner has any tax consequences, but some section 529 plans do not permit a change during the life of the original account owner. *See* Mervin M. Wilf, *§529 Plans: Update & Planning Alternatives (Excluding Investments),* Advanced Estate Planning Techniques, SG062 ALI-ABA 307, 311 (ALI-ABA Continuing Legal Education, Feb. 21-23, 2002).

26. Section 529 considers the contribution a completed gift to the designated beneficiary when the contribution is made, in spite of the fact that the owner of the account (who might be the noncontributing parent) may have the power to reclaim the property. The power sounds much like a general power of appointment. However, the statute states that the tuition fund is not to be included in anyone's estate, except in the event of the death of a donor who is spreading a gift over five years or on the death of the beneficiary and upon the receipt of the funds by the beneficiary's estate. If the parent as owner does reclaim the money, it is clear that the money is a part of the parent's potential taxable estate at that time. However, the money apparently escapes a gift tax on the original transfer to the account, using the annual gift exclusion, which ultimately goes to the owner/parent.

27. The Pension Protection Act of 2006 authorizes the IRS to issue regulations that would clarify the tax treatment of section 529 plans and provide answers to some of these questions. The Bankruptcy Abuse Prevention and Consumer Protection Act of 2005 (Pub. L. No. 109-8, 119 Stat. 23 (2005)) also created a limited bankruptcy exemption for 529 plan assets and education IRAs. *See* 11 U.S.C. §§541(b)(5) & (6).

28. *See, e.g.*, Susan T. Bart, *The Best of Both Worlds: Using a Trust to Make Your 529 Savings Accounts Rock*, 34 ACTEC J. 106 (2008).

simplicity offered by section 529 plans is sacrificed by the adoption of this additional measure.

5. Coverdell Education Savings Accounts[29]

Originally misnamed the "Education IRA" in the Taxpayer Relief Act of 1997, it has nothing to do with retirement, so it was renamed the "Coverdell Education Savings Account,"[30] which generally permits aggregate contributions from all sources except rollovers of up to $2,000 for each child under age 18.[31] The wealth transfer tax rules are similar to those imposed on section 529 plans.[32] The contribution limits are subject to phaseouts if the income of the contributor exceeds certain limits ($190,000 adjusted gross income for those filing joint returns and $95,000 for other taxpayers, which amounts are not adjusted annually for inflation). Those income limits might be avoided if the gift is made directly to the child, who then makes a contribution to the account, although the step transaction doctrine and the inability of a minor to deal with the account could be concerns. Much like the section 529 plan, the distributions are free of tax if used for education expenses,[33] but those expenses may also include elementary and secondary education expenses.[34] The account must be used for education expenses by the time the individual reaches age 30,[35] but the statute permits a change of designated beneficiary to other family members in a manner resembling the section 529 plan. Unused contributions are subject to income tax plus an additional 10 percent penalty.

The Coverdell Education Savings Account is preferable to the section 529 plan if active control over the investment choices or the payment of elementary or secondary education expenses is desired. Otherwise, the $2,000 limits on contributions, the 30-year age limit on the beneficiary, and the contribution phase-outs for higher-income contributors make this a less attractive option. However, while the $2,000 annual limit is small, it can accumulate. For example, $2,000 per year invested at 8 percent over 20 years would grow to $98,171.

There are potential uncertainties about the operation of these accounts. These are not addressed in section 530, so a close examination of the account agreement is required, with particular attention to the rights and powers of the owner, custodian, and designated beneficiary. Section 530, like section 529, is a federal creation, but it requires state legal

29. *See* savingforcollege.com, http://www.savingforcollege.com/coverdell_esas/ (last visited Mar. 8, 2011).

30. The name change was made in July 26, 2001, legislation untitled Pub. L. No. 107-22, 115 Stat. 196 (2001), §§1(a)(1)-(5), which renamed the savings account in honor of Senator Paul D. Coverdell (R-Ga.), who had passed away on July 18, 2000.

31. *See* IRC §530(b)(1).

32. *See* IRC §530(d)(3).

33. *See* IRC §530(d)(2).

34. *See* IRC §530(b)(2).

35. *See* IRC §530(b)(1)(E).

vehicles for its implementation. The IRS has issued model agreements, Forms 5305-EA and 5305-E, for Coverdell accounts that clarify some of these issues. The two forms are substantially the same.[36] This discussion focuses on Form 5305-E, which follows as Exhibit 8.1.

In the absence of an account provision to the contrary, it appears that the unexpended funds must be paid to the estate of a deceased beneficiary. A minor[37] generally may not execute a Will, so the funds would pass by intestate succession. In the situation of divorced parents, with unequal post-divorce contributions or contributions primarily from one set of grandparents, the equal splitting of the account in the event of the child's death could be an undesired consequence. Article III of Form 5305-E, however, provides that a "designated death beneficiary" who is a family member of the designated beneficiary and is under the age of 30 on the date of death of the designated beneficiary shall become the designated beneficiary as of the date of death.

In the absence of an account provision to the contrary, it is uncertain, as a matter of state law, who has the power to designate new beneficiaries. If an adult beneficiary does so, few questions are raised. However, changes by a guardian or custodian on behalf of a minor could raise issues of misapplication of assets. Article VI of Form 5305-E, however, provides an election for the "responsible individual" (i.e., the family member custodian) to be empowered to change or precluded from changing the beneficiary to another member of the designated beneficiary's family. The fine print of Article V of Form 5305-E also permits a responsible individual's naming of a successor.

If the minor owns the account, then, taxes and penalties aside, there is no apparent obstacle to the child spending the funds, particularly upon reaching adulthood, for noneducational purposes. Article V of Form 5305-E provides that unless the grantor of the account makes an election to the contrary, the designated beneficiary becomes the responsible party under the account upon reaching the age of majority.

We have devoted more time to the Coverdell Education Savings Account than it probably deserves, which reflects our concerns about the uncertainties surrounding this financial product. Ironically, questions about these uncertainties are often resolved by lower-level account representatives at the sponsoring financial institution—without the input of an

36. Form 5305-EA is used with a Coverdell custodial account. The contributor to the account is referred to as the "depositor." The financial institution is the "custodian." The "responsible individual" is akin to a trustee or custodian. The "designated beneficiary" is the student. Form 5305-E is used with a Coverdell trust account. The contributor to the account is referred to as the "grantor." The financial institution is the "trustee." The "responsible individual" and "designated beneficiary" are the same parties as in the custodial account arrangement.

37. The most common age of legal capacity is 18. *See* McGovern et al., Wills, Trusts and Estates §7.1 (4th ed. 2010). *See also* UPC §2-501 (an individual 18 or more years of age can make a Will).

attorney. Indeed, what client can reasonably justify legal fees in planning for the modest level of contributions permitted by the statute?

6. Section 2503(c) Trusts

This structure is an older creation of federal wealth transfer taxation law. It is intended to qualify gifts in trust for the full annual gift exclusion without the involvement (or possible awareness) of the intended beneficiary.[38] However, with the alternatives available to the planner today, this is a less commonly used device: As a trust it may require the filing of a separate trust income tax return as well as trust registration at the state level.[39] The trust property must be distributed by the time the beneficiary reaches age 21, and, as with the UGMA/UTMA custodial account, this is not always desirable.[40] If the beneficiary passes away, the property may become an asset of the minor's intestate probate estate. That risk may be mitigated through the inclusion of a testamentary power of appointment, purportedly exercisable by the minor but not exercised in practice, which designates alternate takers upon the nonexercise of the power.[41] Finally, strictly limiting the use of the trust assets for education may jeopardize IRC §2503(c) status.[42] Nevertheless, some clients do choose this form in order to create a "secret" trust of which the beneficiary is unaware, at least until they are 21. If the trust accumulates all income, the trust income tax return reports the investment income without an impact on the beneficiary's individual income tax return. By comparison, income from an UGMA/UTMA custodianship must be reported on the minor's individual income tax return, possibly raising questions by the minor.[43]

38. No *Crummey* notice to the beneficiary is necessary. See Part B.8 *infra*.

39. *See, e.g.*, UPC §7-101.

40. Some practitioners use a device where the beneficiary is given a period after attaining age 21 to demand the trust property. Upon notice to the beneficiary of this right and subsequent failure of the beneficiary to demand distribution, the property remains in trust for a longer period than prescribed by the trust instrument. *See* Rev. Rul. 74-43, 1974-1 C.B. 285 (approving an arrangement where the instrument requires affirmative action on the part of the beneficiary to request the trust assets within 90 days of attaining age 21). Also, if the accumulated income is required to be distributed at age 21 (but not the principal), the value of the income interest can qualify as a present interest under section 2503(c). *See, e.g.*, Herr v. Commissioner, 303 F.2d 780 (3rd Cir. 1962).

41. "[T]he fact that under the local law a minor is under a disability to exercise an inter vivos power or to execute a will does not cause the transfer to fail to satisfy the conditions of section 2503(c).... Further, a transfer does not fail... by reason of the mere fact that... [t]he governing instrument contains a disposition of the property or income not expended during the donee's minority to persons other than the donee's estate in the event of the default of appointment by the donee." Treas. Reg. §25.2503-4(b) (1958).

42. The issue is whether, under the regulations, there are "substantial restrictions" on the use of the income or property for the benefit of the minor. *See* Treas. Reg. §25.2503-4(b)(1) (1958). Strict limitations on the use of trust funds solely for education purposes could run afoul of this provision. For example, in Faber v. United States, 439 F.2d 1189 (6th Cir. 1971), "accident, illness or other emergency" was held too restrictive. However, Rev. Rul. 67-270, 1967-2 C.B. 349 (1967), provided that "support, care, education, comfort, and welfare" was not too limiting.

43. *See* George M. Turner, Irrevocable Trusts, apps. 2 & 2A (3d ed. 1996 & Supp. 2010) (sample IRC §2503(c) trust language).

EXHIBIT 8.1

Form **5305-E** (Rev. October 2010) Department of the Treasury Internal Revenue Service	**Coverdell Education Savings Trust Account** (Under section 530 of the Internal Revenue Code)	**Do not** file with the Internal Revenue Service

Name of grantor	**Grantor's identification number**	Check if amendment . . ▶ ☐
Name of designated beneficiary	**Designated beneficiary's identification number**	
Address of designated beneficiary	Date of birth of designated beneficiary	
Name of responsible individual (generally the parent or guardian of the designated beneficiary)		
Address of responsible individual		
Name of trustee	Address or principal place of business of trustee	

The grantor named above is establishing a Coverdell education savings trust account under section 530 for the benefit of the designated beneficiary exclusively to pay for the qualified elementary, secondary, and higher education expenses, within the meaning of section 530(b)(2), of such designated beneficiary.

The grantor has assigned the trust ______________________ dollars ($__________) in cash.

The grantor and the trustee make the following agreement:

Article I

The trustee may accept additional cash contributions provided the designated beneficiary has not attained the age of 18 as of the date such contributions are made. Contributions by an individual contributor may be made for the tax year of the designated beneficiary by the due date of the beneficiary's tax return for that year (excluding extensions). Total contributions that are not rollover contributions described in section 530(d)(5) are limited to $2,000 for the tax year. In the case of an individual contributor, the $2,000 limitation for any year is phased out between modified adjusted gross income (AGI) of $95,000 and $110,000. For married individuals filing jointly, the phase-out occurs between modified AGI of $190,000 and $220,000. Modified AGI is defined in section 530(c)(2).

Article II

No part of the trust account funds may be invested in life insurance contracts, nor may the assets of the trust account be commingled with other property except in a common trust fund or a common investment fund (within the meaning of section 530(b)(1)(D)).

Article III

1. Any balance to the credit of the designated beneficiary on the date on which he or she attains age 30 shall be distributed to him or her within 30 days of such date.

2. Any balance to the credit of the designated beneficiary shall be distributed within 30 days of his or her death **unless** the designated death beneficiary is a family member of the designated beneficiary and is under the age of 30 on the date of death. In such case, that family member shall become the designated beneficiary as of the date of death.

Article IV

The grantor shall have the power to direct the trustee regarding the investment of the above-listed amount assigned to the trust (including earnings thereon) in the investment choices offered by the trustee. The responsible individual, however, shall have the power to redirect the trustee regarding the investment of such amounts, as well as the power to direct the trustee regarding the investment of all additional contributions (including earnings thereon) to the trust. In the event that the responsible individual does not direct the trustee regarding the investment of additional contributions (including earnings thereon), the initial investment direction of the grantor also will govern all additional contributions made to the trust account until such time as the responsible individual otherwise directs the trustee. Unless otherwise provided in this agreement, the responsible individual also shall have the power to direct the trustee regarding the administration, management, and distribution of the account.

Article V

The "responsible individual" named by the grantor shall be a parent or guardian of the designated beneficiary. The trust shall have only one responsible individual at any time. If the responsible individual becomes incapacitated or dies while the designated beneficiary is a minor under state law, the successor responsible individual shall be the person named to succeed in that capacity by the preceding responsible individual in a witnessed writing or, if no successor is so named, the successor responsible individual shall be the designated beneficiary's other parent or successor guardian. Unless otherwise directed by checking the option below, at the time that the designated beneficiary attains the age of majority under state law, the designated beneficiary becomes the responsible individual. If a family member under the age of majority under state law becomes the designated beneficiary by reason of being a named death beneficiary, the responsible individual shall be such designated beneficiary's parent or guardian.

☐ **Option** (*This provision is effective only if checked*): The responsible individual shall continue to serve as the responsible individual for the trust after the designated beneficiary attains the age of majority under state law and until such time as all assets have been distributed from the trust and the trust terminates. If the responsible individual becomes incapacitated or dies after the designated beneficiary reaches the age of majority under state law, the responsible individual shall be the designated beneficiary.

Cat. No. 25205V Form **5305-E** (Rev. 10-2010)

Article VI

The responsible individual ☐ may or ☐ **may not** change the beneficiary designated under this agreement to another member of the designated beneficiary's family described in section 529(e)(2) in accordance with the trustee's procedures.

Article VII

1. The grantor agrees to provide the trustee with all information necessary to prepare any reports required by section 530(h).
2. The trustee agrees to submit to the Internal Revenue Service (IRS) and responsible individual the reports prescribed by the IRS.

Article VIII

Notwithstanding any other articles which may be added or incorporated, the provisions of Articles I through III will be controlling. Any additional articles inconsistent with section 530 and the related regulations will be invalid.

Article IX

This agreement will be amended as necessary to comply with the provisions of the Code and the related regulations. Other amendments may be made with the consent of the grantor and trustee whose signatures appear below.

Article X

Article X may be used for any additional provisions. If no other provisions will be added, draw a line through this space. If provisions are added, they must comply with applicable requirements of state law and the Internal Revenue Code.

Grantor's signature ______________________ Date ______________

Trustee's signature ______________________ Date ______________

Witness' signature ______________________ Date ______________

(Use only if signature of the grantor or the trustee is required to be witnessed.)

General Instructions

Section references are to the Internal Revenue Code unless otherwise noted.

What's New

Military death gratuity. Families of soldiers who receive military death benefits may contribute, subject to certain limitations, up to 100 percent of such benefits into an educational savings account. Publication 970, Tax Benefits for Education, explains the rules for rolling over the military death gratuity and lists eligible family members.

Purpose of Form

Form 5305-E is a model trust account agreement that meets the requirements of section 530(b)(1) and has been pre-approved by the IRS. A Coverdell education savings account (ESA) is established after the form is fully executed by both the grantor and the trustee. This account must be created in the United States for the exclusive purpose of paying the qualified elementary, secondary, and higher education expenses of the designated beneficiary.

If the model account is a custodial account, see **Form 5305-EA,** Coverdell Education Savings Custodial Account.

Do not file Form 5305-E with the IRS. Instead, the grantor must keep the completed form in its records.

Definitions

Trustee. The trustee must be a bank or savings and loan association, as defined in section 408(n), or any person who has the approval of the IRS to act as trustee. Any person who may serve as a trustee of a traditional IRA may serve as the trustee of a Coverdell ESA.

Grantor. The grantor is the person who establishes the trust account.

Designated beneficiary. The designated beneficiary is the individual on whose behalf the trust account has been established.

Family member. Family members of the designated beneficiary include his or her spouse, child, grandchild, sibling, parent, niece or nephew, son-in-law, daughter-in-law, father-in-law, mother-in-law, brother-in-law, or sister-in-law, and the spouse of any such individual. A first cousin, but not his or her spouse, is also a "family member."

Responsible individual. The responsible individual, generally, is a parent or guardian of the designated beneficiary. However, under certain circumstances, the responsible individual may be the designated beneficiary.

Identification Numbers

The grantor and designated beneficiary's social security numbers will serve as their identification numbers. If the grantor is a nonresident alien and does not have an identification number, write "Foreign" in the block where the number is requested. The designated beneficiary's social security number is the identification number of his or her Coverdell ESA. If the designated beneficiary is a nonresident alien, the designated beneficiary's individual taxpayer identification number is the identification number of his or her Coverdell ESA. An employer identification number (EIN) is required only for a Coverdell ESA for which a return is filed to report unrelated business income. An EIN is required for a common fund created for Coverdell ESAs.

Specific Instructions

Note: *The age limitation restricting contributions, distributions, rollover contributions, and change of beneficiary are waived for a designated beneficiary with special needs.*

Article X. Article X and any that follow may incorporate additional provisions that are agreed to by the grantor and trustee to complete the agreement. They may include, for example, provisions relating to: definitions, investment powers, voting rights, exculpatory provisions, amendment and termination, removal of the trustee, trustee's fees, state law requirements, treatment of excess contributions, and prohibited transactions with the grantor, designated beneficiary, or responsible individual, etc. Attach additional pages as necessary.

Optional provisions in Article V and Article VI. Form 5305-E may be reproduced in a manner that provides only those optional provisions offered by the trustee.

7. The Testamentary Trust

A grandparent or other transferor wishing to gift significant amounts of wealth could make the gifts upon death in the form of a bequest to a testamentary trust for the benefit of the grandchildren.[44] If the grandparent's estate is subject to the federal estate taxes, bequests to or for the benefit of grandchildren may also be subject to the GSTT.

There are several potential drawbacks to this approach, as compared to a systematic plan or program for annual lifetime gifts to the beneficiaries. First, the grandchildren or other intended beneficiaries may need the benefits of the gift at an earlier point than the death of the transferor. Second, from a federal wealth transfer tax perspective, lifetime transfers permit use of the annual gift exclusion, and, unlike testamentary transfers, outright lifetime transfers can be excluded from the GSTT under IRC §2642(c). Third, from a federal wealth transfer tax perspective, lifetime transfers of wealth shift any future appreciation of the gifted property away from the transferor's estate. Nevertheless, if federal wealth transfer taxes are not a consideration, donors frequently insist upon testamentary gifts simply because the clients require the use of these assets during their lifetimes and cannot afford to transfer them prior to death.

8. The Inter Vivos Irrevocable Trust

Assuming that lifetime gifts are intended as a planning measure, the gifts may be made either outright to the beneficiary, with the attendant advantages and disadvantages of outright gifts discussed above, or to an irrevocable trust. The transfer to the trust would generally be a taxable gift for federal wealth transfer tax purposes and also would have the potential for a GSTT if the only beneficiaries of the trust are all two or more generations below the generation of the transferor. (Chapter 16 presents an overview of the federal wealth transfer taxes.) The transferor could use all or a portion of his or her GSTT exemption (which is equal to the estate tax applicable exclusion amount)[45] to reduce or eliminate the GSTT. Likewise, the transferor could use all or a portion of his or her gift tax applicable exclusion amount to reduce or eliminate the gift tax (and if the transferor is married, gift splitting could effectively double the available exemption amount). However, many clients prefer that their lifetime applicable credit amount be preserved[46] unless its use is absolutely necessary, and other

44. If the income taxation and federal wealth transfer taxation consequences to the donee are not a consideration and the transferor is comfortable with the potential misapplication of the gift or the possible loss of the gift to the donee's creditors, the transferor may consider an outright inter vivos or testamentary gift to the parent of the minor, with precatory language suggesting a specific use of the funds for the minor's benefit. For a discussion of this approach and suggested language, *see* Thomas M. Featherston, Jr., et al., Drafting for Tax and Administration Issues 129 (2000).

45. *See* IRC §2631.

46. The use of the gift tax applicable exclusion amount provided by IRC §2505 effectively reduces the estate tax applicable exclusion amount provided by IRC §2010. In computing the estate tax, cumulative post-1976 taxable gifts (i.e., gifts exceeding the IRC §§2503(b) and

considerations may tend to discourage taxable gifts.[47] Donors often prefer using their annual gift exclusion for outright gifts, which, while a modest amount, is free of all wealth transfer taxes.[48]

Indeed, most clients want to use the annual gift exclusion to the greatest degree possible. Gifts to an irrevocable trust, however, generally do not qualify for the annual gift exclusion because they are considered an ineligible "future interest" under the parenthetical language of IRC §2503(b)(1). However, at the price of added complexity and some ritualistic measures (e.g., the sending of notices to beneficiaries), the annual gift tax exclusion may be claimed for gifts to an irrevocable trust by using so-called *Crummey*[49] powers, inter vivos general powers of appointment, which permit withdrawals of trust property by the *Crummey* power holders for a limited period of time following a gift to the trust. By holding such a power to withdraw, even for a limited period of time, the beneficiary is deemed to have received a gift of "a present interest" qualifying it for the §2503(b) annual gift tax exclusion. This alternative is the most expensive to create and supervise, but it is the most flexible. Form L in the Forms Supplement includes these powers.

While some potentially adverse income tax issues are raised by the use of *Crummey* powers,[50] there are many distinct advantages. The most

2503(e) exclusions) are added to the estate in computing a tentative estate tax (*see* IRC §2001(b)(1)), and an offsetting deduction from that tentative tax is permitted only for gift taxes that would have been payable (*see* IRC §§2001(b)(2) & (g)). Accordingly, if taxable gifts were made but no gift tax was paid due to use of the applicable exclusion amount, the estate tax computation will implicitly include a tax on those gifts.

47. Prior to the enactment of the Economic Growth and Tax Relief Reconciliation Act of 2001 (EGTRRA), the lifetime exclusion for gifts was equal in amount to the estate tax exclusion, as is again the case under the Tax Relief, Unemployment Insurance Reauthorization, and Job Creation Act of 2010. EGTRRA temporarily unlinked the applicable exclusion amount prescribed by IRC §2010 and pertaining to the estate tax, from the lifetime gift applicable exclusion amount prescribed by IRC §2505. Accordingly, an individual dying in 2009 with a $3,500,000 taxable estate would pay no federal estate taxes, but an inter vivos gift of the same $3,500,000 would require the payment of a gift tax.

For an explanation of the "de-unification" of the wealth transfer taxes with numerical examples, *see* Ira Mark Bloom et al., Federal Taxation of Estates, Trusts and Gifts 39-40 (rev. 3d ed. 2003). There are other considerations in making an inter vivos gift. First, any payment of gift taxes involves the payment of money today, rather than in the future. That is generally not advantageous except for some individuals anticipating imminent death and wishing to exclude the gift taxes paid from the estate tax base (but *see* IRC §2035, which limits this strategy for gifts made within three years of death). Second, if the gifted asset is certain to appreciate greatly or if valuation discounts may be produced for the remainder of the taxable estate, the payment of a gift tax may still be advantageous, although that may not be attractive to many clients (or possible due to liquidity concerns) if the cash outlay is substantial. Furthermore, an inter vivos gift of appreciated property loses the IRC §1014 basis adjustment available under current law. Third, if it is determined that a married couple should maximize their lifetime gifts to third parties, then even ignoring the impact of additional gifts permitted by the annual gift exclusion provided by IRC §2503(b) or the educational and medical transfers permitted by IRC §2503(e), $10,000,000 in gifts can be made free of tax if each spouse gifts $5,000,000, or by the couple electing gift splitting. *See* IRC §2513.

48. As discussed previously, an outright annual exclusion gift will usually be exempt from the GSTT due to IRC §2642(c).

49. Crummey v. Commissioner, 397 F.2d 82 (9th Cir. 1968).

50. At first blush most *Crummey* trusts are taxable as a separate taxpayer at the high trust income tax rates prescribed by IRC §1(e). However, the *Crummey* power holders may potentially be taxed on a portion of the trust income pursuant to IRC §678. *See, e.g.*, Laura H. Peebles, Crummey *Powers Can Increase Your Income Tax*, 145 Tr. & Est. 35 (Nov. 2006). *Crummey* powers are routinely included in irrevocable life insurance trusts, discussed in Chapter 11; the

significant advantage is that the distribution scheme of the trust is absolutely flexible — there are no prescribed dates or ages of beneficiaries. Particularly with respect to educational uses, the settlor often wishes to specify the type of education permissible (e.g., private versus public universities, graduate school, or professional school) as well as the timing. In addition to crafting the primary purpose of the trust, the settlor can dictate the disposition of unused accumulations so the trust can serve broader family purposes and not be confined just to education, medical, or support needs of the primary beneficiary. As for investment flexibility, the trustee can select from a broad universe of investments, and, unlike a section 529 plan or education savings account, the trust can accept noncash contributions of property.

Still, as compared with a section 529 tuition plan in the special context of education expenses, there are some drawbacks. First, the sending of *Crummey* gift notices is a supervisory burden, often performed by the trustee with the input of the attorney. Second, as a separate taxpayer, the trust must file income tax returns and is subject to the sharply progressive trust income tax rates. Third, the legal fees for drafting the trust instrument may be significantly greater than for other options. Fourth, in the context of grandparent funding of such a trust, if a *Crummey* power is used for the gift tax exclusion, a portion of the GSTT exemption will probably be consumed.[51] Fifth, with respect to the income taxation of the beneficiaries, they will be taxed on distributions to the extent of distributable net income of the trust, while the beneficiary of a section 529 plan or education savings account will be taxed only on distributions not used for education costs.

The increased and broad flexibility of a *Crummey* trust comes at a price. If the client absolutely only wants the gifts to be used for educational purposes, a 529 plan is a good choice. However, in the authors' experience, once the limitations and restrictions of a 529 plan are discussed with and understood by clients, most usually prefer to use the more flexible *Crummey* trust, or, alternatively, create a *Crummey* trust in addition to establishing a 529 plan.

income tax issues presented by the *Crummey* powers to the holders of those powers, as well as IRC §677(a)(3), are sometimes minimized by confining the trust assets to life insurance policies that do not produce taxable income. Alternatively, with appropriate language, the trust settlor could be taxed on the trust income as a grantor trust (thus removing even more assets from the donor's estate). *See* Section C.6, *infra*.

51. If the *Crummey* gift is to qualify for the GSTT exclusion for annual gifts under IRC §2642(c), a very restrictive trust share must be created on behalf of each grandchild. *See* IRC §2642(c)(2). For example, each grandchild must be granted a testamentary general power of appointment over the trust property, which can be inappropriate for estate plans based on the marshaling of family assets or plans in which the trust will play a long-term role in the accumulation of family wealth spared from federal wealth transfer taxes. On the other hand, if it is likely that the trust assets will be consumed during the grandchild's lifetime for the purposes of the trust, the inclusion of the general power of appointment may have few estate tax consequences to the grandchild under IRC §2041.

9. Life Insurance Trusts

Life insurance on the life of the donor[52] can be a means for transferring significant amounts of wealth to younger generations, including grandchildren. An important benefit is derived from the leveraging of the GSTT exemption[53] which need only be allocated to the cash gifts made to the trust (for the payment of the life insurance premiums). Eventually, the much larger death proceeds can pass GSTT free. Large life insurance policies are often held by irrevocable life insurance trusts created for that purpose. This topic is discussed in more detail in Chapter 11.

10. Dynasty Trusts

The limitation or elimination of the Rule Against Perpetuities, coupled with permanent immunity of trusts from the imposition of the GSTT through allocations of the IRC §2631 GSTT exemption,[54] has stirred great interest in the creation of trusts, so-called "dynasty trusts," that will endure for multiple generations. These vehicles are discussed in Chapter 13.

C. Federal Wealth Transfer Tax Considerations (Part II)[55]

Chapter 16 presents an overview of the federal wealth transfer tax. However, several aspects of the federal wealth transfer taxes particularly pertinent to grandparents' gifts are discussed below.

1. The Generation-Skipping Transfer Tax (GSTT)

As a complement to the federal gift and estate taxes, the Internal Revenue Code imposes a GSTT on transfers of wealth to individuals two or more generations below the generation of the transferor — "skip persons." The GSTT — after an exemption per individual equal to the estate tax basic exclusion amount[56] — is imposed at the highest federal estate tax rate.

52. Although insurance on the life of the donor is a typical situation, one might consider the purchase of insurance on the life of a newborn grandchild, inexpensively creating a future pool of wealth for the grandchild's spouse or descendants.

53. *See, e.g.*, Jon J. Gallo, *The Use of Life Insurance in Estate Planning: A Guide to Planning and Drafting, Part II*, 34 Real Prop. Prob. & Tr. J. 55, 58 (1999); Jeffrey K. Eisen, *Planning to Minimize GST: Tools & Traps*, 27 Est. Plan. 73, 75 (2000).

54. *See, e.g.*, Robert L. Moshman, *Avoiding a GSTT Asteroid*, 13 Prob. & Prop. 24 (Mar./Apr. 1999); Richard W. Nenno, *Perpetual Dynasty Trusts: Tax Planning and Jurisdiction Selection*, Planning Techniques for Large Estates, SS010 ALI-ABA 253 (ALI-ABA Continuing Legal Education, Nov. 15-19, 2010).

55. Part I of "Federal Wealth Transfer Tax Considerations" appeared in Chapter 5, Part E.

56. *See* IRC §2631 (linking the GSTT exemption amount to the basic exclusion amount under IRC §201(c)).

In this discussion we will refer to the skip persons as grandchildren, although the GSTT has no familial requirement; it could apply to the child of a neighbor. The GSTT may apply to (1) an outright inter vivos gift to a grandchild; (2) a bequest to a grandchild; (3) a gift to a trust, all of the beneficiaries of which are grandchildren or younger generations; (4) a distribution from a trust to a grandchild; and (5) the shifting of interests in a trust at a point where the interests of older generations lapse, such that the only remaining trust beneficiaries are grandchildren or younger generations.

For outright inter vivos gifts to grandchildren of a modest amount, the GSTT is not a concern, because the annual gift exclusion also extends to the GSTT.[57] However, gifts to a *Crummey* trust do not qualify unless (1) during the life of the *Crummey* interest holder, no portion of the corpus or income of the trust may be distributed to any other person; and (2) if the trust does not terminate before the *Crummey* interest holder dies, the assets of the trust will be included in the gross estate of the individual.[58] With respect to the first requirement, one can fashion a single trust that includes separate trust shares for each grandchild or can create a separate trust for each grandchild that meets this requirement. The second requirement is typically satisfied through the creation of a testamentary general power of appointment in favor of the grandchild. One drawback is that the required includability of the trust assets produces potentially adverse federal wealth transfer consequences to the *Crummey* interest holder, assuming that the trust assets will not be consumed for the purposes of the trust during the lifetime of the power holder. Even if those consequences are not a concern, the restrictions on the diversion of trust assets to other individuals limit the marshaling of family assets. Accordingly, as a practical matter, the donor of gifts subject to a *Crummey* power may instead apply a portion of his or her GSTT exemption to exempt the transfer from the GSTT.

2. Lapses of a General Power of Appointment and *Crummey*

A *Crummey* power is a general power of appointment. The failure to exercise the *Crummey* withdrawal right will be treated as the lapse of a general power of appointment. That lapse will potentially be treated as a taxable gift to the other trust beneficiaries to the extent the value of the property that could be withdrawn exceeds the so-called "5 × 5" or "5 or 5" exception[59] of IRC §2514(e). Most attorneys seek to avoid such a "gift over" by the *Crummey* holder. The gift is avoided by limiting the

57. *See* IRC §2642(c)(3).

58. *See* IRC §2642(c)(2).

59. There is no gift if the value of the property subject to withdrawal under the *Crummey* withdrawal right does not exceed the greater of $5,000 or 5 percent of the trust assets. The IRS maintains that the holder of a power is entitled to only one IRC §2514(e) exception amount per year irrespective of the number of powers held. *See* Rev. Rul. 85-88, 1985-2 C.B. 201.

withdrawal right to the IRC §2514(e) amount, which, for trusts holding corpus worth less than $100,000, effectively limits the *Crummey* gift annual exclusion. And, limiting the withdrawal right to the §2514(e) amount reduces the amount of the gift that can be conveyed to the trust free of gift tax under §2503(b).

One drafting response to this concern is the so-called "hanging *Crummey*," which creates *Crummey* annual withdrawal rights equal to the full annual gift exclusion but spreads the lapse of those rights over several years, permitting only $5,000 to lapse in a given year. Another response is the formation of separate trusts for each donee such that the lapse of the *Crummey* power produces no gift, inasmuch as the beneficiary of the lapse and the holder of the power are the same individual.[60] As noted above, the separate trust solution also avoids the GSTT issues.

3. *Crummey* After *Cristofani*

The withdrawal powers in the *Crummey* case were exercisable by the primary beneficiaries of the trust, Mr. and Mrs. Crummey's children. Some planners believed that in the absence of collusion or an understanding that the withdrawal rights would never be exercised, an absolute stranger to the trust (i.e., someone without any beneficial interest in the trust, a so-called "naked *Crummey*") could be given withdrawal rights. Of course, the predictable IRS position is that, in the absence of collusion or such an understanding, why would a person not exercise the withdrawal right and grab the money? In *Estate of Cristofani*[61] the contingent beneficiaries of a trust, the settlor's five grandchildren, were given withdrawal rights, and the IRS asserted that the *Crummey* exclusions were improperly claimed. The Tax Court upheld the application of the result in *Crummey* to those withdrawal rights, relying on a finding of fact that no understanding by the beneficiaries existed to not exercise the rights. Drafting agreements outside the contours of *Cristofani* introduces an element of risk.[62] If the nonexercise by a beneficiary of his or her *Crummey* withdrawal rights is found to be the product of a prearranged understanding, the gift may not qualify for the annual gift exclusion and would, therefore, subject the donor to liability for the gift tax.

60. Some planners give the *Crummey* power holder a testamentary special power of appointment, which suspends the gift produced by the lapse of the withdrawal right. *See, e.g.*, LAWRENCE BRODY, THE IRREVOCABLE LIFE INSURANCE TRUST—FORMS WITH DRAFTING NOTES 17, 22-23 (2d ed. 1999).

61. 97 T.C. 74 (1991), *acq. in result*, 1992-2 C.B. 1; 1996-2 C.B. 1.

62. Even following its acquiescence in the result in *Cristofani*, the IRS will scrutinize these arrangements. *See, e.g.*, Tech. Adv. Mem. 97-31-004 (Aug. 1, 1997) (refusal to recognize rights of contingent beneficiaries in a reciprocal gift structure). The IRS' argument that beneficiaries had an understanding to not exercise their withdrawal rights was rejected in another Tax Court case involving 16 beneficiaries with contingent remainder interests, Estate of Kohlsaat v. Commissioner, 73 T.C.M. (CCH) 2732 (1997). *Compare* Heyen v. U.S., 945 F.2d 359 (10th Cir. 1991) (gift tax exclusion disallowed for a donor's transfer of property to friends followed by their gifts of the property to the donor's family members).

In addition to its holding concerning the validity of withdrawal rights held by contingent beneficiaries, the *Cristofani* opinion is a valuable review of the doctrine produced by *Crummey.*

Estate of Cristofani v. Commissioner of Internal Revenue 97 T.C. 74 (1991)

RUWE, JUDGE:

Respondent determined a deficiency in petitioner's Federal estate tax in the amount of $49,486. The sole issue for decision is whether transfers of property to a trust, where the beneficiaries possessed the right to withdraw an amount not in excess of the section 2503(b) exclusion within 15 days of such transfers, constitute gifts of a present interest in property within the meaning of section 2503(b).

FINDINGS OF FACT

Petitioner is the Estate of Maria Cristofani, deceased, Frank Cristofani, executor. Maria Cristofani (decedent) died testate on December 16, 1985. At the time of her death, decedent resided in the State of California. Petitioner's Federal estate tax return (Form 706) was timely filed with the Internal Revenue Service Center in Fresno, California, on September 16, 1986.

Decedent has two children, Frank Cristofani and Lillian Dawson. Decedent's children were both born on July 9, 1948. They were in good health during the years 1984 and 1985.

Decedent has five grandchildren. Two of decedent's five grandchildren are Frank Cristofani's children. They are Anthony Cristofani, born July 16, 1975, and Loris Cristofani, born November 30, 1978. Decedent's three remaining grandchildren are Lillian Dawson's children. They are Justin Dawson, born December 1, 1972, Daniel Dawson, born August 9, 1974, and Luke Dawson, born November 14, 1981. During 1984 and 1985, the parents of decedent's grandchildren were the legal guardians of the person of their respective minor children. There were no independently appointed guardians of decedent's grandchildren's property.

On June 11, 1984, decedent executed a durable power of attorney which named her two children, Frank Cristofani and Lillian Dawson, as her Attorneys in Fact. On that same day, decedent executed her will.

On June 12, 1984, decedent executed an irrevocable trust entitled the Maria Cristofani Children's Trust I (Children's Trust). Frank Cristofani and Lillian Dawson were named the trustees of the Children's Trust.

In general, Frank Cristofani and Lillian Dawson possessed the following rights and interests in the Children's Trust corpus and income. Under Article Twelfth, following a contribution to the Children's Trust, Frank Cristofani and Lillian Dawson could each withdraw an amount not to exceed the amount specified for the gift tax exclusion under section 2503(b). Such withdrawal period would begin on the date of the contribution and end on the 15th day following such contribution. Under Article Third, Frank Cristofani and Lillian Dawson were to receive equally the entire net income of the trust quarter-annually, or at more frequent intervals. After decedent's death, under Article Third, the Trust Estate was to be divided into as many equal shares as there were children of decedent then living or children of decedent then deceased but leaving issue. Both Frank Cristofani and Lillian Dawson survived decedent, and thus the Children's Trust was divided into two equal trusts. Under Article Third, if a child of decedent survived decedent by 120 days, that child's trust would be distributed to the child. Both Frank Cristofani and Lillian Dawson survived decedent by 120 days, and their respective trusts were distributed upon the expiration of the 120-day waiting period. During the waiting period, Frank Cristofani and Lillian Dawson received the entire net income of the separate trusts as provided for in Article Third.

In general, decedent's five grandchildren possessed the following rights and interests in the Children's Trust. Under Article Twelfth, during a 15-day period following a contribution to the Children's Trust, each of the grandchildren possessed the same right of withdrawal as described above regarding the withdrawal rights of Frank Cristofani and Lillian Dawson. Under Article Twelfth, the trustee of the Children's Trust was required to notify the beneficiaries of the trust each time a contribution was received. Under Article Third, had either Frank Cristofani or Lillian Dawson predeceased decedent or failed to survive decedent by 120 days, his or her equal portion of decedent's Children's Trust would have passed in trust to his or her children (decedent's grandchildren).

Under Article Third, the trustees, in their discretion, could apply as much of the principal of the Children's Trust as necessary for the proper support, health, maintenance and education of decedent's children. In exercising their discretion, the trustees were to take into account several factors, including "The Settlor's desire to consider the Settlor's children as primary beneficiaries and the other beneficiaries of secondary importance."

Decedent intended to fund the corpus of the Children's Trust with 100 percent ownership of improved real property, on which a warehouse was located, identified as the 2851 Spring Street, Redwood City, California, property (Spring Street property). Decedent intended that a one-third undivided interest in the Spring Street property be transferred to the Children's Trust during each of the 3 taxable years 1984, 1985, and 1986. The Spring Street property was unencumbered property at all times pertinent to this case.[63]

Consistent with her intent, decedent transferred, on December 17, 1984, an undivided 33-percent interest in the Spring Street property to the Children's Trust by a quitclaim deed.[64] Similarly, in 1985, decedent

63. [If the property had been encumbered, the amount of the taxable gift would be reduced by the amount of the debt. However, if the debt exceeded the adjusted basis of the property, taxable gain for income tax purposes could be produced by the transfer. *See, e.g.*, Estate of Levine v. Commissioner, 634 F.2d 12 (2d Cir. 1980); Treas. Reg. 1. 1001-1(e) (1996)—Eds.]

64. [A one-third interest was apparently conveyed to reduce the amount of the annual gift to not exceed the sum of the annual gift exclusions. However, the transfer of an undivided interest in property could also produce a fractional interest discount that would reduce the value of the gift, at least with respect to the first installment. Subsequent transfers of the remaining ownership

transferred a second undivided 33-percent interest in the Spring Street property to the Children's Trust by a quitclaim deed which was recorded on November 27, 1985. Decedent intended to transfer her remaining undivided interest in the Spring Street property to the Children's Trust in 1986. However, decedent died prior to making the transfer, and her remaining interest in the Spring Street property remained in her estate.

The value of the 33-percent undivided interest in the Spring Street property that decedent transferred in 1984 was $70,000. The value of the 33-percent undivided interest in the Spring Street property that decedent transferred in 1985 also was $70,000.

Decedent did not report the two $70,000 transfers on Federal gift tax returns. Rather, decedent claimed seven annual exclusions of $10,000 each under section 2503(b) for each year 1984 and 1985. These annual exclusions were claimed with respect to decedent's two children and decedent's five grandchildren.

There was no agreement or understanding between decedent, the trustees, and the beneficiaries that decedent's grandchildren would not exercise their withdrawal rights following a contribution to the Children's Trust. None of decedent's five grandchildren exercised their rights to withdraw under Article Twelfth of the Children's Trust during either 1984 or 1985. None of decedent's five grandchildren received a distribution from the Children's Trust during either 1984 or 1985.

Respondent allowed petitioner to claim the annual exclusions with respect to decedent's two children. However, respondent disallowed the $10,000 annual exclusions claimed with respect to each of decedent's grandchildren claimed for the years 1984 and 1985. Respondent determined that the annual exclusions that decedent claimed with respect to her five grandchildren for the 1984 and 1985 transfers, of the Spring Street property, were not transfers of present interests in property. Accordingly, respondent increased petitioner's adjusted taxable gifts in the amount of $100,000.

OPINION

. . . Section 2503(b) provides that the first $10,000 of gifts to any person during a calendar year shall not be included in the total amount of gifts made during such year. A trust beneficiary is considered the donee of a gift in trust for purposes of the annual exclusion under section 2503(b). Sec. 25.2503-2(a), Gift Tax Regs.; Helvering v. Hutchings, 312 U.S. 393 (1941). The section 2503(b) exclusion applies to gifts of present interests in property

of the property would place all of the property under the ownership of the trust, which could invite the IRS' application of aggregation doctrine to deny any discounts. That doctrine is still developing, particularly in the aftermath of Rev. Rul. 93-12, 1993-1 C.B. 202 in which the IRS dropped its position that gifts of minority stakes in a corporation to family members must be aggregated on the basis of the family relationship of the parties. *See* JOHN A. BOGDANSKI, FEDERAL TAX VALUATION §4.03[4] (2006 & Cum. Supp. No. 2 2010). In terms of estate tax consequences, when Mrs. Cristofani passed away still owning an undivided one-third interest in the property, the estate might claim a fractional interest discount on the retained interest. Valuation discounts are discussed in the next section and in Chapter 16—EDS.]

and does not apply to gifts of future interests in property. Sec. 2503(b); sec. 25.2503-3(a), Gift Tax Regs.; United States v. Pelzer, 312 U.S. 399 (1941); Estate of Kolker v. Commissioner, 80 T.C. 1082 (1983); Quatman v. Commissioner, 54 T.C. 339 (1970). The regulations define a future interest to include "reversions, remainders, and other interests or estates, whether vested or contingent, and whether or not supported by a particular interest or estate, which are limited to commence in use, possession or enjoyment at some future date or time." Sec. 25.2503-3(a), Gift Tax Regs.; see Commissioner v. Disston, 325 U.S. 442 (1945); Fondren v. Commissioner, 324 U.S. 18 (1945). The regulations further provide that "An unrestricted right to the immediate use, possession, or enjoyment of property or the income from property (such as a life estate or term certain) is a present interest in property. An exclusion is allowable with respect to a gift of such an interest (but not in excess of the value of the interest)." Sec. 25.2503-3(b), Gift Tax Regs.; see *United States v. Pelzer*, supra.

In the instant case, petitioner argues that the right of decedent's grandchildren to withdraw an amount equal to the annual exclusion within 15 days after decedent's contribution of property to the Children's Trust constitutes a gift of a present interest in property, thus qualifying for a $10,000 annual exclusion for each grandchild for the years 1984 and 1985. Petitioner relies upon Crummey v. Commissioner, 397 F.2d 82 (9th Cir. 1968), revg. on this issue T.C. Memo. 1966-144.

In Crummey v. Commissioner, T.C. Memo. 1966-144, affd. in part and revd. in part 397 F.2d 82 (9th Cir. 1968), the settlors created an irrevocable living trust for the benefit of their four children, some of whom were minors. The trustee was required to hold the property in equal shares for the beneficiaries. Under the terms of the trust, the trustee, in his discretion, could distribute trust income to each beneficiary until that beneficiary obtained the age of 21. When the beneficiary was age 21 and up until age 35, the trustee was required to distribute trust income to each beneficiary. When the beneficiary was age 35 and over, the trustee was authorized, in his discretion, to distribute trust income to the beneficiary or his or her issue. Upon the death of a beneficiary, his or her trust share was to be distributed to that beneficiary's surviving issue subject to certain age requirements. If a beneficiary died without issue, then his or her trust share was to be distributed equally to the trust shares of the surviving children of the grantors. In addition, each child was given an absolute power to withdraw up to $4,000 in cash of any additions to corpus in the calendar year of the addition, by making a written demand upon the trustee prior to the end of the calendar year.

Relying on these powers, the settlors claimed the section 2503(b) exclusion on transfers of property to the trust for each trust beneficiary.[65]

65. During the years in *Crummey*, 1962 and 1963, the sec. 2503(b) annual exclusion was $3,000.

Respondent permitted the settlors to claim the exclusions with respect to the gifts in trust to the beneficiaries who were adults during the years of the additions. However, respondent disallowed exclusions with respect to the gifts in trust to the beneficiaries who were minors during such years. Respondent disallowed the exclusions for the minor beneficiaries on the ground that the minors' powers were not gifts of present interests in property.

In deciding whether the minor beneficiaries received a present interest, the Ninth Circuit specifically rejected any test based upon the likelihood that the minor beneficiaries would actually receive present enjoyment of the property.[66] Instead, the court focused on the legal right of the minor beneficiaries to demand payment from the trustee. The Ninth Circuit, relying on Perkins v. Commissioner, 27 T.C. 601 (1956), and Gilmore v. Commissioner, 213 F.2d 520 (6th Cir. 1954), revg. 20 T.C. 579 (1953), stated:

All exclusions should be allowed under the *Perkins* test or the "right to enjoy" test in *Gilmore*. Under *Perkins*, all that is necessary is to find that the demand could not be resisted. We interpret that to mean legally resisted and, going on that basis, we do not think the trustee would have any choice but to have a guardian appointed to take the property demanded. [Crummey v. Commissioner, 397 F.2d at 88.] The court found that the minor beneficiaries had a legal right to make a demand upon the trustee, and allowed the settlors to claim annual exclusions, under section 2503(b), with respect to the minor trust beneficiaries.

The Ninth Circuit recognized that there was language in a prior case, Stifel v. Commissioner, 197 F.2d 107 (2d Cir. 1952), affg. 17 T.C. 647 (1951), that seemed to support a different test.

As we read the *Stifel* case, it says that the court should look at the trust instrument, the law as to minors, and the financial and other circumstances of the parties. From this examination it is up to the court to determine whether it is likely that the minor beneficiary is to receive any present enjoyment of the property. If it is not likely, then the gift is a "future interest." [*Crummey v. Commissioner*, supra at 85.]

As previously stated, the Ninth Circuit rejected a test based on the likelihood that an actual demand would be made. Respondent does not rely on or cite *Stifel* in his brief. We believe that the test set forth in *Crummey v. Commissioner*, supra, is the correct test.

66. The Ninth Circuit stated:

Although under our interpretation neither the trust nor the law technically forbid a demand by the minor, the practical difficulties of a child going through the procedures seem substantial. In addition, the surrounding facts indicate the children were well cared for and the obvious intention of the trustors was to create a long term trust.... As a practical matter, it is likely that some, if not all, of the beneficiaries did not even know that they had any right to demand funds from the trust. They probably did not know when contributions were made to the trust or in what amounts. Even had they known, the substantial contributions were made toward the end of the year so that the time to make a demand was severely limited.... We think it unlikely that any demand ever would have been made. [Crummey v. Commissioner, 397 F.2d 82, 87-88 (9th Cir. 1968).]

Subsequent to the opinion in *Crummey*, respondent's revenue rulings have recognized that when a trust instrument gives a beneficiary the legal power to demand immediate possession of corpus, that power qualifies as a present interest in property. See Rev. Rul. 85-24, 1985-1 C.B. 329, 330 ("When a trust instrument gives a beneficiary the power to demand immediate possession of corpus, the beneficiary has received a present interest. Crummey v. Commissioner, 397 F.2d 82 (9th Cir. 1968)"; Rev. Rul. 81-7, 1981-1 C.B. 474 ("The courts have recognized that if a trust instrument gives a beneficiary the power to demand immediate possession and enjoyment of corpus or income, the beneficiary has a present interest. Crummey v. Commissioner, 397 F.2d 82 (9th Cir.... [1968])." While we recognize that revenue rulings do not constitute authority for deciding a case in this Court, ... we mention them to show respondent's recognition that a trust beneficiary's legal right to demand immediate possession and enjoyment of trust corpus or income constitutes a present interest in property for purposes of the annual exclusion under section 2503(b).... We also note that respondent allowed the annual exclusions with respect to decedent's two children who possessed the same right of withdrawal as decedent's grandchildren.

In the instant case, respondent has not argued that decedent's grandchildren did not possess a legal right to withdraw corpus from the Children's Trust within 15 days following any contribution, or that such demand could have been legally resisted by the trustees. In fact, the parties have stipulated that "following a contribution to the Children's Trust, each of the grandchildren possessed the SAME RIGHT OF WITHDRAWAL as ... the withdrawal rights of Frank Cristofani and Lillian Dawson." (Emphasis added.) The legal right of decedent's grandchildren to withdraw specified amounts from the trust corpus within 15 days following any contribution of property constitutes a gift of a present interest. *Crummey v. Commissioner*, supra.

On brief, respondent attempts to distinguish *Crummey* from the instant case. Respondent argues that in *Crummey* the trust beneficiaries not only possessed an immediate right of withdrawal, but also possessed "substantial, future economic benefits" in the trust corpus and income. Respondent emphasizes that the Children's Trust identified decedent's children as "primary beneficiaries," and that decedent's grandchildren were to be considered as "beneficiaries of secondary importance."

Generally, the beneficiaries of the trust in *Crummey* were entitled to distributions of income. Trust corpus was to be distributed to the issue of each beneficiary sometime following the beneficiary's death. See Crummey v. Commissioner, T.C. Memo. 1966-144. Aside from the discretionary actions of the trustee, the only way any beneficiary in *Crummey* could receive trust corpus was through the demand provision which allowed each beneficiary to demand up to $4,000 in the year in which a transfer to the trust was made. The Ninth Circuit observed:

In our case . . . if no demand is made in any particular year, the additions are forever removed from the uncontrolled reach of the beneficiary since, with exception of the yearly demand provision, the only way the corpus can ever be tapped by a beneficiary, is through a distribution at the discretion of the trustee. [Crummey v. Commissioner, 397 F.2d at 88.]

In the instant case, the primary beneficiaries of the Children's Trust were decedent's children. Decedent's grandchildren held contingent remainder interests in the Children's Trust. Decedent's grandchildren's interests vested only in the event that their respective parent (decedent's child) predeceased decedent or failed to survive decedent by more than 120 days. We do not believe, however, that Crummey requires that the beneficiaries of a trust must have a vested present interest or vested remainder interest in the trust corpus or income, in order to qualify for the section 2503(b) exclusion.

As discussed in *Crummey*, the likelihood that the beneficiary will actually receive present enjoyment of the property is not the test for determining whether a present interest was received. Rather, we must examine the ability of the beneficiaries, in a legal sense, to exercise their right to withdraw trust corpus, and the trustee's right to legally resist a beneficiary's demand for payment. Crummey v. Commissioner, 397 F.2d at 88. Based upon the language of the trust instrument and stipulations of the parties, we believe that each grandchild possessed the legal right to withdraw trust corpus and that the trustees would be unable to legally resist a grandchild's withdrawal demand. We note that there was no agreement or understanding between decedent, the trustees, and the beneficiaries that the grandchildren would not exercise their withdrawal rights following a contribution to the Children's Trust.

Respondent also argues that since the grandchildren possessed only a contingent remainder interest in the Children's Trust, decedent never intended to benefit her grandchildren. Respondent contends that the only reason decedent gave her grandchildren the right to withdraw trust corpus was to obtain the benefit of the annual exclusion.

We disagree. Based upon the provisions of the Children's Trust, we believe that decedent intended to benefit her grandchildren. Their benefits, as remaindermen, were contingent upon a child of decedent's dying before decedent or failing to survive decedent by more than 120 days. We recognize that at the time decedent executed the Children's Trust, decedent's children were in good health, but this does not remove the possibility that decedent's children could have predeceased decedent.

In addition, decedent's grandchildren possessed the power to withdraw up to an amount equal to the amount allowable for the 2503(b) exclusion. Although decedent's grandchildren never exercised their respective withdrawal rights, this does not vitiate the fact that they had the legal right to do so, within 15 days following a contribution to the Children's Trust. Events might have occurred to prompt decedent's children and grandchildren (through their guardians) to exercise their withdrawal rights. For example, either or both of decedent's children and their respective families might have suddenly and unexpectedly been faced with economic hardship; or, in the event of the insolvency of one of decedent's children, the rights of the grandchildren might have been exercised to safeguard their interest in the trust assets from their parents' creditors. In light of the provisions in decedent's trust, we fail to see how respondent can argue that decedent did not intend to benefit her grandchildren.[67]

Finally, the fact that the trust provisions were intended to obtain the benefit of the annual gift tax exclusion does not change the result. As we stated in *Perkins v. Commissioner*, supra, regardless of the petitioners' motives, or why they did what they in fact did, the legal rights in question were created by the trust instruments and could at any time thereafter be exercised. Petitioners having done what they purported to do, their tax-saving motive is irrelevant. [Perkins v. Commissioner, 27 T.C. at 606.]

Based upon the foregoing, we find that the grandchildren's right to withdraw an amount not to exceed the section 2503(b) exclusion, represents a present interest for purposes of section 2503(b). Accordingly, petitioner is entitled to claim annual exclusions with respect to decedent's grandchildren as a result of decedent's transfers of property to the Children's Trust in 1984 and 1985.

Decision will be entered for the petitioner.

Reviewed by the Court.

4. Valuation Discounts

As discussed in Chapter 16, because the federal wealth transfer taxes are imposed on the value of the property transferred, much of estate planning involves attempts to minimize the appraised value of the property. Lifetime gifts play an important role in this planning. For example, if a grandparent dies owning 100 percent of Blackacre, the full value of Blackacre will be included in the grandparent's estate. However, if the grandparent gifts a 50 percent interest in Blackacre to a grandchild, it is well established that the 50 percent interest received by the grandchild is worth less than 50 percent of the value of 100 percent of Blackacre. (However, *how much* less it is worth

67. We note that the facts of the instant case are very similar to the facts that respondent was presented with in Priv. Ltr. Rul. 90-30-005 (Apr. 19, 1990), wherein A created a trust for the benefit of B, in which B was entitled to receive trust income during A's lifetime. Upon A's death, trust corpus was to be distributed to B. If B predeceased A, one-half of the corpus was to be distributed to B's children and the other one-half was to be distributed to A's children. Within 30 days of receiving notice of a contribution to corpus, both B and B's children had the power to withdraw from corpus a proportionate amount of the contribution not to exceed the sec. 2503(b) exclusion. Citing *Crummey*, respondent allowed A to claim annual gift exclusions for both B and B's children. Although private letter rulings are not precedent, sec. 6110(j)(3), they "do reveal the interpretation put upon the statute by the agency charged with the responsibility of administering the revenue laws." Hanover Bank v. Commissioner, 369U.S. 672, 686 (1962)....

is not well established.) This "fractional interest discount" recognizes that it is more difficult to sell an undivided 50 percent interest in a parcel than a 100 percent fee simple interest in the parcel. A hypothetical purchaser buys a potential partition lawsuit. In addition, using the same reasoning, when the grandparent dies, the 50 percent interest included in his or her estate will also be eligible for such a discount.

In a slightly different vein, the grandparent could have formed a limited partnership or limited liability company (real estate is generally not a good candidate for closely held corporate ownership for income tax reasons) by transferring the real estate to the entity followed by periodic transfers of fractional entity ownership interests to the grandchild as gifts. The valuation of the grandchild's cumulative ownership interest is arguably much less than the ownership percentage of the underlying asset because the asset is now an asset of the entity, and the entity's formation documents as well as state law may impose limitations on transfers of interests, voting, and liquidation. The gift tax value of the grandchild's ownership interest might consequently reflect a substantial minority and marketability discount, possibly permitting larger fractional entity gifts to the grandchild than a straight percentage of the underlying assets would indicate. At the same time, the grandparent's estate may also claim valuation discounts with respect to the ownership interests retained by the grandparent.

Although the theory of valuation discounts is relatively simple and compelling, the application is more involved and uncertain. First, the valuation discount generally should be supported by professional appraisals, which may be quite expensive. Clients and their advisors often have an exaggerated opinion of the degree of discounts that can be claimed. Second, the IRS may contest the claimed discount; a number of valuation cases are pending in the courts at any given time. Third, for quite aggressive discount claims, the taxpayer must weigh the risk of the imposition of penalties.[68] Fourth, structuring ownership to establish the discount (e.g., through the use of multiple entities) may require costly attorney and accounting fees to create and maintain the structures. A review of the litigated cases demonstrates the importance of the terms of the entity agreements and the owner's continuous compliance with those terms, as well as the sequencing of the transfers of property into the entities. Fifth, perhaps most importantly, clients should be prepared to demonstrate the legitimate business purposes to be achieved by the formation of an entity, purposes that must go well beyond mere tax minimization. And finally, the client must appreciate that the structures may have state law consequences, such as a loss of control, and a failure to respect those consequences may jeopardize the asserted discounts.

68. *See* IRC §6662.

5. Below-Market Loans

A below-market loan from one family member to another may bestow a benefit on the borrower to the extent the interest rate is below a market rate of interest. IRC §7872 governs the income tax and gift tax consequences of below-market loans in many contexts; here our focus is on a below-market loan intended as a gift.

Very generally, IRC §7872 requires the payment of interest at the "applicable Federal rate" tied to U.S. Treasury securities. If the interest rate on the loan is below that amount, the forgone interest is treated as a gift from the lender to the borrower, and the lender must treat the forgone interest as taxable income. Still, the statute provides some flexibility. First, if the loan amount is less than $10,000, the loan may be excluded from the statute.[69] Second, if the borrower has little investment income and the loan amount does not exceed $100,000, the lender must treat the forgone interest as taxable income only to the extent of the borrower's net investment income.[70] This exception is valuable for young adults borrowing from family members to purchase a home. Third, the applicable federal rate is tied to U.S. Treasury securities and generally is the lowest domestic rate of interest for a given maturity, reflecting the creditworthiness of the federal government. Most commercial lenders would not lend at that rate, so borrowing from family will almost always be a bargain. Fourth, because the lender and borrower are related, the borrower might be able to take risks with the money that a commercial loan would not permit, possibly permitting exploitation of business relationships that the lender/family member has established over the years. Fifth, the IRS has, for now, retreated from its position that gratuitous loan guarantees produce a gift for the value of the guarantee. So long as that is the case, IRC §7872 can be skirted by having the younger generation borrow from a commercial lender but with a favorable interest rate (in addition to the loan itself that might not have otherwise been offered to a potentially inexperienced or otherwise less creditworthy borrower) produced by the elder generation's guarantee of the loan.

6. Grantor Trust Income Tax Rules

The selection of trustees for a testamentary trust is discussed in Chapter 7. The selection of trustees for an irrevocable trust involves most of the same considerations. However, the settlor of an irrevocable trust must also consider the application of the "grantor trust" income tax rules prescribed in IRC §§671-679. The application of the grantor trust rules may cause the settlor of the trust to be taxed on some portion of the trust income.

69. *See* IRC §7872(c)(2).

70. *See* IRC §7872(d)(1). The statute uses the term "forgone" interest, rather than the more common "foregone." *See generally* Francis W. Dubreuil & Christopher J. Clarkson, *CLATs and Intra-Family Loans Provide Wealth Transfer Opportunities*, 37 Est. Plan. 29 (Aug. 2010).

This may be advantageous. For example, some settlors intentionally plan for such a result through the use of "defective trusts," which are structured to avoid inclusion in the settlor's federal wealth transfer tax taxable estate at death but which are not treated as a separate taxpayer for income tax purposes.[71] There are three principal reasons for doing this: (1) to avoid the highly progressive income tax rates applicable to trusts;[72] (2) to avoid the dissipation of the trust's resources that would otherwise be required to pay the trust's income taxes; furthermore, by paying the income taxes, the settlor/donor is able to remove even more assets from his or her taxable estate; and (3) to permit a settlor's value-freezing sale of assets to the trust that avoids treatment as a taxable sale for income tax purposes.[73]

The following ruling addresses the second reason.

Rev. Rul. 2004-64
2004-2 C.B. 7

ISSUES

With respect to a trust whose grantor is treated as the owner of the trust under subpart E, part I, subchapter J, chapter 1 of the Internal Revenue Code (subpart E), what are the gift tax consequences when the grantor pays the income tax attributable to the inclusion of the trust's income in the grantor's taxable income, and what are the estate tax consequences if, pursuant to the governing instrument or applicable local law, the grantor may or must be reimbursed by the trust for that income tax?

FACTS

In Year 1, *A*, a United States citizen, establishes and funds Trust, an irrevocable inter vivos trust, for the benefit of *A*'s descendants. The governing instrument of Trust requires that the trustee be a person not related or subordinate to *A* within the meaning of §672(c) of the Internal Revenue Code. *A* appoints a trustee that satisfies this requirement. Trust is governed by the laws of State. Under the terms of Trust, *A* retains no beneficial interest in or power over Trust income or corpus that would

71. *See, e.g.*, Rev. Rul. 2008-22, 2008-16 I.R.B. 796 (a grantor's power, exercisable in a nonfiduciary capacity, to acquire property held in trust by substituting other property of equivalent value did not result in inclusion of the trust property in the grantor's estate under IRC §§2036 & 2038); IRC §675(4)(C) (The settlor shall be treated as the owner of any portion of a trust in which a power of administration is exercisable in a nonfiduciary capacity without the approval or consent of any person in a fiduciary capacity; a power of administration includes "a power to reacquire the trust corpus by substituting other property of an equivalent value."); Stephen R. Akers et al., *Creating Intentional Grantor Trusts*, 44 REAL PROP. TR. & EST. L.J. 207 (2009).

72. *See* IRC §1(e).

73. *See generally*, Ronald D. Aucutt, *Installment Sales to Grantor Trusts*, Planning Techniques for Large Estates, SS010 ALI-ABA 1681 (ALI-ABA Continuing Legal Education, Nov. 15-19, 2010); Stuart M. Horwitz & Jason S. Damicone, *Creative Uses of Intentionally Defective Irrevocable Trusts*, 35 EST. PLAN. 35 (2008); Michael D. Mulligan, *Fifteen Years of Sales to IDITs—Where Are We Now?*, 35 ACTEC J. 227 (Winter 2009); Mark S. Poker, *A Primer on Sales to Intentionally Defective Grantor Trusts*, 14 ALI-ABA EST. PLAN. COURSE MATERIALS J. 39 (Oct. 2008).

cause the transfer to Trust to constitute an incomplete gift for federal gift tax purposes, or that would cause Trust corpus to be included in *A*'s gross estate for federal estate tax purposes on *A*'s death. However, *A* retains sufficient powers with respect to Trust so that *A* is treated as the owner of Trust under subpart E.

During Year 1, Trust receives taxable income of $10*x*. Pursuant to §671, *A* includes the $10*x* in *A*'s taxable income. As a result, *A*'s personal income tax liability for Year 1 increases by $2.5*x*. *A* dies in Year 3. As of the date of *A*' s death, the fair market value of Trust's assets is $150*x*.

Situation 1: Neither State law nor the governing instrument of Trust contains any provision requiring or permitting the trustee to distribute to *A* amounts sufficient to satisfy *A*'s income tax liability attributable to the inclusion of Trust's income in *A*'s taxable income. Accordingly, *A* pays the additional $2.5*x* liability from *A*'s own funds.

Situation 2: The governing instrument of Trust provides that if *A* is treated as the owner of any portion of Trust pursuant to the provisions of subpart E for any taxable year, the trustee shall distribute to *A* for the taxable year, income or principal sufficient to satisfy *A*'s personal income tax liability attributable to the inclusion of all or part of Trust's income in *A*'s taxable income. Accordingly, the trustee distributes $2.5*x* to *A* to reimburse *A* for the $2.5*xxx* income tax liability.

Situation 3: The governing instrument of Trust provides that if *A* is treated as the owner of any portion of Trust pursuant to the provisions of subpart E for any taxable year, the trustee may, in the trustee's discretion, distribute to *A* for the taxable year, income or principal sufficient to satisfy *A*'s personal income tax liability attributable to the inclusion of all or part of Trust's income in *A*'s taxable income. Pursuant to the exercise of the trustee's discretionary power, the trustee distributes $2.5*x* to *A* to reimburse *A* for the $2.5*x* income tax liability.

LAW AND ANALYSIS

Under §671, if the grantor of a trust is treated as the owner of any portion of the trust under subpart E, those items of income, deductions, and credits against tax of the trust that are attributable to that portion of the trust must be included in computing the taxable income of the grantor.... Section 25.2511-1(c)(1) provides that the gift tax applies with respect to any transaction in which an interest in property is gratuitously passed or conferred on another regardless of the means or device employed. Thus, the gift tax may apply if one party forgives or fails to collect on the indebtedness of another.... Similarly, the gift tax applies if one person gratuitously pays the tax liability of another. *Doerr v. United States*, 819 F.2d 162 (7th Cir. 1987) (donor's payment of the donee's state gift tax liability constitutes an additional gift to the donee).

Section 2036(a)(1) provides that the value of the gross estate shall include the value of all property to the extent of any interest therein of which the decedent has at any time made a transfer (except in the case of a *bona fide* sale for an adequate and full consideration in money or money's worth), by trust or otherwise, under which the decedent has retained for life or for any period not ascertainable without reference to the decedent's death or for any period that does not in fact end before death the possession or enjoyment of, or the right to the income from, the property.

Section 20.2036-1(b)(2) of the Estate Tax Regulations provides that the use, possession, right to income, or other enjoyment of transferred property is treated as having been retained by the decedent to the extent that the transferred property is to be applied towards the discharge of a legal obligation of the decedent.... On the other hand, §2036 generally does not apply when trust property may be used to satisfy the decedent's legal obligations only in the discretion of the trustee, whether or not the discretion is exercised by the trustee....

In the present situations, Trust includes provisions that cause *A* to be treated as the owner of Trust under subpart E and, as a result, to be liable for any income tax attributable to Trust's income. Thus, even though *A* is not a Trust beneficiary, any income tax *A* pays that is attributable to Trust's income is paid in discharge of *A*'s own liability, imposed on *A* by §671.

In *Situation 1*, *A*'s payment of the $2.5*x* income tax liability does not constitute a gift by *A* to Trust's beneficiaries for federal gift tax purposes because *A*, not Trust, is liable for the taxes. In contrast, in the situation presented in *Doerr v. United States*, cited above, the donor's payment was for the donee's tax liability and, as a result, the payment constituted an additional gift to the donee. In addition, no portion of Trust is includible in *A*'s gross estate for federal estate tax purposes under §2036, because *A* has not retained the right to have trust property expended in discharge of *A*'s legal obligation.

In *Situation 2*, the governing instrument of Trust requires the trustee to reimburse *A* from Trust's assets for the amount of income tax *A* pays that is attributable to Trust's income. *A*'s payment of the $2.5*x* income tax liability does not constitute a gift by *A*, because *A* is liable for the tax. The trustee's distribution of $2.5*x* to *A* as reimbursement for the income tax payment by *A* is not a gift by the trust beneficiaries to *A*, because the distribution from Trust is mandated by the terms of the trust instrument.

However, *A* has retained the right to have trust property expended in discharge of *A*'s legal obligation. *A*'s retained right to receive reimbursement attributable to Trust's income causes the full value of Trust's assets at *A*'s death ($150*x*) to be included in *A*'s gross estate under §2036(a)(1). The result would be the same if, under applicable state law, the trustee must, unless the governing instrument provides otherwise, reimburse *A* for *A*'s personal income tax liability attributable to the inclusion of all or part of the Trust's income in *A*'s taxable income, and the governing instrument does not provide otherwise.

In *Situation 3*, the governing instrument of Trust provides the trustee with the discretion to reimburse *A* from Trust's assets for the amount of income tax *A* pays that is attributable to Trust's income. As is the case in *Situation 1* and *Situation 2*, *A*'s payment of the $2.5*x* income tax liability does not constitute a gift by *A* because *A* is liable for the income tax. Further, the $2.5*x*xx paid to *A* from Trust as reimbursement for *A*'s income tax payment was distributed pursuant to the exercise of the trustee's discretionary authority granted under the terms of the trust instrument. Accordingly, this payment is not a gift by the trust beneficiaries to *A*. In addition, assuming there is no understanding, express or implied, between *A* and the trustee regarding the trustee's exercise of discretion, the trustee's discretion to satisfy *A*'s obligation would not alone cause the inclusion of the trust in *A*'s gross estate for federal estate tax purposes. This is the case regardless of whether or not the trustee actually reimburses *A* from Trust assets for the amount of income tax *A* pays that is attributable to Trust's income. The result would be the same if the trustee's discretion to reimburse *A* for this income tax is granted under applicable state law rather than under the governing instrument. However, such discretion combined with other facts (including but not limited to: an understanding or pre-existing arrangement between *A* and the trustee regarding the trustee's exercise of this discretion; a power retained by *A* to remove the trustee and name *A* as successor trustee; or applicable local law subjecting the trust assets to the claims of *A*'s creditors) may cause inclusion of Trust's assets in *A*'s gross estate for federal estate tax purposes.

HOLDINGS

When the grantor of a trust, who is treated as the owner of the trust under subpart E, pays the income tax attributable to the inclusion of the trust's income in the grantor's taxable income, the grantor is not treated as making a gift of the amount of the tax to the trust beneficiaries. If, pursuant to the trust's governing instrument or applicable local law, the grantor must be reimbursed by the trust for the income tax payable by the grantor that is attributable to the trust's income, the full value of the trust's assets is includible in the grantor's gross estate under §2036(a)(1). If, however, the trust's governing instrument or applicable local law gives the trustee the discretion to reimburse the grantor for that portion of the grantor's income tax liability, the existence of that discretion, by itself (whether or not exercised) will not cause the value of the trust's assets to be includible in the grantor's gross estate.

If, however, the settlor wishes that the trust be treated as a separate income taxpayer, the grantor trust rules dictate that certain individuals, usually family members, may not serve as trustees if those trustees wield certain discretionary powers.[74] In particular, note that siblings of the settlor are considered related parties.[75] To avoid grantor trust status, those individuals must also hold an adverse party interest in the trust. The creation of such an interest may add undesirable complexity to the trust structure or simply be undesirable in terms of what powers the settlor would like those individuals to possess. The use of an institutional trustee usually solves that concern.[76] Apart from the selection of a trustee, under some circumstances the settlor may be taxed on trust income that is used to purchase life insurance on the settlor's life or is applied for the benefit of the settlor's spouse or to meet the settlor's support obligations.[77]

D. Specialized Tax Planning Structures

In Part B, "Selecting the Form of the Gift," tax considerations strongly influenced, but were not entirely determinative of, the choice of structures to be used (e.g., the section 529 plan, the §2503(c) trust, and the *Crummey* trust). This section addresses some structures that are almost entirely the product of inter vivos tax planning.

1. GRATs and GRUTs

If an individual gifts property to another but retains some interest in the gifted property, such as an income stream for a period of years, the value of the retained interest may be deducted from the value of the gift. IRC §2702 imposes limits on this principle if the gift is for the benefit of the donor's family members, by requiring that the retained interest, to be valued, must generally be (a) a right to receive a fixed amount payable at least annually (an annuity interest); or (b) a right to receive an amount payable at least annually as a fixed percentage of the fair market value of property determined annually (a unitrust interest). As a general matter, the retention of a simple life estate will not reduce the value of the gift unless the limited exception of IRC §2702(c)(4) applies. The use of a grantor-retained annuity trust (GRAT) or grantor-retained unitrust (GRUT), even of relatively short duration,[78] may significantly reduce the taxable value of

74. *See, e.g.*, IRC §§672 & 674. *See generally* Samuel A. Donaldson, *Understanding Grantor Trusts*, 40 INST. ON EST. PLAN. ¶200 (2006).

75. *See* IRC §672(c).

76. As discussed in Chapter 7, the selection of an institutional trustee presents other issues, principally costs, responsiveness, and investment performance. *See generally* TURNER, *supra* note 43, ch. 3, *Choosing a Trustee*.

77. *See* IRC §677.

78. If any portion of the retained annuity interest is still outstanding and unpaid at the time of the settlor's death, IRC §2036(a) will generally require the inclusion of a portion, or all, of the property in the settlor's gross estate for federal estate taxation purposes. Consequently, the choice

a gift, such as corporate stock. These structures are discussed in more detail in Chapter 16.

2. Qualified Personal Residence Trusts

Applying the same principles as those found in GRATs and GRUTs, IRC §2702 permits a grantor to gift a personal residence. A personal residence in this context is not limited to a "principal" residence, so vacation properties may qualify. The gift is made to a qualified personal residence trust (QPRT), retaining the use of the residence for a term of years that can be valued and therefore deducted from the value of the gift, using the standard tables at Treas. Reg. §20.2031-7. Other family members are usually the remainderpersons. Assuming that the settlor outlives the term of years, so that IRC §2036 does not include the property in the settlor's estate, this permits the transfer of potentially appreciating residential properties to other family members at a reduced federal wealth transfer taxation cost.[79]

E. Using Form Documents (Part IV)[80]

Below is a brief checklist of the fundamental clauses and drafting issues that one often finds in trust forms. Chapter 7 addressed the use of a contingent trust for minors, and Form G of the Forms Supplement contains an example of such a trust. Chapter 15 addresses the use of a revocable trust, and Form J is an example of a revocable trust. Form L is an example of a complex irrevocable trust of the type used for the gifts discussed in this chapter. You may wish to review Form L at this time. Chapter 13 discusses some additional trust clauses that are typically included in more sophisticated long-term trust arrangements.

of the term of the retained interest must be approached with care—and a little luck. On June 7, 2007, the IRS issued proposed regulations concerning, in part, IRC §§2036 & 2039 and the required inclusion amounts for GRAT, GRUT, and QPRT interests. *See* Reg. 119097-05, 72 Fed. Reg. 31487 (June 7, 2007). The regulations were adopted in final form in 2008. *See* Treas. Reg. §§20.2036-1(c) & 20.2039-1(e) (as amended in 2008). *See generally* Lawrence P. Katzenstein, *Regs. Clarify Estate Tax Inclusion of Trust Property, But Issues Remain*, 36 EST. PLAN. 3 (June 2009); Michael D. Whitty, *GRAT Expectations: Questioning, Challenging, and Litigating the Service Position on Estate Tax Inclusion of Grantor Retained Annuity Trusts*, 36 ACTEC J. 87 (Summer 2010).

79. *See* TURNER, *supra* note 43, app. 81 (sample QPRT language). The IRS issued a revenue procedure that provides annotated examples of QPRT trust language. *See* Rev. Proc. 2003-42, 2003-1 C.B. 993.

80. Part I appeared in Chapter 3, Part G. Part II appeared in Chapter 4, Part F. Part III appeared in Chapter 5, Part F. For an interesting overview of drafting trusts (with sample language) see Benjamin H. Pruett, *Tales from the Dark Side: Drafting Issues from the Fiduciary's Perspective*, 35 ACTEC J. 331 (Spring 2010).

1. Description of the Settlor and the Initial Trustee

In an inter vivos irrevocable trust one would generally find the opening lines of the trust expressing an agreement between the settlor and the initial trustee.

2. Description of the Trust Property

The initial trust property is generally described in an exhibit. If the contribution of additional property to the trust is appropriate,[81] the trust instrument should address the degree of formality required to designate additional contributions as trust property and provide for the acceptability of the property by the trustee.

3. Name of the Trust

This name will be used in federal tax returns, state trust registrations, and other filings.

4. Information Statement

Information should be included concerning family, full legal names of beneficiaries, their current addresses, and, if minors or if distributions are contingent on beneficiaries attaining certain ages, dates of birth. This section may describe the current spouse and children of the settlor. If one is dealing with a lifetime irrevocable trust, care must be exercised in describing the settlor's spouse, in the event of subsequent termination of the marriage by divorce, annulment, or death, and possible remarriage. Generally one does not describe more remote beneficiaries, such as grandchildren (unless they are primary beneficiaries), because they are left to the definition of "descendants" or any other applicable term used by the instrument. Any other family members that do not qualify as descendants, such as collateral relatives or sons-in-law or daughters-in-law, who would be eligible for current distributions should also be identified.

EXERCISE 8-1

ANTICIPATING CHANGES IN MARITAL STATUS

Draft language describing the spouse of the settlor that would be flexible enough to exclude the current spouse from any rights under the agreement if a judicial decree of dissolution of marriage or legal annulment is granted but that would include any future spouses of the settlor.

81. For example, contribution of additional property after formation of a GRAT is not permissible.

5. Statement Concerning Revocability

Both revocable trusts and irrevocable trusts are common estate planning tools. Thus, the instrument should clearly state whether the trust is revocable or irrevocable. The presumption at common law is that trusts are irrevocable where there is no provision in the instrument reserving a power of amendment or revocation.[82] The statutes of several states create a presumption of revocability unless the trust is expressly irrevocable.[83]

6. Distribution Schemes

The structure of the distribution provisions is probably the most significant trust drafting issue. Although the desires of the client and the creativity of the attorney may produce numerous refinements, there are some common approaches.

a. *Sprinkle trust.* This language *permits* the trustee to exercise discretion in varying the timing and the amounts of income and/or principal distributed to particular members of a class of beneficiaries. A simple example of sprinkle language would be:

> *Trustee may, from time to time, pay to or apply for the benefit of any one or more of Settlor's descendants, such amounts of the income and principal of the trust as trustee deems advisable, without the necessity of equalization among them at any time.*

b. *Spray trust.* This language is generally applicable to trust income, and *directs* the trustee to distribute income among a class of beneficiaries. In a so-called "vertical" spray trust, the beneficiaries might be limited to a certain beneficiary and his or her descendants, while a "horizontal" spray trust might direct the distribution of income among all generations of the designated class of beneficiaries (spouse, children, grandchildren, great-grandchildren, etc.). A simple example of vertical spray language would be:

> *Trustee shall distribute all of the income of the trust, in such amounts as trustee deems advisable to or for the benefit of any one or more of Settlor's descendants, without the necessity of equalization among such beneficiaries at any time.*

82. *See* Jesse Dukeminier et al., Wills, Trusts, and Estates 658-659 (8th ed. 2009).

83. *See, e.g.*, Cal. Prob. Code §15400 (West 1991); Mont. Code Ann. §72-33-401 (2009). The Uniform Trust Code §602(a) changes the common law rule by providing that a trust is revocable unless the terms of the trust expressly provide that it is irrevocable. The rapidly growing influence of the Uniform Trust Code, which has been adopted by at least 22 states and the District of Columbia, will continue to erode the common law presumption. *See* Table of Jurisdictions Wherein Act Has Been Adopted, 7C U.L.A. 362 (2006 & Supp. 2010).

c. *Accumulation trust.* This trust does not anticipate the distribution of income and/or principal for a period. A simple example of accumulation language would be:

> *Trustee may distribute to such child, or apply for such child's sole benefit, such amounts of income or principal, or both, as trustee may from time to time, in trustee's sole and absolute discretion, deem necessary or advisable. Any undistributed income shall be added to principal.*

d. *Unitrust or total return trust.* Traditional fiduciary accounting involves the division of trust receipts into income or principal. Many distribution schemes provide for the distribution of income but are less generous in distributions of principal. Some clients prefer that the beneficiaries receive distributions of a certain percentage of the total value of trust assets, irrespective of whether the value base is the product of income, capital appreciation, or both.[84] A simple example of unitrust language would be:

> *Trustee shall pay to or apply for Settlor's children's benefit in each taxable year of the trust a Unitrust Amount equal to Five Percent (5%) of the net fair market value of the trust property as of the date of Settlor's death (as finally determined for federal tax purposes) and as subsequently valued as of the first business day of the first calendar month in each taxable year of the trust (the Valuation Date).*[85]

e. *Holdback clause.* This provision reduces or suspends all distributions to a given beneficiary on the occurrence of certain events or circumstances related to the beneficiary such as criminal behavior or bankruptcy (see Chapter 13).

f. *Incentive clause.* This provision increases or conditions distributions to a given beneficiary upon the occurrence of desired behavior, such as graduating Phi Beta Kappa, completing graduate school, birth of children, public service activities, matching income earned by the beneficiary, etc. (see Chapter 13).[86]

84. *See, e.g.*, Jerold I. Horn, *Prudent Investor Rule, Modern Portfolio Theory and Private Trusts: Drafting and Administration Including the "Give-Me-Five" Unitrust*, 33 REAL PROP. PROB. & TR. J. 1, 36-37, 40-41 (Spring 1998) (examples of unitrust distribution clauses). Effective January 2, 2004, the IRS issued final regulations that approve total return and unitrust allocations of trust income. *See generally* Margaret E.W. Sager, *Litigation and the Total Return Trust*, 35 ACTEC J. 206 (Winter 2009); Adam J. Wiensch & L. Elizabeth Beetz, *The Liberation of Total Return*, TR. & EST. 44 (Apr. 2004); Robert B. Wolf & Stephan R. Leimberg, *Total Return Trusts Approved by New Regs, but State Law Is Crucial*, 31 EST. PLAN. 179 (2004).

85. Should the trustee's determination of the net fair market value of the trust assets for subsequent years be conclusive, or should other safeguards be considered?

86. *See, e.g.*, John J. Scroggin, *Protecting and Preserving the Family: The True Goal of Estate Planning, Part II—Some of the Tools*, 16 PROB. & PROP. 34, 40 (July/Aug. 2002) (examples of incentive clause language); Ellen Evans Whiting, *Controlling Behavior by Controlling the Inheritance: Considerations in Drafting Incentive Provisions*, 15 PROB. & PROP. 6 (Sept./Oct. 2001).

g. *Powers of appointment.* Powers of appointment are often included in irrevocable trusts to permit additional input by family members. Simple power of appointment language might be:

> *Trustee shall distribute the trust property, including accumulated income, to Settlor's descendants, in such amounts and proportions and for such estates and interests, outright or in trust, upon such terms, trusts, conditions and limitations as [insert name of donee of power of appointment] shall appoint during her lifetime in a writing referring to this Section ______ delivered to Trustee.*

h. Crummey *withdrawal rights.* See the discussion in Part C above.

7. Identity of Trustee, Successor Trustees

The trust instrument should designate the initial trustee. The removal of trustees (e.g., for cause or without cause, and who can exercise the removal right), the right of resignation, and the selection and qualifications of successors are important issues in drafting the trust instrument.[87] Article 6 of Form L provides examples of typical language of this nature. As discussed in Chapter 16, the structure of a settlor's power to select successor trustees must consider the federal wealth transfer tax consequences because retention of such powers may produce inclusion of the trust assets in the settlor's taxable estate.

8. Trustee Powers and Responsibilities; Exculpatory Clauses

The types of potential investments should be spelled out. Required reports by the trustee should be addressed.[88] Compensation of the trustee is addressed, but usually in a general manner. The trustee, particularly an institutional trustee, may insist on the inclusion of language limiting liability for many situations, including environmental hazards associated with real property, errors or omissions short of gross negligence, or for errors committed by any predecessor trustee.[89]

87. *See generally* Robert A. Vigoda, *Powers to Replace Trustees: A Key Element of (and Risk to) Dynasty Trusts*, 35 Est. Plan. 20 (June 2008).

88. A related issue is the amount of trust information to which beneficiaries are entitled. *See generally* Dana G. Fitzsimons Jr., *Navigating the Trustee's Duty to Disclose*, 23 Prob. & Prop. 40 (Jan./Feb. 2009); Anne J. O'Brien, *The Trustee's Duty to Provide Information to Beneficiaries: When Can the Settlor Say "Don't Ask, Won't Tell"?*, 40 Inst. on Est. Plan. ¶500 (2006); Robert Whitman, *Providing Information to Beneficiaries (With Sample Forms)*, 15 ALI-ABA Est. Plan. Course Materials J. 5 (Feb. 2009).

89. *See, e.g.*, Charles W. Pieterse & Charles E. Coates III, *Exculpatory Clauses May Give Trustees Extra Protection from Liability*, 37 Est. Plan. 26 (Mar. 2010).

9. Spendthrift Clauses

Most settlors wish to include a spendthrift clause for the protection from creditors of the beneficiary and the trust property. This is a common provision. However, a traditional spendthrift clause may limit estate planning flexibility of the beneficiary in terms of precluding an assignment or disclaimer of the beneficial interest to other family members.[90]

10. Saving Clause

The Rule Against Perpetuities (RAP) lurks in the background of trusts, and a saving clause is generally included. As discussed in Chapter 13, state law developments curtailing application of the RAP dictate additional care in the structuring of such clauses.

11. Applicable Law

Generally the law of the state where the trust is created applies in resolving questions of the validity of the trust and trust formation, while the law of the state where the trust is administered applies in resolving questions concerning administration. However, as discussed in Chapter 12, certain states provide special protections against creditors. Further, as discussed in Chapter 13, some states have limited or eliminated the common law RAP. The state of administration may not be clear, particularly if there are family member cotrustees who live in different states. Accordingly, the trust instrument should directly specify the applicable law, and the trust relationships (e.g., situs of trustee, where tax returns are filed) should be arranged, or allowed to be changed, in a consistent manner.[91]

12. Trust Protector

This concept is commonly found in sophisticated long-term trusts, but it is increasingly found in other inter vivos and testamentary irrevocable trusts. It envisions a third party, not a trustee, who wields certain powers to protect the settlor's intent. The protector might be empowered to appoint and remove trustees, to move the situs of the trust (e.g., if tax laws change, if the country of original situs is invaded), to modify the trust provisions to comply with future tax code provisions so as to carry out the settlor's

90. Some spendthrift clauses expressly permit the exercise of a disclaimer. *See, e.g.*, Sebastian V. Grassi, Jr., *Drafting Flexibility into Estate Planning Documents After the 2001 Tax Act (With Sample Clauses)*, 17 No. 2 PRAC. TAX LAW. 7, 9 (Winter 2003) (example of flexible spendthrift language). However, the Uniform Probate Code and the Uniform Disclaimers of Property Interests Act both expressly allow disclaimers in situations where a spendthrift provision has been imposed. *See* UPC §2-1105(a); UNIF. DISCLAIMERS OF PROP. INTERESTS ACT §5(a) (amended 2002), 8A U.L.A. 166 (2003); COLO. REV. STAT. §15-11-801(1) (2010) (based on a former (1993) version of the Uniform Probate Code).

91. *See generally* Malcolm A. Moore, *Choice of Law in Trusts: How Broad Is the Possible Spectrum?*, 36 INST. ON EST. PLAN. ¶600 (2002); Richard W. Nenno, *Choosing and Rechoosing the Jurisdiction for a Trust*, 40 INST. ON EST. PLAN. ¶400 (2006).

intent in that regard (e.g., to minimize taxes), to terminate the trust (e.g., if tax laws change or administration becomes burdensome) (see Chapter 13),[92] or even, most broadly, to "decant" or transfer the trust assets to a new or existing trust.

13. Definitions

Most trusts do not rely on state statutes or common law for definitions of all terms used in the trust agreement. Instead a trust will set out, often in great detail, definitions of important terms such as "descendants" (the status of adoptees, particularly adult adoptees, is a recurring issue) or "by representation" or "education" and so forth.

14. General Provisions

There are a number of miscellaneous provisions included in most trusts. While they may appear to be of little consequence, they may be of great significance if the envisioned event does indeed arise.

a. *Merger.* While this might be permitted without such a clause with the approval of a court, this clause expressly permits the merger of a given trust with other trusts created by the same settlor, but only under certain circumstances.[93]
b. *Division.* As with merger, this could also be permitted by a court if not included in the trust agreement. However, this clause expressly permits the division of a trust into multiple trusts under certain circumstances.
c. *Situs Change.* This provides the steps that need to be taken to move the place of trust administration.
d. *Termination.* While this might also be permitted with the approval of a court, this clause expressly permits the termination of a trust under certain circumstances (e.g., if the trust assets become too small for efficient administration).
e. *Decanting.* A decanting provision permits the trustee, or perhaps a trust protector, to appoint, or otherwise transfer, all or a portion of the trust's property to a different (often newly formed) trust. This permits an extensive amendment (including, if desired, a change of trust situs) of the existing trust (see Chapter 13).[94]

92. *See, e.g.*, David R. Hodgman, *Drafting Flexible Irrevocable Trusts—Whom Do You Trust?*, 23 Est. Plan. 221 (1996) (example of trust protector language); Stewart E. Sterk, *Trust Protectors, Agency Costs, and Fiduciary Duty*, 27 Cardozo L. Rev. 2761 (2006).

93. Merger of trusts can raise income tax concerns. *See, e.g.*, Priv. Ltr. Rul. 2002-36-030 (Sept. 6, 2002) (the IRS ruled that a merger of trusts would not produce gain or loss to the trust or beneficiaries because the beneficiaries would hold the same income and remainder interests before and after the transaction).

94. *See, e.g.*, William R. Culp, Jr. & Briani Bennett Mellen, *Trust Decanting: An Overview and Introduction to Creative Planning Opportunities*, 45 Real Prop. Tr. & Est. L.J. 1 (2010); Thomas E. Simmons, *Decanting and Its Alternatives: Remodeling and Revamping Irrevocable Trusts*, 55 S.D. L. Rev. 253 (2010).

F. CASE STUDY 8-1

Paul and Linda Davis (Part III)

PROVIDING FOR THE GRANDCHILDREN'S HIGHER EDUCATION

We continue with Paul and Linda Davis from Case Studies 5-1 and 7-1. Their two children, John and Abigail, are now ages 7 and 4, respectively. Paul's niece and nephew, Jennifer and Thompson, are now ages 14 and 11, respectively. Paul's father, age 69, and Paul's mother, age 67, have a combined estate worth approximately $8.5 million. The Davis family tree from Case Study 5-1 is carried over to this case study. Paul's sister's husband is Davie L. Jones (per Case Study 5-1, the children bear the Davis surname).

While Paul's parents have been generous in funding family trips and making annual exclusion gifts to Paul and his sister, they have made no other significant gifts. Paul's father sees Paul and his sister as relatively comfortable; in his words, "both of you are well on your way." His current planning focus is on the grandchildren and their future needs, with particular concern for Paul's niece and nephew, one of whom is already a teenager.

Paul's parents have reviewed their assets and have concluded that significant gifts would not jeopardize their standard of living, which involves major expenditures for travel and recreation. They currently have no debts, and their principal assets are set forth below.

Asset	Adjusted Basis	Value
Personal residence	$500,000	$1,500,000
Vacation condominium	$300,000	$750,000
Publicly traded stocks	$300,000	$1,800,000
Municipal bonds	$500,000	$525,000
Treasury securities & money market funds	$700,000	$710,000
Rollover IRAs (from corporate pension plans)	$0	$2,500,000
Tanglewood Farms	$300,000	$800,000
Totals	$2,600,000	$8,585,000

Tanglewood Farms explains a lot about Paul's parents and their view that Paul and his sister should not rely on their parents' wealth. Paul's grandparents originally purchased Tanglewood Farms during the 1930s. Paul's grandparents were salaried people (his grandfather was a railroad foreman and his grandmother worked for the local utility company) who accumulated enough savings to purchase Tanglewood Farms in the depths of the Great Depression at a real estate tax lien sale. Paul's father lived a hardscrabble existence of long hours and hard work at Tanglewood Farms during his youth, which contributed to his burning resolve to achieve something better. Paul's father was an only child because his parents were concerned about being able to support their children. Paul's father attended a public university on an academic scholarship, majoring in marketing (marrying Paul's mother in his senior year) and joined the ranks of a Fortune 500 company as a salesman. He steadily ascended the corporate ladder and retired as the executive vice president of sales.

Paul's father is a proud man who loves his family, yet he has a controlling and "prickly" side as a product of his driven nature and background. Tanglewood Farms is dear to him (all but the family compound is leased for a cash rental), and it is his wish that it remain in the family. Moreover, retention of the property might prove a good long-term investment due to the advancing suburbs of a nearby city.

Part A: If Tanglewood Farms was purchased in the 1930s for unpaid taxes, how can its adjusted basis be $300,000?

Part B: Assume that Paul's parents are willing to make a gift of at least $200,000 immediately for the higher education of the grandchildren. Discuss the planning structure that you would suggest.

Part C: Assume that Paul's parents also plan to make a lifetime gift of Tanglewood Farms to their descendants. Discuss the wisdom of this plan and the planning structure that you would suggest.

Part D: Using Form L from the Forms Supplement as a starting point, draft a single irrevocable trust for Paul's parents that would both provide for the higher education of all of their grandchildren and create an accumulation vehicle for additional gifts that would provide for the discretionary support and welfare of future generations. Draft it in a fashion that would make maximum use of the *Crummey* doctrine. Unless your teacher gives other directions, assume that the state of formation follows the common law Rule Against Perpetuities. Assume that the trustee would be the American Trust Company, 1200 Albany Way, MyCity, MyState 80000.

G. Reference Materials

Treatises

- A. JAMES CASNER & JEFFREY N. PENNELL, ESTATE PLANNING §5.11 (6th ed. 1995 & Supp. 2009-2010) (grantor trust rules); §6.3.2 (kiddie tax); §6.3.3.5 (*Crown* loans); §7.1.1.2, 7.1.1.3 & 7.1.1.4 (*Crummey* power); §7.1.1.10 (qualified minors' trusts); §7.1.1.11 (exclusion for education and medical expenses); §11.4 (federal generation-skipping transfer tax).

- FREDERICK K. HOOPS ET AL., FAMILY ESTATE PLANNING GUIDE §8:21 (4th ed. 1994 & Supp. 2010-2011) (interest-free loans); §§9:2 to 9:4 (annual exclusion and transfers for minors); §9:8 (unlimited exclusion for educational or medical expenses); ch. 15, *The Generation-Skipping Transfer Tax*; §§16:28 & 16:29 (grantor trusts in general and planning opportunities).
- WILLIAM M. MCGOVERN ET AL., WILLS, TRUSTS AND ESTATES 688 (4th ed. 2010) (*Crummey* trusts); 390-391 (UGMA/UTMA); 687 (§2503(c) trusts).
- JOHN R. PRICE & SAMUEL A. DONALDSON, PRICE ON CONTEMPORARY ESTATE PLANNING §2.5.3 (2011) (*Crummey* trusts); §7.38 (*Crummey* trusts); §9.43 (GRATs and GRUTs); §§7.24 & 9.44 (QPRTs); §7.20 (below-market loans); §7.35 (UGMA/UTMA accounts); §§2.5.4 & 7.37 (§2503(c) trusts); §7.9.1 (kiddie tax).
- CHARLES E. ROUNDS, JR. & CHARLES E. ROUNDS, III, LORING AND ROUNDS: A TRUSTEE'S HANDBOOK §9.18 (2010 ed.) (*Crummey* trusts); §8.9.2 (generation-skipping transfer tax, generally); §8.2.1.10 (dynasty trusts); §8.23 (gifts to minors, generally); §9.1 (grantor trusts); §9.17 (§2503(c) trusts); §9.15 (QPRTs).
- RICHARD B. STEPHENS ET AL., FEDERAL ESTATE AND GIFT TAXATION: INCLUDING THE GENERATION-SKIPPING TRANSFER TAX ¶9.04(3)(f) (8th ed. 2002 & Supp. 2011) (*Crummey* powers); ¶10.01(2)(f) (below-market loans); ¶9.04(3)(g) (Coverdell Education Savings Accounts and section 529 plans); ¶9.04(6) (medical expenses and tuition); ¶10.01(3)(j) (section 529 plans); ¶13.01(2)(a) (transfers for educational and medical expenses); ¶¶9.04(4)-9.04(5) (§2503(c) trusts); pt. IV (generation-skipping transfers, generally).
- GEORGE M. TURNER, IRREVOCABLE TRUSTS §8:10 (3d ed. 1996 & Supp. 2010) (§2503(c) trusts); ch. 10 (*Crummey* trusts); ch. 11 (comparing *Crummey* trusts to statutory trust under 2503(b)); ch. 14 (overview of gift exclusions); ch. 16 (sprinkling or spray trusts); ch. 17 (accumulation trust); ch. 21 (generation-skipping trust); ch. 38 (section 529); ch. 41 (QPRTs).
- HAROLD WEINSTOCK & MARTIN NEUMANN, PLANNING AN ESTATE: A GUIDEBOOK OF PRINCIPLES AND TECHNIQUES §§8:36 to 8:37 (4th ed. 2002 & Supp. 2010) (*Crummey* trusts and minor's trusts); §§8:49 to 8:57 (section 529 plans); §8:58 (Coverdell Education Savings Account); §§9:2 to 9:5 (GRITs and QPRTs); §9:6 (GRATs); §§10:1 to 10:5 & §§10:33 to 10:39 (estate planning with life insurance).

Articles

Crummey Trusts and Annual Exclusion Giving

- Marc A. Chorney, *Transfer Tax Issues Raised by* Crummey *Powers*, 33 REAL PROP. PROB. & TR. J. 755 (1999).

- Ted Englebrecht et al., *Section 2038 Can Pull Lifetime Gifts Back into the Estate*, 71 PRAC. TAX STRATEGIES 331 (Dec. 2003).
- Jonathan E. Gopman & Marc H. List, *Impact of the Generation-Skipping Tax and Trusts Using* Crummey *Powers*, 26 EST. PLAN. 169 (1999).
- Sebastian V. Grassi, Jr., *Tax Aspects of* Crummey *Withdrawal Rights*, 18 NO. 1 PRAC. TAX LAW. 21 (Fall 2003).
- Nancy G. Henderson, *Maximizing the Benefits of the Gift Tax Annual Exclusion: How It Works and How It Doesn't*, Estate Planning in Depth, SR042 ALI-ABA 1101 (ALI-ABA Continuing Legal Education, June 13-18, 2010).
- Andrew M. Katzenstein & David P. Schwartz, *Tax Court Limits Annual Gift Tax Exclusion for Gratuitous Transfers of LLC Interests*, 96 J. TAX'N 290 (2002).
- Michael A. Kirtland, *Benefiting Grandchildren Through Lifetime and Testamentary Transfers*, 34 EST. PLAN. 30 (2007).
- Hannah W. Munch, *A "Gift" from the IRS: A Guide to the Gift Tax Annual Exclusion*, 33 EST. PLAN. 16 (2006).
- Laura H. Peebles, Crummey *Powers Can Increase Your Income Tax*, 145 TR. & EST. 35 (Nov. 2006).
- David Pratt & Elaine M. Bucher, *Updated Practical Planning with* Crummey *Powers*, 29 EST. PLAN. 73 (2002).
- John R. Price, Crummey v. Commissioner (1968) *Revisited; Opportunities and Pitfalls of Trust Withdrawal Powers*, 33 INST. ON EST. PLAN. ¶800 (1999).
- Stanley L. Ruby, *Inter Vivos Transfers—Gift Taxation*, Estate Planning 101: Practical Strategies for Estate and Gift Planning SS014 ALI-ABA 73 (ALI-ABA Continuing Legal Education, Oct. 27-29, 2010).
- Walter P. Schwidetzky, *Estate Planning: Hyperlexis and the Annual Exclusion Rule*, 32 SUFFOLK L. REV. 211 (1998).
- Constance D. Smith, *Retaining Control of Gifts to Minors: UTMA and IRC 2503(c) Trust Options*, 34 COLO. LAW. 39 (Nov. 2005).

Overall Wealth Transfer Tax Planning

- Myron Kove & James M. Kosakow, *Techniques That Maximize the Advantage of Lifetime Giving*, 25 EST. PLAN. 463 (1998).
- Michael D. Mulligan, *Formula Transfers: McCord Is Pro-Taxpayer, But Other Developments Are Likely*, 34 EST. PLAN. 3 (2007).
- Stanley L. Ruby, *Fundamentals of Estate Tax and Gift Tax*, Estate Planning 101: Practical Strategies for Estate and Gift Planning SS014 ALI-ABA 5 (ALI-ABA Continuing Legal Education, Oct. 27-29, 2010).

Section 529 Plans & Other Education Planning

- Susan T. Bart, *The Best of Both Worlds: Using a Trust to Make Your 529 Savings Account Rock*, 34 ACTEC J. 106 (2008).

- Susan T. Bart, *No Taxpayer Left Behind: Tax-Wise Techniques for Funding Education*, Planning Techniques for Large Estates, SS010 ALI-ABA 63 (ALI-ABA Continuing Legal Education, Nov. 15-19, 2010).
- Herb Braverman, *Estate Planning Opportunities with Section 529 Plans*, 17 OHIO PROB. L.J. 115 (Jan./Feb. 2007).
- Beverly R. Budin, *Section 529 Plans: What They Are and Who Should Use Them*, 35 INST. ON EST. PLAN. ¶800 (2001).
- Ellen D. Cook, *Navigating the Muddy Waters of College Financial Planning*, 69 PRAC. TAX STRATEGIES 286 (Nov. 2002).
- Chad C. Coombs & Boyd D. Hudson, *Section 529 Plans Offer Another Way to Save for College*, 25 L.A. LAW. 16 (Apr. 2002).
- Jim Hamilton, *Notice 2001-55 and the Rapid Growth of 529 Plans*, 45 RES GESTAE 29 (Apr. 2002).
- Rachel Riede James, *529 Plans: An Education Savings Alternative*, 30 COLO. LAW. 113 (July 2000).
- Cynthia Sharp Myers, *Tax Breaks for Education Savings*, 214 N.J. LAW. 23 (Apr. 2002).
- David M. Pfefferkorn, *The Investment of Custodial Funds in Section 529 Qualified Tuition Programs: Tax Advantages and Fiduciary Concerns*, 30 EST. PLAN. 571 (2003).
- Regina Rathnau, Note, *College Prep: What Every Consumer Should Know About Education Expenses and the Economic Growth & Tax Relief Act of 2001*, 14 LOY. CONSUMER L. REV. 57 (2001).
- savingforcollege.com, *Compare 529 Plans*, http://www.savingforcollege.com (last visited Aug. 20, 2011).
- savingforcollege.com, *The Internet Guide to Coverdell Education Savings Accounts* http://www.savingforcollege.com/coverdell_esas/ (last visited Aug. 20, 2011).
- Michael Schlesinger, *Qualified State Tuition Programs: More Favorable After 2001 Act*, 28 EST. PLAN. 412 (2001).
- Martin M. Shenkman, *Planning Opportunities to Help Families Fund a Child's Education*, 30 EST. PLAN. 24 (2003).
- Barbara A. Taylor & Joseph A. Cipparone, *New Tax Breaks Compete with Traditional Wealth-Transfer Strategies*, 68 PRAC. TAX STRATEGIES 141 (Mar. 2002) (comparisons to UTMA/UGMA accounts and *Crummey* trusts).

Family Trustees (*See also* "Selection of Fiduciaries" in Ch. 7 reference materials.)

- Steve R. Akers, *Selection of Trustees: A Detailed Review of Gift, Estate and Income Tax Effects and Non-tax Effects*, 38 INST. ON EST. PLAN. ¶300 (2004).
- Sheldon G. Gilman, *How and When to Use Trust Advisors Most Effectively*, 35 EST. PLAN. 30 (Feb. 2008).
- Sheldon G. Gilman, *Effective Use of Trust Advisors Can Avoid Trustee Problems*, 35 EST. PLAN. 18 (Mar. 2008).

- Kenneth W. Kingma, *A Beneficiary Serving as Trustee May Affect Asset Protection*, 38 Est. Plan. 22 (Apr. 2011).
- Laura H. Peebles, *Tax Aspects of Choice of Trustee*, 31 Est. Plan. 43 (2004).
- Renee M. Raithel, *Avoiding Tax Pitfalls and Family Conflicts When a Child Is Trustee*, 25 Est. Plan. 218 (1998).
- Kimbrough Street, *Growls or Gratitude? Practical Guidelines for Selection of Individual Trustees and Design of Trustee Succession Plans*, 40 Inst. on Est. Plan. ¶300 (2006).

Generation-Skipping Transfer Tax Planning (*See also* same heading in Ch. 11 and Ch. 13 reference materials.)

- Jonathan G. Blattmachr & Diana S.C. Zeydel, *Adventures in Allocating GST Exemption in Different Scenarios*, 35 Est. Plan. 3 (Apr. 2008).
- Jeffrey K. Eisen, *Planning to Minimize GSTT: Tools & Traps*, 27 Est. Plan. 73 (2000).
- Sebastian V. Grassi Jr., *Generation Skipping Transfer Tax Aspects of* Crummey *Powers After the 2001 Tax Act, Part 1*, 18 Prob. & Prop. 37 (Jan./Feb. 2004).
- Sebastian V. Grassi Jr., *Generation Skipping Transfer Tax Aspects of* Crummey *Powers After the 2001 Tax Act, Part 2*, 18 Prob. & Prop. 50 (Mar./Apr. 2004).
- Stephanie E. Heilborn, *The Complete Guide to Trust Severances for GST Tax Purposes*, 36 Est. Plan. 8 (June 2009).
- Julie K. Kwon, *Generation-Skipping Transfer Tax Planning and Update*, Estate Planning in Depth, SR042 ALI-ABA 1551 (ALI-ABA Continuing Legal Education, June 13-18, 2010).
- Robert L. Moshman, *Avoiding a GSTT Asteroid*, 13 Prob. & Prop. 24 (Mar./Apr. 1999).
- James R. Robinson, *When to Opt Out of the Automatic GST Exemption Allocation Provisions*, 31 Est. Plan. 287 (2004).
- R. Eric Viehman, *Current Issues in Generation-Skipping Tax Planning*, Planning Techniques for Large Estates, SS010 ALI-ABA 1 (ALI-ABA Continuing Legal Education, Nov. 15-19, 2010).

Life Insurance (*See also* "Irrevocable Life Insurance Trusts and Life Insurance" in Ch. 11 reference materials.)

- Jon J. Gallo, *The Use of Life Insurance in Estate Planning: A Guide to Planning and Drafting, Part II*, 34 Real Prop. Prob. & Tr. J. 55 (1999).
- James C. Magner, *What Is Life Insurance? The Evolution of Financial Products*, 35 Est. Plan. 24 (Apr. 2008).

Retained Interest Giving

- Dennis I. Belcher, *The Care and Feeding of GRATs: Enhancing GRAT Performance Through Careful Structuring, Investing and Monitoring*, 39 INST. ON EST. PLAN. ¶700 (2005).
- Jonathan G. Blattmachr et al., *Drafting and Administration To Maximize GRAT Performance*, 20 PROB. & PROP. 16 (Nov./Dec. 2006).
- Daniel L. Daniels & Michael N. Delgass, *Design GRATs to Reap Court-Approved Extra Tax Savings*, 71 PRAC. TAX STRATEGIES 324 (Dec. 2003).
- Samuel A. Donaldson, *Understanding Grantor Trusts*, 40 INST. ON EST. PLAN. ¶200 (2006).
- Denver S. Gilliand, *Fractional Interests Make a Better QPRT*, 32 REAL PROP. PROB. & TR. J. 145 (1997).
- T. Randolph Harris, *GRIT's, GRAT's & Grantor Trusts: Be Graciously Greedy While the Grass Is Green, Before It Gradually Grows Grisly & Grim*, 29 INST. ON EST. PLAN. ¶900 (1995).
- Lawrence P. Katzenstein, *Running the Numbers: An Economic Analysis of GRATs and QPRTs*, 32 INST. ON EST. PLAN. ¶1400 (1998).
- Lawrence P. Katzenstein, *Regs. Clarify Estate Tax Inclusion of Trust Property, But Issues Remain*, 36 EST. PLAN. 3 (June 2009).
- Grayson M.P. McCouch, *Rethinking Section 2702*, 2 FLA. TAX REV. 99 (1994).
- Peter J. Melcher, *Are Short-Term GRATs Really Better Than Long-Term GRATs?*, 36 EST. PLAN. 23 (Mar. 2009).
- Robert T. Napier, *GRAT Expectations*, 149 TR. & EST. 18 (Sept. 2010).
- William Scanlan, Jr., *GRITs, GRATs & GRUTs: A Phoenix Rises from the Ashes of Section 2036(c)*, 27 INST. ON EST. PLAN. ¶1400 (1993).
- David L. Weinreb & Gregory D. Singer, *An Analysis of GRAT "Immunization"*, 34 ACTEC J. 200 (2008).

Trust Distribution Schemes (*See also* "Dynasty Trusts" and "The Drafting of Trusts" in Ch. 13 reference materials.)

- Ronald D. Aucutt, *Structuring Trust Arrangements for Flexibility*, 35 INST. ON EST. PLAN. ¶900 (2001).
- Alexander A. Bove, Jr., *The Letter of Wishes: Can We Influence Discretion in Discretionary Trusts?*, 35 ACTEC J. 38 (2009).
- Christopher P. Cline, *Drafting and Administering Discretionary Trusts: Can Beneficiary Happiness and Trusts Coexist?*, 16 ALI-ABA EST. PLAN. COURSE MATERIALS J. 49 (Oct. 2010).

- Quentin G. Heisler, Jr. & William J. Butler, *Discretionary Distributions*, Ill. Inst. Continuing Legal Educ. Handbook §5.26 (1999) (examples of spray trust language).
- Jerold I. Horn, *Prudent Investor Rule, Modern Portfolio Theory and Private Trusts: Drafting and Administration Including the "Give-Me-Five" Unitrust*, 33 REAL PROP. PROB. & TR. J. 1, 36-37, 40-41 (1998) (examples of unitrust distribution clauses).
- Richard M. Horwood & Jeffrey A. Zaluda, *A Trustee's Balancing Act: Income and Remainder Beneficiaries' Rights*, 30 EST. PLAN. 12 (2003).
- Seth W. Krasilovsky, *Exercising Discretion in Administering Discretionary Trusts*, 36 EST. PLAN. 32 (June 2009).
- Mark Merric, *How to Draft Discretionary Dynasty Trusts—Part 1*, 36 EST. PLAN. 3 (Feb. 2009).
- Mark Merric, *How to Draft Distribution Standards for Discretionary Dynasty Trusts*, 36 EST. PLAN. 3 (Mar. 2009).
- Mark Merric, *How to Draft Discretionary Dynasty Trusts—Part 3*, 36 EST. PLAN. 13 (Apr. 2009).
- Peter B. Tiernan, *Drafting Trusts That Include Broad Invasion Powers*, 77 FLA. B.J. 74 (Nov. 2003).
- Peter B. Tiernan, *Issues to Consider When Drafting Pure Discretionary Trusts*, 80 TAX STRAT. 281 (May 2008).
- Anthony F. Vitiello & Daniel B. Kessler, *The Fully Discretionary Ascertainable Standard*, 149 TR. & EST. 21 (Mar. 2010).
- Carol Warnick et al., *Discretionary Distribution Standards: Full Speed Ahead*, 39 COLO. LAW. 53 (Mar. 2010).
- Adam J. Wiensch & L. Elizabeth Beetz, *The Liberation of Total Return*, TR. & EST. 44 (Apr. 2004).
- Robert B. Wolf & Stephan R. Leimberg, *Total Return Trusts Approved by New Regs, But State Law Is Crucial*, 31 EST. PLAN. 179 (2004).

Trust Protectors and Incentive Clauses

- Richard C. Ausness, *The Role of Trust Protectors in American Trust Law*, 45 REAL PROP. TR. & EST. L.J. 319 (2010).
- Judy Barber, *The Psychology of Conditional Giving: What's the Motivation?*, 21 PROB. & PROP. 57 (Nov./Dec. 2007).
- Nancy G. Henderson, *Managing the Benefits and Burdens of New Wealth with Incentive Trusts (Part 2) (With Sample Provisions)*, 47 No. 7 PRAC. LAW. 11 (Oct. 2001).
- David R. Hodgman, *Drafting Flexible Irrevocable Trusts—Whom Do You Trust?*, 23 EST. PLAN. 221 (1996) (sample protector language).

- David R. Hodgman & Debra L. Stetter, *Can Incentive Trusts Encourage Children to Behave Responsibly?*, 27 EST. PLAN. 459 (2000).
- John H. Lahey, *International and Offshore Trusts: Resolving Conflicting Beneficiary and Fiduciary Interests*, Representing Estate and Trust Beneficiaries and Fiduciaries, SE87 ALI-ABA 277, 280-281 (ALI-ABA Continuing Legal Education, June 29, 2000) (discussing the powers of the protector).
- Howard M. McCue III, *Planning and Drafting to Influence Behavior*, 34 INST. ON EST. PLAN. ¶600 (2000).
- Anne-Marie Rhodes, *Consequences of Heirs' Misconduct: Moving From Rules to Discretion*, 33 OHIO N.U. L. REV. 975 (2007).
- Philip J. Ruce, *The Trustee and the Trust Protector: A Question of Fiduciary Power: Should a Trust Protector Be Held to a Fiduciary Standard?*, 59 DRAKE L. REV. 67 (2010).
- John J. Scroggin, *Protecting and Preserving the Family: The True Goal of Estate Planning, Part II—Some of the Tools*, 16 PROB. & PROP. 34, 40 (July/Aug. 2002) (examples of incentive clause language).
- Stewart E. Sterk, *Trust Protectors, Agency Costs, and Fiduciary Duty*, 27 CARDOZO L. REV. 2761 (2006).
- Joshua C. Tate, *Conditional Love: Incentive Trusts and the Inflexibility Problem*, 41 REAL PROP. PROB. & TR. J. 445 (2006).
- Ellen Evans Whiting, *Controlling Behavior by Controlling the Inheritance: Considerations in Drafting Incentive Provisions*, 15 PROB. & PROP. 6 (Sept./Oct. 2001).

CHAPTER 9

Remarriage (with Children)

A. Common Scenarios

At the risk of making a broad generalization, there are at least three distinct remarriage (with children) situations. First, one or both spouses may have young children from prior marriages, and there remains some likelihood that additional children will be produced from the new union. This couple may consider all of the children on an equal footing for all purposes, including inheritance. Second, one or both spouses may have teenaged or older children, and it is unlikely that additional children will be produced from the new union. This couple may view the higher education of the children as a primary objective, and they will share those costs. While inheritance issues are of secondary importance, there may be a preference by each spouse for his or her respective children. Third, one or both spouses may have emancipated adult children. The support of the surviving spouse will be the couple's primary estate planning objective in this situation, but preserving the inheritance of their respective children will be an important consideration.

B. Pitfalls of the Unplanned Estate

In advising one or both of the spouses, the attorney needs to be extremely mindful of the ethical issues presented by a joint representation. Because of the likely presence of competing sets of heirs and devisees, the conflicts are often much more pronounced. Estate planners commonly encounter spouses who are characterized by significant differences in age, wealth, or status. While separate representation of each spouse is the safest route, it is often more costly, more complicated, and less confidential. In our experience, very few clients prefer separate representation. However, this is not solely the clients' decision, and the attorney, applying his or her broader experience with such matters, must be satisfied that he or she can adequately represent both of the parties. As discussed in Chapter 1, a candid discussion of possible problems and the informed execution of a joint representation agreement are two basic steps in creating such an engagement. However, as discussed in Chapter 4, if the clients' situation calls for the execution of a marital agreement, joint representation of both spouses may not be possible.

The attorney needs to be fully aware of the default rules that apply to these remarriage situations in the absence of planning.

1. Intestate Succession

If either spouse passes away intestate, under many intestate succession statutes, the surviving spouse will not receive all of the decedent's property. The Uniform Probate Code (UPC), for example, gives the surviving spouse the first $150,000 (adjusted for inflation) of the estate plus one half of any balance of the probate estate if one or more of the decedent's surviving descendants are not descendants of the surviving spouse.[1] This would probably be a particularly undesired consequence of the first scenario in Part A above. This result can be altered by the execution of Wills.

2. Elective Share

In a common law property state, the surviving spouse may be entitled to demand a portion of the decedent's estate. The UPC, for example, entitles the survivor to as much as 50 percent of the decedent's augmented estate, depending upon the length of the marriage.[2] The amount of the elective portion in non-UPC states may not depend on the length of marriage, thus permitting a surviving spouse of a three-month marriage the same amount as a surviving spouse of a twenty-five-year marriage. Again, this would probably be an undesirable and unintended consequence in the second and third scenarios in Part A. This result may be altered by the execution of a marital agreement (discussed in Chapter 4).

1. *See* UPC §2-102(4). The dollar amounts in UPC §2-102 are subject to increase or decrease for changes in the Consumer Price Index. *See* UPC §1-109.

2. *See* UPC §2-202.

3. Omitted Spouse

Where a Will exists that was executed before the marriage, statutes often provide a share of the probate estate not otherwise devised to the descendants of the testator for the new spouse even if he or she was not mentioned in the Will.[3]

4. Property Division and Maintenance on Dissolution of Marriage

In a common law property state, a divorcing spouse is usually entitled to a share of the marital property. However, marital property may also include the appreciation during the marriage in assets acquired prior to the marriage.[4] In a handful of states, assets acquired prior to marriage and gifts and inheritances may be subject to division upon dissolution of marriage,[5] a particularly unintended consequence in all three of the scenarios in Part A. Furthermore, a divorcing spouse may be entitled to spousal maintenance, support, or alimony, which also could be a particularly unintended consequence in the second and third scenarios in Part A. Both results may be altered through the use of a marital agreement.

In a community property state, most of the premarital property will remain the separate property of each spouse. However, the couple may wish to address the treatment of community property acquired during their marriage, as well as the issues of spousal maintenance upon dissolution of the marriage.

5. "I Love You" Wills

The decedent may give all or the bulk of his or her property outright to the survivor, perhaps with some modest bequests to the children, with the expectation that the survivor will divide the proceeds equally among all of the children upon his or her subsequent death. This expectation is often reflected in the contingent bequests of the couple's Wills (e.g., "... and if my spouse does not survive me, then to ..."). However, in the absence of proof of a Will contract or an enforceable marital agreement, this expectation may not be implemented because the survivor is free to amend his or her Will to the possible detriment of the decedent's children. The UPC, for example, requires written evidence of such a contract, and the execution of joint or mutual Wills does not create a presumption of a contract not to revoke the Will or Wills.[6] This result can be altered through the use

3. *See, e.g.*, UPC §2-301.
4. These principles are discussed in detail in Chapter 4.
5. *Id.*
6. *See* UPC §2-514. In spite of the statute's negation of a presumption of a contract, it is desirable to insert a clause in the Will that expressly rejects the existence of any contract.

of a Will contract, a more uncertain measure that we generally do not recommend,[7] or through the use of the so-called "QTIP trust" discussed below.

6. Guardianship and Custody of Stepchildren

If one of the legal parents of minor children passes away, the surviving legal parent may insist on sole custody of the children, particularly if the prior arrangement was shared custody. The decedent's wish, as expressed in his or her Will, that a stepparent serve as guardian and conservator of the children in question will generally not control against the desires of a surviving legal parent. While older children may often have a voice in this decision, the desires of the surviving legal parent usually dictate the custody of younger children. This result is tempered in some states, where stepparents are allowed to participate in proceedings for the allocation of parental responsibilities.[8]

C. Planning Measures

There are traditional planning measures that may be used to address most of the concerns identified above. Before implementing any of the measures, the attorney must be conversant with the legal details of the spouses' current situations. For example, existing documents from prior marriages, such as property division agreements and child support orders, may contain legal obligations of one spouse or the other that continue after the death of that spouse as claims against the decedent's estate. In addition, existing Wills, trusts, and nonprobate transfers, such as life insurance and retirement funds, and financial account beneficiary designations must be carefully examined.

1. Remaining Unmarried: Cohabitation

For couples in the third scenario described in Part A, a choice might be not to legally marry. The claims of a survivor or a parting partner would be limited to a contractual claim of "palimony" (discussed in Chapter 6) or

7. "Most commentators think they are a bad idea." WILLIAM M. MCGOVERN ET AL., WILLS, TRUSTS AND ESTATES 252 (4th ed. 2010). *But see* David R. Hodgman, *Using a Contract to Make a Will to Protect Children's Inheritance*, 36 EST. PLAN. 3 (Sept. 2009). Even if a Will contract is implemented, there is a split of authority as to whether the elective share claims of a subsequent surviving spouse will be subordinated to the claims of the Will contract beneficiaries. *See, e.g.*, Via v. Putnam, 656 So. 2d 460 (Fla. 1995) (holding that a "new" surviving spouse's claims prevail). A Will contract may also produce adverse wealth transfer tax consequences in terms of the estate tax marital deduction. *See generally* Amy Morris Hess, *The Federal Transfer Tax Consequences of Joint and Mutual Wills*, 24 REAL PROP. PROB. & TRUST J. 469 (1990).

8. *See, e.g.*, COLO. REV. STAT. §14-10-123(1)(c) (2010) (a person other than a parent who has had the physical care of a child for a period of six months or more may commence such proceedings).

the possible existence of a common law marriage. In this event, the couple should be encouraged to execute a cohabitation agreement (discussed in Chapter 6) outlining the details and financial consequences of their living arrangement to defeat unfounded subsequent claims of palimony, common law marriage where applicable, or a Will contract.

2. Marital Agreements

The marital agreement is discussed in Chapter 4, so we will only summarize that discussion. Briefly, a marital agreement may alter the default rules as to division of property and the award of maintenance upon dissolution of marriage, whether in a common law or community property state. It may also alter the limitations imposed by marriage, such as the elective share, on the testamentary transfer of property. Marital agreements satisfy two general estate planning goals: (a) fixing the financial obligations of each spouse during marriage and in the event of dissolution of marriage; and (b) permitting each spouse to transfer his or her own assets at death as he or she desires.

3. Lifetime Gifts

If either spouse has emancipated adult children not of their current marriage, many of the concerns of those children may be allayed through lifetime measures such as outright gifts of property and tailored life insurance beneficiary designations[9] to and for the benefit of those children. If there is not enough property to implement outright lifetime gifts, a life estate in selected property can be conveyed to the new spouse, with a remainder to the transferor's children.[10] A typical candidate for this treatment in modest estates would be the marital home. That said, a life estate created by deed may raise a number of issues, such as the operation of the IRC §121 exclusion on any gain from the sale of a personal residence. Other issues are, for example, how sales, replacements, and improvements of the residence are accommodated, and possible waste by the life tenant. These issues have the potential to create an adversarial relationship between the stepchildren remainderpersons and the surviving spouse. Moreover, any such transfers should be approved in writing by the non-donor spouse, so that the elective share does not apply to such property.[11]

9. Outright lifetime gifts to nonspousal donees may be taxable gifts for federal (and possibly state) wealth transfer taxation purposes, if the gift exceeds the donor's annual gift tax exclusion amount. Such gifts will require the filing of a gift tax return and the payment of gift and possibly generation-skipping transfer taxes. See Chapter 8. If the donor parent is subject to potential federal wealth transfer taxation, he or she could create an irrevocable life insurance trust to which existing policies could be transferred or in which new policies could be acquired. Such trusts are discussed in Chapter 11.

10. Although this discussion assumes a modest estate, federal wealth transfer taxation considerations do complicate matters, as the transfer of the property will create a potentially taxable gift. *Id.* A lifetime qualified terminable interest property election could, however, eliminate the gift. *See* IRC §2523(f) and the discussion in Section C.4 below.

11. *See, e.g.*, UPC §2-208(a).

While this piecemeal planning may be effective for some estates, it is dangerous if not pursued under the umbrella of an existing marital agreement, inasmuch as it leaves the deceased spouse's other property subject to spousal claims.

4. The QTIP Trust

The care of the surviving spouse is typically the desire of all married couples, including the three couples in the scenarios in Part A. A classic measure to accomplish that result, while preserving the inheritance of the first-to-die's children,[12] would be the creation of a trust interest for the benefit of the surviving spouse, perhaps with limited powers to invade principal, with the remainder passing to persons designated by the decedent.

Property given *outright* to the surviving spouse qualifies for the federal estate tax marital deduction and will not be subject to estate taxation on the death of the transferor spouse. (Chapter 16 discusses the federal wealth transfer taxes.) However, property placed in trust for the benefit of a surviving spouse may also qualify for the federal estate tax marital deduction if certain requirements are satisfied. In dealing with remarriage planning, the "qualified terminable interest property" (hence the "QTIP" acronym) structure described in IRC §2056(b)(7) is often recommended.

Essentially, the QTIP requirements are that: (a) the surviving spouse is entitled to all the income from the property held in trust,[13] payable annually or at more frequent intervals (under the regulations, the use of a personal residence qualifies under this standard); (b) an election of this treatment must be made by the estate of the decedent; and (c) no person, including the surviving spouse, may have a power to appoint any part of the property to any person other than the surviving spouse during the surviving spouse's lifetime. While only "income" is *required* to be distributed, that could prove to be insufficient for the financial needs of the surviving spouse,[14] and thus the trust instrument often provides for supplemental distributions of principal to the surviving spouse pursuant to a designated standard. Of course, it must be kept in mind that this could

12. Balancing the needs of the surviving spouse with the needs of the decedent's children is difficult enough under the three scenarios described in Part A. However, there is another remarriage scenario: Consider young spouses in a first marriage, with children only of that union. There is a great probability that if one spouse passes away, the survivor may remarry. If that occurs, there will be stepchildren of the surviving spouse, there may be stepchildren of the new spouse, and there may be half-siblings produced by the new union. Although this may be difficult to discuss with a young couple, if there are significant separate assets involved (e.g., from inherited wealth), the wealthy spouse's concerns and planning may resemble that for the couples in the third scenario in Part A. The estate plan may require a combination of tools such as a marital agreement, irrevocable trusts for descendants, and a QTIP trust for the surviving spouse.

13. The QTIP may also apply to life estates created by deed, but such a plan may be messy in terms of delineating the rights of the life tenant versus the remainderpersons. A trust generally is a better solution. For a critical comparison of life estates created by deed (legal life estates) with trusts see DUKEMINIER ET AL., WILLS, TRUSTS, AND ESTATES 554-555 (8th ed. 2009).

14. This is particularly true if prevailing interest rates are quite low.

invite the dissipation of the trust funds. If this is a great concern, invasion of the trust principal by the surviving spouse could be expressly prohibited or subject to the discretion of an independent or adverse cotrustee.

QTIP planning is a fixture of estates with federal wealth transfer tax consequences. However, the same concept may be used in estates that do not have such tax concerns. While the QTIP is typically encountered in the context of a testamentary trust, the attorney should not overlook the lifetime QTIP trust. IRC §2523 permits the lifetime creation of a QTIP interest for the benefit of a spouse with no immediate federal gift tax consequences. This can be an attractive tool for clients who wish to implement planning measures while they are living, particularly so they can observe how the arrangements operate. Absent a Will contract or marital agreement, this also can provide the QTIP beneficiary spouse with some security. Of course, all of this assumes that the client owns assets that he or she is willing and able to part with during his or her lifetime.[15] The testamentary or lifetime QTIP is not, however, a complete solution, because by itself it does not address the dissolution of marriage or elective share concerns that could upset the structure. Moreover, unlike a Will contract, it does not promise reciprocal treatment.[16] A marital agreement consequently remains an important part of the planning solution.

The identity of the trustee of the QTIP trust is a common issue. Most clients want their surviving spouse to be the trustee. However, if the surviving spouse and the decedent's children (stepchildren of the surviving spouse) do not get along or there is the potential for such ill will, perhaps a better choice for trustee is a neutral third party who is not aligned with either faction. As noted above, this is particularly true if the QTIP trust permits the invasion of principal in the exercise of the trustee's discretion.

Here is an example of language from a QTIP trust that provides only for the distribution of income to the surviving spouse:

> *My trustee shall pay to or apply for the sole benefit of my spouse, at least annually, all income from the Marital Trust from the date of my death. My trustee shall have no authority to invade the trust principal for any purpose during the life of my spouse.*

15. To qualify for QTIP wealth transfer taxation treatment the spousal beneficiary designation must be irrevocable.

16. Reciprocal treatment is primarily a concern if both spouses have significant assets that will be ultimately devoted to a group of beneficiaries comprised of both stepchildren and children. A single joint trust that becomes irrevocable upon the death of the first spouse is a possible solution to the lack of assured reciprocal treatment, at least for assets held in the trust. However, federal (and possibly state) wealth transfer tax and income tax consequences to both spouses must be considered in the structure of the trust. *See generally* BNA Estates, Gifts and Trusts Portfolios: Trusts, Howard M. Zaritsky, Portfolio 860-1st: Revocable Inter Vivos Trusts §VI.C. *Special Tax Problems of Joint Revocable Trusts* (2011); Bette Heller et al., *Joint Revocable Trusts*, 26 Colo. Law. 63 (Aug. 1997); John H. Martin, *The Joint Trust: Estate Planning in a New Environment*, 39 Real Prop. Prob. & Tr. J. 275 (2004); Beth A. Turner, *Joint Revocable Trusts*, 19 Prob. & Prop. 49 (July/Aug. 2005).

EXERCISE 9-1

DRAFTING INVASION OF PRINCIPAL POWERS

Assume that the client is concerned that his or her spouse might be unable to live comfortably on just the income from the QTIP trust provision set out above. Draft language that would permit invasion of the trust corpus for the survivor's needs in this event.

EXERCISE 9-2

THE QTIP'S UNFAIRNESS

Some commentators have asserted that a QTIP trust is fundamentally unfair to female surviving spouses (*see* the articles collected in Part E below). If this is so, may an attorney ever fairly represent both spouses if a testamentary QTIP trust is to be implemented?

D. CASE STUDY 9-1

John Roberts and Alice Turley

THE SECOND MARRIAGE

John Roberts (age 59) and Alice Turley (age 57) are to be married. This will be the second marriage for each of them. John has two adult children, and Alice has one adult child. John and Alice have been residing in a home owned by John worth approximately $200,000. They plan to purchase a new home after they are married, to be titled in joint tenancy. Each will contribute equally to the purchase price of $300,000 from other funds, and it will not be subject to a mortgage. John plans to gift the current home to his adult children, outright, prior to his marriage to Alice.

Part A: Evaluate John's plan to gift the current home to his children in light of the elective share under the UPC.

Part B: Evaluate the federal tax consequences of John's plan to gift the current home to his children.

Part C: Assuming they live in a common law property state, evaluate John and Alice's plan for ownership of the new home.

Part D: Assuming they live in a community property state, evaluate their plan for ownership of the new home.

Part E: Assume that there is instead a mortgage on their new home in the principal amount of $100,000, and both John and Alice are liable as co-mortgagors. Assume further that the new home is titled in tenancy in common, not in joint tenancy. What consequences follow from that development? Should John anticipate this? What alternatives might he consider?

Part F: Assume further that John and Alice each have significant amounts invested in traditional and Roth IRAs and employer 401(k) plans. They plan to designate one another as the primary beneficiary, with John's children as the secondary beneficiaries of his accounts and with Alice's child as the secondary beneficiary of her accounts. Assuming they live in a common law property state, evaluate their plan for the ownership of the retirement accounts.

E. Reference Materials

Treatises

General Planning for Remarriage

- Frederick K. Hoops et al., Family Estate Planning Guide §§33:13 to 33:16 (4th ed. 1994 & Supp. 2010-2011) (mixed child households); §33.17 (second marriages for the elderly).

Cohabitation (*See also* "Unmarried Households" in Ch. 6 reference materials.)

- Hoops et al., *supra*, §33:18 (elderly companionships).

Marital Agreements (*See also* same heading in Ch. 4 reference materials.)

- William M. McGovern et al., Wills, Trusts and Estates §3.9 (4th ed. 2010).
- Laura W. Morgan & Brett R. Turner, Attacking and Defending Marital Agreements (2001).

QTIP Trusts

- A. James Casner & Jeffrey N. Pennell, Estate Planning §§13.5.6 & 13.6.1.1 (6th ed. 1995 & Supp. 2009-2010) (QTIP trusts).
- Hoops et al., *supra*, §§13:31 & 13:32 (QTIP trusts).
- Charles E. Rounds, Jr. & Charles E. Rounds, III, Loring and Rounds: A Trustee's Handbook §8.9.1.3 (2010) (marital deduction and QTIP).
- George M. Turner, Revocable Trusts ch. 27, *Qualified Terminal Interest Property Trust (QTIP Trust)* (5th ed. 2003 & Supp. 2010).
- Harold Weinstock & Martin Neumann, Planning an Estate: A Guidebook of Principles and Techniques §§4:20 to 4:24 (4th ed. 2002 & Supp. 2010).

Articles

General Planning for Remarriage

- Richard E. Barnes, *Till Death Do Us Part (Again) — Estate Planning for Second Marriages*, 21 Prob. & Prop. 34 (Mar./Apr. 2007).
- Charles Cahn II, *Estate Planning to Avoid Complications of Remarriage*, 19 Est. Plan. 268 (1992).
- Leon Fieldman & Mary D. Fieldman, *Estate Planning for the Second Marriage*, 74 Ill. B.J. 92, 95 (Oct. 1985).
- Randall J. Gingiss, *Second Marriage Considerations for the Elderly*, 45 S.D. L. Rev. 469 (2000).
- Joseph Gorman, Jr., *Estate Planning During Divorce and Remarriage*, 18 Inst. on Est. Plan. ¶¶400, 403 (1984).
- Andrew H. Hook & Thomas D. Begley, Jr., *Estate Planning for Blended Families*, 33 Est. Plan. 47 (2006).
- Eric A. Manterfield, *Marital Planning While the Rules Are Changing*, 40 Inst. on Est. Plan. ¶700 (2006).
- Dan C. Peare & Hugh W. Gill, *Estate Planning for the Second Marriage (or Third . . . or Fourth)*, 24 J. Tax'n Inv. 300 (2007).
- Carol A. Rhees, *How to Plan for a Divorced Client Who Is Preparing to Remarry*, 14 Est. Plan. 168 (1987).
- Nancy Boxley Tepper, *Estate Planning for Second Marriages*, 120 Tr. & Est. 16 (Sept. 1981).
- Jeffrey A. Zaluda, *Estate Planning with Respect to Divorce*, 22 Est. Plan. 352 (1995).

Marital Agreements (*See also* same heading in Ch. 4 reference materials.)

- Dennis I. Belcher & Laura O. Pomeroy, *A Practitioner's Guide for Negotiating, Drafting and Enforcing Premarital Agreements*, 37 Real Prop. Prob. & Tr. J. 1 (2002).
- Virginia F. Coleman, *Selected Issues in Planning for the Second Marriage*, Planning Techniques for Large Estates, SR016 ALI-ABA 151 (ALI-ABA Continuing Legal Education, Nov. 16-20, 2009).
- P. Andre Katz & Amanda Clayman, *When Your Elderly Clients Marry: Prenuptial Agreements and Other Considerations*, 16 J. Am. Acad. Matrim. Law. 445 (2000).
- Harry S. Margolis, *Prenuptial Agreements for Older Clients*, 10 Elder L. Rep. 10 (May 1997).
- Judith E. Siegel-Baum & Joshua W. Averill, *Postnuptial Agreements Can Resolve Personal and Estate Planning Issues*, 29 Est. Plan. 405 (2002).

Cohabitation (*See also* "Unmarried Households" in Ch. 6 reference materials.)

- Frank S. Berall, *Tax Consequences of Unmarried Cohabitation*, 18 No. 2 Prac. Tax Law. 55 (Winter 2004).

- Dianne S. Burden, *Remarriage vs. Cohabitation*, 16 FAM. ADVOC. 31 (1993).

Stepchildren

- Kim A. Feigenbaum, Note, *The Changing Family Structure: Challenging Stepchildren's Lack of Inheritance Rights*, 66 BROOK. L. REV. 167 (2000).
- Thomas M. Hanson, Note, *Intestate Succession for Stepchildren: California Leads the Way, But Has It Gone Far Enough?*, 47 HASTINGS L.J. 257 (1995).
- Cathy J. Jones, *Stepparent Adoption and Inheritance, a Suggested Review of the UPC §2-114*, 8 W. NEW ENG. L. REV. 33 (1993).
- Margaret M. Mahoney, *Stepparents as Third Parties in Relation to Their Stepchildren*, 40 FAM. L.Q. 81 (2006).
- Jean A. Martland, *Intent as to Stepchildren, Remarriage Construed*, 11 EST. PLAN. 121 (1984).
- Andrew L. Noble, Note, *Intestate Succession for Stepchildren in Pennsylvania: A Proposal for Reform*, 64 U. PITT. L. REV. 835 (2003).

QTIP Trusts

- Vicki L. Anderson, *How to QTIP an IRA: New Rules*, 50 RES GESTAE 28 (2006).
- Jeffrey A. Baskies & Brian J. Samuels, *The Marital Unitrust: A New Planning Strategy for the Remarried Spouse*, 27 EST. PLAN. 480 (2000).
- David A. Berek, *Taxes, Marital QTIP Trusts, and Anti-Apportionment Clauses*, 93 ILL. B.J. 418 (Aug. 2005).
- Marc A. Chorney, *Using QTIP Trusts in Conjunction with Marital Agreements*, 28 COLO. LAW. 85 (Oct. 1999).
- Joseph M. Dodge, *A Feminist Perspective on the QTIP Trust and the Unlimited Marital Deduction*, 76 N.C. L. REV. 1729 (1998).
- Mary Louise Fellows, *Wills and Trusts: "The Kingdom of the Fathers,"* 10 LAW & INEQ. J. 137, 156-159 (1991).
- Wendy C. Gerzog, *The Marital Deduction QTIP Provisions: Illogical and Degrading to Women*, 5 UCLA WOMEN'S L.J. 301 (1995).
- Wendy C. Gerzog, *The Illogical and Sexist QTIP Provisions: I Just Can't Say It Ain't So*, 76 N.C. L. REV. 1597 (1998).
- Wendy C. Gerzog, *Solution to the Sexist QTIP Provisions*, 35 REAL PROP. PROB. & TR. J. 97 (2000).
- James F. Gulecas, *Drafting the Lifetime QTIP Trust (with Sample Provisions)*, 13 No. 3 PRAC. TAX LAW. 13 (Spring 1999).
- Christopher R. Hoyt, *Funding Bypass and QTIP Trusts in the Crossfire of Conflicting Estate Tax, Income Tax and ERISA Laws*, 39 INST. ON EST. PLAN. ¶400 (2005).
- Dana R. Irwin, *Removing the Scaffolding: The QTIP Provisions and the Ownership Fiction*, 84 NEB. L. REV. 571 (2005).
- Lawrence Zelenak, *Taking Critical Tax Theory Seriously*, 76 N.C. L. REV. 1521 (1998).

CHAPTER 10 Migratory Married Couples

A. State Law Considerations

1. Domicile

As a general rule the laws of a decedent's place of domicile govern the disposition of his or her estate. A notable exception is the disposition of real estate, which is governed by the laws of the state where the real property is located. The determination of the place of domicile is principally a function of physical residence at the place of a claimed domicile and the intent of the decedent to make a particular locale his or her domicile. A decedent's intent in this matter is determined through a weighing of many factors, such as the place of voter registration, the state that issues the decedent's driver's license and automobile registration, the filing of resident state income tax returns, the ownership of a residence, and so forth.[1]

A person has only one legal domicile, but can simultaneously have many residences. As a result, the issue of domicile may be murky in a number of situations. For example, some individuals maintain personal residences in several states or countries, sometimes referring to a residence as "my winter home" or "my summer home." Other individuals, particularly those employed in construction activities, may maintain a string of residences, each of which they would consider to be temporary. Finally, with elderly individuals, there can be a transition period during which they

1. *See generally* Ronald S. Kochman, *Moving Is a Family Decision*, 127 Tr. & Est. 522 (May 1988).

gradually move from their longtime residence to a new retirement location or to living arrangements closer to family.

From a planning perspective one would generally not alter these activities solely to preserve a particular state of domicile for estate planning purposes, although there might be other driving factors, such as state and local tax burdens, climate, medical services, and recreation opportunities. In this situation the planner needs to be aware of the potential consequences of the moves, and the concomitant need for alterations of the estate plan, such as the drafting of a new Will or powers of attorney. If preserving the application of the laws of a particular state is important to the plan, the planner might consider the use of a revocable trust as a Will substitute. (See Chapter 15.) Generally, the laws of the state of administration of a trust govern rather than the laws of the settlor's domicile, so some affirmative selection of applicable law can usually be achieved.

2. Wills

As noted above, the laws of the state of domicile at death generally apply. However, the decedent's Will may have been executed under the different laws of another state. For example, the other state may require more or fewer witnesses,[2] recognize interested witnesses, or recognize holographic Wills. However, statutes such as Uniform Probate Code (UPC) §2-506, and courts even in the absence of such a statute, may still deem a Will valid if it is shown to have been executed in compliance with the then applicable law of the place of execution.[3]

Beyond Will execution requirements, the degree of spousal protections (e.g., the elective share) may also differ dramatically from state to state.[4] For example, a statute drafted along the lines of the pre-1990 UPC would give the surviving spouse a one-third share of the augmented estate irrespective of the duration of the marriage, while the revised UPC would give the surviving spouse an increasing 1.5 percent to 50 percent share based on marriage durations of from one to fifteen years.[5]

2. Vermont law until recently required three witnesses; however, like many other states, it now requires two. *See* VT. STAT. ANN. tit. 14 §5 (2010).

3. UPC §2-506 provides that a Will is valid if execution complies with the UPC or "complies with the law at the time of execution of the place where the will is executed, or of the law of the place where at the time of execution or at the time of death the testator is domiciled, has a place of abode, or is a national." This type of provision can have international consequences if any of these locations are outside the United States.

4. Consider also the possibility that (i) opposite-gender unmarried couples may relocate their domicile to a state that recognizes traditional common law marriage, or (ii) same-sex couples may relocate their domicile to a state that recognizes marriage or some other civil relationship between such persons. In both of these situations certain spousal protections that were previously unavailable to these couples may arise as a result of such relocation and need to be considered. Changes to or from a community property state also introduce planning considerations (See Part A.5, *infra.*)

5. The percentages in the text are the product of two interrelated UPC sections. UPC §2-202(a) provides for an elective share amount equal to 50 percent of the value of the "marital-property portion" of the augmented estate. The marital-property portion is computed by multiplying the value of the augmented estate by an increasing percentage, which spans from 3 percent to 100 percent, depending on the duration of the marriage. *See* UPC §2-203(b).

Aside from questions of the *validity* of the Will, there remain questions about the *interpretation* of the Will. For example, a Will that relied on the prevailing state law at the time and place of execution for definitions, fiduciary powers, and obligations could be subject to interpretations that shift with the change in the state of domicile. However, that is not an absolute rule, and a court may apply the law of the jurisdiction where the testator was domiciled when the Will was executed.[6] Accordingly, the attorney needs to draft choice of law clauses with care and anticipate possible changes. The overriding concern generally is to carry out the testator's intent, and the attorney's attention to the choice of law provisions in the Will can be a significant factor in this determination.

3. Trusts

As noted above, the law applicable to a trust is generally that of the place of administration. This rule provides predictability with respect to the impacts of a change of domicile, particularly if a revocable trust separate from the decedent's Will is used as the principal instrument. Without careful drafting, the place of administration as a practical matter might end up being the place of the decedent's final domicile. Attorneys who draft testamentary trusts often assume that the laws of the state of domicile will govern both the Will and the testamentary trust created under the Will. While this is often the expectation, careful drafting can make the choice of law more certain.

4. Ancillary Probate

The ownership of multiple personal residences as well as the accumulation of various real estate interests over the course of a decedent's various moves may produce the need for "ancillary probate" of the assets located outside the state of administration of the estate. Each state's own real property laws govern the ownership and transfer of real property located within the state's boundaries. As a result, a probate administered in State A cannot unilaterally direct or effect how real property located in State B is to be transferred. Thus, there is a need to open an ancillary probate in State B, usually for the sole purpose of conveying the real property owned by the decedent in State B under State B's laws.

There are several planning measures that should be considered to minimize the need for ancillary probate. First, the decedent could create joint tenancies with survivorship rights, but this solution suffers from the same drawbacks already noted in Chapters 3 and 5 (finality of the gift, potential loss of IRC §121 benefits, etc.) and is at best a deferral of the ancillary probate administration for the survivor unless the applicable state

6. *See, e.g.*, UPC §2-703, which permits the selection of governing law by the testator unless it is contrary to the provisions of the elective share, exempt property and family allowances, or public policy.

law permits transfer-on-death deeds. Second, the decedent could title the assets in a revocable trust so that they are not subject to probate administration in the situs state.[7] Third, the decedent could title the assets in an entity, such as a limited partnership or limited liability company, which transmutes the indirect interest in the real estate into intangible personal property, the administration of which is generally governed by the laws of the state of domicile.[8]

5. Community Property

We refer the reader to the discussion of community property in Chapter 4. There are several general aspects of community property that are well known to most students in a Wills and Trusts course. First, if a married couple moves from a common law property state to a community property state, both partners may lose the benefits of the elective share or other spousal protection of the common law property state. Second, if a married couple moves from a community property state to a common law property state, the elective share, rules for the division of property upon dissolution of marriage, or other spousal protection of the common law property state may be an overlay on the community property.

The first issue may be mitigated somewhat if the destination community property state applies a "quasi-community property" doctrine. California, Idaho, and Washington, for example, apply this doctrine. Very generally speaking, the spouse who owned the assets under the common law property system still retains ownership. However, quasi-community property principles provide that upon the death of the spouse who owns the assets, the survivor may be entitled to a share. However, if the non-owning spouse predeceases, the decedent has no rights of disposition in the assets owned by the surviving spouse, unlike the rights the decedent would enjoy if the property were true community property.[9] The second issue is more complex and defies a state by state summary. Nevertheless, both of these issues can be addressed through the use of marital agreements or changes in the titling of assets to rearrange spousal protection.

A very common problem is the transmutation of community property into common law property, particularly with couples who have made multiple interstate moves. Some may not see this as a problem, particularly if the property is subsequently titled in joint tenancy in a common law property state such that each spouse holds a one-half interest in the

7. Property in State B owned by a revocable trust created by a settlor who died in State A usually remains owned by the trust upon the death of the settlor, so no legal transfer or probate is required in State B. The trustee may distribute the property by executing a deed.

8. Property in State B owned by a business entity that is in turn owned by a decedent who died in State A will remain owned by the business entity upon the decedent's death, so no legal transfer of real property is required in State B.

9. Quasi-community property may have an inter vivos impact in some states. For example, California law extends quasi-community property principles to property division upon dissolution of marriage. *See* Grace Ganz Blumberg, Community Property in California 574-576 (4th ed. 2003).

property resembling their rights under a community property regime.[10] One drawback to this arrangement is that the Internal Revenue Code provides a special basis rule for community property that adjusts the basis for both halves of the community property upon the death of the first spouse, not just the half owned by the decedent.[11] This full step-up in basis could be lost, however, if the property is held in joint tenancy, as the rule of IRC §2040(b) would be invoked providing an adjustment only for one-half of the property.

Another problem is the conversion of separately owned property under a community property system to jointly owned property in a common law property state, which may cause the separate property to lose that status upon a return to a community property state. These issues can be addressed in a marital agreement. Short of that, 14 states[12] have adopted the Uniform Disposition of Community Property Rights at Death Act of 1971[13] (UDCPRDA). UDCPRDA recognizes that property acquired in a common law property state while a domiciliary of the common law property state may retain community property status if acquired with community funds. If the protection of the UDCPRDA is sought, titling of real estate and other assets should be made with express recognition of the statute and the retained community property nature of the asset. However, the UDCPRDA is couched in terms of testamentary transfers, so its application in other contexts, such as dissolution of marriage, is uncertain.

UDCPRDA does not deal with the issue of whether property purchased in a common law property state with community funds by a couple residing in a community property state remains community property: It is reasonably well settled that the new property will be community property.[14]

6. State Estate, Inheritance, and Succession Taxes

The federal estate tax credit for state estate taxes paid expired in 2005 and was replaced by a deduction.[15] Many state estate tax levies were previously an insignificant planning concern because they were structured as a "sponge" or "pick-up" tax imposed only in the amount, and to the extent, of the available federal credit. With the anticipated repeal of the federal credit, more states moved to impose separate estate taxes. With couples who change domicile, the state estate tax regime of the new state of

10. While holding property in joint tenancy does protect the surviving tenant against the loss of interest in property, it does so at the cost of effectively "unprotecting" the heirs or beneficiaries of the first-to-die tenant. They may eventually receive nothing. Contrast this to community property, where the first-to-die spouse's heirs/beneficiaries could receive the first-to-die's interest in the property while still protecting the second-to-die's interest. Is tenants-in-common a better way to hold such transmuted property?

11. *See* IRC §1014(b)(6).

12. The adopting states include Alaska, Arkansas, Colorado, Connecticut, Florida, Hawaii, Kentucky, Michigan, Montana, New York, North Carolina, Oregon, Virginia, and Wyoming.

13. Unif. Disposition of Community Prop. Rights at Death Act, 8A U.L.A. 213 (2003).

14. *See* Blumberg, *supra* note 9, at 567-571.

15. *See* IRC §2011(f). A new estate tax deduction was created for state estate taxes. *See* IRC §2058.

domicile was always a concern. However, with the rise of separate state estate tax levies, a review of the current Will and overall estate plan can be even more pertinent.[16] This can also be a concern for couples who may have established their domicile in one state, but own property subject to estate taxes in another state, or couples who complete their planning in one state and later move to another state that has different state estate, inheritance and succession tax laws.[17]

B. International Wills

The Uniform International Wills Act (UIWA) is found in UPC §§2-1001 through 2-1010. The principal objective of the act is the creation of uniform rules for the recognition of the validity of Wills executed abroad and administered in the United States and vice versa, irrespective of the "location of the assets and of the nationality, domicile, or residence of the testator. . . ."[18] Only 15 states and the District of Columbia[19] (and relatively few foreign countries)[20] have adopted statutes incorporating provisions of the UIWA in whole or in part. The UIWA is not the only relevant international convention, but it is the most important one that speaks to the form of instruments.[21]

The UIWA requirements are that (1) the Will is in writing; (2) the testator declares that the document is his or her Will and that he or she knows the contents thereof in the presence of two witnesses *and* a person authorized to act in connection with international Wills; (3) the testator in

16. There is also the possibility that federal estate tax exclusion levels could be large enough to significantly or entirely exempt a decedent's estate from federal estate taxes, but because of less generous state estate and inheritance tax exclusion levels, an estate could be required to pay state estate or inheritance taxes that exceed the federal estate taxes payable.

17. *See generally* Anthony E. Woods, *Decoupling's Dilemma*, 143 TR. & EST. 50 (Apr. 2004); Richard B. Covey & Dan T. Hastings, *Recent Developments in Transfer and Income Taxation of Trusts and Estates and State Trust and Estate Law*, 40 INST. ON EST. PLAN. ¶¶ 145-145.1 (2006) (survey of state wealth transfer taxes); and Elizabeth C. McNichol, *Many States Are Decoupling from the Federal Estate Tax Cut* at http://www.cbpp.org/files/5-23-02sfp.pdf (last visited Aug. 20, 2011). For a policy overview, *see* Jeffrey A. Cooper, *Interstate Competition and State Death Taxes: A Modern Crisis in Historical Perspective*, 33 PEPP. L. REV. 835 (2006).

18. *See* UIWA §2.

19. Alaska, California, Colorado, Connecticut, Delaware, District of Columbia, Illinois, Michigan, Minnesota, Montana, Nevada, New Hampshire, New Mexico, North Dakota, Oregon, and Virginia. *See* 8 U.L.A. 476 (1998 & Supp. 2010).

20. One commentator identifies the following countries as adopting the Washington Convention which provides for international Wills: Belgium, Bosnia-Herzegovina, Canada, Cyprus, Ecuador, France, Italy, Libya, Niger, Portugal, and Slovenia. *See* M. Read Moore, *Advising U.S. Clients Who Own Foreign Property*, 40 INST. ON EST. PLAN. ¶903.2 (2006).

21. The Hague Convention Relating to the Form of Testamentary Dispositions of 1961 has been adopted by a greater number of countries than the UIWA and it speaks more broadly to choice of law rules, rather than prescribing a manner for executing a Will. *Id.*, ¶903.3. There are several other Hague conventions that have yet to gain significant numbers of signatories. *Id.*, ¶904.6 (discussing 1989 Hague Convention on the Law Applicable to Succession to the Estates of Deceased Persons and 1985 Hague Convention on the Law Applicable to Trusts and on Their Recognition).

the presence of the witnesses and the authorized person signs the Will or if he or she previously signed it, acknowledges his or her signature; (4) if the testator is unable to sign, the authorized person makes a note of the reason for the testator's inability to sign on the Will;[22] and (5) the witnesses and the authorized person attest the Will by signing in the testator's presence.

As additional "points of form," section 4 of the UIWA directs that (1) the signatures be placed at the end of the Will; (2) if the Will consists of several sheets, each sheet must be numbered and signed by the testator; (3) the date of the Will is noted at the end of the Will by the authorized person; and (4) the authorized person shall ask the testator whether he or she wishes to make a declaration concerning the safekeeping of the Will; if the testator so desires, the location of the Will is set forth in a certificate completed by the authorized person. Failure to comply with these points of form will not, however, invalidate the Will as an international Will.

The "authorized person" referred to in the UIWA is limited to individuals who have been admitted to practice law and are currently licensed to so do before the courts of the state where the Will is signed.[23]

EXERCISE 10-1

COMPARING THE UPC AND UIWA EXECUTION FORMALITIES

Compare the execution requirements of UPC §§2-502 and 2-504 to the UIWA, noting any differences. Should an attorney representing a U.S. resident who owns foreign real estate follow the execution rules of the UIWA as well as those of the state of domicile?

C. Foreign Property Holdings

Clients often own foreign bank accounts[24] and real property. This is typically the consequence of their immigration into the United States, with naturalized citizenship or permanent residency, or the receipt of inheritances from family members who resided abroad. Other clients may simply wish to own a second or retirement home outside the United States.[25]

22. It is permissible for any other person present to sign the testator's name at the testator's direction if the authorized person makes note of this on the Will.

23. *See* UIWA §9.

24. Foreign bank accounts present a number of potential concerns. *See generally* Alexander A. Bove, Jr. & Melissa Langa, *Handling the Risks of Foreign Bank Accounts and Avoiding the Penalties*, 35 EST. PLAN. 27 (July 2008); Andrew H. Weinstein & Kevin E. Packman, *What Private Wealth Attorneys Need to Know About Money Laundering*, 37 EST. PLAN. 28 (June 2010).

25. *See, e.g.*, Theresa H. Marx, *A Step-by-Step Guide to Purchasing a Home in France*, 36 EST. PLAN. 24 (Sept. 2009).

1. Foreign Law Issues

In some cases, the laws of the foreign country limit the types of property that may be owned by nationals of other countries, and local counsel should be retained. Foreign inheritance and other taxes will often be a concern.[26] In almost all cases, the client's U.S. Will must be reviewed in connection with any treaties or other conventions of the foreign country to confirm that no administration problems in the United States or the foreign country will be encountered, particularly if foreign beneficiaries are a factor.[27] Indeed, upon death, the U.S. estate of an individual owning foreign situs property may be faced with an ancillary proceeding in the foreign country.[28] The estate could be required to appoint a U.S. personal representative as well as a foreign personal representative, and the U.S. Will may address the nomination of both.[29] In some cases, clients are advised to execute multiple Wills, one in the United States and others in the foreign countries in which property is situated, so-called "situs Wills."[30] Or, in some countries, clients may merely affirmatively state in their U.S. Will that the law of their U.S. domicile is to govern the administration of their estate.[31] In any event, the services of local counsel in the foreign country should be retained when foreign Wills are being drafted or

26. *See, e.g.*, Mark W. Smith, *An Introduction to Estate Planning in the United Kingdom*, 37 EST. PLAN. 10 (Apr. 2010) (in part discussing inheritance and related tax laws).

27. Although beyond the scope of this book, distributions to foreign beneficiaries who are residents of certain countries may encounter state or federal restrictions on transfers of property to countries such as Cuba. *See, e.g.*, ROBERT C. LAWRENCE III, INTERNATIONAL TAX AND ESTATE PLANNING: A PRACTICAL GUIDE FOR MULTINATIONAL INVESTORS §8:6.3, *Release of the Assets* (Practising Law Institute 2001).

28. In civil law jurisdictions, which encompass much of Europe, assets and liabilities of the decedent may pass by universal succession, minimizing the impact of a Will. *See, e.g.*, William H. Newton III, *Estate Administration and Postmortem Planning Considerations for the International Client*, reprinted as ch. 4 of A GUIDE TO INTERNATIONAL ESTATE PLANNING—DRAFTING, COMPLIANCE, AND ADMINISTRATION STRATEGIES (Jeffrey A. Schoenblum ed., 2000); Moore, *supra* note 20, ¶901.2 ("As a result, individuals who live in civil law countries tend not to use wills to the same extent as individuals who live in common law countries . . .").

29. One finds suggestions in planning literature that the executor in the primary jurisdiction should be given authority to appoint or remove, as the case may be, executors or other representatives in the other jurisdictions.

30. *See, e.g.*, Barbara Hauser, *The Use of Multiple ("Situs") Wills, reprinted as* ch. 3 of A GUIDE TO INTERNATIONAL ESTATE PLANNING—DRAFTING, COMPLIANCE AND ADMINISTRATION STRATEGIES, *supra* note 28; Moore, *supra* note 20, ¶902 ("Should You Use a Situs Will?"). The coordination of the multiple instruments in terms of revocation, amendments, and the extent of disclosure to the particular government authorities is an important facet of this strategy. *See also* Michael W. Galligan, *International Estate Planning for U.S. Citizens: An Integrated Approach*, 36 EST. PLAN. 11 (Oct. 2009) (discussing the use of limited liability companies to hold foreign property of U.S. citizens).

31. For example, language similar to the following could be inserted into the U.S. Will for a client owning property in Switzerland: "Notwithstanding the place of my residence or domicile at the time of my death, in the event I am deemed to be a resident or domiciliary of the Swiss Confederation at the time of my death, or otherwise possess property of any nature which is deemed to be subject to the laws of the Swiss Confederation, then pursuant to RS 291, Chapter 6 of the Swiss Federal Act on International Private Law of 1987, and the Hague Convention Concerning Conflict of Laws in Matters of Will and Testamentary Dispositions dated 5 October 1961, I hereby elect, and it is my express intention and desire, to have any and all aspects of the probate, administration, enforcement, execution and/or disposition of my foregoing Will and estate to be governed by the laws of my domicile/country of origin (United States of America), and hereby submit my foregoing Will and estate in its entirety thereto."

significant foreign property issues are involved.[32] Local counsel will almost always be necessary if ancillary proceedings are required.

2. U.S. Income Tax Issues

A U.S. citizen or resident[33] is taxed on worldwide income for U.S. income tax purposes, but any foreign taxes might be reduced if a tax treaty applies. Also, a credit against the U.S. income tax might be available for income taxes paid to other countries.[34] A U.S. citizen or resident with a principal residence located abroad may still use the benefits of IRC §121.[35] However, a U.S. citizen or resident may not use an IRC §1031 like-kind exchange of real estate if foreign real estate is one of the properties. A nonresident alien is generally subject to U.S. income taxation only on U.S. source income.[36] Complicated additional issues, beyond the scope of this book, exist for all taxpayers if property is held by an entity.[37]

3. U.S. Federal Wealth Transfer Tax Issues

The estate of a U.S. citizen or resident[38] is taxed on worldwide assets.[39] The estates of noncitizen nonresidents are subject to the federal estate tax only on the value of property situated in the United States.[40] Property situated in the United States generally includes real property located in the United States, most tangible personal property located in the United

32. The use of local counsel for significant assets would seem to be the rule rather than the exception, particularly if there are foreign taxation issues. *See, e.g.*, Moore, *supra* note 20, ¶901.4 (discussing foreign estate and inheritance tax rules).

33. See IRC §7701(b) (income tax definition of "residence").

34. *See* IRC §§901 & 903.

35. However, if the U.S. citizen or resident becomes a nonresident "expatriate" for income tax purposes, the impact of provisions such as IRC §§877 & 877A must be considered. *See, e.g.*, Stephen Liss, *HEART-ache: Expatriation Under the New Inheritance Tax*, 37 EST. PLAN. 18 (Apr. 2010) (discussing IRC §877A).

36. *See generally* Sanford H. Goldberg, *The Taxation of Nonresident Aliens*, 14 ALI-ABA EST. PLAN. COURSE MATERIALS J. 11 (Oct. 2008) (discussing income and wealth transfer tax implications). A nonresident alien individual may be taxable on income "effectively connected with the conduct of a trade or business within the United States." *See* IRC §871(b). The disposition of U.S. real property interests is generally treated as trade or business income. *See* IRC §897(a). Income from U.S. sources that is not connected with a U.S. business is generally subject to a flat tax rate. *See* IRC §871(a) (30 percent tax rate unless a treaty imposes a different rate). Nonresident aliens who were once U.S. citizens or resident aliens may be subject to special expatriation provisions. *See supra* note 35.

37. *See, e.g.*, Paula Charpentier & Lucy S. Lee, *Foreign Trust Reporting and Compliance*, 14 ALI-ABA EST. PLAN. COURSE MATERIALS J. 5 (Apr. 2008); Samuel A. Donaldson, *A Hitchhiker's Guide to International Estate Planning: Estate Planning for United States Citizens with Assets Abroad and for Nonresidents with United States Assets*, 33 ACTEC J. 228 (Spring 2008) (in part discussing ownership of foreign corporations and U.S. beneficiaries of foreign estates and trusts); John F. Meigs & Ryan R. Gager, *Using a U.S. Qualified Personal Residence Trust in Cross-Border Planning*, 35 EST. PLAN. 22 (July 2008); Alexander M. Popovich, *Avoiding the Disadvantageous Tax Consequences of a Foreign Nongrantor Trust*, 36 EST. PLAN. 29 (May 2009); James R. Robinson, *U.S. Trusts with Foreign Beneficiaries: Issues and Observations*, 35 EST. PLAN. 25 (Aug. 2008).

38. Residency for wealth transfer tax purposes is governed by different rules than for the income tax. *See* Treas. Reg. §20.0-1(b) (as amended in 1994).

39. IRC §2014 provides a credit toward the U.S. estate tax on account of death taxes paid to foreign countries. The death taxes payable to the foreign country may be influenced by an applicable estate tax treaty with the United States.

40. *See* IRC §2106. *See generally* Goldberg, *supra* note 36; Mark W. Smith, *Careful Pre-Immigration Planning Can Save Significant Taxes*, 34 EST. PLAN. 30 (2007).

States, shares of stock in domestic corporations, and deposits in U.S. banks.[41] Barring the application of a tax treaty that would provide for a larger credit,[42] the estate of a noncitizen nonresident subject to the federal estate tax is otherwise allowed a unified credit of $13,000, which would shelter taxable assets valued at $60,000.[43]

D. The Alien Spouse

Property transfers to a noncitizen spouse must be handled with special care; otherwise an estate tax marital deduction is denied.[44] If an estate tax marital deduction is desired, the bequest must be in the form of a qualified domestic trust, a so-called "QDOT," the requirements for which are established by IRC §2056A. A standard domestic marital trust will usually not contain all of the necessary language to include a noncitizen spouse, so this is a specialized drafting issue.

EXERCISE 10-2

QDOT LANGUAGE

Read IRC §2056A and then review the language in Form M. Does it qualify for QDOT treatment?

E. CASE STUDY 10-1

Eric and Tatiana Osborn

THE NONCITIZEN SPOUSE

Eric Osborn (age 29) is a Foreign Service officer with the State Department stationed in Washington, D.C., and residing in Virginia. His wife, Tatiana (age 27), has permanent U.S. residency but is not a citizen. At this

41. *See* Treas. Reg. §20.2104-1 (as amended in 1974). Because of the limited unified credit allowed noncitizen nonresidents, even a modest second home could generate a U.S. estate tax. Consequently, it is sometimes recommended that the noncitizen nonresident create a foreign corporation to own the U.S. real estate, a topic beyond the scope of this book.

42. *See* IRC §2102(b)(3).

43. *See* IRC §2102(c)(1).

44. *See* IRC §2056(d). A trap for the unwary "mixed-citizenship" couple is that inter vivos gifts from a U.S. citizen spouse to a non-U.S. citizen spouse may be subject to gift taxes. While the marital deduction for inter vivos gifts to a U.S. citizen spouse is unlimited, the marital deduction for inter vivos gifts to a non-U.S. citizen spouse is limited to an annual amount of $100,000 (plus cost-of-living adjustments, which produced an adjusted amount of $136,000 for calendar year 2011. *See* IRC §2523(i).

time she is a full-time homemaker. They have one child, Anna (age 2), who is a U.S. citizen.

Part A: Assume that Eric's Will contains the following provision: "Without regard to my domicile at my death, Virginia law shall govern the rights of all persons interested in my estate and the validity and construction of this Will."

How will this clause be applied if Eric and Tatiana establish a new domicile in California? For example, what if there is a partial intestacy under the Will? What if Tatiana wishes to exercise spousal rights?

Would your answer change if Eric's Will read as follows: "The validity and construction of my Will and all trusts created under my Will shall be governed by the laws of the State of Virginia. Questions relating to the administration of a trust shall be governed by the law of the situs of administration of that trust."

Part B: Assume that Eric and Tatiana own their Virginia home, valued at $350,000 (subject to a $200,000 mortgage), in joint tenancy with rights of survivorship. They purchased the home for $250,000 with a $25,000 down payment from an inheritance Eric received from his grandmother. Assume that Eric is killed in a traffic accident. After Eric's death, what is the income tax basis of the home in Tatiana's hands?

Part C: Assume that the Virginia home is titled solely in Eric's name, and that because of the line of work he is in, the State Department provides Eric a $10,000,000 life insurance policy on his life, payable to his estate. If Eric's Will leaves his entire estate to Tatiana, will there be any estate tax due upon Eric's death? If not, why not? If so, how would you advise Eric and Tatiana so as to avoid this outcome?

F. Reference Materials

Treatises

- Barbara Hauser, International Estate Planning: A Reference Guide (2010).
- Frederick K. Hoops et al., Family Estate Planning Guide ch. 19 (4th ed. 1994 & Supp. 2010-2011) (multi-state estates); ch. 31 (foreign trust taxation).
- Robert C. Lawrence, III & Elisa Shevlin Rizzo, *Basic Conflict of Laws Principles*, in A Guide to International Estate Planning (Jeffrey A. Schoenblum ed., 2000).
- John R. Price & Samuel A. Donaldson, Price on Contemporary Estate Planning §3.22-3.39 (2011) (community property).
- Douglas L. Siegler & Lloyd Lena Plaine, *Planning for Transfers to Non-Citizen Spouses, in* A Guide to International Estate Planning (Jeffrey A. Schoenblum ed., 2000).

- George M. Turner, Revocable Trusts ch. 28 (5th ed. 2003 & Supp. 2010) (QDOTs); ch. 29 (choice of laws).

Articles

Planning for Interstate Moves

- Karen E. Boxx, *Community Property Across State Lines*, 19 Prob. & Prop. 9 (Jan./Feb. 2005).
- Jackson M. Bruce Jr., *Multistate Uniformity in Trust and Estate Substantive Law and Some New Wrinkles and Concepts: Revised Articles II and VI of the Uniform Probate Code*, 26 Inst. on Est. Plan. ¶¶ 600, 609 (1992).
- Anne K. Hilker, *Planning for the Married Couple Moving into or out of a Community Property State*, 14 Est. Plan. 212 (1987).
- Stanley M. Johanson, *The Migrating Client: Estate Planning for the Couple from a Separate Property State*, 9 Inst. on Est. Plan. ¶800 (1975).
- Jack M. Kinnebrew, *Texas Community Property: Moving to or from a Community Property State May Create Special Problems*, 121 Tr. & Est. 15 (June 1982).
- Ronald S. Kochman, *Moving Is a Family Decision*, 127 Tr. & Est. 22 (May 1988).
- Malcolm A. Moore, *Migration and Property in the 1990's: The Increasing Importance of Community Property—Separate Property Recognition and Resolution*, 25 Inst. on Est. Plan. ¶1100 (1991).
- Richard W. Nenno, *Choosing and Rechoosing the Jurisdiction for a Trust*, 40 Inst. on Est. Plan. ¶400 (2006).
- J. Thomas Oldham, *Management of the Community Estate During an Intact Marriage*, 56 Law & Contemp. Probs. 99 (1993).
- J. Thomas Oldham, *Tracing, Commingling, and Transmutation*, 23 Fam. L.Q. 219 (1989).
- John Paul Parks, *Special Estate Planning Strategies to Fit the Needs of the Mobile Client*, 18 Est. Plan. 150 (1991).
- David Pratt & Lisa M. Stern, *Estate Planning Considerations for Migratory Clients*, 34 Est. Plan. 16 (2007).
- Jeremy T. Ware, *Section 1014(b)(6) and the Boundaries of Community Property*, 5 Nev. L.J. 704 (2005).
- John A. Warnick & Sergio Pareja, *Selecting a Trust Situs in the 21st Century*, 16 Prob. & Prop. 53 (Mar./Apr. 2002).
- Wiley, *Community Property in a Common Law State*, 21 Prac. Law. 81 (June 1975).

Planning for the Multinational Estate

- Vicky Levy Eskin & Bryan John Driscoll, *Estate Planning with Foreign Property*, 28 Gpsolo 43 (Apr./May 2011).

- Michael W. Galligan, *International Estate Planning for U.S. Citizens: An Integrated Approach*, 36 EST. PLAN. 11 (Oct. 2009).
- Robert C. Lawrence, III, *Multinational Estate Planning Headaches and the Panacea Therefor*, 29 INST. ON EST. PLAN. ¶1800 (1995).
- M. Read Moore, *Advising U.S. Clients Who Own Foreign Property*, 40 INST. ON EST. PLAN. ¶900 (2006).
- M. Read Moore, *Answers to Your Questions About International Estate Planning*, Estate Planning in Depth, SP053 ALI-ABA 27 (ALI-ABA Continuing Legal Education, June 14-19, 2009).
- M. Read Moore, *Tax and Estate Planning Issues for U.S. Clients Who Own Foreign Property*, Planning Techniques for Large Estates, SS010 ALI-ABA 1885 (ALI-ABA Continuing Legal Education, Nov. 15-19, 2010).
- G. Warren Whitaker & Jean-Marc Tirard, *Des Americains en France*, 146 TR. & EST. 34 (Aug. 2007).

Planning for Transfers to the Noncitizen Spouse

- Stephen R. Akers, *Stirring the Alphabet Soup: ABC's Through XYZ's of QTIP's and QDOT's*, 28 INST. ON EST. PLAN. ¶300 (1994).
- Rachna D. Balakrishna, *Using a Spousal Access Trust as a QDOT Alternative for a Noncitizen Spouse*, 35 EST. PLAN. 15 (June 2008).
- William T. Diss, *QDOT's to the Rescue: Complications and Solutions*, 132 TR. & EST. 56 (Oct./Nov. 1993).
- Richard M. Fijolek & J. Mitchell Miller, *Marital Deduction Planning for Noncitizen Spouses*, 20 EST. PLAN. 20 (1993).
- M. Read Moore, *Practical Estate Planning Techniques for Noncitizen Spouses*, 26 EST. PLAN. 205 (1999).
- M. Read Moore, *Practical Estate Planning for Non-Citizens Who Reside in the United States*, Estate Planning in Depth, SK093 ALI-ABA 493 (ALI-ABA Continuing Legal Education, June 19-24, 2005).
- Maria E. Nunez, *Planning for the Payment of Estate Tax Attributable to Transfers to Non-U.S. Citizen Spouses*, International Trust and Estate Planning, SM033 ALI-ABA 329 (ALI-ABA Continuing Legal Education, Oct. 5-6, 2006).
- Mark W. Smith, *Careful Pre-Immigration Planning Can Save Significant Taxes*, 34 EST. PLAN. 30 (2007).
- Robin Rose Stiller, *International Estate Planning 101: A Basic Guide to Estate Planning for Non-Citizen Clients*, 15 AKRON TAX J. 121 (2000).
- G. Warren Whitaker & Michael J. Parets, *My Client Married an Alien: Ten Things Everyone Should Know About International Estate Planning*, 18 PROB. & PROP. 25 (Mar./Apr. 2004).

CHAPTER 11 The Wealthy Married Couple

A. The Taxation Factor

With the exception of the discussion in Chapter 8 (Gifts from Grandparents), taxation issues have not yet played a leading role in the planning alternatives discussed in this book. That will dramatically change with this chapter, which deals with wealthy married couples. Many planners will tell you that the federal wealth transfer tax consequences of marriage are the most significant issues they encounter in planning. Ownership of businesses is a common factor in the accumulation of significant household wealth, so this chapter also deals with estate planning for family businesses.

At the time the second edition of this book was published we wrote that "the future of the federal wealth transfer taxes remained quite uncertain." That remains equally true as we complete this edition because the provisions of the current law, the Tax Relief, Unemployment Insurance Reauthorization, and Job Creation Act of 2010[1] (2010 Act), will no longer apply to the estates of decedents dying, gifts made, or generation-skipping transfers after December 31, 2012. If the federal wealth transfer taxes are eliminated or the exemptions are further increased to a point that the taxes apply to even fewer individuals, tax issues will recede in importance for many people. However, the other issues of estate planning will remain. We hope that the variety of case studies in this book demonstrates the importance of these other issues, such as dissolution of

1. Pub. L. No. 111-312, 124 Stat. 3296 (2010).

marriage, asset preservation, and planning for incapacity. However, we now need to deal with the federal wealth transfer tax consequences of marriage. (Chapter 16 provides an overview of the federal wealth transfer taxes.)

B. The Economic Growth and Tax Relief Reconciliation Act of 2001 (EGTRRA) and Tax Relief, Unemployment Insurance Reauthorization, and Job Creation Act of 2010 (2010 Act)

To fully understand the impact of the 2010 Act (and the consequences of a failure to extend its December 31, 2012, sunset date) it is necessary to revisit the implications of the prior, albeit likewise temporary, law. In that regard, the Economic Growth and Tax Relief Reconciliation Act of 2001[2] (EGTRRA) introduced several frustrating planning wrinkles[3] that required belated remedial action in the 2010 Act.

First, under EGTRRA, the estate tax and the generation-skipping transfer tax, but not the gift tax, which was retained as a backstop to income tax avoidance planning, were set to terminate for decedents dying and for generation-skipping transfers made after December 31, 2009. Contrary to the prevailing expectations of most estate planners, Congress did not act prior to December 31, 2009, so the estates of decedents dying in 2010 and generation-skipping transfers made in 2010 were not subject to tax. The 2010 Act implemented a compromise regime for 2010. The default option for estates offered a more generous $5,000,000 applicable exclusion amount, a reduced tax rate, and an IRC §1014 step-up in basis. Alternatively, estates could elect no estate tax, but with a modified carryover basis for assets.

Second, EGTRRA's repeal of the estate and generation-skipping transfer tax, plus all of the phased-in changes described below, were subject to sunset for decedents dying and gifts made after December 31, 2010, such that the exemptions, rates, and other features of the tax would revert to their pre-EGTRRA 2001 status. Along with adding its own amendments, the 2010 Act extended the overall sunset date to December 31, 2012. Although one might again expect that Congress will extend the 2010 Act changes or fashion some other compromise, one cannot predict that,

2. Pub. L. No. 107-16, 155 Stat. 38 (2001).

3. *See, e.g.*, Richard B. Covey, *Recent Developments (2001) in Transfer Taxes & Income Taxation of Trusts & Estates*, 36 Inst. on Est. Plan. ¶¶ 100, 101.5 (2002); Steve R. Akers, *Estate Planning Under the 2001 Act—Planning and Drafting in an Uncertain Environment*, Planning Techniques for Large Estates, SH022 ALI-ABA 903 (ALI-ABA Continuing Legal Education, Nov. 18-22, 2002). In Section B.2 of Chapter 16 we discuss in greater detail some of the possible drafting responses to the still uncertain future of the estate tax.

particularly in light of the years of impasse that preceded the enactment of the 2010 Act.

Third, EGTRRA gradually reduced the maximum rate of estate and generation-skipping transfer taxes from 50 percent to 45 percent. The maximum gift tax rate declined from 50 percent to 45 percent, and was scheduled to further decline to 35 percent for gifts made after 2009. The 2010 Act adopted a 35 percent maximum rate for estates of decedents dying, gifts made, or generation-skipping transfers made in 2010-2012.

Fourth, EGTRRA increased the applicable exclusion amount (formerly referred to as the unified credit) for estates to $1,000,000 for decedents dying in 2003, $1,500,000 in 2004 and 2005, $2,000,000 in 2006-2008, and $3,500,000 in 2009. These increases in the applicable exclusion amount significantly reduced the number of individuals subject to federal wealth transfer taxes.[4] As discussed in Section D.2.a below, those increases (as well as subsequent increases in the 2010 Act) affected marital deduction formula clauses. However, in preserving the gift taxes as a backstop, the applicable exclusion amount was no longer unified, and the exclusion for gift taxes was limited to $1,000,000. The 2010 Act increased the applicable exclusion amount to $5,000,000, which can rise in multiples of $10,000 for cost-of-living adjustments.[5] The 2010 Act also re-unified the applicable exclusion amount for estate and gift taxes, effective for gifts made after December 31, 2010.

Fifth, under EGTRRA, a modified carryover basis regime supplanted IRC §1014 for property acquired from a decedent dying in 2010.[6] Although this carryover basis regime was retained for the estates of decedents dying in 2010 that elected that treatment (along with the imposition of no estate or generation-skipping transfer tax), the 2010 Act otherwise abolished it, so this book does not focus on the details of the 2010 transitional year election or carryover basis.

While the enactment of EGTRRA added new and competing uncertainties, rather than stability and certainty, to the tax landscape, the enactment of the 2010 Act continues many of these same uncertainties. For example, will the estate tax revert to its 2001 rates and exemptions in 2013? Will the 2010 Act be extended? Or will the estate tax be modified to some other scheme? Will it perhaps be abolished altogether? In Section B.2 of Chapter 16, "Planning After the 2010 Act," we discuss in greater detail some of the possible drafting responses to the still uncertain future of the estate tax.

4. EGTRRA also repealed the Family-Owned Business Interest Deduction (IRC §2057) as of 2004. The number of estate tax returns filed decreased from 108,071 in 2001 to 45,070 in 2005. However, the number of returns for estates with gross assets in excess of $3,500,000 increased, with the largest percentage increase reported for estates in excess of $20,000,000, where 628 returns were filed in 2001 and 760 in 2005. In spite of the large overall decrease in the number of estate tax returns (58%), the estate tax revenues declined by 8 percent from $23,500,000,000 in 2001 to $21,700,000,000 in 2005. *See* Brian G. Raub, *Recent Changes to the Estate Tax Exemption Level and Filing Population*, STATISTICS OF INCOME BULLETIN (Summer 2007).

5. *See* IRC §2010(c).

6. *See* IRC §1022.

C. The Deceased Spousal Unused Exclusion Amount (DSUEA)

While most of the 2010 Act was devoted to merely extending and modifying EGTRRA, it did introduce an important, new marital estate tax planning tool, the "deceased spousal unused exclusion amount" (DSUEA).[7]

1. An Overview of Marital Estate Tax Planning Before the DSUEA

Prior to the 2010 Act, the applicable exclusion amount was personal to each spouse (except for amounts applied to IRC §2513 gift-splitting elections), and any unutilized amount evaporated with that spouse's death. Consequently, a common estate planning structure for married couples was to set aside a share (the nonmarital share) of the estate that would not pass to the surviving spouse (to disqualify it for the IRC §2056 marital deduction), so that the available applicable exclusion amount could be utilized to reduce the net estate tax on the nonmarital share to zero. The nonmarital share that passed free of estate tax (if limited to the amount of the applicable exclusion amount) could be given outright to beneficiaries other than the surviving spouse, but in many cases (particularly where the estate was relatively modest so the surviving spouse might need access to those funds) it would be given to a so-called "bypass" or "family" trust. The surviving spouse would typically have some rights to income (and perhaps corpus) of the trust, but the ultimate beneficiaries would be other family members.

The division of the first spouse's estate between the nonmarital share and the marital share was typically accomplished through the use of a "formula clause" in the spouse's governing instrument, the primary purpose of which was to maximize the amount of assets that would pass "tax free" to the nonspousal share.

The bypass trust and formula clause structure introduced additional complexity in the planning for a married couple. From a drafting standpoint, the governing instrument needed to express the formula clause, rules for funding the nonmarital and marital shares, and the provisions of the trusts. Those issues are addressed in some detail later in this chapter. From a postmortem administration standpoint, if a bypass trust was utilized, that required a fiduciary (i.e., a trustee, who could be a family member), fiduciary income tax returns, and other details. Also, existing simple nonprobate survivorship Will substitutes (such as joint tenancies, joint accounts, and beneficiary designations) often needed to be severed or

7. *See* IRC §2010(c)(4).

re-directed to ensure that that were enough probate or nonprobate assets to satisfy the full formula amount of the nonmarital share.

A less technical alternative employed a disclaimer Will or revocable trust, under which the surviving spouse would receive all of the estate assets, but would be free to timely disclaim, to the extent necessary, a portion of those assets, which would then pass as a nonspousal gift, to use the applicable exclusion amount. Typically, the disclaimed portion would pass to a disclaimer trust to which the surviving spouse would have access[8] but for which the marital deduction was unavailable (thus, those assets would be subject to estate tax, but by use of the decedent's applicable exclusion amount, the tax due at the first spouse's death would be zero).

A planned estate consequently required a governing instrument drafted with care and attentiveness to the wealth transfer tax rules, the possible maintenance of one or more (if a marital trust was used) trusts, and coordination of Will substitutes (including nonprobate property designated beneficiaries) to ensure that enough assets passed to the non-marital share. An unplanned estate might still be saved through the informed use of disclaimers to create a nonmarital share, but aside from technical considerations, a drawback was the possibility of the surviving spouse's complete loss of the disclaimed property. While these issues were routine for an experienced estate planner, it created additional planning complexity and costs and had the potential to confuse clients.

2. Operation of the DSUEA

The promise of the DSUEA is that a married couple ostensibly does not need to use a bypass trust in the applicable governing instrument; instead, everything can simply pass to the survivor. Generally speaking, the applicable exclusion amount is "portable," and if it is not fully utilized by the first spouse to die, the remainder can be utilized by the survivor. The simplicity of the DSUEA must, however, be considered in light of some subtle, but important, limitations the 2010 Act imposed upon its use and availability,[9] as well as the fact that the DSUEA is a new concept, in a new law, that is otherwise set to expire at the end of 2012.

a. *Assuming One Marriage, the Rules Seem Simple.*

Example 1. Husband 1 dies in 2011, having made taxable gifts of $3,000,000 during his lifetime (and leaving no taxable estate), or having made no taxable gifts and leaving a $3,000,000 taxable

8. The surviving spouse would need to heed the timing rules of IRC §2518 as well as other technical considerations, such as the "passage without direction" rules that permit only certain surviving spouse powers over the disclaimer trust. *See* Treas. Reg. §25.2518-2(e) (1997).

9. For example, while the gift tax exclusion, estate tax exclusion, and GSTT exemption are unified at $5,000,000 under the 2010 Act, only the unused gift and estate tax exclusions are portable; the GSTT exemption is not portable to the surviving spouse.

estate.[10] *Assuming a proper election by the estate of Husband 1,*[11] *Wife*[12] *has an applicable exclusion amount equal to the basic exclusion amount ($5,000,000)*[13] *plus a DSUEA of $2,000,000,*[14] *or $7,000,000. Wife may use all or any portion of the $7,000,000 for lifetime gifts, because the section 2505(a) credit refers to the section 2010(c) applicable credit amount. Wife's estate may use any unused portion for estate taxes otherwise due at her death.*

Although the DSUEA is not inflation-adjusted, the Wife's $5,000,000 basic exclusion amount in Example 1 will continue to increase with any inflation, assuming that Wife lives that long and the two-year term of the 2010 Act is extended.

b. With Multiple Marriages and Planning, This Can Become Complicated. The DSUEA is received only from the "*last such deceased spouse of such surviving spouse,*"[15] so a surviving spouse cannot stack DSUEAs from multiple deceased spouses.

Example 2. Assuming the same facts from Example 1, Wife subsequently marries Husband 2, and Husband 2 also predeceases Wife. Husband 2 made $4,000,000 in taxable gifts and left no taxable estate. Recall that the tentative DSUEA from Husband 1 was $2,000,000. However, Wife is eligible only for a $1,000,000 DSUEA from Husband 2 because the DSUEA is limited to the lesser of the $5,000,000 basic exclusion amount or the unused exclusion of the last deceased spouse (Husband 2). Consequently, Wife's applicable exclusion amount is $6,000,000, which she may use for lifetime gifts or for transfers at death.[16]

However, until Husband 2 dies, Husband 1 remains Wife's "last such deceased spouse." Wife can apparently make lifetime gifts prior to

10. This example is drawn from Example 1 in the "Technical Explanation of the Revenue Provisions Contained in the 'Tax Relief, Unemployment Insurance Reauthorization, and Job Creation Act of 2010' Scheduled for Consideration by the United States Senate," prepared by the Staff of the Joint Committee on Taxation (Dec. 10, 2010) (Joint Committee Explanation).

11. *See* IRC §2010(c)(5)(A).

12. To retain comparability with the Joint Committee Explanation, this discussion also uses the Husband 1, Husband 2, and Wife designations of the parties.

13. A notable change introduced by the 2010 Act is that the applicable exclusion amount is indexed for inflation, with calendar year 2010 as the base year. These examples use the unadjusted $5,000,000 amount.

14. The DSUEA is calculated under IRC §2010(c)(4) as the lesser of: $5,000,000; or $5,000,000 minus "the amount with respect to which the tentative tax is determined under section 2001(b)(1) on the estate of such deceased spouse." The 2001(b)(1) amount is comprised of the amount of the taxable estate plus any adjusted taxable gifts (which are gifts made by the decedent after 1976 that are not includible in the gross estate of the decedent). Consequently, when Husband 1 made $3,000,000 in gifts, that increased the 2001(b)(1) amount to $3,000,000, solely on account of the adjusted taxable gifts. Under the no-gift alternative, the 2001(b)(1) amount would include no adjusted taxable gifts, but would still become $3,000,000 due to the inclusion of the $3,000,000 taxable estate.

15. IRC §2010(c)(4)(B)(i) (emphasis added).

16. This example is drawn from Example 2 in the Joint Committee Explanation, *supra* note 10.

Husband 2's death, from her assets (or from assets gifted to her by Husband 2 using the section 2523 marital deduction for gifts), and use all of her $7,000,000 applicable exclusion amount that includes the DSUEA from Husband 1. A literal reading of the Code suggests that she can do this.[17] If she predeceases Husband 2, it would appear that there are no adverse consequences. Indeed, if she didn't use all of the $7,000,000 applicable exclusion amount for lifetime gifts, it may be available to her estate.

There is, however, another consideration. Unless Wife is much older or terminally ill, it is not assured that she will predecease Husband 2. If Husband 2 instead predeceases Wife, his estate could pass a DSUEA of $5,000,000, assuming no prior taxable gifts by Husband 2. Wife's estate would then be eligible for a basic exclusion amount of $5,000,000, plus a DSUEA of $5,000,000 from Husband 2. If Wife made gifts of $7,000,000 in order to fully utilize the applicable exclusion amount that included a $2,000,000 DSUEA from Husband 1, Wife's estate would start with adjusted taxable gifts of $7,000,000. Her estate would be taxable if it included other assets in excess of $3,000,000.

In any event, it appears to be a "use it or lose it" proposition for Wife with the DSUEA from Husband 1, as it appears that Husband 2 cannot succeed to it if Wife were to predecease him. In that respect, the result in Example 3 of the Joint Committee Explanation appears to not be supported by the language of the statute, as it can be read as confusing the language of the basic exclusion amount with the applicable exclusion amount. Example 3 below is drawn from the Joint Committee Explanation verbatim.

> *Example 3. Assume that same facts as in Examples 1 and 2, except that Wife predeceases Husband 2. Following Husband 1's death, Wife's applicable exclusion amount is $7 million (her $5 million basic amount plus $2 million deceased spousal exclusion amount from Husband 1). Wife made no taxable transfers and has a taxable estate of $3 million. An election is made on Wife's Estate tax return to permit Husband 2 to use Wife's deceased spousal unused exclusion amount, which is $4 million (Wife's $7 million applicable exclusion amount less her $3 million taxable estate). Under the provision, Husband 2's applicable exclusion amount is increased by $4 million, i.e., the amount of deceased spousal unused exclusion amount of Wife.*

Although Example 3 could be interpreted as supplying an answer, it is unclear from the statute how the applicable exclusion amount is allocated, in Wife's estate, between the basic exclusion amount and the DSUEA from

17. This result would appear even more unremarkable if Wife had made the gifts prior to marrying Husband 2.

Husband 1. This uncertainty will need to be resolved by clarification from Congress or the IRS.

Example 4. Assume that Wife from Example 3 has a taxable estate of $3,000,000 and an applicable exclusion amount of $7,000,000 (which includes a $2,000,000 DSUEA from Husband 1). Wife transfers $2,000,000 to a bypass trust in order to utilize Husband 1's DSUEA. In calculating Husband 2's DSUEA from Wife, one would hope for $5,000,000. Section 2010(c)(4) provides, however, that Husband 2's DSUEA is the lesser of: $5,000,000; or $5,000,000 minus the section 2001(b)(1) amount of $2,000,000, i.e., $3,000,000. Consequently, the mechanics don't seem to permit first using the DSUEA from Husband 1 to preserve the balance of Wife's basic exclusion amount. If that is correct, Wife could consider using all of the $7,000,000 applicable exclusion amount to sidestep this issue.

The ultimate consequences turn on the amount of wealth that Husband 1, Husband 2, and Wife possess and the order of deaths. Marriage (and remarriage) has always had estate tax consequences due to the confluence of the applicable exclusion amount (even before it was portable) and the marital deduction. For example, a wealthy person (A) could marry a poorer person with an unused applicable exclusion amount (B). (A) could make unlimited nontaxable lifetime or testamentary gifts to (B), and (B) could ultimately transfer those assets to (A)'s other beneficiaries, using (B)'s applicable exclusion amount.[18] On the other hand, if (A) and (B) are both wealthy, that planning is limited. Moreover, (A) or (B) might have already used some or all of their respective applicable exclusion amounts for inter vivos gifts made before their marriage. The portability option, and the implications of using the DSUEA from prior spouses, adds even more complications to the planning picture.

c. The Election Requirement. Portability requires an election made in an estate tax return of the first spouse to die.[19] Who can predict the future of clients' wealth, longevity, remarriages, tax laws, and the like? And, putting oneself in the shoes of the fiduciary of the first spouse's estate, how does one balance the specter of hindsight liability for failing to file an election to preserve the unused exclusion amount against the waste of estate resources in filing the return and election? The easier path may be to simply file the return and the DSUEA election in all estates of significant value. Attorneys will need to give thought to the fiduciary powers expressed in the governing instrument (which may now need to include

18. The section 2056(b)(7) QTIP assures (A) that the remainder will pass to (A)'s intended beneficiaries.

19. *See* IRC §2010(c)(5)(A).

instructions in this regard) and provide guidance to (and exculpation of) the fiduciary in making these decisions.

3. The DSUEA's Impact on Marital Estate Planning

The apparently benign DSUEA rules might suggest that simple "I Love You" Wills and nonprobate survivorship structures (such as JTWROS, POD designations, retirement account beneficiary designations, etc.) that transfer the bulk of family wealth to the surviving spouse will become acceptable measures for estate tax-sensitive plans for the death of the first spouse.[20] Indeed, the DSUEA is a boon for the unplanned estate, as it supplements the disclaimer as a postmortem planning tool. Of course, this assumes perhaps unreasonably, that there was enough planning to make the DSUEA election upon the death of the first spouse.

There are several benefits to be gained through the use of the DSUEA as a substitute for a bypass trust structure:

- **Reduced Costs**. The additional costs of funding (such as appraisals) and administering a bypass trust (such as fiduciary fees and trust income tax reporting) are avoided. Such costs (particularly the appraisal costs) may nonetheless be incurred in the first-to-die spouse's estate anyway as part of the process of electing the DSUEA and filing the required returns with the IRS in the first-to-die spouse's estate.
- **More Control**. The surviving spouse may prefer outright ownership of the assets, rather than ownership and control through a trust. But such ownership and control also subject these assets to the claims of creditors of the surviving spouse.
- **Avoidance of Lifetime Equalizing Transfers**. Full utilization of the applicable exclusion amount without the DSUEA requires that the assets be held and equalized between the spouses (because it is unknown who will die first) or at least that the first spouse to die has assets sufficient to utilize to the fullest the then available applicable exclusion amount. As discussed later in this chapter, without the DSUEA, lifetime transfers to "equalize" the spouses' estates are necessary, and those transfers can have other desirable or undesirable consequences.
- **Less Retitling of Will Substitute Assets**. Related to the immediately preceding point, without the DSUEA, the estate planner and client will often need to change how clients' property is held, (such as JTWROS, POD designations, retirement account beneficiary designations, etc.) to ensure that the first spouse to die owns enough assets at the time of his or her death so that the applicable exclusion

20. Of course, Wills and revocable trusts will not go away, as the governing instruments need to account for disposition of the property upon the death of the second spouse, particularly in simultaneous death circumstances.

amount can be fully utilized. While completing all of these changes may add to the planning costs at the outset and administration costs upon the death of the first spouse, most of these tasks are undertaken by the clients themselves.

- **Second Step Up in Basis**. The income tax basis of property placed in a bypass trust receives an IRC §1014 adjustment based on the fair market value at the time of the first spouse's death. If those assets are instead passed to the surviving spouse, they will not only receive a basis adjustment at the death of the first spouse, but also receive a (hopefully higher) second section 1014 adjustment at the time of the surviving spouse's death (assuming the surviving spouse still owns the assets).

There are, however, several continuing benefits to be gained through the use of the bypass trust structure:

- **DSUEA Future Uncertain**. The DSUEA and the other increased applicable exclusion amounts are creations of the 2010 Act, and that legislation is scheduled to sunset after December 31, 2012. Thus, the future availability and applicability of the DSUEA is unknown.
- **Reduction of the DSUEA on Remarriage.** If a deceased client's spouse remarries, there is the possibility that the planned for DSUEA could be partially or entirely lost, thus subjecting those assets to estate taxes that otherwise could have eventually passed entirely estate tax free to nonspousal beneficiaries.[21] This risk can be avoided using a bypass trust to hold those assets for the benefit of the surviving spouse.
- **Protecting Assets for Future Beneficiaries**. The decedent may prefer that his or her spouse not hold the bypass trust assets outright for several reasons, including but not limited to spendthrift protection, protection against creditors of the surviving spouse, investment management (particularly upon the surviving spouse's incapacity), and assurance that the assets of the bypass trust will pass to the decedent's desired beneficiaries (and not, e.g., to a successor spouse) and how and when those beneficiaries may eventually receive such assets. If these are significant concerns of the decedent, a trust for the marital share may also be desired.
- **Avoiding Future Estate Taxes on Appreciation**. While the assets held by the surviving spouse will receive a (hopefully) larger section 1014 basis adjustment, this also means that there will be a larger value

21. How is this possible? Suppose the surviving spouse receives outright $5,000,000 in assets from the first-to-die spouse, with both spouses assuming that the DSUEA will entirely shelter these assets from estate tax in the surviving spouse's estate someday. If the surviving spouse were to remarry a new spouse who had no exclusion remaining (e.g., the new spouse previously made lifetime gifts of $5,000,000 to other beneficiaries, such as children) and that new spouse dies before the surviving spouse, the DSUEA vanishes because the DSUEA of the "last" spouse was zero. Should this be a question matchmaking services start asking? ("How much estate tax exclusion amount do you currently have?").

in the surviving spouse's estate subject to the estate tax. A bypass trust "freezes" the estate tax value of those assets at the death of the first spouse — the value of future appreciation of those assets is not subject to estate tax on the death of the second spouse.

- **Full Use of Generation-Skipping Transfer Tax Exemption**. The exemption for the generation-skipping transfer tax (GSTT) is linked to the $5,000,000 "basic exclusion amount under section 2010,"[22] not to the applicable exclusion amount that includes the DSUEA. So, the first spouse's unused GSTT exemption is not portable to the surviving spouse. If the spouses plan on eventually making gifts to skip persons (such as grandchildren or the like) in excess of the surviving spouse's GSTT exemption, the decedent may wish to make nonspousal gifts to such skip persons at the death of the first spouse or to a bypass trust for later distribution to such skip persons, using the GSTT exclusion of the first spouse to die.[23]
- **State Estate Taxes**. Most states do not have portability, which may require a "taxable" bypass trust in the estate of the first spouse, in order to maximize exemptions and exclusions at the state level. This can be a very important consideration.
- **Reduced Income Tax Rate**. Unless the bypass trust is structured to require all of the distribution of income to the surviving spouse, the income can be "sprinkled" among other beneficiaries who may be in lower income tax brackets.

The estate planner and clients will need to balance the benefits of the DSUEA against those of the bypass trust. We anticipate that the degree of client concern about non-tax issues will play a larger role in the ultimate selection of the structure to be employed. Before the DSUEA, it was often a straightforward matter to accept the restrictions (and protections) of a bypass trust "to save taxes." Creating a bypass trust may not be as clearly compelling now, as compared with the landscape prior to the 2010 Act. In the end, however, as is often the case, the decision will lie with which path provides the greatest likelihood of certainty and effectiveness in achieving the clients' non-tax-related goals, when cast against a backdrop of minimizing taxes. It is probably a fair statement that the estate planner must now balance more competing considerations than ever before.

Next, we address the technical aspects of marital deduction planning, largely in the context of a bypass trust and a marital trust. The impact of the DSUEA is a part of the discussion.

22. IRC §2631(c).

23. If a 2056(b)(7) trust is used for the marital trust to the survivor, a reverse QTIP election permitted by section 2652(a)(3) could be utilized to address this issue. However, reverse QTIP planning usually requires a proliferation of trusts (or subtrusts) on the marital share, a significantly greater planning effort requirement than the passive DSUEA application being discussed here.

D. Form of Marital Gift, Formula Clauses, and Funding Alternatives

At the risk of oversimplification, marital deduction planning boils down to a handful of pivotal issues. What form will the gift to the surviving spouse take? How much property should pass to the surviving spouse or for his or her benefit? How will the bequest to the surviving spouse be funded?

1. Form of Gift

Selecting the form of the marital gift is a primary consideration. Should it be outright, in trust, or a combination of the two? As discussed in Chapter 9, second marriages often call for the use of a marital trust to protect the interests of children from the prior marriage. In a very long-term marriage one might expect to find increased use of outright gifts, and one usually does if modest wealth is involved. However, trusts are often used for the marital share in light of their other benefits, such as asset management by the trustee and asset protection for the surviving spouse's benefit, including spendthrift protection at least as to the principal of the trust. Spendthrift provisions must be drafted with care if a suspension of payment approach is used, so as not to violate the marital deduction requirement that the surviving spouse be entitled to all income for his or her lifetime.[24]

The DSUEA is another factor in this analysis. If a bypass trust is not utilized for a portion of the estate assets, relying instead on the DSUEA, a trust may nonetheless be desired to receive the assets passing to the surviving spouse. For example, if a valuation freeze is not desired as of the death of the first spouse and there are no GSTT concerns, the bulk of the first spouse's assets could still pass to a marital trust. The trustee of the marital trust would apply the surviving spouse's applicable exclusion amount (which includes the DSUEA) toward the estate tax liability created by the inclusion of the marital trust in the taxable trust. One would expect that among other considerations in the choice of a marital trust, there would be included the possibility of multiple marriages, asset management in the event of the disability of the surviving spouse, and asset protection considerations described in the preceding paragraph.

If a trust is used for the marital gift, the planner must be sure that it qualifies for the estate tax marital deduction.[25] With respect to the estate

24. *Compare* Tech. Adv. Mem. 82-48-008 (Aug. 18, 1982) (a suspension of payment spendthrift clause violated the required income requirement for a marital deduction trust); Treas. Reg. §20.2056(b)-5(f)(7) (as amended 2004) ("An interest passing in trust will not fail to satisfy the condition that the spouse be entitled to all the income merely because its terms provide that the right of the surviving spouse to the income shall not be subject to assignment, alienation, pledge, attachment or claims of creditors.").

25. *See* IRC §2056.

tax marital deduction, summarized below are five types of trusts that can qualify for the marital deduction.

(1) ***Power of Appointment Trust (IRC §2056(b)(5)).*** Generally speaking, this trust requires a lifetime income interest in the property for the benefit of the surviving spouse, plus a general power of appointment in the spouse. The required general power of appointment, even if confined to a testamentary exercise, can make this alternative unattractive to some testators.[26]

(2) ***Qualified Terminable Interest Property Trust (IRC §2056(b)(7)).*** Like the power of appointment trust, this trust[27] requires a "qualifying income interest" for the life of the surviving spouse. However, there is no required general or special power of appointment.[28] The so-called "QTIP trust" has proved to be popular because the decedent can control the disposition of the remainder. Chapter 9 discusses the use of the QTIP trust for remarriage situations.

(3) ***Charitable Remainder Trust (IRC §2056(b)(8)).*** Chapter 14 discusses the use of charitable remainder trusts. Generally speaking, a charitable remainder trust is structured to create an interest in private beneficiaries, usually family members, with a remainder passing to charity. If the surviving spouse is the only noncharitable beneficiary of a charitable remainder trust, the interest for the benefit of the surviving spouse can qualify for the marital deduction. In this case the marital deduction provisions bow to the very detailed charitable remainder trust rules in delineating the interest of the surviving spouse. One might especially encounter this type of trust when married couples have no children or other natural objects of their bounty and wish to have all or the bulk of their estate pass to charity upon the death of the surviving spouse.

26. In a manner resembling the general power of appointment structure of IRC §2056(b)(5), IRC §2056(b)(6) permits a marital deduction for insurance or annuity proceeds, not necessarily in trust, provided that the surviving spouse is given a lifetime interest in payments from the contract and has a general power to appoint the remaining amounts payable under the contract.

27. Although this provision is usually implemented by a trust, it is not confined to a trust structure. It could, for example, apply to a life estate by deed for the benefit of a surviving spouse or to survivor annuities.

28. No person may have a power to appoint any part of the property to any person other than the surviving spouse during his or her life. *See* IRC §2056(b)(7)(B)(ii)(II). Extreme care must be exercised in connection with this restriction. For example, Treas. Reg. §20.2056(b)-5(j), interpreting IRC §2056(b)(5), states that "[A] power to distribute corpus to the spouse for the support of minor children will not disqualify the trust if she is legally obligated to support such children." However, Example 4 of Treas. Reg. §20.2056(b)-7(h), interpreting IRC §2056(b)(7), casts some doubt on a trustee's power to distribute marital trust property for the maintenance and support of the surviving spouse's minor child, although the Example states that the distribution does not necessarily relieve the surviving spouse of his or her obligation to support the child. While we mention this issue to alert the reader to this thread in the regulations, we do not recommend that any planner engage in this type of drafting brinksmanship for so little gain in terms of the estate tax marital deduction. In our view, the best practice is to include only the surviving spouse in the distribution provisions of the marital trust.

(4) ***Estate Trust.*** The forms of trust discussed above are all exceptions to the "terminable interest" rule announced by IRC §2056(b)(1). The so-called "estate trust" is a product of the treasury regulations.[29] It satisfies the terminable interest rule because, although distributions may be restricted during the surviving spouse's lifetime, all of the trust property, including accumulated income, is ultimately paid to the surviving spouse's estate. This approach was more desirable when an accumulation trust could shelter the surviving spouse from income taxes on trust income distributions. That background factor has shifted with the current highly progressive trust income tax rate structure. The estate trust may still remain useful as a receptacle for non-income-producing assets, such as closely held stock, raw land, or collectibles, for which the income distribution requirements of the other alternatives can be avoided.

(5) ***Qualified Domestic Trust (IRC §2056A).*** As discussed in Chapter 10, the marital deduction is generally disallowed if the surviving spouse is not a U.S. citizen.[30] However, the marital deduction will be allowed if the property is placed in a "qualified domestic trust" complying with the requirements of IRC §2056A, a so-called "QDOT." Form M in the Forms Supplement provides an example of QDOT language.

EXERCISE 11-1

MARITAL DEDUCTION QUALIFYING LANGUAGE

Review the following language found in a marital deduction trust. Does it qualify for the marital deduction? If so, under what IRC provision?

11-1.1. Disposition of Income. My trustee shall pay to or apply for the sole benefit of my spouse, at least annually, all income from this trust from the date of my death.

11-1.2. Disposition of Principal. My trustee shall distribute to my spouse such amounts of the principal of this trust as my spouse may request from time to time by a writing delivered to my trustee during my spouse's lifetime. My trustee may also distribute to my spouse, or apply for my spouse's sole benefit, such amounts of principal as my trustee deems necessary or advisable for my spouse's happiness, support, health, comfort and welfare.

11-1.3. Termination and Disposition. This trust shall terminate upon the death of my spouse. I hereby grant to my spouse, alone and in all events, the power to appoint by Will which makes specific reference to this power and which shall have been admitted to probate in a formal or informal proceeding,

29. *See* Treas. Reg. §20.2056(c)-2(b)(1)(iii) (as amended in 1994).
30. *See* IRC §2056(d).

the entire remaining principal and all undistributed income of the trust to my spouse's estate or in favor of any other person or persons. To the extent that my spouse does not validly exercise this power to appoint by Will, the property then remaining in this trust, if any, shall be distributed... [insert contingent distribution instructions here].

EXERCISE 11-2

MORE MARITAL DEDUCTION QUALIFYING LANGUAGE

Review the following language found in a marital deduction trust. Does it qualify for the marital deduction? If so, under what IRC provision?

11-2.1. Disposition of Income. My trustee shall pay to or apply for the sole benefit of my spouse, at least annually, all income from this trust from the date of my death.

11-2.2. Disposition of Principal. My trustee may distribute to, or apply for the sole benefit of, my spouse, such amounts of the principal as my trustee may from time to time in its discretion deem necessary or advisable for my spouse's health, education, support, and maintenance. In making such determination, my trustee shall consider all resources that are available to my spouse outside the trust that are known to my trustee.

11-2.3. Termination and Disposition. On the death of my spouse, this trust shall terminate and my trustee shall distribute to the personal representative of my spouse's estate all the net income received or accrued during the period between the date of the last income distribution and the date of my spouse's death. The assets then remaining in this trust shall be, subject to paragraph 11-2.4 below, distributed to... [insert distribution instructions here].

11-2.4. Payment of Taxes. If any federal estate taxes are incurred by my spouse's estate as a result of the inclusion of any part or all of this trust in my spouse's estate for estate tax purposes, my trustee shall distribute to the personal representative of my spouse's estate, unless my spouse's Will specifically refers to this trust and directs otherwise, that amount of principal necessary to reimburse my spouse's estate for the tax so incurred, including interest and penalties thereon, computed under the provisions of Section 2207A(a) of the Code and any successor statute of similar purpose. In addition, my Trustee shall distribute to the personal representative of my spouse's estate, unless my spouse's Will specifically refers to this trust and directs otherwise, that amount of principal necessary to reimburse my spouse's estate for all other inheritance, estate, or death taxes payable by reason of my spouse's death, together

continued on next page

with interest and penalties thereon, which taxes are attributable to the inclusion of any part or all of the principal of this trust in my spouse's gross estate for such tax purposes, computed in accordance with the provisions of Section 2207A(a) of the Code, as if such taxes were federal estate taxes. My trustee may rely conclusively upon the statements of my spouse's personal representative in determining the amount of any reimbursement to be made hereunder.

EXERCISE 11-3

UNPRODUCTIVE PROPERTY

What is the purpose of including the following language in a marital deduction trust?

> *Unproductive property shall not be held as an asset of this trust for more than a reasonable time without to my spouse's written consent.*

EXERCISE 11-4

PAYMENT OF TAXES

What is the purpose of paragraph 11-2.4 in the trust provision in Exercise 11-2?

a. Trust Drawbacks. The principal disadvantage of using a trust for the marital deduction amount is its complexity. This complexity stems from (1) the drafting complications of the trust in terms of qualifying it for the estate tax marital deduction; (2) drafting complications in terms of management of the trust assets once the trust is funded (e.g., how much access the surviving spouse should have to the trust assets); and (3) complexity in the management of the trust in terms of selection and compensation of trustees, preparation of required income tax returns, and so forth. A broader disadvantage discussed below is the potential inflexibility of the trust solution, particularly with respect to the QTIP trust.

The QTIP trust is often selected due to the decedent's power to dictate the disposition of the remainder, coupled with a minimum statutory requirement of only income to the surviving spouse. However, the estate planner should consider whether this absolute power is desirable from an overall family estate planning standpoint or from an estate tax planning standpoint. With respect to overall family estate planning, the decedent may wish to give the surviving spouse a testamentary special power of appointment over some portion of the trust assets. Similarly, the decedent may wish to give the surviving spouse some absolutely discretionary withdrawal rights from the trust corpus.[31] Consider the following language in that regard:

> *My trustee shall distribute from the principal of the trust such amount or amounts as my spouse may request be withdrawn by a writing delivered to my trustee during the month of January of each calendar year specifically electing my spouse's right of withdrawal under this paragraph and specifying the amount of such withdrawal requested, provided, however, the total of such withdrawals with respect to any calendar year shall not exceed the greater of $5,000.00 or five percent (5%) of the principal of the trust at the end of the preceding calendar year.*

The right of the surviving spouse to withdraw assets from the QTIP trust for any purpose can permit him or her to make nontaxable inter vivos gifts using his or her annual gift tax exclusions,[32] thereby whittling away the remainder of the QTIP trust, which will be subject to estate taxation upon the survivor's death.[33] Of course, while these planning refinements move in the direction of the flexibility enjoyed by outright marital deduction gifts, they move away from the restrictions of the QTIP, which may be an important part of the decedent's overall plan where preservation of the remainder is a paramount consideration.

b. Total Return Trusts. As discussed above, trust interests that qualify for the marital deduction generally must distribute all income to the surviving spouse. Traditionally, applicable state law divided trust receipts between "income" and "principal." For example, cash dividends from a publicly traded stock would be considered income, but gains realized on the sale of the stock would generally be considered principal. This division scheme often conflicted with modern investment strategies that focus on the expected total return of the invested portfolio as a whole, derived both from current income and appreciation of capital.[34] In addition, during periods of low interest rates, income beneficiaries could receive only very modest trust payouts if the traditional distinctions were applied.

31. As in the sample language below, this would often be structured as a "5 or 5" power or "5 × 5" power complying with IRC §2514(e) and IRC §2041(b)(2), which is the typical approach in a family trust. However, if all of the QTIP remainder will nevertheless be included in the surviving spouse's estate, as a technical matter the surviving spouse's failure to exercise the general power of appointment would not seem to invoke IRC §2514 or §2041. However, one does encounter partial QTIP elections, so if the power of appointment in part applies to the non-marital share, the lapse problem reemerges. Consequently, by custom or through an abundance of caution, one sees "5 or 5" powers in this context.

32. The annual gift exclusion is $13,000 per donee as of 2011 (IRC §2503(b)). In addition, the exclusion for certain medical and educational expenses is potentially unlimited (IRC §2503(e)).

33. To promote the "whittling away" of the remainder of the marital trust, some planners prohibit distributions of principal from the family trust to the surviving spouse until the marital trust is exhausted. For sample withdrawal right language addressing many varied situations, *see* Jeffrey A. Schoenblum, Page on the Law of Wills, vol. 7 (Forms) ch. 87F (2010).

34. *See, e.g.*, Unif. Prudent Investor Act, §2.

Many states have modified the traditional approach. Some have adopted statutes that permit the trustee to adjust the allocations between income and principal to reflect the return from the portfolio as a whole.[35] Others have adopted statutes that permit the definition of income as a unitrust amount, expressed as a percentage of the value of the trust.[36] Some states have adopted both approaches.[37]

The IRS responded to these changes in state law by issuing final regulations that reflect these concepts. In connection with the overall income taxation of trust income, the regulations now define "income" as including total return or unitrust concepts.[38] With respect to marital deduction trusts specifically, the regulations also permit broader definitions of "income," including total return or unitrust amounts.[39] The regulations do not define what a reasonable apportionment of the trust's total return is between the income and principal beneficiaries. However, an example in the regulations and a statement in the preamble to the regulations suggest that an apportionment to income of 3 to 5 percent of trust assets will be considered reasonable, and planners consider that range as a safe harbor.[40]

2. The Amount of the Bequest

a. Computing the Amount of the Bequest. Prior to EGTRRA, marital deduction planning was deceptively simple. Most formula clauses provided for so-called "maximum deferral," and an amount designed to fully use the decedent's unified credit was transferred outright to non-spousal beneficiaries or to a trust, commonly referred to as a "credit shelter trust," "bypass trust," or "family trust." Under this scheme, there was a risk of making the marital share largely irrelevant, because most of the estate could pass to the family trust. In response to that issue, some planners eschewed formula clauses and substituted a so-called "disclaimer Will," under which the bulk of the estate passes outright to the surviving spouse or to a marital trust for the benefit of the surviving spouse. He or she individually, however, or perhaps as trustee of the marital trust, may disclaim a portion of those assets, which will then fund the family trust.[41]

35. *See, e.g.*, UNIF. PRINCIPAL AND INCOME ACT, §§103 & 104.

36. *See, e.g.*, COLO. REV. STAT. §15-1-404.5 (2010).

37. *See, e.g.*, COLO. REV. STAT. §§15-1-403 & 404 (2010) (trustee's power to adjust) & 15-1-404.5 (2010) (total return trusts). *See generally* Adam J. Wiensch & L. Elizabeth Beetz, *The Liberation of Total Return*, 143 TR. & EST. 44 (Apr. 2004).

38. *See* Treas. Reg. §1.643(b)-1 (2004).

39. *See* Treas. Reg. §§20.2056(b)-5(f)(1) & 20.2056(b)-7(d)(1) (2004).

40. *See generally* Wiensch & Beetz, *supra* note 37, at 46; Robert B. Wolf & Stephan R. Leimberg, *Total Return Trusts Approved by New Regs, But State Law Is Crucial*, 31 EST. PLAN. 179, 180-181 (2004).

41. Form N in the Forms Supplement is a sample disclaimer Will. *See generally* Jonathan G. Blattmachr & Michael L. Graham, *Thinking About the Impossible for 2010—No Estate Tax and Carryover Basis*, 21 PROB. & PROP. 12 (May/June 2007); Jerold I. Horn, *The Chief Uncertainty in Estate Planning*, 21 No. 5 PRAC. TAX LAW. 57 (Spring 2007); John J. Scroggin, *Estate Planning to Cope with the Current Legislative Uncertainty*, 34 EST. PLAN. 10 (2007); Barbara A. Sloan, *Disclaimer Planning Revitalized Under EGTRRA*, Advanced Estate Planning Techniques, SG062 ALI-ABA 369, 371-372 (ALI-ABA Continuing Legal Education, Feb. 21-23, 2002); Michael J.

An intermediate position was to use a formula clause but anticipate a possible disclaimer by the surviving spouse that would pare back a portion of the sums otherwise passing to him or her.

With EGTRRA's substantial increases in the applicable exclusion amount, reaching $3,500,000 in 2009, there was increased concern about the possible overfunding of the family trust, to the detriment of the surviving spouse. That concern had planners focusing on measures such as the expanded use of disclaimers, possible caps on the traditional formula clause, and increased access to the family trust by the surviving spouse.

The 2010 Act's increase in the applicable exclusion amount to $5,000,000, coupled with inflation adjustments, further contributes to possible overfunding and spousal access concerns if a family trust structure that excludes the surviving spouse as a beneficiary is used. Those concerns, however, are tempered by the DSUEA, which could eliminate the use of the family or bypass trust in favor of a marital trust. Accordingly, the formula clause after the 2010 Act could assume several forms:

- **Maximum to Bypass Trust, Remainder to Marital Trust**. A client with GSTT or state estate tax concerns, concerns that the DSUEA or the increased applicable exclusion amount may not be extended or might be reduced, or desiring a valuation freeze of the bypass assets share, might choose a formula clause that sets aside a full applicable exclusion amount in the bypass trust, with the balance passing to the marital share. The degree of access by the surviving spouse to the bypass trust (mandatory or discretionary income distributions, discretionary corpus distributions, powers of invasion of corpus) will be dictated typically by the size of the marital share; that is, if the marital share is small, or non-existent, the surviving spouse is likely to have the greatest access to the bypass trust assets.
- **All Marital Trust, Disclaimer to Bypass Trust**. A client without the concerns described in the preceding structure (but with concerns about asset protection, asset management, or assured transmission of the remainder), might choose to forego a bypass trust and pass the bulk of the assets to a marital trust. This plan assumes the continued applicability of the DSUEA. However, the trustee of the marital trust may be empowered to disclaim a portion of the assets, which would then pass to a contingent bypass trust if changes in the law or the nature of the estate assets require this.
- **All to Surviving Spouse, Disclaimer to Bypass Trust**. A client might choose a formula clause that foregoes a bypass trust and passes

Howell, *Disclaimer Trusts—A Wait and See Approach to Estate Planning in Light of EGTRRA*, 15 S.C. LAW. 42 (Nov. 2002); Sebastian V. Grassi, Jr., *Drafting the Marital Deduction Disclaimer Trust after the 2001 Tax Act (with Sample Clauses and Trust Form)*, (Part 1), 16 No. 3 PRAC. TAX LAW. 29 (Spring 2002); (Part 2), 16 No. 4 PRAC. TAX LAW. 7 (Summer 2002) (the two-part Grassi article is a very comprehensive treatment and includes sample language).

the bulk of the assets to the surviving spouse outright. However, if the surviving spouse disclaims all or a portion of those assets, the disclaimed assets pass to a contingent bypass trust for the surviving spouse's indirect benefit.[42]

- **All to Surviving Spouse**. A client might choose a formula clause that passes the bulk of the assets to the surviving spouse outright and does not provide for a contingent bypass trust as a receptacle for assets disclaimed by the surviving spouse. This is the simple estate for which the DSUEA was created, and it would be rarely appropriate unless the value of the combined marital assets assures that no estate tax is possibly due for federal or state purposes. In Section B.2 of Chapter 16, "Planning After the 2010 Act," we discuss in greater detail some of the possible drafting responses to the uncertain future of the estate tax.

EXERCISE 11-5

DISCLAIMER WILLS

In light of the 2010 Act, why shouldn't formula clauses generally be supplanted by disclaimer Wills?

b. Equalization Clauses. Although the maximum deferral strategy works for most estates, it can be disadvantageous if the surviving spouse passes away soon after the death of the other spouse, and the estate tax rates are progressive. If estate tax rates are progressive, spreading the assets between the two spousal estates can reduce the combined estate tax that is payable. A so-called "equalization clause" reduces the amount of the marital share upon the occasion of serial deaths (serial deaths upon which federal estate taxes are imposed twice also raise the potential application of IRC §2013 to mitigate a portion of the combined tax burden). EGTRRA incrementally decreased the maximum estate tax rate from 50 percent in 2002 to 45 percent in 2007-2009. The scheduled estate tax rate on an amount of assets equal to a $2,000,000 or $3,500,000 applicable exclusion amount was 45 percent, so as a practical matter progressivity in the estate tax rates no longer existed after EGTRRA. The 2010 Act compounded this state of affairs by decreasing the maximum estate tax rate to 35 percent, while increasing the applicable exclusion amount to $5,000,000. However, with the continuing uncertainty surrounding the future of the federal wealth transfer taxes, it would seem that inclusion of an equalization clause remains prudent.

42. The surviving spouse would need to heed the timing rules of IRC §2518 as well as other technical considerations such as the "passage without direction" rules that permit only certain surviving spouse powers over the disclaimer trust. *See* Treas. Reg. §25.2518-2(e) (1997).

An example of such a clause is set out below:

> *If my spouse survives me, but dies within six months following the date of my death, my personal representative shall distribute from my residuary estate to my trustee, to be held in a trust, the largest amount that, after making allowance for the marital deduction allowed with respect to all interests in property that pass or have passed to my spouse other than under this section, will result in the lowest aggregate federal estate taxes computed for my estate and for my spouse's estate pursuant to Section 2001(b) of the Code (in each case reduced by the available applicable credit amount*[43] *against federal estate tax, but no other credit), on the assumptions that my spouse died after me, but on the date of my death.*

EXERCISE 11-6

SURVIVAL PERIODS

Why is six months chosen for the survival period rather than twelve months, for example? Could the phrase "but on the date of my death" create a potential problem?

EXERCISE 11-7

EQUALIZATION CLAUSES

Is the inclusion of an equalization clause necessary to achieve the equalization result?

c. The Pecuniary Amount and Fractional Share Formula Clauses.[44] The marital deduction bequest ultimately needs to be described as an amount of property that will pass to the surviving spouse or will fund the marital trust. There are generally two forms of "formula" clauses that make this calculation, the "pecuniary amount" marital formula clause and the "fractional share" marital formula clause. However, a formula clause is not necessary in all cases, and some planners use a disclaimer Will or a *Clayton* contingent QTIP election to divide the estate into marital and non-marital shares through postmortem actions. With the DSUEA now available, these issues may be less important for some clients. However, in spite of the DSUEA, many clients will continue to utilize a

43. The Taxpayer Relief Act of 1997 introduced some confusion by retaining the old terminology "unified credit" in the title of IRC §2010, while using "the applicable credit amount" in the text of IRC §2010(a), but with the amount of the credit determined in IRC §2010(c) with reference to the estate tax computed on "the applicable exclusion amount." This confusion is continued with the 2010 Act.

44. *See* John R. Price & Samuel A. Donaldson, Price on Contemporary Estate Planning, ch. 5 (2011), for examples of formula clause language and a discussion of funding methods.

bypass trust for the reasons previously discussed and thus this discussion assumes that a bypass trust is being utilized.

(1) The pecuniary amount formula clause. The pecuniary amount marital formula clause is more widely used than the fractional share approach because it is generally easier to understand and apply. An example of a pecuniary amount marital formula clause is set out below. It is reasonably self-explanatory:

> *If my spouse survives me, my trustee shall set aside from my residuary estate a marital deduction amount, to be held in trust for my spouse under Article XX and to be known as the Marital Trust. Except as otherwise provided below, the marital deduction amount shall be the least amount necessary to obtain a marital deduction sufficient to reduce the federal estate tax payable by reason of my death to the lowest possible amount.*[45] *The marital deduction amount shall be reduced by the value of any interest in property which qualifies for the marital deduction and which passes or has passed from me to my spouse other than by this gift.*

This is not magic—it is simply language that sets the amount of a bequest. However, it is a fundamental principle of Wills law that bequests can be specific, demonstrative, general, or residuary; and those distinctions must be weighed in selecting the form of the marital bequest. The language in the example above is often referred to as a "pre-residuary pecuniary" amount; it is a general bequest determined before the residue is calculated. The residue of the estate passes to the family trust. The order can be reversed, with the family trust carved out as a general bequest and the marital bequest receiving the residue.

Unfortunately, the decision whether to use a pre-residuary pecuniary marital amount or a residuary marital amount is not uncomplicated. When a decedent dies, the amounts of all general bequests, including the marital share or the family share, are fixed as of the date of death, or alternate

45. Prior to 2005, IRC §2011 permitted a federal estate tax credit for a scheduled amount of the state estate taxes paid. In 2005, the credit was replaced by a deduction. *See* IRC §2058. In response, states have modified their estate tax structures to varying degrees. *See infra* notes 68-69 and accompanying text. Prior to 2005, it was accepted practice to include a saving clause in the marital deduction formula clause to avoid an adverse interaction between the federal estate tax marital deduction and the state estate taxes. The concern was that in an otherwise nontaxable federal estate (produced by zeroing out the estate through the use of the marital deduction), a state estate tax nevertheless could be produced if the federal estate tax marital deduction was reduced to reflect that any remaining federal tax would be absorbed by the available credit for state estate taxes. While the federal return would have no net tax due, there could be an unnecessary tax created at the state level. The mathematics was a bit challenging and required an analysis of the structure of the state estate tax, with an emphasis on so-called "sponge" or "pick-up" state tax approaches. Here is an example of typical saving language: "provided, however, that the state death tax credit shall be taken into account for this purpose only to the extent that it does not increase the amount of state death taxes payable." With the elimination of the federal credit for state estate taxes, this language no longer has any effect. However, if the estate is potentially subject to state estate taxes, the marital deduction formula (as well as tax apportionment clauses and disclaimer planning) must consider the structure of the applicable state tax regime (e.g., exemption amounts and references to the federal credit or deduction). It is probably a fair statement that this issue now requires even more thoughtful state-by-state tailoring.

valuation date, if elected. However, those bequests may not be funded until months later, after the personal representative has collected the estate assets, sold some of the assets, paid creditors, etc. Consequently, the values of assets at the time of funding may be more or less than the date-of-death values. Thus, generally speaking, if the marital or family share is expressed as a fixed amount, it is a general bequest for state law purposes, computed at the time of death or on the alternate valuation date, and would remain the same irrespective of fluctuations in value.[46] The "fixing" referred to in the following examples is a function of the allocation of postmortem appreciation (or depreciation) of the estate assets during the administration of the estate. It is sometimes referenced as "freezing" the value of the gift (e.g., the marital share) at the values existing at the decedent's death; it is not to be confused with the concept that the assets that pass to the bypass trust are "frozen," in the sense that after the trust is funded, the bypass trust assets and all appreciation in those assets escape inclusion in the taxable estate of the surviving spouse.

EXAMPLE

"FIXING" THE MARITAL SHARE IN AN APPRECIATING ESTATE

Assume that the estate is worth $8,000,000 as of date of death. The formula, following a maximum deferral strategy, creates a $3,000,000 marital trust, expressed as a general bequest, and a $5,000,000 residuary family trust (ignoring possible inflation adjustments of the applicable exclusion amount). If the estate increases in value to $8,300,000 during administration, the marital share remains fixed at $3,000,000, and the family trust share increases to $5,300,000. That $5,300,000 is viewed for estate tax purposes as simply the appreciated $5,000,000 assets, and accordingly passes free of any additional estate taxes. If the objective is to pass the maximum amount of property free of estate tax to accumulate in the future free of estate tax, the pre-residuary marital gift is usually the preferred approach. One must keep in mind, however, the possibility that the estate could diminish in value during administration, with the result being an undesirable "under-funding" of the residuary family trust. Indeed, if the estate were to decrease in value to $7,700,000 during administration, only $4,700,000 would pass to the residuary family trust—the marital share as a general bequest remains fixed at $3,000,000.

46. This is the generally accepted interpretation of the mechanics. However, an Arizona case dealing with the abatement of competing general bequests suggests that pre-residuary bequests may not be fixed as of the time of death, but can reflect postmortem fluctuations in value. The facts of the case are arguably distinguishable from the clear cut competing general and residuary bequests described in the text. And, the case could be wrong on this point of the law (it has not been embraced in other jurisdictions). *See* In re Estate of Goldman, 158 P.3d 892 (Ariz. Ct. App. 2007).

EXAMPLE

DIMINISHING THE FAMILY SHARE IN A DECLINING ESTATE

Assume that we are dealing with a larger estate, with a gross value of $11,000,000. The pre-residuary marital share would be $6,000,000, and the residuary family trust share would be $5,000,000 (ignoring possible inflation adjustments of the applicable exclusion amount). The general bequest is $6,000,000, a large amount to set aside during administration, and it exacerbates the income tax consequences, as discussed below in Part D.3, "Funding the Marital Share." Further assume that the assets of the estate decline by 20 percent during administration, not an impossibility for certain asset classes. The marital share remains at $6,000,000, but the tax-exempt family trust share bears all of the depreciation in the estate, and becomes $2,800,000. While this is an extreme example, it demonstrates the leverage that a large pre-residuary marital share exerts on a lesser residuary family trust.

This, however, is not simply a federal wealth transfer tax issue. In maximizing the size of the family trust, the planner needs to consider the assets of the surviving spouse—are they adequate to support him or her? If there are such concerns, the family trust could also permit the surviving spouse to invade the corpus of the family trust. (If the spouse's withdrawal power is not subject to an ascertainable standard, a trustee other than the surviving spouse should be entrusted with this power so a taxable general power of appointment in favor of the surviving spouse is not created).

While the result in the first example above is quite attractive from a federal wealth transfer tax standpoint because the value of the property passing to the surviving spouse was frozen, the surviving spouse might have preferred to share in some of that appreciation. Again, in lieu of providing for a share of the appreciation, the planner might permit the surviving spouse access to the family trust (either through discretionary distributions made by a trustee other than the surviving spouse, or by distributions made subject to an ascertainable standard by the surviving spouse as trustee). That is generally a more flexible alternative that responds to the *actual* future needs of the surviving spouse, rather than being a response to the *perceived* future needs of the surviving spouse determined during the unsettling period of bereavement following the death of a spouse.

If these alternatives are not acceptable, the formula could be "flipped." That is, the marital trust amount could be expressed as a residuary amount with the family share expressed as a fixed general bequest. The result would be that the marital trust would benefit from increases (and be burdened with declines) in value that occur during the administration of the estate. Because the marital trust assets will someday be subject to estate tax, an increased marital asset base, unless it declines due to consumption or investment reverses, could produce additional estate taxes that would not have been payable had the appreciated value flowed into the family trust.[47] Aside from the estate tax consequences, the state law consequences are not uniformly positive in terms of ensuring the financial well-being of the surviving spouse. The marital share could also suffer from declines in value during administration. This is a two-way proposition: if the marital share is expressed as a residuary amount, it may actually decline in funded value if the estate assets contract. This uncertain dual aspect of a residuary marital gift, with practical disadvantages of a declining estate value at the one extreme, coupled with the possible negative estate tax consequences of an appreciating estate value at the other extreme, makes the pre-residuary pecuniary marital gift alternative compelling for many clients.

(2) The fractional share formula clause. The alternative to the pecuniary marital share (a pre-residuary general gift) is to use a fractional share formula clause (a residuary gift). The language of this clause does not provide for a fixed dollar amount; instead, it produces a numerical fraction, and the marital share is that fraction of the total residue assets of the estate. An example of a fractional share clause is set out below:

> *If my spouse survives me, my trustee shall set aside a fractional share from my residuary estate to be held in trust for my spouse under Article XX and to be known as the Marital Trust. The fractional share shall be computed as follows: The numerator of the fraction shall equal the unlimited federal estate tax marital deduction allowable to my estate. If such amount is more than would be necessary to produce the lowest possible federal estate tax with respect to my gross estate*[48] *then such amount shall be reduced so that it is equal to the minimum marital deduction, if any, that is necessary to produce the lowest possible federal estate tax. In addition, the numerator shall be reduced by the value of any interest in property which qualifies for the marital deduction and which passes or has passed from me to my spouse other than by this Article. The denominator of the fraction shall be the value of my residual estate.*

Because of the nature of the fractional share clause, issues concerning the characterization of the bequest as either a general bequest or a residuary bequest are avoided — a fractional share is a fractional share of the residue. But, with a fractional share clause, one cannot freeze the appreciation in assets during administration. Moreover, some practitioners worry that applying the fractional share rigorously could require a

47. Some commentators disagree with this approach because its benefits are limited to increases or decreases in value during the postmortem administration period, a relatively limited period of time. In addition, it can limit the benefits of alternate valuation under IRC §2032 if values fall. *See* Jerome A. Manning et al., Manning on Estate Planning §2.6 (5th ed. 1995 & Supp. 2009).

48. A saving clause was typically inserted at this point to address the interaction of the federal credit for state estate taxes and the state estate taxes themselves. *See supra* note 45.

fractional share and joint ownership between the marital share and the family share in each and every asset. Some planners avoid it for that reason.[49] However, as discussed in the next section, the fractional share does offer some income tax advantages in funding the marital share.

3. Funding the Marital Share

The executor/personal representative needs instructions as to which assets must be selected for funding the marital share. May it be only those assets that have declined in value since the date of death? If one could include only those assets, one might obtain some estate tax advantage because it is the marital trust that will be taxed on the death of the survivor. On the other hand, what will the surviving spouse think about receiving all of the depreciated assets for the marital trust, tax issues aside? Alternatively, should assets that are fairly representative of appreciation and depreciation of the estate as a whole be used?

a. Revenue Procedure 64-19. Due to the potential estate tax avoidance opportunities posed by funding alternatives, the IRS will deny the marital deduction unless Revenue Procedure 64-19, 1964-1 C.B. 682, is followed. If the marital share is expressed as a fixed pecuniary amount with the family trust as the residuary legatee, then the Revenue Procedure 64-19 funding issues are presented. There are several permitted alternatives in this revenue procedure — including use of a fractional share, using date of funding values, and funding with assets that are fairly representative of appreciation and depreciation experienced by the estate assets. Revenue Procedure 64-19, below, demands close attention by the estate planning attorney. Indeed, the alternatives permitted by the revenue procedure are not readily apparent from a cursory reading.

Rev. Proc. 64-19
1964-1 C.B. 682

The Federal estate tax marital deduction may be allowed where, under the terms of a Will or trust, an executor or trustee is empowered to satisfy a pecuniary bequest or transfer in trust to a decedent's surviving spouse with assets at their value as finally determined for Federal estate tax purposes, subject, however, to prescribed conditions.

49. That technical rigor is usually relaxed through the addition of a funding clause that permits the personal representative to make non-pro rata distributions of assets. Thus, a "pure" fraction (of each asset) becomes a fiction — the fraction is of the gross estate. Rev. Rul. 69-486, 1969-2 C.B. 159 held that a taxable sale or exchange was produced where the executor did not hold an express power to make non-pro rata distributions. However, in a corporate distribution context, Rev. Rul. 83-61, 1983-1 C.B. 78 rejected that conclusion when there was such a power. There are many private letter rulings in the trust and estate context holding that the inclusion of a power to make non-pro rata distributions will eliminate the taxable event. *See, e.g.*, Priv. Ltr. Rul. 2007-23-014 (June 8, 2007). For other complications, see MANNING ET AL., *supra* note 47, §2.7.

SECTION 1. PURPOSE.

The purpose of this Revenue Procedure is to state the position of the Internal Revenue Service relative to allowance of the marital deduction in cases where there is some uncertainty as to the ultimate distribution to be made in payment of a pecuniary bequest or transfer in trust where the governing instrument provides that the executor or trustee may satisfy bequests in kind with assets at their value as finally determined for Federal estate tax purposes.

SEC. 2. BACKGROUND.

.01 The Internal Revenue Service has received inquiries concerning the amount of the marital deduction which should be allowed for a pecuniary bequest in a Will or for a transfer in trust of a pecuniary amount where the governing instrument not only provides that the executor or trustee may, or is required to, select assets in kind to satisfy the bequest or transfer, but also provides that any assets distributed in kind shall be valued at their values as finally determined for Federal estate tax purposes. The question is the same whether the amount of the bequest or transfer is determined by a formula fixing it by reference to the adjusted gross estate of the decedent as finally determined for Federal estate tax purposes, or its amount is determined in some other fashion by which a fixed dollar amount distributable to the surviving spouse can be computed. Any bequest or transfer in trust described in subsection 2.01 is hereinafter referred to as a "pecuniary bequest or transfer" for purposes of this Revenue Procedure.

.02 Where, by virtue of the duties imposed on the fiduciary either by applicable state law or by the express or implied provisions of the instrument, it is clear that the fiduciary, in order to implement such a bequest or transfer, must distribute assets, including cash, having an aggregate fair market value at the date, or dates, of distribution amounting to no less than the amount of the pecuniary bequest or transfer, as finally determined for Federal estate tax purposes, the marital deduction may be allowed in the full amount of the pecuniary bequest or transfer in trust. Alternatively, where, by virtue of such duties, it is clear that the fiduciary must distribute assets, including cash, fairly representative of appreciation or depreciation in the value of all property thus available for distribution in satisfaction of such pecuniary bequest or transfer, the marital deduction is equally determinable and may be allowed in the full amount of the pecuniary bequest or transfer in trust passing to the surviving spouse.

.03 In many instances, however, by virtue of the provisions of the Will or trust, or by virtue of applicable state law (or because of an absence of applicable state decisions), it may not be clear that the discretion of the fiduciary would be limited in this respect, and it cannot be determined that he would be required to make distribution in conformance with one or the other of the above requirements or that one rather than the other is applicable. In such a case, the interest in property passing from the decedent to his surviving spouse would not be ascertainable as of the date of death, if the property available for distribution included assets which might fluctuate in value.

SEC. 3. INSTRUCTIONS TO TAXPAYERS AND SERVICE PERSONNEL.

[This section is omitted. It specifies transitional ameliorative measures applicable to instruments executed prior to the issuance of the revenue procedure.]

SEC. 4. SCOPE.

.01 The problem here considered is restricted to the situation involving bequests and transfers in trust described in sections 1 and 2.01. It does not arise in other cases, for example:

(1) In a bequest or transfer in trust of a fractional share of the estate, under which each beneficiary shares proportionately in the appreciation or depreciation in the value of assets to the date, or dates, of distribution.

(2) In a bequest or transfer in trust of specific assets.

(3) In a pecuniary bequest or transfer in trust, whether in a stated amount or an amount computed by the use of a formula, if:

(a) The fiduciary must satisfy the pecuniary bequest or transfer in trust solely in cash, or

(b) The fiduciary has no discretion in the selection of the assets to be distributed in kind, or

(c) Assets selected by the fiduciary to be distributed in kind in satisfaction of the bequest or transfer in trust are required to be valued at their respective values on the date, or dates, of their distribution.

.02 This Revenue Procedure does not relate to any issue arising under the income tax provisions of the Internal Revenue Code.

SEC. 5. FORM OF AGREEMENTS.

[This section is omitted. It provides forms to comply with the transitional ameliorative measures prescribed by Section 3.]

EXERCISE 11-8

MARITAL SHARE FUNDING LANGUAGE

Some version of the following language is often used in the funding language of marital deduction provisions. What is the role of this language?

> A. *The Personal Representative shall not distribute in satisfaction of the [marital share] any assets that are not capable of qualifying for the marital deduction;*
>
> or
>
> B. *The marital deduction amount shall be composed only of interests in property which qualify for the federal estate tax marital deduction.*

b. Complying with Revenue Procedure 64-19. As noted above, Revenue Procedure 64-19 states that the fractional share qualifies because it will purportedly allocate a slice of each and every asset in the estate, whether appreciated or depreciated. Although theoretically correct, unless the estate contains very simple assets and involves simple distribution schemes, it is difficult as a practical matter to divide each asset between the marital and credit shelter trust share on a pro rata basis. Accordingly, under the "pick and choose" method permitting non–pro rata distributions, some beneficiaries may receive a complete undivided interest in certain assets as their fractional share of the estate. Making those designations may entail the need for new, or revised, value appraisals at the time of funding.

Much of the attention on funding is on pecuniary amount marital bequests because of the pecuniary amount's perceived advantages in shifting postmortem appreciation away from the marital share. Accordingly, funding issues are driven by Revenue Procedure 64-19's acceptance of pecuniary amount funding approaches that use date of funding valuation or valuation that is fairly representative of the overall postmortem appreciation or depreciation in all of the estate assets.

There are many variations on this theme, but generally a planner is presented with three types[50] of funding clauses: (1) so-called *true worth* (date of funding/date of allocation values used rather than date-of-death values — marital trust receives full value); (2) *minimum worth* (lower of date-of-death value or value at time of funding); and (3) *fairly representative* (fair mix of both appreciated and depreciated assets, using date-of-death values).[51]

(1) True worth funding. It has been our experience that true worth funding is the most popular approach, and some commentators confirm

50. There could be a fourth option, the so-called "single fund marital" approach, which does not explicitly fund the marital trust. In our experience this is rarely used. *See* Jeffrey N. Pennell, *Funding Marital Deduction (and Other) Bequests*, 35 Inst. on Est. Plan. ¶¶ 1500, 1505 (2001).

51. For a discussion of marital share funding options, see Laurie L. O'Donnell, *Funding of Marital Trusts, in* Understanding and Using Trusts §11.2.1 (MCLE) (2002); Jeffrey N. Pennell, *Selected Materials Relating to Planning Marital Transfers*, Planning Techniques for Large Estates, SH069 ALI-ABA 461 (ALI-ABA Continuing Legal Education, Apr. 28-May 2, 2003); Julia B. Fisher, *Pecuniary v. Fractional Share: What Are the Considerations?*, Advanced Estate Planning Techniques, SG062 ALI-ABA 117 (ALI-ABA Continuing Legal Education, Feb. 21-23, 2002).

that.[52] The true worth principle, fair market value as of date of funding or allocation, is easy to apply, and it complies with the express directions of Revenue Procedure 64-19. However, particularly in a protracted administration, true worth funding may require a second set of asset appraisals to determine the date of funding or allocation values (the first set being required for the probate inventory and the estate tax return valuations).[53] Another drawback to the true worth method is the estate's potential realization of gain or loss for income tax purposes. That issue is discussed in the next section.

(2) Minimum worth funding. The minimum worth approach applies the lower of the date of death value or the value at the time of funding. While it is not a method expressly addressed by Revenue Procedure 64-19, it is considered as complying with the revenue procedure because its reference to a potentially lower value at time of funding eliminates the prospect of funding the marital share with assets that declined in value during administration. However, that formula may have the effect of overfunding the marital share if the asset in question has appreciated during administration, because the marital bequest is considered satisfied only to the extent of the lesser date of death value. Like the true worth formula, the minimum worth formula may require a second set of appraisals to establish the asset valuations as of time of funding.[54] As compared with the true worth method, its principal advantage lies in avoiding the recognition of gain on funding the marital share.

(3) Fairly representative funding. The fairly representative approach is drawn expressly from Revenue Procedure 64-19. Ostensibly, one may use the date-of-death values in funding the marital share, exercising vigilance that the selected assets fairly represent the postmortem overall appreciation and depreciation in the estate assets. At best, exercising that vigilance is an uncertain task for the personal representative in a complex estate; moreover, it can result in overfunding the marital share. At worst, such vigilance may require a second appraisal of all assets of the estate to ensure that the selected assets are truly representative. As compared with the true worth method, the fairly representative approach may be desirable in terms of avoiding the recognition of gain in funding the marital share.

52. *See, e.g.*, O'Donnell, *supra* note 51, §11.2.1. A survey of members of the American College of Trust and Estate Counsel and attendees at the Miami Institute on Estate Planning found that a pecuniary bequest to the marital trust with date of funding valuation was the most common approach, closely followed by a pecuniary bequest to the family trust with date of funding valuation, and followed by a fractional share clause with discretion in asset allocation. *See* Malcolm A. Moore & Jeffrey N. Pennell, *Practicing What We Preach: Esoteric or Essential?*, 27 INST. ON EST. PLAN. ¶¶ 1200 & 1211 (1993).

53. However, to the extent the estate assets are cash or publicly traded assets (such as securities), determining a "second" date of funding values for such assets is simple and straightforward.

54. Treas. Reg. §26.2642-2(b)(2)(i) suggests that for generation-skipping transfer tax purposes, an allocation of the GSTT exemption to the pecuniary marital trust cannot be accomplished if minimum worth funding is used. *See* O'Donnell, *supra* note 51, §11.2.1(c).

c. Income Tax Impacts of Funding Methods. One drawback of a pecuniary general bequest is judicial authority, principally *Kenan v. Commissioner*,[55] to the effect that the transfer of assets in kind in satisfaction of such a bequest is a taxable sale or exchange of the assets. Ideally one would fund the pecuniary bequest with money rather than in kind, but this is impractical in many cases, particularly if the bequest is quite substantial. Some commentators propose that the use of the fractional share formula avoids this problem.[56] It is also asserted that minimum worth[57] or fairly representative[58] funding of a pecuniary bequest may avoid *Kenan* gain. In any event, it may be an exaggerated problem for many estates unless the decedent owned assets that could substantially appreciate during administration, because under IRC §1014, the gain is limited to postmortem appreciation.

Funding the pecuniary bequest as quickly as possible may minimize any appreciation. Another option is to specifically bequeath significant assets that are expected to appreciate directly to the marital share. The marital formula clause will take that value into account and reduce the amount of the formula bequest, so the amount of the aggregate marital deduction is not a concern. However, specific bequests reduce the flexibility of the personal representative in selecting assets to fund the marital share. Alternatively, if the marital share is very large and *Kenan* is seen as a problem, some practitioners use a residuary marital share — *Kenan* is avoided but at the price of losing the postmortem appreciation valuation freeze enjoyed by the pre-residuary bequest approach.

A careful review of the client's assets, the size of the estate, and the likely appreciation during a future administration is crucial to analyzing the choices presented here. In any event, in considering the amount and selection of assets in funding marital bequests, one needs to consider the impact of asset transfers outside the control and discretion of the personal representative. The two principal asset categories are nonprobate transfers (e.g., life insurance, joint tenancies, transfer-on-death accounts, payable-on-death accounts, retirement accounts, etc.) and other probate-specific gifts (such as tangible personal property and specific bequests) that pass to the surviving spouse.

d. The Retirement Asset Funding Trap. As discussed in Chapter 12, if retirement assets are being used to fund a pecuniary bequest, there is a significant risk that such funding will require the recognition of all of the income in respect of a decedent included in those retirement assets; alternative forms of bequest are strongly advised by most commentators. One simple approach is to designate the surviving spouse or marital trust as the beneficiary of the retirement assets as a nonprobate asset that does not

55. 114 F.2d 217 (2d Cir. 1940).
56. Pennell, *supra* note 51, ¶¶ 1504.3 & 1504.4.
57. *Id.* ¶1502.3.
58. *Id.* ¶1502.2.

pass by reason of any formula clause (although the assets are considered in the aggregate amount of assets, probate and nonprobate, that pass to the surviving spouse under the formula clause).

EXERCISE 11-9

MARITAL SHARE FUNDING AND REV. PROC. 64-19

Three alternative funding approaches are set out below. Identify them and discuss whether they comply with Revenue Procedure 64-19.

A. *My personal representative, in satisfying this gift, may distribute property in cash or in kind, or partly in each, with any property valued at fair market value at the date of allocation to the marital share.*
B. *My personal representative, in satisfying this gift, may distribute property in cash or in kind, or partly in each, provided, however, that the assets so distributed shall be selected by my personal representative in a manner such that they shall have an aggregate fair market value fairly representative of the appreciation or depreciation in value to the date or dates of each distribution of all property that is available for distribution.*
C. *My personal representative, in satisfying this gift, may distribute property in cash or in kind, or partly in each, with any property valued at fair market value at the date of allocation to the marital share unless such fair market value shall be greater than its federal income tax basis, in which event such asset shall be valued at its federal income tax basis.*

EXERCISE 11-10

SELECTING A FUNDING METHOD

Assume that you are drafting the marital deduction clause in the husband's Will. The husband owns $6,200,000 in assets. The wife owns $1,800,000 in assets. In practice, you would need to know much more, such as whether any of the assets consist of nonprobate property (e.g., joint tenancies, insurance, IRA or pension assets), as well as information such as the ages, physical condition, and final wishes of the couple. The husband's desire is that the marital and the family/bypass/credit shelter portions both be placed in trust. The client also desires a pecuniary share, so the fractional share is not to be considered. It is the husband's desire that if the estate increases in value from the time of death to the date of funding the trusts, that the increase inure to the benefit of the beneficiaries of the family/bypass/credit shelter trust. Discuss whether you would use a pre-residuary pecuniary marital bequest or a residuary marital bequest, and discuss the funding method you would select.

EXERCISE 11-11

DRAFTING THE MARITAL DEDUCTION LANGUAGE

Using parts of Form H in the Forms Supplement, draft the marital deduction section of the husband's Will in Exercise 11-10.

EXERCISE 11-12

A COMMON PROBLEM

What is the planning problem demonstrated by the wife's estate in Exercise 11-10?

e. The "Reverse QTIP" Election. For years after 2003 each spouse has a generation-skipping transfer tax (GSTT) exemption equal to the applicable exclusion amount, and the "reverse QTIP" election has largely become a historical artifact. However, much like equalization clauses discussed earlier in this chapter, it remains prudent to retain the option of making this election, particularly in the uncertain federal wealth transfer tax environment, as well as in situations where the decedent may have made large, non-GSTT lifetime gifts that consumed portions of his or her applicable exclusion amount and wishes to create a QTIP trust with skip persons as the remainderpersons.

The GSTT is imposed on the transferor for direct skips, on the transferee for taxable distributions, and on the trustee for taxable terminations.[59] IRC §2652(a)(1) defines "transferor" for these purposes to mean the decedent where the property is subject to estate tax.[60] Until EGTRRA's increase in the estate tax applicable exclusion in 2002 to roughly the amount of the GSTT exemption,[61] a risk of the maximum deferral strategy for marital deduction purposes was that the estate of the first spouse would not pass enough taxable assets to skip persons to fully utilize the GSTT exemption. IRC §2652(a)(3) is a response to this issue. It provides an election, often referred to as the "reverse QTIP," which is made by the estate of the first spouse to die. The reverse QTIP election treats the deceased spouse, not the surviving spouse, as the transferor for

59. *See* IRC §2603(a).

60. *See* Treas. Reg. §26.2652-1(a) (as amended in 1997).

61. The Taxpayer Relief Act of 1997 introduced a phased-in increase in the applicable exclusion amount for estates, ranging from $625,000 in 1998 to $1,000,000 for 2006 and thereafter. EGTRRA increased the applicable exclusion amount to $1,000,000 for 2002 and 2003, $1,500,000 in 2004 and 2005, $2,000,000 in 2006-2008, and $3,500,000 in 2009. The 2010 Act further increased the applicable exclusion amount to $5,000,000, plus indexed increases for inflation (IRC §2010(c)). For years 2004 and beyond, the GSTT exemption and the applicable exclusion amount are equal amounts, thus obviating the need to make a reverse QTIP election if the credit shelter trust is fully funded. If significant GSTT transfers are desired, the 2010 Act creates an incentive for full utilization of the GSTT exemption in the estate of the first spouse to die because the DSUEA does not apply to the GSTT exemption. *See supra* note 22 and accompanying text.

GSTT purposes. This applies the otherwise unused portion of the decedent's GSTT exemption, the difference between the credit shelter gift and the allowable GSTT exemption of the decedent, to those assets, while preserving the impact of the QTIP election for estate tax purposes. This option is unavailable with other marital deduction provisions such as the IRC §2056(b)(5) gift. An example of reverse QTIP language is set out below:

> *All provisions of this Will shall be construed to permit divisions, distributions, other dispositions and the creation of multiple trusts regardless of the number of trusts established hereunder. My fiduciaries may use my available generation-skipping transfer tax exemption (to the extent possible) in order to establish and maintain separate trusts which have generation-skipping inclusion ratios of either zero (the exempt trusts) or one (the nonexempt trusts) by making the election permitted under Section 2652(a)(3) to treat the property of the Marital Trust, or of any or all of the separate trusts into which said Marital Trust may have been divided, with respect to which a marital deduction is allowed to my estate pursuant to the provisions of Section 2056(b)(7), as if the election under Section 2056(b)(7) to treat such property as qualified terminable interest property had not been made, so as to ensure, for purposes of the federal generation-skipping transfer tax, that my estate is treated as the transferor of any such qualified terminable interest property.*

EXERCISE 11-13

REVERSE QTIP TRUSTS

Estates that expect to use the reverse QTIP election usually include two marital trusts, rather than one, or at a minimum permit the division of the marital trust into two subtrusts, commonly referred to as the "exempt QTIP" and the "non-exempt QTIP" (*see, e.g.*, Priv. Ltr. Rul. 2002-26-026 (June 28, 2002), approving the severance of a QTIP trust into two subtrusts, one of which qualified for the reverse QTIP). The assets subject to the election are directed to one of the trusts, with the balance of the marital assets to the other trust. Read IRC §2652(a)(3) to see why this approach is followed.

4. Special Community Property Considerations

The marital formula clauses discussed in the preceding material generally apply in a community property jurisdiction. The formula clauses operate on the decedent's separate property as well as on his or her one-half interest in the community property. However, community property can present special challenges in terms of postmortem property management, inasmuch as the decedent's estate and the survivor will each own a one-half interest in each item of community property. Consequently, it may be desirable for the community property to pass to the marital share and the separate property to pass to the family trust share, so that the community property's management is more congruent with the survivor's management of his or her one-half of the community property. However, postmortem management aside, the decedent may wish to also coordinate the ultimate disposition of the community and separate property, which raises the issues discussed in the next paragraph.

One traditional approach is the "survivor's election," formerly known as the "widow's election." In this planning measure, the decedent's Will purports to dispose of all of the community property, putting the survivor to an equitable election.[62] The survivor may acquiesce in the transfers under the decedent's Will, which often dictates the ultimate disposition of the community property, including the survivor's interest in the community property. In that regard, the survivor relinquishes his or her control of the survivor's one-half of the community property. However, in return, the survivor generally enjoys a life estate in all of the community property. If the survivor rejects the election, he or she will be entitled to his or her one-half of the community property, but not to any income from the decedent's one-half.[63] The survivor's relinquishment of his or her property rights may have income and wealth transfer consequences, which are beyond the scope of this book.[64]

All of these arrangements must be coordinated with the federal estate tax deduction. For example, if the survivor rejects the income interest in the decedent's one-half of the community property, the decedent's estate will not be entitled to a marital deduction with respect to that property. Moreover, if the survivor accepts the election, the amount of the marital deduction may be reduced by the amount of the consideration deemed provided by the survivor in the form of the interest relinquished in the survivor's separate property and one-half interest in the community property.[65] Due to the complexities and uncertain tax consequences of the survivor's election, Professors Price and Donaldson have described it as "not suitable for most clients."[66]

62. *See generally* Stanley M. Johanson, *Revocable Trusts and Community Property: The Substantive Problems*, 47 Tex. L. Rev. 537 (1969); Stanley M. Johanson, *Revocable Trusts, Widow's Election Wills, and Community Property: The Tax Problems*, 47 Tex. L. Rev. 1247 (1969). An equitable election of this nature may be used in a common law property jurisdiction as well, subject to the spouse's rights under the elective share.

63. *See* 13 Texas Forms Legal & Bus. §25:111 (Bancroft-Whitney 2006) (sample form survivor's election).

64. *See generally* A. James Casner & Jeffrey N. Pennell, Estate Planning §§3.6.1 & 3.6.2 (6th ed. 1995 & Supp. 2009-2010).

65. *See* Treas. Reg. §20.2056(b)-4(b), Example 3 (as amended in 1999); United States v. Stapf, 375 U.S. 118 (1963).

66. Price & Donaldson, *supra* note 44, §9.29. *See also* §3.27.

As an alternative to the forced aspects of the survivor's election, the spouses may make voluntary coordinated dispositions of the community and separate property, which can be accomplished through the use of a joint revocable trust. In that case, the attorney drafting the terms of the trust should be careful to preserve the separate and community nature of the contributed property, including income derived from the property, in case the couple divorces or the trust is revoked while both spouses are alive.[67]

5. State Estate, Inheritance, and Succession Taxes

The federal estate tax credit for state estate taxes paid expired in 2005 and was replaced by a deduction.[68] Many state estate tax levies were previously an insignificant planning concern because they were structured as a "sponge" or "pick-up" tax imposed only in the amount of, and to the extent of, the available federal credit. With the repeal of the federal credit, more states are imposing separate estate taxes. The applicable state estate taxes will need to be examined to determine if they coordinate with the applicable exclusion amount and the marital deduction. Otherwise, a bequest to a family trust that is exempt from federal wealth transfer taxes might be taxable for state estate tax purposes if the exclusions and exemptions differ.[69]

E. The Vision for Succession or Cashing Out

Reportedly, more than 80 percent, and possibly as many as 90 percent,[70] of U.S. businesses are family-owned and managed. Many family businesses do not survive through multiple generations of family members; the average family-owned business lasts only 24 years.[71] Federal wealth

67. *See* SCHOENBLUM, *supra* note 33, at vol. 7 (Forms), ch. 19F (example of community property revocable trust language); Bette Heller et al., *Joint Revocable Trusts*, 26 COLO. LAW. 63 (Aug. 1997).

68. *See* IRC §2011(f). A new estate tax deduction was created for state estate taxes. *See* IRC §2058. The new estate tax deduction would sunset with the 2010 Act after December 31, 2012, if not extended.

69. *See generally* Anthony E. Woods, *Decoupling's Dilemma*, 143 TR. & EST. 50 (Apr. 2004); Richard B. Covey & Dan T. Hastings, *Recent Developments in Transfer and Income Taxation of Trusts and Estates and State Trust and Estate Law*, 40 INST. ON EST. PLAN. ¶¶ 145-145.1 (2006) (survey of state wealth transfer taxes); Elizabeth C. McNichol, *Many States Are Decoupling from the Federal Estate Tax Cut*, available at http://www.cbpp.org/5-23-02sfp.pdf (last visited Aug. 8, 2011); Richard S. Rothberg, *The Deductible New York Estate Tax*, 339 PLI/Est 237 (PLI Tax Law and Est. Plan. Course Handbook Series No. 8761, Sept./Oct. 2006); and Daniel B. Evans, *Paying State Death Taxes from the Marital Share*, 21 PROB. & PROP. 54 (Sept./Oct. 2007). For a policy overview, see Jeffrey A. Cooper, *Interstate Competition and State Death Taxes: A Modern Crisis in Historical Perspective*, 33 PEPP. L. REV. 835 (2006).

70. *See* Jon J. Gallo & David A. Hjorth, *Business Succession Planning: A Look at Some of the Financial, Emotional and Estate Planning Issues*, 304 PLI/Est 29 (PLI Tax and Est. Plan. Course Handbook Series No. D0-0075, May 14-15, 2001).

71. *Id.* at 31.

transfer tax burdens are identified as one mortality factor, because payment of the tax introduces liquidity concerns. Business concerns such as competition are another factor. Lack of interest or ability on the part of younger generations is yet another factor.

A full discussion of planning for family business succession is beyond the scope of this book.[72] However, as a general matter the attorney needs to discuss some pivotal issues with the client to gain a sense of the direction of the family business: (1) Are younger family members committed to continuing the business and are they being groomed for management and ownership of the company? (2) If the answer to (1) is yes, how will the ownership pass to them? If the answer is no, the planning will focus on preparation for an eventual sale of the business. Gifts of interests to family members may play an estate tax planning role, as well as S corporation elections, tax-deferred corporate reorganizations, like-kind exchanges, and other income tax planning considerations. (3) Will family members who do not participate in management be given an ownership in the company? (4) If the answer to (3) is no, are there other estate assets that can be given to them?[73] (5) If the answer to (3) is yes, what measures will be taken to assure no interference with the family-member managers, yet avoid oppression of the nonmanaging family members? How will the family-member managers be compensated for their services? Are there family conflicts that must be addressed? (6) If outside managers will be hired or retained, will they be given an ownership in the company? (7) Does the company have the liquidity and cash flow required to pay any federal wealth transfer tax obligations? (8) If the answer to (7) is no, is the acquisition of life insurance, the use of special valuation measures, or the use of deferred payments of estate taxes possible? (9) Will the company simply be sold? (10) If the answer to (9) is yes, can the income tax gain be deferred?

F. Buy-Sell Agreements

Buy-sell agreements serve a number of important functions in structuring succession in family businesses. First, the agreement may provide a

72. *See generally id.*; Michael D. Allen, *Motivating the Business Owner to Act*, Estate Planning for the Family Business Owner, SFA2 ALI-ABA 1 (ALI-ABA Continuing Legal Education, Mar. 15, 2001); Steve R. Akers, *Business Succession Planning and Planning Considerations for Buy-Sell Agreements*, Estate Planning for the Family Business Owner, SFA2 ALI-ABA 679 (ALI-ABA Continuing Legal Education, Mar. 15, 2001).

73. If the parent has nonbusiness assets available for bequests to nonparticipating family members and seeks equal treatment of all beneficiaries, there is a possible tension created by the federal wealth transfer taxation implications. The children inheriting the business will seek to minimize its valuation for federal wealth transfer taxation purposes, but that may have the corollary result of minimizing the value of the nonbusiness assets that the nonparticipating beneficiaries receive. This is particularly troublesome if the heir to the business is also the personal representative of the estate. *See* JEROME A. MANNING ET AL., *supra* note 47, §11:3.6.

mechanism for outside managers to acquire an ownership interest while also providing an exit for family owners. Second, the agreement may provide a mechanism for some family members to acquire an ownership interest while also providing an exit for other family owners, such as the estate of a deceased shareholder. Third, the agreement may play a role in fixing the valuation of the ownership interests for federal wealth transfer taxation purposes.[74] Fourth, the agreement, in conjunction with restricted sale agreements, may help keep the business in the hands of a limited group of individuals. Fifth, the agreement, in conjunction with restricted sale agreements, may ensure that an S corporation election is maintained if the entity is a corporation.[75]

Once it is determined that a buy-sell agreement is to be employed, the identity of the buyer must also be determined: Will it be the business or another owner? Under a "redemption" or "entity purchase" approach, the business enterprise purchases the ownership interest of the deceased or selling owner. Under a "cross-purchase" approach, the other owners purchase the ownership interest. A hybrid agreement is often used.

In a hybrid agreement, the obligation (or option) to acquire the ownership interest of the selling party will first fall on the company or, alternatively, on the other owners. If the company has the first obligation (option) to acquire the seller's interests, then to the extent that the company does not redeem all of the interests, the other shareholders will have the option or obligation to purchase the remaining shares (the "cross-purchase" approach).[76] If, on the other hand, the hybrid agreement gives the nonselling owners the first option (or obligation) to purchase the selling owner's interests, then, to the extent that they do not purchase all of the selling parties' interests, the company is usually obligated to purchase, or redeem, such unpurchased interests.

Structuring the buy-sell agreement involves a number of income tax issues, business entity governance issues, and business issues that are beyond the scope of this book (e.g., what the "trigger" events are for the buy-sell obligation; whether the purchasing obligations are an option, right of first refusal, or formula obligation; how the price is determined—by appraisal, book value, formula, multiple of earnings, set price, etc.; how the purchase will be funded—by operating cash flow, a bank loan, life insurance, etc.).

74. *See* Treas. Reg. §20.2031-2(h) (as amended in 1992) & IRC §2703.
75. *See* IRC §§1361 & 1362.
76. As suggested in the following sentence in the text, the order of the purchases could, of course, be reversed. However, in a corporate ownership structure that sequence and the nature of the purchaser's obligation under the agreement (e.g., is it an option or an unconditional obligation to purchase?) must be approached with care to avoid constructive dividend issues. *See generally* Rev. Rul. 69-608, 1969-2 C.B. 42 (analyzing the constructive dividend implications of seven alternative redemption structures).

The complex and often emotional issues surrounding buy-sell agreements may raise the ever-present issue of professional ethics. There is a strong temptation for the estate planning lawyer to "do it all" and fail to strongly advise others such as unrelated managers and owners of the need to retain independent representation. These planning situations also raise broader issues of conflicts in representing multiple generations. Clients rarely want to spend additional legal fees on independent representation. The attorney who tackles a joint or multiple-party representation without proper safeguards assumes a great risk that will not be appreciated until something goes awry. See Chapter 1 for a discussion of these issues.

G. Grantor-Retained Annuity Trusts and Grantor-Retained Unitrusts

If younger family members are to receive a substantial interest in the business by gift, the amount of the gift may be reduced, and the donor may retain an income stream for retirement purposes, through the use of a grantor-retained annuity trust (GRAT) or a grantor-retained unitrust (GRUT) meeting the requirements of IRC §2702. A limitation to the feasibility of this strategy for the closely held business is that they often do not generate or distribute enough cash or other income to pay the annuity required by the GRAT or GRUT. Further, unlike GRATs or GRUTs of publicly traded securities, in which the stock can be sold to generate liquidity, there often is no market for closely held shares, nor a desire on the part of the family owners for outside ownership, so liquidity is limited.[77]

H. Recapitalizations and Valuation Freezes

Due to federal income tax considerations, many closely held corporations do not pay regular dividends, and returns are instead paid in the form of tax-deductible salaries and benefits to the shareholder employees.

77. If the donor dies before the termination of the GRAT or GRUT interest, IRC §2036(a) will most likely include a portion of the gifted assets in the donor's estate. *See* Lawrence P. Katzenstein, *Economic & Valuation Planning Opportunities: GRITS, GRATS, and QPRTS*, Estate Planning in Depth, SB90 ALI-ABA 1221, 113 (ALI-ABA Continuing Legal Education, June 15, 1997). On June 7, 2007, the IRS issued proposed regulations concerning, in part, IRC §§2036 & 2039 and the required inclusion amounts for GRAT, GRUT, and QPRT interests. *See* Reg. 119097-05, 72 Fed. Reg. 31487 (June 7, 2007). The final regulations were adopted in 2008.

The 15 percent income tax rate on corporate dividends introduced by the Jobs and Growth Tax Relief Reconciliation Act of 2003 (and extended by the 2010 Act), however, has made the receipt of dividends more attractive. Moreover, if a shareholder is contemplating retirement, the lost salary may be supplanted by the payment of regular dividends to the retiring party. A recapitalization is a way to provide for the retirement of a family member and to shift ownership of the business to the younger generation.

Generally, the corporation is recapitalized (this can also be accomplished with partnership-like entities) by the issuance of preferred shares, which pay dividends, to the retiring shareholder. The shift in ownership and future appreciation of the business is accomplished through the issuance of common shares, which do not pay a regular dividend, to the younger shareholders. It was often claimed that the gift of the common shares to the younger shareholders had little or no value because the terms of the preferred shares absorbed all of the existing entity value. To address this, IRC §2701 imposes certain requirements on the preferred stock, or it otherwise is ignored for valuing the gift to the younger generation (thus resulting in a larger gift to the younger generation subject to gift tax). Even if the preferred stock provides for the payment of an appropriate cumulative dividend, the statute still ascribes a minimum value to the common stock making it difficult to avoid a taxable gift to the younger generation.

I. Valuation Discounts

Even if the older generation concludes that it is not desirable to part with all ownership interests in a company, lifetime gifts may produce federal wealth transfer tax savings by utilizing marketability and minority valuation discounts on the gifts, removing future appreciation from the estate, and reducing control premiums that otherwise would apply to the retained interest.[78]

EXERCISE 11-14

DISPOSITION ALTERNATIVES FOR A FAMILY BUSINESS

Parent owns 100 percent of the common stock of Alpine Industries, Inc. (Alpine), a MyState manufacturer of sweaters and other outdoor apparel that sells under a well-known brand name, "Outdoor Duds."

78. *See generally* Richard B. Gregory & William S. Forsberg, *Leveraged Transfers of Business Assets*, 16 Prob. & Prop. 48 (Nov./Dec. 2002).

Alpine is a C corporation for federal income tax purposes. A balance sheet and income statement for Alpine are as follows.

Balance Sheet	
Cash	$200,000
Accounts receivable	800,000
Land and building (net of depn.)	350,000
Machinery and equipment (net of depn.)	800,000
Accrued salaries and taxes	(240,000)
Accounts payable	(300,000)
Net book value (shareholders' equity)	$1,610,000

Income Statement	
Sales	$10,000,000
Cost of goods sold	(7,000,000)
Executive salaries	(300,000)
General and administrative costs	(600,000)
Net income	$2,100,000
Federal & MyState income taxes	(630,000)
Net income after taxes	$1,470,000

A national manufacturer has approached Parent with an offer to purchase Alpine for $15,000,000. This has caused Parent to consider several estate planning alternatives. Discuss how each of the planning alternatives would be structured and the plan's impact on federal wealth transfer taxes.

A. Under this plan, Parent would not sell at this point, but would gift some portion of the Alpine stock to Parent's four adult children. In particular, consider the impact of IRC §2703 and general valuation principles, in particular Rev. Rul. 93-12 (discussed in Chapter 16).

B. Under this plan, Parent would cause Alpine to be recapitalized in a tax-deferred corporate reorganization pursuant to IRC §368(a)(1)(E). Parent would exchange all of the stock of Alpine for two classes of stock, Class A common and Class B common. Fifteen thousand shares of the Class A stock would be issued. Each Class A share would be entitled to $1,000 and no more upon the liquidation of Alpine. Each Class A share would be entitled to an annual $60 dividend, paid on a noncumulative basis. Each holder of the Class A stock would be entitled to "put" the stock to Alpine (i.e., require Alpine to redeem the stock) at $1,100 per share at any time from five to ten years after the issuance of the stock (ignore IRC §305(c)). The Class A stock would be voting. The Class B stock would be nonvoting but would be entitled to all dividends and liquidation proceeds after the Class A requirements are met. Fifteen thousand shares of the Class

continued on next page

B stock would be issued. Parent would retain the Class A stock and gift all of the Class B stock to the children in the same year as the recapitalization. In subsequent years, Parent would gift portions of the Class A stock to the children. In particular, consider the impact of IRC §2701.

C. This is the same plan as B, except that the dividends on the Class A stock are cumulative.

D. This is the same plan as B, except that the voting rights of the Class A stock lapse in 15 years, and the Class B stock at that time becomes voting stock. In particular, consider the impact of IRC §2704.

E. Under this alternative the national manufacturer would change its purchase offer into an offer for a forward triangular merger under IRC §§368(a)(1)(A) and 368(a)(2)(D). The national manufacturer would establish a subsidiary (Newco) that would be merged into Alpine, with the Alpine shareholders receiving publicly traded common stock of Newco's parent. As a result of the merger, Alpine would cease to exist. The corporate income tax aspects of the merger are beyond the scope of the problem and are offered only as background. However, do you have any wealth transfer tax planning suggestions?

F. Under this alternative, Parent would follow plan A or plan E, but would first transfer all of Alpine's stock to Alpine Holdings, Ltd., a limited partnership, in exchange for partnership interests. Parent would subsequently gift limited partnership interests to Parent's adult children. In particular, consider Hackl v. Commissioner, 118 T.C. 279 (2002); Kimbell v. United States, 371 F.3d 257 (5th Cir. 2004); Estate of Bongard v. Commissioner, 124 T.C. 95 (2005); Bryle M. Abbin, *Planning with Family Limited Partnerships in the Current Environment*, 15 ALI-ABA Est. Plan. Course Materials J. 47 (Aug. 2009); Paul S. Lee, *Family Investment Partnerships: Structure, Design, Issues, and Problems (Beyond the Valuation Discount)*, 24 Prac. Tax Law. 16 (2010).

J. Life Insurance

Life insurance plays an important role in estate planning for family businesses because it is a source of liquidity that can provide the funds to purchase the interests of shareholders upon their deaths.[79] Life insurance can provide the funds to purchase estate assets, so that the assets do not need to be sold at a "fire sale" or fall into the hands of outsiders. The funds can also be used to make loans to the estate as necessary to pay estate obligations such as federal wealth transfer taxes. Properly structured, life

79. If the life insurance proceeds are to be used to purchase the business interests owned by the decedent upon his or her death, a policy on the life of only that person might be obtained. However, if the life insurance is primarily for the purpose of paying wealth transfer taxes, the unlimited marital deduction may produce no estate tax until the death of the surviving spouse. In that case, a life insurance policy insuring the lives of both spouses could be acquired that would pay a death benefit only upon the death of the surviving spouse — so-called "second-to-die" life insurance — at a usually lower premium cost.

insurance proceeds may avoid both income taxation[80] and federal wealth transfer taxation,[81] and the original premiums may be sheltered from federal gift tax through the use of the annual gift exclusion.[82]

The estate tax on life insurance proceeds can be easily avoided by having someone other than the insured own the policy and possess its "incidents of ownership."[83] This can also be accomplished by creating an irrevocable trust to own the life insurance policy, a so-called "ILIT," an acronym for "irrevocable life insurance trust." There are several advantages to an ILIT's ownership of the life insurance policy beyond the avoidance of estate tax on the proceeds.[84] First, when the death benefit is paid, it can be held in the trust and managed and distributed in accordance with the insured decedent's wishes expressed in the trust instrument. A second advantage is the general protective quality of trusts in dealing with creditors of a surviving spouse as well as with minor beneficiaries and spendthrift behavior. Third, if the ILIT purchases assets from the decedent's estate, those assets may be subject to management and distribution under the trust instrument rather than outright distribution from the estate. Fourth, complications can be avoided that would arise in connection with the simultaneous death of both spouses when one spouse is the owner and beneficiary of a life insurance policy insuring the life of the other spouse. The fifth advantage is that distributing the death benefit outright to a surviving spouse or other family member could create a potential future federal wealth transfer tax problem for him or her, which can generally be avoided by trust ownership, as well as by providing some level of asset protection to the life insurance proceeds.

There is little that distinguishes an ILIT from a typical irrevocable trust. One can simply add provisions that address the life insurance functions of the trust to the basic irrevocable trust in Form L of the Forms Supplement. Among other provisions, one typically includes a *Crummey* withdrawal right to shelter the contribution of funds to the trust to pay premiums.[85] The following language may be included to deflect IRS claims that the withdrawal right is illusory because the trust has no assets other than the life insurance policy:

> *Trustee may, in Trustee's discretion, satisfy any withdrawal demand, in whole or in part, by distributing to such beneficiary*

80. *See* IRC §101.
81. *See* IRC §2042.
82. *See* IRC §2503(b).
83. In community property jurisdictions, care must be exercised with respect to the source of the premium payments to avoid an unintended ownership interest in the life insurance policy. *See generally* Grace Ganz Blumberg, Community Property in California 546-547, at n.4 (4th ed. 2003); Price & Donaldson, *supra* note 44, §6.16.
84. Generally, the trust is both the owner and the beneficiary of the life insurance policy. On the insurance company documents the ownership is usually described in terms of the trustee, such as "Susan T. Brown, Trustee, Under Declaration of Trust dated April 1, 2011," or "Susan T. Brown, as Trustee of the Green Irrevocable Life Insurance Trust, dated April 1, 2011." One sees "Under Declaration of Trust" abbreviated as "U/D/T," while the date of a trust agreement is often preceded by "u/a/d," meaning "under agreement dated."
85. *Crummey* withdrawal rights are discussed at some length in Chapter 8.

cash or property of equivalent fair market value, including an interest in any life insurance policy held as part of the trust estate.

Further, the trust would generally include language dealing with the trustee's responsibilities as to the ownership of life insurance policies, such as:

Trustee (1) may purchase and/or hold insurance of any type or nature, including permanent; term, or group insurance or a combination thereof, upon the terms and conditions as Trustee determines, in Trustee's sole discretion, to be in the best interests of this trust and the beneficiaries hereof; (2) may obtain, by way of assignment from Settlor or others, insurance policies of any type and nature; (3) may pay premiums on insurance purchased by or assigned to Trustee; (4) shall, on behalf of the trust, have all incidents of ownership and exercise all rights and privileges under any insurance policy or group plan certificate, as the case may be,[86] *including but not limited to the right to name the trust or any beneficiary of the trust as beneficiary of the policies involved, the right to convert or substitute said insurance in any manner permitted by the insurer or by law, the right to elect any optional mode of payment, and the right to borrow against the policies to the extent possible and to pledge the same for any loan or loans.*

Some institutional trustees may also require the inclusion of language similar to the following:

Trustee shall not have any duty to review or exercise judgment, whether from an insurance or an investment point of view, of insurance policies assigned, conveyed, transferred, delivered to or purchased by the trust. Settlor specifically acknowledges that the Trustee would not accept the position of Trustee unless its duties and responsibilities were limited as set out in the previous sentence.[87]

86. This passage addresses the trustee's powers. Elsewhere in the typical ILIT one would find a declaration that the settlor has no rights of any nature in any insurance policies owned by the trust.

87. Life insurance policies may prove to be a poor investment, and the insolvency of an insurer may raise additional issues about the desirability of such policies. The settlor usually makes those decisions at the outset, so the trustee demands exculpation from any related liability. *See generally* William B. Davis, *Life Insurance: A Fiduciary Time Bomb*, 131 Tr. & Est. 35 (May 1992). In a broader sense, the attorney needs to be aware of the possible concerns of the proposed trustee and communicate with the trustee before finalizing the document.

EXERCISE 11-15

ILIT LANGUAGE

What is the role of the following clause, which is often included in an ILIT?

Following Settlor's death, if any part of the assets of the trust, including the proceeds of any life insurance policies, is included in Settlor's gross estate for federal estate tax purposes, Trustee shall deliver those assets to the trustee named under Settlor's Will or, if none has been appointed, to Settlor's personal representative to be distributed as part of Settlor's residuary estate. Any other trust property (including the proceeds of any life insurance policies on the life of Settlor which Trustee may receive) shall be held for the uses and purposes set forth hereafter.

EXERCISE 11-16

MORE ILIT LANGUAGE

What is the role of the following clause in an ILIT and what is a risk of including it?

Trustee may purchase any or all of the assets of, and may make loans to, the estate of any decedent (including Settlor) or any other trust created by any person (including Settlor).

K. Special Considerations for Agriculture

While other closely held businesses may use the special valuation provisions of IRC §2032A, agriculture is the intended principal beneficiary. We refer the reader to other resources for a complete discussion of that section;[88] however, there are several observations that can be made as an overview. First, IRC §2032A does not answer completely the federal wealth transfer tax concerns of a large estate because it can reduce valuation by no more than $750,000 (plus increases for inflation). Second, the election limits the use of the property to farming for another ten years after the decedent's death, often not a desirable outcome for the heirs or younger generation. Third, even if the agricultural property is very valuable as an absolute matter, IRC §2032A is unavailable unless the asset represents

88. *See* Dennis I. Belcher, *Estate Planning for Family Business Owners: Section 2032A, Section 6166, and Section 303*, Estate Planning in Depth, SH092 ALI-ABA 449 (ALI-ABA Continuing Legal Education, June 15-20, 2003); Michael C. Hodes & David A. Cagle, *Estate Planning Strategies Specifically for the Family Farm*, 30 EST. PLAN. 211 (May 2003).

roughly one half of the value of the estate. A valuable bona fide farm that is nevertheless part of a much larger financial empire, or estate, may not qualify. Fourth, although "real" farmers may not face qualifying problems, retiring farmers or absentee lessors of farmland must satisfy various participation rules for the property to be eligible for special valuation. The planner must be particularly careful in dealing with the degree and form of participation by the owner of the property.

Beyond IRC §2032A issues, agricultural planning often involves techniques that can be used in other contexts as well. As discussed in Chapter 14, conservation easements may be used to generate an income tax deduction and estate tax savings. In addition, agricultural land can be gifted to the next generation using the cumulative impact of the annual gift exclusion. As with non-agricultural planning, life insurance may also provide a source of liquidity to pay estate taxes and other obligations.

Finally, one does not often encounter farms owned in fee simple by individuals. Rather, a common planning tool is to use family corporations, family limited liability companies, or family limited partnerships as owners in order to provide a continuity of ownership of critical assets beyond the real estate, such as water rights and grazing leases, and a degree of protection from liabilities arising from the agricultural activities.[89] In addition, these entities may produce valuation discounts for gifts of ownership interests made during life, as well as discounted values of ownership interests held at death.

EXERCISE 11-17

QUALIFYING FOR SPECIAL VALUATION

Considering Tanglewood Farms in Case Study 8-1, could Paul's parents take advantage of the special valuation provisions of IRC §2032A with respect to that asset?

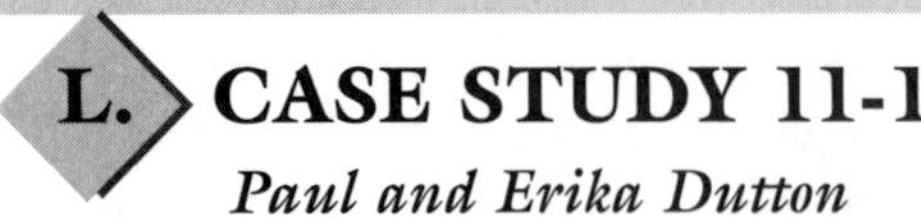

L. CASE STUDY 11-1

Paul and Erika Dutton

THE MARRIED SMALL BUSINESS OWNER

Paul Edward Dutton (born January 15 and currently age 57) and Erika Jones Dutton (born April 10 and currently age 53) have been married 31 years. Paul and Erika have two children, Cindy Elizabeth Dutton (born July 8 and currently age 29), and Stephen Jones Dutton (born May 10 and currently age 26).

89. See Chapter 12 for a discussion of asset protection strategies.

Paul is the 50 percent owner of Acme Auto Parts, Inc. (AAPI), a MyState corporation, which is a profitable retail auto parts company with five stores. Stan Sparks (45 percent) and his son Jack Sparks (5 percent) own the other 50 percent. Stan is 45 years old and Jack is 22 years old. AAPI leases all of its store locations from third-party landlords, but AAPI has retained earnings of approximately $500,000 to carry out plans for the acquisition of the real estate for several of the stores. AAPI pays Paul an annual salary of approximately $165,000, while Stan and Jack receive $115,000 and $55,000 respectively. AAPI is a C corporation and has never paid a dividend. Paul estimates that AAPI's business could be sold for approximately $10,000,000.

Erika has been primarily a homemaker for much of their marriage. Five years ago she renewed her secondary school teaching certificate and has since been working as a high school math teacher. She earns an annual salary of approximately $38,000.

Paul and Erika own a home, in joint tenancy, valued at $600,000 (purchased for $200,000). They have joint bank accounts and investments valued at approximately $350,000. Erika separately owns $175,000 in investments that she purchased for $100,000 with an inheritance from her parents.

Paul's interest in the corporation's retirement plan is worth $400,000, and Erika is the primary beneficiary. Erika will probably not have enough years of service for a full retirement benefit, but she could withdraw her contributions from the school district's plan, and that would produce a sum of approximately $30,000.

The corporation leases a new automobile for Paul. Erika owns an almost new luxury sport utility vehicle valued at approximately $40,000.

Part A: Assume that Paul and Erika have asked you to update their Wills. Paul is a very controlling person by nature and has requested that any marital share be placed in trust. Because of the relatively modest size of the estate, he has requested that the credit shelter amount be placed in a family trust. With respect to the family trust (and the marital trust), after Erika's death he would distribute one-half of the trust assets to the children when the then living oldest child reaches age 45, and the remaining assets when then living oldest child reaches age 50. In reviewing the Duttons' objectives and their situation, how will you approach this drafting project in terms of the marital formula clause and choice of fiduciaries? Are there any other issues you should raise?

Part B: Draft Paul's Will based on the facts in Part A.

Part C: Assume that Paul also wishes to acquire a whole life insurance policy on his life, with a death benefit of $1,000,000. After discussing this matter with you, he wishes to place the policy in an ILIT. The proceeds would be held in the trust, with the income sprinkled among Paul's wife, children, and grandchildren. The corpus would be distributed at the same time as the family and marital trusts described above, but equally among all descendants living at that time. Draft this ILIT, using Form L in the Forms Supplement as a starting point.

Part D: Assume that Paul is concerned about Erika's remarriage after his death. Assume that the Will in Part A would otherwise provide for a QTIP marital trust with discretionary distributions of corpus, and a family trust with a discretionary sprinkling of income or corpus among Paul's family, including Erika. Discuss how Paul's concerns can be addressed.

Part E: Assume that Paul wishes to divide a token amount, no more than $15,000 total, among several of his long-term employees, to be distributed by his personal representative. Discuss how Paul's wishes can be implemented.

M. Reference Materials

Treatises

- Dirk R. Dreux IV & Joe M. Goodman, Business Succession Planning and Beyond: A Multidisciplinary Approach to Representing the Family-Owned Business (1997).
- Frederick K. Hoops et al., Family Estate Planning Guide, Appendix 12 (4th ed. 1994 & Supp. 2010-2011) (irrevocable life insurance trust form).
- John R. Price & Samuel A. Donaldson, Price on Contemporary Estate Planning §2.9 (2011) (gift tax marital deduction generally); §2.28 (reverse QTIP election); §2.46.1 (valuation discounts); §2.47 (valuation freezes); ch. 5 (marital deduction generally); §5.7.1 (equalization clauses); §§5.34-5.37 (formula pecuniary amount gifts); §§5.38-5.39 (formula fractional gifts); §5.40 (choosing between formula methods); §6.24 (ILITs); §7.16 (valuation discounts); §9.1 (valuation freezes); §9.43 (GRATs and GRUTs); §9.44 (QPRTs); §11.1.2 (valuation discounts); §11.1.8 (recapitalizations); §11.32 (recapitalizations); §§11.6-11.12 (buy-sell agreements); §11.13 (IRC §303 redemptions); §12.19 (special use valuation); §12.23 (reverse QTIP election).
- Martin M. Shenkman & Stephen R. Akers, Estate Planning after the Tax Relief and Job Creation Act of 2010 (2011).
- Richard B. Stephens et al., Federal Estate and Gift Taxation—Including the Generation-Skipping Transfer Tax ¶4.02[4] (8th ed. 2002 & Supp. 2011) (valuation discounts and premiums); ¶4.04 (special use valuation); ¶5.06 (marital deduction generally); ¶17.02[1][c][i] (reverse QTIP election); ch. 19 (estate freezes generally).

Articles

Planning Under EGTRRA

- Steve R. Akers, *Estate Planning Under the 2001 Act—Planning and Drafting in an Uncertain Environment*, Planning Techniques for Large Estates, SH022 ALI-ABA 903 (ALI-ABA Continuing Legal Education, Nov. 18-22, 2002).
- Jonathan G. Blattmachr, Georgiana J. Slade & Bridget J. Crawford, *Estate Planning for Persons With Less Than $5 Million*, 34 Est. Plan. 18 (2007).
- Richard B. Covey, *Recent Developments (2001) in Transfer Taxes & Income Taxation of Trusts & Estates*, 36 Inst. on Est. Plan. ¶100, 101.5 (2002).
- Sebastian V. Grassi, Jr., *Drafting the Marital Deduction Disclaimer Trust after the 2001 Tax Act (with Sample Clauses and Trust Form)* (Part 1), 16 No. 3 Prac. Tax Law. 29 (Spring 2002); (Part 2), 16 No. 4 Prac. Tax Law. 7 (Summer 2002).
- Sebastian V. Grassi, Jr., *Drafting Flexibility into Estate Planning Documents after the 2001 Tax Act (with Sample Clauses)*, 17 No. 2 Prac. Tax Law. 7 (Winter 2003).
- Jerold I. Horn, *Estate Planning and Drafting for the Economic Growth and Tax Relief Reconciliation Act of 2001 ("EGTRRA") (with Forms)*, ALI-ABA Est. Plan. Course Materials J. 33 (Dec. 2001).
- Paula M. Jones, *Planning for the 10-year Phase Out of Estate Tax (with Form)*, 17 No. 2 Prac. Tax Law. 57 (Winter 2003).
- Timothy B. Lewis, *How the Economic Growth & Tax Relief Act of 2001 Affects Basic Estate Planning Strategy—Tax & Non-Tax Considerations*, 15 Utah B.J. 21 (Mar. 2002).
- Eric A. Manterfield, *Marital Planning While the Rules Are Changing*, 40 Inst. on Est. Plan. ¶700 (2006).

Planning Under the 2010 Act

- Ronald D. Aucutt, *Interpreting 2010 Estate Planning Documents*, 25 Prac. Tax Law. 9 (Spring 2011).
- Marc S. Bekerman, *Credit Shelter Trusts and Portability—Does One Exclude the Other?*, 25 Prob. & Prop. 10 (May/June 2011).
- Alan S. Gassman & Christopher J. Denicolo, *The Role of Credit Shelter Trusts Under the New Estate Tax Law*, 38 Est. Plan. 10 (June 2011).
- Marvin D. Hills, *Subsequent Remarriage Complicates Exclusion Amount Portability*, 38 Est. Plan. 3 (May 2011).
- Michael J. Jones, *The 2010 Tax Election—Opt In or Opt Out?*, 150 Tr. & Est. 18 Apr. 2011).
- John A. Miller & Jeffrey A. Maine, *The Fundamentals of Wealth Transfer Tax Planning: 2011 and Beyond*, 47 Idaho L. Rev. 385 (2011).

Disclaimers and Postmortem Planning

- Francis J. Antonucci & Robert Whitman, *Using Disclaimers in Post-Mortem Planning*, 18 No. 3 PRAC. TAX LAW. 5 (Spring 2004).
- B. Dane Dudley & Darren M. Wallace, *A Client's Death Doesn't Mean All Planning Must Rest in Peace — Qualified Disclaimers and Other Keys to Post-Mortem Planning Opportunities*, 17 PROB. & PROP. 42 (May/June 2003).
- Philip A. Di Giorgio & Louis W. Pierro, *Postmortem Planning Allows Fine-Tuning of a Client's Estate Plan*, 34 EST. PLAN. 31 (2007).
- Adam J. Hirsch & Richard R. Gans, *Disclaimer Reform and UDPIA: The Disappointing Amendments of 2006*, 33 EST. PLAN. 24 (2006).
- Adam J. Hirsch, *Disclaimer Law and UDPIA's Unintended Consequences*, 36 EST. PLAN. 34 (Apr. 2009).
- Jerold I. Horn, *Enhancing the Use of Spousal Disclaimers that Salvage Exemptions But Do Not Forgo Enjoyment*, 29 ACTEC J. 265 (2004).
- Barbara A. Sloan, *Disclaimer Planning Revitalized under EGTRRA*, Advanced Estate Planning Techniques, SG062 ALI-ABA 369 (ALI-ABA Continuing Legal Education, Feb. 21-23, 2002).

Marital Deduction Formula Clauses

- Len Cason, *IRS Ruling Approves "Poorer Spouse Funding Technique,"* 31 EST. PLAN. 234 (2004).
- Lauren Y. Detzel, *The Heart of the Matter — Efficient Use of Formula Clauses in Estate Planning*, 30 INST. ON EST. PLAN. ¶1600 (1996).
- Reed W. Easton, *How to Fully Fund a Credit-Shelter Trust Without Transferring Assets or Using Retirement Plans*, 105 J. TAX'N 349 (Dec. 2006).
- Julia B. Fisher, *Pecuniary v. Fractional Share: What Are the Considerations?*, Advanced Estate Planning Techniques, SG062 ALI-ABA 117 (ALI-ABA Continuing Legal Education, Feb. 21-23, 2002).
- Alvin J. Golden, *It's Déjà Vu All Over Again: Recent Developments in Marital Deduction Planning*, 31 INST. ON EST. PLAN. ¶1600 (1997).
- Sebastian V. Grassi, Jr., *Summary of Marital Deduction Funding Formulas and Methods (With Checklist and Chart)*, 22 PRAC. TAX LAW. 5 (2008).
- Bertram L. Levy & Michelle L. Harris, *Planning for Estate Equalization in the Face of Jumbo Exclusions*, 37 EST. PLAN. 16 (Feb. 2010) (Part 1 of 2).

- Donna Litman, *The Interrelationship Between the Elective Share and the Marital Deduction*, 40 Real Prop. Prob. & Tr. J. 539 (2005).
- Barry M. Nudelman & Athena A. Panos, *Choosing the Most Appropriate Marital Deduction Formula Clause*, 23 Est. Plan. 256 (1996).
- Laurie L. O'Donnell, *Funding of Marital Trusts, in* Understanding and Using Trusts §11 (MCLE) (2001).
- Jeffrey N. Pennell, *Funding Marital Deduction (and Other) Bequests*, 35 Inst. on Est. Plan. ¶1500 (2001).
- Jeffrey N. Pennell, *Selected Materials Relating to Planning Marital Transfers*, Planning Techniques for Large Estates, SH069 ALI-ABA 461 (ALI-ABA Continuing Legal Education, Apr. 28-May 2, 2003).
- Charles D. Rubin, *Tax Results of Settling Trust Litigation Involving QTIP Trusts*, 36 Est. Plan. 23 (Jan. 2009).
- Peter B. Tiernan, *Using Gifts from a Marital Trust to Reduce the Second Tax*, 90 J. Tax'n 210 (1999).

Non-marital Trusts

- Bruce L. Stout, *Should the Surviving Spouse Serve as Trustee of the Nonmarital Trust?*, 17 Est. Plan. 168 (1990).

Total Return Trusts

- Mackenzie P. McNaughton & Stephanie Anne Lipinski Galland, *What You Need to Know About Recent Changes to the Concept of "Trust Income" Under State Law and the Code*, 21 No. 3 Prac. Tax Law. 31 (Spring 2007).
- Margaret E.W. Sager, *Litigation and the Total Return Trust*, 35 ACTEC J. 206 (2009).
- Adam J. Wiensch & L. Elizabeth Beetz, *The Liberation of Total Return*, 143 Tr. & Est. 44 (Apr. 2004).
- Robert B. Wolf & Stephan R. Leimberg, *Total Return Trusts Approved by New Regs, But State Law Is Crucial*, 31 Est. Plan. 179 (2004).

State Estate, Inheritance, and Succession Taxes

- Jeffrey A. Cooper, John R. Ivimey, & Donna D. Vincenti, *State Estate Taxes After EGTRRA*, 17 Quinnipiac Prob. L.J. 90 (2003).
- Jeffrey A. Cooper, *Interstate Competition and State Death Taxes: A Modern Crisis in Historical Perspective*, 33 Pepp. L. Rev. 835 (2006).
- Richard B. Covey & Dan T. Hastings, *Recent Developments in Transfer and Income Taxation of Trusts and Estates and State Trust and Estate Law*, 40 Inst. on Est. Plan. ¶145-145.1 (2006) (survey of state wealth transfer taxes).
- Daniel B. Evans, *Paying State Death Taxes from the Marital Share*, 21 Prob. & Prop. 54 (Sept./Oct. 2007).

- Charles D. Fox, IV & Adam M. Damerow, *The ACTEC State Death Tax Chart—Still Going Strong After Seven Years*, 35 ACTEC J. 53 (2009).
- Robert C. Pomeroy & Susan L. Abbott, *Deathbed Opportunities*, 146 TR. & EST. 22 (June 2007) (planning strategies in decoupled states).
- Richard S. Rothberg, *The Deductible New York Estate Tax*, 339 PLI/Est 237 (PLI Tax Law and Est. Plan. Course Handbook Series No. 8761, Sept./Oct. 2006).
- Debra L. Stetter, *Deathbed Gifts: A Savings Opportunity for Residents of Decoupled States*, 31 EST. PLAN. 270 (2004).
- Anthony E. Woods, *Decoupling's Dilemma*, 143 TR. & EST. 50 (Apr. 2004).

Buy-Sell Agreements and Business Succession

- Steve R. Akers, *Family Business Succession Planning and Planning Considerations for Buy-Sell Agreements*, Estate Planning for the Family Business Owner, SFA2 ALI-ABA 679 (ALI-ABA Continuing Legal Education, Mar. 15, 2001).
- Steve R. Akers, *Estate Administration—A Summary of Practical Tax-Planning Ideas*, Estate Planning for the Family Business Owner, SF09 ALI-ABA 995 (ALI-ABA Continuing Legal Education, Aug. 10, 2000).
- Steve R. Akers, *An Overview of Post-Mortem Tax Planning Strategies*, 34 INST. ON EST. PLAN. ¶1200 (2000).
- Michael D. Allen, *Motivating the Business Owner to Act*, Estate Planning for the Family Business Owner, SFA2 ALI-ABA 1 (ALI-ABA Continuing Legal Education, Mar. 15, 2001).
- Dennis I. Belcher, *Estate Planning for Family Business Owners: Section 2032A, Section 6166, and Section 303*, Estate Planning in Depth, SH092 ALI-ABA 449 (ALI-ABA Continuing Legal Education, June 15-20, 2003).
- Travis L. Bowen, *The Use of Trusts in Business Continuation and Succession*, 17 PROB. & PROP. 30 (May/June 2003).
- Stephanie B. Casteel, *Drafting Buy-Sell Agreements After True and Blount*, 20 PROB. & PROP. 67 (Jan./Feb. 2006).
- Mike Cohn, *Integrating Family Governance and Legal Architecture for Family Business Clients*, 40 INST. ON EST. PLAN. ¶1300 (2006).
- Frederic G. Corneel, *Dealing with Conflict in Family Corporations*, 15 INST. ON EST. PLAN. ¶1800 (1981).
- Dave L. Cornfeld, *Non-Tax Considerations in Preparing Buy-Sell Agreements*, 28 INST. ON EST. PLAN. ¶1000 (1994).
- James G. Dickinson, *Terms to Consider When Drafting Corporate Buy-Sell Agreements*, 37 EST. PLAN. 3 (Sept. 2010).
- Scott A. Dondershine, *Planning for the Transfer of a Successful Closely Held Business*, 29 EST. PLAN. 335 (2002).

- Charles D. Fox, *Non-Tax Considerations in the Succession of Closely Held Businesses*, 36 Inst. on Est. Plan. ¶900 (2002).
- Jon J. Gallo & David A. Hjorth, *Handling the Nontax Issues in Business Succession Planning*, 25 Est. Plan. 226 (1998).
- Sebastian V. Grassi, Jr., *New Rules Concerning Employer-Owned Life Insurance Affect Buy-Sell Agreements (With Sample Drafting Language)*, 21 Prac. Tax Law. 7 (Winter 2007).
- Sebastian V. Grassi, Jr. & Julius H. Giarmarco, *The Five Levels of Practical Succession Planning for the Family-Owned Business*, 23 Prac. Tax Law. 39 (2009).
- Edward F. Koren, *Preserving the Patriarch's Patrimony for the Prodigal and Other Paranormal (or Normal) Progeny: Non-Tax Considerations in Family Business Succession Planning*, 31 Inst. on Est. Plan. ¶1200 (1997).
- Gerald LeVan, *Passing the Family Business to the Next Generation Handling Conflict*, 22 Inst. on Est. Plan. ¶1400 (1988).
- Stephen R. Looney & Ronald A. Levitt, *Shareholder Agreements for Closely Held Corporations*, 5 Bus. Entities 20 (Jan./Feb. 2003).
- John W. Meara, *Valuation Issues for the Family Business*, Estate Planning for the Family Business Owner, SG020 ALI-ABA 841 (ALI-ABA Continuing Legal Education, July 5-7, 2001).
- Eric A. Manterfield, *Select Planning Strategies for the Family Business Owner (With Forms)*, 24 Prac. Tax Law. 45 (2010).
- Gregory F. Monday, *Business Continuation Planning for the Loss of a Family Business Owner*, 37 Est. Plan. 22 (Apr. 2010).
- Richard B. Robinson, *Business Succession Planning, Profits Interests and §2701*, 34 ACTEC J. 243 (2009).
- James D. Spratt Jr., *The Art of Crafting Business Succession Arrangements*, 17 Prob. & Prop. 20 (Nov./Dec. 2003).
- Lauren J. Wolven & Susan T. Bart, *Human Issues in Estate Planning for the Family Business Owner*, 14 ALI-ABA Est. Plan. Course Materials J. 5 (Aug. 2008).
- Howard M. Zaritsky, *Forgotten Provisions in Buy-Sell Agreements*, 19 Inst. on Est. Plan. ¶600 (1985).
- Michael H. Zuckerman & John G. Grall, *Corporate Buy-Sell Agreements as Estate and Business Planning Tools*, 28 Est. Plan. 599 (2001).

Business Entity Planning

- N. Todd Angkatavanich & Edward A. Vergara, *Preferred Partnership Freezes*, 150 Tr. & Est. 20 (May 2011).
- Ronald D. Aucutt, *Using C Corporations in Estate Planning*, 33 Inst. on Est. Plan. ¶1000 (1999).
- Richard L. Dees, *Using a Partnership to Freeze the Value of Pre-IPO Shares*, 33 Inst. on Est. Plan. ¶1100 (1999).

- Martin A. Goldberg, *Family Investment LLC: Planning Opportunities and Guidelines*, 30 Est. Plan. 227 (May 2003).
- Paul S. Lee, *Family Investment Partnerships: Structure, Design, Issues, and Problems (Beyond the Valuation Discount)*, 24 Prac. Tax Law. 16 (2010).
- Burnell E. Steinmeyer Jr. & Todd D. Turner, *Second-Generation Planning—The Corporate Division Alternative*, 20 Prob. & Prop. 49 (Nov./Dec. 2006).

Generation-Skipping Transfer Tax Planning (See also same heading in Ch. 8 and Ch. 13 reference materials.)

- John B. Atkins, *Balancing the GSTT Exemption and the Marital Deduction*, 14 Prob. & Prop. 16 (July/Aug. 2000).
- Jeffrey K. Eisen, *Planning to Minimize GST: Tools & Traps*, 27 Est. Plan. 73 (2000).
- Ellen K. Harrison, *Generation-Skipping Planning in Light of EGTRRA*, 39 Inst. on Est. Plan. ¶1000 (2005).
- Robert L. Moshman, *Avoiding a GSTT Asteroid*, 13 Prob. & Prop. 24 (Mar./Apr.1999).
- Thomas E. Peckham, Harry F. Lee & Darien K. S. Fleming, *The GST Tax and Various Planning Issues, Post-Mortem Planning and Estate Administration*, SK070 ALI-ABA 149 (ALI-ABA Continuing Legal Education, Oct. 28-30, 2004).
- Lloyd Leva Plaine & Pam H. Schneider, *Generation-Skipping Transfer Tax Planning in 2002*, 36 Inst. on Est. Plan. ¶700 (2002).

Irrevocable Life Insurance Trusts and Life Insurance

- Bradley E.S. Fogel, *Using Life Insurance Trusts to Hold Group Term Life Insurance*, 11 Prob. & Prop. 30 (Sept./Oct. 1997).
- Bradley E.S. Fogel, *Life Insurance and Life Insurance Trusts: Basics and Beyond*, 16 Prob. & Prop. 8 (Jan./Feb. 2002).
- Jon J. Gallo, *Life Insurance Due Diligence: Or Everything You've Always Wanted to Know About Life Insurance But Were Afraid to Ask*, 40 Inst. on Est. Plan. ¶1500 (2006).
- Julius H. Giarmarco, *The Tax Consequences of* Crummey *Clauses in Irrevocable Life Insurance Trusts*, 75 Mich. B.J. 1278 (Dec. 1996).
- Sebastian V. Grassi, Jr., *Checklist for Drafting the Irrevocable Life Insurance Trust (with Sample Forms)*, 15 No. 1 Prac. Tax Law. 13 (Fall 2000).
- Sebastian V. Grassi, Jr., *Key Issues to Consider When Drafting Life Insurance Trusts*, 20 Est. Plan. 217 (2001).
- Sebastian V. Grassi, Jr., *Selected Issues in Drafting the Irrevocable Life Insurance Trust after the 2001 Tax Act*, 28 ACTEC J. 277 (2003).

- Sebastian V. Grassi, Jr., *Using Life Insurance for Business Succession/ Estate Planning for Closely Held Businesses (With Sample Provisions)*, 22 PRAC. TAX LAW. 7 (2008).
- Joshua E. Husbands, *Life Insurance Planning for Closely Held Businesses*, 36 EST. PLAN. 3 (Oct. 2009).
- Patrick J. Lannon, *Planning Opportunities with Irrevocable Life Insurance Trusts*, 34 EST. PLAN. 26 (2007).
- Stephen R. Leimberg & Albert E. Gibbons, *Performing Due Diligence with Respect to Life Insurance Trusts Is Crucial*, 30 EST. PLAN. 248 (2003).
- Mary Ann Mancini, *Water, Water Everywhere: Life Insurance as the Life Preserver for the Closely-Held Business*, 36 INST. ON EST. PLAN. ¶800 (2002).
- Donald O. Jansen, *Giving Birth to, Caring for, and Feeding the Irrevocable Life Insurance Trust*, 41 REAL PROP. PROB. & TR. J. 571 (2006).
- Marya P. Robben & Bob Cohen, *Estate Planning with Life Insurance Policies: Reduce Potential Liability Claims While Improving a Client's Estate Plan*, 24 PROB. & PROP. 59 (Jan./Feb. 2010).
- Melvin A. Warshaw, *ILIT Trustees: Bridge Out Ahead... Lock in Your Navigation System Now*, 24 PROB. & PROP. 32 (July/Aug. 2010).
- Diana S.C. Zeydel, *How to Create and Administer a Successful Irrevocable Life Insurance Trust*, 34 EST. PLAN. 3 (June 2007-Part I).
- Diana S.C. Zeydel, *A Complete Tax Guide for Irrevocable Life Insurance Trusts*, 34 EST. PLAN. 13 (July 2007-Part II).
- Gary A. Zwick, *Building Flexibility Into the Irrevocable Life Insurance Trust*, 24 J. TAX'N INV. 211 (Spring 2007).

GRATs and GRUTs

- Jonathan G. Blattmachr & Diana S.C. Zeydel, *Comparing GRATs and Installment Sales*, 41 INST. ON EST. PLAN. ¶200 (2007).
- Lawrence P. Katzenstein, *Economic & Valuation Planning Opportunities: GRITs, GRATs, GRUTs, and QPRTs*, Estate Planning in Depth, SB90 ALI-ABA 1221 (ALI-ABA Continuing Legal Education, June 15, 1997).
- Carlyn S. McCaffrey, *The Care and Feeding of GRATs—Enhancing GRAT Performance Through Careful Structuring, Investing and Monitoring*, 39 INST. ON EST. PLAN. ¶700 (2005).
- Michael D. Whitty, *Heresy or Prophecy: The Case for Limiting Estate Tax Inclusion of GRATs to the Annuity Payment Right*, 41 REAL PROP. PROB. & TR. J. 381 (2006).

Valuation Discounts

- Byrle M. Abbin, *Recent Valuation Decisions*, Planning Techniques for Large Estates, SM077 ALI-ABA 1001 (ALI-ABA Continuing Legal Education, Apr. 23-27, 2007).

- Bruce M. Di Cicco, *Controlling the FLP—Is the Taxpayer a Safe Choice?*, 37 EST. PLAN. 13 (Dec. 2010).
- *Tony Garvy, Recent Cases Shed Light on the Use of Valuation Discounts*, 37 EST. PLAN. 27 (July 2010).
- Richard H. Greenberg, *How to Handle Issues Raised by the IRS in the Family Limited Partnership Arena*, 5 BUS. ENTITIES 42 (Jan./Feb. 2003).
- Brant J. Hellwig, *Estate Tax Exposure of Family Limited Partnerships under Section 2036*, 38 REAL PROP. PROB. & TR. J. 73 (2003).
- Susan K. Smith & Alfred J. Olsen, *Fractionalized Equity Valuation Planning: Preservation of Post-Mortem Valuation Discounts*, 34 INST. ON EST. PLAN. ¶1100 (2000).

Special Use Valuation

- Orville W. Bloethe, *Special Use Valuation—$$ Savings for the Family Farm But For Others, Land Mines and Pot Holes*, 26 INST. ON EST. PLAN. ¶800 (1992).
- J. Chrys Dougherty, *Application of I.R.C. Section 2032A to Business Real Estate Other than a Farm or Ranch*, 17 INST. ON EST. PLAN. ¶1300 (1983).
- Roger A. Mceowen, *Farmland Estate Valuation in an Era of Rising Land Values*, 35 EST. PLAN. 31 (Oct. 2008).

Other

- Robert J. Durham, Jr., *When the Milk of Human Kindness Does Not Flow: To Give or Not to Give, and If to Give, Then When?*, 30 INST. ON EST. PLAN. ¶400 (1996).

CHAPTER 12

Asset Protection and Retirement Planning

A. Planning for Wealth Accumulations from Services

Physicians, investment advisors, and other highly paid professionals share several prominent planning concerns. Preserving their assets in the face of potential claims arising from malpractice and other errors or omissions is an important goal.[1] Furthermore, in response to income tax incentives, a significant portion of their net worth is invested in retirement plan assets, which also present special planning challenges. While the wealthy professional is the focus of this chapter, asset protection planning may be desirable for a number of other wealthy individuals such as owners of rental real estate, business operators, entertainment businesses, and so forth.

B. Basic Asset Protection

Asset protection encompasses a broad set of measures and elements, including some basic techniques, plus advanced applications discussed in Parts C and D, some of which are implemented by specialists.[2]

1. Corporate officers and directors also may need asset protection. *See* Gideon Rothschild, *Protecting the Estate from In-Laws and Other Predators*, 35 INST. ON EST. PLAN. ¶¶ 1700, 1701 (2001).

2. The attorney must appreciate the professional ethics and legal implications of his or her involvement in the planning transactions and may request certain representations and financial

1. Choice of Professional Services Entity

Professionals often practice in a business relationship with other professionals. The traditional professional general partnership not only subjects a partner to liability for his or her own actions but also the actions of his or her partners. Although the degree of protection varies by state, the use of the professional corporation, limited liability company, or limited liability partnership can often limit a professional's liability for nonprofessional claims (e.g., contract or lease obligations) and the actions of others, although it is difficult to limit the personal liability of the actor himself or herself.[3]

2. Insurance

Asset protection often suggests an extreme "last ditch" posture aimed at discouraging litigation, encouraging a favorable settlement of litigation, or ultimately avoiding creditor collection remedies. Those measures are no substitute for insurance, including adequate casualty and business insurance, as well as professional liability insurance, particularly because an important function of insurance is to fund the costs of defending against a claim. However, because in some cases the claim may exceed the insurance coverage, there may be significant exclusions from coverage (such as intentional torts or punitive damages), the optimal coverage is unavailable or prohibitively expensive, or the insurer may become insolvent, additional asset protection strategies should also be employed.

3. Titling of Assets

The details of the law of fraudulent conveyances are beyond the scope of this book.[4] Generally speaking, however, fraudulent conveyance law permits creditors to reclaim assets that were transferred by a debtor under certain circumstances that vary according to state law,[5] ranging from insolvency at the time of the transfer, to anticipated insolvency, to possible insolvency based on undercapitalization in view of the risks of an enterprise. Nonetheless, fraudulent conveyance doctrine tends to allow asset transfers at an early stage, before a potential problem arises.[6] Mindful of

information from the client at the outset. *See generally* Henry J. Lischer, Jr., *Professional Responsibility Issues Associated with Asset Protection Trusts*, 39 REAL PROP. PROB. & TR. J. 561 (2004); David J. Slenn, *Has the Warning Bell Sounded for Asset Protection Planners?*, 24 PROB. & PROP. 48 (Mar./Apr. 2010); Lisa M. Stern & Leonard S. Baum, *What Private Wealth Attorneys Need to Know About Money Laundering*, 37 EST. PLAN. 28 (June 2010); BARRY S. ENGEL ET AL., ASSET PROTECTION PLANNING GUIDE, ch. 16, *Ethical, Civil, and Criminal Considerations for the Asset Protection Planner* (2000).

3. *See generally* PETER SPERO, ASSET PROTECTION: LEGAL PLANNING, STRATEGIES AND FORMS ¶¶ 11.01 & 11.05 (2001 & Supp. 2011).

4. *See generally id.* at ch. 3; Barry S. Engel et al., *Asset Protection for the Business and Professional Practice*, 35 EST. PLAN. 16 (Feb. 2008).

5. Section 548 of the federal Bankruptcy Code also includes a fraudulent conveyance provision. *See generally* W. HOMER DRAKE, JR. & CHRISTOPHER S. STRICKLAND, CHAPTER 11 REORGANIZATIONS §9.22 (2d ed. 2010-2011).

6. The appearance of an "intent to delay, hinder, or defraud creditors" (a common test of whether a transfer is fraudulent) is more compelling if the transfer and insolvency are proximate in

the fraudulent conveyance backdrop, the titling of assets presents asset protection opportunities. First, if the professional is married, earnings and inheritances received by the other spouse and other property of that spouse brought to the marriage should be kept separate from the professional's assets. Marital agreements (see Chapter 4) can play a role in determining which spouse owns particular assets. Likewise, debts and obligations of the other spouse should also be kept separate whenever possible.[7] Second, important personal use assets, such as the family home (assuming homestead exemptions do not exempt it) might be titled from the outset, solely in the name of the other spouse (although the non-owning spouse may need to co-make the loan) unless the other spouse has his or her own risk issues that would make such a plan imprudent. Third, inasmuch as protection of the spouse and children is often of first priority, periodic gifts to an irrevocable trust solely for their benefit could be considered in lieu of investments titled solely in the professional's name. Indeed, one traditional planning device for professionals is the formation of an irrevocable trust for the benefit of the professional's children, which would own the professional's building, furniture, and equipment, and lease them to the professional.[8]

EXERCISE 12-1

DISSOLUTION OF MARRIAGE IMPLICATIONS

With respect to the second and third planning suggestions in the preceding paragraph, how does one protect the professional against consequences stemming from the dissolution of a marriage?

4. Accumulation of Exempt Assets

Another strategy of the professional who is at risk might be the accumulation of assets that may be exempt from claims of creditors. Florida[9] and

time. Moreover, the Uniform Fraudulent Transfer Act, which is applicable in most states, provides four-year and one-year statutes of limitation. *See generally* Jacob Stein, *Asset Protection May Risk Fraudulent Transfer Violations*, 37 Est. Plan. 12 (Aug. 2010).

7. On the other hand, if both spouses are potential debtors or the assets cannot otherwise be so cleanly separated, the creation of joint tenancies or tenancies by the entirety may frustrate the claims of some creditors. *See* Duncan E. Osborne et al., *Asset Protection Trust Planning*, Planning Techniques for Large Estates, SF79 ALI-ABA 543, 561 (ALI-ABA Continuing Legal Education, Apr. 23, 2001) (arguing that joint ownerships as a practical matter discourage creditors); Alan S. Gassman, *Practical Asset Protection Strategies and Considerations*, Sophisticated Estate Planning Techniques, SE09 ALI-ABA 641, 677-678 (ALI-ABA Continuing Legal Education, Sept. 16, 1999) (discussing tenancies by the entirety); Fred Franke, *Asset Protection and Tenancy by the Entirety*, 34 ACTEC J. 210 (2009).

8. *See generally* George M. Turner, Irrevocable Trusts, ch. 15, *Educational Trusts with Use of Gift and Lease Arrangement* (3d ed. 1996 & Supp. 2010); John R. Price & Samuel A. Donaldson, Price on Contemporary Estate Planning §§9.17-9.22.2 (2011).

9. Fla. Const. Art. X, §4(a)(1) (West 2010) (homestead exemption not to exceed 160 acres in rural areas or one-half acre in municipalities, if the property is the residence of the owner or his or her family).

Texas[10] are famous for their liberal homestead exemptions for personal residences that shield them from creditor claims. Other states provide less generous amounts.[11] Similarly, state laws often protect life insurance policies from creditors of the insured.[12] However, the Bankruptcy Abuse Prevention and Consumer Protection Act of 2005[13] (BAPCPA) introduced several new limitations on the homestead exemption, including longer waiting periods to establish domicile in the homestead state, disallowance of the exemption to the extent the property is attributable to certain property disposed of within a ten-year period preceding the filing of the bankruptcy petition, and limits on the value of the homestead if acquired within the 1,215 days prior to the filing of the bankruptcy petition or if the bankrupt engaged in certain illegal behavior.[14]

Retirement plan assets have also generally enjoyed protection against creditors of the plan participant. In analyzing the treatment of claims of creditors against retirement plan assets, one must consider at least three scenarios: (1) the rights of judgment creditors directly against the plan assets; (2) the rights of judgment creditors against the beneficiary when he or she is receiving distributions from the plan; and (3) the rights of creditors upon the beneficiary's bankruptcy. The third situation is often the most important in application.

The Employee Retirement Income Security Act of 1974 (ERISA) broadly protects the assets of applicable retirement plans from the claims of judgment creditors, garnishment, or voluntary assignment.[15] Not all retirement plans enjoy this exemption. Plans governed by IRC §§401(a) and 401(k) generally do protect the beneficiary against the claims of all creditors except a spouse under certain conditions, the Internal Revenue Service, and the retirement plan itself in certain situations. Plans governed by IRC §403(b) may be protected, depending on the structure of the plan.[16] Traditional and Roth Individual Retirement Accounts (IRAs) generally do not qualify for this protection.[17] However, some

10. TEX. PROP. CODE ANN. §§41 & 42 (Vernon 2000 & Supp. 2010) (homestead exemption for 200 acres of rural property on which a family resides, 100 acres of rural property on which a single person resides, or ten acres for urban property).

11. *See, e.g.*, CAL. CODE CIV. PROC. §§704.720 & 704.730 (West 2009 & Supp. 2011) (providing for an exemption of $75,000, $100,000, or $175,000, depending on the circumstances of the debtor); 735 ILL. COMP. STAT. 5/12-901 (West 2003 & Supp. 2010) ($15,000 exemption for an individual, $30,000 if owned by two or more people); MASS. ANN. LAWS ch. 188, §§1 & 1A (LexisNexis 1994 & Supp. 2007) ($500,000 homestead exemption for the principal residence of the debtor); N.Y. C.P.L.R. 5206 (McKinney 1997 & Supp. 2011) ($50,000 exemption).

12. *See* Duncan E. Osborne et al., *supra* note 7, at 560; ENGEL ET AL., *supra* note 2 at 565-568 (table of the state exemption statutes and exempt amounts).

13. Pub. L. No. 109-8, 119 Stat. 23 (2005).

14. *See generally* Lawerence R. Ahern, III, *Homestead and Other Exemptions Under the Bankruptcy Abuse Prevention and Consumer Protection Act: Observations on "Asset Protection" after 2005*, 13 AM. BANKR. INST. L. REV. 585 (2005).

15. *See* SPERO, *supra* note 3, ¶13.03[1].

16. *See id.*, ¶13.03[1][a].

17. *See id.*, ¶13.03[1][a][v].

state statutes provide separate exemptions, in whole or in part, for assets such as IRAs.[18]

The ERISA exemption does not apply after retirement benefits are distributed,[19] and the interplay of state exemption and garnishment statutes will determine whether amounts paid out are also exempt, in whole or in part, from creditor claims.[20]

In a worst case scenario, the beneficiary may find himself or herself in bankruptcy. The BAPCPA expanded the existing exclusion[21] of retirement assets from the bankruptcy estate, extending to almost all tax-deferred accounts recognized by IRC §§401, 403, 408, 408A, 414, 457, and 501(a).[22] However, the exclusion for IRAs (excluding Simplified Employee Pension and Simple IRAs) is limited to $1,000,000 (adjusted for inflation[23]), but certain rollovers to IRAs from other plans do not count against that cap.[24] With the enactment of the BAPCPA, retirement funds are an even more preferred asset class from a creditor protection standpoint.

C. More Advanced Asset Protection Options

1. Family Limited Partnerships and Limited Liability Companies

As discussed in Chapter 8, the formation of a family limited partnership or limited liability company can be an effective federal wealth transfer tax planning measure through the creation of valuation discounts. Wealthy professionals often use this type of entity to own business assets, real estate, or other investments. Other family members, or trusts for their benefit, may also be partners or members of the entities.

Aside from the federal wealth transfer tax implications, limited partnerships and limited liability companies are also often recommended for their asset protection features. First, if the underlying investment, such as real estate, poses certain risks of legal liability for the owner, the creation of

18. *See id.*, ¶13.03[6]; William L. Norton, Jr. & William L. Norton, III, Norton Bankruptcy Law and Practice §56:5 (3d ed. 2008 & Supp. 2011); Spero, *supra* note 3, ¶13.03[3]; Alson R. Martin, *Protecting Qualified Plan and IRA Benefits from Creditors (Recent Developments in the Post-*Patterson v. Shumate *Era)*, Professional Organizations, Qualified Plans, Health Care, and Welfare Benefits, SC58 ALI-ABA 75 (ALI-ABA Continuing Legal Education, Feb. 21-23, 1998).

19. *See* Spero, *supra* note 3, ¶13.03[1][a][ii].

20. *See* Engel et al., *supra* note 2, ch. 15, *Protection of Retirement Benefits.*

21. *See, e.g.*, Patterson v. Shumate, 504 U.S. 753 (1992) (excluding ERISA plan benefit from the bankruptcy estate); Rousey v. Jacoway, 544 U.S. 320 (2005) (excluding IRA from the bankruptcy estate).

22. BAPCPA §224, amending 11 U.S.C. §522.

23. As of April 1, 2010, the adjusted exclusion amount was $1,171,650. *See* 11 U.S.C. §522(n).

24. *See generally* Mark A Bogdanowicz, *Pension Funds Are Protected Post-BAPCPA — Or Are They?* 2007 No. 7 Norton Bankr. L. Adviser 1 (July 2007); Ahern, *supra* note 14.

a limited liability vehicle will be prudent. The potential risks of these so-called "internal liabilities" may also suggest that the attorney create a separate entity for each risky venture.[25] Further, if the owner employs competent independent contractor managers, the risks of acts or omissions being attributed to the owner are reduced. These measures address potential liabilities stemming from the particular investment or business activity. Second, if a judgment is entered against a partner or member individually (so-called "external liabilities"), the creditor may be entitled to proceed only against the partnership or limited liability company interest with a charging order, rather than foreclosing against the partnership or membership interest or proceeding against the underlying assets of the entity.[26] Third, the right of the creditor (or anyone) to become a partner or member may be limited under the terms of the partnership or operating agreement or otherwise be subject to buy-sell agreements or other restrictions on transfer.[27] The second and third measures address potential liabilities that could arise from activities apart from the partnership or LLC against which the charging order is sought. How all of this plays out is very specific to state law.

2. Inter Vivos QTIP Trusts

As discussed in Chapters 9 and 11, the Internal Revenue Code permits a marital deduction for federal wealth transfer tax purposes, in the event of a transfer to a so-called "QTIP trust" for the benefit of the transferor's spouse. IRC §2056(b)(7) establishes the technical requirements of the

25. The Internal Revenue Service will permit a partnership, limited partnership, or limited liability company owned solely by a husband and wife as community property to be treated as a disregarded entity for federal income tax purposes or as a partnership. *See* Rev. Proc. 2002-69, 2002-45 I.R.B. 831. On a related note, §8215 of the U.S. Troop Readiness, Veteran's Care, Katrina Recovery, and Iraq Accountability Appropriations Act, 2007, Pub. L. No. 110-28, 121 Stat. 112 (2007), amended IRC §761(f), to permit a partnership owned solely by a husband and wife to elect out of partnership income tax status, thus eliminating the need to file a federal partnership income tax return. The effectiveness of a single-member entity against creditor claims of the sole member is far from certain. *See, e.g.*, ENGEL ET AL., *supra* note 2, at 133-134; Carter G. Bishop, *Reverse Piercing: A Single Member LLC Paradox*, 54 S.D. L. REV. 199 (2009). In part, the bankruptcy trustee might be permitted to sell the assets of a single-member LLC rather than settling for a charging order. *See, e.g.*, In re Ashley Albright, 203 Bankr. LEXIS 291 (Bankr. D. Colo. Apr. 4, 2003).

26. *See generally* SPERO, *supra* note 3, ¶¶ 9.02, 10.04[4]; Elizabeth M. Schurig & Amy P. Jetel, *Fact or Fiction? A Charging Order Is the Exclusive Remedy Against a Partnership Interest*, 17 PROB. & PROP. 57 (Nov./Dec. 2003); Jacob Stein, *Building Stumbling Blocks*, BUS. ENTITIES 28 (Sept./Oct. 2006); Alan S. Gassman & Sabrina M. Moravecky, *Charging Orders: The Remedy for Creditors of Debtor Partners*, 36 EST. PLAN. 21 (Dec. 2009); Myron Kove & James M. Kosakow, *Asset Protection Advantages of a Family Limited Partnership*, 37 EST. PLAN. 34 (June 2010); Carter G. Bishop, *LLC Charging Orders: A Jurisdictional and Governing Law Quagmire*, 12 BUS. ENTITIES 14 (May/June 2010). In a minority of states, creditors may be able to foreclose on the partnership interest rather than be limited to a charging order. *See* ENGEL ET AL., *supra* note 2, at 111-117.

27. Significantly, the annual gift exclusion under IRC §2503(b) may be jeopardized if the partnership provisions governing matters such as transfers of interests, withdrawal of capital contributions, and distribution of profits are too restrictive. *See generally* Hackl v. Commissioner, 118 T.C. 279 (2002), *aff'd*, 335 F.3d 664 (7th Cir. 2003); Robert E. Madden & Lisa H. R. Hayes, *Tax Court Disallows Transfers of LLC Interests as Gifts of Present Interest*, 29 EST. PLAN. 352 (2002).

testamentary QTIP trust, and IRC §2523(e) establishes the rules for the inter vivos QTIP trust. The principal requirement of both forms is that the donee spouse be entitled to all of the income from the trust property for his or her lifetime and that no one, including the donee spouse, during the donee spouse's lifetime may distribute the property to anyone other than the beneficiary spouse. However, the donor spouse may designate the remainderpersons. Assuming that fraudulent conveyance concerns are addressed,[28] as well as the characterization of the gift in the event of dissolution of marriage, the inter vivos QTIP trust can be an attractive vehicle for lifetime transfers of assets for the benefit of one's spouse (and ultimately one's descendants).

In the event of dissolution of marriage, the inter vivos QTIP trust shares drawbacks with other transfers directly to or for the benefit of the donee spouse. While a marital agreement may mitigate these drawbacks in terms of adjusting other aspects of the property division if the transferor spouse has other assets, the beneficiary of the inter vivos QTIP trust may not be changed as a result of the dissolution; he or she must irrevocably remain the same person who was the transferor's spouse at the time of the trust's creation. By comparison, a broader irrevocable trust for the benefit of spouse and descendants may provide flexibility in the event of dissolution of marriage through a careful definition in the instrument of the term "spouse."

D. Other Advanced Asset Protection Options

The asset protection measures discussed below will usually require more specialized knowledge and experience on the part of the attorney.

1. Domestic Asset Protection Trusts

The majority rule, with some exceptions, is that creditors may attach the beneficial interest of a settlor in a self-settled trust. However, a growing number of states (notably Alaska, Delaware, Nevada, and South Dakota, among others) have enacted legislation that protects the interest of a settlor/beneficiary against the claims of creditors, provided that the settlor's interest in the trust is discretionary, the trustee is an unrelated and unsubordinate party, and the trust has some situs in the particular state (usually requiring a local trustee and the location of some trust assets).[29]

28. *See generally* Spero, *supra* note 3, ¶4.08[1] (transfers of property pursuant to a property settlement in dissolution of marriage may be subject to fraudulent conveyance law).

29. For a general overview, see http://www.oshins.com/images/DAPT_Rankings.pdf (last visited June 4, 2011); *See generally* Richard W. Nenno, *Planning with Domestic Asset-Protection Trusts: Part I,* 40 Real Prop. Prob. & Tr. J. 263 (2005); Richard W. Nenno, *Planning with Domestic Asset-Protection Trusts: Part II,* 40 Real Prop. Prob. & Tr. J. 477 (2005); Duncan

An attraction of these trusts is their location in the United States, which gives them the protection and convenience of U.S. laws, regulations, and customs, while making the federal income tax consequences routine. However, some writers have criticized these trusts, inasmuch as they are largely untested and are subject to the full faith and credit, contract, and supremacy (e.g., in bankruptcy proceedings) clauses of the U.S. Constitution, which may require the recognition of judgments from other states.[30]

Although created principally for their asset protection qualities, domestic asset protection trusts present tax issues, including status as grantor trusts, the gift tax consequences of their funding, and the estate tax consequences upon the death of the settlor/beneficiary. Although the advice is limited to the requesting taxpayer,[31] the following Private Letter Ruling provides some answers to these questions as well as a glimpse into the basic structure of a self-settled Alaska trust.[32]

PLR 200944002
October 30, 2009

...Grantor proposes to create an irrevocable trust (Trust) for the benefit of Grantor, his spouse and descendents [sic]. Trust will be initially funded with $X. Trust Company will serve as trustee.

Article Second, paragraph A of Trust provides, in part, that trustee will pay over the income and principal of Trust in such amounts and proportions as trustee in its sole and absolute discretion may determine for the benefit of one or more members of the class consisting of Grantor, Grantor's spouse and Grantor's descendants. Any income not paid will be accumulated and added to principal.

Under the terms of Article Second, paragraph B, upon termination of Trust, no part of the income or principal of Trust may be transferred or

E. Osborne & Jack E. Owen, Jr., *Asset Protection: Trust Planning*, Planning Techniques for Large Estates, SM077 ALI-ABA 301, 330-345 (ALI-ABA Continuing Legal Education, Apr. 23-27, 2007) (comparing domestic asset protection trust statutes); David G. Shaftel, *A Comparison of the Various State Domestic Asset Protection Trust Statutes*, 35 Est. Plan. 3 (Mar. 2008) (Part 1); David G. Shaftel, *A Comparison of the Various State Domestic Asset Protection Trust Statutes*, 35 Est. Plan. 14 (Apr. 2008) (Part 2); David G. Shaftel, *Comparison of the Twelve Domestic Asset Protection Statutes*, 34 ACTEC J. 293 (2009).

30. *See* Osborne & Owen, *id.*, at 335-346 (discussing full faith and credit, supremacy clause, and contract clause concerns); Michael A. Passananti, *Domestic Asset Protection Trusts: The Risks and Roadblocks Which May Hinder Their Effectiveness*, 32 ACTEC J. 260 (2006). One commentator has pointed out that some domestic asset protection trust statutes do not explicitly exculpate the trustee from personal liability. *See* Erin C. V. Bailey, Asset *Protection Trusts Protect the Assets: But What About the Trustees?*, 21 Prob. & Prop. 58 (Jan./Feb. 2007). The statutes of leading domestic asset protection trust jurisdictions such as Alaska, Delaware, and South Dakota do include such protections. *Id.* at 59. The BAPCPA permits the bankruptcy trustee to avoid transfers made by the debtor to self-settled trusts within ten years of the filing of the bankruptcy petition if intent to hinder, delay, or defraud creditors can be established. Certain violations of securities laws or misbehavior as a fiduciary will contribute to such finding of intent. *See* Ahern, *supra* note 14, at 607-608.

31. *See* IRC §6110(j)(3).

32. *See generally* Gideon Rothschild et al., *IRS Rules Self-Settled Alaska Trust Will Not Be in Grantor's Estate*, 37 Est. Plan.3 (Jan. 2010).

paid to Grantor, Grantor's estate, Grantor's creditors or the creditors of Grantor's estate. Article Second, paragraph B, also provides that upon the death of Grantor and Grantor's spouse, the entire principal together with any accrued income shall be distributed to any descendant of Grantor then living to be held in separate trusts. If there is no descendant then living, the principal and income shall be disposed of in accordance with the terms and conditions of Article Fourth, which provides that the property shall be transferred, conveyed and paid over to one or more organizations described in §§170, 2055 and 2522 of the Internal Revenue Code.

Article Eighth, paragraph B, provides that the following persons may not be a trustee of Trust or any other trust created under Trust: (1) Grantor; (2) the spouse or a former spouse of Grantor; (3) any individual who is a beneficiary of Trust or a trust created under Trust; (4) the spouse or a former spouse of a beneficiary of any trust hereunder; (5) anyone who is related or subordinate to Grantor within the meaning of §672(c).

Article Eleventh, paragraph B, provides Grantor with the power, exercisable in a nonfiduciary capacity, without the approval or consent of any person in a fiduciary capacity, to acquire property held in the trust by substituting other property of an equivalent value. Grantor will exercise the power by certifying in writing that the substituted property and the trust property for which it is substituted are of equivalent value and Trustee shall have a fiduciary obligation to ensure Grantor's compliance with the terms of the power to substitute property. Before the substitution of property is completed, the trustee must be satisfied that the properties acquired and substituted are in fact of equivalent value. In addition, the power can not be exercised in a manner that can shift benefits among the trust beneficiaries.

Article Twelfth, paragraph B, provides that Grantor may not be a trustee of Trust or remove any trustee of trust. Article Twelfth, paragraph D, provides that trustee shall not pay Grantor or Grantor's executors any income or principal of Trust in discharge of Grantor's income tax liability. Trustee is not a related or subordinate party within the meaning of §672(c).

Grantor is a resident of State and the situs of Trust is State. State Statute provides that a person who in writing transfers property in trust may provide that the interest of a beneficiary of the trust, including a beneficiary who is the settlor of the trust, may not be either voluntarily or involuntarily transferred before payment or delivery of the interest to the beneficiary by the trustee. Under State Statute, if the trust instrument contains this transfer restriction, it prevents a creditor existing when the trust is created or a person who subsequently becomes a creditor, from satisfying a claim out of the beneficiary's interest in the trust unless, (1) the trust provides that the settlor may revoke or terminate all or part of the trust without the consent of a person who has a substantial beneficial interest in the trust and the interest would be adversely affected by the exercise of the power held by the settlor to revoke or terminate all or part of the trust; (2) the settlor intends to defraud a creditor by transferring the assets to the trust; (3) the settlor is currently in default of a child support obligation by more than 30 days; or (4) the trust requires that all or a part of the trust's income or principal, or both, must be distributed to the settlor.

You have requested the following rulings:

1. A completed taxable gift will occur when Grantor makes a contribution to Trust.
2. No portion of Trust's assets will be includible in Grantor's gross estate.

RULING 1

. . . Section 25.2511-2(c) provides, in part, that a gift is incomplete in every instance in which a donor reserves the power to revest the beneficial title to the property in himself. A gift is also incomplete if and to the extent that a reserved power gives the donor the power to name new beneficiaries or to change the interests of the beneficiaries as between themselves.

In this case, Grantor has retained no power to revest beneficial title or reserved any interest to name new beneficiaries or change the interests of the beneficiaries. Consequently, we conclude that Grantor's transfer of $X to trust will be a completed gift of $X.

RULING 2

Section 2036(a)(1) provides that the value of the gross estate shall include the value of all property to the extent of any interest therein of which the decedent has at any time made a transfer (except in the case of a bona fide sale for an adequate and full consideration in money or money's worth), by trust or otherwise, under which the decedent has retained for life or for any period not ascertainable without reference to the decedent's death or for any period that does not in fact end before death the possession or enjoyment of, or the right to the income from, the property.

Section 20.2036-1(b)(2) of the Estate Tax Regulations provides that the use, possession, right to income, or other enjoyment of transferred property is treated as having been retained by the decedent to the extent that the transferred property is to be applied towards the discharge of a legal obligation of the decedent.

Rev. Rul. 2008-16, 2008 I.R.B. 796, provides guidance regarding whether the corpus of an *inter vivos* trust is includible in the grantor's gross estate under §2036 or §2038 if the grantor retained the power, exercisable in a nonfiduciary capacity, to acquire property held in the trust by substituting other property of equivalent value. The ruling provides that, for estate tax purposes, the substitution power will not, by itself, cause the value of the trust corpus to be includible in the grantor's gross estate, provided the trustee has a fiduciary obligation (under local law) to ensure the grantor's compliance with the terms of this power by satisfying itself that the properties acquired and substituted by the grantor are in fact of equivalent value and further provided that the substitution power cannot be exercised in a manner that can shift benefits among the trust beneficiaries.

Based on Rev. Rul. 2008-16, we conclude that in this case the substitution power, by itself, will not cause the value of the trust corpus to be includible in Grantor's gross estate.

Rev. Rul. 2004-64, 2004-2 C.B. 7, considers situations in which the trustee reimburses the grantor for taxes paid by the grantor attributable to the inclusion of all or part of the trust's income in the grantor's income. In Rev. Rul. 2004-64, a grantor created an irrevocable inter vivos trust for the benefit of the grantor's descendants. The grantor retained sufficient powers with respect to the trust so that the grantor is treated as the owner of the trust under subpart E, part I, subchapter J, of chapter 1 of the Code. When the grantor of a trust, who is treated as the owner of the trust under subpart E, pays the income tax attributable to the inclusion of the trust's income in the grantor's taxable income, the grantor is not treated as making a gift of the amount of the tax to the trust beneficiaries. If, pursuant to the trust's governing instrument or applicable local law, the grantor had to be reimbursed by the trust for the income tax payable by the grantor that was attributable to the trust's income, the full value of the trust's assets would be includible in the grantor's gross estate under §2036. If, however, the trust's governing instrument or applicable local law gave the trustee the discretion to reimburse the grantor for that portion of the grantor's income tax liability, the existence of that discretion, by itself, whether or not exercised, would not cause the value of the trust's assets to be includible in the grantor's gross estate. However, such discretion combined with other facts (including but not limited to: an understanding or pre-existing arrangement between grantor and the trustee regarding the trustee's exercise of this discretion; a power retained by Grantor to remove the trustee and name grantor as successor trustee; or applicable local law subjecting the trust assets to the claims of grantor's creditors) may cause inclusion of Trust's assets in grantor's gross estate for federal estate tax purposes.

In this case, under the terms of Article Twelfth, paragraph D, the trustee is prohibited from paying Grantor or Grantor's executors any income or principal of Trust in discharge of Grantor's income tax liability. Although, Rev. Rul. 2004-64 does not consider this situation, it is clear from the analysis, that because the trustee is prohibited from reimbursing Grantor for taxes Grantor paid, that Grantor has not retained a reimbursement right that would cause Trust corpus to be includible in Grantor's gross estate under §2036. See Rev. Rul. 2004-64. In addition, the trustee's discretionary authority to distribute income and/or principal to Grantor, does not, by itself, cause the Trust corpus to be includible in Grantor's gross estate under §2036.

We are specifically not ruling on whether Trustee's discretion to distribute income and principal of Trust to Grantor combined with other facts (such as, but not limited to, an understanding or pre-existing arrangement between Grantor and trustee regarding the exercise of this discretion) may cause inclusion of Trust's assets in Grantor's gross estate for federal estate tax purposes under §2036.

We are specifically not ruling on whether or not Trust is a trust described in subpart E, part I, subchapter J, of chapter 1 of the Code.

---

2. Foreign Asset Protection Trusts

At the price of increased complexity and cost, a client may establish trusts in certain foreign jurisdictions that have enacted debtor-friendly laws and offer the privacy and creditor inconvenience of a foreign locale. Some foreign jurisdictions commonly noted in this regard include the Jersey Channel Islands, the Turks and Caicos islands, the Cook Islands, the Cayman Islands, Bermuda, and the Bahamas.[33] The U.S. Constitution does not limit these foreign sovereigns, and, as a practical matter, geographical distance and privacy laws may lend an additional measure of protection (although these may be of less benefit due to developments in connection with efforts to expose money centers supporting terrorist activity). On the other hand, the trust assets are subject to the laws of a foreign country that could prove to be unstable,[34] and a foreign trust raises some U.S. income tax issues.[35] Of note, these techniques do not necessarily require that the protected assets be transferred to the foreign jurisdiction. Indeed, it is not physically possible to do that with some assets, notably real estate. Consequently, a related technique can include designating a foreign trust as a member of a limited liability entity, such as the general partner of a family limited partnership, to add an additional layer of creditor protection to U.S.-based family limited partnership assets.[36]

3. Expatriation

An extreme and somewhat impractical measure outside the scope of this book is the renunciation of U.S. citizenship, coupled with domicile in, and a transfer of assets to, a locale that affords immunity from creditor collection remedies.[37]

33. *See* Osborne & Owen, *supra* note 29, at 364-381 (comparing the laws of leading foreign asset protection jurisdictions).

34. This is commonly referred to as "importing the law." On the other hand, moveable assets such as stocks and securities may use the "exporting the assets" approach where the assets are invested offshore. One planning book notes that most assets, although titled in a foreign trust, may remain in the United States so long as there are no threatened or actual claims. *See* ENGEL ET AL., *supra* note 2, at 265.

35. *See, e.g.*, IRC §679.

36. The prior discussion assumes that assets are transferred to an offshore trust. Under the "importing the law approach" the trust assets remain in the United States, but the laws of the foreign country are invoked through the use of a foreign trust that holds the U.S. assets. *See* Osborne, *supra* note 7, at 586.

37. *See generally* ENGEL ET AL., *supra* note 2, ch. 14, *Expatriation as an Asset Protection Tool*.

4. Fraudulent Conveyance Law in Action — An Example

As noted above, potential application of the law of fraudulent conveyances is a consideration in many asset protection structures, and the analysis is highly factual with reference to the debtor's behavior and so-called "badges of fraud." The case below is an example of a debtor's tangled web of transfers, entities, and transactions that was ultimately unraveled by the courts.

In re Gary E. Krause, Debtor. United States of America, Plaintiff–Appellee, v. Gary E. Krause; Richard L. Krause, Defendants, and Linda S. Parks, Intervenor–Appellee, v. Drake Krause; Rick Krause, Intervenors–Appellants. __ F.3d __(10th Cir. 2011)

GORSUCH, Circuit Judge.

Can a taxpayer avoid the IRS by moving money to a "diet cookie" company and then destroying records that might show the company to be a sham? Or by transferring assets to his "children's trusts" only to use the trusts to pay for his country club membership, buy cars, and fund his lifestyle? The answer, of course, is no. Why this is so takes a bit more explanation.

I

Gary Krause's feud with the IRS traces back decades. Beginning in the 1970s, Mr. Krause developed public housing projects and promoted tax-shelter partnerships. It didn't take long, however, before the IRS challenged his attempts to deduct a variety of claimed losses. As happens in these things, litigation soon broke out and proceeded to consume the better part of a decade. At the end of it all, the two sides reached a settlement in which Mr. Krause agreed that he owed taxes for 1975, 1978, 1979, 1980, 1981, 1982, 1983, and 1986, and the IRS calculated his liability at $3.5 million.

But as it turned out the settlement settled nothing. In 2005, Mr. Krause declared bankruptcy under Chapter 7, claiming that he had no meaningful assets and seeking a discharge of his federal tax liabilities. The IRS responded by initiating an adversarial proceeding in bankruptcy court. The agency sought a declaration that Mr. Krause's tax debts were not dischargeable in bankruptcy, that Mr. Krause had fraudulently conveyed various of his assets to other entities, and that the IRS's pre-existing tax lien should attach to the assets held by those entities. Yet more litigation over these questions followed, but when the dust finally settled the bankruptcy court had decided two things.

First, the bankruptcy court held that two companies — Drake Enterprises and PHR, LLC — were the nominees or alter egos of Mr. Krause and that the IRS's tax lien attached to their assets. What these companies actually did and whether they enjoyed any existence independent of

Mr. Krause was never quite clear. Drake Enterprises claimed to market a so-called "diet cookie." PHR appeared to do no more than hold title to the family residence. What was clear, however, was this. During discovery Mr. Krause intentionally erased computer hard drives containing the records of both companies. And in the process he violated court orders compelling production of the materials. For this misconduct and after an exhaustive three-day evidentiary hearing, the court entered a sanctions order declaring that it would treat PHR and Drake Enterprises as the "nominees or the alter ego[s] of Krause and ... thus [the] property of [Mr. Krauses's bankruptcy] estate and subject to turnover" to the IRS....

Second, the bankruptcy court held that Mr. Krause had fraudulently conveyed certain assets to trusts nominally created for the benefit of his now-adult children, Drake and Rick Krause. Given this, the bankruptcy court held, the IRS tax lien attached to those assets as well. Unlike its holding with respect to Drake Enterprises and PHR, however, the bankruptcy court reached its conclusions about the trust assets on the merits and after a nine-day trial at which the court allowed Drake and Rick to intervene and participate along with their father.

After the bankruptcy court issued its final judgment, Drake and Rick, along with their father, appealed to the district court. The district court, however, affirmed the bankruptcy court's judgment, and it is this decision that Drake and Rick, now proceeding without their father, ask us to reconsider and reverse.

II

Turning to second things first, we begin with the bankruptcy court's judgment that assets Mr. Krause transferred to the children's trusts are subject to the IRS's lien under 26 U.S.C. §6321. The scope of our review here is governed by that familiar formulation: we assess legal questions *de novo* but will reverse the bankruptcy court's factual findings only if they are proven to be clearly erroneous.... Because the facts found by the bankruptcy court in this case aren't meaningfully disputed, we proceed directly to our own analysis of the law's application to those facts.

On that score, §6321 allows the IRS to satisfy a tax deficiency by attaching a lien on any "property" or "rights to property" belonging to the taxpayer. To determine whether a particular asset falls within the reach of a §6321 lien, we and any court must engage in a two-part inquiry. First, we must ask what rights under state law, if any, the taxpayer has in the asset the IRS seeks to attach. This step is necessary at the outset because it is, after all, "state law [that] creates legal interests and rights" in things ... Second, now with a sense of what state legal entitlement the taxpayer enjoys in the asset at issue—with a sense of the bundle of rights state law gives him to the thing or *res* at issue—we must ask, under federal law, whether those "state-delineated rights qualify as 'property' or 'rights to property' within the compass of the federal tax lien legislation." ...

A

In Kansas, as in most states, a debtor cannot evade his creditors by fraudulently conveying his property to someone else. Such conveyances are, as a matter of state law, "deemed utterly void and of no effect." *See* K.S.A. §33–102. Put differently, the transferor retains equitable ownership of the assets and those assets remain subject to attachment by his creditors.... To determine whether a conveyance is fraudulent and so void as a matter of state law, Kansas law directs us to look for "six badges or indicia of fraud": "(1) a relationship between the grantor and grantee; (2) the grantee's knowledge of litigation against the grantor; (3) insolvency of the grantor; (4) a belief on the grantee's part that the contract was the grantor's last asset subject to a Kansas execution; (5) inadequacy of consideration; and (6) consummation of the transaction contrary to normal business procedures." ...

Mr. Krause wears these badges boldly. In setting up the "children's trusts," he transferred money first to his wife who, in turn, transferred them to the trusts, all for no consideration. Mr. Krause also transferred various insurance policies to the trusts, again for no consideration. Each of these transfers took place after Mr. Krause knew the IRS was conducting an audit of his taxes and after the IRS issued a notice disallowing certain of his claimed losses. And while Mr. Krause's brother, Richard, served as trustee for the children's trusts, both he and Mrs. Krause have admitted that Mr. Krause controlled the assets in question at all times. Indeed, Mr. Krause maintained no personal bank account after 2000 but instead used the children's trusts to pay for his country-club memberships, car loans, and other personal expenses. And Mr. Krause did all this without objection from Richard, who candidly described his philosophy toward the trusts as "stick your head in the sand and then you don't know what is going on." ... In light of these remarkable and undisputed facts, badges of fraud all, it is plain that Mr. Krause remained the owner of the transferred assets; that the children's trusts held those assets simply as his nominees; and that those assets are subject to attachment by Mr. Krause's creditors under Kansas law....

When the facts are bad, they say, argue the law. And with the facts so badly against them, that's exactly what Rick and Drake do here. According to the brothers, our analysis and the bankruptcy court's necessarily rest on "reverse veil piercing." And this is legally problematic, they say, because Kansas courts haven't yet adopted that doctrine. Neither, the brothers predict, are Kansas courts likely to do so if and when confronted with the question.

But as it happens we don't need to gaze into the crystal ball to divine what Kansas courts might do about reverse veil piercing doctrine. We don't because the doctrine has nothing to do with our decision. In a classic veil piercing scenario, of course, a court pierces the corporate form to hold an individual responsible for acts done in the name of the corporation because the court finds that the individual and corporation are one and the same, no more than alter egos. Analogously, in a reverse veil piercing case, a court permits a creditor to recover a debt from the assets of a corporation determined to be the alter ego of an individual debtor, the two being so intermixed as to be essentially indistinguishable. But none of this is necessary to our resolution of this case. To reach the result we do, we need and do hold only that Kansas law recognizes fraudulent conveyance doctrine; that Mr. Krause fraudulently conveyed certain particular assets (cash and insurance policies) to the children's trusts; that the trusts held those particular assets as Mr. Krause's nominees; and that, for purposes of Kansas law, those assets still belonged to Mr. Krause and so were lawfully subject to attachment to satisfy his debts.

The difference between finding an entity to be a nominee holding fraudulently conveyed assets and finding an entity to be the debtor's alter ego under reverse veil piercing doctrine may be a subtle one. But it is no less significant for its subtlety. Under reverse veil piercing doctrine, the IRS would have needed to show that the trusts at issue were not just Mr. Krause's nominees with respect to the particular assets in question but his alter ego for all purposes. *See Bollore S.A. v. Import Warehouse, Inc.*, 448 F.3d 317, 325 (5th Cir. 2006) (recognizing that "courts can reverse pierce a corporation's veil based on a finding of alter ego"). As reward for making this more onerous showing, the IRS might have seized all the assets in the trusts without regard to their original source. *See Oxford Capital Corp. v. United States*, 211 F.3d 280, 284 (5th Cir. 2000) ("Under the alter ego doctrine, ... *all* the assets of an alter ego corporation may be levied upon to satisfy the tax liabilities of a delinquent taxpayer-shareholder if the separate corporate identity is merely a sham.") (emphasis added). By contrast, a nominee holding a fraudulently conveyed asset may maintain an independent legal identity and lawfully hold other assets of its own. Finding that an entity is a nominee of the debtor only requires a showing that the nominee holds bare or apparent title to a particular asset that actually belongs to the debtor. And it is only the particular assets held in this fashion (not others the nominee may possess in its own right) that the debtor's creditor may reach. *See* Elliott, *Federal Tax Collection, Liens and Levies* ¶9.10[1]; Internal Revenue Manual §5.17.2.5.7 (Dec. 14, 2007); Internal Revenue Manual §5.17.2.5.7.2 (Dec. 14, 2007).

By way of example, suppose that someone besides Mr. Krause had legitimately donated money to the children's trusts. Those funds would not have been held by the trusts as nominees, and a nominee lien would not have attached to those assets. To obtain those funds, the IRS might have sought to attach liens on *all* trust assets. But to succeed in doing so under a reverse veil piercing theory, the IRS would have had to show that the trusts and Mr. Krause were effectively alter egos. That, of course, would have been a harder row to hoe, and it is one the government has not even attempted in this case. In this case, the IRS has sought only a nominee lien on particular assets Mr. Krause fraudulently conveyed to the trusts. And it is on that basis alone that we rest our decision, allowing the IRS to attach liens only to the assets Mr. Krause fraudulently conveyed to the trusts. Whether or not Kansas might allow or prohibit the IRS to do more than this through alter ego reverse veil piercing is beside the point.

B

That leaves us to answer the second half of the §6321 inquiry. Here we must ask whether Mr. Krause's rights to and interest in the particular assets he fraudulently conveyed, as defined by Kansas law, qualify as "property" or "rights to property" under the federal tax lien statute.

The answer to that question is easy and affirmative. Section 6321's language "is broad and reveals on its face that Congress meant to reach every interest in property that a taxpayer might have." *Drye*, 528 U.S. at 56 (internal quotation omitted). Indeed, the Supreme Court has held that "[w]hen Congress so broadly uses the term 'property,' we recognize . . . that the Legislature aims to reach every species of right or interest protected by law and having an exchangeable value." *Id.* (internal quotation omitted). From this it follows ineluctably, we hold, that the terms "property" and "rights to property" for purposes of federal law under §6321 embrace not only rights or interest with exchangeable value that the taxpayer holds formal legal title to, but also those that the taxpayer (as here) is found under state law to have fraudulently conveyed to a nominee.

The Supreme Court's decision in *Drye* illustrates the expanse of the terms "property" and "rights to property" under federal law and why they necessarily embrace Mr. Krause's interests. In *Drye*, the taxpayer was the sole heir to his mother's estate. Under state law, however, he was permitted to and did disclaim any interest in the estate, allowing the estate to pass to his daughter as the next lineal descendant. *See Drye*, 528 U.S. at 52. And once the estate was disclaimed, state law went a step further, prohibiting the taxpayer's creditors from touching the estate. Despite these notable features of state law restricting the interests enjoyed by the taxpayer and his creditors after a disclaimer, the Supreme Court did not hesitate in holding that the taxpayer had nonetheless received "property" or a "right to property" for purposes of federal law at the time of his mother's death. *See id.* Whether or not denominated as "property" or a "right to property" for purposes of state law, the taxpayer's bundle of interests and rights guaranteed by state law — allowing him the choice either to keep the estate or channel it to another family member — were enough, the Court held, to render it "property" or a "right to property" for purposes of federal law. Similar situations where §6321 has been read to embrace interests and rights that may not be formally defined or thought of as "property" for purposes of state law abound. *See, e.g., United States v. Craft*, 535 U.S. 274, 276, 122 S. Ct. 1414, 152 L. Ed. 2d 437 (2002) (holding that even though the state statute doesn't create a separate interest in entireties property, the federal tax lien statute still reaches such interest); *21 West Lancaster Corp. v. Main Line Rest., Inc.*, 790 F.2d 354, 357-58

(3d Cir. 1986) (ruling that while a liquor license didn't constitute "property" under state law, it was still "property" under the federal tax lien statute). Of course, our case is far easier. Even as a matter of Kansas law, Mr. Krause retained full equitable ownership over the fraudulently transferred assets, all of which possessed exchangeable value. And that is easily and more than enough to render his state law interests "property" or "rights to property" for purposes of federal law under §6321.

. . . Once Mr. Krause's rights and interests were defined under state law, the remaining question under §6321 wasn't whether the trusts were Mr. Krause's "nominees" for purposes of federal tax law but whether the rights and interests Mr. Krause enjoyed under state law were "property" or "rights to property" under §6321. And given the expansiveness of those latter terms, there simply is no doubt of the answer: the liquid cash assets and various insurance policies Mr. Krause fraudulently conveyed and so still equitably owned for purposes of Kansas law indubitably possessed exchangeable value and thus qualified as "property" or "rights to property" for purposes of federal law.

III

That still leaves us with the diet cookie company, the house holding corporation, Mr. Krause's destruction of their corporate records, and the bankruptcy court's sanctions order declaring both entities to be Mr. Krause's nominees or alter egos.

To the extent the brothers seek to challenge the court's order with respect to the cookie company, Drake Enterprises, we hold they lack standing. Long ago and for many years, the Bankruptcy Code permitted only a "person aggrieved" by a bankruptcy court order to challenge it on appeal. *Kane v. Johns-Manville Corp.*, 843 F.2d 636, 641-42 (2d Cir. 1988); *In re DBSD N. Am., Inc.*, ____ F.3d ____, 2011 WL 350480, at *4-5 (2d Cir. Feb. 7, 2011). To qualify as a "person aggrieved," courts held, the putative appellant had to show that his rights or interests were "directly and adversely affected pecuniarily" by a bankruptcy court's order. *Kane*, 843 F.2d at 642. While the Code has since been amended many times and the "person aggrieved" phrase no longer appears, *see* 28 U.S.C. §158(d)(1); *id.* §158(a)(1), many courts, including this one, have continued for decades to enforce the person aggrieved requirement as a matter of prudential standing. . . .

They have done so because, without such a requirement, bankruptcy litigation could easily "become mired in endless appeals brought by a myriad of parties who are indirectly affected by every bankruptcy court order." *Holmes*, 881 F.2d at 940 (internal quotation marks omitted). . . .

Our case proves the problem. Those affected by the bankruptcy court's order — Mr. Krause and his wife — do not seek to appeal the sanction order. Only the sons Drake and Rick are before us, and neither they nor the trusts of which they claim to be the beneficiaries have *any* interest in Drake Enterprises. In fact, even Drake and Rick's brief concedes that their father and mother were and are the sole shareholders of Drake Enterprises, just as the bankruptcy court found. Nor do Drake and Rick identify any other way in which they might be affected by an adverse decision against Drake Enterprises. Plainly, they lack prudential standing under our controlling precedent.

With respect to PHR, the story is slightly different. PHR is a limited liability company, and the trusts created for the benefit of Rick and Drake Krause are listed as members of that company. The government doesn't dispute that this is enough to afford them prudential standing to appeal the bankruptcy court's sanction order and, following the government's tack here, we will also assume without deciding that it is. Unlike certain other statutory or constitutional jurisdictional questions, the resolution of a sticky prudential standing question may be bypassed in favor of deciding the case on the merits when it's clear that the appellant will lose there anyway. . . .

And that's exactly the case we have before us. The only merits argument Drake and Rick level against the bankruptcy court's sanction order is one we have already addressed and rejected. The brothers simply and again accuse the bankruptcy court of having defied Kansas law by engaging in reverse veil piercing to find PHR and Mr. Krause alter egos. As it happens, however, the sanctions order declared PHR to be the "nominee" *or* the alter ego of Krause and are thus property of the estate and subject to turnover." . . . So even assuming Drake and Rick are correct in surmising that Kansas is likely to prohibit reverse veil piercing, the bankruptcy court's order remains independently and separately justified under nominee theory. And, as we have already explained and so won't repeat at length here, nominee theory is analytically distinct from reverse veil piercing theory. To defeat the bankruptcy court's sanction order, Drake and Rick must knock out each of the legs on which it rests. Even assuming they might succeed in knocking out one, they make no effort to displace the other. So it is that the bankruptcy's order necessarily remains standing, and the judgment in this case must be

Affirmed.

E. Tax Planning for Retirement Plan Assets

Retirement plans offer a number of federal income tax incentives. First, the contributions are generally deductible from the income of the contributor when made (the Roth 401(k) and Roth IRA are notable exceptions). Second, while the appreciation in retirement assets is generally taxable when withdrawn (the Roth accounts again are exceptions to the preceding statement), the retirement plan and the participant generally incur no federal (and usually no state) income taxes during the accumulation period. Third, loan provisions may permit limited access to the retirement funds prior to the ordinary retirement withdrawal period, although loans are unavailable under some plans, such as IRAs. Fourth, the participant may be in a lower income tax bracket in the retirement withdrawal period, when the retirement income is taxed, than during the accumulation period.

Because the retirement plan is a tax-sheltered environment for the earnings on the invested amounts and a deferral of tax on the original deducted contributions and because the primary purpose of the plans is to furnish retirement income, tax law generally forces an eventual end to the shelter by imposing a minimum distribution requirement when the participant reaches a certain age that assumes retirement (the Roth IRA is not subject to this rule until the participant dies[38]). Subject to a number of exceptions, that date is generally April 1 of the calendar year following the calendar year in which the participant reaches age 70½.[39] For some employer-sponsored plans, the date may be extended to the calendar year in which the participant retires, if later.[40] This date is the "required beginning date," commonly referred to as the "RBD." Starting with the RBD, the participant is required to withdraw minimum distributions from the retirement plan, which are computed with respect to the participant's life expectancy or the life expectancy of the participant and a designated joint beneficiary. This minimum sum is the "required minimum distribution," commonly referred to as the "RMD."[41] Failure to withdraw the RMD may subject the participant to a 50 percent penalty on the undistributed RMD amount![42]

Although the agony is in the excruciating details and technical traps of these provisions, the gist of income tax planning for retirement plan benefits is to prolong the income tax deferral under the plan by keeping the RMD to the smallest possible amount.[43] Because the RMD for a participant and a designated beneficiary is generally smaller than that solely

38. A Roth 401(k) (technically a "designated Roth account" governed by IRC §402A) is subject to the minimum distribution rules, so a rollover to a Roth IRA, which is otherwise exempt from these rules during the participant's lifetime, can be a planning consideration. *See* Natalie B. Choate, Life and Death Planning for Retirement Benefits §5.2.02 (7th ed. 2011).

39. If the participant defers receipt of the RMD until the following year (but no later than April 1), the participant will generally report two RMDs for that year, one for the prior year which was postponed until the current year, and a second for the current year itself. *See id.* §1.4.07.

40. *See* IRC §401(a)(9).

41. If the participant holds interests in multiple plans, the RMD is calculated separately for each plan (including IRAs). For IRA and 403(b) accounts the RMD, although calculated separately for each account, can be withdrawn from any combination of the accounts. For other types of plans, the RMD must be paid only from the pertinent plan. *See* Choate, *supra* note 38, §1.3.04. This discussion assumes a defined contribution plan. The RMDs for defined benefit plans are subject to additional rules. *See id.* §1.1.05.

42. *See* IRC §4974.

43. While this is generally true, a participant with a shortened life expectancy might wish to accelerate the recognition of the retirement plan income (or convert to a Roth IRA if possible) so that the payment of the income taxes on the distribution or conversion depletes his or her taxable estate.

for the participant,[44] planning often focuses on including a designated beneficiary, ideally one who is younger than the participant and therefore has a greater life expectancy.

When a participant dies, the planning shifts to prolonging the income tax deferral for the retirement assets to be received by the designated beneficiary. As discussed in point 4 below, the failure to designate a beneficiary will generally produce adverse income tax consequences by accelerating the recognition of the retirement asset income.

Generally, if the participant had not yet reached his or her RBD on death, distributions must be made over the life expectancy of a nonspouse designated beneficiary, starting with the participant's death (payments must begin no later than the end of the year following the year of the participant's death), not when the beneficiary reaches, or the participant would have reached, his or her RBD.[45]

If the participant had already reached his or her RBD, generally distributions must be made to a nonspouse designated beneficiary (again, payments must commence by the end of the year following the year of the participant's death) over the life expectancy of the designated beneficiary or over what would have been the participant's life expectancy if that is longer.[46]

If the participant dies before his or her RBD and the spouse is the sole designated beneficiary, distributions over the life expectancy of the surviving spouse are not required to commence until the later of the end of the year following the year of the participant's death (the normal rule) or the year in which the participant would have reached age 70½.[47] If the participant dies after his or her RBD, the surviving spouse is treated like a nonspouse designated beneficiary and must commence receipt of distributions by the end of the year following the year of the participant's death. However, as discussed in point 6 below, a surviving spouse has additional alternatives available in dealing with the retirement assets.

Mastering the planning for retirement plan benefits is beyond the scope of this book. Generalizations are dangerous; the law is in a constant state of administrative flux. There are entire books devoted to this sole topic (see the references in Part G). However, there are some crucial planning points to be gleaned from this area, which we present with little citation to primary authority, although we will provide citations to a

44. Even if the participant has no designated beneficiary, the Uniform Lifetime Table prescribed by the IRS assumes the joint life expectancy of a participant and a hypothetical beneficiary who is ten years younger, so the calculated RMD is understated in purely actuarial terms. *See* Choate, *supra* note 38, §1.3.02.

45. *See id.* §1.5.03. However, if the plan permits, the designated beneficiary can elect between the life expectancy method and the five-year method described in point 4 of the text that follows. *See id.* §1.5.07.

46. *See id.* §1.5.04.

47. *See id.* §1.6.04.

leading practitioner guide.[48] We caution readers not to rely on this broad overview without significant further contemporaneous research.

1. Outright Beneficiary Designations of Humans Are Simplest

As discussed in point 4 below, the designation of an estate as a beneficiary is not desirable. Trusts may be beneficiaries, however, it must be understood that trusts will pay income tax at the highest marginal rates above a very low threshold. Thus, the income tax burden may be greater than if the individual beneficiaries receive the income directly. If the income is distributed to the individual beneficiaries so that the trust receives an income tax deduction not to exceed the trust's "distributable net income," the trust instrument's definitions of fiduciary "principal" and "income" must be studied to determine whether all of the RMD received by the trust will be treated as distributable net income for trust accounting purposes.[49]

2. It Is Preferable That a Marital Trust Pay Income Taxes on the RMD Rather than a Family Trust

Because the payment of the income tax depletes trust assets, one would rather pay with marital trust assets, which will otherwise be subject to estate tax on the survivor's death. However, this is a closer question if the beneficiaries of the family trust have much longer life expectancies (producing a much lower RMD) than the surviving spouse.[50]

3. Don't Fund a Pecuniary Bequest with Retirement Assets

Pecuniary and fractional bequests are discussed in Chapter 11. Income from a retirement account (other than a Roth account) is income in respect of a decedent (IRD) under IRC §691. It is commonly believed that the transfer of an item of IRD in satisfaction of a pecuniary obligation may trigger immediate recognition of the IRD. Accordingly, retirement account assets should be disposed of using a fractional or residuary formula bequest or, preferably, as a specific bequest of the IRD item itself.[51]

48. *See generally id.*

49. *See id.* §§6.1.02 & 6.1.03.

50. *See id.* §3.3.02. If the spouse is a beneficiary of both trusts and his or her life expectancy determines the RMD for both trusts, all of the RMD apparently may not be withdrawn from the marital trust. *See id.* §1.5.09.

51. *See id.* §6.5.08.

4. Designate a Beneficiary and Avoid Designating an Estate as a Retirement Plan Beneficiary

The IRS asserts that if an estate is a retirement plan beneficiary, any individual beneficiaries of the estate will not be considered designated beneficiaries for purposes of computing the RMD.[52] If there is no designated beneficiary and the participant has not yet begun receiving the RMD under the plan, the plan assets must be distributed within five years after the death of the participant (because a Roth IRA has no RBD, this five-year rule will apply to most Roth IRAs if there is no designated beneficiary).[53] If there is no designated beneficiary and the participant has been receiving the RMD, the plan assets must continue to be distributed using the participant's RMD.[54]

5. A Trust May Provide Designated Beneficiaries

If a trust has human beneficiaries, their life expectancies are considered in computing an RMD for the trust, provided that they are identifiable from the trust instrument (which can be satisfied by class descriptions such as "my children"), and certain technical requirements are fulfilled (such as irrevocability, validity under state law, and the provision of documentation to the plan administrator).[55]

6. A Spousal Trust as a Beneficiary Requires Special Marital Deduction Planning

As discussed in Chapter 11, a trust that qualifies for the marital deduction must provide the surviving spouse with a right to income for life. The interaction of the RMD rules and the marital deduction rules is not seamless, inasmuch as the RMD distributed to the trust may be less or more than all of the income earned on the retirement fund. Although there are several approaches, a common solution is to distribute an amount equal to the income of the retirement plan, even if it exceeds the RMD.[56] This frustrates the objective of achieving maximum deferral. If the benefits are instead payable directly to the surviving spouse, this problem is avoided.[57]

52. *See* Treas. Reg. §1.401(a)(9)-4 (as amended in 2002).

53. "The [participant's] entire interest must be distributed by the end of the calendar year which contains the fifth anniversary of the date of the [participant's] death." Treas. Reg. §1.401(a)(9)-3, A-2 (as amended in 2004). *See* CHOATE, *supra* note 38, §§1.5.03, 1.5.06 & 5.2.02.

54. *See* CHOATE, *supra* note 38, §§1.5.08 & 1.7.04.

55. *See id.* §§6.2.03 & 6.2.07.

56. *See id.* §§3.3.01-3.3.08. The primary IRS guidance addressing the structuring of a marital trust as a beneficiary of an IRA is Rev. Rul. 2006-26 (reproduced in this chapter). It expands on the approach of Rev. Rul. 2000-2, 2001-1 C.B. 305, which allowed the surviving spouse to have a power to compel distributions from the IRA, as opposed to requiring mandatory distributions, which was the approach of obsolete Rev. Rul. 89-89, 1989-2 C.B. 231.

57. *See* CHOATE, *supra* note 38, §3.3.11. The designation of a nonspousal beneficiary of community property retirement assets is fraught with problems. *See generally* Michael J. Jones, *There's an IRA Trap in Community Property States*, 146 TR. & EST. 32 (Nov. 2007).

Designating the surviving spouse as the beneficiary would also permit the surviving spouse to use the special spousal election to convert an inherited IRA to an account of his or her own[58] or to roll over other inherited retirement plans into the surviving spouse's retirement plan.[59] Furthermore, if the surviving spouse has not yet attained the RBD, the RMD on the inherited account is postponed.[60]

7. Charitable Bequests of Retirement Plan Assets May Be Useful

It may be useful to designate a charity as the primary beneficiary of a retirement plan such as an IRA. The estate may receive a charitable deduction for the value of the account for federal wealth transfer taxes, and recognition of IRD by private beneficiaries is avoided (see the articles on this topic collected at Part G).[61]

8. Roth IRA Conversions Are More Accessible for Wealthy Individuals

Effective for 2010 and later years, a taxpayer can convert distributions from certain retirement plans (including §§401(a), 403(a), 403(b) & 457(b) retirement plans and IRAs)[62] to a Roth IRA without regard to his or her income.[63] Although ordinary income taxes must be paid on the conversion, this option provides an additional planning option to be considered in connection with a rigorous calculation of the overall financial implications.[64]

58. *See* IRC §408(d); CHOATE, *supra* note 38, §3.2.03.

59. *See* CHOATE, *supra* note 38, §3.2. The Pension Protection Act of 2006, Pub. L. No. 109-280 (2006) permits nonspouse beneficiaries of inherited retirement plan accounts to transfer the assets into an IRA by a trustee-to-trustee transfer. The nonspouse beneficiary must begin taking the RMD, albeit based on the beneficiary's life expectancy, by the end of the year following the year of the participant's death, even if the beneficiary is younger than 70½. This is to be contrasted with a spousal rollover, where the surviving spouse can defer the RMD until he or she reaches age 70½. *See* Lee A. Snow, *The Pension Protection Act's Retirement Provisions Affecting Individuals*, 34 EST. PLAN. 3 (2007); Diana S.C. Zeydel, Mitchell M. Gans, & Jonathan G. Blattmachr, *What Estate Planners Need to Know About the New Pension Protection Act*, 105 J. TAX'N 199 (Oct. 2006); Howard M. Esterces, *A Great New Option: The Nonspousal Rollover*, 146 TR. & EST. 50 (Apr. 2007).

60. The surviving spouse under age 59½ has additional concerns, because if the assets are transferred to a retirement account that is his or her own account, the surviving spouse will become subject to a possible 10 percent penalty on premature distributions. *See* CHOATE, *supra* note 38, §3.2.08.

61. *See generally id.* ch. 7; SPERO, *supra* note 3, ¶13.01A.

62. *See* CHOATE, *supra* note 38, §5.4.01. However, the conversion may be precluded by the plan's terms unless the participant is separating from the employer or has reached retirement age. *See id.*, §5.4.08.

63. *See id.*§5.4.02.

64. *See Id.*, §5.8.02, 5.8.03 & 5.8.04 (discussing considerations in the conversion); R. Kevin Trout & Deborah W. Thomas, *Conversion to a Roth IRA Becomes a Powerful Estate Planning Strategy*, 24 PRAC. TAX LAW. 57 (2010).

EXERCISE 12-2

POST-MORTEM RETIREMENT BENEFIT PLANNING OPTIONS

Rachel is 35 years old, and her elder sister, Pam, passed away at age 45. Rachel is the designated beneficiary of Pam's IRA, which has a date of death value of $225,000. How must Rachel treat the IRA for federal income tax purposes, and what are her options?

Assume that Pam was also a participant in a qualified defined contribution retirement plan governed by IRC §401(a), and Rachel is the designated beneficiary of a vested benefit with a value of $75,000. How must Rachel treat the retirement benefit for federal income tax purposes, and what are her options?

As explained in point 6 above, the designation of a marital trust as a retirement plan beneficiary introduces additional complexity that is avoided if the surviving spouse is directly the beneficiary. The IRS's current approach to this issue is expressed in Revenue Ruling 2006-26 below. While the ruling is a bit complex and buttresses the point about added complexity of a marital trust in this situation, it also addresses the impact of fiduciary accounting rules on the marital deduction.

Rev. Rul. 2006-26
2006-22 I.R.B. 939

This ruling clarifies circumstances under which the surviving spouse is considered to have a qualifying income interest for life in an IRA where a marital trust is designated as the IRA beneficiary for purposes of electing to have the IRA treated as qualifying terminable interest property under section 2056(b)(7) of the Code. . . .

ISSUE

If a marital trust described in *Situations 1*, *2*, or *3* is the named beneficiary of a decedent's individual retirement account (IRA) or other qualified retirement plan . . . that is a defined contribution plan, under what circumstances is the surviving spouse considered to have a qualifying income interest for life in the IRA (or qualified retirement plan) and in the trust for purposes of an election to treat both the IRA and the trust as qualified terminable interest property (QTIP) under 2056(b)(7) of the Internal Revenue Code?

FACTS

A dies in 2004, at age 68, survived by spouse, *B*. Prior to death, *A* established an IRA described in 408(a). *A*'s will creates a testamentary marital trust (Trust) that is funded with assets in *A*'s probate estate. . . . Prior to death, *A* named Trust as the beneficiary of all amounts payable from the IRA after *A*'s death.... The IRA is currently invested in productive assets and *B* has the right (directly or through the trustee of Trust) to compel the investment of the IRA in assets productive of a reasonable income. The IRA document does not prohibit the withdrawal from the IRA of amounts in excess of the annual required minimum distribution amount under 408(a)(6). The executor of *A*'s estate elects under 2056(b)(7) to treat both the IRA and Trust as QTIP.

Under Trust's terms, all income is payable annually to *B* for *B*'s life, and no person has the power to appoint any part of the Trust principal to any person other than *B* during *B*'s lifetime. *B* has the right to compel the trustee to invest the Trust principal in assets productive of a reasonable income. On *B*'s death, the Trust principal is to be distributed to *A*'s children, who are younger than *B*. Under the trust instrument, no person other than *B* and *A*'s children has a beneficial interest in Trust (including any contingent beneficial interest). Further, as in Rev. Rul. 2000-2, 2000-1 C.B. 305, under Trust's terms, *B* has the power, exercisable annually, to compel the trustee to withdraw from the IRA an amount equal to all the income of the IRA for the year and to distribute that income to *B*. If *B* exercises this power, the trustee is obligated under Trust's terms to withdraw the greater of all of the income of the IRA or the annual required minimum distribution amount under 408(a)(6), and distribute currently to *B* at least the income of the IRA. The Trust instrument provides that any excess of the required minimum distribution amount over the income of the IRA for that year is to be added to Trust's principal. If *B* does not exercise the power to compel a withdrawal from the IRA for a particular year, the trustee must withdraw from the IRA only the required minimum distribution amount under 408(a)(6) for that year.

... Because the requirements of A-4 and A-5 of 1.401(a)(9)-4 of the Income Tax regulations are satisfied and there are no beneficiaries or potential beneficiaries that are not individuals, the beneficiaries of the trust may be treated as designated beneficiaries of the IRA. In accordance with 408(a)(6) and the terms of the IRA instrument, the trustee of Trust elects to receive annual required minimum distributions using the exception to the five year rule in 401(a)(9)(B)(iii) for distributions over a distribution period equal to a designated beneficiary's life expectancy. Because amounts may be accumulated in Trust for the benefit of *A*'s children, *B* is not treated as the sole beneficiary and, thus, the special rule for a surviving spouse in 401(a)(9)(B)(iv) is not applicable. Accordingly, the trustee of Trust elects to have the annual required minimum distributions from the IRA to Trust begin in 2005, the year immediately following the year of *A*'s death. The amount of the annual required minimum distribution from the IRA for each year is calculated by dividing the account balance of the IRA as of December 31 of the immediately preceding year by the remaining distribution period. Because *B*'s life expectancy is the shortest of all of the potential beneficiaries of Trust's interest in the IRA (including remainder beneficiaries), the distribution period for purposes of 401(a)(9)(B)(iii) is *B*'s life expectancy, based on the Single Life Table in A-1 of 1.401(a)(9)-9, using *B*'s age as of *B*'s birthday in 2005, reduced by one for each calendar year that elapses after 2005. On *B*'s death, the required minimum distributions with respect to any undistributed balance of the IRA will continue to be calculated in the same manner and be distributed to Trust over the remaining distribution period.

Situation 1—Authorized Adjustments Between Income and Principal. The facts and the terms of Trust are as described above. Trust is governed by the laws of State *X*. State *X* has adopted a version of the Uniform Principal and Income Act (UPIA) including a provision similar to section 104(a) of the UPIA providing that, in certain circumstances, the trustee is authorized to make adjustments between income and principal to fulfill the trustee's duty of impartiality between the income and remainder beneficiaries. More specifically, State *X* has adopted a provision providing that adjustments between income and principal may be made, as under section 104(a) of the UPIA, when trust assets are invested under State *X*'s prudent investor standard, the amount to be distributed to a beneficiary is described by reference to the trust's income, and the trust cannot be administered impartially after applying State *X*'s statutory rules regarding the allocation of receipts and disbursements to income and principal. In addition, State *X*'s statute incorporates a provision similar to section 409(c) of the UPIA providing that, when a payment is made from an IRA to a trust: (i) if no part of the payment is characterized as interest, a dividend, or an equivalent payment, and all or part of the payment is required to be distributed currently to the beneficiary, the trustee must allocate 10 percent of the required payment to income and the balance to principal; and (ii) if no part of the payment made is required to be distributed from the trust or if the payment received by the trust is the entire amount to which the trustee is contractually entitled, the trustee must allocate the entire payment to principal. State *X*'s statute further provides that, similar to section 409(d) of the UPIA, if in order to obtain an estate tax marital deduction for a trust a trustee must allocate more of a payment to income, the trustee is required to allocate to income the additional amount necessary to obtain the marital deduction.

For each calendar year, the trustee determines the total return of the assets held directly in Trust, exclusive of the IRA, and then determines the respective portion of the total return that is to be allocated to principal and to income under State *X*'s version of section 104(a) of the UPIA in a manner that fulfills the trustee's duty of impartiality between the income and remainder beneficiaries. The amount allocated to income is distributed to *B* as income beneficiary of Trust, in accordance with the terms of the Trust instrument. Similarly, for each calendar year the trustee of Trust determines the total return of the assets held in the IRA and then determines the respective portion of the total return that would be allocated to principal and to income under State *X*'s version of section 104(a) of the

UPIA in a manner that fulfills a fiduciary's duty of impartiality. This allocation is made without regard to, and independent of, the trustee's determination with respect to Trust income and principal. If *B* exercises the withdrawal power, Trustee withdraws from the IRA the amount allocated to income (or the required minimum distribution amount under 408(a)(6), if greater), and distributes to *B* the amount allocated to income of the IRA.

Situation 2—Unitrust Income Determination. The facts, and the terms of Trust, are as described above. Trust is governed by the laws of State *Y*. Under State *Y* law, if the trust instrument specifically provides or the interested parties consent, the income of the trust means a unitrust amount of 4 percent of the fair market value of the trust assets valued annually. In accordance with procedures prescribed by the State *Y* statute, all interested parties authorize the trustee to administer Trust and to determine withdrawals from the IRA in accordance with this provision. The trustee determines an amount equal to 4 percent of the fair market value of the IRA assets and an amount equal to 4 percent of the fair market value of Trust's assets, exclusive of the IRA, as of the appropriate valuation date. In accordance with the terms of Trust, trustee distributes the amount equal to 4 percent of the Trust assets, exclusive of the IRA, to *B*, annually. In addition, if *B* exercises the withdrawal power, Trustee withdraws from the IRA the greater of the required minimum distribution amount under 408(a)(6) or the amount equal to 4 percent of the value of the IRA assets, and distributes to *B* at least the amount equal to 4 percent of the value of the IRA assets.

Situation 3—"Traditional" Definition of Income. The facts, and the terms of Trust, are as described above. Trust is governed by the laws of State *Z*. State *Z* has not enacted the UPIA, and therefore does not have provisions comparable to sections 104(a) and 409(c) and (d) of the UPIA. Thus, in determining the amount of IRA income *B* can compel the trustee to withdraw from the IRA, the trustee applies the law of State *Z* regarding the allocation of receipts and disbursements to income and principal, with no power to allocate between income and principal. As in *Situations 1* and *2*, the income of Trust is determined without regard to the IRA, and the income of the IRA is separately determined based on the assets of the IRA.

LAW AND ANALYSIS

... Section 2056(b)(7) provides that QTIP, for purposes of 2056(a), is treated as passing to the surviving spouse and no part of the property is treated as passing to any person other than the surviving spouse. Section 2056(b)(7)(B)(i) defines QTIP as property that passes from the decedent, in which the surviving spouse has a qualifying income interest for life, and to which an election under 2056(b)(7) applies. Under 2056(b)(7)(B)(ii), the surviving spouse has a qualifying income interest for life if, *inter alia*, the surviving spouse is entitled to all the income from the property, payable annually or at more frequent intervals.

Section 20.2056(b)-7(d)(2) provides that the principles of 20.2056(b)-5(f), relating to whether the spouse is entitled for life to all of the income from the property, apply in determining whether the surviving spouse is entitled for life to all of the income from the property for purposes of 2056(b)(7).

Section 20.2056(b)-5(f)(1) provides that, if an interest is transferred in trust, the surviving spouse is entitled for life to all of the income from the entire interest if the effect of the trust is to give the surviving spouse substantially that degree of beneficial enjoyment of the trust property during the surviving spouse's life that the principles of the law of trusts accord to a person who is unqualifiedly designated as the life beneficiary of a trust. In addition, the surviving spouse is entitled for life to all of the income from the property if the spouse is entitled to income as determined by applicable local law that provides for a reasonable apportionment between the income and remainder beneficiaries of the total return of the trust and that meets the requirements of 1.643(b)-1.

Section 20.2056(b)-5(f)(8) provides that the terms "entitled for life" and "payable annually or at more frequent intervals" require that under the terms of the trust the income referred to must be currently (at least annually) distributable to the spouse or that the spouse must have such command over the income that it is virtually the spouse's. Thus, the surviving spouse will be entitled for life to all of the income from the trust, payable annually, if, under the terms of the trust instrument, the spouse has the right exercisable annually (or at more frequent intervals) to require distribution to the spouse of the trust income and, to the extent that right is not exercised, the trust income is to be accumulated and added to principal.

Generally, 1.643(b)-1 provides that, for purposes of various provisions of the Code relating to the income taxation of estates and trusts, the term "income" means the amount of income of the estate or trust for the taxable year determined under the terms of the governing instrument and applicable local law. Under 1.643(b)-1, trust provisions that depart fundamentally from traditional principles of income and principal generally will not be recognized. Under these traditional principles, items such as dividends, interest, and rents are generally allocated to income and proceeds from the sale or exchange of trust assets are generally allocated to principal.

However, under 1.643(b)-1, the allocation of an amount between income and principal pursuant to applicable local law will be respected if local law provides for a reasonable apportionment between the income and remainder beneficiaries of the total return of the trust for the year, including ordinary and tax-exempt income, capital gains, and appreciation. For example, a state statute providing that income is a unitrust amount of no less than 3 percent and no more than 5 percent of the fair market value of the trust assets, whether determined annually or averaged on a multiple year basis, is a reasonable apportionment of the total return of the trust. Similarly, under 1.643(b)-1, a state statute that permits the trustee to make adjustments between income and principal to fulfill the trustee's duty of impartiality between the income and remainder beneficiaries is generally a reasonable apportionment of the total return of the trust.

Rev. Rul. 2000-2, 2000-1 C.B. 305, concludes that a surviving spouse has a qualifying income interest for life under 2056(b)(7)(B)(ii) in an IRA and in a marital trust named as the beneficiary of that IRA if the spouse has the power, exercisable annually, to compel the trustee to withdraw the income earned on the IRA assets and to distribute that income (along with the income earned on the trust assets other than the IRA) to the spouse. Therefore, assuming all other requirements of 2056(b)(7) are satisfied, and provided the executor makes the election for both the IRA and the trust, the IRA and the trust will qualify for the marital deduction under 2056(b)(7). The revenue ruling also concludes that the result would be the same if the terms of the trust require the trustee to withdraw an amount equal to the income earned on the IRA assets and to distribute that amount (along with the income earned on the trust assets other than the IRA) to the spouse.

In *Situation 1*, under section 104(a) of the UPIA as enacted by State *X*, the trustee of Trust allocates the total return of the assets held directly in Trust (*i.e.*, assets other than those held in the IRA) between income and principal in a manner that fulfills the trustee's duty of impartiality between the income and remainder beneficiaries. The trustee of Trust makes a similar allocation with respect to the IRA. The allocation of the total return of the IRA and the total return of Trust in this manner constitutes a reasonable apportionment of the total return of the IRA and Trust between the income and remainder beneficiaries under 20.2056(b)-5(f)(1) and 1.643(b)-1. Under the terms of Trust, the income of the IRA so determined is subject to *B*'s withdrawal power, and the income of Trust, so determined, is payable to *B* annually. Accordingly, the IRA and Trust meet the requirements of 20.2056(b)(7)(B)(ii) and therefore *B* has a qualifying income interest for life in both the IRA and Trust because *B* has the power to unilaterally access all of the IRA income, and the income of Trust is payable to *B* annually.

Depending upon the terms of Trust, the impact of State *X*'s version of sections 409(c) and (d) of the UPIA may have to be considered. State *X*'s version of section 409(c) of the UPIA provides in effect that a required minimum distribution from the IRA under Code section 408(a)(6) is to be allocated 10 percent to income and 90 percent to principal. This 10 percent allocation to income, standing alone, does not satisfy the requirements of 20.2056(b)-5(f)(1) and 1.643(b)-1, because the amount of the required minimum distribution is not based on the total return of the IRA (and therefore the amount allocated to income does not reflect a reasonable apportionment of the total return between the income and remainder beneficiaries). The 10 percent allocation to income also does not represent the income of the IRA under applicable state law without regard to a power to adjust between principal and income. State *X*'s version of section 409(d) of the UPIA, requiring an additional allocation to income if necessary to qualify for the marital deduction, may not qualify the arrangement under 2056. Cf. Rev. Rul. 75-440, 1975-2 C.B. 372, using a savings clause to determine testator's intent in a situation where the will is ambiguous, but citing Rev. Rul. 65-144, 1965-1 C.B. 422, for the position that savings clauses are ineffective to reform an instrument for federal transfer tax purposes. Based on the facts in *Situation 1*, if *B* exercises the withdrawal power, the trustee is obligated under Trust's terms to withdraw the greater of all of the income of the IRA or the annual required minimum distribution amount under 408(a)(6), and to distribute at least the income of the IRA to *B*. Thus, in this case, State *X*'s version of section 409(c) or (d) of UPIA would only operate to determine the portion of the required minimum distribution amount that is allocated to Trust income, and (because Trust income is determined without regard to the IRA or distributions from the IRA) would not affect the determination of the amount distributable to *B*. Accordingly, in *Situation 1*, the requirements of 2056(b)(7)(B)(ii) are satisfied. However, if the terms of a trust do not require the distribution to *B* of at least the income of the IRA in the event that *B* exercises the right to direct the withdrawal from the IRA, then the requirements of 2056(b)(7)(B)(ii) may not be satisfied unless the Trust's terms provide that State *X*'s version of section 409(c) of the UPIA is not to apply.

In *Situation 2*, the trustee determines the income of Trust (excluding the IRA) and the income of the IRA under a statutory unitrust regime pursuant to which "income" is defined as a unitrust amount of 4 percent of the fair market value of the assets determined annually. The determination of what constitutes Trust income and the income of the IRA in this manner satisfies the requirements of 20.2056(b)-5(f)(1) and 1.643(b)-1. The Trustee distributes the income of Trust, determined in this manner, to *B* annually, and *B* has the power to compel the trustee annually to withdraw and distribute to *B* the income of the IRA, determined in this manner. Accordingly, in *Situation 2*, because *B* has the power to unilaterally access all income of the IRA, and the income of Trust is payable to *B* annually, the IRA and Trust meet the requirements of 20.2056(b)(7)(B)(ii). The result would be the same if State *Y* had enacted both the statutory unitrust regime and a version of section 104(a) of the UPIA and the income of Trust is determined under section 104(a) of the UPIA as enacted by State *Y*, and the income of the IRA is determined under the statutory unitrust regime (or *vice versa*). Under these circumstances, Trust income and IRA income are each determined under state statutory provisions applicable to Trust that satisfy the requirements of 20.2056(b)-5(f)(1) and 1.643(b)-1, and therefore *B* has a qualifying income interest for life in both the IRA and Trust.

In *Situation 3*, *B* has the power to compel the trustee to withdraw the income of the IRA as determined under the law (whether common or statutory) of a jurisdiction that has not enacted section 104(a) of UPIA. Under the terms of Trust, if *B* exercises this power, the trustee must withdraw the greater of the required minimum distribution amount or the income of the IRA, and at least the income of the IRA must be distributed to *B*. Accordingly, in *Situation 3*, the IRA and Trust meet the requirements of 2056(b)(7)(B)(ii), and therefore *B* has a qualifying income interest for life in both the IRA and Trust, because *B* receives the income of Trust (excluding the IRA) at least annually and *B* has the power to unilaterally access all of the IRA income determined in accordance with 20.2056(b)-5(f)(1). The result would be the same if State *Z* had enacted section 104(a) of the UPIA, but the trustee decided to make no adjustments pursuant to that provision.

In *Situations 1*, *2*, and *3*, the income of the IRA and the income of Trust (excluding the IRA) are determined separately and without taking into account that the IRA distribution is made to Trust. In order to avoid any duplication in determining the total income to be paid to *B*, the portion of the IRA distribution to Trust that is allocated to trust income is disregarded in determining the amount of trust income that must be distributed to *B* under 2056(b)(7).

The result in *Situations 1*, *2*, and *3* would be the same if the terms of Trust directed the trustee annually to withdraw all of the income from the IRA and to distribute to *B* at least the income of the IRA (instead of granting *B* the power, exercisable annually, to compel the trustee to do so). Furthermore, if, instead of Trust being the named beneficiary of a decedent's interest in the IRA, Trust is the named beneficiary of a decedent's interest in some other qualified retirement plan described in section 4974(c) that is a defined contribution plan, the same principles would apply regarding whether *B* is considered to have a qualifying income interest for life in the qualified retirement plan.

HOLDING

If a marital trust is the named beneficiary of a decedent's IRA (or other qualified retirement plan described in section 4974(c) that is a defined contribution plan), the surviving spouse, under the circumstances described in *Situations 1, 2*, and *3* in this revenue ruling, will be considered to have a qualifying income interest for life in the IRA (or qualified retirement plan) and in the trust for purposes of an election to treat both the IRA (or qualified retirement plan) and the trust as QTIP under 2056(b)(7). If the marital deduction is sought, the QTIP election must be made for both the IRA and the trust.

Taxpayers should be aware, however, that in situations such as those described in this revenue ruling in which a portion of any distribution from the IRA to Trust may be held in Trust for future distribution rather than being distributed to *B* currently, *B* is not the sole designated beneficiary of

A's IRA. As a result, both *B* and the remainder beneficiaries must be taken into account as designated beneficiaries in order to determine the shortest life expectancy and whether only individuals are designated beneficiaries. See A-7(c) of 1.401(a)(9)-5.

EFFECT ON OTHER REVENUE RULINGS

Rev. Rul. 2000-2, 2000-1 C.B. 305, is modified, and as modified, is superseded.

F. CASE STUDY 12-1

John and Susan Able

PLANNING FOR RETIREMENT AND ASSET PROTECTION

John and Susan Able are husband and wife, ages 62 and 59 respectively. They have been happily married for 37 years. Susan inherited $800,000 from her parents several years ago, and she has invested those funds in a combination of certificates of deposit, U.S. Treasury securities, and equity mutual funds. On their accountant's advice, Susan is the sole owner of these accounts, but John is a TOD or POD beneficiary on most of them. Her portfolio is currently worth approximately $1,250,000. John and Susan own a home as joint tenants that is worth approximately $700,000. They also own, as joint tenants, three rental properties worth approximately $800,000 in total. None of their real estate properties is encumbered by a mortgage. Aside from automobiles, home furnishings, and some modest cash reserves, their only other assets of any significance are their retirement plans.

Susan owns regular IRAs valued at $95,000, and her adjusted basis in those accounts is $5,000.

Susan also owns a Roth IRA valued at $4,500.

John owns regular IRAs valued at $2,200,000, in which his adjusted basis is zero. This large sum was produced from the rollover of a retirement plan benefit from a civil engineering firm in which he was a partner. John is now semi-retired, is doing some consulting from time to time, and has begun drawing Social Security benefits.

Their house has been free and clear of debt for some time, their two children are adults and independent, and the rental properties produce approximately $3,100 per month cash flow. Consequently, their basic living needs are covered by the rental income. In addition, Susan's investments and John's Social Security benefits provide additional funds for travel, gifts, and special occasions.

John and Susan have come to you for estate planning advice. They currently have Wills that were executed over 20 years ago, before Susan received her inheritance, before the increase in the value of their retirement plan assets, and before their real estate assets had appreciated. Accordingly, they believe that some attention needs to be given to their overall planning. Inasmuch as they can live off their current income for the foreseeable future, they are particularly concerned about the income taxes that must be paid in connection with the IRAs, which will deplete their other invested assets. As John noted, "I don't want to withdraw the money and pay taxes. We don't need it. However, our accountant told us that we need to do that when I reach age 70½."

The income tax concern about the IRAs brought them to your office. Otherwise, their planning goals are as follows, in order of priority:

1. To provide assets that maintain the survivor in comfort and security;
2. With respect to the remainder that will be transferred to their children, to prevent dissipation of the funds by possible future divorces or other events (although the children are now happily married);
3. To accomplish the foregoing objectives with minimal costs, including federal and state taxes as well as legal fees.

Please discuss the following issues:

A. Do John and Susan require any asset protection planning at this time?

B. In terms of minimizing federal wealth transfer taxes, what planning measures would you propose to John and Susan? State your assumptions, if any are required, and indicate what other facts you would like to know.

C. With respect to the IRAs in particular, what should be done? How should the beneficiary designations be handled? If a QTIP marital trust will be the beneficiary, what language would you include to resolve the RMD/QTIP income problem?

G. Reference Materials

Treatises

Asset Protection

- Mark A Bogdanowicz, *Pension Funds Are Protected Post-BAPCPA—Or Are They?*, 2007 No. 7 NORTON BANKR. L. ADVISER 1 (July 2007).
- W. HOMER DRAKE, JR. & CHRISTOPHER S. STRICKLAND, CHAPTER 11 REORGANIZATIONS §9:22 (2d ed. 2010-2011) (discussing fraudulent conveyances under the Bankruptcy Code).
- BARRY S. ENGEL ET AL., ASSET PROTECTION PLANNING GUIDE (2000).
- WILLIAM L. NORTON, JR. & WILLIAM L. NORTON, III, NORTON BANKRUPTCY LAW AND PRACTICE §56:23 (3d ed. 2010) (discussing state retirement plan creditor exemptions).

- Peter Spero, Asset Protection: Legal Planning, Strategies and Forms ¶¶ 11.01 & 11.05 (2001 & Supp. 2011) (discussing professional corporations); ch. 3(discussing fraudulent conveyance law); ¶¶ 13.03[1][a] & 13.03[3] (discussing retirement plan creditor exemptions); ¶¶ 9.02, 9.02[1][b] & 10.04[4] (discussing charging orders).

Retirement Asset Tax Planning

- Natalie B. Choate, Life and Death Planning for Retirement Benefits (7th ed. 2011).
- John R. Price & Samuel A. Donaldson, Price on Contemporary Estate Planning, ch. 13 (2011) (chapter devoted to planning for retirement plan assets).

Articles

Asset Protection

- Lawerence R. Ahern, III, *Homestead and Other Exemptions Under the Bankruptcy Abuse Prevention and Consumer Protection Act: Observations on "Asset Protection" After 2005*, 13 Am. Bankr. Inst. L. Rev. 585 (2005).
- Richard C. Ausness, *The Offshore Asset Protection Trust: A Prudent Financial Planning Device or the Last Refuge of a Scoundrel?*, 45 Duq. L. Rev. 147 (2007).
- Erin C. V. Bailey, *Asset Protection Trusts Protect the Assets: But What About the Trustees?*, 21 Prob. & Prop. 58 (Jan./Feb. 2007).
- Carter G. Bishop, *LLC Charging Orders: A Jurisdictional and Governing Law Quagmire*, 12 Bus. Entities 14 (May/June 2010).
- Alexander A. Bove, Jr., *Protecting Assets Through Insurance and Annuities*, 31 Est. Plan. 270 (2004).
- Alexander A. Bove, Jr., *Moving the Immovable: Protecting Real Estate from Creditors' Claims*, 27 Est. Plan. 302 (2000).
- Alexander A. Bove, Jr., *The Swiss Annuity: Is It as Good as Their Chocolate? When Asset Protection Estate Planning and Tax Deferral Come in One Box*, 146 Tr. & Est. 52 (2007).
- Robert T. Danforth, *Rethinking the Law of Creditors' Rights in Trusts*, 53 Hastings L.J. 287 (2002).
- J. Richard Duke, *Offshore, Legitimately*, 145 Tr. & Est. 42 (Nov. 2006).
- John K. Eason, *Policy, Logic, and Persuasion in the Evolving Realm of Trust Asset Protection*, 27 Cardozo L. Rev. 2621 (2006).
- Barry S. Engel, *Integrated Estate Planning with Foreign-Situs Trusts*, 31 Tax Adviser 102 (Feb. 2000).
- Barry S. Engel & David L. Lockwood, *Domestic Asset Protection Trusts Contrasted with Foreign Trusts*, 29 Est. Plan. 288 (2002).

- Barry S. Engel et al., *Asset Protection for the Business and Professional Practice*, 35 Est. Plan. 16 (Feb. 2008).
- Fred Franke, *Asset Protection and Tenancy by the Entirety*, 34 ACTEC J. 210 (2009).
- Alan S. Gassman, *Common Mistakes Estate Planners Make Regarding Asset Protection*, 29 Est. Plan. 518 (2002).
- Alan S. Gassman, *Practical Asset Protection Strategies and Considerations*, Sophisticated Estate Planning Techniques, SE09 ALI-ABA 641 (ALI-ABA Continuing Legal Education, Sept. 16, 1999).
- Alan S. Gassman & Sabrina M. Moravecky, *Charging Orders: The Remedy for Creditors of Debtor Partners*, 36 Est. Plan. 21 (Dec. 2009).
- Alvin J. Golden, *Asset Protection for QRPs and IRAs*, 142 Tr. & Est. 40 (Nov. 2003).
- Alvin J. Golden, *Piercing Shield Laws to Garnish SEP-IRAs*, 141 Tr. & Est. 51 (Aug. 2002).
- Alvin J. Golden, *Retirement Benefits and Creditor's Rights*, Sophisticated Estate Planning Techniques, SS007 ALI-ABA 289 (ALI-ABA Continuing Legal Education, Sept. 13-14, 2010).
- Kenneth Goldstein, *Most Common Estate Planning and Asset Protection Mistakes: A Practitioner's Lists*, 23 J. Tax'n Inv. 319 (2006).
- Charles Harris & Tye J. Klooster, *Beneficiary-Controlled Trusts Can Lose Asset Protection*, 145 Tr. & Est. 37 (Dec. 2006).
- Adam J. Hirsch, *Fear Not the Asset Protection Trust*, 27 Cardozo L. Rev. 2685 (2006).
- Richard M. Horwood & Jeffrey A. Zaluda, *Current Trends in Asset Protection*, 19 J. Tax'n Inv. 307 (2002).
- Richard M. Horwood & Jeffrey A. Zaluda, *Custom Designing Domestic Asset Protection Strategies*, 25 J. Tax'n Inv. 42 (2007).
- Denis A. Kleinfeld, *Rules of Engagement*, 145 Tr. & Est. 54 (Nov. 2006) (contempt proceedings and asset protection).
- Myron Kove & James M. Kosakow, *Asset Protection Advantages of a Family Limited Partnership*, 37 Est. Plan. 34 (June 2010).
- Henry J. Lischer, Jr., *Professional Responsibility Issues Associated with Asset Protection Trusts*, 39 Real Prop. Prob. & Tr. J. 561 (2004).
- Henry J. Lischer, Jr., *Domestic Asset Protection Trusts: Pallbearers to Liability?*, 35 Real Prop. Prob. & Tr. J. 479 (2000).
- Alson R. Martin, *Protecting Qualified Plan and IRA Assets from Creditors (Recent Developments in the Post-*Patterson v. Shumate *Era*), Professional Organizations, Qualified Plans, Health Care, and Welfare Benefits, SC58 ALI-ABA 75 (ALI-ABA Continuing Legal Education, Feb. 21-23, 1998).
- Mario A. Mata, *Frequently Asked Questions Regarding Offshore Wealth Preservation Trusts*, 18 No. 3 Prac. Tax Law. 27 (Spring 2004).

- Mario A. Mata, *Use of FLPs and LLCs in Asset Protection Planning*, 18 No. 2 PRAC. TAX LAW. 15 (Winter 2004).
- Richard A. Naegele & Mark P. Altieri, *How Safe Is Your Pension? Creditor Protection for Retirement Plans and IRAs*, 22 PRAC. TAX LAW. 33 (2008).
- Richard W. Nenno, *Delaware Law Offers Asset Protection and Estate Planning Benefits*, 26 EST. PLAN. 3 (1999).
- Richard W. Nenno, *Planning with Domestic Asset-Protection Trusts: Part I*, 40 REAL PROP. PROB. & TR. J. 263 (2005).
- Richard W. Nenno, *Planning with Domestic Asset-Protection Trusts: Part II*, 40 REAL PROP. PROB. & TR. J. 477 (2005).
- Duncan E. Osborne & Jack E. Owen, Jr., *Asset Protection: Trust Planning*, Planning Techniques for Large Estates, SM077 ALI-ABA 301, 330-345 (ALI-ABA Continuing Legal Education, Apr. 23-27, 2007).
- Duncan E. Osborne, Leslie C. Giordani & Arthur T. Catterall, *Asset Protection and Jurisdiction Selection*, 33 INST. ON EST. PLAN. ¶1400 (1999).
- Steven J. Oshins, *The Nevada Asset Protection Trust—An Alternative to the Offshore Trust*, 21 J. TAX'N INV. 288 (2004).
- Michael A. Passananti, *Domestic Asset Protection Trusts: The Risks and Roadblocks Which May Hinder Their Effectiveness*, 32 ACTEC J. 260 (2006).
- John W. Porter, *Asset Protection Other Than Self-Settled Trusts: Beneficiary Controlled Trusts, FLPs, LLCs, Retirement Plans and Other Creditor Protection Strategies*, 39 INST. ON EST. PLAN. ¶300 (2005).
- Randall W. Roth, *Protecting Assets from Creditors Legally, Ethically, and Morally*, Advanced Estate Planning Techniques, SG062 ALI-ABA 75 (ALI-ABA Continuing Legal Education, Feb. 21-23, 2002).
- Gideon Rothschild, *Protecting the Estate from In-Laws and Other Predators*, 35 INST. ON EST. PLAN. ¶1700 (2001).
- Gideon Rothschild & Daniel S. Rubin, *Ninth Circuit Treads on an Established Right*, 145 TR. & EST. 48 (Nov. 2006) (fraudulent transfer doctrine).
- Gideon Rothschild et al., *IRS Rules Self-Settled Alaska Trust Will Not Be in Grantor's Estate*, 37 EST. PLAN. 3 (Jan. 2010).
- Dennis M. Sandoval, *Drafting Trusts for Maximum Protection from Creditors*, 30 EST. PLAN. 290 (2003).
- David G. Shaftel, *Alaska's Experience with Self-Settled Discretionary Spendthrift Trusts*, 29 EST. PLAN. 506 (2002).
- David G. Shaftel & Jonathan G. Blattmachr, *Alaska's 2006 Amendments to Its Trust and Estate Statutes*, 34 EST. PLAN. 10 (2007).
- David G. Shaftel, *A Comparison of the Various State Domestic Asset Protection Trust Statutes*, 35 EST. PLAN. 3 (Mar. 2008) (Part 1);

David G. Shaftel, *A Comparison of the Various State Domestic Asset Protection Trust Statutes*, 35 EST. PLAN. 14 (Apr. 2008) (Part 2).

- David G. Shaftel, *Comparison of the Twelve Domestic Asset Protection Statutes*, 34 ACTEC J. 293 (2009).
- David J. Slenn, *Has the Warning Bell Sounded for Asset Protection Planners?* 24 PROB. & PROP. 48 (Mar./Apr. 2010).
- Peter Spero, *How to Arrange a Client's Property for Asset Protection*, 22 EST. PLAN. 226 (1995).
- Jacob Stein, *Asset Protection May Risk Fraudulent Transfer Violations*, 37 EST. PLAN. 12 (Aug. 2010).
- Jacob Stein, *Practical Primer and Radical Approach to Asset Protection*, 38 EST. PLAN. 21 (June 2011).
- Lisa M. Stern & Leonard S. Baum, *What Private Wealth Attorneys Need to Know About Money Laundering*, 37 EST. PLAN. 28 (June 2010).

Retirement Asset Tax Planning (See also "Retirement Plan Beneficiary Designations" in Ch. 3 reference materials and "Retirement Plan Spousal Beneficiary Designations" in Ch. 5 reference materials.)

- Jean T. Adams, *Solving the 3-D Puzzle: Working with Retirement Benefits in Estate Planning*, 34 EST. PLAN. 22 (2007).
- John B. Atkins, *Individual Retirement Accounts and Prohibited Transactions*, 25 PROB. & PROP. 34 (May/June 2011).
- Edward V. Atnally, *Estate Planning and Retirement Benefits—An Approach Toward Simplification*, Part 2, 23 PROB. & PROP. 56 (Sept./Oct. 2009).
- Edward V. Brennan, *Planning for Community Property Retirement Benefits and IRAs*, 29 EST. PLAN. 187 (2002).
- Len Cason, *Maximizing Funding of Credit Shelter Trust with Non-IRA Assets*, 29 EST. PLAN. 282 (2002).
- Natalie B. Choate, *Sticky Situations*, 146 TR. & EST. 48 (Sept. 2007) (executor's challenges in dealing with retirement benefits).
- Richard Coppage & Sidney J. Baxendale, *Roth IRA Conversion Rules Shed Income Limit in 2010*, 84 TAX STRATEGIES 132 (Mar. 2010).
- Bradford N. Dewan, *Update on Estate Planning for IRAs and Pension Plans*, 38 EST. PLAN. 8 (July 2011).
- Reed W. Easton, *How to Fully Fund a Credit-Shelter Trust Without Transferring Assets or Using Retirement Plans*, 105 J. TAX'N 349 (2006).
- Howard M. Esterces, *A Great New Option: The Nonspousal Rollover*, 146 TR. & EST. 50 (Apr. 2007).
- Mary C. Hester & Jacquelyn Morton, *Using Retirement Plans to Make Charitable Gifts*, 50 LA. B.J. 269 (Dec. 2002/Jan. 2003).

- Marcia Chadwick Holt, *Roth IRAs and You*, 146 Tr. & Est. 39 (Sept. 2007).
- Christopher R. Hoyt, *When the Estate Is the IRA Beneficiary*, 141 Tr. & Est. 17 (Nov. 2002).
- Christopher R. Hoyt, *Charitable Gifts and Bequests of IRD Assets (Including IRAs, Stock Options, and Savings Bonds)*, Charitable Giving Techniques, SE093 ALI-ABA 345 (ALI-ABA Continuing Legal Education, May 30-31, 2002).
- Christopher R. Hoyt, *How to Structure Charitable Bequests from IRAs and Retirement Plan Accounts*, Charitable Giving Techniques, SE86 ALI-ABA 325 (ALI-ABA Continuing Legal Education, June 1, 2000).
- Jay W. Miller & James L. Mohr, *Consider Annuities and Roth IRAs in Retirement Planning*, 37 Est. Plan. 33 (July 2010).
- Sanford J. Schlesinger, *Charitable Estate Planning with Retirement Benefits and Related Life Insurance Planning*, 69 N.Y. B.J. 14 (Jan. 1997).
- Sandra Brown Sherman et al., *Apply Tax Planning Ideas to Improve Retirement Distributions*, 71 Prac. Tax Strategies 27 (July 2003).
- Martin Silfen, *Retirement Plan Fundamentals for Estate Planners*, Fundamentals of Retirement and IRA Distributions, VLR999 ALI-ABA 1 (ALI-ABA Continuing Legal Education, Mar. 16, 2000).
- Lee A. Snow, *Final IRA Distribution Rules Expand and Clarify Tax-Saving Opportunities*, 29 Est. Plan. 395 (2002).
- Lee A. Snow, *The Pension Protection Act's Retirement Provisions Affecting Individuals*, 34 Est. Plan. 3 (2007).
- Steven E. Trytten, *To My Wife, I Leave My IRA*, 141 Tr. & Est. 42 (Sept. 2002).
- Steven E. Trytten, *Estate Planning for Retirement Assets*, Estate Planning in Depth, SR042 ALI-ABA 651 (ALI-ABA Continuing Legal Education, June 13-18, 2010).
- Leslie J. Wilsher, *Estate Planning Strategies for Retirement Benefits*, 31 Est. Plan. 226 (2004).
- Diana S. C. Zeydel, Mitchell M. Gans & Jonathan G. Blattmachr, *What Estate Planners Need to Know About the New Pension Protection Act*, 105 J. Tax'n 199 (Oct. 2006).

CHAPTER 13

The Generation-Skipping Trust and Other Wealth Perpetuation Measures

In recent years state laws have emerged that have weakened or eliminated the limits imposed by the common law Rule Against Perpetuities (RAP) on the structuring of long-term trusts. These changes have in turn produced more interest by clients of relatively moderate wealth in the creation of generation-skipping trusts and so-called "perpetual" or "dynasty" trusts. With the RAP receding in importance, the planner's focus has shifted to creating trusts that can successfully function in such a long-term, unpredictable environment while also planning for the federal generation-skipping transfer tax (GSTT). In addition to minimizing the capital-depleting impact of wealth transfer taxes, a generation-skipping trust has the potential to contribute to the perpetuation of the wealth of a family group, guarding it against dissipation through investment or financial mismanagement, dissolution of marriage, creditors, and spendthrift behavior.

This chapter introduces other family wealth perpetuation measures that complement the generation-skipping trust, such as family mission statements, family offices, and family trust companies.

A. The Rule Against Perpetuities

A discussion of the fundamental doctrine of the RAP is beyond the scope of this book. We will instead focus on the overall drafting challenges. As of 1999, at least seven states had effectively eliminated the common law rule,[1] and by 2003, that number had increased to roughly 19 states and the District of Columbia.[2] The variations in approach and the pace of amendments defy a tidy summary, but a 2007 commentary identified 21 states and the District of Columbia as eliminating the common law rule altogether or in certain contexts (such as trusts), or modifying it to approach practical repeal.[3] Since then, several more states have parted ways with the RAP.[4] At least 26 states and the District of Columbia have adopted the Uniform Statutory Rule Against Perpetuities[5] (USRAP). Several states that adopted USRAP made significant modifications.[6]

1. *See* Angela M. Vallario, *Death by a Thousand Cuts: The Rule Against Perpetuities*, 25 J. LEGIS. 141 (1999) (referring to ALASKA STAT. §34.27.050(a)(3) (Michie 1998); DEL. CODE ANN. tit. 25, §503(a) (1989 & Supp. 2000); IDAHO CODE tit. 55-111 (2003); 765 ILL. COMP. STAT. 305/2-6 (West 1993 & Supp. 1998); MD. CODE ANN., EST. & TRUSTS, §11-102 (2001 & Supp. 2002); S.D. CODIFIED LAWS §43-5-8 (Michie 1997); WIS. STAT. ANN. §700.16 (West 2000)).

2. A 2003 article identified 16 states that abolished the rule. Five states abolished the rule entirely: Idaho, New Jersey, Rhode Island, South Dakota, and Wisconsin. Eight states made the rule optional: Arizona, Colorado, Illinois, Maine, Maryland, Nebraska, Ohio, and Virginia. Delaware abolished the rule only with respect to personal property. Florida extended the wait-and-see period to 360 years, effectively abolishing the rule. Alaska abolished the rule except with respect to certain powers of appointment. *See* T.P. Gallanis, *The Future of Future Interests*, 60 WASH. & LEE L. REV. 513, 544-556 (2003). Due to the variations in the statutory measures, the number of abolishing states may vary based on one's criteria. For example, another 2003 article added Missouri, Washington, and Wyoming to the list of abolishing states, increasing the number to 19. *See* Stewart E. Sterk, *Jurisdictional Competition to Abolish the Rule Against Perpetuities: R.I.P. for the R.A.P.*, 24 CARDOZO L. REV. 2097, 2101-2103 (2003). Professors Dukeminier and Krier in yet another 2003 article suggested that the total was 20 states, and at least 5 others were considering repeal or liberalization legislation. *See* Jesse Dukeminier & James E. Krier, *The Rise of the Perpetual Trust*, 50 UCLA L. REV. 1303, 1313-1314 (2003).

3. *See* Frederick J. Schneider, *A Rule Against Perpetuities for the Twenty-First Century*, 41 REAL PROP. PROB. & TR. J. 743, 748-749 (2007). The author identified Alaska, Idaho, New Jersey, South Dakota, and Wisconsin as states that eliminated the rule entirely. *Id.* at n.26. Arizona, the District of Columbia, Illinois, Maine, Maryland, Missouri, Nebraska, New Hampshire, Ohio, and Virginia repealed the rule at it applied to trusts. *Id.* at n.27. Delaware, Florida, Washington, and Wyoming adopted a modified rule applicable to trusts. *Id.* at n.28. Nevada adopted a 365-year rule, *Id.* at n.24, while Colorado and Utah adopted 1,000-year terms. *Id.* at n.25. The Colorado 1,000-year limit applies only to interests in trusts. *See* Wayne M. Gazur, *Colorado Revisits the Rule Against Perpetuities*, 35 COLO. LAW. 75 (Nov. 2006).

4. *See* http://www.oshins.com/dynastytruststates.html (last visited June 4, 2011) for a currently maintained list. During the 2007 legislative session, North Carolina effectively eliminated the rule for interests in trust if the trustee has the power to sell. *See* N.C. GEN. ST. §41-23, 2007 N.C. H.B. 1384 (Aug. 19, 2007). During the 2010 legislative session, Kentucky also effectively abolished the rule for interests in trust if the trustee has the power to sell. *See* 2010 KY. ACTS 21.

5. *See* UNIF. STATUTORY RULE AGAINST PERPETUITIES (1990), Table of Jurisdictions Wherein Act Has Been Adopted, 8B U.L.A. 223 (2001 & Supp. 2010). USRAP is incorporated into the Uniform Probate Code (UPC) as §§2-901 through 2-907.

6. *See* Dan W. Holbrook, *The Rule Against Perpetuities: Time to Re-Examine?*, 38 TENN. B.J. 31 (Apr. 2002) (e.g., Florida increased the USRAP vesting period to 360 years). Although considered a USRAP state, Colorado has adopted a 1,000-year limit on interests in trusts. *See* Gazur, *supra* note 3.

As a consequence of this legislative activity, the common law RAP still applies in only a handful of states.[7]

1. Seeking Absolute Freedom

If a client desires freedom from the RAP, then formation of the trust under the laws of a state that has eliminated the RAP may be advisable. Although this is an increasingly routine matter and trust departments can be helpful in providing necessary forms and some direction, assistance of local counsel may be required.[8] If the client does not reside in one of the growing number of states that have eliminated the RAP or wishes to use family member trustees, the maintenance of a trust situs[9] in another state may produce additional costs.

2. USRAP

USRAP provides that a nonvested property interest is invalid unless the common law RAP is satisfied upon creation of the interest or the interest vests or terminates within 90 years after its creation.[10] USRAP expressly excludes a number of transactions from the RAP, many of which were already excluded under the common law rule.[11] USRAP further permits a court to reform an interest that would violate USRAP.[12] Either reformation under USRAP or failure of the interest through application of the RAP in a jurisdiction not adopting USRAP provides unpredictable results in the disposition of the property. A longstanding response to the RAP has been the inclusion of saving clauses in instruments. One challenge is assessing the impact of USRAP on such clauses.

7. Alabama, Arkansas, Louisiana, Mississippi, Oklahoma, Texas, and Wyoming still followed the common law RAP without substantial modifications. *See* Vallario, *supra* note 1, and Holbrook, *supra* note 6. However, in 2003, Wyoming joined the ranks of states effectively abolishing the rule by increasing the vesting period to 1,000 years. *See* Sterk, *supra* note 2, at 2103 n.31.

8. ABA Model Rule of Professional Conduct 5.5(a) states that a lawyer shall not practice law in a jurisdiction where doing so violates the regulation of the legal profession in that jurisdiction. *See* Model Rules of Prof'l Conduct R. 5.5 (2003). *See generally* Gerard E. Wimberly, Jr., *The Unauthorized Practice of Law by Licensed Attorneys: A Perilous Paradox*, 37 Ariz. Att'y 29 (June 2001).

9. Maintaining the situs in a foreign state may require administration of the trust in that foreign jurisdiction, at least one resident trustee, and the deposit of some trust assets in that foreign jurisdiction. *See generally* Stephen E. Greer, *The Alaska Dynasty Trust*, 18 Alaska L. Rev. 253, 284 (2001) (Alaskan trust situs requirements); Merwin (Trey) Grayson III, *A Comparison of Dynasty Trusts in Alaska, Delaware, and Ohio from the Perspective of the Ohio Practitioner*, 27 N. Ky. L. Rev. 669, 680 (2000) (qualified Delaware trustee requirement); Thomas H. Foye, *Using South Dakota Law for Perpetual Trusts*, 12 Prob. & Prop. 17, 18-19 (Jan./Feb. 1998).

10. *See* UPC §2-901. The general comments to USRAP state that the 90-year period "represents a reasonable approximation of . . . the period of time that would, *on average*, be produced through the use of an actual set of measuring lives identified by statute and then adding the traditional 21-year tack-on period after the death of the survivor." General Comment §C.1., Unif. Statutory Rule Against Perpetuities (1990) §1, 8B U.L.A. 245 (2001).

11. *See* the official comments to UPC §2-904 for a technical discussion of the exceptions. *Id.*

12. *See* UPC §2-903.

EXERCISE 13-1

SAVING CLAUSES AND USRAP

Discuss whether the following clauses are appropriate, particularly in a state that has adopted USRAP. In particular, why doesn't the clause expressly incorporate the 90-year wait-and-see limitation of USRAP?

A. *All trusts created hereunder shall in any event terminate no later than 21 years after the death of the last survivor of the group composed of settlor, settlor's spouse, and those of settlor's issue living at settlor's death. The property held in trust shall be discharged of any trust and shall immediately vest in and be distributed to the persons then entitled to the income therefrom in the proportions in which they are beneficiaries of the income, and for this purpose only, any person then eligible to receive discretionary payments of income of a particular trust shall be treated as being entitled to receive the income, and if two or more persons are so treated, the group of such persons shall be treated as being entitled to receive such income as a class, to be distributed among them by representation.*

B. *All trusts created hereunder shall in any event terminate no later than 21 years after the death of the last survivor of the group composed of settlor, settlor's spouse, and those of settlor's issue living at settlor's death. In that event, the property held in trust shall be discharged of any trust and the assets and any accrued and undistributed income shall immediately vest in and be distributed to the then current beneficiaries of the trust in the proportions in which they are then eligible to receive distributions from the trust, and for this purpose only, it should be presumed that any person then eligible to receive any distribution from the trust is entitled to receive the full distribution, and if more than one person are so treated, the group of such persons shall be treated as being entitled to receive such distribution as a class, to be distributed among them, by representation.*

C. *All trusts created under this agreement shall in any event terminate not later than 21 years after the death of the last survivor of all natural persons living at the time of the execution of this agreement who are beneficiaries under this agreement. If any trust is terminated under this section, the property held in trust shall be discharged of any trusts, and shall immediately vest in and be distributed to the persons then entitled to receive the income, in the same shares as those in which the income is then being distributed to them. For this purpose it shall be presumed that any person entitled to receive discretionary distributions from the income of any trust is entitled to receive the full income, and that any group or class of persons so entitled is entitled to receive the income in equal shares by representation.*

EXERCISE 13-2

EXTENDING THE MEASURING LIVES

How would you modify clause A, B, or C in Exercise 13-1, if at all, to take advantage of the "twelve-healthy-babies-ploy" frequently discussed in connection with the RAP?

EXERCISE 13-3

OTHER CONCERNS

Ignoring USRAP, do you have any other concerns about the use of clauses A, B, or C above in a common law RAP state?

Although the focus of the exercises above is on the interaction of saving clauses and USRAP, a greater challenge has emerged from the disintegration of RAP doctrine. For example, the use of saving clauses along the lines of those in Exercise 13-1 in a jurisdiction that has eliminated the RAP or has extended the RAP limitation period would prematurely terminate the trust. On the other hand, if one is establishing the trust in a jurisdiction that has eliminated the RAP, should one draft for the possibility (this is typically an irrevocable trust that can't be subsequently amended without judicial process) that the trust situs could change to a more restrictive RAP jurisdiction? Should and, if so, how does one draft an "all weather" saving clause?[13] Is there another approach to this problem of uncertainty?

B. The Generation-Skipping Transfer Tax

Federal wealth transfer taxes are discussed in Chapter 16. Long-term generation-skipping trusts are a special focus of the GSTT, which has generally applied to irrevocable trusts created since September 25, 1985.[14] Many of the trusts created by very wealthy families are exempt because they were created prior to the 1985 effective date. Moreover, from September 25, 1985, through December 31, 1989, a so-called "Gallo exemption" permitted transfers free of the GSTT in aggregate amounts not to exceed

13. *See, e.g.*, Jule E. Stocker et al., Stocker and Rikoon on Drawing Wills and Trusts §5.6.4 (Practising Law Institute, current through Release 6, Nov. 2005) (example of a comprehensive multi-jurisdiction saving clause). *Compare* Joel C. Dobris et al., Estates and Trusts 914-921 (3d ed. 2007) (discussing the impact of highly flexible saving clauses such as "for as long a period as is legally possible"); Gazur, *supra* note 3, at 79 ("In light of the difficulty of drafting such an all-inclusive clause, practitioners instead might see highly flexible provisions that simply limit the duration of the trust 'to the longest period permitted by the law applicable to the trust.'"). Paragraph 4.7 of Form J in the Forms Supplement offers an alternate RAP saving clause.

14. Although enacted in 1976 as part of the Tax Reform Act of 1976, Pub. L. No. 94-455, 90 Stat. 1520 (1976), the pre-1986 version was retroactively repealed with the adoption of the 1986 amendments.

$2,000,000 per grandchild. Spousal gift splitting permitted transfers up to $4,000,000 per grandchild.[15]

In spite of the GSTT's stumbling start, there are taxpayers who do pay the tax. Based on estate and gift tax returns filed in 2006, roughly $126,000,000 in GSTT was paid.[16] It remains a significant obstacle to the long-term viability of dynasty trusts, assuming that the GSTT is not ultimately repealed with the other federal wealth transfer taxes or otherwise significantly liberalized.

1. The General Application of the GSTT

As discussed in Chapter 16, the GSTT is imposed at the highest rate of estate tax on the value of property transferred under three types of generation-skipping transfers: "direct skips," "taxable distributions," and "taxable terminations." As applied to a trust, a direct skip will arise through a gift, lifetime or testamentary, to an irrevocable trust, all of the beneficiaries of which are at least two or more generations below the generation assignment of the settlor. If the settlor's children are also beneficiaries of the trust, the gift to the trust is not a direct skip.[17] However, the two other types of generation-skipping transfers could apply. For example, if the transfer to the trust was not a direct skip, but distributions can be made to grandchildren or great-grandchildren, the amount of the actual distributions made to those second (or more) generation descendants would be subject to the GSTT as a taxable distribution at the time of distribution. And, even if the distributions to the grandchildren or great-grandchildren are minimal, upon the termination of the interest of the older generation (in this case the level of the children of the settlor), the value of the trust property in which the older generation held an interest will be subject to the GSTT as a taxable termination. A taxable termination will occur with each shift of generations, not only upon the first shift.

15. *See* Laura K. Sundberg & Edward F. Koren, *The Gallo Exclusion: It Must Be Used Before Its Time*, 63 FLA. BAR J. 51 (Nov. 1989).

16. This total amount was produced by adding unpublished IRS data for gift and estate tax returns. The GSTT paid with taxable gift tax returns filed in 2006 was $25,978,589. *See* http://www.irs.gov/pub/irs-soi/06gf01gr.xls (last visited Aug. 27, 2011). The GSTT paid with taxable estate tax returns filed in 2006 was $100,067,000. *See* http://www.irs.gov/pub/irs-soi/06es01fy.xls (last visited Aug. 27, 2011). This is a decrease from the $157,900,000 in GSTT officially reported for estate and gift tax returns filed in 2000. *See* IRS Statistics of Income Bulletin, Spring 2002, Publication 1136. A survey asked estate planning attorneys the following question: "As your estimate, how frequently do situations arise in which taxpayers . . . actually pay a GSTT?" Thirty percent of the respondents replied "never," 55.9 percent replied "seldom," 13 percent replied "sometimes," and 1.2 percent replied "often." None replied "very often." *See* Wayne M. Gazur, *Do They Practice What We Teach?: A Survey of Practitioners and Estate Planning Professors*, 19 VA. TAX REV. 1, 46-47 (1999).

17. One planning structure includes a charitable beneficiary in a trust that would otherwise be a skip person. This strategy must weigh the impact of IRC §2652(c)(2) under which "an interest which is used primarily to postpone or avoid any [GSTT] shall be disregarded." *See, e.g.*, Roy Adams, David Handler & Deborah Dunn, *The HEET Trust: A New Twist on Section 2503(e)*, 139 TR. & EST. 18 (July 2000); Michael Delgass & Deborah Gordon, *HEET Wave*, 144 TR. & EST. 20 (Mar. 2005).

2. The GSTT Exemption

IRC §2631 allows an aggregate GSTT exemption equal to the estate tax applicable exclusion amount for each transferor.[18] With gift splitting, married couples may transfer twice that amount. However, if one spouse dies, unlike the deceased spousal unused exclusion amount that applies to the estate tax,[19] the survivor does not accede to the decedent's unused GSTT exemption.[20]

There are three separate taxes that need to be considered. If the value of the property transferred to an irrevocable trust does not exceed the GSTT exemption available to the transferor, and there are no additional nonexempt contributions made to the trust, the irrevocable trust is exempt from the GSTT forever because the IRC §2642 inclusion ratio remains 0. The use of the GSTT exemption, coupled with formation of a trust in a jurisdiction that has abolished the RAP, has given rise to the so-called "dynasty trust," which can theoretically endure forever. However, a transfer of property to the trust during the donor's lifetime will still be a taxable gift, and will be subject to potential gift tax. Likewise, if the transfer is made by a testamentary gift from a decedent, the gift will be subject to potential estate tax in the decedent's estate. The gift tax and estate tax may be avoided (or reduced) depending on the amount of gift or estate tax applicable exclusion available to the transferor at the time of the transfer.

While the GSTT exemption may not be an extremely significant sum for the exceptionally wealthy, dynasty trusts that are created free of all federal wealth transfer taxes (GSTT and gift or estate taxes) can accumulate a handsome amount. The "Rule of 72" is a quick method of estimating the period in which a sum will double. Assuming a robust annual growth rate of 10 percent (approximating the historic long-term performance of a diversified 100 percent equity portfolio), $5,000,000 placed in such a trust would double within roughly seven years, and would double again in another seven years, and so forth.[21]

In addition, the transfer tax and GSTT exemption amounts are applied after the donor may have claimed various valuation discounts, such as fractional interest, minority interest, and marketability discounts, to the property interests transferred to the trust. For example, a settlor could first create a family limited partnership or family limited liability company to which property would be transferred. Partnership or limited liability

18. *See* IRC §2631(c).

19. *See* IRC §2010(c). See also Chapter 11, Part C.

20. IRC §2631 refers only to the "basic exclusion amount" in section 2010(c), which excludes the deceased spousal unused exclusion amount.

21. One commentator compared the growth of $1,000,000 placed in a dynasty trust with $1,000,000 passed outright to a child, which is then passed on generation to generation. At a 7 percent net growth rate, the trust will have grown to $159,800,000 by the time of the great-great-grandchild, while the outright plan would pass only $14,500,000 to the great-great-grandchild. *See* Brian Layman, *Perpetual Dynasty Trusts: One of the Most Powerful Tools in the Estate Planner's Arsenal*, 32 Akron L. Rev. 747, 756 (1999).

company interests, for which valuation discounts might be claimed, would then later be gifted to the irrevocable trust. The result is the potential transfer of assets with an underlying value (i.e. pre-discounted value) greater than the GSTT exemption to the trust.

3. GSTT Drafting Issues

a.* Crummey *Clauses. The *Crummey* withdrawal clause discussed in Chapter 8 is difficult to use in a GSTT environment because IRC §2642(c) places restrictions on the *Crummey* clause that otherwise limit its utility for overall federal wealth transfer taxation planning. As discussed at greater length in Chapter 8, IRC §2642(c)(3) denies GSTT annual gift exclusions for transfers in trust unless: (1) during the life of the beneficiary, no portion of the corpus or income of the trust may be distributed to or for the benefit of any other person; and (2) if the trust does not terminate before the individual dies, the assets of such trust will be includable in the gross estate of such individual.

The first limitation precludes marshaling of assets for the benefit of a class of individuals, but that may not be entirely objectionable if the purpose of the trust is strictly accumulation during the lives of those individuals. In that case a practical solution is the creation of separate trusts or shares of a common trust for the benefit of each skip person.

The second limitation is a greater obstacle, because to satisfy it, a testamentary general power of appointment in favor of the individual is often utilized. This increases the risk that a federal estate tax will be paid on the trust assets that are thereby included in the taxable estate of the individual by operation of IRC §2041. As discussed in Part B.3.d. below, a general power of appointment may be included in a generation-skipping trust to reduce future GSTT, aside from immediate *Crummey* issues.

After considering the planning alternatives, the dynasty trust may be rendered absolutely GSTT-exempt through the simple use of a portion of the donor's GSTT exemption. However, the *Crummey* clause may still be desirable to exempt the dynasty trust gifts from gift tax.

b. Payment of GSTT. The administrative provisions of a dynasty trust usually address the payment of the GSTT. Generally, the recipient of a taxable distribution is liable for the GSTT and must file the required tax return.[22] On the other hand, the trustee usually bears those responsibilities for a taxable termination.[23] If the trust instrument provides for payment of the transferee's GSTT on a taxable distribution, the taxes paid by the trust increase the amount of the taxable distribution.[24] In the case of a taxable termination, the trust instrument may specify which trust shares bear the GSTT tax.

22. *See* Treas. Reg. §26.2662-1(c)(1)(i) (1995).
23. *See* Treas. Reg. §26.2662-1(c)(1)(ii) (1995).
24. *See* IRC §2621(b).

c. Inclusion Ratio Planning. Common GSTT planning maintains that for efficient use of exemptions and simplified tax management of the trusts, the "inclusion ratio" computed under IRC §2642 should be either 0 (total exemption) or 1 (total inclusion), without intermediate positions.[25] A common administrative provision authorizes the trustee to create subtrusts with each subtrust having an inclusion ratio of 0 or 1. Section 2642(a)(3) provides rules for a "qualified severance" in connection with this technique.

In addition, many trusts include language permitting the trustee to: (a) make GSTT-exempt distributions to any nonskip persons, such as a child of the settlor, from subtrusts with the greatest inclusion ratio; (b) make GSTT-exempt distributions to any skip person for IRC §2613(a) medical and tuition expenses from subtrusts with the greatest inclusion ratio; (c) make distributions to any skip person that are taxable from subtrusts with the lowest inclusion ratio; and (d) decline non-exempt additions to an otherwise totally exempt trust, permitting the trustee to administer the non-exempt additions as a separate trust with provisions identical to the exempt trust.[26]

d. General Power of Appointment Authority. In some cases it may be more tax-efficient to subject trust assets to the estate tax of a beneficiary rather than to the GSTT. One approach is to give authority to the trustee to grant a general testamentary power of appointment to the beneficiary of portions of any trust with an inclusion ratio greater than 0. In this manner, the assets would be subject to estate taxation in the estate of the beneficiary.[27] This increases the risk that a federal estate tax will be paid on the appointable trust assets because they will be included in the taxable estate of the beneficiary by operation of IRC §2041. However, because the estate tax rate will be equal to or less than the applicable GSTT tax rate, there is no additional tax risk, and the grant of such a power to appoint could in fact result in reduced taxes. The planner must consider that this does introduce a risk that the appointable assets could, as a result of the actual exercise of the general power of appointment, pass outside the intended family and multigenerational stream, a result that may be contrary to the settlor's intent.[28] Indeed, this ultimately involves a trade-off between minimization of taxes and the loss of control over the appointable assets.

25. *See, e.g.*, Richard W. Nenno, *Planning with Dynasty Trusts*, Planning Techniques for Large Estates, SG041 ALI-ABA 1597, 1613 (ALI-ABA Continuing Legal Education, Nov. 12-16, 2001).

26. *See, e.g.*, JULE E. STOCKER ET AL., *supra* note 13, at §5.6.6 (sample language for division of trust assets into exempt and nonexempt portions).

27. *See* Lloyd Leva Plaine & Pam H. Schneider, *Planning Beyond the GST Exemption — To Skip or Not to Skip, That Is the Question*, 32 INST. ON EST. PLAN. ¶¶ 400, 403.3 (1998).

28. If this is truly of concern, one technique to reduce this possibility may be to create a general power of appointment that permits the beneficiary to appoint the assets only to the "creditors of the estate of the beneficiary."

e. Deemed Allocations of the GSTT Exemption. EGTRRA added IRC §2632(c), which provides for automatic allocations of the GSTT exemption to certain gifts in trust. Taxpayers may elect to be excluded from the statute. However, the intent of the provision is to save taxpayers from inadvertent failures to affirmatively allocate the GSTT exemption to gift transfers. IRC §2632(a) already provided for a deemed allocation of the GSTT exemption to lifetime direct skips. If, for example, only the grandchildren or other skip persons were beneficiaries of the trust (a withdrawal right, such as a *Crummey* power, does not alone count as a trust interest), IRC §2632(a) would have made a deemed allocation of the GSTT exemption, because the trust would be treated as a skip person and the gift to the trust would be a direct skip. However, if nonskip persons were beneficiaries in the trust, making the trust a nonskip person, GSTT transfers could still later occur upon a distribution from the trust to a skip person or upon a taxable termination. A gift to such a trust was a trap for the unwary, because it reportedly was common for taxpayers to fail to file a gift tax return allocating a portion of the GSTT exemption to such types of gifts.

IRC §2632(c) now creates a deemed allocation of the GSTT exemption in some of these circumstances. However, if it is likely that the proceeds of the trust will be ultimately distributed to nonskip beneficiaries (e.g., to the parents of the grandchildren rather than to the grandchildren themselves) the deemed allocation could be seen as wasting that portion of the GSTT exemption. In that case the taxpayer might reject the automatic allocation.[29]

EXERCISE 13-4

GSTT BASICS

Identify the gift tax and GSTT implications of each of the following transactions:

(Where GP = Grandparent; C = Grandparent's Child; GC = Grandparent's Grandchildren; and GGC = Grandparent's Great-grandchildren)

A. GP (unmarried) makes a lifetime gift of $22,000 to GC.
[See IRC §§2611(a)(3); 2612(c); 2613(a)(1); 2623; 2631; 2632(b); 2641; 2642(a)(1) & (2); 2642(c)(3); 2651(b)(1) & 2515.]

B. GP (married) makes a lifetime gift equal to [double the annual gift tax exclusion] to GC. GP's spouse consents to gift splitting.
[See the sections in Exercise A, plus §2652(a)(2).]

29. *See, e.g.*, JEROME A. MANNING ET AL., MANNING ON ESTATE PLANNING, §6:10.3 (5th ed. 1995 & Supp. 2009). *See generally* Diana S.C. Zeydel, *Handling Affirmative and Deemed Allocations of GST Exemption (Part I)*, 34 EST. PLAN. 12 (2007); Diana S.C. Zeydel, *Deemed Allocations of GST Exemption to Lifetime Transfers (Part II)*, 34 EST. PLAN. 3 (2007).

C. GP (unmarried), age 85, makes a testamentary bequest by Will of $22,000 to the 19-year old son of GP's driver.
[See the sections in Exercise A, plus §2651(d).]

D. GP (unmarried) gifts $200,000 to a discretionary inter vivos irrevocable trust, the beneficiaries of which are GC and GGC. Assume no *Crummey* withdrawal rights. The trustee subsequently distributes property among GC and GGC. C is still alive; why is this important? Should a *Crummey* right have been included anyway in spite of the restrictions imposed by IRC §2642(c)(2)?
[See the sections in Exercise A, plus §§2613(a)(2), 2651(e) & 2653(a).]

E. Same facts as in Exercise D, but GP's child, C, also holds a current, non-discretionary, right to .001% of the fiduciary income of the trust.

F. Same facts as in Exercise E, but the trust subsequently distributes $5,000 to each of the GC.
[See the sections in Exercise A, plus §§2611(a)(1); 2612(b) & 2621.]

G. Same facts as in Exercise F, except the trust distributes the $5,000 directly to educational institutions for tuition and required fees.
[See the sections in Exercise A, plus §2611(b)(1).]

H. Same facts as in Exercise E, but GP's child, C, later passes away, when the trust corpus is worth $300,000.
[See the sections in Exercise A, plus §§2611(a)(2); 2612(a) & 2622.]

C. Beneficiary Conduct

A true dynasty trust will include unborn beneficiaries and others whose future conduct or circumstances cannot be predicted with certainty or reliability. Due to the possible adverse federal estate tax consequences, the irrevocable trust is usually created with little or no continuing power retained by the settlor to adjust for these uncertainties (see Chapter 16). Moreover, at some point a long-term, perpetual trust will "outlive" its creator and the members of his or her immediate family.[30] Accordingly, the settlor must rely on the trustee's judgment and the terms of the trust instrument to guide the trustee.

30. It was a common observation about the RAP that the "lives in being" rule implicitly recognized a common sense notion that the creator of a future interest could do so only with regard to descendants that he or she could observe at that time. Of course, who could predict the future behavior of, for example, a one-year old great-grandchild?

1. Trustee Discretion

While one often sees more discretion placed in the trustee with respect to distributions of principal, that discretion could be extended to all distributions. Although it is often stated that a trustee may never exercise absolute[31] discretion that excludes the power of the courts, discretion short of that may be directed by the language of the trust instrument.

EXERCISE 13-5

DISCRETIONARY DISTRIBUTION LANGUAGE

Compare the following distribution standards:

A. *The trustee shall distribute to any one or more of my descendants as much of the net income or principal, or both, of the trust as the trustee determines advisable to provide for their health, education, maintenance, and support.*

B. *The trustee may distribute to any one or more of the settlor's descendants, as much of the net income or principal, or both, of the trust as the trustee determines advisable, in the exercise of the trustee's free and absolute discretion, to provide for their health, education, support, maintenance, comfort, and welfare, but not so as to discharge or satisfy any legal obligation of the settlor to support such beneficiaries.*

C. *The trustee shall distribute to or apply for the benefit of settlor's descendants as much of the net income and principal of the trust as the trustee deems necessary or advisable for their education, health, maintenance, and support.*

D. *The trustee shall distribute to or apply for the benefit of settlor's descendants as much of the net income and principal of the trust as the trustee deems necessary or advisable, in the exercise of the trustee's reasonable discretion, for their education, health, maintenance, and support.*

E. *The trustee may distribute to any one or more of the settlor's descendants, as much of the net income or principal, or both, of the trust as the trustee determines advisable, in the exercise of the trustee's free and absolute discretion.*

Evaluate the desirability of the language in clauses A-E from the standpoint of directing or guiding the trustee as to the use of trust funds, yet

31. For example, according to the Restatement of Trusts (Second) §187, comment j, the adjectives "absolute," "unlimited," or "uncontrolled" modifying "discretion" are not "interpreted literally but are ordinarily construed as merely dispensing with the standard of reasonableness." A trustee may not act dishonestly upon some motive other than accomplishing the purposes of the trust, or "act arbitrarily without an exercise of his judgment." The Uniform Trust Code provides that discretion that is "absolute," "sole," or "uncontrolled" must nevertheless be exercised "in good faith" and in accordance with the terms and purposes of the trust and the interests of the beneficiaries. *See* UNIF. TRUST. CODE §814(a).

preserving a measure of discretion in the trustee. Also, what is the purpose of the language in clause B "but not so as to discharge or satisfy any legal obligation of the settlor to support such beneficiaries"?

2. Holdback Clauses

Some trusts suspend distributions to a beneficiary upon the occurrence and continuation of certain events related to the beneficiary such as imprisonment, substance abuse, bankruptcy, being a defendant in a lawsuit or party to a dissolution of marriage proceeding, and disability, among others (disability is discussed in Chapter 15).[32] Depending upon the degree of discretion the settlor wants to grant to the trustee, these holdback provisions may either permit the trustee to suspend distributions in the trustee's discretion (a permissive holdback) or require the trustee to suspend distributions (a restrictive holdback).

Aside from providing guidance to the trustee, the purpose of permissive holdback provisions is to provide support to the trustee by way of expressing the settlor's intent in the trust agreement, in any dispute with the beneficiary on this issue, for making such discretionary holdbacks. The restrictive provisions take a harder stance by attempting to remove most of the trustee's discretion. Such holdbacks are mandatory—there is no discretion. The trustee is absolutely prohibited from making distributions for as long as a holdback condition continues. Of course, even in the restrictive holdback clauses the trustee retains some degree of discretion, as it is usually the trustee[33] who ultimately decides when a holdback condition exists. However, once it is determined that a holdback situation exists, the trustee is prohibited from making the distribution. In this manner, any beneficiary dispute is limited to whether a holdback situation exists, not whether the trustee should have exercised such a suspension of distribution. Holdback provisions may encompass a broad array of circumstances. However, suspension of distributions in connection with some events, such as marriage or remarriage, may be subject to public policy limitations and should be drafted with care.[34]

32. *See* Malcolm A. Moore, *New Horizons in the Grant and Exercise of Discretionary Powers*, 15 Inst. on Est. Plan. ¶¶ 600, 606.1-606.9 (1981) (discussing potential holdback events).

33. To further insulate the trustee from such disputes with the beneficiary, an independent, third-party nontrustee (such as a trust protector) could be designated solely for the purpose of determining if such a holdback condition exists or continues to exist. See Section D.2 below.

34. *See* Ellen Evans Whiting, *Controlling Behavior by Controlling the Inheritance: Considerations in Drafting Incentive Provisions*, 15 Prob. & Prop. 6 (Sept./Oct. 2001).

EXERCISE 13-6

HOLDBACK EVENTS

While clients may sometimes have certain holdback events in mind, it is usually the attorney's role to suggest some triggering events. Prepare a list of the types of events that should trigger and sustain the holdback of trust distributions.

3. Incentive Clauses

In contrast to, but not in exclusion of, holdback provisions, some settlors wish to provide incentives to their descendants such that *positive* actions are rewarded by *increases* in trust distributions. While this is very subjective and difficult to draft, milestones could include marriage, the attainment of an educational degree, outstanding student performance, continued sobriety, birth of a child, achievement of specified earnings levels (e.g., a matching formula), or election to public office.[35]

4. Spendthrift Clauses

Protection from dissipation of trust assets to satisfy the claims of the trust beneficiaries' creditors is an important role of long-term trusts.[36] Spendthrift clauses are upheld in most states,[37] and most dynasty trusts include such a clause. The drafting attorney, however, must carefully consider the consequences of including such clauses because they can produce unintended situations in terms of estate planning flexibility (e.g., they may preclude an otherwise desirable future transfer of an asset by direct gift or disclaimer by a beneficiary).[38]

35. *Id.*; Howard M. McCue III, *Planning and Drafting to Influence Behavior*, 34 INST. ON EST. PLAN. ¶¶ 600, 606.1 (2000); Paul A. Meints, *Using Trusts to Provide Incentives, Rewards, Remembrances, and other Benefits to Chosen Beneficiaries*, 15 No. 2 PRAC. TAX LAW. 25 (Winter 2001).

36. In a jurisdiction that robustly recognizes the validity of spendthrift clauses, the spendthrift clause can permit the trustee to ignore a garnishment order, permitting payments to or on behalf of a beneficiary. The spendthrift clause, of course, cannot protect the beneficiary from creditors outside of the trust (e.g., if the creditor has garnished personal bank accounts or commenced collection proceedings against other personal assets).

37. A small minority of states do not enforce spendthrift clauses to any degree, while a larger minority will recognize them but limit their effect in circumstances such as intentional torts, claims of a spouse or children, providers of necessities, etc. *See generally* WILLIAM M. MCGOVERN ET AL., WILLS, TRUSTS AND ESTATES 417-422 (4th ed. 2010). The Uniform Trust Code generally allows the claims of a beneficiary's child, spouse, former spouse, judgment creditors who provided services for the protection of the beneficiary's interest in the trust, and governments. *See* UNIF. TRUST CODE §503.

38. *See, e.g.*, Sebastian V. Grassi, Jr., *Drafting Flexibility into Estate Planning Documents after the 2001 Tax Act (with Sample Clauses)*, 17 No. 2 PRAC. TAX LAW. 7, 9 (Winter 2003) (example of flexible spendthrift language). Like the predecessor Uniform Disclaimer of Property Interests Act, the Uniform Disclaimer of Property Interests Act provision found at UPC §2-1105(a) permits a person to disclaim an interest or power even if its creator imposed a spendthrift provision or similar restriction on transfer or a restriction or limitation on the right to disclaim.

D. Drafting for the Unpredictable

Chapter 8 includes a discussion of fundamental clauses that are typically included in a trust. The very long-term existence of the dynasty trust makes certain clauses even more important, and the drafter of a dynasty trust must be creative in attempting to anticipate and mitigate unforeseen and unpredictable events.

1. Merger or Termination of Trusts

Developments such as changes in tax laws, declines in asset values, or operating efficiencies may make it desirable for a trust to be terminated or merged with another trust. Clauses that empower an independent trustee or a separate trust protector, to take these measures are often included in trust instruments. Such clauses may include thresholds (measured, e.g., by the size of trust or the number of beneficiaries) that can both limit and empower such a person to exercise discretion, depending on the circumstances.

2. Trust Protectors

A trustee may be subject to a number of influences, such as fiduciary duties owed to beneficiaries, self-interest in continuing to earn a trustee fee, and possible loyalty to a given jurisdiction where the trust is administered. Some trusts appoint a so-called "trust protector" who is not a trust fiduciary but is nonetheless given broad powers to alter, decant, or even terminate the trust in the event that certain unforeseen circumstances arise that may frustrate the trust's purpose or defeat the settlor's intent in creating the trust.[39] For example, a trust protector may be empowered, but not required, to alter the language and terms of the trust in order to correct ministerial drafting errors, to respond to changes in the pertinent laws, to terminate the trust, to remove a trustee, or to move the situs of the trust to another state or country.[40]

While some of this oversight possibly could be accomplished through the use of multiple trustees who are each given different decision-making powers, designation of an independent, nonbeneficiary, nontrustee, trust protector is often a better approach.[41] Trustees are fiduciaries, and their

39. For an example of trust protector language, see David Hodgman, *Drafting Flexible Irrevocable Trusts—Whom Do You Trust?*, 23 Est. Plan. 221 (1996).

40. *See, e.g.*, David Hayton, *Letters of Wishes and Protectors as Devices to Further the Settlor's Purposes*, reprinted as ch. 14 of A Guide to International Estate Planning—Drafting, Compliance, and Administration Strategies (Jeffrey A. Schoenblum ed., 2000); Madeline J. Rivlin, *Dynasty Trusts*, 319 PLI/Est 909, 919 (PLI Tax Law and Est. Plan. Course Handbook Series No. D0-009B, Sept.-Oct. 2002); Alexander A. Bove, Jr., *The Trust Protector: Trust(y) Watchdog or Expensive Exotic Pet?*, 30 Est. Plan. 390 (2003).

41. If the trust protector is also a beneficiary and the powers of the protector are quite broad, one must avoid characterization of the protector powers as a taxable general power of appointment for federal wealth transfer taxation purposes.

exercise of such powers to modify the trust must be measured against fiduciary standards. If the trustee were involved in a hostile situation with a beneficiary, such conduct could be deemed to be self-serving and could present serious conflict of interest issues.

By comparison, a trust protector is generally not considered a fiduciary[42] and *may* act but generally has no obligation to do so. Thoughtful consideration in the designation of the initial trust protector and successor trust protectors, as well as carefully drafted language in the trust instrument authorizing, but not requiring, the exercise of specific powers by a trust protector, may ensure that the protector has no self-interest to promote and increase the likelihood that the trust protector remains insulated in the event of a trustee-beneficiary dispute.

3. Decanting Powers

Decanting powers permit someone (perhaps an independent trustee or a trust protector) to distribute all or a portion of the assets of one trust to another trust (often a newly formed trust) for the benefit of the beneficiaries of the former trust. This power streamlines the modification of irrevocable trusts that have been found to be deficient in some respect. Express provision of decanting powers in a trust may overlap with the outcomes that could be achieved through an outright modification of the trust or merger with another trust (particularly if the instrument expressly permits mergers).

Decanting in the absence of an express clause in the trust agreement is a more uncertain endeavor. Some states have enacted statutes that permit decanting without the inclusion of any language authorizing decanting in the trust agreement.[43] In the absence of an enabling statute, or express

42. Due to limited U.S. experience with trust protectors, it is unclear at this time whether protectors will be found to owe fiduciary duties to the trust beneficiaries. One commentator has concluded that no fiduciary duty is so owed absent bad faith by the protector. *See* Grassi, *supra* note 38, at 9. *Compare* Edward C. Halbach, Jr., *Uniform Acts, Restatements, and Trends in American Trust Law at Century's End*, 88 CAL. L. REV. 1877, 1916 (2000) (predicting that absent an expression of strong settlor intent to the contrary, protectors will probably be deemed to hold fiduciary powers). The Uniform Trust Code acknowledges that a trust instrument may confer upon a trustee or "other person" a power to direct the modification or termination of the trust. *See* UNIF. TRUST CODE §808(c) (2000), 7C U.L.A. 362, 604 (2006 & Supp. 2007). However, a person who holds a power to direct is presumptively a fiduciary who is required to act in good faith with regard to the purposes of the trust. *Id.* at §808(d). The status of protectors is not on the list of mandatory rules, so the terms of the trust could override this. *Id.* at §105(b). Indeed, the comments to section 808 provide: "A settlor can provide that the trustee must accept the decision of the power holder without question. Or a settlor could provide that the holder of the power is not to be held to the standards of a fiduciary." *See generally* Gregory S. Alexander, *Trust Protectors: Who Will Watch the Watchmen?*, 27 CARDOZO L. REV. 2807 (2006); Stewart E. Sterk, *Trust Protectors, Agency Costs, and Fiduciary Duty*, 27 CARDOZO L. REV. 2761 (2006); Richard C. Ausness, *The Role of Trust Protectors in American Trust Law*, 45 REAL PROP. TR. & EST. L.J. 319 (2010); Philip J. Ruce, *The Trustee and the Trust Protector: A Question of Fiduciary Power. Should a Trust Protector Be Held to a Fiduciary Standard?*, 59 DRAKE L. REV. 67 (2010).

43. See William R. Culp, Jr. & Briani Bennett Mellen, *Trust Decanting: An Overview and Introduction to Creative Planning Opportunities*, 45 REAL PROP. TR. & ESTATE L.J. 1, 37 n.242 (2010) (citation of decanting statutes from Alaska, Arizona, Delaware, Florida, Nevada, New Hampshire, New York, North Carolina, South Dakota, and Tennessee).

decanting authority provided in the trust agreement, one may be able to rely on a trustee's power to make discretionary distributions for the benefit of a beneficiary. Decanting also presents a number of tax issues beyond the scope of this book.[44]

4. Powers of Appointment

A power of appointment is a well-known way to introduce family input into the distribution of trust assets.[45] It can create an incentive for members of the younger generation to curry favor with, or indeed continue to treat with honor and respect, the older generation holder of such a power.

Property subject to a general power of appointment will generally be included in the holder's federal taxable estate,[46] so most powers are structured as special powers to avoid that result,[47] with a notable exception for GSTT planning, as discussed earlier in this chapter.

Special powers in particular enjoy protection from the donee's creditors and may complement the asset protection features of a spendthrift trust.[48]

PRACTICE POINTER: In drafting a special power of appointment, the following issues must be considered: (a) the identity of the holder of the power; (b) the identity of the permissible appointees or objects of the power; (c) the property that will be subject to the power; (d) the time and manner of exercise, including the possible requirement of an express reference in any document exercising the power to the originating document, and its date, granting or authorizing the power; (e) whether the property can be appointed outright or in further trust; (f) whether the power can be exercised exclusively with respect to only certain possible appointees; and (g) disposition of the property in default of exercise.

44. *See generally* William R. Culp, Jr. & Briani L. Bennett, *Use of Trust Decanting to Extend the Term of Irrevocable Trusts*, 37 Est. Plan. 3 (June 2010); Thomas E. Simmons, *Decanting and Its Alternatives: Remodeling and Revamping Irrevocable Trusts*, 55 S.D. L. Rev. 253 (2010).

45. *See generally* John R. Price, *Powers to the Right People: Flexibility without Taxability or Drafters Desiderata: Nontaxable Flexibility*, 25 Inst. on Est. Plan. ¶700 (1991); William S. Forsberg, *Special Powers of Appointment: The Key to Flexibility in Planning*, 27 Est. Plan. 13 (2000); William R. Culp, Jr. & Mark L. Richardson, *Lifetime Special Powers of Appointment Offer Unique Planning Opportunities*, 33 Est. Plan. 34 (2006).

46. *See* IRC §2041.

47. *See* Jule E. Stocker et al., *supra* note 12, at §5.6.4 (typical dynasty trust dispositive scheme with special power of appointment).

48. *See* William M. McGovern et al., *supra* note 37, 476-477 (discussing creditor remedies applied to powers of appointment); Alexander A. Bove, Jr., *Using the Power of Appointment to Protect Assets—More Power Than You Ever Imagined*, 36 ACTEC J. 333 (2010).

EXERCISE 13-7

EVALUATING A POWER OF APPOINTMENT

Evaluate the efficacy of the following power of appointment:

> *The trustee shall distribute to any one or more of the settlor's descendants such amounts or proportions of the net income or principal, or both, of the trust as [insert holder's name] may from time to time direct in a writing delivered to the trustee or by Will, in either case specifically referring to this special power of appointment.*

E. Organizing the Family to Create and Perpetuate Wealth

This chapter has emphasized selected structures for preserving family wealth, such as the use of long-term trusts with the inclusion of spendthrift and holdback provisions. However, there are additional measures that can promote a more focused and cohesive family group.

1. Family Mission Statements

It is common for organizations to compose mission statements as a path to future action. Author Stephen R. Covey suggests that families adopt a mission statement.[49] The objective is to identify goals and common values, and to chart progress and strengthen family cohesiveness through measures such as scheduled meetings (the "family council"). The mission statement can encourage a shared personal investment by all generations in common plans and outcomes, hopefully reducing dissension that detracts from happiness as well as encouraging positive behaviors and wealth creation. A significant component is an expression of gratitude for the work and vision of prior and current generations.[50]

49. *See* Stephen R. Covey, 7 Habits of Highly Effective Families 70 (paperback ed. 1999) (Habit 2 is the family mission statement).

50. *See generally* Gerald Le Van, *Family Mission Statements: What Estate Advisors Need to Know*, 35 Est. Plan. 33 (Mar. 2008); Linda C. McClain, *Family Constitutions and the (New) Constitution of the Family*, 75 Fordham L. Rev. 833 (2006) (discussing the implications of family mission statements and constitutions from a family law perspective).

EXERCISE 13-8

MISSION STATEMENT

Write a mission statement for your family.

2. Family Offices

Family offices are generally divided between single-family offices (SFOs) and multi-family offices (MFOs). By one account there are over 5,000 SFOs and approximately 100 MFOs.[51]

An SFO can be as simple as a wealthy family member who maintains a small office and full- or part-time employees who perform various management functions such as recordkeeping, reporting, investment oversight, and scheduling meetings with other family members and outside advisors (attorneys, accountants, investment advisors, property managers, and so forth). However, the SFO for an extremely wealthy family (typically with assets in excess of $100,000,000[52]) would generally serve multiple members of the same family (who would share the costs in some fashion), and the activities of the SFO would not only further coordinated wealth building, but also family cohesiveness and a sense of shared purpose and destiny.

The SFO will typically be structured as an entity, in many cases as a limited liability company. In this context the SFO may employ a manager, in-house advisors, and employees (with consultation of outside advisors when necessary) who will coordinate, for the family, areas and functions such as estate planning, business succession planning, tax planning and preparation, investment management,[53] trust administration, family meetings, administration (recordkeeping, banking, bill paying, employment of household and security staff), risk management, and philanthropy.

An MFO generally offers the same functions as the SFO, but it offers them to multiple families. Due to the scale of operations, the MFO may be able to offer a broader and deeper menu of services.[54]

51. *See* Patricia M. Soldano, *When to Use and How to Choose a Family Office*, 35 EST. PLAN. 20 (Dec. 2008).

52. *See* Mark B. Edwards, *The Family Office: What It Is and What It Does*, Estate Planning for the Family Business Owner, SM003 ALI-ABA 1539 (ALI-ABA Continuing Legal Education July 19-21, 2006) ("Most commentators indicate that a single family office requires about $100,000,000 as the threshold amount for its creation."). *Compare* Soldano, *id.*, ("A single-family office must usually have assets in excess of $400 million to support the professional personnel that are needed to manage the assets.").

53. *See* Audrey C. Talley, *Family Offices: Securities and Commodities Law Issues*, 34 ACTEC J. 284 (2009).

54. *See generally* Patricia M. Soldano, *Collaboration from the Family Office Perspective*, 150 TR. & EST. 49 (Mar. 2011) (speaking to the benefits of collaboration among MFO advisors).

3. Family Trust Companies

The trust is the central component in a plan for long-term transmission of wealth, and the trustee's administration of the trust is a critical feature in that plan. While independent institutional trustees can be the norm, some families use their own trust company to manage the trust assets. One benefit of a family trust company is that the interposition of an entity affords some asset protection to the family members who would otherwise assume a trustee role, and unlike a single individual trustee, a trust company assures a level of continuity.[55] Beyond that, it is asserted that family control of the trustee function permits more flexible (and perhaps less conservative) investment plans.[56] Family control of a trust, however, presents a number of tax issues, as reflected in the length of a comprehensive proposed revenue ruling on this subject.[57]

F. CASE STUDY 13-1

***Paul and Linda Davis* (Part IV)**

PROTECTING FUTURE GENERATIONS

We continue with the case of Paul and Linda Davis from case studies 5-1, 7-1, and 8-1. Case Study 8-1 described Paul's parents and their gift of $200,000 for the grandchildren's education and the gift of Tanglewood Farms. Paul's parents are now considering additional gifts.

Paul's father is an avid reader of financial planning publications, and one day he read an article discussing the benefits of dynasty trusts. Paul's father recalled his own humble beginnings and the many turns in the road of life that could have changed his course for the worse. Paul's father is particularly worried about his descendants' investment practices (Paul suffered a drubbing in some speculative stock investments), and his descendants' behavior (Paul's father is concerned about divorce and spendthrift behavior). In his words, "kids these days don't understand the value of thrift, accumulation instead of spending, and the miracle of patient compounding." Further, Paul's father firmly believes that all situations, including families, "revert to the mean," and that he has been very smart, very lucky, and very driven; he fears that his descendants

55. *See, e.g.*, Robert R. Galloway, *Private Trust Companies: An Informal Primer*, 19 Ohio Prob. L.J. 233 (July/Aug. 2009) (benefits include liability protection, discretionary distributions by committee rather than by a single individual, permanence, and family control). *See generally* Carol A. Harrington & Ryan M. Harding, *Private Trust Companies and Family Offices: What Every Estate Planner Needs to Know*, Sophisticated Estate Planning Techniques, SP020 ALI-ABA 675 (ALI-ABA Continuing Legal Education Sept. 4-5, 2008).

56. *See, e.g.*, Iris J. Goodwin, *How the Rich Stay Rich: Using a Family Trust Company to Secure a Family Fortune*, 40 Seton Hall L. Rev. 467 (2010).

57. *See* Notice 2008-63, 2008-31 I.R.B. 261.

may not fare as well. In his words, "it is from lunch pail to lunch pail by the third generation."

Accordingly, Paul's father and mother have decided to contribute an undivided one-half interest in their vacation condominium to a dynasty trust (with the expectation that the entire condominium will be sold in the near future) plus cash from the liquidation of other investments, with an aggregate value of $1,000,000. Because the grandchildren's higher education is already provided for by the plan in Part III of the case study (see Chapter 8), and because Paul's father believes that Paul and his sister are already comfortable (and will receive bequests when both parents have passed away), Paul's father envisions that the trust will accumulate income for at least the next 20 years. Distributions of income or corpus in the interim would be an extraordinary event. It is Paul's father's hope that the trust corpus will grow and be something that future generations of the Davis family can "fall back on if necessary to ensure their success."

Using Form L from the Forms Supplement as a starting place, draft a lifetime dynasty trust for Paul's parents that responds to the settlors' concerns. Unless your teacher gives other directions, assume that the RAP does not apply. Assume that the initial trustee is the American Trust Company, 1200 Albany Way, MyCity, MyState 80000.

G. Reference Materials

Treatises

- Lawrence Brody, The Irrevocable Life Insurance Trust—Forms with Drafting Notes 88-91 (2d ed. 1999) (example of trust protector language).
- Barry S. Engel et al., Asset Protection Planning Guide 481-483 (2000) (example of trust protector language).
- William M. McGovern et al., Wills, Trusts and Estates (4th ed. 2010).
- John R. Price & Samuel A. Donaldson, Price on Contemporary Estate Planning (2011).
- Charles E. Rounds, Jr. & Charles E. Rounds, III, Loring and Rounds: A Trustee's Handbook (2010 ed.).
- Austin Wakeman Scott et al., Scott and Ascher on Trusts (5th ed. 2006 & Supp. 2010)
- Richard B. Stephens et al., Federal Estate and Gift Taxation: Including the Generation-Skipping Transfer Tax (8th ed. 2002 & Supp. 2011) (GSTT generally).
- George M. Turner, Irrevocable Trusts (3d ed. 1996 & Supp. 2010).

Articles

Rule Against Perpetuities

- Jesse Dukeminier & James E. Krier, *The Rise of the Perpetual Trust*, 50 UCLA L. Rev. 1303 (2003).
- Lynn Foster, *Fifty-One Flowers: Post-Perpetuities War Law and Arkansas's Adoption of USRAP*, 29 U. Ark. Little Rock L. Rev. 411 (2007).
- Wayne M. Gazur, *Colorado Revisits the Rule Against Perpetuities*, 35 Colo. Law. 75 (Nov. 2006).
- Amy Morris Hess, *Freeing Property Owners from the RAP Trap: Tennessee Adopts the Uniform Statutory Rule Against Perpetuities*, 62 Tenn. L. Rev. 267 (1995).
- Dan W. Holbrook, *The Rule Against Perpetuities: Time to Reexamine?*, 38 Tenn. B.J. 31 (Apr. 2002).
- Ronald C. Link & Kimberly A. Licata, *Perpetuities Reform in North Carolina: The Uniform Statutory Rule Against Perpetuities, Nondonative Transfers, and Honorary Trusts*, 74 N.C. L. Rev. 1783 (1996).
- Note, *Dynasty Trusts and the Rule Against Perpetuities*, 116 Harv. L. Rev. 2588 (2003).
- Frederick R. Schneider, *A Rule Against Perpetuities for the Twenty-First Century*, 41 Real Prop. Prob. & Tr. J. 743 (2007).
- Stewart E. Sterk, *Jurisdictional Competition to Abolish the Rule Against Perpetuities: R.I.P. for the R.A.P.*, 24 Cardozo L. Rev. 2097 (2003).
- Angela M. Vallario, *Death by a Thousand Cuts: The Rule Against Perpetuities*, 25 J. Legis. 141 (1999).

Dynasty Trusts

- Ronald D. Aucutt, *Structuring Trust Arrangements for Flexibility*, 35 Inst. on Est. Plan. ¶900 (2001).
- Kevin W. Blanton & Rachna D. Balakrishna, *Dynasty Trusts and Life Insurance: New Opportunities for Leverage*, 30 Est. Plan. 407 (2003).
- Daniel L. Daniels & David T. Leibell, *Dynasty Trusts: The Basics*, 146 Tr. & Est. 36 (Apr. 2007).
- Jesse Dukeminier, *Dynasty Trusts: Sheltering Descendants from Transfer Taxes*, 23 Est. Plan. 417 (1996).
- Jesse Dukeminier & James E. Krier, *The Rise of the Perpetual Trust*, 50 UCLA L. Rev. 1303 (2003).
- Julia B. Fisher, *Dynasty Trusts: Problems and Drafting Considerations*, Advanced Estate Planning Techniques, SG062 ALI-ABA 53 (ALI-ABA Continuing Legal Education, Feb. 21-23, 2002).
- Mary Louise Fellows, *Why the Generation Skipping Transfer Tax Sparked Perpetual Trusts*, Symposium: Trust Law in the 21st Century, 27 Cardozo L. Rev. 2511 (2006).

- Thomas H. Foye, *Using South Dakota Law for Perpetual Trusts*, 12 PROB. & PROP. 17 (Jan./Feb. 1998).
- Jon J. Gallo, *I Won't; I Might; I Will: Drafting Strategies for Generation-Skipping Trusts*, 26 INST. ON EST. PLAN. ¶1500 (1992).
- Merwin (Trey) Grayson III, *A Comparison of Dynasty Trusts in Alaska, Delaware, and Ohio from the Perspective of the Ohio Practitioner*, 27 N. KY. L. REV. 669 (2000).
- Stephen E. Greer, *The Alaska Dynasty Trust*, 18 ALASKA L. REV. 253 (2001).
- Brian Layman, *Perpetual Dynasty Trusts: One of the Most Powerful Tools in the Estate Planner's Arsenal*, 32 AKRON L. REV. 747 (1999).
- Elizabeth L. Mathieu, *How to Choose and Evaluate a Corporate Trustee for Long-Term Trusts*, 27 EST. PLAN. 80 (2000).
- Mark Merric, *How to Draft Discretionary Dynasty Trusts—Part 1*, 36 EST. PLAN. 3 (Feb. 2009).
- Mark Merric, *How to Draft Distribution Standards for Discretionary Dynasty Trusts*, 36 EST. PLAN. 3 (Mar. 2009).
- Mark Merric, *How to Draft Discretionary Dynasty Trusts—Part 3*, 36 EST. PLAN. 13 (Apr. 2009).
- Richard W. Nenno, *Dynasty Trusts from the Client's Perspective*, 33 INST. ON EST. PLAN. ¶1300 (1999).
- Richard W. Nenno, *Planning with Dynasty Trusts*, Planning Techniques for Large Estates, SG041 ALI-ABA 1597 (ALI-ABA Continuing Legal Education, Nov. 12-16, 2001).
- Madeline J. Rivlin, *Dynasty Trusts*, 319 PLI/Est 909 (PLI Tax Law and Est. Plan. Course Handbook Series No. D0-009B, Sept.-Oct. 2002).
- Judith Kish Ruud, *When Enough Is Enough & What to Do with the Excess*, 41 ADVOC. 12 (Aug. 1998).
- Robert H. Sitkoff, *The Lurking Rule Against Accumulations of Income*, 100 NW. U. L. REV. 501 (2006).
- Robert A. Vigoda, *Powers to Replace Trustees: A Key Element of (and Risk to) Dynasty Trusts*, 35 EST. PLAN. 20 (June 2008).
- Riley Wilson, *Perpetual Trusts: You Can't Take It With You (But You Can Still Have Your Say)*, 24 J. TAX'N INV. 99 (2007).

The Drafting of Trusts (See also "Trust Distribution Schemes" and "Trust Protectors and Incentive Clauses" in Ch. 8 reference materials.)

- Ronald D. Aucutt, *Structuring Trust Arrangements for Flexibility*, 35 INST. ON EST. PLAN. ¶¶900, 904.3B (2001).
- Richard C. Ausness, *The Role of Trust Protectors in American Trust Law*, 45 REAL PROP. TR. & EST. L.J. 319 (2010).
- Alexander A. Bove, Jr., *Using the Power of Appointment to Protect Assets—More Power Than You Ever Imagined*, 36 ACTEC J. 333 (2010).

- Mary Clarke & Diana S.C. Zeydel, *Directed Trusts: The Statutory Approaches to Authority and Liability*, 35 Est. Plan. 14 (Sept. 2008).
- Mark Cohen, *The Top Fourteen Things You Need to Know About the Uniform Trust Code*, II NAELA J. 259 (2006).
- Jeffrey A. Cooper, *Speak Clearly and Listen Well: Negating the Duty to Diversify Trust Investments*, 33 Ohio N.U. L. Rev. 903 (2007).
- William R. Culp, Jr. & Mark L. Richardson, *Lifetime Special Powers of Appointment Offer Unique Planning Opportunities*, 33 Est. Plan. 34 (2006).
- William R. Culp, Jr. & Briani Bennett Mellen, *Trust Decanting: An Overview and Introduction to Creative Planning Opportunities*, 45 Real Prop. Tr. & Estate L.J. 1 (2010).
- William R. Culp, Jr. & Briani L. Bennett, *Use of Trust Decanting to Extend the Term of Irrevocable Trusts*, 37 Est. Plan. 3 (June 2010).
- Jo Ann Engelhardt, *Avoiding Problems with Trust Agreements and Fiduciary Administration*, 49 No. 5 Prac. Law. 37 (Oct. 2003).
- Michael G. Ferguson, *Wills and Trusts: Meeting the Drafting Challenges (With Sample Clauses)*, 43 No. 6 Prac. Law. 31 (Sept. 1997).
- Sheldon G. Gilman, *How and When to Use Trust Advisors Most Effectively*, 35 Est. Plan. 30 (Feb. 2008).
- Sheldon G. Gilman, *Effective Use of Trust Advisors Can Avoid Trustee Problems*, 35 Est. Plan. 18 (Mar. 2008).
- Sebastian V. Grassi, Jr., *Drafting Flexibility into Trusts Helps Cope with Uncertainty*, 29 Est. Plan. 347 (2002).
- David A. Handler & Alison E. Lothes, *The Case for Principle Trusts and Against Incentive Trusts*, 147 Tr. & Est. 30 (Oct. 2008).
- Nancy G. Henderson, *Managing the Benefits and Burdens of New Wealth with Incentive Trusts) (with Sample Provisions)*, (Part 1), 47 No. 6 Prac. Law. 51 (Sept. 2001); (Part 2), 47 No. 7 Prac. Law. 11 (Oct. 2001).
- Paul R. Lipton & Susan Fleischner Kornspan, *Expansion of Trustee's Authority May Not Relax the Standard of Care*, 29 Est. Plan. 343 (2002).
- Matthew P. Matiasevich, *Hog-Tying the Contumacious Beneficiary: The Disentitlement Doctrine in Estate and Trust Litigation*, 21 Prob. & Prop. 46 (Mar./Apr. 2007).
- Howard M. McCue III, *Planning and Drafting to Influence Behavior*, 34 Inst. on Est. Plan. ¶600 (2000).
- Richard W. Nenno, *Choosing and Rechoosing the Jurisdiction for a Trust*, 40 Inst. on Est. Plan. ¶400 (2006).
- Richard W. Nenno, *Directed Trusts: Can Directed Trustees Limit Their Liability?*, 21 Prob. & Prop. 45 (Nov./Dec. 2007).
- Alan Newman, *Spendthrift and Discretionary Trusts: Alive and Well Under the Uniform Trust Code*, 40 Real Prop. Prob. & Tr. J. 567 (2005).

- John Jeffrey Pankauski & Robert E. Conner, *Looking for the Exits: A Fiduciary's Sell Strategy Under the Prudent Investor Act*, 20 Prob. & Prop. 40 (Nov./Dec. 2006).
- Anne-Marie Rhodes, *Consequences of Heirs' Misconduct: Moving from Rules to Discretion*, 33 Ohio N.U. L. Rev. 975 (2007).
- Philip J. Ruce, *The Trustee and the Trust Protector: A Question of Fiduciary Power. Should a Trust Protector Be Held to a Fiduciary Standard?*, 59 Drake L. Rev. 67 (2010).
- John J. Scroggin, *Protecting and Preserving the Family: The True Goal of Estate Planning, Part I—Reasons and Philosophy*, 16 Prob. & Prop. 29 (May/June 2002).
- John J. Scroggin, *Protecting and Preserving the Family: The True Goal of Estate Planning, Part II—Some of the Tools*, 16 Prob. & Prop. 34 (July/Aug. 2002).
- Thomas E. Simmons, *Decanting and Its Alternatives: Remodeling and Revamping Irrevocable Trusts*, 55 S.D. L. Rev. 253 (2010).
- Peter B. Tiernan, *Evaluate and Draft Helpful Trust Protector Provisions*, 38 Est. Plan. 24 (July 2011).
- Suzanne Brown Walsh, *Drafting Under the Uniform Trust Code (With Sample Provisions)*, 21 Prac. Tax Law. 23 (Winter 2007).
- Ellen Evans Whiting, *Controlling Behavior by Controlling the Inheritance: Considerations in Drafting Incentive Provisions*, 15 Prob. & Prop. 6 (Sept./Oct. 2001).

Spendthrift Clauses

- Anne S. Emanuel, *Spendthrift Trusts: It's Time to Codify the Compromise*, 72 Neb. L. Rev. 179 (1993).
- William S. Huff, *Spendthrift Clauses: Legality and Effect on Post-Transfer Estate Planning*, 18 Inst. on Est. Plan. ¶1200 (1984).

Generation-Skipping Transfer Tax Planning

(See also same heading in Ch. 8 and Ch. 11 reference materials.)

- Jon J. Gallo, *I Won't; I Might; I Will: Drafting Strategies for Generation-Skipping Trusts*, 26 Inst. on Est. Plan. ¶¶1500, 1505.1 (1992) (sample language for provisions for distributions); 1505.2 (sample language for estate and GSTT provisions); 1505.3 (provisions for trust administration); 1507 (sample Will provisions).
- Julie K. Kwon, *Advanced Generation-Skipping Transfer Tax Issues (With Forms) (Part 1)*, 13 ALI-ABA Est. Plan. Course Materials J. 5 (Dec. 2007).
- Lloyd Leva Plaine, *Planning Beyond the GST Exemption—To Skip or Not to Skip, That Is the Question*, 32 Inst. on Est. Plan. ¶¶400, 404.6 (1998) (sample language for trust with one inclusion ratio for nonskip persons, skip persons, and charities, plus other GSTT planning techniques).

- Gideon Rothschild, *Understanding the Generation-Skipping Transfer Tax*, 321 PLI/Est 305 (PLI Tax Law and Est. Plan. Course Handbook Series No. D0-009F, Nov. 2002).
- Pam H. Schneider, *GST Planning with Irrevocable Insurance Trusts: Putting It All Together After the Final GST Regulations*, 31 INST. ON EST. PLAN. ¶¶ 300, 301.4 (1997) (not wasting the GSTT exemption on otherwise exempt transfers—using the predeceased child exemption, trust tuition, and medical expenses exemption); 302.3 (assets to be transferred, valuing hard-to-value property—sample language included); 302.5 (withdrawal powers as a transfer in trust, using gift tax exclusion); 304.2 (funding provisions).
- Georgiana J. Slade, *Inter Vivos Generation-Skipping Transfer Tax Planning*, 34 INST. ON EST. PLAN. ¶¶ 500, 504.3) (2000) (making assets available for nonskip person—trustee could purchase the asset such as a business, then operate the business with the nonskip person, on death of nonskip person, business remains asset of GSTT exempt trust and is held for the benefit of the skip persons).
- Laura K. Sundberg & Edward F. Koren, *The Gallo Exclusion: It Must Be Used Before Its Time*, 63 FLA. B.J. 51 (Nov. 1989).
- R. Eric Viehman, *Current Issues in Generation-Skipping Tax Planning*, Planning Techniques for Large Estates, SS010 ALI-ABA 1 (ALI-ABA Continuing Legal Education Nov. 15-19, 2010).
- Diana S.C. Zeydel, *Handling Affirmative and Deemed Allocations of GST Exemption (Part I)*, 34 EST. PLAN. 12 (2007).
- Diana S.C. Zeydel, *Deemed Allocations of GST Exemption to Lifetime Transfers (Part II)*, 34 EST. PLAN. 3 (2007).

Unauthorized Practice of Law

- Jeffrey A. Baskies, *Florida Ethics Opinion Highlights Multi-Jurisdictional Practice Landmine*, LAW. WEEKLY USA 4, 2004 LWUSA 180 (Mar. 15, 2004) (discussing a Florida bar ethics opinion suggesting that a lawyer outside of Florida advising a client about Florida law may be practicing law in Florida).
- Quintin Johnstone, *Multijurisdictional Practice of Law: Its Prevalence and Its Risks*, 74 CONN. B.J. 343 (Dec. 2000).
- Raymond J. Werner, *Licensed in One State, But Practicing in Another: Multijurisdictional Practice*, 17 PROB. & PROP. 6 (Mar./Apr. 2003).
- Gerard E. Wimberly, Jr., *The Unauthorized Practice of Law by Licensed Attorneys: A Perilous Paradox*, 37 ARIZ. ATT'Y 29 (June 2001).

Family Mission Statements, Offices, and Trust Companies

- STEPHEN R. COVEY, 7 HABITS OF HIGHLY EFFECTIVE FAMILIES 70 (paperback ed. 1999).
- Mark B. Edwards, *The Family Office: What It Is and What It Does*, Estate Planning for the Family Business Owner, SM003

ALI-ABA 1539 (ALI-ABA Continuing Legal Education July 19-21, 2006).

- Robert R. Galloway, *Private Trust Companies: An Informal Primer*, 19 OHIO PROB. L.J. 233 (July/Aug. 2009).
- Iris J. Goodwin, *How the Rich Stay Rich: Using a Family Trust Company to Secure a Family Fortune*, 40 SETON HALL L. REV. 467 (2010).
- Carol A. Harrington & Ryan M. Harding, *Private Trust Companies and Family Offices: What Every Estate Planner Needs to Know*, Sophisticated Estate Planning Techniques, SP020 ALI-ABA 675 (ALI-ABA Continuing Legal Education Sept. 4-5, 2008).
- Gerald Le Van, *Family Mission Statements: What Estate Advisors Need to Know*, 35 EST. PLAN. 33 (Mar. 2008).
- Linda C. McClain, *Family Constitutions and the (New) Constitution of the Family*, 75 FORDHAM L. REV. 833 (2006).
- Carleen L. Schreder, *The IRS Issues Guidance on Private Trust Companies*, 36 EST. PLAN. 8 (Jan. 2009).
- Patricia M. Soldano, *When to Use and How to Choose a Family Office*, 35 EST. PLAN. 20 (Dec. 2008).
- Patricia M. Soldano, *Collaboration from the Family Office Perspective*, 150 TR. & EST. 49 (Mar. 2011).
- Audrey C. Talley, *Family Offices: Securities and Commodities Law Issues*, 34 ACTEC J. 284 (2009).

CHAPTER 14 Charitable Gifts

A. Weighing Client Objectives

Planning for charitable giving requires careful consideration of federal and state income, gift, and estate tax consequences, although any one of these areas may be the driving force of the client's planning. A number of charitable gift alternatives are available, each with its own special requirements, advantages, and disadvantages, and it is easy for a planner to become confused. It has been our experience that as a starting point, five general questions for a client can establish a direction for the planning.

1. Why does the client want to make charitable gifts? Does the client have a significant charitable intent?
2. Is there a client preference for, or do client circumstances dictate (e.g., liquidity concerns), a lifetime gift or a testamentary gift?
3. Is there a client preference, or need, for some degree of retained income, use, or enjoyment of the gifted property by the client or family members?
4. Is there a client preference for a federal income tax deduction for the gifted property?
5. Is there a client preference for continuing input about the application of the gifted property?

The answers to these questions clearly suggest some planning measures and exclude others. Question 1 might seem silly, but many clients have heard stories that one can increase wealth by the use of charitable donations. While that might be the case in a few circumstances (e.g., very highly appreciated property contributed to a charitable remainder trust), most charitable structures will, at best, leave the client with tax savings and/or income streams that don't fully compensate for the complete loss of the gifted property.[1] After examining the alternatives, some clients walk away because "the numbers just don't work." It is a matter of expectations.[2]

With respect to question 5, for example, a donor-advised fund[3] or the formation of a private foundation might be considered for substantial charitable gifts. With respect to questions 2 and 4 in tandem, a federal income tax deduction for the donor is generally available only if a lifetime gift is made. A client preference for the type of retained benefits described in question 3 will invoke the "split-interest" principles, which rule out a simple outright charitable gift.

B. Outright Testamentary Bequests

The simple testamentary bequest to charity is often overlooked in the glare of the other more complex structures. The donor may be unmarried or may be a childless widow or widower. Even if the donor has natural objects of his or her bounty, the donor may believe that they have already been treated fairly through lifetime giving or other bequests. The donor may have a very specific charitable purpose in mind beyond selecting the charitable organization, such as "for scholarships to needy students of Irish descent."[4] A condition subsequent may be imposed, such as "so long as the Albertson School continues its program of art education." As discussed in the following paragraphs, conditional bequests may present tax complications.

A testamentary bequest may be chosen because the donor does not want to part with the particular asset, such as an art collection, during the donor's life, or the donor does not want to part with the financial security represented by the gift. A testamentary bequest may be also preferred

1. Some "wealth replacement" structures use the income tax savings to fund a purchase of life insurance to replace the lost wealth. This assumes that the proposed insured is still insurable at acceptable premium costs.

2. *See, e.g.*, Byrle M. Abbin, *No More "Gravy Train": 1997 Law Revisions Dramatically Affect the Economics of CRT's — Only Those With True Charitable Motivation Should Create Them*, 34 INST. ON EST. PLAN. ¶1400 (2000).

3. Fidelity Investments was a pioneer of these arrangements. Very generally, the donor contributes money to the fund, which is invested by the sponsor. The sponsor receives a fee for its services. The donor's privileges could include nonbinding recommendations or advice concerning the recipient of the funds, the timing of the gift to the recipient (although the donor can claim an immediate income tax deduction), and the manner in which the funds are invested in the interim. *See, e.g.*, Tanya D. Marsh, *A Dubious Distinction: Rethinking Tax Treatment of Private Foundations and Public Charities*, 22 VA. TAX REV. 137, 174-178 (2002) (describing the operation of a for-profit donor-advised fund). Traditional charities, such as university charitable foundations, may offer donor-advised opportunities. However, as discussed later in this chapter, the Pension Protection Act of 2006 introduced a number of restrictions on donor-advised funds.

4. Charitable gifts that discriminate on the basis of race or gender raise issues of enforceability, particularly if a public organization is involved. *See generally* CHARLES E. ROUNDS, JR. & CHARLES E. ROUNDS, III, LORING AND ROUNDS: A TRUSTEE'S HANDBOOK §9.4.3 (2010 ed.); WILLIAM M. MCGOVERN ET AL., WILLS, TRUSTS AND ESTATES 439-440 (4th ed. 2010). It is also dangerous if the donor wishes to earmark a certain person — for example, a missionary — for the gift. *See, e.g.*, Conrad Teitell, *Earmarking Charitable Gifts for Individuals? Don't*, 142 TR. & EST. 40 (Supp., Apr. 2003).

because the donor does not desire the publicity or family pressures produced by a lifetime charitable gift.

The donor will not receive an income tax deduction for a testamentary gift (in some cases an estate can claim an income tax deduction for charitable gifts), but in most cases a federal estate tax deduction will be allowed for the value of the gift, without any limitations on amounts (i.e., one could give all of the taxable estate to charity and receive a deduction).[5]

There are, however, potential pitfalls in even this simple structure. First, from a federal estate tax standpoint, the status of the charitable organization must be reviewed in advance to determine if it is a qualifying organization under IRC §§2055(a), 2055(e)(1), and 2055(g).[6] Second, the possibility must be addressed, particularly with a testamentary gift, that the named charitable organization will not exist or be a qualifying organization at the time of funding.[7] Third, conditional bequests and gifts with reverter clauses must be handled with care, otherwise the federal estate tax deduction might be denied even if the condition is ultimately satisfied.[8] Fourth, with the proliferation of organizations with similar names, the charitable organization must be identified with great care and specificity. For example, it is good practice to include the charitable organization's legal name, address, telephone number, and tax identification number in the gift language. Fifth, the tax apportionment clause of the Will must consider the impact of estate taxes and other costs on charitable gifts, because estate taxes and certain other costs apportioned to and reducing the charitable gift will reduce the amount the charitable organization receives, as well as reduce the estate tax charitable gift deduction.[9] Sixth, the use of the gift by the charitable organization is restricted to certain purposes or is it an unrestricted gift (e.g., "for any purpose . . .")? Finally, confirm the applicability, albeit remote, of any Mortmain restrictions.[10]

5. *See* IRC §2055. Even with a simple gift to charity of the residue, care must be exercised in drafting so that the expenses of administration are nonetheless expressly provided for.

6. To search for IRS approved charitable organizations listed in *Publication 78, Cumulative List of Organizations described in Section 170(c) of the Internal Revenue Code of 1986*, see http://www.irs.gov/charities/article/0,id=96136,00.html (last visited Aug. 27, 2011). Another consideration is whether a contribution will be a source of terrorist financing. The U.S. Treasury has issued recommendations. *See Anti-Terrorist Financing Guidelines: Voluntary Best Practices for U.S.-Based Charities*, http://www.treasury.gov/resource-center/terrorist-illicit-finance/Pages/protecting-charities-intro.aspx (last visited Aug. 27, 2011)

7. The doctrine of cy pres is not an acceptable solution. The instrument should name an alternate organization or give the personal representative the power to substitute another similar qualifying organization (if the testator desires that; he or she, in that case, may wish that the gift simply lapse).

8. *See* Treas. Reg. §20.2055-2(b) Example 2 (as amended in 2001); Alan F. Rothschild Jr., *Planning and Documenting Charitable Gifts*, 20 PROB. & PROP. 53 (July/Aug. 2006).

9. *See* Treas. Reg. §20.2055-3 (as amended in 1999). *See generally* Jerald David August, *Final Hubert Regulations Fix Boundaries for Administrative Expenses*, 27 EST. PLAN. 195 (2000). *See also* Estate of Marion P. Bradford, 84 T.C.M. (CCH) 337 (2002) (charitable deduction reduced by federal estate and state inheritance taxes apportioned to the charitable bequest).

10. A 1992 law review article singled out three jurisdictions (Idaho, Georgia, and Mississippi) that had not either repealed or had their Mortmain restriction found to be unconstitutional. *See* Shirley Norwood Jones, *The Demise of Mortmain in the United States*, 12 MISS. COLL. L. REV. 407 (1992). Our research suggests that the last of the applicable statutes and constitutional provisions was repealed in 1996, effective as of January 1, 1998.

EXERCISE 14-1

EVALUATING TESTAMENTARY CHARITABLE GIFT LANGUAGE

Evaluate the desirability of the following clauses for state law as well as federal wealth transfer tax purposes.

A. *I give all the rest and residue of my estate to my personal representative, to be distributed to whatever charities she may deem worthy.* (*See* Rev. Rul. 69-285, 1969-1 C.B. 222.)

B. *My personal representative shall distribute the residue of my estate to or for the use of those organizations to which gifts of income or principal shall qualify as tax-free under the laws relating to income, estate, inheritance, or gifts, of the United States or any state having jurisdiction.* (*See* Rev. Rul. 71-200, 1971-1 C.B. 272.)

Draft a clause authorizing the personal representative to select charitable organizations to receive the sum of $50,000. Tax issues aside, how can a pecuniary sum (as compared with a fractional or percentage share) to charity be potentially dangerous?

C. Outright Lifetime Gifts

An outright lifetime gift offers a number of benefits. First, the asset and any future appreciation are removed from the donor's estate, producing eventual estate tax savings on the donor's death. Second, if desired, the donor and his or her family can enjoy the gratitude of the donee and positive publicity and accompanying prestige.[11] Third, the donor is able to judge the donee's use of initial funds as a prelude to additional gifts. Fourth, the donor will usually enjoy a federal, and often state, income tax deduction at the time of the gift.[12]

However, there are a number of potential pitfalls as well. First, the charitable organization must be a qualifying charitable organization for gift tax purposes[13] and for income tax purposes.[14] While there are substantial overlaps, the income tax requirements, for example, are

11. A charitable pledge is a promise to make a charitable gift in the future—lifetime or testamentary. From a state law standpoint, with some exceptions the promise is generally not enforceable against the donor. The donor generally is not entitled to a tax deduction until the property is actually transferred to the charity. *See, e.g.*, Priv. Ltr. Rul. 2002-41-044 (Oct. 11, 2002) (treating a pledge as an incomplete charitable gift). *See generally* JOHN R. PRICE & SAMUEL A. DONALDSON, PRICE ON CONTEMPORARY ESTATE PLANNING §8.6 (2011).

12. *See* IRC §170.

13. *See* IRC §2522.

14. *See* IRC §170.

narrower in terms of foreign charities. The IRS maintains a list of approved charities.[15] Second, unlike the estate tax and gift tax charitable deductions, which are unlimited, the income tax deduction amount for lifetime gifts is limited to certain percentages of adjusted gross income, with some modifications, which may never exceed 50 percent and may be limited to far less (for example, 30 percent if donating to certain private foundations or even less for certain contributions of capital gain property[16]). While the unused contributions may be carried over for five years, those carryovers expire with the death of the donor.[17] Third, gifts of $250 or more generally must be acknowledged in writing by the charitable organization.[18] Fourth, special appraisal requirements are imposed for contributions of property other than cash or publicly traded securities having a value in excess of $5,000 ($10,000 for certain property).[19] Fifth, deductions for charitable contributions of tangible personal property exceeding $5,000 must be reduced or recaptured if the donee disposes of the property within three years.[20]

If the donor wishes to retain interests in the gifted property for the benefit of the donor or other noncharitable beneficiaries, the technical split-interest rules discussed in the next section must be followed for both gift tax and income tax purposes. Those rules often require that

15. *See* note 6, *supra.*

16. Some private foundations are 50 percent charities, while others are 30 percent charities. Eligibility turns on the manner of operation. *See generally* BORIS I. BITTKER & LAWRENCE LOKKEN, FEDERAL TAXATION OF INCOME, ESTATES AND GIFTS ¶35.3.2 (3d ed. 2000 & Cum. Supp. 2011).

17. The Pension Protection Act of 2006 added a 15-year carryover period for certain qualified conservation contributions made during 2006 and 2007. *See* IRC §§170(b)(1)(E) & (b)(2)(B). That provision was extended through 2009 by the Food Conservation and Energy Act of 2008, and further extended through 2011 by the Tax Relief, Unemployment Insurance Reauthorization, and Job Creation Act of 2010. In any event, the possible expiration of the contribution deduction carryover must be a consideration if the donor is elderly or in poor health.

18. *See* IRC §170(f)(8). The Pension Protection Act of 2006 added a recordkeeping requirement that precludes any deduction for the contribution of a cash, check, or other monetary gift unless the donor maintains as a record of such contribution, a bank record or a written communication from the donee showing the name of the donee organization, the date of the contribution, and the amount of the contribution. *See* IRC §170(f)(17).

19. *See* Treas. Reg. §1.170A-13 (as amended in 1996). The Pension Protection Act of 2006 added a more restrictive definition of "qualified appraisal" and "qualified appraiser" for charitable contribution purposes. *See* IRC §170(f)(11)(E); John A. Bogdanski, *For Appraisers, New Tax Qualification Rules and Special Penalty*, 34 EST. PLAN. 16 (2007).

20. If a taxpayer contributes tangible personal property, the use of which is unrelated to the donee's charitable function, the income tax deduction is essentially limited to the taxpayer's adjusted basis in the property. *See* IRC §170(e)(1)(B)(i). The regulations already provided that a painting, for example, contributed to a charity that sells the painting (as opposed to using the painting in its functions) would be subject to this rule. *See* Treas. Reg. §1.170A-4(b)(3)(i). The Pension Protection Act of 2006, however, added an additional provision that requires a reduction in the income tax deduction if the donee organization disposes of the contributed property within three years of the contribution. *See* IRC §170(e)(1)(B)(i)(II). Consequently, even if a taxpayer donates museum-quality art to an art museum and the museum displays the art in its charitable function, there is the risk that the museum will dispose of the art within three years, reducing the taxpayer's deduction. Although this issue is beyond the scope of this book, taxpayer-imposed restrictions on the museum's sale of the painting within three years could reduce the value of the contribution. *See generally* Richard L. Fox, *Charitable Limitations and Reforms of the Pension Protection Act [Part I]*, 33 EST. PLAN. 3, 15-16 (Nov. 2006); Paul R. Comeau & Alexander M. Popovich, *Giving and Loaning Art to Charity*, 147 TR. & EST. 38 (May 2008).

the contributions be placed in trust. However, there are two notable exceptions to those rules.

1. Remainder Interests in a Personal Residence or Farm

The gift of a remainder interest in a personal residence or farm may qualify for the gift tax charitable deduction and the income tax charitable deduction, even if free of trust.[21] While the income tax deduction is only for the value of the remainder interest, this remainder interest structure permits the donor's continued use of the property, even for life, overcoming possible donor objections to parting with its use. If the donor dies while enjoying the use of the property, the value of the property will be included in the estate by IRC §2036(a)(1), but that inclusion is offset by the estate tax deduction for the value of the property passing to the charitable organization.

2. Undivided Outright Interests in Property

The split-interest limitations generally apply to uses divided by time (e.g., life estates, terms of years, and remainders). An exception is created for gifts of undivided interests in property such that the donor can gift, for example, an undivided one-half interest in Blackacre by deed, not limited to a personal residence or farm, and qualify for the charitable deduction.[22] The donor will not own the gifted undivided interest at the time of death, so an estate tax saving is produced. In addition, if the donor still retains the remaining undivided interests in the property, the value of those interests may be further reduced by fractional interest discounts (see Chapter 16).

A gift of undivided interests is not without its potential complications. First, the donor and the charitable organization are co-owners of the property, and as co-owners they will need to cooperate in paying for the upkeep, real property taxes, and so forth. Second, the donor must understand that the charitable organization could dispose of its interest to a stranger. Third, the donor must be aware that the gift of the undivided interest will result in a loss of control with respect to the overall property interest. Fourth, as to the charitable organization, the direct ownership of such an asset may have undesirable income tax consequences such as the need to report unrelated business taxable income.[23] Fifth, the donor must weigh the stringent limitations on gifts of partial interests in tangible personal property imposed by the Pension Protection Act of 2006.[24]

21. *See* IRC §§170(f)(3)(B) & 2522(c)(2). If the property consists of a combination of both depreciable and nondepreciable property or depletable and nondepletable property, different valuation factors will be applied to the depreciable/depletable assets and the nondepreciable/nondepletable assets. *See* Treas. Reg. §1.170A-12 (as amended in 2000).

22. *See* IRC §§170(f)(3)(B) & 2522(c)(2).

23. *See* IRC §511.

24. In general, the Pension Protection Act of 2006 (as amended by the Technical Corrections Act of 2007) provides that, with some exceptions, an income or gift tax deduction for a partial interest in tangible personal property is precluded unless the remaining interests in the

EXERCISE 14-2

GIFTING A PERSONAL RESIDENCE

An elderly widow owns a stately personal residence valued at approximately $1,000,000, the basis of which is $400,000. She plans to gift the residence to a local university for use as an alumni center. Evaluate her alternatives in structuring the gift.

D. Lifetime Split-Interest Gifts

The general rule is that deductions for split-interest gifts are denied unless they are structured in a certain format.[25] These rules were introduced by the Tax Reform Act of 1969 to counter certain abuses that sometimes left the charitable donee with little value.

1. Contributions of Remainders

In the case of property transferred in trust, no deduction is allowed for the value of a contribution of a remainder interest to a charitable organization unless it is in the form of a charitable remainder annuity trust, a charitable remainder unitrust, or a pooled income fund. The benefits of these arrangements include: (a) an immediate income tax deduction for the value of the remainder; (b) estate tax savings, because the value of the property and future appreciation of that property is effectively removed from the estate; (c) the creation of an assured income stream for the donor or other family members, although the receipt of interests by beneficiaries other than the donor will be a taxable gift, which may compare favorably with the economic result that could otherwise be obtained by selling the

property are owned by the donor and/or the donee. For income tax purposes the valuation of the subsequent donations of fractional interests is subject to a special rule referring to the lesser of the property's value at the time of the first gift or the value at the time of the additional gift — the upshot is that the donor does not benefit from any appreciation in the property but could suffer from a decline in value. For income and gift tax purposes the charitable deduction can be recaptured if the donor does not gift the remaining fractional interests in the property within the earlier of ten years from the first gift or the donor's date of death. *See generally* Avi Z. Kestenbaum & Jeffrey Perelman, *Numerous Pension Act Changes Affect Charitable and Estate Planning*, 78 PRAC. TAX STRATEGIES 204, 208 (Apr. 2007); Richard L. Fox, *Charitable Limitations and Reforms of the Pension Protection Act [Part II]*, 33 EST. PLAN. 3, 3-6 (Dec. 2006) ("donors will likely be reluctant to contribute fractional interests in tangible personal property").

25. The IRS has issued various revenue rulings and other pronouncements that provide drafting guidance, including sample language, for split-interest gifts in trust. These pronouncements provide a starting place in the drafting of these instruments. However, several of the forms include well-known traps for the unwary and cannot be used without modifications. *See generally* PRICE & DONALDSON, *supra* note 11, at §8.23; Richard L. Fox, *A Guide to the IRS Sample Charitable Lead Trust Forms-Part 1*, 36 EST. PLAN. 7 (Apr. 2009); Richard L. Fox, *A Guide to the IRS Sample Charitable Lead Trust Forms-Part 2*, 36 EST. PLAN. 13 (May 2009); Richard L. Fox, *A Guide to the IRS Sample Charitable Remainder Trust Forms*, 33 EST. PLAN. 13 (Jan. 2006).

property in a taxable transaction and investing the proceeds; and (d) the donor can change the charitable beneficiary during his or her lifetime, and keep the existence of the trust confidential during the donor's lifetime.

Point (c) is very important to the structure of these arrangements. Even with a current income tax rate of 15 percent[26] on most capital gain income, the primary advantage of these charitable remainder structures is the donor's avoidance of the tax on capital gains from the contributed property. The charitable trust is permitted to sell the property without paying income taxes on that gain,[27] freeing more after-tax assets for the income stream that is paid to the donor or the donor's private beneficiaries.[28] If the contributed assets are not highly appreciated or if the income tax rate on long-term capital gains were further reduced, much of the economic advantage of these arrangements would be lost.[29] If the donor's primary objective is donative, then this factor recedes in importance.

The federal income and estate tax requirements have produced several split-interest charitable gift vehicles discussed below.

a. Charitable Remainder Annuity Trust. A charitable remainder annuity trust (CRAT) must comply with rules announced in Treas. Reg. §§1.664-1, 1.664-2, and 1.664-3. Due to statutory amendments that may not be reflected in the regulations, one should begin with an examination of IRC §664. Generally, the trust must pay a sum certain not less than annually to individuals living at the time of the creation of the trust. The sum may be paid for a fixed term of years up to 20 years, or for the lives of the designated recipients. The value of the income interest is treated as a taxable gift to the individual beneficiaries, but the value of the charitable remainder is deductible for income tax and gift tax purposes. The total amount payable annually to the private beneficiaries cannot be less than 5 percent, nor more than 50 percent, of the initial fair market value of the property placed in trust. No additional contributions may be made after the initial contribution. A qualifying charitable organization must be the remainderperson,[30]

26. The 15 percent rate introduced by the Jobs and Growth Tax Relief Reconciliation Act of 2003 would apply only to gains recognized prior to 2009, and, unless extended, the previous 20 percent capital gains rate would again apply. *See* Jobs and Growth Tax Relief Reconciliation Act of 2003, §303, Pub. L. No. 108-27, 117 Stat. 752, 764 (2003). However, the Tax Relief, Unemployment Insurance Reauthorization, and Job Creation Act of 2010 extended the 15 percent rate through 2012.

27. To avoid an IRS argument that a sale by the trust is attributed to the donor, the trustee should not be obligated to sell the asset. *See, e.g.*, Rev. Rul. 60-370, 1960-2 C.B. 203; Blake v. Commissioner, 697 F.2d 473 (2d Cir. 1982).

28. Although the donor avoids the direct impact of the capital gains tax, under complex ordering rules the distributions to the private beneficiaries may be in large part taxable income. *See* Bruce R. Hopkins, The Tax Law of Charitable Giving §12.5 (4th ed. 2010 & Supp. 2011).

29. Based on 1992 statistics, the median amount of charitable remainder trust gifts was approximately $160,000. *See* Christopher Weems, *Charitable Giving in America*, 139 Tr. & Est. 72 (Dec. 2000).

30. The regulations permit concurrent or successive remainderpersons, and the instrument must provide for alternative remainderpersons in case a designated remainderperson no longer is a qualified charitable organization.

and the value of the remainder must be at least 10 percent of the initial fair market value of all property contributed to the trust.

The CRAT has three principal advantages: (1) it provides the private beneficiaries, who may include the donor, with a fixed income amount; (2) while there are initial transaction costs for appraisals and forming the trust, there is no annual appraisal requirement in subsequent years; and (3) as discussed above, it provides a measure of capital gains tax avoidance.[31]

The CRAT has two principal disadvantages: (1) the fixed income amount may erode in relative value in a high-inflation environment; and (2) the fixed income amount may draw down the trust fund and exhaust it prematurely, to the detriment of the private beneficiaries, because the remainder is required to be protected for at least 10 percent of the initial fair market value of the property.

b. Charitable Remainder Unitrust. A charitable remainder unitrust (CRUT) must comply with the rules of Treas. Reg. §§1.664-1 and 1.664-3. The requirements resemble those of the annuity trust, except that in lieu of a fixed payment, the unitrust must distribute at least annually a fixed percentage, which cannot be less than 5 percent nor more than 50 percent, of the net fair market value of the trust assets, determined annually. The remainder interest cannot be less than 10 percent of the net fair market value of property when contributed to the trust. Additional contributions, however, are not precluded, as the fair market value of the trust must be determined each year. A discussion of more complex planning structures such as the so-called "NIMCRUT,"[32] "NICRUT,"[33] and "FLIPCRUT"[34] is beyond the scope of this book.

The CRUT has two principal advantages: (1) it can provide an inflation hedge for the individual beneficiaries because the annual payments increase with the value of the underlying trust assets; and (2) additional contributions are not precluded, thereby permitting additional planning flexibility without the need to create additional charitable structures.

The CRUT has two principal disadvantages: (1) if the trust assets decline in value, the income stream to the private beneficiaries will be reduced, although the trust assets will never be exhausted; and (2) annual appraisals of the assets of the trust are required, which may or may not be

31. *See supra* note 28.

32. NIMCRUT is an acronym for net income makeup charitable remainder unitrust. *See, e.g.*, Abbin, *supra* note 2. The NIMCRUT can be useful in gifting non-income-producing and illiquid assets (like closely held business interests) that will not support the payment of the regular unitrust amount in early years, but with a "makeup" of the missed payments in later years. *See* IRC §664(d)(3).

33. The NICRUT acronym refers to a "Net-Income CRUT" that modifies the fixed percentage payout to be the lesser of a fixed percentage or the trust's annual income. *See* Bruce R. Hopkins, *supra* note 28, §12.3.

34. *See id.* The Flip Unitrust (FLIPCRUT) permits a onetime conversion from a NICRUT or NIMCRUT to a standard fixed percentage, but only if "triggered on a specific date or by a single event whose occurrence is not discretionary with, or within the control of, the trustees or any other persons." Treas. Reg. §1.664-3(a)(1)(i)(c) (as amended in 2003).

burdensome depending on the asset mix (e.g., publicly traded securities are not difficult to value; land would generally require an appraisal).

c. Pooled Income Fund. The details of the pooled income fund structure are explained in Treas. Reg. §1.642(c)-5. A pooled income fund is an investment fund maintained by the public charitable organization that is the remainderperson. Unlike the CRAT and the CRUT, which are private trusts that permit the donor to serve as a trustee, the pooled income fund provisions forbid the donor or private beneficiary from serving as a trustee. The donor contributes property to the fund, and the property is required to be commingled with other property contributed to the fund. The donor generally recognizes no taxable gain or loss with respect to the contribution. The donor gifts an irrevocable remainder interest to the charitable organization and retains or creates a life income interest for one or more beneficiaries, each of whom must be living at the time of the gift. At the time of the property contribution, the donor receives units of participation in the fund based on the value of the contribution in comparison with the value of total fund assets. The income interest is subsequently based on the annual income of the fund assigned to each unit of participation, and distributions to the donor are treated as ordinary income. Upon the termination of the income interests, the units of the remainderperson charity are severed from the investment pool.

The pooled income fund has two principal advantages: (1) the formation entails fewer transaction costs, because the charitable organization has usually established the fund in advance; and (2) the arrangement can promote investment diversification and a higher level of professional investment management.

The pooled income fund suffers from two principal disadvantages: (1) the donor does not have the same degree of control over the details of tailoring the arrangement, including the ability to change the designated remainder charitable organization;[35] and (2) the donor may not manage the pooled income fund assets.[36]

35. IRS guidance interpreting IRC §642(c)(5)(E) (which requires that the pooled income fund be maintained by the charitable beneficiary), is relatively strict in policing the designation of the charitable remainderperson. For example, Treas. Reg. §1.642(c)-5(b)(5) (as amended in 1979) and Rev. Rul. 92-107, 1992-2 C.B. 120, permit the inclusion of multiple charities that share a common identity of purpose in certain cases (e.g., where a national charity includes its local supervised affiliates as beneficiaries), and the model form provided by Rev. Proc. 88-53, 1988-2 C.B. 712, permits the trustee's designation of a substitute charitable remainderperson if the designated charity ceases to exist or no longer qualifies as a public charity. Otherwise, it is our impression that pooled income funds generally do not permit the donor to subsequently change the designation of the charitable beneficiary. *Compare* Rev. Rul. 76-8, 1976-1 C.B. 179 (permitting the donor to substitute another charity as the remainderperson of a charitable remainder trust).

36. *See generally* Michael G. May, *Choosing the Trustee of a Charitable Remainder Trust*, 24 Est. Plan. 172 (1997).

2. Contributions of Income Interests

No charitable deduction is allowed for the value of any interest in property other than a remainder, transferred in trust, unless the interest is a guaranteed annuity, known as a charitable lead annuity trust (CLAT), or a fixed percentage, known as a charitable lead unitrust (CLUT), of the fair market value of the trust property, determined and distributed annually. These interests are often referred to as "charitable lead" interests because the charitable organization is gifted the income interest, with the individual beneficiaries receiving the remainder. An income tax deduction of the value of the charitable interest is not permitted unless the trust is treated as a grantor trust such that the donor remains taxable on income earned by the trust. Consequently, this structure is not generally used to gain an income tax deduction.

The attraction of charitable lead trusts is that the donor can fulfill charitable expectations with the gift of the lead interest, enjoying gratitude from the charitable donee during the donor's life while transferring the remainder and its future appreciation to private beneficiaries. For example, a parent of a young child could make a charitable gift of the income from an apartment building for 20 years and then have the remainder pass tax-free to the child as a young adult. Because the amount of the taxable gift to the private beneficiaries is generally computed by deducting the value of the lead interest from the value of the contributed property, this structure is able to produce gift tax savings by minimizing the amount of the gift made to the private remainderpersons upon the funding of the charitable gift. The lead trust structure is attractive only if the underlying property will appreciate at a rate in excess of the discount rate used to value the lead interest, thereby increasing the value of the remainder. A low interest rate environment is beneficial in terms of setting the applicable IRC §7520 discount rate.[37]

a. Charitable Lead Annuity Trust. The CLAT is described in Treas. Reg. §20.2055-2(e)(2)(vi). It resembles the income interest payable to the individual beneficiaries of a charitable remainder annuity trust except that in this structure the charitable organization is the income beneficiary. It requires that a determinable fixed amount, be paid at least annually, for a specified term of years or for the lives of certain individuals, who must be living on the date of transfer and who are certain relatives. If the charitable interest is not in trust it will not qualify unless paid by an insurance company or organization regularly engaged in issuing annuity contracts.

b. Charitable Lead Unitrust. The CLUT is described in Treas. Reg. §20.2055-2(e)(2)(vii). The income interest resembles that of the charitable remainder unitrust. The unitrust interest is the right to receive

37. *See, e.g.*, Lawrence P. Katzenstein, *Drafting Charitable Lead Trusts and A Look at the IRS Lead Trust Forms (With Samples)*, 16 ALI-ABA Est. Plan. Course Materials J. 5 (Oct. 2010) (mathematical demonstration of lead trust benefits).

payment, at least annually, of a fixed percentage of the net fair market value, determined annually, of the property that funds the unitrust interest. Payments may be made for a specified term of years or for the lives of the same circumscribed group of relatives described in the guaranteed annuity interest. Similarly, if the property is not held in trust, the interest must be paid by an insurance company or by an organization regularly engaged in issuing interests otherwise meeting the requirements of a unitrust interest.

3. Gift Annuities

In this structure the donor purchases an annuity from a charitable organization in exchange for a contribution of property. If the value of the contributed property exceeds the value of the annuity received, an income tax charitable deduction may be obtained for the difference. On the other hand, if appreciated property is used to purchase the annuity, the donor may be required to recognize gain, which is spread over the term of the annuity. The advantage here is the deferral, but not the avoidance, of capital gain tax. If the annuity is extinguished by the donor's death, nothing is included in his or her estate except for any unconsumed annuity payments. If the annuity provides a survivor benefit, IRC §2039 will include the value of the survivor annuity in the estate (however, if the survivor is a spouse, the marital deduction may apply).

E. Testamentary Split-Interest Gifts

All of the split-interest gifts described in the preceding section can be structured in a testamentary fashion such that the estate of the donor plays the described role of the donor. The creation of a testamentary CRAT or CRUT with the surviving spouse as the sole noncharitable beneficiary satisfies the marital deduction requirements.[38] As noted several times above, a significant drawback to the testamentary approaches is the donor's loss of the income tax charitable deduction.[39]

38. *See* IRC §2056(b)(8).

39. Special planning considerations are presented in dealing with an IRA and other retirement accounts. For example, a charitable organization may be a designated beneficiary of an IRA. See Chapter 12, Section E.7, *supra*. The charity as a tax-exempt entity generally will not be required to recognize the income in respect of a decedent (IRD; *see* IRC §691) captured in the retirement account, yet the donor will receive an estate tax deduction for the value of the gift, permitting gifts of non-IRD property to other private beneficiaries. In some cases, this arrangement may involve the charitable organization's receipt of the IRA but with the creation of an annuity for the benefit of a private beneficiary. *See, e.g.*, Priv. Ltr. Rul. 2002-30-018 (July 26, 2002).

F. Conservation Contributions

There are a number of tax incentives for gifts that further environmental concerns.

1. Qualified Conservation Contributions

An income tax charitable deduction for a "qualified conservation contribution" is not required to be in trust.[40] Very generally, a qualified conservation contribution requires the contribution of a qualified real property interest, including the entire interest of the donor, a remainder interest, or a perpetual qualifying restriction to a qualified organization exclusively for conservation purposes. "Conservation purposes" include preservation of land for the general public, protection of a habitat, historic preservation, and preservation of open space for the scenic enjoyment of the general public.[41] A correlative gift tax deduction is provided by IRC §2522(c)(2). However, an additional gift tax deduction is provided for the grant of perpetual conservation restrictions that do not meet all of the requirements for an income tax deduction.[42] A testamentary conservation contribution will not provide the same income tax benefits, but IRC §2055 provides correlative estate tax deductions.[43] The Pension Protection Act of 2006 imposed additional limitations on the deductibility of so-called "facade easements" and for inclusion of property in registered historic districts.[44]

2. Qualified Conservation Easements

A drawback to a conservation easement is that the subject land is still subject to estate taxation upon the death of the donor, although the value of the land included in the estate is lower because of the prior conservation easement. The Taxpayer Relief Act of 1997 added IRC §2031(c), which permits a limited additional exclusion from the estate with reference to the value of land that is subject to a qualified conservation easement.

G. Private Foundations

Some individuals may desire greater continuing influence on the policies of the charitable organizations to which they are donating. Wealthy individuals may benefit from the creation of a private foundation, as compared with a public foundation, which draws a certain level of support from the

40. *See* IRC §170(f)(3)(B)(iii).
41. *See* IRC §170(h).
42. *See* IRC §2522(d).
43. *See* IRC §§2055(e)(2) & 2055(f).
44. *See generally* Fox, *supra* note 24, at 6-7.

general public.[45] Income tax deductible contributions may be made to the private foundation, subject to percentage limitations in IRC §170, which may be lower than the deductions allowed for gifts to public foundations and charities.[46] The charitable gift also removes those assets from the donor's estate.[47] The creator of a private foundation is able to exercise significant control in the selection of the foundation's managers, who ultimately will create and execute the foundation's charitable policies. Some parents see private foundations as a means to not only make charitable gifts and maintain some control over those gifts but as a measure to involve their adult children in philanthropic activities by making them trustees or directors of the family foundation(s).

While a private foundation can afford a significant degree of donor control over the use of the gifted funds, it has its drawbacks. First, as previously noted, the federal income tax deduction for contributions to private foundations may be limited to 30 percent of the contribution base (adjusted gross income excluding net operating losses) compared to 50 percent for other charities. Second, the formation and operation of a private foundation may involve significant legal and maintenance costs. Third, private foundations may be subject to an excise tax on investment income.[48] Fourth, private foundations may be subject to minimum distribution requirements, generally speaking, calculated as 5 percent of investment assets.[49]

H. Donor-Advised Funds

In response to the drawbacks of private foundations, private financial services companies began offering so-called "donor-advised" funds. Traditional charities, such as universities, have also begun offering donor-advised gift alternatives. Generally speaking, in this arrangement a donor contributes to a charitable conduit fund maintained by a sponsor. The donor enjoys the privilege to make nonbinding recommendations or give advice concerning the recipient of the gift, the manner in which the funds are invested pending distribution, and the timing of the distribution.[50] The sponsor usually receives a fee for its services, but the economies of scale produced by the pooling of funds from many donors make the cost structure and simplicity attractive to many donors. The donors claim a charitable income tax deduction subject to the

45. *See* IRC §509.
46. *See supra* note 16.
47. One commentary notes that almost 10 percent of Americans' gifts to nonprofit organizations in 1998 were to private foundations. *See* Sanford J. Schlesinger & Dana L. Mark, *The Private Foundation: Back in Vogue as a Charitable Giving Vehicle*, 26 Est. Plan. 386 (1999).
48. *See* IRC §4940.
49. *See* IRC §4942.
50. *But see* Richard L. Fox, *Nevada Supreme Court Lets Donor-Advised Fund Ignore Donor's Advice*, 38 Est. Plan. 9 (May 2011).

50 percent limitation when the property is contributed to the fund.[51] The donor-advised fund is an attractive alternative to the private foundation, unless the charitable gift is substantial[52] and the client desires an enduring philanthropic presence by his or her family.[53]

However, the Pension Protection Act of 2006 imposed a number of restrictions on donor-advised funds. While the legislation provides guidance in an area that was largely governed by general tax principles, it also makes the structure more restrictive (particularly in terms of donor control), complicated, and subject to the imposition of penalties. Indeed, some of the new restrictions resemble those imposed on private foundations, significantly diminishing the competitive edge once enjoyed by donor-advised funds.[54]

I. CASE STUDY 14-1

***Paul and Linda Davis* (Part V)**

ADDING PHILANTHROPY TO THE ESTATE PLAN

We continue with Paul and Linda Davis from case studies 5-1, 7-1, 8-1, and 13-1. This study focuses on Tanglewood Farms, described in Case Study 8-1. You should review those facts.

Paul's parents are considering a shift in their proposed plans for disposition of Tanglewood Farms, and they have asked you for recommendations that incorporate lifetime charitable gifts. They are particularly interested in the income tax advantages of charitable giving in light of the significant income that they will be required to report in connection with Paul's father's IRA once he attains age 70½.

Part A: Tanglewood Farms (which includes a family compound) would remain in the family as a private recreation area in spite of the advancing suburbs of a nearby city. Discuss structures that would accomplish these objectives as well as providing tax savings.

51. *See* Tanya D. Marsh, *supra* note 3, for a discussion of the operation of donor-advised funds.

52. What is substantial? Many advisors had generally recommended a minimum contribution of $5 million dollars to establish a private foundation. However, third-party professional service companies are now available that can handle the legal and administrative burdens of private foundations such that many clients are now considering establishing private foundations with assets of $1,000,000 or less.

53. *See generally* Joel M. Breitstein, *Donor-Advised Funds: A Good Vehicle for Charitable Planning*, 29 Est. Plan. 81 (2002) (comparing the advantages and disadvantages of donor-advised funds and private foundations); Janet Nava Bandera, *Summarizing the Differences Between Private Foundations and Donor-Advised Funds*, 25 J. Tax'n Inv. 90 (2008).

54. *See generally* John V. Woodhull, *Major Changes for Donor-Advised Funds*, 18 Tax'n of Exempts 217 (Mar./Apr. 2007); Gerald B. Treacy, Jr., *Cold Snap for DAFs*, 146 Tr. & Est. 49 (Jan. 2007); Kestenbaum & Perelman, *supra* note 24 at 205-206; Fox, *supra* note 24 at 9-12.

Part B: As an alternative plan, Tanglewood Farms would be donated to charity, but Paul's parents desire some economic return to family members, particularly in light of Tanglewood Farms' escalating real estate development value.

J. Reference Materials

Treatises

- BORIS I. BITTKER & LAWRENCE LOKKEN, FEDERAL TAXATION OF INCOME, ESTATES, AND GIFTS, ¶82.1.2 (3d ed. 2003 & Cum. Supp. 2011) (charitable remainder annuity trusts and unitrusts); ¶82.1.3 (pooled income funds); ¶82.1.4 (charitable lead trusts).
- BRUCE HOPKINS, THE TAX LAW OF CHARITABLE GIVING (4th ed. 2010 & Supp. 2011) (current law regarding charitable giving, including *Hubert*, and CRTs).
- WILLIAM M. MCGOVERN ET AL., WILLS, TRUSTS AND ESTATES §9.10 (4th ed. 2010) (charitable trusts).
- JOHN R. PRICE & SAMUEL A. DONALDSON, PRICE ON CONTEMPORARY ESTATE PLANNING §4.16 (2011) (testamentary cash gift to charity); ch. 8 (gifts to charitable organizations).
- RICHARD B. STEPHENS ET AL., FEDERAL ESTATE AND GIFT TAXATION: INCLUDING THE GENERATION-SKIPPING TRANSFER TAX ¶5.05 (8th ed. 2002 & Supp. 2011) (testamentary gifts to charity); ¶11.02 (inter vivos gifts to charity).

Articles

Overview of Charitable Giving Planning

- Vaughn W. Henry & Johni Hays, *How to Avoid Costly Mistakes in Charitable Planning*, 30 EST. PLAN. 78 (2003).
- Thomas F. Horton, *Effective Charitable Planning Strategies After the 2001 Tax Act*, 29 EST. PLAN. 580 (2002).
- Kathryn W. Miree, *Navigating the Landmines in Charitable Gift Planning*, 41 INST. ON EST. PLAN. ¶1000 (2007).
- Carolyn M. Osteen, *Charitable Gift Rules*, 15 ALI-ABA EST. PLAN. COURSE MATERIALS J. 17 (Aug. 2009).
- Conrad Teitell, *Charitable Giving Tax Strategies: Windfalls and Pitfalls*, 27 INST. ON EST. PLAN. ¶1100 (1993).
- Christopher Weems, *Charitable Giving in America*, 136 TR. & EST. 72 (Dec. 2000) (discussing trends in American charitable giving).

Charitable Remainder and Other Split-Interest Giving

- Byrle M. Abbin, *No More "Gravy Train": 1997 Law Revisions Dramatically Affect the Economics of CRT's—Only Those with True*

Charitable Motivation Should Create Them, 34 INST. ON EST. PLAN. ¶1400 (2000) (a comprehensive article discussing CRTs).

- Martyn S. Babitz & Lisa Susanto, *Charitable Lead Annuity Trusts: A Useful, but Neglected, Planning Tool*, 34 EST. PLAN. 21 (2007).
- Paul D. Callister, *Charitable Remainder Trusts: An Overview*, 51 TAX. LAW. 549 (1998).
- Paul D. Callister, *Charitable Remainder Trusts: An Overview*, 16 No. 2 GP SOLO & SMALL FIRM LAW. 52 (Mar. 1999).
- Carolyn C. Clark, *I Get a Kick Out of Unitrusts and Flip over NIM-CRUT's*, 32 INST. ON EST. PLAN. ¶1600 (1998).
- Christopher P. Cline, *Accelerated Charitable Trusts Provide New Gift Giving Opportunities*, 26 EST. PLAN. 59 (1999) (discussing planning to circumvent IRS regulations restricting CRTs.).
- Richard L. Fox, *A Guide to the IRS Sample Charitable Remainder Trust Forms*, 33 EST. PLAN. 13 (Jan. 2006).
- Richard L. Fox, *A Guide to the IRS Sample Charitable Lead Trust Forms—Part 1*, 36 EST. PLAN. 7 (Apr. 2009).
- Richard L. Fox, *A Guide to the IRS Sample Charitable Lead Trust Forms—Part 2*, 36 EST. PLAN. 13 (May 2009).
- Francis W. DuBreuil & Christopher J. Clarkson, *CLATs and Intra-Family Loans Provide Wealth Transfer Opportunities*, 37 EST. PLAN. 29 (Aug. 2010).
- Lawrence P. Katzenstein, *Charitable Remainder Trusts: Charity Can Begin at Home (with Form)*, 13 ALI-ABA EST. PLAN. COURSE MATERIALS J. 27 (Aug. 2007).
- Lawrence P. Katzenstein, *Drafting Charitable Lead Trusts and A Look at the IRS Lead Trust Forms (With Samples)*, 16 ALI-ABA EST. PLAN. COURSE MATERIALS J. 5 (Oct. 2010).
- David T. Leibell & Daniel L. Daniels, *CRTs and Difficult Assets*, 142 TR. & EST. 44 (Apr. 2003).
- Stephan R. Leimberg & Albert E. Gibbons, *Life Insurance as a Charitable Planning Tool, Part I*, 29 EST. PLAN. 132 (2002) (discussing use of life insurance gifts to a CRT).
- Michael G. May, *Choosing the Trustee of a Charitable Remainder Trust*, 24 EST. PLAN. 172 (1997).
- Scott M. Nelson, *Charitable Remainder and Lead Trusts: An Advisor's Thoughts*, 25 J. TAX'N INV. 30 (2007).
- Sanford J. Schlesinger, *Split Interest Charitable Trusts*, 39 INST. ON EST. PLAN. ¶1600 (2005).
- Sanford J. Schlesinger & Dana L. Mark, *Revisiting the Charitable Lead Trust*, 26 EST. PLAN. 86 (1999) (discussing charitable lead trusts as alternatives to a CRT).
- Pam H. Schneider, *The Intersection Between the Generation-Skipping Transfer Tax and Charitable Planning*, 41 INST. ON EST. PLAN. ¶1100 (2007).

- Roger D. Silk, *Charitable Remainder Trusts vs. Selling Assets and Funding a Private Foundation*, 139 TR. & EST. 36 (Oct. 2000) (evaluating differences between CRTs and private foundations).
- Sandra Brown Sherman & Daltesh D. Patel, *Pointers in Selecting Assets to Fund Charitable Trusts*, 29 EST. PLAN. 132 (2002) (discussing types of assets to fund CRTs).
- Winton C. Smith, *Charitable Giving Exit Strategies*, 40 INST. ON EST. PLAN. ¶800 (2006).
- Daniel Glen Worthington, *Revised Charitable Trust Rules: Rethinking Short-Term Trusts*, 139 TR. & EST. 20 (Mar. 2000) (discussing innovative ways to look at CRTs).

Donor-Advised Funds and Private Foundations

- Janet Nava Bandera, *Summarizing the Differences Between Private Foundations and Donor-Advised Funds*, 25 J. TAX'N INV. 90 (2008).
- Michael V. Bourland & Michelle Coleman-Johnson, *Public Charities and Private Foundations: Planning Alternatives*, Estate Planning for the Family Business Owner, SJ002 ALI-ABA 131 (ALI-ABA Continuing Legal Education, July 10-12, 2003).
- Michael V. Bourland et al., *Charitable Lead Trusts*, 15 ALI-ABA EST. PLAN. COURSE MATERIALS J. 19 (Feb. 2009).
- Joel M. Breitstein, *Donor-Advised Funds: A Good Vehicle for Charitable Planning*, 29 EST. PLAN. 81 (2002).
- Joel C. Dobris, *A Letter About Investing to a New Foundation Trustee, with Some Focus on Socially Responsible Investing*, 34 ACTEC J. 234 (2009).
- Richard L. Fox, *Nevada Supreme Court Lets Donor-Advised Fund Ignore Donor's Advice*, 38 EST. PLAN. 9 (May 2011).
- Jonathon E. Gopman & Harry J. Friedman, *A Primer on Foundations and Charitable Trusts*, 139 TR. & EST. 20 (May 2000) (overview of the use of private foundations).
- Tanya D. Marsh, *A Dubious Distinction: Rethinking Tax Treatment of Private Foundations and Public Charities*, 22 VA. TAX REV. 137 (2002).
- Jerry J. McCoy, *Property Contributions and Nontrust Techniques*, Charitable Giving Techniques, SM089 ALI-ABA 213 (ALI-ABA Continuing Legal Education, May 31-June 1, 2007).
- Kathryn W. Miree, *The Family Foundation: An Owner's Manual*, 35 INST. ON EST. PLAN. ¶1600 (2001).
- Carolyn M. Osteen, *More Than You Ever Wanted to Know about Private Foundations and Public Charities*, 30 INST. ON EST. PLAN. ¶1300 (1996).
- Doris Rubenstein, *Considering a Family Foundation? Consider This First*, 139 TR. & EST. 26 (Dec. 2000) (discussing private foundation planning).

- Sanford J. Schlesinger & Dana L. Mark, *The Private Foundation: Back in Vogue as a Charitable Giving Vehicle*, 26 Est. Plan. 386 (1999) (current trends in use or private foundations for charitable purposes).
- Sanford J. Schlesinger & Dana L. Mark, *Unrelated Business Income and the Charitable Organization*, 27 Est. Plan. 177 (2000) (impact on private foundations).
- Roger D. Silk, *When Is a Private Foundation an Appropriate Strategy?*, 27 Est. Plan. 87 (2000).
- Gerald B. Treacy, Jr., *Cold Snap for DAFs*, 146 Tr. & Est. 49 (Jan. 2007).
- John V. Woodhull, *Major Changes for Donor-Advised Funds*, 18 Tax'n of Exempts 217 (Mar./Apr. 2007).

Conservation Easements

- Shea B. Airey, *Conservation Easements in Private Practice*, 44 Real Prop. Tr. & Est. L.J. 745 (2010).
- Katherine S. Anderson & Marybeth K. Jones, *Conservation Easements: An Essential Tool in the Practitioner's Estate Planning Toolbox*, 35 Land & Water L. Rev. 183 (2000).
- Alexander R. Arpad, *Private Transactions, Public Benefits, and Perpetual Control Over the Use of Real Property: Interpreting Conservation Easements as Charitable Trusts*, 37 Real Prop. Prob. & Tr. J. 91 (2002).
- Brenda J. Brown, *Land Preservation Provides Estate Tax Benefits: Section 2031(c)*, 17 UCLA J. Envtl. L. & Pol'y 117 (1998-1999).
- John G. Cameron, Jr., *What You Should Know About Conservation Easements (With Form)*, 26 Prac. Real Est. Law. 9 (July 2010).
- Frederico Cheever, *Public Good and Private Magic in the Law of Land Trusts and Conservation Easements: A Happy Present and a Troubled Future*, 73 Denv. U. L. Rev. 1077 (1996).
- Laura Jean Kreissl & Karyn Bybee Friske, *IRS Takes a Hard Stance on Deductions for Conservation Easements*, 84 Prac. Tax Strategies 86 (Feb. 2010).
- Dominic P. Parker, *Land Trusts and the Choice to Conserve Land with Full Ownership or Conservation Easements*, 44 Nat. Resources J. 483 (2004).
- John C. Sawyer, *Conservation Easements Help Preserve Real Estate for an Owner's Family*, 26 Est. Plan. 68 (1999).
- James S. Sligar, *Estate Planning for Major Family Real Estate Holdings*, 133 Tr. & Est. 48 (Dec. 1994).

Income in Respect of Decedent and Retirement Plan Assets

- Christopher R. Hoyt, *The Family Wins When IRD Is Used for Charitable Bequests. How to Do It*, 36 Inst. on Est. Plan. ch. 4 (2002).

- Christopher R. Hoyt, *Treacherous Waters*, 148 Tr. & Est. 15 (Jan. 2009) (charitable bequests of IRD).
- Philip M. Lindquist, *Tax-Deferred Variable Annuities: 25% Economic Loss? 100% Taxation?*, 12 Prob. & Prop. 11 (Nov./Dec. 1998).

Miscellaneous Charitable Giving Issues

- Paul R. Comeau & Alexander M. Popovich, *Giving and Loaning Art to Charity*, 147 Tr. & Est. 38 (May 2008).
- Shane T. Hamilton, *Ethical Considerations When Representing Nonprofit and Tax-Exempt Organizations*, 21 Prac. Tax Law. 37 (2007).
- Lawrence P. Katzenstein, *Estates with Charities as Beneficiaries: How Do We Protect Their Interests?*, 15 ALI-ABA Est. Plan. Course Materials J. 45 (Feb. 2009).
- Jay W. Miller, *Donating Life Insurance to Charities Is Worth the Effort*, 36 Est. Plan. 22 (Oct. 2009).
- John C. Sawyer, *Problems in Administering Estates Having Charitable Beneficiaries*, 35 Est. Plan. 24 (Feb. 2008).

CHAPTER 15 Planning for Incapacity

A. Alternatives

As discussed in Chapter 3, the possibility of becoming incapacitated is not confined just to the elderly.[1] Young adults may become incapacitated as a result of illness or accidental injuries, so they too need protective planning measures such as durable powers of attorney, health care powers of attorney, and living wills. Nevertheless, as a practical matter, incapacity will be a greater and increasing likelihood for older clients, and the attorney must evaluate possible approaches to those problems. Although clients usually find this to be a surprise, many states do not repose any "default" legal authority in these matters to the spouse of the incapacitated individual. That places a premium on advance planning.

1. Conservatorship and Guardianship

Where an individual has not dealt with the issue through estate planning, a conservatorship will probably be necessary to manage the financial affairs of an incapacitated individual. As discussed in Chapter 7, conservatorships are subject to court supervision and can be costly and cumbersome. Even with other planning structures in place, a conservatorship may be unavoidable for some matters, such as, under Uniform Probate Code (UPC) §5-411(a)(7), the making, amending, or revocation of a protected person's Will or revocable trust. Likewise, if health care issues are not fully

1. "You are four to six times more likely to become incapacitated than you are to die in the next year, according to insurance industry morbidity statistics." RENNO L. PETERSON ET AL., 21ST CENTURY WEALTH: ESSENTIAL FINANCIAL PLANNING PRINCIPLES 136 (2000).

dealt with by health care powers of attorney, a judicially appointed guardian may be necessary.

2. Durable Power of Attorney

A durable power of attorney largely avoids the need for a conservatorship in dealing with the financial affairs of the incapacitated person. However, its authority may be limited. UPC §5B-108 (part of the Uniform Power of Attorney Act (2006)), for example, provides that if a conservator or guardian is subsequently appointed, the agent under the durable power of attorney is accountable to any court-appointed fiduciaries. In any event, the authority granted to an agent under a durable power of attorney varies from state to state.

3. Health Care Power of Attorney and Living Will

As discussed in Chapter 3, the health care power of attorney and a living will can provide coordinated guidance with respect to the medical care of the incapacitated person. Furthermore, encouraging a client to prepare such instruments usually leads to the client discussing these matters with his or her spouse, children, or designated agents, something they may otherwise postpone or never do.

4. Revocable Trust

A revocable trust is not confined to planning for incapacity; it can play a number of roles. The revocable trust can provide for the ultimate disposition of the protected person's assets, fulfilling the function of a Will. It can also provide for the lifetime management of assets, fulfilling the functions of a durable power of attorney and most of the functions of a conservatorship, as discussed in more detail in the next section.

B. The Revocable Trust

1. The Continuing Debate

While a revocable trust, often referred to as a "living trust," may serve an important role in the management of a protected person's assets during his or her lifetime, it also enjoys wide acceptance as a Will substitute that avoids probate or estate administration. The debate over the advantages and disadvantages of the Will and probate versus the revocable trust became a mainstream topic nearly a half-century ago,[2] and continues to this day. One still finds articles and commentary on why a particular side of

2. *See* Norman F. Dacey, How to Avoid Probate (1st ed. 1966).

the debate is or is not correct. We don't intend to repeat that debate, so we have included citations to some of those articles in the background materials listed in Part G below.[3]

Opinions on the desirability of a revocable trust as a Will substitute vary with the burdens imposed by the applicable probate laws. In a UPC state, for example, the attorneys, personal representatives, and other fiduciaries are compensated only for the value of time actually spent on a probate case. Most probate cases proceed from start to finish without the input of a judge. On the other hand, a person from a state in which compensation for any of those people is based on a percentage of the value of the assets of the estate, irrespective of time spent, or in a state where probate is a more protracted judicial process, would have a more jaundiced view of probate.

2. Advantages of the Revocable Trust

While we leave the full debate to others of the pros and cons of revocable trusts, in our view there are some advantages to be gained by their use.

a. Cost. If the state of administration permits attorney fees or personal representative commissions that are computed as a percentage of the value of the probate estate, the use of a revocable trust may reduce or eliminate the probate estate and the concomitant statutory fees. On the other hand, however, a trustee of a revocable trust will generally be eligible for compensation for services rendered, and in some jurisdictions these commissions are computed as a percentage of the trust estate, thus negating any cost advantage of the revocable trust. Even in jurisdictions where statutory "percentage fees" are the custom, family members serving as personal representatives could waive such commissions. Finally, while statutory attorney fees may be avoided if there is no probate estate, an attorney will usually be necessary to deal with the operation of the revocable trust in any event.

b. Speed. In UPC states, even a simple probate administration cannot be "closed" in fewer than six to nine months.[4] In states with more traditional probate, which requires court supervision or cumbersome appraisal procedures, that process may be significantly extended. The wait can seem like an eternity to the estate beneficiaries: they understandably want their inheritance. Moreover, the beneficiaries may see any delay as due to the attorneys "taking their cut."

3. *See, e.g.*, George M. Turner, Revocable Trusts ch. 64 (5th ed. 2003 & Supp. 2010) (reviewing the revocable trust versus probate debate).

4. Although, to be fair, in a simple estate the "closing" of the estate may have little practical significance. Because there are few, if any, statutory restrictions on the distribution of estate assets, assets may be distributable from the simple probate estate just as quickly as from a revocable trust, usually in a matter of weeks, if not days.

In comparison, a revocable trust becomes irrevocable with the death of the settlor, and provided that a successor trustee is in place, the distribution provisions of the trust could become operative immediately. If the estate is principally composed of simple assets such as bank accounts or publicly traded securities, the distributions could begin within weeks.[5]

However, distributions may still be delayed even if a revocable trust is used. Most personal representatives and trustees are wisely reluctant to distribute assets before the close of the period for filing claims against the estate. The potential liability of the fiduciary for unpaid taxes may also discourage early distributions. Consider that if a federal or state estate tax return is required, it may be filed up to nine months after the decedent's death (or later if automatic extensions are requested). Distributions of any significance may not be forthcoming until the return is accepted by the IRS, which may not occur until at least an additional 18 months or longer after the filing of the estate tax return. And, if the estate or trust holds complex assets such as real estate or collectibles that need to be sold, the distribution process may be further delayed.

It should also be appreciated that the advantage the revocable trust may have, if any, assumes that all of the important assets were titled in the name of the revocable trust prior to the death of the settlor—otherwise the probate process must be followed to transfer assets from the probate estate to the trust, an additional step further delaying distributions from the trust to the beneficiaries.

c. Closely Held Businesses. Although businesses can, as a practical matter, run for days without anyone inquiring about the authority of employees, a sole proprietorship is a particularly good asset to be held in a revocable trust.[6] Although many probate courts would permit an expedited appointment of a personal representative to operate the business, the trustee of a revocable trust may be authorized to operate the business as of the moment of the decedent's death. On the other hand, poor (or no) estate planning and the less sophisticated sole proprietorship business form in particular are often fellow travelers, so the revocable trust may not be a planned measure.

d. Ancillary Probate. Titling real property assets located in a state other than the decedent's state of domicile in a revocable trust may avoid ancillary probate in the foreign jurisdiction. This cannot be accomplished with a Will, but other approaches, such as the use of joint tenancies, transfer-on-death or beneficiary deeds (where available), and the

5. One commentator advises registration of any safe deposit box in the name of the revocable trust, so that the trustee has ready access to it after the decedent's death. *See* TURNER, *supra* note 3, §18:7.

6. If an entity such as a corporation or limited liability company is the business owner, the death of an officer/shareholder or manager/member will not paralyze operations if other officers or managers are already in place to serve in the operations roles of the deceased individual.

ownership of real property by an entity such as a limited liability company or limited partnership may just as effectively avoid ancillary probate.

*e. **Privacy.*** A Will may become a public document. A nontestamentary trust is generally a private document, although there may be some public filings of a registration form or the like.[7] Third parties, such as financial institutions, may require a copy of the revocable trust instrument during the settlor's lifetime, particularly when establishing title in the trust. However, this is often deflected through the preparation of a summary "certification" or "affidavit" document that makes representations as to the existence of a trust in lieu of delivering a full copy of the trust instrument.[8]

*f. **Management of Property.*** If the revocable trust is funded, it can provide a platform for management of the assets even if the settlor is not yet deceased or even incapacitated. If the settlor in fact becomes incapacitated, the detailed trustee powers spelled out in the trust will almost always be preferable to the costs and inflexibility of a judicial conservatorship or the possible gaps of authority for an agent acting under a durable power of attorney. A settlor who provides ongoing financial support for a child with special needs may be concerned about providing for both the needs of the settlor and the child in the event of the settlor's incapacity.[9]

*g. **Claims of Undue Influence or Lack of Capacity.*** If the decedent created a revocable trust and held assets in it for some time, some attorneys believe that this course of dealings may diminish claims of undue influence or lack of capacity regarding the disposition of the decedent's assets as compared to a Will.[10]

*h. **Choice of Law.*** The law of the decedent's domicile at death generally governs the probate administration. Language in a revocable trust instrument may, however, choose the applicable law and the site of administration of the trust.

3. Disadvantages of the Revocable Trust

There are several asserted disadvantages of the revocable trust.[11]

7. *See, e.g.*, UPC §7-101 (duty to register trusts but not necessarily the trust instrument itself).

8. *See, e.g.*, Unif. Trust Code §1013 (certification of trust procedure for disclosures to persons other than beneficiaries).

9. *See, e.g.*, Katherine N. Barr et al., *Top 15 Tips for Estate Planners When Planning for Special Needs*, 24 PROB. & PROP. 38, 40-41 (Mar./Apr. 2010) (example of special language for parent's revocable trust).

10. Although the revocable trust does provide more opportunity for establishing a settlor's course of dealings, the fundamental standard for capacity may not differ from that for a Will. *See, e.g.*, Unif. Trust Code §601 (capacity to create, amend, revoke, or add property to a revocable trust is the same as that required to make a Will).

11. The list of possible drawbacks is not exhaustive. Others include obscure issues such as liability for environmental contamination. *See, e.g.*, Thomas L. Stover, *Ten Good Reasons Not to*

a. Cost. A Will is usually less expensive to draft than a revocable trust[12] and a revocable–trust–based plan may be more expensive over time to maintain, particularly if the revocable trust is funded and the assets keep turning over. The greater cost might be justified for clients nearing life's end, but often revocable trusts are suggested for younger married couples. With decades of the trust's existence ahead of them, the lifelong costs of maintaining the trust must also be considered.[13]

b. Barring Creditors' Claims. If the estate is not probated because of the revocable trust, the claims of unknown creditors may not be barred as quickly as they would be under the probate approach of a general notice to creditors.

c. Tax Issues. There are possible tax drawbacks, such as IRC §2032 alternate valuation eligibility,[14] S corporation issues,[15] and the ability of an estate to use any fiscal year-end.[16]

d. Lifetime Complexity. Because assets need to be ultimately titled in the name of the revocable trust, transfers to the trust may raise practical property law issues, such as the impact on title insurance coverage and potential violation of due on transfer clauses in loan documents. Once the assets are titled in the revocable trust, further dealings, such as lending and insurance transactions, may be more complicated than if the property were held free of trust.

Avoid Colorado Probate, 25 COLO. LAW. 69 (Sept. 1996); Clifton B. Kruse, Jr., *Twenty-Six Reasons for Caution in Using Revocable Trusts*, 21 COLO. LAW. 1131 (June 1992); TURNER, *supra* note 3, ch. 64, *Practical, Ethical, and Persistent Objections in the Use of Revocable Living Trusts.* If the settlor of the trust has minor children, the attorney must confirm that a signed writing by a parent in the form of a revocable trust may appoint a guardian. Otherwise the pourover Will must serve that purpose. *Compare* UPC §5-202(a), which permits appointment "by will or other signed writing by a parent."

12. Compare the length and complexity of the simple Will (Form B) with the revocable trust (Form J) in the Forms Supplement. The latter is significantly more complex.

13. Proponents of the revocable trust, however, would point to the reduced costs of probate resulting from the use of revocable trusts. One publication asserts that a revocable trust for an estate valued under $675,000 would produce administration costs of less than one half of 1 percent, as compared with 5 to 6 percent average costs for probate, with the costs for larger revocable trust–based estates approaching three quarters of 1 percent. *See* ROBERT A. ESPERTI ET AL., THE LIVING TRUST WORKBOOK 18 (2001).

14. If the revocable trust divides the property into separate trusts upon the death of the settlor, the division may constitute a distribution under IRC §2032(a)(1). *See, e.g.*, C. Douglas Miller & R. Allan Rainey, *Dying with the "Living" (or "Revocable") Trust: Federal Tax Consequences of Testamentary Dispositions Compared*, 37 VAND. L. REV. 811, 819 (1984). This may be avoided if the assets are not distributed or allocated to trusts within six months of death, but that detracts from the claimed speed of administration.

15. In general, an estate may hold S corporation stock for the duration of its existence, while a nongrantor trust may do so only for two years following the decedent's death. *See* IRC §1361(c)(2). There are exceptions for "qualified Subchapter S" and "electing small business" trusts, but those present complications beyond the scope of this book.

16. The Taxpayer Reconciliation Act of 1997 added IRC §645, which permits an elective inclusion of the revocable trust in the decedent's estate for federal income tax purposes, thus solving one of the principal tax-related shortcomings of the revocable trust. *See, e.g.*, Myron Kove & James S. Kosakow, *Prop. Regs. Clarify Treating Revocable Trust as Part of Estate*, 28 EST. PLAN. 169 (2001); Amy K. Kanyuk, *IRC Section 645 Is Your Friend*, 142 TR. & EST. 26 (Dec. 2003).

e. Likelihood of Probate Anyway. It is our experience that many clients do not diligently and completely fund the revocable trust with all of their otherwise probate assets or, if they do, they neglect to rigorously acquire and hold all future acquisitions and transfers in the trust. Thus, a probate administration will be required anyway to "pour" or fund the omitted assets into the revocable trust, thus negating many of the expected benefits of the trust.

4. Mechanics

Form J in the Forms Supplement is a sample revocable trust.[17] There are some issues that need to be taken into account in creating a revocable trust.

a. Funding. A revocable trust can only operate on assets that are owned by the trust as of the date of death.[18] Due to perceived drawbacks of having assets titled in the trust during the settlor's lifetime (such as dealing with insurance, banks, etc.) or through simple inadvertence, many revocable trusts are not fully funded at death. If the settlor is incompetent, a preexisting durable power of attorney that specifically permits such conveyance becomes an important funding tool.[19]

b. Incapacity. Revocable trusts often state that the settlor remains the sole trustee so long as he or she is competent. The trust instrument often states that a trustee who becomes incompetent shall be deemed to have resigned and shall cease serving as a trustee. While the trust instrument will generally designate several alternate trustees in that event, the difficulty is in determining if the settlor, or a successor trustee, is, or has become, incompetent.

One solution is to have the settlor adjudicated incompetent, but this can involve a public proceeding at the price of the settlor's dignity and family harmony, and it partially defeats the objectives in creating a revocable trust to avoid judicial involvement, reduce costs, and maintain privacy.

Another solution may be to initially name cotrustees, with the settlor and the other trustee each able to act alone. While it is often intended that the nonsettlor cotrustee's power is to be used by the nonsettlor cotrustee only in the event of the settlor's incapacity, and the settlor could retain the

17. Form J is a revocable trust for an unmarried settlor. For an example of a revocable trust for a married individual, *see* FREDERICK K. HOOPS ET AL., FAMILY ESTATE PLANNING GUIDE, Appendix 4 (4th ed. 1994 & Supp. 2010-2011).

18. New York law provides that listing untitled assets in the trust agreement is not enough to subject them to the operation of the trust. *See* N.Y. EST. POWERS & TRUSTS §7-1.18 (West 2002). For a sample client reminder letter regarding funding, see Robert H. Feldman, *What to Look for in Reviewing Estate Plans (with Forms)*, 17 NO. 3 PRAC. TAX LAW. 53, 59 (Spring 2003).

19. Some attorneys advise the client not to sign a general power of attorney but to confine the power of attorney only to transferring property to the revocable trust. *See, e.g.*, ESPERTI ET AL., *supra* note 13, at 11-12.

power to remove the cotrustee for misdeeds committed prior to the settlor's incapacity, the possibility that the cotrustee may act alone in advance of incapacity could be unacceptable to the settlor.[20]

In many cases a settlor for whom imminent incapacity is foreseeable will voluntarily resign his or her trustee position in advance of becoming incapacitated. However, looming incapacity is not always presented—accidents and sudden illnesses could instead precipitate the incapacity. And, even for settlors with gradually deteriorating capacity, the nature of the illness, the settlor's personality, or sheer neglect of the legal aspects of the situation may preclude a voluntary resignation by the settlor.

A common solution was to provide an express procedure for the determination of the settlor's incompetency in the trust agreement itself, such as the following language:[21]

> *If at any time, in the written opinion of the trustee's attending physician and one other licensed physician nominated by a majority of the group composed of any other trustee then acting and settlor's living adult children, a trustee acting hereunder is physically or mentally incapacitated to such an extent that the trustee is unable to give prompt and intelligent attention to trust affairs, then, as of the date of the later of the two physician's letters, such trustee shall be deemed to have given written notice of trustee's resignation in such manner as required hereunder to properly effect such a resignation. By agreeing to serve, the individual trustee waives any physician/patient privilege that might prevent any physician from expressing an opinion in writing as to the trustee's physical or mental condition.*

This solution was never without complications, because at a minimum it required letters from two physicians. The stringent patient privacy provisions of the Health Insurance Portability and Accountability Act of 1996 (HIPAA)[22] have contributed to difficulties in obtaining medical information about the settlor. These HIPAA considerations have produced a number of suggested measures such as: the settlor's delivery to the other beneficiaries of a continuing waiver of his or her HIPAA privacy rights at the time of executing the trust agreement (coupled with immediate removal as trustee upon the settlor's revocation of the waiver); requests for a HIPAA waiver by the trustee at the time of alleged incompetency (coupled with immediate removal as trustee upon failure to furnish such

20. *But see* Martin M. Shenkman, *Planning for Clients with Multiple Sclerosis*, 146 Tr. & Est. 19 (July 2007) (recommending a co-trustee from inception, with exceptions for significant decisions for settlors suffering from chronic illnesses, such as multiple sclerosis, where the settlor can experience temporary debilitating flare-ups of the illness).

21. A self-help guide to drafting revocable trusts provides for three individuals (other than the successor trustee) who will determine, by a majority vote, whether the trustee is incapacitated. *See* Denis Clifford, Make Your Own Living Trust, 83, 131-132 & Form 1, Section III(D) (10th ed. 2011).

22. Pub. L. No. 104-191, 110 Stat. 1936 (1996).

waiver); and the settlor's delivery of letters from two physicians at the time of alleged incompetency concluding that the settlor is not incapacitated (coupled with immediate removal as trustee upon failure to furnish the letters at all or failure to furnish a "clean" trustee-is-competent letter).[23]

Form J in the Forms Supplement uses a more streamlined approach to this issue by permitting a majority of the other trustees and beneficiaries to remove the settlor as trustee upon an asserted disability. At first blush this would appear to place unacceptable levels of control in the other parties. However, if the settlor is incompetent, this provides a simplified way to remove him or her — that shouldn't be overlooked. In addition, the trust document's selection of successor trustees can dictate who will take his or her place upon removal. Moreover, if the settlor is still competent, he or she can simply revoke the trust or provide evidence of capacity.

And, finally, a non-interested person, or perhaps a trust protector, could be given the power to remove a trustee (or any fiduciary) at any time for no reason whatsoever. While clearly this style of process should result in the most efficient, timely, and seamless management of the trust, many settlors may be uncomfortable giving such a broad, unbridled power to anyone.

The importance of this issue extends beyond the obvious need for continuity in management authority; it also recognizes that the trust instrument's provisions for distributions are often modified during the settlor's incompetence, shifting from an open-ended approach that assumes the settlor is the trustee to one governed by a standard, such as the health, education, support, and maintenance of the settlor, the settlor's spouse, and the settlor's descendants (see Form J, paragraph 2.2, for an example).

c. Pourover Wills. As noted above, it is possible, if not probable, that significant assets owned by the settlor will not be titled in the revocable trust as of his or her death. It is standard practice to have the settlor execute a Will that "pours over" all such assets to the revocable trust (see Form I in the Forms Supplement).[24] Accordingly, a standard revocable trust "package" includes the revocable trust, a pourover Will, and a durable

23. *See generally* Martin M. Shenkman, *Estate Planning Documents Need to Address HIPAA Issues*, 36 Est. Plan. 14 (Mar. 2009); Jacqueline Myles *Crain*, *HIPAA-A Shield for Health Information and a Snag for Estate Planning and Corporate Documents*, 40 Real Prop. Prob. & Tr. J. 357 (2005); Daniel B. Evans, *What Estate Lawyers Need to Know About HIPAA and "Protected Health Information,"* 18 Prob. & Prop. 20 (July/Aug. 2004); Michael L. Graham, *Important HIPAA Compliance Issues for the Estates and Trusts Lawyer*, 39 Inst. on Est. Plan. ¶800 (2005); Michael L. Graham & Jonathan G. Blattmachr, *Planning for the HIPAA Privacy Rule*, 29 ACTEC J. 307 (2004); Thomas J. Murphy, *Drafting Health Care Proxies to Comply with the New HIPAA Regs.*, 30 Est. Plan. 559 (2003); Thomas J. Murphy, *Dealing with HIPAA: Powers of Attorney, Record Releases, Court Orders, and Subpoenas*, 5 Marq. Elder's Advisor 183 (2004).

24. If the revocable trust does not contain special dispositions such as a marital deduction subtrust or a protective trust for other beneficiaries, some attorneys question the wisdom of pouring over the leftover assets into the revocable trust. The probate of the pourover assets can delay the distribution of the revocable trust. The use of a backup Will instead that does not pour over into the revocable trust would, arguably, confine the distribution delay to just the probated assets. *See, e.g.*, Clifford, *supra* note 21, at 219-220.

power of attorney (which, at a minimum, will allow for funding the trust in the event of the settlor's incapacity).

d. Tax Issues. Because the trust remains revocable until the settlor's death, its creation and funding do not result in a completed gift for federal gift tax purposes.[25] It is generally a "grantor trust" for federal income tax purposes, so the settlor reports all of the trust income directly on his or her individual income tax return.[26] The trust property is included in the settlor's estate for federal estate tax purposes.[27] There are no estate tax advantages to holding or disposing of assets by either a Will (through probate) or by revocable trust (outside of probate). Like a Will, a revocable trust executed by a married individual may contain language and instructions creating marital and family trust shares at the death of the settlor.

While most revocable trusts are grantor trusts for federal income tax purposes during the settlor's lifetime, upon the settlor's death the trust becomes a taxable entity that files an annual Form 1041 federal income tax return.[28] An estate is also a taxable entity, and it too files a Form 1041 federal income tax return. Although similar, the income tax rules for estates and trusts are different in some respects. IRC §645 permits the executor of an estate and the trustee of certain revocable trusts to elect to treat the trust as part of the estate for federal income tax purposes. If no estate and no executor exist, the trustee of the revocable trust may still execute this election.[29]

C. Long-Term Care Alternatives

The preceding material emphasized the treatment of the financial affairs of the disabled or incompetent individual. However, with the inevitable consequences of the aging process the daily care of the individual eventually may become the primary concern, eclipsing the strictly financial and asset disposition planning. That said, long-term care in the United States has an unavoidable financial aspect to it as well. As discussed in the next section, paying for that care is a concern for most individuals.

A number of long-term care alternatives are available for elderly or disabled clients, and the aging of the general U.S. population would suggest that the number of offerings will expand.[30]

25. *See* Treas. Reg. §25.2511-2(c) (as amended in 1999).
26. *See* IRC §676.
27. *See* IRC §2038.
28. Some grantor trusts are not required to file income tax returns during the settlor's lifetime. However, if the trust earns postmortem income, an income tax return may be required.
29. *See supra* note 16.
30. *See generally* Lawrence A. Frolik, *Housing Options for the Older Client*, 13 ALI-ABA Est. Plan. Course Materials J. 23 (Feb. 2007).

1. Family Members

Care by family members in their homes or that of the client is an option if there is an available and willing family caregiver. Indeed, one account reports that family members and friends are the sole caregivers for approximately 70 percent of the elderly.[31] Even if there is such a family caregiver, the needs of the ward may exceed the ability or training of the caregiver.

2. Sporadic Home Health Care

In many cases the elderly individual requires only limited help in their own home. There are many forms of assistance, including weekly housecleaning; weekly visits from a nurse; daily visits from a health worker, who helps with dressing, bathing, meals, and scheduling medications; use of a portable medical alert device; and daily deliveries of prepared meals under the auspices of the government-sponsored "Meals on Wheels" program. Modifications to the individual's home may be necessary, such as construction of a walk-in shower, installation of handrails, grab bars, ramps, and so forth. At some point, the condition of the individual may require more intensive care. Some individuals' financial resources and the nature of their care requirements may permit them to remain in their home and to use the services of a full-time in-home caregiver. For others, circumstances may dictate a move out of their current residence.

3. Congregate and Assisted Living

There are many variations on this theme. At one extreme the individual may move to an "adult community" where there is little focus on personal care inasmuch as the congregate living is intended for "young," active retired individuals. The focus is on smaller, low-maintenance residences, recreational facilities, available group dining events, convenient transportation, and planned social activities.

If personal care and safety issues become a greater concern, the individual may move to an "assisted living" area designed for the elderly or disabled, but where the individual may still occupy a separate apartment. The bathroom facilities are typically handicapped-accessible and include an emergency call cord; there are convenient elevators and ramps where necessary; the hall corridors have handrails; and so forth. The assisted living facility usually provides and coordinates transportation for the tenants plus offers exercise and recreation programs, as well as optional group dining programs.

If the individual requires additional assistance, he or she may still occupy a separate apartment, but the facility will provide more comprehensive services such as all meals, laundry, and housekeeping. In some cases the facility may also provide assistance with dressing, bathing, and

31. *See* Robert R. Pohls, *Long Term Care Insurance*, 32 Brief 28 (Fall 2002).

using the toilet. Alternatively, the individual may become a boarder in a group home, where meals and some supervision are available, but the level of care is not as broad as is the case with a skilled nursing facility.

4. Skilled Nursing Facility

Some assisted living complexes include a "skilled nursing" wing or other facility. These facilities are staffed with health care providers around the clock and provide not only basic medical care to the tenants, but often full surgical facilities. The condition of the individual may ultimately require this level of care, which is similar to, but generally below, that provided by hospitals. By one account, approximately 15 percent of long-term care is in a nursing home setting.[32]

5. Hospice Care

Hospice care is designed for terminally ill patients who are entering the final stages of the dying process. Emphasis is often on palliative care to reduce the signs and symptoms the patient may be experiencing and to make the patient as comfortable as possible. While such care often is provided in the individual's home, the level of care necessary may require transfer to a residential hospice facility.

D. Financing Long-Term Care

Under the current structure of the U.S. health care and entitlement system, the primary burden of paying for long-term care falls on the individual unless he or she qualifies for Medicaid assistance.[33]

1. Private Income and Savings

Although the costs vary widely by locale, the annual cost of care in a skilled nursing facility may approach $70,000 or more. If both spouses require such care, the costs are potentially doubled. The reported average stay in a nursing home is roughly two years, but a significant percentage will stay for five years or more.[34] Women on average have longer stays than men. Factors such as preexisting conditions and family medical history will

32. *See* Michael A. Kirtland, *Considerations in Purchasing Long-Term Care Insurance*, 64 ALA. LAW. 188, 189 (May 2003).

33. *See generally* Michael Wytychak III, *Payment of Nursing Home Bills Through the Medicaid Program*, 36 IDAHO L. REV. 243 (2000); Lawrence A. Frolik, *Paying for Long-Term Care*, EXPERIENCE 35 (Fall 2006); Richard L. Kaplan, *Retirement Planning's Greatest Gap: Funding Long-Term Care*, 11 LEWIS & CLARK L. REV. 407 (2007).

34. One account states that the average stay is more than two years, with 10 to 20 percent of the patients staying for five years or more. *See* Pohls, *supra* note 31, at 28. Another account places the average stay at 2.4 years. *See* Kirtland, *supra* note 32, at 189.

adjust these probabilities. Wealthier individuals will have the income and/or assets available to fund those expenses. Less wealthy individuals may not, in which case Medicaid assistance, discussed in Part E below, supplies the funding. The most difficult planning questions are those of the "middle class," who have some income or assets but are unwilling to exhaust those resources before resorting to Medicaid assistance. That issue is briefly discussed in the next section.

2. Long-Term Care Insurance

Certain long-term care insurance contracts qualify for federal income tax treatment comparable to accident and health care insurance. Generally speaking, premium payments are treated as medical expense itemized deductions, and the benefit payments are generally excluded from income.[35] Only "qualified long-term care insurance contracts" receive this treatment, and that status is accorded only to contracts providing for certain services and consumer protections.

The price of long-term care insurance is generally a function of the individual's age at the time of acquiring the insurance. Thus, premiums will be higher the later the insurance is obtained. The price is also a function of the individual's overall health, and the price may be increased or coverage denied altogether for some preexisting conditions such as kidney dialysis treatments, receipt of disability payments, or diagnosis of diseases such as Alzheimer's or Parkinson's.[36]

The Patient Protection and Affordable Care Act[37] created a new, voluntary long-term care insurance program, the Community Living Assistance Services and Supports (CLASS) program. For employees who do not opt out, employers choosing to participate in CLASS will withhold premiums that vary with the employee's age. An alternative program will be developed for self-employed individuals and individuals with non-participating employers. It is expected that CLASS will be implemented in 2012 or 2013.[38]

3. Accelerated Death Benefits and Viatical Settlements

It is increasingly common for life insurance contracts to include "living benefit" or "accelerated death benefit" provisions that permit the payment of life insurance proceeds to a terminally or chronically ill individual prior

35. *See generally* IRC §7702B; Vorris J. Blankenship, *Tax Issues Complicate the Costs of Chronic Illness and Long-Term Care Insurance*, 107 J. TAX'N 216 (Apr. 2007).

36. *See generally* Kirtland, *supra* note 32; Cynthia L Barrett, *Long Term Care Insurance and the Elder Law Practice (with Questionnaires for Clients and Fiduciaries)*, 13 ALI-ABA EST. PLAN. COURSE MATERIALS J. 51 (Feb. 2007); Lawrence A. Frolik, *Points to Consider Before Buying Long-Term Care Insurance*, 37 EST. PLAN. 20 (July 2010). *See also* http://www.longtermcareinsurance.org (last visited Aug. 27, 2011).

37. Pub. L. No. 111-148.

38. *See generally* Paul N. Van de Water, *CLASS: A New Voluntary Long-Term Care Insurance Program*, Center on Budget and Policy Priorities (Apr. 16, 2010), http://www.cbpp.org/cms/index.cfm?fa=view&id=3156 (last visited Aug. 27, 2011).

to his or her death. These accelerated death benefits can be a source of funding for the costs of the individual's care. The receipt of the benefit may be exempt, wholly or in part, from federal income tax.[39]

In some cases the insured will sell his or her future death benefits to a private party in return for immediate funds. These "viatical" or "life" settlements are generally sought by individuals who own policies that do not contain an accelerated death benefit provision, or the individual does not meet the "terminally ill" or "chronically ill" requirements of the policy.[40]

4. Reverse Mortgages

Elderly individuals who own a home may consider a so-called "reverse mortgage." Generally speaking, the individuals borrow against their homes, receiving a periodic or monthly payment, or only as needed, for their living expenses (which may include health care costs but could include the cost of other items, such as vacations). The home is sold upon the death of the owners, and the mortgage principal and accrued interest are repaid with the sales proceeds. The amount that the owners may borrow is largely a function of the home's value and the owners' life expectancies.[41]

5. Medicare and Medicaid

Medicare pays only for very limited stays in a skilled nursing facility. Medicaid, a welfare program predicated on the individual's lack of significant income or assets, is the primary government assistance for long-term care.[42]

This area is full of pitfalls for the client and attorney alike. Clients may engage in some attempts at self-help through the transfers of property to

39. Accelerated death benefits for a terminally ill insured may generally be received free of income tax, but benefits for a chronically ill insured are free of income tax only if used to defray costs of care. *See generally* IRC §101(g).

40. *See generally* Andrew Spurrier, *The Death of Death Futures: The Effects of the Health Insurance Portability and Accountability Act of 1996 on the Insurance and Viatical Settlement Industries*, 4 Conn. Ins. L.J. 867 (1997-1998) (discussing background and federal income tax treatment of accelerated death benefits and viatical settlements); Bernard Eizen & Victor S. Levy, *New and Expanded Uses of Viatical Settlements in Insurance Planning*, 26 Est. Plan. 475 (1999); Morton P. Greenberg & C. Andrew Graham, *Life Settlements: A New Option for Excess Life Insurance*, 31 Colo. Law. 99 (Oct. 2002); Jessica Maria Perez, *You Can Bet Your Life on It! Regulating Senior Settlements to Be a Financial Alternative for the Elderly*, 10 Elder L.J. 425 (2002); James C. Magner & Stephan R. Leimberg, *Life Settlement Transactions: Important Tax and Legal Issues to Consider*, 34 Est. Plan. 3 (2007); Stephan R. Leimberg et al., *Life Settlements: How to Know When to Hold and When to Fold*, 35 Est. Plan. 3 (Aug. 2008).

41. *See generally* Reverse Mortgages: A Lawyer's Guide to Housing and Income Alternatives (David A. Bridewell & Charles Nauts eds., 1997); Celeste M. Hammond, *Reverse Mortgages Can Provide Cash Up Front*, 86 ABA J. 62 (May 2000); http://www.aarp.org/money/credit-loans-debt/reverse_mortgages/ (last visited Aug. 27, 2011); http://assets.aarp.org/www.aarp.org_/articles/revmort/AARPmodelspecifications.pdf (last visited Aug. 27, 2011); D. Steve Boland, *Reverse Mortgages Can Help Seniors Meet Their Financial Needs*, 36 Est. Plan. 29 (Sept. 2009).

42. Medicaid assistance is not limited to nursing home care and can include costs such as home health aides and supplies under some circumstances. *See* Kaplan, *supra* note 33, at 422-423.

family members before applying for benefits. In addition to the loss of the property and its benefits, such transfers may disqualify the client for Medicaid benefits. For the attorney, some traditional estate planning techniques, such as the use of revocable trusts for home ownership, may have potentially adverse consequences in terms of Medicaid benefits.[43] This technical and somewhat state-specific area is overviewed in the next section.

E. Public Assistance Issues

The impact of public assistance on estate planning is a complex and shifting overlay of federal rules on an additional layer of state and local rules and enforcement. An attorney practicing in this area needs to have an affinity for administrative detail, and a background in social work is a plus.

> *[Note: The discussion below is an extremely broad and nontechnical overview of the area and should not be relied on without further research, particularly because the legal issues are constantly evolving and are subject to wide variations under differing state laws.]*

The issues in this area are produced by the intersection of a public assistance system that assumes little or no assets or income by a qualifying person, usually someone who is age 65 or older, blind, or disabled, with situations in which there is private wealth available for the benefit of the person who desires public assistance. For example, an independent mentally disabled individual may be eligible for a modest stipend under Social Security Disability (SSD)[44] or Supplemental Security Income (SSI),[45] food stamps assistance, subsidized "Section 8" housing, and Medicaid benefits. Medicaid is a welfare system for medical care administered by the states under a federal umbrella. Only Medicaid provides for long-term care. Eligibility is in part tied to income and asset levels. Planning generally focuses on maintaining eligibility by not exceeding the income or asset limits.[46] While the financial aspects of the disabled person's care are important, planning must also address matters such as medical treatment decisions, selection of caregivers, and education.[47]

43. *See infra* note 62.

44. This is a disability benefit for the disabled child of a worker covered by Social Security. The disability must have arisen prior to the child's 22nd birthday.

45. This is the more commonly applied benefit available to (1) citizens age 65 and older and (2) blind or disabled individuals of any age.

46. Medicare, on the other hand, is a system of medical insurance primarily for the elderly without means-testing. It allows only short-term stays in nursing home facilities.

47. *See* Sebastian V. Grassi, Jr., *Estate Planning for a Family with a Special Needs Child*, 23 Prob. & Prop. 15 (July/Aug. 2009).

A common concern for clients who have a condition requiring long-term institutional care is qualifying for Medicaid so that it will pay for much of the cost. The planner often encounters at least four different scenarios, although this is by no means an exhaustive list.

First, in establishing a trust or drafting a Will for a client, the attorney must consider the impact on a potential beneficiary who is not then receiving nor is expected to receive public assistance but nonetheless may require it sometime in the future due to some unforeseen event that produces debilitating injuries, or the onset of illness. The drafting solution is typically a contingent trust, the terms of which anticipate the public assistance considerations.

Second, in dealing with the future care of an incapacitated person who is currently or is expected to be on public assistance, the attorney may be asked by other family members (often parents or siblings) to create a trust, often referred to interchangeably as a "supplemental care trust," "supplemental needs trust," or sometimes as a "special needs trust,"[48] for the benefit of the incapacitated person.

Third, an individual with special needs may have his or her own resources, typically from the settlement of a personal injury lawsuit (but not enough for complete support), that will be placed in a special needs trust for the individual's benefit, but without significantly impairing eligibility for public assistance.

Fourth, in dealing with the care of a person who requires institutional care, whether due to age, illness, or incapacity, the attorney may be faced with questions about eligibility for public assistance and possible transfers of assets, such as to other family members, so that they are not consumed by the costs of the care.

All four scenarios have public assistance concerns as a background issue. In the first situation the settlor or testator usually does not want to gift property to a person on public assistance only to see it considered an available resource of the individual to be consumed in replacing funds that otherwise would be provided by public assistance. The second and third situations differ in terms of the source of the assets. If someone other than the disabled person is providing the assets (a "third-party trust"), the planning will resemble that for the first situation above. On the other hand, if the planning involves the transfer of the disabled person's own assets (e.g., proceeds of a tort judgment or the property of a person who becomes disabled) to a trust or other structure, the planning goal is often to preserve the assets as a future source of *additional* support of the disabled person without disqualifying the person for public assistance. In the fourth situation, the individual wishes to dispose of his or her property

48. As demonstrated by the titles of articles cited in this chapter, the "Supplemental Needs Trust" and "Special Needs Trust" descriptions are used interchangeably. In some cases the local practice of the public assistance agency will dictate the selection of a title.

before applying for public assistance so that the assets are not consumed by the costs of his or her own care.

1. Scenario #1—Third-Party Supplemental Needs Trusts for Contingent Disability or Long-Term Care of a Beneficiary

This scenario addresses general drafting measures for an unpredictable future event, such as if the beneficiary of a Will or trust unexpectedly becomes disabled after the applicable instrument is executed.[49] Indeed, "anyone can become a special needs child in just a matter of seconds."[50]

Common drafting responses include a combination of: (a) instructing the fiduciary to retain any property for the disabled beneficiary in a continuing trust until the disability has ceased (if ever), making distributions of principal or income only in the trustee's sole and absolute discretion not pursuant to a support standard, and in a manner so as to maximize medical or public assistance benefits; (b) including a strong statement of the settlor's intent that the trust assets be used only to supplement, not supplant or diminish, public assistance benefits that would otherwise be available to the beneficiary, coupled with authority to amend or reform the trust if necessary to fully carry out such intent; (c) inclusion of a strong spendthrift provision denying trust assets to the beneficiary's creditors, including government agencies (although spendthrift clauses generally are not enforced against government agencies); and (d) directing the disposition of the trust's corpus (typically to other family members) upon the disabled beneficiary's death. These drafting measures evolved, along with the judicial and legislative responses to them, into a topic that is outside the scope of this book.[51] However, examples of sample language for this purpose are widely available.[52]

2. Scenario #2—Third-Party Supplemental Needs Trusts for a Beneficiary with Known or Expected Disability or Long-Term Care Requirements

The drafting measures here are very similar to those in Scenario #1, except that this situation often employs a specially designed trust for the benefit of an individual who is already disabled or expected to be disabled in the future. The planning challenge is consequently much more immediate, and the instrument will likely be more comprehensive than the contingent

49. The beneficiary, or a conservator acting in his or her behalf, could disclaim the interest, but the disclaimed assets would generally still be considered a resource of the beneficiary. *See* Joel C. Dobris et al., Estate and Trusts 158-159 (3d ed. 2007).

50. Grassi, *supra* note 47, at, 17.

51. For a discussion of the development of the law in this area from feudal England to the present day, *see* Joseph A. Rosenberg, *Supplemental Needs Trusts for People with Disabilities: The Development of a Private Trust in the Public Interest*, 10 B.U. Pub. Int. L.J. 91 (2000).

52. *See, e.g.*, Grassi, *supra* note 47, at 18 (sample contingent trust language).

provisions in Scenario #1.[53] The settlor of the trust is a person other than the beneficiary, and the trusts consequently are often referred to as "third-party" arrangements. The trust may be a free-standing inter vivos trust or a testamentary trust, depending upon the timing of the transfers and other considerations. While these complications could be avoided through an outright gift to another family member, with a precatory request that the funds be utilized for the benefit of the disabled individual, the protections of a trust are lost in terms of dissipation of the funds for other purposes, lack of successor management if the family member predeceases the disabled individual, and lack of assured transmission of any remainder upon the death of the disabled individual.

As with Scenario #1, the trust needs to navigate the sometimes asymmetrical shoals of disqualifying the beneficiary for the applicable types of public assistance, principally SSI and Medicaid. Indeed, the trust will often be created for a beneficiary who is already eligible for such assistance. The preservation of eligibility is accomplished primarily by ensuring that the trust assets are not considered a resource of the beneficiary, and that distributions are not considered as disqualifying income. The trust instrument provides that the trust assets are to provide only for additional needs (consequently the "supplemental" care or needs trust description) of the beneficiary beyond what would otherwise be provided by public assistance. The instructions to the trustee generally reflect that distributions may be made that only supplement, but do not supplant, benefits otherwise available from public assistance (e.g., the trust usually will not permit distributions to the beneficiary for basic food, clothing, or housing). The beneficiary does not have the power to revoke the trust, or the trust assets will be considered a financial resource of the beneficiary. The beneficiary or his or her spouse should not serve as the trustee.[54]

As a practical matter, the types of "needs" that may be supplied by this kind of trust are extremely limited, and the types of needs may have different impacts for SSI or Medicaid purposes. For example, distributions from the trust may be treated as income for SSI purposes, and cash distributions will usually be counted as income unless a specific exclusion applies.[55] However, in-kind distributions, such as a nonrefundable airline ticket, that cannot be converted into food, clothing, or shelter are not treated as an income resource for SSI purposes.[56] In-kind distributions, even for food, clothing, and shelter, may not reduce SSI benefits to the same degree as cash distributions[57] but may disqualify the recipient for

53. *See, e.g.*, Jeffrey N. Pennell, *Special Needs Trusts: Reflections on Common Boilerplate Provisions*, 6 NAELA J. 89 (2010) (commentary on an extensive, inter vivos, supplemental needs trust instrument).

54. *See* Sterling I. Ross, Jr., *The Special Needs Trust: A New Wrinkle No More*, 36 Inst. on Est. Plan. ¶¶ 1600, 1602.2D (2002).

55. *Id.* at 1601.1D.5.

56. *Id.*

57. *Id.* at 1601.1D.6.

Medicaid assistance. Careful and informed drafting is of paramount importance.[58]

EXERCISE 15-1

PAUL AND LINDA DAVIS (PART VI)

We continue with Paul and Linda Davis from case studies 5-1, 7-1, 8-1, 13-1, and 14-1. Linda and Paul added to their family from Case Study 8-1, with the birth of Amanda Rebecca Davis, age 2 (born May 15, two years ago). The other children, John and Abigail, are now ages 17 and 14, respectively. Amanda is a Down's child, and it is Paul and Linda's plan that she reside with them as long as possible, with a transition to a group home if necessary.

A. What planning measures should Paul and Linda consider in light of Amanda's special needs?
B. Assuming that Paul and Linda choose a testamentary trust to provide for Amanda, draft the provisions of the trust that would be included in their Wills.

3. Scenario #3 — First-Party (Self-Settled) Trusts by a Known Beneficiary

A first-party trust is distinguished from the third-party arrangements discussed above by the fact that the beneficiary (or someone acting on his or her behalf) is the settlor of the trust. Trusts of this type established after August 10, 1993, are subject to specific federal law, which generally will not consider the trust assets as a resource of the beneficiary if certain requirements are satisfied. If the requirements are not satisfied, federal law otherwise generally treats the assets of self-settled trusts as resources of the settlor, regardless of whether the trust is discretionary. Some commentators prefer the "special needs trust" description for this type of trust due to favorable name recognition with government agencies.[59] In that regard, a new attorney working in this area should not rely on labels attached to trusts because there are overlaps and local differences in the use of terminology.

Generally, the beneficiary may not revoke the trust, or the trust assets will be considered an immediately available resource. The trust must be

58. *Id.* at 1604 (sample trust language provisions). For an example of a special needs trust governed by Michigan law, see HOOPS ET AL., *supra* note 17, Appendix 32. *See generally* Ira S. Wiesner, *Special Needs Trusts*, 142 TR. & EST. 24 (June 2003); Sebastian V. Grassi, Jr., *Estate Planning for a Special Needs Child Requires Special Planning (With Sample Forms)*, 22 No. 1 PRAC. TAX LAW. 23 (Fall 2007); Marcia J. Boyd & J. David Seay, *Special Needs Trusts to Benefit the Mentally Ill Client or Family Member*, EXPERIENCE 25 (Summer 2007); Grassi, *supra* note 47, at 18 (sample trust language); JEFFREY A. SCHOENBLUM, PAGE ON THE LAW OF WILLS, ch. 76AF (2d ed. 2010) (special needs clauses); L. RUSH HUNT, ESTATE PLANNING FORMS (2009) (includes drafting for beneficiaries with special needs); STEPHEN ELIAS, SPECIAL NEEDS TRUSTS (rev. ed. 2007).

59. *See* Ross, *supra* note 54, at 1600.3D.

established while the beneficiary is under the age of 65, although the trust may continue after age 65 if properly qualifying at the outset. Finally, upon the death of the beneficiary, the trust must pay to the state an amount equal to the total medical assistance (i.e., Medicaid) paid on behalf of the beneficiary.[60] In contrast, third-party trusts generally do not include this payback requirement; they would instead pass any residue to other remainderpersons.

4. Scenario #4 — Other First-Party Dispositions to Qualify for Assistance

An unmarried individual generally cannot qualify for Medicaid unless he or she is practically destitute.[61] However, some assets may not be considered resources, such as a primary residence,[62] cars, and funeral plots ("exempt" assets).[63] Medicaid also has maximum qualifying income levels that must be considered. Consequently, the transfer of nonexempt assets can be used as a planning tool.

Usually the transfer is made to family members (usually adult children or grandchildren)[64] by the individual well in advance of seeking assistance. Prior to the enactment of the Deficit Reduction Act of 2005[65] (DRA 2005) discussed below, Medicaid law generally imposed a lookback period of 36 months such that any assets disposed of within 36 months of the application for assistance were considered as assets of the applicant that must be spent down for care before public assistance would commence.[66] If the assets were in trust (possibly including a revocable trust) the

60. *Id.* at 1603.1.

61. This general overview assumes an unmarried individual. If only one spouse is institutionalized, the other spouse is referred to as the "community spouse." He or she is permitted to retain a residence and automobile with no limits on value, plus other assets referred to as the "community spouse resource allowance." The treatment of the community spouse's income is subject to rules beyond the scope of this overview. *See* Kaplan, *supra* note 33, at 425-427 (discussing the community spouse rules). The assets of the community spouse may be subject to estate recovery claims by the state when the community spouse dies. *Id.* at 429.

62. Under certain conditions, the individual's equity in a principal residence may be an exempt asset for purposes of Medicaid eligibility (subject to caps discussed in the text that follows) so long as the individual intends to return home (which intent is typically interpreted quite liberally), subject to a potential recovery action by the state upon the individual's death to collect the benefits paid. However, the individual may lose the Medicaid eligibility exemption for the home if it is transferred to a revocable trust. *See generally* Gary Mazart, *Protecting the Home in Government Benefits Planning*, 164 N.J. LAW. 34 (Oct. 1994); Lilian M. Jacquard, *Preserving and Planning for the Principal Residence*, 51 R.I. B.J. 11 (Jan./Feb. 2003); Dennis M. Sandoval, *Get Medicaid, Keep the House*, 142 TR. & EST. 29 (July 2003). For a discussion of the loss of the home exemption upon transfer to a revocable trust, see HOOPS ET AL., *supra* note 17, §30:13; Clifton B. Kruse, J. *The Untoward Effect of Revocable Trusts on Medicaid Eligibility*, 26 COLO. LAW. 83 (Sept. 1997).

63. *See* Clifton B. Kruse, Jr., *Medicaid Considerations for Lawyers Representing the Upper Crust*, 33 INST. ON EST. PLAN. ¶700, 701.2 (1999). Some assets that are "exempt" for purposes of qualifying for Medicaid may nevertheless later be subject to recovery claims by the state upon the individual's death for the cost of care. *See* Kaplan, *supra* note 33, at 429-430 (describing Medicaid estate recovery rules).

64. If the individual is married, the spouse's assets and income are a consideration, subject to the "community spouse" rules. *See supra* note 61.

65. Pub. L. No. 109-171, 120 Stat. 4 (2005).

66. The 36 months was only the period of the lookback. The spend-down period could be a shorter or longer period, depending on the value of the asset transferred and the cost of care.

lookback period could be extended to 60 months before the application for assistance.

One hoped that if the individual transferred all of his or her property outright to family members more than 36 months prior to applying for Medicaid benefits, he or she would be considered to have little countable income or asset resources.[67] This structured poverty might strike some as fraudulent — or at least unethical. Congress apparently shared that view to a limited degree, and in the Health Insurance Portability and Accountability Act of 1996 added criminal penalties for asset transfers within 36 or 60 months, as the case may be, prior to an application for Medicaid benefits. Those provisions were repealed and replaced by 1997 legislation[68] that apparently made attorneys criminally liable for counseling clients to partake in such transfers. Although the Department of Justice is currently not bringing criminal prosecutions under this provision, the existence of the statute still warrants caution on the part of attorneys.[69]

Congress again responded to Medicaid planning measures in DRA 2005, effective as of February 8, 2006. DRA 2005 significantly restricts the planning measures described above. For example, DRA 2005 generally imposes a cap on the amount of the personal residence exemption.[70] DRA 2005 also generally extends the lookback period to 60 months for all transfers.[71] In addition, if a transfer falls within the lookback period, the period of ineligibility does not begin to run until the individual applies for Medicaid. The legislation addresses a number of other issues[72] beyond the scope of this discussion. Still, some planning opportunities remain, particularly if transfers are made outside of the lookback period.[73]

This type of planning remains a serious matter that requires special knowledge much beyond this general overview.

67. Some planning involves the client's formation of an irrevocable trust with other family members as remainderpersons, but with the client retaining an income-only interest in the trust (no distributions of principal) that complies with the Medicaid income tests. The initial transfer to the trust, however, was subject to the 60-month lookback period. *See, e.g.*, David Goldfarb, *Use of Trusts in Medicaid Planning in New York, reprinted in* Martin Petroff, *Medicaid Qualifying Trusts & Medicaid Supplemental Needs Trusts: Planning Options for the Elderly and the Disabled*, (320 PLI/Est 375, 381 PLI Tax Law and Est. Plan. Course Handbook Series No. D0-009L, Sept. 2002) (discussing New York law and providing sample trust forms).

68. *See* Balanced Budget Act of 1997, Pub. L. No. 105-33, 111 Stat. 251, 522 (1997).

69. *See, e.g.*, New York State Bar Ass'n v. Reno, 999 F. Supp. 710 (N.D.N.Y. 1998) (granting preliminary injunction against enforcement of the provisions; in 1999, the government's appeal was dismissed by the Court of Appeals for the Second Circuit); Magee v. United States, 93 F. Supp. 2d 161 (D.R.I., 2000) (denying motion for preliminary injunction).

70. *See* Michael Gilfix & Bernard A. Krooks, *Asset Preservation and Long-term Care*, 20 Prob. & Prop. 34, 35-36 (Nov./Dec. 2006) ($500,000 limit on eligible home equity, but each state has the option to increase the cap up to $750,000); Michael Gilfix, *Planning for the Home Under Tougher Medicaid Rules*, 35 Est. Plan. 27 (Mar. 2008).

71. Gilfix & Krooks, *supra* note 70, at 36-37.

72. *Id.* at 37-39 (discussing the implications for annuities, partial months of ineligibility, the community spouse resource allowance, continuing care retirement communities, and long-term care insurance). *See also* Michael Gilfix & Bernard A. Krooks, *Screwed*, 146 Tr. & Est. 45 (Jan. 2007).

73. *See, e.g.*, Shirley B. Whitenack et al., *The Revival of the Income-Only Trust in Medicaid Planning*, 36 Est. Plan. 32 (Jan. 2009); Matthew J. Marcus, *Many Effective Medicaid Planning Strategies Still Exist after the DRA*, 35 Est. Plan. 24 (Oct. 2008).

F. CASE STUDY 15-1

Janice Green

THE ELDERLY CLIENT IN PHYSICAL DECLINE

Janice Matilda Green, age 85, never married and is childless. Her closest living relatives are two nieces, Ellen Chase Summers, age 50, and Isabel Bertin-White, age 46, both of whom live in other states approximately 1,200 miles away. Ellen and Isabel have not visited or seen their aunt in at least 20 years.

Ellen is married and has two children: Ellen Ashley Summers, age 25, and Jack Stewart Summers, age 20. Isabel is married and has three children: Victoria Bertin-White, age 20; Sarah Bertin-White, age 15; and Foster Robert Bertin-White, age 10.

Janice retired at age 70 after a 50-year career with various corporate iterations of a regional telephone company. She receives a monthly pension of approximately $1,500 and a monthly Social Security benefit of $800. She owns a small house that she bought in 1954 for $12,000. It is now appraised at $150,000 and is unencumbered. Janice has always been extremely thrifty and was a consistent and savvy investor. The value of her investments in certificates of deposit, Treasury securities, equity mutual funds, and some selected "Blue Chip" stocks is approximately $2,000,000. She dips into her investments on rare occasions, such as to purchase a new car (in recent years she drives only short distances) or to travel (she has not traveled much in recent years, particularly after the death of her sister, the mother of Ellen and Isabel).

Janice has always been good with numbers and detail, but she has increasingly been having difficulty in keeping track of her investments and balancing her checkbook. Her broker has been helping her with those tasks but has recently indicated that it is becoming a burden. Janice has also noticed that she is increasingly forgetful. Her physician attributes her difficulties as being part of the normal aging process. However, it concerns Janice. Some friends have suggested that Janice might consider an assisted living situation. Janice rejects that idea. She has always led an independent life, is very comfortable with her home and surroundings, and doesn't want to be "surrounded by old people." On the other hand, she doesn't relish the intrusion, nor the cost, of an in-home caregiver or domestic. For her financial matters at least, she might consider the advisory services of a local trust company, Independent Trust Advisors, 1200 Pine Blvd., MyCity, MyState 80000.

Janice has a Will that she executed in 1955. It passes all of her property to her sister or her sister's descendants, "per stirpes."

Part A: Evaluate the use of a joint tenancy for Janice's home and POD and TOD designations for her investments to minimize the probate of her estate.

Part B: Based on Janice's overall circumstances, discuss what planning documents you would suggest in updating her 1955 Will.

Part C: Using Forms I and J from the Forms Supplement as a guide, draft a pourover Will and revocable trust for Janice.

G. Reference Materials

Treatises

- Denis Clifford, Make Your Own Living Trust (10th ed. 2011).
- Stephen Elias, Special Needs Trusts (rev. ed. 2007).
- Robert A. Esperti et al., The Living Trust Workbook (2002) (a book designed for consumers that offers a number of forms, particularly for funding the revocable trust).
- Carla Neeley Freitag, The Funding of Living Trusts (2004).
- Lawrence A. Frolik & Melissa C. Brown, Advising the Elderly or Disabled Client: Legal, Health Care, Financial and Estate Planning (2d ed. 1992 & Supp. 2011).
- L. Rush Hunt & Lara Rae Hunt, A Lawyer's Guide to Estate Planning—Fundamentals for the Legal Practitioner, §5.24 (3d ed. 2004) (special needs trust); §15.8 (Will form containing special needs trust language).
- L. Rush Hunt, Estate Planning Forms (2009) (includes drafting for beneficiaries with special needs).
- Clifton B. Kruse, Jr., Third-Party and Self-Created Trusts—Planning For The Elderly and Disabled Client (3d ed. 2001).
- William M. McGovern et al., Wills, Trusts and Estates ch. 14 (4th ed. 2010) (planning for incapacity).
- Doug H. Moy, Living Trusts (3d ed. 2003).
- John R. Price & Samuel A. Donaldson, Price on Contemporary Estate Planning §§10.07-10.17 (2011) (revocable trusts).
- Margaret S. Price, The Special Needs Child and Divorce: A Practical Guide to Evaluating and Handling Cases (2009).
- George M. Turner, Revocable Trusts (5th ed. 2003 & Supp. 2010).

Articles

Overall Planning Issues

- D. Steve Boland, *Reverse Mortgages Can Help Seniors Meet Their Financial Needs*, 36 Est. Plan. 29 (Sept. 2009).
- Raymond Bornhoft, *Estate Planning, An Opportunity to Map the Future for an Elderly Client*, 35 Ark. Law. 12 (Spring 2000).

- Lawrence A. Frolik, *The Challenges of Estate Planning with a Very Old Client*, 34 EST. PLAN. 3 (2007).
- Stephan R. Leimberg et al., *Life Settlements: How to Know When to Hold and When to Fold*, 35 EST. PLAN. 3 (Aug. 2008).
- Wayne Moore & Monica Kolasa, *AARP's Legal Services Network: Expanding Legal Services to the Middle Class*, 32 WAKE FOREST L. REV. 503 (1997).
- Ken Ransford, *Financial Abuse of Elderly Adults*, 23 COLO. LAW. 1077 (May 1994).

Planning for Incapacity

- Maureen S. Bateman & Mark W. Smith, *The Incapacitated Trustee*, 145 TR. & EST. 28 (Feb. 2006) (drafting trusts with the possibility that the fiduciary becomes mentally incapacitated or otherwise unavailable).
- Lawrence A. Frolik, *Points to Consider Before Buying Long-Term Care Insurance*, 37 EST. PLAN. 20 (July 2010).
- Sebastian V. Grassi, Jr., *Estate Planning for a Special Needs Child Requires Special Planning (with Sample Forms)*, 22 NO. 1 PRAC. TAX LAW. 23 (Fall 2007).
- Sebastian V. Grassi, Jr., *Estate Planning for a Family with a Special Needs Child*, 23 PROB. & PROP. 15 (July/Aug. 2009).
- Michael A. Kirtland, *Dealing with Mental Capacity Issues in Estate Planning*, 30 EST. PLAN. 192 (2003).
- Judith W. McCue, *Planning for the Elderly Disabled*, 29 INST. ON EST. PLAN. ¶1600 (1995) (discussing the considerations in planning an estate for a disabled or possibly disabled person).
- Abraham J. Perlstein, *Comprehensive Future Care Planning for Disabled Beneficiaries*, 27 EST. PLAN. 358 (2000).
- Michael Schuster, *Planning for Incapacity*, 279 PRAC. LAW INST. 411 (July 1999) (discussing living wills and health care proxies, as well as consequences of lack of planning).
- Martin M. Shenkman & Joshua Rubenstein, *Chronic Illness: Practical Planning and Drafting, Part 2*, 25 PROB. & PROP. 48 (Mar./Apr. 2011).
- Martin M. Shenkman, *Estate Planning Documents Need to Address HIPAA Issues*, 36 EST. PLAN. 14 (Mar. 2009).
- Ronald T. Staeball, *Securing the Future of a Child with a Disability*, 139 TR. & EST. 43 (Aug. 2000) (discussing minors and disabilities).
- Peter J. Strauss, *The Geri-Hat-Trick: Three Goals of Estate Planning for the Elderly*, 24 INST. ON EST. PLAN. ¶1300 (1991) (discussing management of an elderly decedent's estate).

Deathbed Planning

- Jonathan G. Blattmachr & Mitchell M. Gans, *Deathbed Planning*, 24 TR. & EST. 23 (Dec. 2002).

- Richard M. Horwood & Jeffrey A. Zaluda, *Planning Strategies When a Client's Death Is Imminent*, 20 EST. PLAN. 168 (1993).
- Suzanne Tucker Plybon & James R. Robinson, *Estate Planning for Procrastinators: Those Who Wait Until the Last Minute*, (Part I) 28 EST. PLAN. 422, (Part II) 28 EST. PLAN. 486 (2001).

Durable Powers of Attorney

- Russell E. Haddleton, *The Durable Power of Attorney: An Evolving Tool*, 14 PROB. & PROP. 58 (May/June 2000) (overview of the durable power of attorney).
- Russell E. Haddleton, *The Durable Power of Attorney Is on the Way*, 24 PROB. & PROP. 50 (May/June 2010).
- Andrew H. Hook & Thomas D. Begley, Jr., *The Elder Law Durable Power of Attorney, 29* EST. PLAN. 538 (2002).
- Michael S. Insel, *Durable Power of Attorney Can Alleviate Effects of Client's Incapacity*, 22 EST. PLAN. 37 (1995).
- Jerry L. Lerman, *Make Sure That a Durable Power of Attorney Is Truly Durable*, 33 TAX ADV. 222 (Apr. 2002) (general discussion of powers of attorney).
- Peter B. Tiernan, *Gift-Giving by an Agent Under a Durable Power of Attorney*, 26 EST. PLAN. 372 (1999).
- Peter B. Tiernan, *Florida Durable Powers of Attorney: Exploring the Limits of an Agent's Authority*, 76 FLA. B.J. 34 (July/Aug. 2002) (durable power of attorney considerations for Florida practitioners).
- Daniel A. Wentworth, *Durable Powers of Attorney*, 17 PROB. & PROP. 37 (Nov./Dec. 2003).

Revocable Trusts

- Roy M. Adams, *The Revocable Trust*, 139 TR. & EST. 57 (Jun. 2000) (discussing current considerations for revocable trusts).
- Ralph M. Engel, *The Pros and Cons of Living Trusts as Compared to Wills*, 29 EST. PLAN. 155 (2002).
- Bette Heller et al., *Joint Revocable Trusts*, 26 COLO. LAW. 63 (Aug. 1997).
- Myron Kove & James S. Kosakow, *Prop. Regs. Clarify Treating Revocable Trust as Part of Estate*, 28 EST. PLAN. 169 (Apr. 2001) (brief discussion of recent tax law changes regarding revocable trusts).
- Robert E. Madden & Lisa H.R. Hayes, *Administration Expense from Revocable Trust Not Deductible*, 27 EST. PLAN. 124 (2000) (discussing tax treatment of administration expenses in the context of revocable trusts).
- L. William Schmidt, Jr., *How to Fund a Revocable Living Trust Correctly*, 20 EST. PLAN. 67 (1993).

- Jay D. Waxenberg & Henry J. Leibowitz, *Comparing the Advantages of Estates and Revocable Trusts*, 22 EST. PLAN. 265 (1995).

Public Assistance Planning

- Katherine N. Barr et al., *Top 15 Tips for Estate Planners When Planning for Special Needs*, 24 PROB. & PROP. 38 (Mar./Apr. 2010).
- Cynthia Barret, *Family Member Liability for Nursing Home Costs*, EXPERIENCE 24 (Winter 2007).
- Thomas D. Begley, Jr. & Andrew H. Hook, *The Reason for Medicaid Planning*, 29 EST. PLAN. 642 (2002).
- Martha A. Churchill & Patricia E. Kefalas Dudek, *Adults with Disabilities: Prepare for the Future with a Special Needs Trust*, 79 MICH. B.J. 1360 (Oct. 2000) (discussing special needs trusts for adults).
- David J. Correira, *Disability Trusts that Allow a Client to Qualify for Medicaid*, 30 EST. PLAN. 233 (2003).
- Bradley E.S. Fogel, Scylla *and* Charybdis *Attack: Using Trusts for Medicaid Planning and Non-Medicaid Asset Protection*, 35 ACTEC J. 45 (2009).
- Lawrence A. Frolik, *Paying for Long-Term Care*, EXPERIENCE 35 (Fall 2006).
- Lawrence A. Frolik, *Basic Medicaid: Paying for Nursing Home Care*, 13 ALI-ABA EST. PLAN. COURSE MATERIALS J. 11 (Apr. 2007).
- Michael Gilfix & Bernard A. Krooks, *Asset Preservation and Long-Term Care*, 20 PROB. & PROP. 34, 35-36 (Nov./Dec. 2006).
- Michael Gilfix, *Planning for the Home Under Tougher Medicaid Rules*, 35 EST. PLAN. 27 (Mar. 2008).
- Sebastian V. Grassi, Jr. & Nancy H. Welber, *Estate Planning with Retirement Benefits for a Special Needs Child: Part 1—Understanding Retirement Plan Distribution Rules*, 23 PROB. & PROP. 28 (July/Aug. 2009).
- Sebastian V. Grassi, Jr., *Estate Planning for a Family with a Special Needs Child*, 23 PROB. & PROP. 15 (July/Aug. 2009).
- Diana C. Jacque et al., *Gerontology and the Law: A Selected Annotated Bibliography: 1999-2001 Update*, 76 S. CAL. L. REV. 699 (2003) (includes references to materials on long-term care and Medicaid estate planning).
- Katrina S. Jones & Marco D. Chayet, *Resolving a Medicaid Claim in a Decedent's Probate Estate*, 37 COLO. LAW. 31 (Feb. 2008).
- Richard L. Kaplan, *Retirement Planning's Greatest Gap: Funding Long-Term Care*, 11 LEWIS & CLARK L. REV. 407 (2007).
- Clifton B. Kruse, Jr., *Medicaid Considerations for Lawyers Representing the Upper Crust*, 33 INST. ON EST. PLAN. ¶700 (1999).
- Carole C. Lamson, *Supplemental Needs Trusts Offer Planning Options for the Disabled*, 320 PRAC. L. INST. 417 (Sept. 2002) (summary of special needs trusts and their benefits).

- Matthew J. Marcus, *Many Effective Medicaid Planning Strategies Still Exist after the DRA*, 35 EST. PLAN. 24 (Oct. 2008).
- Jeffrey N. Pennell, *Special Needs Trusts: Reflections on Common Boilerplate Provisions*, 6 NAELA J. 89 (2010).
- Abraham J. Perlstein, *Comprehensive Future Care Planning for Disabled Beneficiaries*, 27 EST. PLAN. 358 (2000) (brief discussion of special needs trusts).
- Joseph A. Rosenberg, *Supplemental Needs Trusts for People with Disabilities: The Development of a Private Trust in the Public Interest*, 10 B.U. PUB. INT. L.J. 91 (2000) (tracing the history and effectiveness of special needs trusts).
- Sterling I. Ross, Jr., *The Special Needs Trust: A New Wrinkle No More*, 36 INST. ON EST. PLAN. ¶1600 (2002).
- Shirley B. Whitenack et al., *The Revival of the Income-Only Trust in Medicaid Planning*, 36 EST. PLAN. 32 (Jan. 2009).

Professional Ethics (See also "Client Conflicts" in Ch. 1 reference materials.)

- Teresa Stanton Collett, *The Ethics of Intergenerational Representation*, 62 FORDHAM L. REV. 1453 (1994).

The Client Interview (See also same heading in Ch. 1 reference materials.)

- Marla Lyn Mitchell-Cichon, *What Mom Would Have Wanted: Lessons Learned from an Elder Law Clinic About Achieving Clients' Estate Planning Goals*, 10 ELDER L.J. 289 (2002).

CHAPTER 16

Federal Wealth Transfer Tax Principles and Planning Strategies

A. An Overview of the Federal Wealth Transfer Taxes

1. A Brief Overview

The Internal Revenue Code imposes an excise tax, separate from the income tax, on the transfer of wealth from one individual to another. Based on the amount of tax revenues produced, the principal tax is the federal estate tax imposed on the value of a decedent's estate.[1] A federal gift tax is imposed on the donor of lifetime gifts of property.[2] With the enactment of the Tax Reform Act of 1976, the estate and gift taxes were "unified" in the sense that the same rate schedule was applied, post-1976 gifts were factored into the computation of the estate tax, and a single credit, with some exceptions, could be applied to the payment of either or both.[3] However, the Economic Growth and Tax Relief Reconciliation Act of 2001[4] (EGTRRA) temporarily unlinked the applicable exclusion amount prescribed by IRC §2010 for the estate tax from an applicable exclusion amount of $1,000,000 per individual prescribed by IRC §2505 for the gift tax. The Tax Relief, Unemployment Insurance Reauthorization,

1. *See* IRC §2001.
2. *See* IRC §2501.
3. *See* IRC §§2505 & 2010.
4. Pub. L. No. 107-16, 155 Stat. 38 (2001).

and Job Creation Act of 2010[5] (2010 Act) re-unified the applicable exclusion amount for estate and gift taxes, effective for gifts made after December 31, 2010.

The gift and estate taxes are imposed on the transfer of wealth, which usually occurs on transfers of property from one generation to another. Aware of this, planners attempted to avoid the sequential, generation-by-generation imposition of those taxes by skipping generations (that the donor deemed already had, or would receive, sufficient wealth) and transferring wealth to younger or future generations (such as grandchildren or beyond). A principal feature of this generation-skipping planning was the creation of long-term trusts that employed beneficial interests (sometimes accompanied by powers of appointment) that were structured to be exempt from gift or estate taxes otherwise imposed on the beneficiaries. Such tax avoidance planning was belatedly addressed by the enactment of the third federal wealth transfer tax, the generation-skipping transfer tax (GSTT).[6] The operation of the GSTT is also discussed in connection with dynasty trusts in Chapter 13.

2. A Summary of the Gift Tax

a. Defining "Property" and "Gift." The gift tax is imposed on the "transfer of property by gift."[7] While some planning skirts the definition of "property" and accordingly the gift tax (e.g., gratuitous provision of personal services, introductions to business opportunities, and loan guarantees), most transfers of money, securities, collectibles, and real estate fall squarely within the definition such that valuation is usually the pivotal issue.[8] While the regulations suggest that donative intent is not a factor in determining whether a gift has occurred (outside of transfers made in the ordinary course of business[9]), most gifts in family situations do indeed demonstrate donative intent.

b. Completion of the Gift. While there is much doctrine dealing with whether gifts are "complete" and therefore taxable, or incomplete and therefore not taxable,[10] most gifts in a planning context are complete; although the requirements for completeness in terms of the gift tax versus

5. Pub. L. No. 111-312, 124 Stat. 3296 (2010).
6. *See* IRC §2601
7. *See* IRC §2501.
8. Below-market loans are a special category dealt with by IRC §7872.
9. One is to simply compare the value of what was relinquished with the value, in money or money's worth, of what was received. *See* IRC §2512(b) ("Where property is transferred for less than an adequate and full consideration in money or money's worth, then the amount by which the value of the property exceeded the value of the consideration shall be deemed a gift."); Treas. Reg. §25.2511-1(g)(1) (as amended in 1997) ("Donative intent on the part of the transferor is not an essential element in the application of the gift tax to the transfer."); and Treas. Reg. §25.2512-8 (as amended in 1992) ("However, a sale, exchange, or other transfer of property made in the ordinary course of business (a transaction which is bona fide, at arm's length, and free from any donative intent), will be considered as made for an adequate and full consideration in money or money's worth.").
10. *See* Treas. Reg. §25.2511-1 (as amended in 1997) & Treas. Reg. §25.2511-2 (as amended in 1999).

the estate tax are not entirely consistent, incomplete gifts generally will not avoid the later imposition of the estate tax and may be less favored for that reason.

Planners regularly encounter three common situations for which completion doctrine plays a role, and for which they must understand the gift tax consequences. First, a creation of a joint bank account is generally not a gift to the noncontributing owner, while the creation of a joint tenancy in real estate is generally a completed gift.[11] The different outcomes turn on the donor's power to undo the former (by a complete withdrawal of the account funds), while lacking that power with respect to the latter. Second, the funding of a revocable trust, sometimes referred to as a "living trust," is not a completed gift because of the retained power of revocation.[12] Third, because of the donor's power to undo a gift (due to a lack of legal consideration), a gift by regular check to a noncharitable donee is not complete until the donee presents the check for payment, the check is paid by the drawee bank when first presented, and the donor is alive when the check is paid by the drawee bank.[13] Timing of the completion is very important in this context, because the annual gift exclusion may not be effective in the year desired or the exclusion may be lost altogether if the donor prematurely dies.

c. The Annual Exclusion. As discussed in the planning strategy discussion, which follows in Part B, gift planning focuses on maximizing use of the annual gift exclusion, and that exclusion is generally unavailable for gifts in trust unless the formalities of the *Crummey* doctrine are followed. Annual gifts and *Crummey* withdrawal powers are discussed in Chapter 8.

d. Lapse of Powers of Appointment. While crafting powers of appointment has an important estate tax component,[14] there is a technical gift tax aspect as well. If a person is given a general power of appointment, the lapse of that power is not considered a gift of property to the extent that the value of the property that could have been appointed does not exceed the greater of $5,000 or 5 percent of the assets from which the exercise of the power could be satisfied.[15] General powers of appointment in nonmarital trusts, for example, are almost always drafted in compliance with these so-called "5 or 5" guidelines. As discussed in Chapter 8, a *Crummey* withdrawal power is a general power of appointment, so the structure and extent of the power must consider this gift tax rule so as to avoid a deemed taxable gift by the *Crummey* powerholder.

11. *Compare* Treas. Reg. §25.2511-1(h)(4) & (5) (as amended in 1999). With two owners, the donor and the donee, the completed gift is of an undivided one-half interest in the property rather than an interest in the entire property.

12. *See* Treas. Reg. §25.2511-2(c) (as amended in 1999). Revocable trusts are discussed in Chapter 15.

13. *See* Rev. Rul. 96-56, 1996-2 C.B. 161 (adopting a multi-part test for determining completion and the year of the gift).

14. *See* IRC §2041.

15. *See* IRC §2514(e).

e. Value Reduction and Shifting. Again, as demonstrated by the estate planning discussion in Part B, many of the remaining gift tax issues involve valuation (particularly discounts), freeze structures (e.g., self-canceling installment notes (SCINs), private annuities, and sales to defective trusts), retained interest deductions (i.e., GRATs, GRUTs, and QPRTs) and the use of disclaimers.

f. The Applicable Exclusion Amount. Each donor has a lifetime $5,000,000 inflation-adjusted applicable exclusion amount.[16] Married couples can each fully utilize that amount, even if only one of the spouses is the donor, by using a gift-splitting election.[17] The maximum gift tax rate is 35 percent, but it is scheduled to increase to 55 percent for gifts made after 2012 if the 2010 Act is not extended or replaced.[18] The future of rates and the applicable exclusion amounts is subject to a great deal of uncertainty, as discussed later in Part B.2 of this chapter.

g. The Gift Tax Return. The federal gift tax return, Form 709, is an annual filing, due by April 15 of the year following the year of the completed gift.[19] An extension of the time for filing the individual's individual income tax return generally extends the time period for filing the gift tax return for that year.[20]

3. A Summary of the Estate Tax

The estate tax is imposed on the decedent's taxable estate,[21] which is determined by subtracting certain deductions from the gross estate. Compared with the gift tax, there are more available deductions.

a. Gross Estate. For a U.S. citizen or resident alien, IRC §2033 provides that the gross estate includes the value of all property, worldwide, to the extent of the decedent's interest at the time of his or her death.[22] For the most part, this is a simple category, but it may include a significant amount of wealth in the form of financial assets and real estate. It roughly resembles the probate estate of the decedent plus nonprobate assets such as certain interests in trusts (e.g., reversions or remainders) and employee benefits. Other nonprobate assets, such as joint bank accounts or life insurance insuring the decedent, are addressed by more targeted sections of the Internal Revenue Code, such as IRC §§2040 and 2042, respectively.

16. *See* IRC §2505 referencing IRC §2010.
17. *See* IRC §2513. A gift tax deduction is also available for transfers between spouses. *See* IRC §2523.
18. *See* IRC §2502(a).
19. *See* IRC §6075(b)(1).
20. *See* IRC §6075(b)(2) & (3).
21. *See* IRC §2001(a).
22. *See* IRC §2033. The wealth transfer taxation of nonresident aliens is briefly discussed in Chapter 10.

Much of the complexity of the estate tax lies in the special provisions that include the value of interests that would not otherwise be included in the probate estate. We address those sections in their numerical order.

1. IRC §2034 expressly confirms that dower or curtesy interests (as well as the elective share in a common law property jurisdiction) are property of the decedent's estate. However, the transfer of assets to the surviving spouse in satisfaction of those interests may produce an estate tax marital deduction (described below) for the decedent's estate. In comparison, the surviving spouse's interest in community property is not subject to this rule and is excluded from the decedent's estate from the outset because the decedent does not own the surviving spouse's interest.

2. IRC §2035(a)(2) includes in the estate transfers of interests within three years of death that otherwise, if retained, would have been included in the estate under four sections discussed below: §§2036, 2037, 2038, and 2042. This section precludes the release or other extinguishment of the affected interests shortly before death in an attempt to avoid their inclusion in the taxable estate.

3. IRC §2035(b) includes in the estate gift taxes paid on any gifts made within three years prior to death. This section precludes deathbed gifts, which would exploit the fact that the estate tax is otherwise not "gift tax-inclusive" with respect to gift taxes previously paid by the decedent (that is, the wealth that was dissipated by paying the gift tax on inter vivos gifts is not otherwise subject to the estate tax on death).

4. IRC §2036(a)(1) includes in the estate the value of property in which the donor/decedent retained a life estate, a term of years that had not expired as of the date of death, or any other interest that cannot be ascertained without reference to the decedent's death.[23] Sloppy planning or careless implementation of lifetime gifts, such as gifting of real estate with the donor/decedent's retention of rights to occupancy, rents, or crops, may invite unwanted application of this section. It may affect trusts that satisfy a donor/decedent's legal obligations, so trusts for the benefit of the donor/decedent's dependent children must be handled with care.[24] This section may also affect sophisticated gift-leveraging structures such as the GRAT, GRUT, or QPRT, discussed in Part B, if the donor/decedent dies while the retained interest is still in effect.[25]

5. IRC §2036(a)(2) includes property in which the donor/decedent retained the right to designate the persons who will possess or enjoy the property or its income. This section is usually encountered in

23. The final requirement is a technical provision aimed at interests that would otherwise evaporate "one hour before the time of my death" so as to otherwise circumvent this section.

24. *See, e.g.*, Treas. Reg. §20.2036-1(b)(2) (1958); Estate of Chrysler v. Commissioner, 44 T.C. 55 (1965); Estate of Gokey v. Commissioner, 735 F.2d 1367 (7th Cir. 1984).

25. On June 7, 2007, the IRS issued proposed regulations concerning, in part, IRC §§2036 & 2039 and the required inclusion amounts for GRAT, GRUT, and QPRT interests. *See* Reg. 119097-05, 72 Fed. Reg. 31487 (June 7, 2007). *See generally* Stephanie G. Rapkin, *How Will the New Prop. Regs. Affect Grantor Retained Trusts?*, 34 Est. Plan. 25 (2007). Final regulations were issued in 2008.

connection with transfers in trust when the donor/decedent retained these powers, usually as a trustee, or in custodianships for minors when the donor/decedent acted as the custodian. For example, this section applies if the donor/decedent had the discretionary power to sprinkle trust property to one beneficiary rather than to another. The section has been broadly construed to include the power to simply postpone, but not divert, enjoyment.[26] Section 2036(a)(2) cannot be avoided by including (with the donor) independent cotrustees or cotrustees with a significant economic interest that would be adversely affected by the donor/decedent's exercise of the powers.[27] Even if the donor/decedent was not acting as a trustee at the time of death, the power to appoint himself or herself as a trustee would still invoke the section.[28] *Although there are several exceptions, which are discussed in the next paragraph, a settlor who acts as the trustee of the irrevocable trust so created generally does so at his or her peril from an estate tax planning standpoint.*

From a planning and drafting standpoint, there are relatively clear solutions to these concerns: (1) the donor/decedent may act as a trustee if there is absolutely no discretion exercisable by the trustee over distributions, but this is still dangerous because it requires a conclusion that no impermissible discretion is present. In addition, one loses the discretion and flexibility that most settlors desire; (2) the donor/decedent may act as a trustee if there is no discretion exercised over distributions because the trustee must follow an ascertainable standard,[29] but this too may be dangerous if the standard is considered to lack ascertainability, and this approach also involves a loss of flexibility; (3) independent trustees may make distributions in any manner, but the donor/decedent may not, in any event, appoint himself or herself as a trustee or ever serve in that capacity (the trust instrument should expressly prohibit the settlor from serving as a trustee); and (4) as an embellishment to point (3), the donor/decedent should leave the appointment or removal of trustees to other persons; if the donor/decedent wishes to retain such powers, he or she should comply with Estate of Wall v. Commissioner, 101 T.C. 300 (1993), and Rev. Rul. 95-58, 1995-2 C.B. 191, which limit the settlor's choices in that regard.

Rev. Rul. 95-58
1995-2 C.B. 191

The Internal Revenue Service has reconsidered whether a grantor's reservation of an unqualified power to remove a trustee and appoint a new

26. *See, e.g.*, Struthers v. Kelm, 218 F.2d 810 (8th Cir. 1955).

27. The language of IRC §2036(a)(2) states that the right is "either alone or in conjunction with *any* person" (emphasis added). *See* Helvering v. City Bank Farmers Trust Co., 296 U.S. 85 (1935).

28. *See* Estate of Farrel v. United States, 553 F.2d 637 (Ct. Cl. 1977).

29. *See, e.g.*, Old Colony Trust Co. v. United States, 423 F.2d 601 (1st Cir. 1970).

trustee (other than the grantor) is tantamount to a reservation by the grantor of the trustee's discretionary powers of distribution. This issue is presented in Rev. Rul. 79-353, 1979-2 C.B. 325.... An analogous issue is presented in Rev. Rul. 77-182, 1977-1 C.B. 273. The reconsideration is caused by the recent court decision in Estate of Wall v. Commissioner, 101 T.C. 300 (1993)....

Section 2036(a) of the Internal Revenue Code, in general, provides that the value of the gross estate includes the value of all property to the extent of any interest in the property that was transferred by the decedent (for less than adequate consideration) if the decedent has retained for life the right, alone or in conjunction with any person, to designate the person who shall possess or enjoy the property or the income therefrom.

Section 2038(a)(1), in general, provides that the value of the gross estate includes the value of all property to the extent of any interest in the property that was transferred by the decedent (for less than adequate consideration) if the decedent held a power, exercisable alone or in conjunction with any person, to change the enjoyment of the property through the exercise of a power to alter, amend, revoke, or terminate....

For purposes of 2036 and 2038, it is immaterial in what capacity the power was exercisable by the decedent. Thus, if a decedent transferred property in trust while retaining, as trustee, the discretionary power to distribute the principal and income, the trust property will be includible in the decedent's gross estate under 2036 and 2038. The regulations under 2036 and 2038 explain that a decedent is regarded as having possessed the powers of a trustee if the decedent possessed an unrestricted power to remove the trustee and appoint anyone (including the decedent) as trustee. Sections 20.2036-1(b)(3) and 20.2038-1(a) of the Estate Tax Regulations.

Rev. Rul. 79-353 concludes that, for purposes of 2036(a)(2) and 2038(a)(1), the reservation by a decedent-settlor of the unrestricted power to remove a corporate trustee and appoint a successor corporate trustee is equivalent to the decedent-settlor's reservation of the trustee's discretionary powers....

Rev. Rul. 77-182 concludes that a decedent's power to appoint a successor corporate trustee only in the event of the resignation or removal by judicial process of the original trustee did not amount to a power to remove the original trustee that would have endowed the decedent with the trustee's discretionary control over trust income.

In *Estate of Wall*, the decedent had created a trust for the benefit of others and designated an independent corporate fiduciary as trustee. The trustee possessed broad discretionary powers of distribution. The decedent reserved the right to remove and replace the corporate trustee with another independent corporate trustee. The court concluded that the decedent's retained power was not equivalent to a power to affect the beneficial enjoyment of the trust property as contemplated by 2036 and 2038....

. . . Rev. Rul. 79-353 [is] revoked. Rev. Rul. 77-182 is modified to hold that even if the decedent had possessed the power to remove the trustee and appoint an individual or corporate successor trustee that was not related or subordinate to the decedent (within the meaning of 672(c)), the decedent would not have retained a trustee's discretionary control over trust income.

QUESTION

You have been asked to draft the trustee appointment provisions of an irrevocable trust in which the settlor will hold a power to remove the trustee and appoint a new trustee. Would you reference IRC §672(c)?

The application of IRC §2036 is not confined to interests in the trusts. The IRS has met some success in applying it to interests in family limited partnerships created for, among other reasons, valuation discount planning purposes.[30]

6. IRC §2037, an obscure section, includes the value of property where possession or enjoyment of the property may be obtained only by surviving the decedent[31] and the decedent has retained a reversionary interest the value of which exceeds 5 percent of the value of the property. Subtle future interest traps may satisfy the survival requirement, so the surest way to avoid this section is to absolutely avoid the required reversion. Certainly, one objective of estate tax-driven drafting is to strictly eschew any type of reversion, no matter how remote.

7. IRC §2038 overlaps significantly with IRC §2036. Section 2038 includes the value of property that the decedent has at any time transferred, where the enjoyment at the time of the decedent's death is subject to change by the decedent through the exercise of a power to "alter, amend, revoke, or terminate." This section includes the assets of a typical revocable trust in the settlor's estate, but that is generally an accepted facet of revocable trusts. The section has also been applied to irrevocable trusts

30. *See, e.g.*, Read W. Easton, *Court Applies Section 2036 Favorably to Family Partnership*, 84 Tax Strategies 153 (Mar. 2010); Byrle M. Abbin, *A Practical Checklist for Planning with Family Limited Partnerships*, 33 Est. Plan. 10 (2006) (describing the relevant cases); Jerald David August & Casey Scott August, *Income Tax Aspects of Forming Operating, and Exiting FLPs*, 34 Est. Plan. 13 (2007) ("hurdles include . . . Chapter 14 provisions, valuation disputes . . . and assertions of retained control or enjoyment"); Walter D. Schwidetzky, *Family Limited Partnerships: The Beat Goes On*, 60 Tax Law. 277 (2007); Robert E. Madden & Lisa H.R. Hayes, *Assets Held in Family Limited Partnerships Were Includable in Decedent's Estate*—Estate of Strangi ("Strangi III"), T.C.M. 2003-145, 30 Est. Plan. 455 (2003); David L. Keligian, *Family Partnerships and Code Sec. 2036—Judicial Activism Targets Family Entities*, 81 Taxes 35 (Sept. 2003).

31. For helpful interpretative examples, see Treas. Reg. §20.2037-1 (1958).

where the donor/decedent has attempted to retain powers of this type. The power to accelerate or postpone enjoyment but not shift it to another also has been held to invoke this section.[32] However, the power of the settlor to terminate the trust with the consent of all beneficiaries has been held outside the scope of the section.[33] Although the overlap between IRC §§2036 and 2038 is imperfect, the four planning and drafting guidelines described above for §2036 apply to IRC §2038 as well.

8. IRC §2039 includes annuities or other payments receivable by any beneficiary by reason of surviving the decedent if, under the contract or agreement, an annuity or other payment was payable to the decedent (i.e., the decedent was currently receiving payments), or the decedent possessed the right to receive such annuity or payment. This section effectively includes in the estate IRAs, 401(k) plan benefits, and other retirement benefits enjoyed by the decedent, but for which a survivor would enjoy a benefit as well. These types of interests can also present income tax disadvantages to the recipient. With the exception of Roth accounts, all or a portion of these investments typically constitute "income in respect of a decedent" that will be taxable income to the recipient. See Chapter 12 for a discussion of the planning considerations in dealing with retirement accounts.

9. IRC §2040 deals with joint interests in property with rights of survivorship, whether in real estate or personal property.

(a) IRC §2040(a) provides that if a decedent created a joint interest in property with a noncontributing party, even if a taxable gift was produced, as would be the case with real estate, the value of all the property is included in the decedent's estate. If the decedent had used instead a tenancy in common, then barring application of another section (e.g., IRC §2036(a)(1) if the decedent had retained the right to the income from all the property), only the percentage interest owned by the decedent would be included in the estate, and a fractional interest discount might be available as well. Generally, IRC §2040(a) is not a wealth transfer tax planning tool and is a consequence of Will substitute probate avoidance.[34]

(b) IRC §2040(b) provides a special rule for survivorship tenancies solely between spouses. Upon the death of the first spouse, the value of

32. *See* Lober v. United States, 346 U.S. 335 (1953).

33. *See* Helvering v. Helmholz, 296 U.S. 93 (1935); Treas. Reg. §20.2038-1(a) (as amended in 1962). *Compare* Unif. Trust Code §411(a) (a noncharitable irrevocable trust may be modified or terminated upon consent of the settlor and all beneficiaries).

34. IRC §2040(a) can play an income tax planning role in a simple estate where the donor wants a completed inter vivos gift of property such as real estate, but wants the donee to receive the adjusted tax basis benefits of IRC §1014 upon the donor's death, rather than the carryover basis result generally prescribed for inter vivos gifts by IRC §1015. A joint tenancy with rights of survivorship will pass all the property to the donee upon the donor's death with a minimum of paperwork, but the IRC §2040(a) string will pull all of the property back into the donor's estate tax estate, producing the desired income tax basis adjustment. The creation of the joint interest will be a completed gift that often will require the filing of a gift tax return if the value exceeds the gift tax annual exclusions, even if no gift tax is due because of the $5,000,000 gift tax applicable exclusion amount. If the property is located in a state that permits transfer on death deeds (see Chapter 3) that would generally be a better solution.

one half of the property is included in the decedent's estate. However, because that one half passes to the surviving spouse by operation of law upon the death of the first spouse, that inclusion is offset by the estate tax marital deduction, discussed below.[35] The overall estate tax result is consequently benign for most married couples.[36] A planning focus that will recede with the passage of time has been on avoiding IRC §2040(b) for tenancies created prior to 1977 such that IRC §2040(a) would apply to include all the property in the contributing spouse's estate, securing an income tax basis adjustment in all of the property under IRC §1014.[37]

10. IRC §2041 includes in the estate property that is subject to the exercise of a general power of appointment. Different rules apply to powers created before October 21, 1942; this discussion focuses on powers created after this time, although one must be aware of this crucial timeline when dealing with old trusts. The definition of a "general" power of appointment is crucial. It is a "power which is exercisable in favor of the decedent, his estate, his creditors, or the creditors of his estate."[38] A nontaxable "special" power of appointment may be exercisable in favor of anyone *but* the decedent, his or her creditors, his or her estate, or creditors of his or her estate.

There are several other exceptions to this general rule, the principal exception for drafting purposes being that a general power does not include "a power to consume, invade, or appropriate property for the benefit of the decedent which is limited by an ascertainable standard relating to the health, education, support, or maintenance of the decedent."[39] The regulations give examples of language that satisfies the statutory standard. There are a number of cases dealing with deviations from the language—a risky endeavor, considering the likely small gain when it comes to practical application of the language by a trustee.

11. IRC §2042 deals with insurance on the decedent's life.[40] The proceeds of insurance on the life of the decedent are included in the decedent's estate in two instances. First, the proceeds will be included if the amounts are receivable by the executor, which would also include insurance proceeds expended for the benefit of the estate, such as insurance earmarked to satisfy debts of the decedent. Second, the proceeds will be included if the decedent possessed at the time of his or her death "any of the incidents of ownership."[41] The regulations state that "incidents of ownership" is a broader concept than ownership of the policy and includes "the power to change the beneficiary, to surrender or cancel the

35. *See* IRC §2056. However, if the surviving spouse is not a citizen of the United States, IRC §2040(b) and 2056 may not apply. *See* IRC §2056(d).

36. Only the one-half included in the decedent's estate will qualify for the IRC §1014 basis adjustment. In comparison, if the property is community property, both the decedent's one-half and the survivor's one-half are eligible for the basis adjustment. *See* IRC §1014(b)(6).

37. *See, e.g.*, Gallenstein v. United States, 975 F. 2d 286 (6th Cir. 1992).

38. *See* IRC §2041(b)(1).

39. *See* IRC §2041(b)(1)(A).

40. The value of life insurance owned by the decedent on the life of another is included in the decedent's estate under IRC §2033.

41. *See* IRC §2042(2).

policy, to assign the policy, to revoke an assignment, to pledge the policy for a loan, or to obtain from the insurer a loan against the surrender value of the policy."[42] The simplest planning measure is to place all incidents of ownership in someone other than the decedent/insured. An irrevocable life insurance trust is often used in this planning environment as a substitute owner of the policy. See Chapter 11. If the decedent/insured wishes to transfer by gift incidents of ownership in an existing policy, planners must be aware that IRC §2035(a)(2) would nevertheless include the insurance proceeds in the decedent/insured's estate if he or she dies within three years of the transfer.[43] Moreover, the value of the policy at the time of transfer will be a taxable gift. If the decedent/insured survives the three-year period, the insurance proceeds should be excluded from the estate.

12. IRC §2044 is a housekeeping provision that operates in conjunction with the marital deduction, discussed below. It ensures that property passing from the estate of the first spouse to die and for which a marital deduction was claimed under the QTIP provisions of IRC §2056(b)(7) is then included in the estate of the surviving spouse to the extent that the property was not consumed during the surviving spouse's life. The marital deduction is designed to provide a deferral, not a permanent exemption, of estate tax. This provision is necessary because, as discussed below, the QTIP does not require a general power of appointment that would otherwise require inclusion in the surviving spouse's estate.

In a similar vein, IRC §2519 produces a taxable gift if the donee spouse disposed of all or part of the qualifying income interest that was created in an inter vivos QTIP under IRC §2523 or in a testamentary QTIP under IRC §2056(b)(7). The regulations interpreting IRC §2519 are helpful in understanding the provision.

b. Deductions.

1. IRC §2053 provides a deduction for funeral and administration expenses, claims against the estate, and unpaid mortgages or other indebtedness encumbering property that is included in the gross estate. There are a number of conditions applied to these deductions that are beyond the scope of this overview.

2. IRC §2054 permits a deduction for losses not compensated for by insurance or otherwise that are suffered during administration by the estate arising from fires, storms, shipwrecks, or other casualties, or from theft.

42. *See* Treas. Reg. §20.2042-1(c)(2) (as amended in 1979). An incident of ownership includes "a reversionary interest (whether arising by the express terms of the policy or other instrument or by operation of law) only if the value of such reversionary interest exceeded 5 percent of the value of the policy immediately before the death of the decedent." *See* IRC §2042(2). However, the regulations provide that the reversionary interest does not include the possibility that the decedent might receive a policy or its proceeds by inheritance through the estate of another person, or as a surviving spouse under a statutory right of election of a similar right. *See* Treas. Reg. §20.2042-1(c)(3) (as amended in 1979). That limitation is important because some estate plans place the incidents of ownership in a loved one of the insured.

43. *See, e.g.*, Lawrence I. Richman, *Sidestepping 2035*, 146 Tr. & Est. 32 (Apr. 2007) (sale of a life insurance policy to an irrevocable grantor trust to avoid IRC §2035).

3. IRC §2055 permits an unlimited deduction for the value of gifts to designated qualified public, charitable, and religious organizations. See Chapter 14.

4. IRC §2056 permits an unlimited deduction for the value of property passing from the decedent to the surviving spouse. It correlates with the marital deduction permitted by IRC §2523 for inter vivos gifts. The marital deduction is not allowed if the surviving spouse is not a U.S. citizen,[44] but the deduction may be allowed if a qualified domestic trust is created to receive the marital gift. A qualified domestic trust is required in this situation to ensure the ultimate collection of the estate tax upon the death of the surviving spouse.[45] See Chapter 10.

Testamentary gifts made outright to the surviving spouse are generally eligible for the marital deduction provided that (a) the property passes or has passed from the decedent to the surviving spouse; (b) the property is included in determining the value of the gross estate; (c) the property is not a nondeductible terminable interest; and (d) the noncitizen surviving spouse requirements described above are satisfied.

With respect to the first requirement, IRC §2056(c) qualifies a broad group of transactions as satisfying the passing requirement (e.g., by testate or intestate succession, by dower, through joint ownership with right of survivorship, or through exercise or lapse of a power of appointment).

The second requirement is a commonsense prohibition against a potential windfall deduction for property not subject to the estate tax in the first place.

The third requirement, dealing with terminable interests, is prescribed by IRC §2056(b)(1) and is the most complex aspect of the marital deduction. In general, a property interest is a nondeductible terminable interest if three requirements are met: (1) on the lapse of time, the occurrence of an event or contingency, or the failure of an event or contingency to occur, the interest terminates or fails; (2) an interest in such property passes or has passed for less than full and adequate consideration in money or money's worth from the decedent to any person other than the surviving spouse or the estate of the surviving spouse; and (3) by reason of such passing that person, or his or her heirs or assigns, may possess or enjoy any part of such property after such termination or failure of the surviving spouse's interest.

A patent (which expires with the lapse of time), while terminable, is still eligible for the marital deduction because requirements (2) and (3) above are not satisfied. On the other hand, a life estate in the surviving spouse with a remainder to the children will meet all three requirements, and the deduction will fail unless some other exception applies, such as the QTIP, described below. The regulations offer helpful examples applying these principles. However, a terminable interest meeting only requirement

44. *See* IRC §2056(d).
45. *See* IRC §2056A. See Chapter 10.

(1) will still be nondeductible if it is acquired for the surviving spouse pursuant to directions of the decedent, by the executor, or by the trustee of a trust.[46] One must accordingly exercise care in drafting marital bequest provisions that direct the acquisition of certain investments. Likewise, in funding the share passing to the surviving spouse, it is important to include language that assets not qualifying for the marital deduction are not eligible (see Form H, paragraph 3.2(a)). Otherwise, IRC §2056(b)(2) provides that if the ineligible assets are in the pool of assets from which the marital share can be funded, the marital deduction is reduced by the value of those assets, irrespective of whether they are in fact included in the funded assets.

The prohibition against certain terminable interests would apparently preclude the use of survival clauses (e.g., "to my wife if she survives me for 30 days") in marital bequests, but a limited exception is provided by IRC §2056(b)(3) that permits a survival period not to exceed six months after the decedent spouse's death or lapse upon a common disaster resulting in the death of the decedent and the surviving spouse. However, as discussed in Chapter 11, great care must be exercised in using such a survival clause. If the surviving spouse does not survive for the required period such that no property passes to him or her, double probate of assets may be avoided, but the estate of the surviving spouse may not include enough property to fully utilize his or her applicable exclusion amount. Moreover, in estates at the highest marginal estate tax rates, this could subject the estate of the first spouse to die to tax at higher rates than if the assets were divided between the two estates. The so-called "equalization clause" discussed in Chapter 11 is a solution to this problem. However, as discussed in more detail in Chapter 11, the current highest marginal estate tax rate (35 percent) together with the rate of tax applied on an estate valued at the applicable exclusion amounts for years 2011-2012 (35 percent) has eliminated, for now at least, the rate progressivity of the estate taxes.

While outright gifts are a relatively simple matter, the decedent may wish to place the marital bequest in trust. Unless the remainderperson is the estate of the surviving spouse, creating the so-called "estate trust," most trust arrangements would violate the terminable interest prohibitions. However, three marital trust exceptions to the terminable interest rule are available:

(1) IRC §2056(b)(5) permits a marital deduction for property placed in trust if the surviving spouse is entitled for life to all the income from the property, payable at least annually, and the surviving spouse has a general power of appointment to appoint the remainder (inter vivos or testamentary or both) alone and in all events.

(2) IRC §2056(b)(7), which was added to the Internal Revenue Code in 1981, permits a marital deduction if the surviving spouse is entitled to all the income from the property, payable at least annually, and no person

46. *See* IRC §2056(b)(1)(C).

has a power to appoint any part of the property to any person other than the surviving spouse, although a power exercisable only at or after the death of the surviving spouse is permitted. This property is referred to in the Code as "qualified terminable interest property," producing the "QTIP" acronym regularly used by estate planners. Unlike the IRC §2056(b)(5) bequest, the QTIP is an election made on the estate tax return of the first spouse to die. This permits an added measure of postmortem planning. However, aside from the electivity aspects of the QTIP, its popularity in larger part stems from the absence of any requirement that the surviving spouse hold a general power of appointment over the trust assets, thus assuring the first spouse's wishes as to how the remainder is to be disposed upon the death of the surviving spouse. This assured disposition of the remainder may be particularly attractive in providing for children from prior marriages of the decedent. See Chapter 9.

(3) IRC §2056(b)(8) simplifies the rules by making the terminable interest rule inapplicable if the surviving spouse is the beneficiary of a charitable remainder trust. The charitable remainder trust tax rules require certain levels of income distributions to the private beneficiary, and those apply to protect the surviving spouse. The provision otherwise resembles a QTIP in the sense that the first spouse designates the remainderperson, here a charitable organization. See Chapter 11 for a discussion of marital deduction planning issues and techniques and Chapter 14 for a discussion of charitable giving.

c. Computing the Estate Tax. If the decedent has made no taxable gifts,[47] the rates at IRC §2001 are applied to the amount of the taxable estate, and that tax is reduced by the full applicable exclusion amount allowed by IRC §2010. If the decedent has made taxable gifts, the computation is more complicated. Gifts made prior to 1977 are ignored.[48] Otherwise, a "tentative tax" is computed on the sum of the taxable estate plus post-1976 taxable gifts. The tax payable on the post-1976 gifts (computed at the rates applying as of the decedent's date of death but reduced by any lifetime uses of the applicable exclusion amount under IRC §2505) is subtracted from the first tentative tax, and that net amount is reduced by the full applicable exclusion amount allowed by IRC §2010. The maximum rate of estate tax is 35 percent in 2010-2012. The applicable exclusion amount, formerly referred to as the unified credit, is $5,000,000 for those years, with inflation indexing in 2012.[49] The future of rates and the applicable exclusion amounts, as well as the entire estate tax, are subject to a great deal of uncertainty, as discussed later in Part B.2 of this chapter.

47. "Taxable gifts" do not include gifts made pursuant to IRC §2503(b) using the annual gift exclusion or gifts made pursuant to IRC §2503(e) for certain education and medical costs.

48. A pre-1977 gift could enter into the calculation if it is included in the gross estate due to the decedent's retained interest in the gifted property (e.g., as an IRC §2040(a) joint tenancy). In that event, a modified credit for the gift taxes paid may be allowed. *See* IRC §2012.

49. *See* IRC §2010(c).

d. Paying the Estate Tax. The federal estate tax return is due nine months after the decedent's death,[50] and the tax due is payable at that time.[51] Extensions of time to file the return[52] and pay the tax[53] can be granted upon timely written application to the IRS. However, failure to pay the estate tax by the nine-month deadline will subject the estate to interest on the tax due. Installment payment of estate tax bearing a lower rate of interest is available for estates that consist largely of interests in qualifying closely held businesses.[54] The estate tax produced by the inclusion of reversions or remainders can be postponed until after the termination of the preceding interest in the property.[55]

4. A Summary of the Generation-Skipping Transfer Tax

The generation-skipping transfer tax (GSTT) was not enacted until 1976. It was significantly reconfigured in 1986, and taxpayers paying the tax in the prior ten-year period were granted refunds. Because this is a particularly complex taxation scheme, this summary only skims the most salient points.

The GSTT imposes a tax on generation-skipping transfers at the maximum federal estate tax rate.[56] There are three types of generation-skipping transfers: direct skips, taxable distributions, and taxable terminations.[57] A "direct skip" is a transfer, subject to either the gift or estate tax, that is made to a skip person.[58] A "skip person" includes a natural person in a generation that is two or more generations below the generation of the transferor.[59] An outright inter vivos gift of property by a grandparent to a grandchild, or an outright bequest of property from a grandparent's estate to a grandchild would be simple examples of direct skips. Generation assignments are dictated by IRC §2651. Spouses are assigned to the same generation.[60]

A "skip person" may include a trust if all interests in the trust are held by skip persons or there is no person holding an interest in the trust and at no time after the transfer may a distribution be made to a nonskip person.[61] The concept of a trust with no person holding an interest in the trust is produced by the definition of "interest," which generally

50. *See* IRC §6075(a).
51. *See* IRC §6151(a).
52. *See* IRC §6081.
53. *See* IRC §6161.
54. *See* IRC §6166.
55. *See* IRC §6163.
56. *See* IRC §2641(a).
57. *See* IRC §2611(a).
58. *See* IRC §2612(c).
59. *See* IRC §2613(a)(1).
60. *See* IRC §2651(c).
61. *See* IRC §2613(a)(2). A "trust" can include legal property interests such as a life estate, estate for years, and insurance and annuity contracts that have "substantially the same effect as a trust." *See* IRC §2652(b)(1) & (3). For example, assume that Grandmother's estate devises a life estate in Blackacre to Son, with the remainder passing to Grandchild. That could be analyzed for GSTT purposes as not a direct skip to a skip person trust, because the arrangement includes an interest held by a skip person. However, upon Son's death, a "taxable termination" (discussed in the text paragraphs that follow) would occur. In addition, if Son were to properly disclaim his interest (*see* IRC §2518), an immediate direct skip would be created.

excludes future rights to income or corpus.[62] An accumulation trust, for example, falls into this category.

A "taxable distribution" is a distribution from a trust to a skip person other than a taxable termination, discussed next, or a direct skip. A distribution of income or corpus to a grandchild from a trust established by a grandparent is a simple example. However, if the transfer of the property to the grandchildren's trust is itself taxable as a direct skip, then another GSTT on a distribution of corpus to the grandchildren would seem to produce a double tax. This concern is addressed by IRC §2653(a), which treats the transferor as only one generation higher than the highest generation of any person who has an interest in the trust immediately after the transfer. That provision would move the grandchildren up one generation so that distributions from the trust to them would not be subject to the GSTT.[63]

A "taxable termination" includes the termination of interests in a trust unless immediately after such termination a nonskip person has an interest in the trust property, or if at no time after such termination may a distribution be made from such trust to a skip person. A simple example is a trust that sprinkles income among children, grandchildren, and great-grandchildren of the settlor. A taxable termination occurs upon the death of the last surviving child. IRC §2653(a) will, however, apply to the trust so that the grandchildren are moved up to the generation immediately below the transferor, such that distributions to them will not be taxable distributions.[64] But, as was the case with the death of the last surviving child, a taxable termination occurs upon the death of the last surviving grandchild, and so forth.

If a generation-skipping transfer has occurred, the tax is computed by multiplying the taxable amount by the applicable rate.[65] In a direct skip, the taxable amount is the value of the property received by the skip person.[66] In a taxable distribution, the taxable amount is the value of the property received by the skip person reduced by any expense incurred by the skip person in the determination, collection, or refund of the GSTT imposed on the distribution.[67] However, if the trust pays the GSTT, that is considered an additional taxable distribution. In a taxable termination, the taxable amount is the value of all property with respect to which a taxable termination has occurred, reduced by any applicable administration expenses, claims, or indebtedness applicable to the property.[68] This provision applies most forcefully if the trust itself is terminating.

62. *See* IRC §2652(c).
63. *See* Treas. Reg. §26.2653-1(b), Example 1 (1995).
64. *See* Treas. Reg. §26.2653-1(b), Example 2 (1995).
65. *See* IRC §2602.
66. *See* IRC §2623.
67. *See* IRC §2621.
68. *See* IRC §2622.

The "applicable rate" is the product of the maximum federal estate tax rate and the inclusion ratio.[69] The "inclusion ratio" is 1 minus a fraction, the numerator of which is the amount of the GSTT exemption allocated to the transfer and the denominator of which is, with some exceptions, the value of the property transferred.[70] The GSTT exemption is equal to the estate tax applicable exclusion amount. As an example, assuming that the transferor has used none of his or her GSTT exemption and that the value of the property transferred is less than or equal to the exemption, the value of the fraction is 1, which produces an inclusion ration of 0 and an applicable tax rate of 0.

The GSTT exemption raises important planning issues. First, if a trust is created and transfers to the trust do not exceed the value of the GSTT exemption, that trust is immune forever from the GSTT, whether on taxable terminations or distributions, because the inclusion ratio remains 0. This is crucial to the creation of dynasty trusts, discussed in Chapter 13. Second, spouses can effectively use both of their GSTT exemptions, because gift splitting is allowed for this purpose.[71] Third, for GSTT purposes, the decedent is the transferor in the case of property subject to estate tax.[72] If the first spouse to die bequeaths the bulk of his or her estate to the surviving spouse to defer the estate tax through the use of the marital deduction, the first spouse's unused GSTT exemption is lost. The same results may occur where the decedent made large, non-GSTT lifetime gifts that consumed significant portions of his or her applicable exclusion amount (thereby precluding the creation of a bypass trust that is a skip person) and wishes to create a QTIP trust with skip persons as the remainderpersons.

The so-called "reverse QTIP" election of IRC §2652(a)(3) addresses this problem by permitting the estate of the first spouse to treat the QTIP election as not being made for GSTT purposes, so that the GSTT exemption of the first spouse can be fully utilized. With parity between the amount of the GSTT exemption and the estate tax applicable exclusion, the election is now less significant, but as demonstrated above could still be important if significant GSTT gifts are desired.[73] The reverse QTIP election is discussed in Chapter 11.

The GSTT coordinates with most of the gift tax exclusions. Gifts eligible for the gift tax exclusions under IRC §2503(b) and (e) generally

69. *See* IRC §2641(a).
70. *See* IRC §2642(a).
71. *See* IRC §2652(a)(2). *See generally* Jonathan G. Blattmachr & Diana S.C. Zeydel, *Adventures in Allocation GST Exemption in Different Scenarios*, 35 Est. Plan. 3 (Apr. 2008).
72. *See* IRC §2652(a)(1).
73. It is assumed that the first spouse makes nonmarital gifts equal to the estate tax applicable exclusion amount, coupled with marital gifts that eliminate the taxable estate. When the GSTT exemption exceeded the estate tax applicable exclusion amount, a portion of the GSTT exemption would be unused by the first spouse under this traditional estate planning structure. The reverse QTIP election was a very important solution to this problem. Notwithstanding equalization of the applicable exclusion amount and the GSTT exemption, the election still has a role to play in the situations described in the text.

are also exempt from the GSTT.[74] This exemption, however, does not apply to gifts in trust unless certain rules are followed.[75] See Chapter 8 for a discussion of this issue. Gifts or bequests to a spouse do not produce a GSTT because spouses are considered to be of the same generation.[76]

B. Planning Strategies and Techniques

1. General Planning Strategies

While the federal wealth transfer tax system offers a number of complexities beyond the scope of this overview,[77] the critical aspects that shape the estate planning process can be summarized.

a. Strategy—Minimizing/Reducing Valuations. All three taxes are imposed on the fair market value of property transferred or deemed transferred at the particular relevant time (time of gift, time of death, time of generation-skipping transfer). Several provisions of the Internal Revenue Code explicitly permit a lesser value to be applied. For example, IRC §2032A provides special valuation for the assets of closely held businesses and family farms; IRC §2031(c) permits a reduced valuation for land subject to certain conservation easements; and IRC §2032 permits an alternate valuation of the estate assets as of six months after death.

The regulations define "fair market value" as "the price at which the property would change hands between a willing buyer and a willing seller, neither being under any compulsion to buy or to sell and both having reasonable knowledge of relevant facts."[78] The courts have been receptive to applying general appraisal principles in ascertaining fair market value. On the one hand, property, particularly real estate, is to be valued at its highest and best use. In connection with valuing ownership interests in business entities, a premium may be added for control.[79] On the other hand, the value of property may reflect a reduction or discount[80] for the impact of: fractional interests in the property rather than an undivided whole

74. *See* IRC §2642(c).
75. *See* IRC §2642(c)(2).
76. *See* IRC §2651(c).
77. For a comprehensive treatment of federal wealth transfer taxes, see A. James Casner & Jeffrey N. Pennell, Estate Planning (6th ed. 1995 & Supp. 2009-2010); Richard B. Stephens et al., Federal Estate and Gift Taxation: Including the Generation-Skipping Transfer Tax (8th ed. 2002 & Supp. 2011).
78. Treas. Reg. §20.2031-1(b) (as amended in 1965) (estate tax purposes; second sentence); Treas. Reg. §25.2512-1 (as amended in 1992) (gift tax purposes; second sentence).
79. *See, e.g.*, Estate of Trenchard v. Commissioner, 69 T.C.M. (CCH) 2164 (1995) (40 percent control premium for a 60.92 percent ownership interest).
80. There is a flood of literature on the evolving subject of discounts for federal estate and gift tax purposes. The principles are summarized in John A. Bogdanski, Federal Tax Valuation ch. 4 (1996 & Supp. 2010). *See also* John R. Price & Samuel A. Donaldson, Price on Contemporary Estate Planning §2.14.1 (2011).

interest;[81] minority interests in business entities;[82] impaired marketability of interests in business entities; loss of a key person in a business; built-in capital gains in C corporations;[83] securities law restrictions;[84] and sales of large blocks of stock or other assets, such as collectibles (so-called "blockage" discounts) that would flood the market.[85]

Technique 1—Creating Discounts by Gifts of Property. Fractional interest discounts may be created through gifts of portions of the subject property. For example, Parent could gift an undivided one-half interest in Blackacre to Child. Parent would claim a "fractional interest discount," which values the gift at less than one-half of the value of the entire parcel to reflect the costs of a partition action and the difficulties in managing and selling the property with a co-owner. Parent's estate would argue that the retained one-half should also be discounted for estate tax purposes.

In a similar fashion, Parent could gift interests in a family business to Child and claim that the value of the gifted interests should reflect a "minority discount" for lack of control. If Parent gifts enough interests to Child, Parent's estate may argue that the retained interests lack control of the business (and any control premium), and possibly qualify for a minority discount. Indeed, a drawback to such gifts may be the loss of control over the gifted assets.

Rev. Rul. 93-12
1993-1 C.B. 202

ISSUE

If a donor transfers shares in a corporation to each of the donor's children, is the factor of corporate control in the family to be considered in valuing each transferred interest, for purposes of section 2512 of the Internal Revenue Code?

FACTS

P owned all of the single outstanding class of stock of X corporation. P transferred all of P's shares by making simultaneous gifts of 20 percent of the shares to each of P's five children, A, B, C, D, and E.

81. *See, e.g.*, Williams v. Commissioner, 75 T.C.M. (CCH) 1758 (1998) (allowing an aggregate 44 percent discount on undivided one-half interests in timberland, 24 percent being a product of a lack of control over the parcel).

82. *See, e.g.*, Rev. Rul. 93-12, 1993-1 C.B. 202.

83. *See, e.g.*, Eisenberg v. Commissioner, 155 F.3d 50 (2d Cir. 1998), *acq.*, 1999-1 C.B. xix (allowing discount for income taxes on appreciated assets).

84. *See, e.g.*, Estate of McClatchy v. Commissioner, 147 F.3d 1089 (9th Cir. 1998) (reducing the value of publicly held stock due to securities law resale restrictions that would have applied to the decedent).

85. *See, e.g.*, Treas. Reg. §20.2031-2(e) (as amended in 1992) (describing blockage discount as applied to stock).

LAW AND ANALYSIS

Section 2512(a) of the Code provides that the value of the property at the date of the gift shall be considered the amount of the gift.

Section 25.2512-1 of the Gift Tax Regulations provides that, if a gift is made in property, its value at the date of the gift shall be considered the amount of the gift. The value of the property is the price at which the property would change hands between a willing buyer and a willing seller, neither being under any compulsion to buy or to sell, and both having reasonable knowledge of relevant facts.

Section 25.2512-2(a) of the regulations provides that the value of stocks and bonds is the fair market value per share or bond on the date of the gift. Section 25.2512-2(f) provides that the degree of control of the business represented by the block of stock to be valued is among the factors to be considered in valuing stock where there are no sales prices or bona fide bid or asked prices.

Rev. Rul. 81-253, 1981-1 C.B. 187, holds that, ordinarily, no minority shareholder discount is allowed with respect to transfers of shares of stock between family members if, based upon a composite of the family members' interests at the time of the transfer, control (either majority voting control or de facto control through family relationships) of the corporation exists in the family unit. The ruling also states that the Service will not follow the decision of the Fifth Circuit in Estate of Bright v. United States, 658 F.2d 999 (5th Cir. 1981).

In Bright, the decedent's undivided community property interest in shares of stock, together with the corresponding undivided community property interest of the decedent's surviving spouse, constituted a control block of 55 percent of the shares of a corporation. The court held that, because the community-held shares were subject to a right of partition, the decedent's own interest was equivalent to 27.5 percent of the outstanding shares and, therefore, should be valued as a minority interest, even though the shares were to be held by the decedent's surviving spouse as trustee of a testamentary trust. See also, Propstra v. United States, 680 F.2d 1248 (9th Cir. 1982). In addition, Estate of Andrews v. Commissioner, 79 T.C. 938 (1982), and Estate of Lee v. Commissioner, 69 T.C. 860 (1978), nonacq., 1980-2 C.B. 2, held that the corporation shares owned by other family members cannot be attributed to an individual family member for determining whether the individual family member's shares should be valued as the controlling interest of the corporation.

After further consideration of the position taken in Rev. Rul. 81-253, and in light of the cases noted above, the Service has concluded that, in the case of a corporation with a single class of stock, notwithstanding the family relationship of the donor, the donee, and other shareholders, the shares of other family members will not be aggregated with the transferred shares to determine whether the transferred shares should be valued as part of a controlling interest.

In the present case, the minority interests transferred to A, B, C, D, and E should be valued for gift tax purposes without regard to the family relationship of the parties.

HOLDING

If a donor transfers shares in a corporation to each of the donor's children, the factor of corporate control in the family is not considered in valuing each transferred interest for purposes of section 2512 of the Code. For estate and gift tax valuation purposes, the Service will follow *Bright*, *Propstra*, *Andrews*, and *Lee* in not assuming that all voting power held by family members may be aggregated for purposes of determining whether the transferred shares should be valued as part of a controlling interest. Consequently, a minority discount will not be disallowed solely because a transferred interest, when aggregated with interests held by family members, would be a part of a controlling interest. This would be the case whether the donor held 100 percent or some lesser percentage of the stock immediately before the gift.

Rev. Rul. 81-253 is revoked.

The facts of Revenue Ruling 93-12 are critical—each child received only a 20 percent interest. The IRS in other circumstances has continued to contest valuation discounts where a "swing vote" premium can arise.

TAM 9436005
September 9, 1994

ISSUE

Should the fact that each of three 30 percent blocks of stock transferred has "swing vote" attributes be taken into account as a factor in determining the fair market value of the stock?

FACTS

The donor owned all of outstanding common stock of Corporation, totaling 28,975 shares. On December 18, 1989, the donor transferred 8,592 shares (approximately 30 percent of the outstanding common stock in Corporation) to each of three children. The donor also transferred 1,509 shares (approximately 5 percent of the stock) to his spouse. The donor retained 1,510 shares or approximately 5 percent of the stock....

The ownership of the stock before and after the transfer may be summarized as follows:

SUMMARY OF STOCK HOLDINGS

	Donor	Child 1	Child 2	Child 3	Spouse
Before	100%	0	0	0	0
After	5%	30%	30%	30%	5%

With respect to each gift, the stock was valued at approximately $50 per share representing the net asset value of Corporation, less a 25 percent discount characterized as a discount for minority interest and marketability.

APPLICABLE LAW AND ANALYSIS

Section 2501 provides that a gift tax is imposed for each calendar year on the transfer of property by gift.

Section 2511 provides that the gift tax shall apply whether the transfer is in trust or otherwise, whether the gift is direct or indirect, and whether the property is real or personal, tangible or intangible.

Section 2512(a) provides that the value of the property at the date of the gift shall be considered the amount of the gift.

Section 25.2512-1 of the Gift Tax Regulations provides that, if a gift is made in property, its value at the date of the gift shall be considered the amount of the gift. The value of the property is the price at which the property would change hands between a willing buyer and a willing seller, neither being under any compulsion to buy or sell, and both having reasonable knowledge of relevant facts.

Section 25.2512-2(a) provides that the value of stocks and bonds is the fair market value per share or bond on the date of the gift. Section 25.2512-2(f) provides that all relevant factors are to be taken into account in determining fair market value including the degree of control of the business represented by the block of stock to be valued.

Rev. Rul. 59-60, 1959-1 C.B. 237, provides guidelines for valuing closely held stock. Rev. Rul. 59-60 specifically states that the size of a block of stock is a factor to be considered in determining fair market value. The revenue ruling also holds that all relevant factors must be considered and that no general formula may be used that is applicable to different valuation situations.

In general, in determining the value of shares of stock that represent a minority interest, a discount may be allowed in appropriate circumstances to reflect the fact that the holder of a minority interest lacks control over corporate policy, and thus for example, cannot compel the payment of dividends or the liquidation of the corporation. Ward v. Commissioner, 87 T.C. 78, 106 (1986). Where a donor makes simultaneous gifts of multiple shares of securities to different donees, each gift is valued separately in determining fair market value for gift tax purposes. See, e.g., Whittemore v. Fitzpatrick, 127 F. Supp. 710 (D.C. Conn. 1954); Avery v. Commissioner, 3 T.C. 963 (1944); §25.2512-2(e).

In Rev. Rul. 93-12, 1993-1 C.B. 202, a donor transferred 20 percent of the outstanding shares of a closely-held corporation to each of his five children. The ruling concludes that, if a donor transfers shares in a corporation to each of the donor's children, the factor of corporate control in the family is not considered in valuing each transferred interest for purposes of §2512. Thus, in valuing the shares, a minority discount will not be disallowed solely because a transferred interest, when aggregated with interests held by other family members, would be a part of a controlling interest.

In Estate of Winkler v. Commissioner, TCM 1989-232, the decedent, Clara Winkler, owned 10 percent of the voting stock of a closely-held corporation. Of the balance of the voting stock, 40 percent was owned by other members of the Winkler family and 50 percent was owned by members of the Simmons family. The court recognized that the decedent's block constituted a minority interest in the corporation. However, the court found that, in view of the fact that neither family possessed a controlling interest in the corporation, the decedent's minority block had special characteristics that enhanced its value. The court described these "swing vote" characteristics as follows:

> This 10 percent voting stock could become pivotal in this closely held corporation where members of one family held 50 percent and members of another family held 40 percent. By joining with the Simmons family a minority shareholder could effect control over the corporation and by joining the Winkler family, such a minority shareholder could block action.... Looking at this even split between the two families, the 10 percent block of voting stock, in the hands of a third party unrelated to either family could indeed become critical. While it is difficult to put a value on this factor, we think it increases the value of the Class A voting stock by at least the 10 percent that [respondent's appraiser] found.

The court went on to find that, under the facts presented, the increased value attributable to the swing vote characteristics of the stock offset any minority discount otherwise available. See also, Glenn Desmond and Richard Kelley, Business Valuation Handbook, §11.01 (1991) ("Likewise, if a minority block would enable another minority holder to achieve a majority with control or if the minority were needed to reach the percentage ownership needed to merge or file consolidated statements, the stock would have added value."); Shannon P. Pratt, Valuing Small Businesses and Professional Practices, 527 (2d ed. 1994) ("[I]f two stockholders own 49 percent [of the stock] and a third owns 2 percent, the 49 percent stockholders may be on a par with each other.... The 2 percent stockholder may be able to command a considerable premium over the pro-rata value for that particular block because of the swing vote power.");

Estate of Bright v. United States, 658 F.2d 999, 1007 and 1009 n. 9 (5th Cir. 1981), where the court discussed swing vote analysis in detail.

In the instant case, immediately before the transfers, the donor owned 100 percent of the outstanding stock of Corporation. The donor simultaneously transferred 3 blocks of stock, each constituting 30 percent of the outstanding stock, to each of his three children. As discussed above, the three transfers are valued separately for gift tax purposes. As is evident, each gift, viewed separately, possesses the same swing vote characteristics described by the court in *Estate of Winkler*. That is, as a result of the simultaneous transfer, three individuals each owned a 30 percent block of stock. The owner of any one of the transferred blocks could join with the owner of any of the other transferred blocks and control the corporation. Thus, any one of these 30 percent blocks, whether owned by an individual related or unrelated to the family, could be critical in controlling the corporation. As the court concluded in *Estate of Winkler*, this swing vote attribute of each of the transferred blocks enhances the value of each block and is properly taken into account in determining the fair market value of each block transferred.

The donor argues that attributing a swing vote value to each transferred block in this case produces an arbitrary result. That is, if the donor had not made a simultaneous transfer, but rather had transferred each 30 percent block at different times, the valuation of each block would be different. For example, the first 30 percent block transferred might have no swing vote attributes, since after the initial transfer, the donor would continue to possess control of the corporation through his ownership of the retained 70 percent block.

However, the objection raised by the donor is inapposite. First, donor's assumption that the value of none of the three seriatim gifts would reflect swing vote attributes is incorrect. We agree that the value of the first 30 percent transfer would not reflect any swing vote value. However, the second transfer of 30 percent of the stock would possess swing vote value. Further, as a result of this second transfer, the value of the 30 percent interest held by the first transferee would increase, because that block would acquire enhanced voting control in the form of swing vote value as a result of the second transfer. After that transfer, the value of each of the three blocks would have been equalized, because no one stockholder would possess control of the corporation. This enhancement of value with respect to the first transferee's block at the time of the second transfer would constitute an indirect gift to that transferee at the time of the second transfer. Finally, the third 30 percent block would also have swing vote value both before and after the third transfer. Thus, we believe that, even if the three transfers were made at different times, the total value of the gifts would ultimately be the same as if the three transfers were made simultaneously.

Further, under established case law, gift tax valuation results are often dependent on the nature and timing of the gift. For example, a single transfer of a large block of stock to an individual might be valued differently for gift tax purposes than several independent transfers of smaller blocks at different times. On the other hand, the result might not differ with respect to the swing value approach, or any other valuation principles, in the case of an integrated series of transfers. See, e.g., Citizens Bank and Trust Co. v. Commissioner, 839 F.2d 1249 (7th Cir. 1988); Estate of Murphy v. Commissioner, T.C.M. 1990-472. Accordingly, we do not believe the donor's objections in any way mitigate against applying swing vote analysis to the facts presented here.

As discussed above, all relevant factors are to be considered when valuing closely held stock. As the court concluded in *Estate of Winkler*, swing block potential is one such factor. In this case, each 30 percent block of stock has swing vote characteristics. The extent to which the swing vote potential enhances the value of each block transferred is a factual determination. However, all relevant factors including the minority nature of each block, any marketability concerns, and swing vote potential, should be taken into account in valuing each block.

CONCLUSION

In determining the fair market value of three 30 percent blocks of stock transferred by the donor, the swing vote attributes of each block are factors to be taken into consideration in determining the value of each block.

Technique 2—Creating Discounts by Transferring Assets to Restrictive Entities. If Parent owns all of Blackacre outright, the valuation of Blackacre will be a relatively straightforward matter. However, if Parent contributes Blackacre to a family limited partnership (FLP) or a limited liability company (LLC), Parent will now own an interest in the entity. If Parent subsequently gifts FLP or LLC interests to Child, Parent may claim that the gift valuation should reflect significant "minority interest discounts," plus a "discount for lack of marketability." The marketability discount is buttressed by the FLP and LLC agreement, which typically imposes restrictions on transfers of interests and liquidation of the entity.[86] Parent's estate may later argue that any retained interests also

86. The Omnibus Budget Reconciliation Act of 1990 added IRC §§2703 and 2704 to the Code. IRC §2703 ignores the valuation consequences of restrictions on the sale of property (such as options to purchase property or buy-sell agreements) unless the restriction is a bona fide business arrangement, is not a device to transfer such property to members of the decedent's family as a gift, and is comparable to other arms' length arrangements. While IRC §2703 has made options and buy-sell agreements less effective in limiting the value of property to the purchase-option price, the courts have largely rejected its application to the FLP or LLC agreement itself. In another planning device targeted by the 1990 legislation, taxpayers would claim a discount on gifts of business interests or other property due to a voting right or other restriction retained by the donor, but that right or restriction would subsequently lapse so that the donor's estate would

should reflect minority interest and marketability discounts. The disadvantages of this planning include the costs of forming and maintaining the entities (e.g., attorney fees, appraisal fees, tax return preparation fees) and potential loss of control over or access to the underlying assets.

Taxpayers have been successful in the courts in achieving large combined discounts. However, the courts' evaluation of FLPs and LLCs is still evolving, and the IRS has met with some success in challenging such claimed discounts.[87]

b. Strategy—Transferring and Limiting (Freezing) Future Asset Appreciation. An outright gift of property is a powerful estate planning measure because assuming that the property will appreciate, a transfer of the property today may save a greater future estate tax on this appreciated value. An outright gift of property is also one of the simplest techniques.

Technique 3—Outright Gift of Appreciating Property. Parent is the founder of a start-up company and expects that the company will issue shares to the public (an "initial public offering" or IPO) in the next two years. If the IPO unfolds as planned, Parent's shares will explode in value, perhaps increasing 20-fold. A gift of some of Parent's shares to Child now would be an excellent estate planning technique.

Several countervailing factors must be weighed, however: (1) if the gift is large (that is, in excess of Parent's available gift tax exclusion of $5,000,000), the current payment of a gift tax must be compared with the future possible payment of an estate tax; moreover, Parent may not have the funds available now to pay the tax; (2) the possible increase or decrease in or even elimination of the estate and gift taxes; (3) the loss of the IRC §1014 income tax basis adjustment, because IRC §1015 imposes a "carryover" basis for gifts (on the other hand, the income tax on long-term capital gains is 15 percent, much less than the highest wealth transfer tax rates, and the IPO may be sold for investment reasons long before Parent's death); (4) the possibility that the gifted asset will not appreciate as expected, or depreciate, or even possibly become worthless; and (5) the

not be subject to tax on the value of the right or restriction. IRC §2704(a) addresses this situation by creating a gift or testamentary transfer of the decrease in value at the time of the lapse. Finally, IRC §2704(b) disregards restrictions on the liquidation of an FLP or LLC if they are more restrictive than those imposed by federal or state law. *See* Treas. Reg. §25.2704-2(b) (1992). State legislatures responded by amending FLP and LLC statutes to provide, as a default matter, for very restrictive liquidation rules, which in turn made IRC §2704(b) largely inapplicable. *See, e.g.*, Estate of Jones v. Commissioner, 116 T.C. 121, 128-130 (2001) (rejecting application of IRC §2704(b) to an FLP). *See* Abbin, *supra* note 30 (describing the relevant cases); Brant J. Hellwig, *Estate Tax Exposure of Family Limited Partnerships under Section 2036*, 38 REAL PROP. PROB. & TR. J. 73 (2003). However, the federal annual gift exclusion under IRC §2503(b) may be jeopardized if the partnership or LLC provisions governing matters such as transfers of interests, withdrawal of capital contributions, and distribution of profits are too restrictive. *See generally* Hackl v. Commissioner, 118 T.C. 279 (2002), *aff'd*, 335 F.3d 664 (7th Cir. 2003); Robert E. Madden & Lisa H.R. Hayes, *Tax Court Disallows Transfers of LLC Interests as Gifts of Present Interest*, 29 EST. PLAN. 352 (2002).

87. *See supra* note 30.

practical estate planning considerations of an outright gift to a child must be evaluated.

The $5,000,000 inflation-adjusted applicable exclusion amount introduced by the 2010 Act permits significant nontaxable gifts. Beyond that, some planners would consider payment of gift taxes today to be highly inadvisable against the uncertain backdrop of the 2010 Act and possible permanent repeal of the estate tax.[88] However, for a very elderly client who might not be expected to live until the estate tax is repealed, a taxable gift might not be ruled out due to the tax "exclusivity" of the gift tax. Subject to an exception for gifts made within three years of death, which would undo this advantage[89] the taxes paid on gifts are not subject to wealth transfer taxes.[90] By comparison, the property of an estate that will ultimately be consumed to pay the estate taxes is itself subject to the estate tax. Nevertheless, the justifications for a taxable gift at this point would generally need to be very compelling.

However, Parent in Technique 3 should not be discouraged, because a combination approach may be attractive. For example, Parent might form an irrevocable trust in which Child will be a beneficiary. Although more complex, the trust instrument permits Parent, as settlor (but not as trustee, to avoid IRC §§2036 and 2038 concerns), to indirectly dictate the management and distribution of the gift. Parent might then transfer the stock to an FLP and then gift interests in the FLP to the trust, claiming minority and marketability discounts on the gift. Parent may still avoid the payment of an actual gift tax if Strategy c—maximizing gift deductions, exclusions, and exemptions, discussed below, is followed.

The taxpayer may own property, such as a business, farm, or real estate property that is appreciating rapidly. Unlike Parent in Technique 3 above, however, an immediate gift of the entire asset is not attractive, because it would generate a taxable gift. Indeed, the appreciation is so great that it outstrips the taxpayer's attempts to gift portions of the asset using marketability and minority discounts and the annual gift exclusion. The taxpayer needs to halt the inclusion of the future appreciation of the asset in Parent's estate, which is referred to as "freezing" the asset.

Technique 4—Asset Freeze Structures. The asset freeze concept is relatively simple. The taxpayer wants to retain the asset (or convert the form of the asset to another form) to permit future gifting or other transfers of the

88. With gift tax rates at historic lows under the 2010 Act, and the possibility of higher estate tax rates in the future, there is a planning argument to make gifts in excess of the $5,000,000 exclusion now, before the expiration of the 2010 Act. However, there is also the possibility that future estate tax rates could be *less* than current gift tax rates. With this uncertainty, in our experience most clients will vote with their wallets and find the payment of *any* taxes today to be unacceptable.

89. *See* IRC §2035(b).

90. However, any GSTTs paid in connection with the gift are treated as additional gifted amounts. *See* IRC §2515.

retained interest, but wants to minimize future appreciation. Several approaches are available, but they are not so simple.

Technique 4.1—The Self-Canceling Installment Note (SCIN). Assume that Parent sells Blackacre to Child in exchange for an installment note, the terms of which provide that upon Parent's death, the remaining unpaid balance is extinguished.[91] The principal advantage is that Parent now owns, instead of Blackacre, a debt instrument that will not appreciate. Upon Parent's death and before repayment, the balance of the obligation evaporates. The "winning" taxpayers using SCINs are those who can convince the courts of the bona fides of the original sale and then unexpectedly die. Parent can report the income tax gain using the IRC §453 installment sales method of reporting, and Child will receive an adjusted basis in Blackacre equal to the purchase price. The disadvantages are (1) the price may need to be higher than fair market value to compensate Parent for the possibility of extinguishment of the obligation upon his or her death—if Parent lives to see the obligation repaid, his or her estate may actually be increased; and (2) if Blackacre is appreciated, the gain on the sale will be taxable to Parent or Parent's estate.[92]

Technique 4.2—The Private Annuity. Using this technique, Parent transfers Blackacre to Child in exchange for an annuity paid by Child, the payment amounts and term being calculated with reference to Parent's life expectancy. The annuity provides for extinguishment upon Parent's death (resembling the SCIN). The estate of Parent "wins" if Parent does not achieve his or her life expectancy.

The principal advantages of the private annuity are (1) upon Parent's death nothing is included in Parent's estate from the annuity except for any unconsumed proceeds; and (2) upon Parent's death, unlike with a SCIN, neither Parent nor Parent's estate reports additional income from the annuity obligation. The principal disadvantages are (1) if Parent outlives the life expectancy used to price the annuity, Parent's estate may increase in value; (2) annuities generally must be Child's unsecured promise (for income tax reasons to avoid the accelerated recognition of the gain), as compared to a SCIN, which may be secured; (3) Parent reports income from the sale of Blackacre under the annuity income tax rules of IRC §72 (as discussed below, this treatment is now uncertain in light of proposed regulations); and (4) if the annuity payments too closely

91. We have not included a related technique in which Parent sells Blackacre to Child in exchange for an installment obligation with the intent that Parent would forgive subsequent installments on the note as they become due, using the annual gift exclusion. There is some question as to whether these transactions can be structured to pass muster in the courts if the intent to forgive is clear at the outset. *Compare* Haygood v. Commissioner, 42 T.C. 936 (1964) (transaction respected); Estate of Maxwell v. Commissioner, 3 F.3d 591 (2d Cir. 1993) (transaction treated as a gift).

92. *See, e.g.*, Frane v. Commissioner, 998 F.2d 567 (8th Cir. 1993) (estate taxable on income reportable from the canceled installment obligation).

track the income derived from Blackacre, the IRS may attempt to recast the transaction as a retained life estate subject to IRC §2036.[93] Reflecting upon these issues, in late 2006 the IRS issued proposed regulations that would change the income tax treatment of private annuities, much to the detriment of taxpayers. The proposed regulations would eliminate the spreading of the recognized gain over a period of years and would instead require that the annuity be valued in the year of sale and all of the gain recognized at that time.[94]

Technique 4.3—Sale to a Defective Grantor Trust. Under this technique Parent instead sells Blackacre to an irrevocable trust created for the benefit of Child.[95] The trust is irrevocable to avoid its inclusion in Parent's estate under IRC §2038 of the estate tax. Because Parent sells Blackacre to the trust for full and adequate consideration in money or money's worth (e.g., with an enforceable promissory note), there is no gift if the promissory note is respected by the IRS. Conventional estate planning wisdom, wisdom that has not been affirmed or rejected by the IRS, suggests that Parent contribute "seed money" to the trust in an amount equal to at least one-ninth of the purchase price of the asset (such that the trust assets are composed of 10% cash and 90% purchased property, less the promissory note), in an attempt to cast the transaction in a better posture. The trust now owns Blackacre while Parent owns a "frozen" installment obligation. The trust is made intentionally "defective" under the grantor trust rules.[96] It is treated as a grantor trust, which is ignored as a separate taxpayer for income tax purposes. Parent reports no gain on the sale of Blackacre or interest income on the installment obligation for income tax purposes.[97] The issues of whether Parent's estate must recognize any remaining gain pertaining to outstanding balances of the purchase price and the amount of the trust's adjusted basis in the property are not settled.[98]

Technique 4.4—Entity Freeze. Along the lines of Technique 2, parent transfers Blackacre to an FLP or LLC[99] in exchange for ownership interests that could then be gifted to Child. However, to limit the future

93. *See generally* William P. Elliot & Thomas A. Gavin, *Revisiting the Traditional Private Annuity Transaction*, 81 TAXES 25 (Aug. 2003) (overview of private annuity principles).

94. *See generally* Stephan R. Leimberg, Kevin J. McGrath & Howard Z. Zaritsky, *Deferral of Gain Eliminated in Sales of Appreciated Property for a Private Annuity*, 34 EST. PLAN. 3 (2007).

95. *See generally* Michael D. Mulligan, *Sale to an Intentionally Defective Irrevocable Trust for a Balloon Note—An End Run Around Chapter 14?*, 32 INST. ON EST. PLAN. ¶1500 (1998).

96. Many of the grantor trust rules overlap with inclusionary estate tax rules, so this requires care, but "defects" are often created under the administrative powers of IRC §675, particularly §675(4)(C) dealing with the power to reacquire the trust corpus by substituting other property of an equivalent value. In Rev. Rul. 2008-22, I.R.B. 2008-16, the IRS ruled that a power to substitute trust property would not result in inclusion of the trust under IRC §§2036 & 2038.

97. *See, e.g.*, Rev. Rul. 85-13, 1985-1 C.B. 184.

98. *See, e.g.*, Jonathan G. Blattmachr et al., *Income Tax Effects on Termination of Grantor Trust Status by Reason of the Grantor's Death*, 97 J. TAX'N 149 (2002).

99. A corporation with multiple classes of stock could also be used, but for income tax reasons, real estate is generally held by a passthrough entity such as a FLP or LLC.

appreciation in Blackacre inuring to the benefit of Parent's ownership in the FLP or LLC, at least two economic classes of interests will be created. One class will resemble preferred stock, receiving a cumulative but limited return and a priority in liquidation proceeds, while the other class will resemble common stock, with uncertain but unlimited returns. The limited "preferred" class should not appreciate as much as the other class, but it should also capture much of the current value of the entity, minimizing the gift tax value of the other interests, which will be gifted to Child.

IRC §2701 applies to this technique. For the technique to be effective, the preferred ownership interest must enjoy a payment that is payable on a periodic basis and is cumulative.[100] If Blackacre is a developed property producing a stream of rentals, this structure may be viable.[101] However, even if the preferred interest commands significant value, it cannot absorb all of the entity value. A minimum valuation rule provides that the value of the junior interests cannot be valued at less than 10 percent of the sum of the total value of all equity interests plus the total amount of indebtedness of the entity.[102] IRC §2701 is discussed in Chapter 11.

c. Strategy—Maximizing Gift Deductions, Exclusions, and Exemptions. *Technique 5—Regular Use of the Annual Gift Exclusion, Gift Splitting, and Educational/Medical Gift Exclusion.* Significant amounts of wealth may be transferred simply and free of any wealth transfer taxes by using the annual gift tax exclusion described in IRC §2503(b) on a regular basis over a sustained period of time. Moreover, some assets, such as life insurance, create additional "leverage" in the use of the annual exclusion, because the assets will eventually increase in value so greatly upon receipt of the full death benefit of the policy. Irrevocable life insurance trusts (ILITs) are discussed in Chapter 11.

A married couple using the exclusion in tandem with gift splitting[103] can make significant nontaxable gifts in the aggregate because there is no limit on the number of donees. The availability of the annual exclusion (and the difficulties of asset ownership and management by minors) has produced the widespread use of the so-called "*Crummey* clause" in irrevocable trusts (see Chapter 8).

An individual may also gift unlimited amounts for educational expenses (principally tuition and fees, but excluding living expenses) and medical care, provided that the amounts are paid directly to the

100. *See* IRC §2701(c)(3).

101. *See generally* Stephen M. Breitstone, *Estate Planning Strategy for Leveraged Real Estate*, 68 Prac. Tax Strategies 132 (Mar. 2002); Ann Berger Lesk & Claudio A. De Vellis, *Estate Planning with Real Estate Assets*, 562 PLI/Tax 275 (PLI Tax Law and Est. Plan. Course Handbook Series No. J0-006M Feb. 2003) (discussing GRATs, low-interest loans, installment sales, SCINs, private annuities, and FLPs).

102. *See* IRC §2701(a)(4).

103. *See* IRC §2513.

educational institution or medical care provider.[104] The beneficiary of the payments may be any individual.

For example, Grandparent is pleased that Granddaughter was recently accepted at an exclusive private university, but annual tuition and fees exceed $30,000. So long as Grandparent writes checks directly to the university for the tuition and fees, the payment of all of the $30,000 tuition is not a taxable gift, is not subject to the GSTT,[105] and does not require the filing of a gift tax return.[106] In addition, Grandparent may pay a portion of Granddaughter's living expenses using the annual gift exclusion. A drawback to this plan is that it requires Grandparent to survive while the grandchildren complete their education. Planners usually recommend the creation of a custodial account, irrevocable trust, or a tax-advantaged college savings plan (such as a section 529 plan) to which Grandparent could make gifts in advance of that time. Such alternatives are discussed in Chapter 8.

Technique 6—Creating Gift Tax Deductions with Retained Interests. Property may be gifted at a reduced gift tax by creating retained interests in the donor that reduce the value of the gift. The special rules of IRC §2702 must be considered, and if the donor dies while enjoying the retained interest, a portion or all of the property will be included in the donor/decedent's estate. Nevertheless, if properly structured and if the donor outlives the term of the retained interest, one may substantially leverage the amount that is transferred and almost eliminate the gift in certain situations. This has produced acronyms tracking the various planning structures residing within the confines of IRC §2702, such as the GRAT (grantor-retained annuity trust), GRUT (grantor-retained unitrust), and QPRT (qualified personal residence trust).

As an example, consider Grandmother, who owns a beach house that is a family treasure and wishes that it remain in the family. Because properties in that locale are expected to continue to appreciate greatly, Grandmother has decided to make a gift of the property now. However, an outright gift would consume all of her $5,000,000 applicable exclusion amount for gifts, and she would need to pay some tax. Grandmother is age 70 and in excellent health. If she were to gift the beach house but retain an interest for ten years, the interest retained for the term of years would be valued at approximately 50 percent of the value of the home (assuming a seven percent IRC §7520 interest rate[107]). Thus, Grandmother could gift the beach house to a QPRT and retain the right to use the house for ten

104. *See* IRC §2503(e); Treas. Reg. §25.2503-6 (1984).

105. The GSTT provisions provide an exemption for such gifts. *See* IRC §2642(c)(3).

106. *See* IRC §6019(a)(1).

107. The value of the term of years increases or decreases with the interest rate applied in the valuation tables. In a lower interest rate environment of 4.2 percent, the value of the term of years would decline to approximately 34 percent of the value of the home.

years. The advantage is that the amount of the gift is reduced; thus all of it may be absorbed by her available applicable exclusion amount. The downside to this technique is that if Grandmother dies during the ten-year period, the full value of the property will be included in her estate under IRC §2036(a).[108] However, from an estate tax perspective, there is no risk, as Grandmother is no worse off as compared to doing nothing—her risk is limited to the cost incurred to establish the trust. Another disadvantage is that the IRC §1014 step-up in basis will be lost—the trust will take the property at Grandmother's carryover basis.[109]

As another example, Parent who holds IPO shares such as those in Technique 3 might consider a similar strategy using a GRAT or GRUT, thereby eliminating a significant portion of the gift. Moreover, due to Parent's younger age, such a retained interest is even more compelling in terms of avoiding the application of IRC §2036.

A seminal case, *Walton v. Commissioner*, is included below. It demonstrates the practical applications of a GRAT, particularly one that involved hundreds of millions of dollars. As a result of the decision, the IRS amended a regulation[110] which would have otherwise blocked the use of GRATs that "zero out"[111] or almost completely eliminate any taxable gift on the transfer.

The *Walton* GRAT provided for a payment to the grantor of an annuity for the shorter of two years or her lifetime. If the grantor did not survive the two-year term, the balance of the annuity would be paid to her estate. The IRS regulation at issue provided that the annuity payable to the grantor's estate was not a "qualified interest," such that the only deductible interest was that tied to the grantor's life. If sustained, this position would have precluded the elimination of the taxable gift, the "zeroing out,"

108. On June 7, 2007, the IRS issued proposed regulations concerning, in part, IRC §§2036 and 2039 and the required inclusion amounts for GRAT, GRUT, and QPRT interests. *See* Reg. 119097-05, 72 Fed. Reg. 31487 (June 7, 2007). Final regulations were issued in 2008. *See generally* Mitchell M. Gans & Jonathan G. Blattmachr, *Treatment of GRATs Under the Section 2036 Proposed Regulations—Questions Remain*, 107 J. Tax'n 143 (2007). In valuing Grandmother's term of years, the actuarial valuation tables at Treas. Reg. §20.2031-7 (as amended in 2000) can be utilized. *See* IRC §2702(a)(3)(A)(ii). As yet another exception to the GRAT and GRUT requirements, the fair market value of a term interest in tangible property can be deducted, even if not expressed as a GRAT or GRUT, if the requirements of IRC §2702(c)(4) are satisfied. *See* Treas. Reg. §25.2702-2(c) (as amended in 2005). However, as demonstrated by *Walton*, significant planning involves intangible property such as corporate stock so the GRAT or GRUT requirements must be applied.

109. However, Grandmother doesn't expect that the property would be sold any time soon. Moreover, the new owners might at some point be able to use exchanges under IRC §1031 to defer gain on a disposition, if the asset were someday free of trust someone could establish residency invoking the IRC §121 exclusion, and in any event the capital gain tax under current law, 15 percent, would be far less than the estate tax imposed on Grandmother's estate.

110. The IRS acquiesced in the decision in Notice 2003-72, 2003-2 C.B. 964 and subsequently amended Treas. Reg. §25.2702-3(e) Example 5 in T.D. 91981, 70 Fed. Reg. 9222 (Feb. 21, 2005), 2005-1 C.B. 717.

111. Some commentary notes that aggressive GRAT planning can "avoid virtually all gift taxes," which would have benefits even if the estate tax is ultimately repealed but the gift tax is retained. *See* Carlyn S. McCaffrey et al., *The Aftermath of* Walton: *The Rehabilitation of the Fixed-Term, Zeroed-Out GRAT*, 95 J. Tax'n 325 (2001).

because the actuarial value of the annuity determined with reference to the grantor's life would not be 100 percent of the value of the property. This would be even more troublesome for elderly grantors.

To appreciate this technique, it is important to understand that with a GRAT the grantor is hoping that the transferred property will appreciate in the future at a rate greater than the interest rate prescribed by the IRC §7520 actuarial tables used to calculate and value the annuity payable to the grantor. The desired result is that significant property will remain in the GRAT after the complete payment of the full annuity to the grantor. If this occurs, the property remaining in the GRAT will have been "transferred" out of the grantor's estate without the imposition of any transfer taxes.

In *Walton*, the Wal-Mart stock did not appreciate at a sufficiently vigorous rate, and the GRAT was exhausted by the required payments to the grantor. However, in the example cited earlier regarding Parent's IPO shares, which are expected to explode in value by 20-fold, the result should be considerably better. In practice, planners use multiple GRATs, created in different years and with different types of asset classes. These multiple GRATs can also be structured with staggered annuity termination periods, such that a GRAT is regularly maturing and then "rolled over" to a new GRAT. It is accepted that some of the GRATs will not work out because the expected appreciation does not arise, as was the case in *Walton*, or the grantor does not survive the term of the GRAT. However, by the use of multiple GRATs, staggered terms, and varied asset classes, one increases the likelihood that some of the GRATs will be successful wealth shifting devices.

It should be noted that the Treasury Regulations provide that the annuity payments cannot be made by the issuance of a "note, other debt instrument, option, or other similar financial arrangement"[112] by the trustee. Consequently, if the dividends, interest, rents, or other inflows (such as third-party borrowings) to the trust are insufficient to pay the required annuity payments, the trust may be required to sell trust assets, incurring an income tax. In most cases the grantor of the GRAT will be taxable on such income, because the GRAT is structured as a grantor trust.[113]

112. Treas. Reg. §25.2702-3(d)(6) (as amended 2005).

113. The retained interest might be considered a reversionary interest under IRC §673 or the grantor may retain certain administrative powers under IRC §675 that produce grantor trust status. For an in-depth discussion of the law and mathematics of retained interest gifting strategies, see Lawrence P. Katzenstein, *Estate Planning and Charitable Planning in a Time of Low Interest Rates*, Advanced Planning Techniques, SK059 ALI-ABA 31 (ALI-ABA Continuing Legal Education, Mar. 9-11, 2005). *See generally* Jonathan G. Blattmachr, Diana S.C. Zeydel & Austin W. Bramwell, *Drafting and Administration to Maximize GRAT Performance*, 20 Prob. & Prop. 16 (Nov./Dec. 2006).

Walton v. Commissioner of Internal Revenue
115 T.C. 589 (2000)

NIMS, J.

P established and funded with corporate stock two substantially identical grantor retained annuity trusts (GRAT's). Each GRAT had a 2-year term during which P retained the right to receive an annuity. In the event that P died prior to expiration of the 2-year term, the remaining scheduled annuity payments were to be made to her estate. The balance of the trust property would then be paid to the remainder beneficiaries.

Held: For purposes of determining the value under sec. 2702, I.R.C., of the gift effected upon creation of each GRAT, P's retained qualified interest is to be valued as an annuity for a specified term of years, rather than as an annuity for the shorter of a term certain or the period ending upon P's death.

Held, further, Sec. 25.2702-3(e), *Example* (5), Gift Tax Regs., is an invalid interpretation of sec. 2702, I.R.C.

Respondent determined a deficiency in Federal gift tax against petitioner for 1993 in the amount of $4,532,776.82. The sole issue for decision is the valuation under section 2702 of gifts resulting from petitioner's creation of two grantor retained annuity trusts (GRAT's)....

BACKGROUND

... Prior to April 7, 1993, petitioner was the sole owner of, and held in her name, 7,223,478 shares of common stock of Wal-Mart Stores, Inc., a publicly traded entity. Then, on April 7, 1993, petitioner established two substantially identical GRAT's, each of which had a term of 2 years and was funded by a transfer of 3,611,739 shares of the above Wal-Mart stock. The fair market value of the Wal-Mart stock on that date was $27.6875 per share, and the consequent initial fair market value of each trust was $100,000,023.56.

According to the provisions of each GRAT, petitioner was to receive an annuity amount equal to 49.35 percent of the initial trust value for the first 12-month period of the trust term and 59.22 percent of such initial value for the second 12-month period of the trust term. In the event that petitioner's death intervened, the annuity amounts were to be paid to her estate. The sums were payable on December 31 of each taxable year but could be paid up through the date by which the Federal income tax return for the trust was required to be filed. The payments were to be made from income and, to the extent income was not sufficient, from principal. Any excess income was to be added to principal.

Upon completion of the 2-year trust term, the remaining balance was to be distributed to the designated remainder beneficiary. Petitioner's daughter Ann Walton Kroenke was the beneficiary so named under one trust instrument; petitioner's daughter Nancy Walton Laurie was named in the other.

Each trust was irrevocable, prohibited additional contributions, specified that the grantor's interest was not subject to commutation, and mandated that no payment be made during the trust term to any person other than the grantor or the grantor's estate. The two trustees for each respective trust were petitioner and the daughter for whose benefit the trust was created.

The following payments were made to petitioner from each of the GRAT's:

Date of Payment	Form of Payment	Number of Shares	Value per Share	Amount of Payment
7/9/93	Cash			$ 117,381.52
10/4/93	Cash			117,381.52
7/15/94	Stock	1,434,518	$25.1900	36,135,508.42
1/5/94	Cash			117,381.52
4/14/94	Cash			153,498.91
7/3/94	Cash			153,498.91
10/3/94	Cash			92,531.89
6/26/95	Stock	2,142,517	26.1875	56,107,163.94
1/5/95	Cash			92,531.89
4/14/95	Cash			108,861.05
6/26/95	Stock	34,704	26.1875	908,811.00
		3,611,739		94,104,550.57

The assets of each GRAT were exhausted upon the final payment of stock in June of 1995, as all income and principal had been distributed to petitioner pursuant to the scheduled annuity payments. Since the aggregate amount of annuity payments called for by each trust instrument was $108,570,025.58 (49.35 percent × $100,000,023.56 + 59.22 percent × $100,000,023.56), each GRAT resulted in a $14,465,475.01 shortfall in annuity payments to the grantor and left no property to be delivered to the remainder beneficiary.

Petitioner timely filed a United States Gift (and Generation-Skipping Transfer) Tax Return, Form 709, for the taxable year 1993. Therein, petitioner valued at zero the gifts to her daughters of remainder interests in the GRAT's. Petitioner represented that the value of her retained interests in the GRAT's equaled 100 percent of the value of the Wal-Mart stock on the date of the transfer, thus eliminating any taxable gift to the remaindermen. Respondent subsequently issued a notice of deficiency determining that petitioner had understated the value of the gifts resulting from her establishment of the two GRAT's. Petitioner now concedes on brief that the gift occasioned by each GRAT should be valued at $6,195.10, while respondent asserts that the taxable value of each gift by petitioner is $3,821,522.12.

DISCUSSION

I. GENERAL RULES

Section 2501 imposes a tax for each calendar year on the transfer of property by gift by any taxpayer. Pursuant to section 2512, the value of the transferred property as of the date of the gift "shall be considered the amount of the gift". Generally, where property is transferred in trust but the donor retains an interest in such property, the value of the gift is the value of the property transferred, less the value of the donor's retained interest. See sec. 25.2512-5A(e), Gift Tax Regs.; sec. 25.2512-5T(d)(2), Temporary Gift Tax Regs., 64 Fed. Reg. 23224 (Apr. 30, 1999). However, if the gift in trust is to a family member (as defined in section 2704(c)(2)), the value of the gift is determined subject to the limitations of section 2702. See *id.*

As pertinent herein, section 2702 provides:

Sec. 2702. Special Valuation Rules in Case of Transfers of Interests in Trusts

(a) Valuation Rules.—

(1) In general.—Solely for purposes of determining whether a transfer of an interest in trust to (or for the benefit of) a member of the transferor's family is a gift (and the value of such transfer), the value of any interest in such trust retained by the transferor or any applicable family member . . . shall be determined as provided in paragraph (2).

(2) Valuation of retained interests.—

(A) In general.—The value of any retained interest which is not a qualified interest shall be treated as being zero.

(B) Valuation of qualified interest.—The value of any retained interest which is a qualified interest shall be determined under section 7520 [providing for use of valuation tables prescribed by the Secretary for annuities, life interests, etc.].

(b) Qualified Interest.—For purposes of this section, the term "qualified interest" means—

(1) any interest which consists of the right to receive fixed amounts payable not less frequently than annually,

(2) any interest which consists of the right to receive amounts which are payable not less frequently than annually and are a fixed percentage of the fair market value of the property in the trust (determined annually), and

(3) any noncontingent remainder interest if all of the other interests in the trust consist of interests described in paragraph (1) or (2).

Regulations promulgated under section 2702 define, and expand upon, certain of the terms employed in section 2702. "Retained" denotes "held by the same individual both before and after the transfer in trust." Sec.

25.2702-2(a)(3), Gift Tax Regs. The statutory definition of "qualified interest" is likewise elucidated in the following manner: "Qualified interest means a qualified annuity interest, a qualified unitrust interest, or a qualified remainder interest." Sec. 25.2702-2(a)(5), Gift Tax Regs. A "qualified annuity interest," in turn, is "an interest that meets all the requirements of §25.2702-3(b) and (d)." Sec. 25.2702-2(a)(6), Gift Tax Regs.

The above-referenced paragraph (b) of section 25.2702-3, Gift Tax Regs., requires that a "qualified annuity interest" consist of "an irrevocable right to receive a fixed amount," "payable to (or for the benefit of) the holder of the annuity interest for each taxable year of the term." Sec. 25.2702-3(b)(1)(i), Gift Tax Regs. In this context, a "fixed amount" is either a stated dollar amount or a fixed fraction or percentage (not to exceed 120 percent of the fixed fraction or percentage payable in the preceding year) of the initial fair market value of the property transferred to the trust as finally determined for Federal tax purposes. Sec. 25.2702-3(b)(1)(ii), Gift Tax Regs. In either case, the fixed amount must be payable periodically but not less frequently than annually. See *id.*

Paragraph (d) of section 25.2702-3, Gift Tax Regs., then adds the following requirement dealing with the term of the annuity interest: "The governing instrument must fix the term of the annuity or unitrust interest. The term must be for the life of the term holder, for a specified term of years, or for the shorter (but not the longer) of those periods." Sec. 25.2702-3(d)(3), Gift Tax Regs. Furthermore, the trust instrument must also prohibit distributions from the trust to or for the benefit of any person other than the holder of the qualified annuity interest during the term of the qualified interest. See sec. 25.2702-3(d)(2), Gift Tax Regs.

II. CONTENTIONS OF THE PARTIES

Respondent contends that in establishing each GRAT, petitioner created three separate and distinct interests: (1) The annuity payable to her during her lifetime, (2) the "contingent" interest of her estate to receive the annuity payments in the event of her death prior to expiration of the 2-year trust term, and (3) the remainder interest granted to her daughter. Of these three, it is respondent's position that only the first interest, but not the second, constitutes a qualified retained interest within the meaning of section 2702 and the regulations promulgated thereunder. Respondent particularly relies upon section 25.2702-3(e), *Example* (5), Gift Tax Regs. (hereinafter Example 5), as a valid interpretation of the statute and as governing the issues involved in this case.

Hence, according to respondent, only the value of an annuity payable for the shorter of 2 years or the period ending upon petitioner's death may be subtracted from the fair market value of the stock in calculating the value of the taxable gift made by reason of petitioner's establishment of the GRAT's. Respondent concludes that the present value of the retained qualified interest in each GRAT was $96,178,501.88 and the taxable gift $3,821,522.12 (consisting of the estate's contingent interest of $2,938,000.00 and the remainder interest of $883,522.12).

Conversely, petitioner maintains that for valuation purposes under section 2702, each GRAT is properly characterized as creating only two separate interests: (1) A retained annuity payable for a fixed term of 2 years, and (2) a remainder interest in favor of her daughter. Petitioner further asserts that the former, in its entirety, is a qualified interest within the meaning of the statute. Accordingly, it is petitioner's position that the retained interest to be subtracted in computing the amount of the taxable gift occasioned by each GRAT is to be valued as a simple 2-year term annuity, without regard to any mortality factor. Using this method, petitioner calculates the retained annuity as having a value of $99,993,828.90, such that each GRAT effected a gift of $6,195.10.

To the extent that Example 5 would appear to suggest otherwise, petitioner avers that the example is an invalid and unreasonable interpretation of section 2702. Petitioner argues that the example is unsupported by statutory language or legislative history and is inconsistent with other regulations and examples, especially section 25.2702-3(d)(3), Gift Tax Regs. In the alternative, petitioner claims that even if Example 5 is a permissible interpretation of the statute on substantive grounds, it is procedurally invalid as issued in violation of the notice and comment provisions of the Administrative Procedures Act, 5 U.S.C. sec. 553 (1994).

III. APPLICATION

As pertinent here, section 2702 provides a facially simple formula for valuation: (Value of property transferred in trust) – (value of any qualified interest retained by the grantor) = value of gift. Applying this formula, however, requires resolution of potentially complex subsidiary issues. For instance, in order to determine the amount that may be subtracted, the following are among the questions that must be addressed: The nature of the interest "retained" by the grantor, the extent to which that interest is "qualified," and the actuarial value of the qualified interest.

A. The Nature of the Interest Retained

Commencing with the threshold inquiry of what interest or interests petitioner "retained," we conclude that, even if we were to view the GRAT indentures as creating separate interests in favor of petitioner and petitioner's estate, both such interests must be construed as retained by petitioner. It is axiomatic that an individual cannot make a gift to himself or to his or her own estate. An attempt to do so has long been treated at common law as a retention by the individual of the interest purportedly transferred. For example, 1 Restatement, Trusts 2d, section 127 comment b (1959), states:

> Where the owner of property, whether real or personal, transfers it in trust to pay the income to himself for a period of years and at the expiration of the period to pay the principal to him, he is the sole beneficiary of the trust. He is likewise the sole beneficiary where he transfers property in trust to

> pay the income to himself for life and on his death to pay the principal to his estate, or to his personal representatives. . . .

Hence, because petitioner could not as a matter of law give an interest in property to her estate, she by default retained all interests in the 2-year term annuities set forth in the trust documents. Such interests thus were, as required by the regulations, "held by the same individual both before and after the transfer in trust." Sec. 25.2702-2(a)(3), Gift Tax Regs.

B. The Extent of the Qualified Interest

Having therefore decided that petitioner, either individually or through her estate, retained the 2-year annuities in their entirety, we next consider the extent to which these interests are "qualified." In this connection, section 2702 itself provides only that "qualified interest" means "any interest which consists of the right to receive fixed amounts payable not less frequently than annually." Sec. 2702(b)(1). Since a simple 2-year annuity would appear to fall within this definition, we turn to whether relevant regulations set forth additional restrictions.

The regulatory provision which enumerates the permissible terms for a qualified annuity mandates that the term be "for the life of the term holder, for a specified term of years, or for the shorter (but not the longer) of those periods." Sec. 25.2702-3(d)(3), Gift Tax Regs. Petitioner thus contends that her 2-year annuities are sanctioned by the second of these three options and may be valued as such. Respondent, however, asserts that petitioner's annuities are in fact of the third listed type and cites Example 5 and section 25.2702-3(e), *Example (1)*, Gift Tax Regs., among others, in support of this position. Example 5 states as follows:

> A transfers property to an irrevocable trust, retaining the right to receive 5 percent of the net fair market value of the trust property, valued annually, for 10 years. If A dies within the 10-year term, the unitrust amount is to be paid to A's estate for the balance of the term. A's interest is a qualified unitrust interest to the extent of the right to receive the unitrust payment for 10 years or until A's prior death.

Section 25.2702-3(e), *Example (1)*, Gift Tax Regs., provides: A transfers property to an irrevocable trust, retaining the right to receive the greater of $10,000 or the trust income in each year for a term of 10 years. Upon expiration of the 10-year term, the trust is to terminate and the entire trust corpus is to be paid to A's child, provided that if A dies within the 10-year term the trust corpus is to be paid to A's estate. A's annual payment right is a qualified annuity interest to the extent of the right to receive $10,000 per year for 10 years or until A's prior death, and is valued under section 7520 without regard to the right to receive any income in excess of $10,000 per year. The contingent reversion is valued at zero. The amount of A's gift is the fair market value of the property transferred to the trust less the value of the qualified annuity interest.

We agree with respondent that Example 5, if valid, would preclude the valuation methodology for which petitioner argues. To say that Example 5 is not on point because it involves a unitrust rather than an annuity interest would be to rely on a distinction without a substantive difference. Consequently, we are faced squarely with the question of this regulation's validity.

The regulations at issue here are interpretative regulations promulgated under the general authority vested in the Secretary by section 7805(a). Hence, while entitled to considerable weight, they are accorded less deference than would be legislative regulations issued under a specific grant of authority to address a matter raised by the pertinent statute....

Because section 2702 does not speak to the issue of the permissible term for a qualified annuity, Example 5 does not expressly contradict any statutory language. Accordingly, we focus on the statute's origin and purpose for further guidance. [The Court then examined at length the legislative history of the Omnibus Budget Reconciliation Act of 1990 and the arguments made by the IRS and the taxpayer.]

Thus, given the above authorities, we construe each of the subject GRAT's as creating a single, noncontingent annuity interest payable for a specified term of years to the undifferentiated unit of petitioner or her estate. We further conclude that Congress meant to allow individuals to retain qualified annuity interests for a specified term of years, and that the proper method for doing so is to make the balance of any payments due after the grantor's death payable to the grantor's estate. We hold that Example 5 is an unreasonable interpretation and an invalid extension of section 2702, and we need not reach the issue of whether it was adopted in violation of the Administrative Procedures Act. Accordingly, the qualified interest retained by petitioner in each GRAT here is an annuity payable for a specified term of 2 years....

Technique 7—Creating Gift Tax and Income Tax Deductions with Charitable Gifts. The gift tax and the estate tax offer deductions for gifts to charitable organizations.[114] For very wealthy clients, where family and loved ones are otherwise amply provided for, or for clients without significant family, bequests to charity made upon the donor's death reduce the estate tax while also serving a philanthropic purpose. However, inter vivos gifts to charity are attractive to an even broader group of clients because the gifts, in addition to reducing the taxable estate of the donor, may also provide a current income tax deduction for the value of the charitable interest.[115] Moreover, if the client wishes to benefit other family members with the same gift, split-interest gifts may be used, where much of the value of the transfer to the family members is sheltered by the deduction of the

114. *See* IRC §§2522 & 2055.
115. *See* IRC §170.

value of the charity's interest in the property. This is a charitable version of the retained interest mechanics that are the foundation of the GRATs, GRUTs, and QPRTs, discussed earlier. Furthermore, if appreciated property is transferred to a qualifying charitable trust, it may generally be sold by the trust with no imposition of federal income taxes, so more after-tax wealth is available for the benefits paid to family members and to the charity.

Using this technique, family members might enjoy income from the property for their lives or for a fixed term, with the remainder passing to charity under a charitable remainder trust. Conversely, using a "charitable lead trust," a charity might be gifted the right to income from the property for a fixed number of years, with the remainder passing to family members. Split-interest gifts are subject to overlapping rules that must be complied with for federal income tax purposes, as well as for wealth transfer tax purposes. *See* Chapter 14.

d. Strategy—Avoiding Asset Inclusion in the Taxable Estate and Shifting Wealth to Others *Technique 8—Avoiding Estate Tax Inclusive "Strings."* As demonstrated by Technique 6, which involves QPRTs and GRATs, wealth shifting techniques need to be structured with an understanding of the estate tax consequences of the gift transaction. While an outright gift free of trust is the simplest planning technique in terms of the estate tax consequences, it may have adverse consequences if not planned correctly.

For example, Grandfather wishes to transfer Farmacre to Child outright, using annual real estate deeds for portions of the property.[116] However, Grandfather continues to farm Farmacre as part of a larger agricultural operation. He plants and harvests crops on Farmacre, retains all of the profits, and has not executed any type of lease with Child: in short, he continues to treat Farmacre as his own. It is clear that upon Grandfather's death the gifted portions of Farmacre will be included in his estate because of the de facto life estate he has retained, thereby invoking IRC §2036(a).

Transfers to revocable trusts are usually made for broader estate planning reasons, not for wealth transfer tax avoidance. The revocable nature of the trust dictates its inclusion in the taxable estate under IRC §2038. Revocable trusts are discussed in Chapter 15. However, transfers to irrevocable trusts are often for wealth transfer avoidance and as a receptacle for inter vivos gifts using the annual gift exclusion and/or the applicable exclusion amount. Inclusion in the taxable estate is generally not a desired consequence. The various "retained string" provisions were discussed in greater detail in the summary of the estate tax earlier in this chapter.

116. The IRS in Rev. Rul. 83-180, 1983-2 C.B. 169, accepts this serial gifting of portions of property. The ruling does not address the valuation issues, such as allowing fractional interest discounts if undivided interests in parcels are gifted as compared to gifting entire interests in fewer acres.

Some techniques such as Technique 3 (Outright Gift of Appreciating Property) and Technique 4 (Asset Freeze Structures), focus on limiting the appreciation of assets in an individual's estate. Other techniques exploit the structure of certain estate tax provisions with the desired result that wealth is never included in the individual's estate in the first place and therefore needn't be disposed of, frozen, etc. Techniques 9 through 12, below, are examples of such planning.

Technique 9—Avoiding General Powers of Appointment. Powers of appointment are an important tool in the drafting of Wills and trusts, because they permit someone other than the decedent/settlor—usually a family member or loved one—to exercise some later discretion in how the assets are to be applied for the benefit of others. However, IRC §2041 would include the appointable assets in the estate of the holder of a general power of appointment, and under IRC §2514 the holder of the power treats the exercise of a general power of appointment in favor of another as a gift of the appointed assets. Consequently, there are few situations in which general powers of appointment are desirable from a wealth transfer tax standpoint.[117] In crafting Wills and trusts, one therefore should focus on meeting the technical requirements of the exceptions to general power treatment (generally referred to as a "special power of appointment," although that language is not in the tax code).

There are two principal exceptions used by planners. One exception is a power exercisable in favor of others, not in favor of the holder, "his estate, his creditors, or the creditors of his estate."[118] The other exception is a power "limited by an ascertainable standard relating to the health, education, support or maintenance"[119] of the holder.

Technique 10—Ownership of Life Insurance. Life insurance is an important component of many estate plans. The proceeds are generally exempt from federal income taxation[120] and can be a source of liquidity for the estate in terms of funding business purchases and satisfying debts and other obligations, including estate taxes.[121] The federal estate tax on the life insurance proceeds may be easily avoided with proper structuring:

117. A *Crummey* withdrawal power is a general power of appointment, a necessary drawback to support the doctrine of the case. *Crummey* powers are discussed in Chapter 8. As discussed in Chapter 11, a general power of appointment is a requirement of some marital deduction gifts, such as the IRC §2056(b)(5) requirement. And as discussed in Chapter 13, general powers of appointment may be used for GSTT planning purposes to substitute a possible estate tax on the holder of the power, supplanting a GSTT imposed on the appointable assets. General powers of appointment, including *Crummey* powers, that are included in trusts are usually structured as "5 or 5" powers under IRC §2514(e) to avoid the creation of a gift upon the lapse of the power.

118. IRC §2041(b)(1).

119. IRC §2041(b)(1)(A).

120. *See* IRC §101.

121. If the sole purpose of the life insurance is to provide cash liquidity to pay estate and other taxes, then so-called "second-to-die" insurance policies, which insure the lives of both spouses but only pay the face value on the death of the second insured, are popular because (1) the payment of the proceeds coincides with the time that estate taxes are usually payable, if at all (on the death of the second spouse), and (2) the premiums for such a policy are significantly lower (because two insureds must die to trigger payout).

never have the decedent own the policy on his or her life, directly or indirectly, or otherwise hold any other "incidents of ownership"[122] in the policy. Many estate plans involve the proper configuration of life insurance ownership, including the creation of an ILIT referred to earlier. See Chapter 11.

Technique 11 — Use of Disclaimers. The exercise of a qualified disclaimer in compliance with IRC §2518 is not treated as a taxable gift, although it may trigger a GSTT if the ultimate recipient is two or more generations removed from the donor/decedent. Disclaimers are accordingly an important post-mortem planning device to shift inherited wealth among family members free of gift tax. In light of the uncertainties surrounding the 2010 Act, many planners recommend consideration of "disclaimer Wills," which make the allocation decisions between nonmarital and marital shares of the estate a post-mortem tool effectuated by careful use of disclaimers. (See Form N of the Forms Supplement for a sample disclaimer Will.)

Technique 12 — Below-Market Loans. The use of money is a valuable asset in itself, and below-market loans accomplish the transfer of that asset to other family members. While IRC §7872 has limited the benefits of this technique, some planning is still attractive at the margins, largely because the statutorily required interest rates are generally lower than what would be demanded by most private lenders. Below-market loans are discussed in Chapter 8.

e. Strategy — Optimal Use of Deductions for Spousal Gifts or Bequests. Spouses may transfer unlimited amounts to one another inter vivos[123] or at death.[124] The wealth transfer taxes are simply deferred, because the structural assumption is that wealth transfer taxes will be imposed on the residual estate at the survivor's death.

Although there are exceptions, the marital deduction strategy generally has two components: (1) providing for the maximum deferral of the wealth transfer tax by making marital bequests to reduce the estate tax payable to zero upon the death of the first spouse (an exception is made for spouses dying within months of one another, in which case the estates may be equalized); and (2) providing for the maximum use of each spouse's applicable exclusion amount. The second component was typically accomplished through the creation of a nonmarital gift as a "credit shelter," "family," or "bypass" trust. As discussed in Chapter 11, the 2010 Act introduced the Deceased Spousal Unused Exclusion Amount (DSUEA), which simplifies the second component in some situations. For some estates it could eliminate the need for a bypass or credit shelter trust.

122. *See* IRC §2042.
123. *See* IRC §2523.
124. *See* IRC §2056.

As discussed in Chapter 11 and in the section that follows, there are other considerations in the use of the bypass trust that may still remain compelling after the DSUEA.

2. Planning After the 2010 Act

a. Uncertainty Dominates the Planning Environment. As discussed in greater depth in Chapter 11, EGTRRA dramatically reduced the impact of the wealth transfer taxes, but in the process introduced several new and frustrating planning wrinkles.[125] The estate tax and the GSTT, but not the gift tax, which was retained as a backstop to income tax avoidance planning, were set to terminate for decedents who died after December 31, 2009, and generation-skipping transfers made after December 31, 2009. Contingency planning for this possibility produced a lot of prognostication by commentators, wasted planning activity, and client planning paralysis, while awaiting an outcome. The "unthinkable" happened, and the termination did occur in 2010, until order was restored with the enactment of the 2010 Act on December 17, 2010.

EGTRRA's principal benefits were its gradual reduction in the maximum rate of wealth transfer taxes from 50 percent to 45 percent, and an increase in the applicable exclusion amount, formerly referred to as the unified credit, for estates, reaching $3,500,000 in 2009. EGTRRA did create its share of problems, such as establishing a $1,000,000 exclusion for gifts different from the estate and GSTT exclusions, and flirting with "carryover basis" for 2010. Those flaws were corrected by the 2010 Act, subject to transitional rules for 2010. All of EGTRRA's changes were subject to sunset for decedents dying and gifts made after December 31, 2010, such that the exemptions, rates, and other features of the tax would revert to their pre-EGTRRA, 2001 status. The 2010 Act modified the EGTRRA changes (in general further liberalizing them) and pushed back the sunset date to December 31, 2012.

Planners and their clients consequently have guidance for 2011 and 2012, but not beyond. As discussed below, some actions in 2011 and 2012 (such as large gifts) may have adverse impacts if the 2010 Act is not extended. Further, clients will face a restrictive pre-EGTRRA landscape (including a $1,000,000 applicable exclusion amount and a 55 percent maximum wealth transfer tax rate) in 2013 if the 2010 Act is not extended or replaced. The uncertainties that dogged EGTRRA are continued with the 2010 Act. For example, will the estate tax be reborn at 2001 rates and exemptions in 2013? Or will the estate tax be modified to some other scheme? Will it perhaps be abolished altogether?

125. *See, e.g.*, Richard B. Covey, *Recent Developments* (2001) *in Transfer Taxes & Income Taxation of Trusts & Estates*, 36 Inst. on Est. Plan., ¶¶ 100, 101.5 (2002); Steve R. Akers, *Estate Planning Under the 2001 Act*, Planning Techniques for Large Estates, SG690 ALI-ABA 225 (ALI-ABA Continuing Legal Education, Apr. 22-26, 2002); Paula M. Jones, *Planning for the 10-Year Phase Out of Estate Tax (with Form)*, 17 No. 2 Prac. Tax Law. 57 (Winter 2003).

b. Planning for 2011 and 2012. During this period, the applicable exclusion amount will be \$5,000,000, indexed for inflation in 2012. The DSUEA, discussed in Chapter 11, will be applicable to decedents dying in those years.

(1) The DSUEA's Limited Role. As discussed in Chapter 11, the DSUEA is a response to the concerns of an unplanned estate, but its benefit to more complex estates is questionable.

- The appreciation in property placed in a bypass (also known as a "credit shelter" or "family" trust) escapes estate tax in the estate of the surviving spouse, although the trade-off is a loss of IRC §1014 basis adjustment; the age and health of the surviving spouse, the surviving spouse's financial needs, the size of the estate relative to the amount of the applicable exclusion amount, and the nature of the estate's assets are some of the factors considered in assessing the benefits of a bypass trust.[126]
- Property placed in a bypass trust can benefit from professional management by a trustee, although a competent surviving spouse can also engage similar, if not identical, professional management over the spouse's assets.
- Property placed in a bypass trust can mitigate problems presented by the possible incapacity of the surviving spouse.
- Property placed in a bypass trust can be protected against creditors of the surviving spouse and other beneficiaries.
- Property placed in a bypass trust can be protected against dissipation or misdirection by the surviving spouse (particularly in a second marriage situation).
- Property placed in a bypass trust can be protected against elective share claims or dissipation or misdirection by a new spouse of the surviving spouse.
- The GSTT exemption is not portable, so significant GSTT testamentary gifts by the first spouse can be accommodated by a bypass trust.
- In states that impose an estate tax, the marital or family exemptions may be different amounts than for federal purposes, requiring a more tailored scheme than anticipated by the DSUEA.[127]
- Even if a bypass trust is eliminated, the creation of a marital trust to extend trust protection to the household wealth will introduce much of the complexity that one would seek to avoid by eliminating the bypass trust.

126. *See, e.g.*, Jonathan G. Blattmachr et al., *Estate Planning After the 2010 Tax Relief Act: Big Changes, But Still No Certainty*, 114 J. TAX'N 68, 82-85 (Feb. 2011) (scenarios with different estate sizes and rates of appreciation).

127. *See id.*, at 84-86.

- The DSUEA will sunset with the rest of the 2010 Act on December 31, 2012, so reliance on it in instruments that could remain in effect after that date would not appear to be prudent.

(2) The DSUEA's Impact for Decedents Dying in 2011 or 2012. Apart from its impact on traditional bypass trust planning, the DSUEA does offer inter vivos planning opportunities if a deceased spouse dies during 2011-2012 and did not fully utilize all of his or her applicable exclusion amount. As discussed in Chapter 11, a surviving spouse who does not believe that the DSUEA will be extended beyond 2012, or who plans to remarry, may consider certain inter vivos gifting structures to utilize the DSUEA.

(3) Inter Vivos Planning for the $5,000,000 Applicable Exclusion Amount. The $5,000,000 applicable exclusion amount extends to gifts, GSTT transfers, as well as to decedents dying in 2011 and 2012. If one assumes that the $5,000,000 amount will be extended past 2013, this presents a lot of inter vivos planning opportunities.

- FLPs and QPRTs may no longer be needed for smaller estates for the purpose of minimizing values, and consequently might be unwound.[128]
- Inter vivos gifting schemes of all types, such as sales to IDGTs, GRATs, QPRTs, and life insurance trusts (ILITs),[129] can be implemented for much larger amounts, now that the EGTRRA $1,000,000 gift exclusion has been supplanted by the unified $5,000,000 amount.[130]

A caution is that many of these lifetime gifts will be included in the estate tax computation as an adjusted taxable gift.[131] If the donor used all of the $5,000,000 exclusion for inter vivos gifts, and the IRC §2010 applicable exclusion amount is less than $5,000,000 at the time of the donor's death, the difference will produce an additional estate tax unless Congress clarifies in future law that this was not the intent: It is conceivable that Congress could fashion a grandfather rule for these gifts, even if it decides to decrease the amount of the applicable exclusion amount after

128. *See, e.g.*, Eugene Pollinque & Pauline W. Markey, *Family Partnership Liquidation Presents Tax Issues*, 38 Est. Plan. 25 (May 2011); Martin M. Shenkman & Stephen R. Akers, Estate Planning after the Tax Relief and Job Creation Act of 2010 79 (2011) (discussing unwinding FLPs and QPRTs—the latter by failing to pay a fair rental at the end of the term of years, thereby invoking IRC §§2036 & 1014).

129. *See, e.g.*, Melvin A. Warshaw, *Life Insurance Planning After the 2010 Tax Act*, 150 Tr. & Est. 48 (Apr. 2011); Shenkman & Akers, *supra* note 128, ch. 6 (discussing gift leveraging opportunities for sales to IDGTs, GRATs, QPRTs, etc.).

130. The larger exclusion will allow wealthy, insurable elderly individuals to consider establishing an ILIT to hold a larger, and more expensive, life insurance policy acquired as single premium "paid up" insurance without incurring gift tax at the time of transferring funds to the trust.

131. *See* IRC §2001(b)(1)(B). This assumes that the gift is not otherwise included in the gross estate; such exclusion is generally the desired outcome.

2012.[132] Even if there is the possibility of additional estate tax, the donor's estate will still enjoy the benefits of lifetime gifts in terms of shifting post-gift appreciation away from the estate. In addition, subject to calculations of the net tax impacts under the client's particular circumstances and level of wealth, this could be a "pay me later" proposition as an end result.

(4) Marital Deduction Drafting Considerations for the Increased Applicable Exclusion Amount (or a Decreased Applicable Exclusion Amount). Assuming that the DSUEA does not supplant a formula clause, typical language for a pre-residuary marital bequest formula clause, for example, sets aside to the marital share an amount roughly equal to the decedent's estate, reduced by the amount, if any, needed to increase the decedent's taxable estate to the largest amount that will result in no federal estate tax being payable after allowing for the applicable exclusion amount. Under this formula, the marital share could be eliminated unless the decedent's estate exceeds $5,000,000. The same result should follow if residuary marital bequests[133] or fractional share bequests[134] are used. While a marital bequest will be created if the first spouse to die's estate exceeds $5,000,000 by any amount, unless the value of the estate significantly exceeds $5,000,000, the marital share will be nonetheless relatively small. This is a concern for the surviving spouse if the bypass trust does not provide the same degree of spousal access as a marital trust, as is often the case with second marriages with his and her kids.

On the other hand, if the $5,000,000 applicable exclusion amount is reduced in a Congressional compromise after 2012, or the $1,000,000 pre-EGTRRA amount re-emerges as a default, the marital trust share will increase in comparison with the nonmarital share, so many of these safeguards will no longer be necessary. However, *flexibility* is the watchword, and that attribute is shared by the contingent QTIP election and disclaimer Will options discussed below.

(i) *Limits on the Nonmarital Share.* In planning for EGTRRA's dramatic increases in the applicable exclusion amount, some commentators recommended overall limits ("caps," "ceiling," or "collar") on the size of the nonmarital share expressed in terms of an absolute

132. *See, e.g.*, Blattmachr et al., *supra* note 126, at 78-79, 88 (recommending that very wealthy clients make substantial inter vivos gifts immediately); Marvin D. Hills, *Subsequent Remarriage Complicates Exclusion Amount Portability*, 38 Est. Plan. 3, 7-8 (discussing "claw-back" scenarios).

133. If a residuary marital bequest is used, a bequest to the family trust is created of the largest amount that can pass free of federal estate tax after allowing for the applicable credit amount, with the residue to the marital share. This language creates the same result as a pre-residuary bequest. However, with the marital bequest taking the form of a residue, it does keep open the possibility, however impractical, of a disclaimer by the beneficiaries of the family trust, which could redirect the funds to the marital trust.

134. If a fractional share formula is used, the numerator of the marital share fraction is equal to the smallest amount that will result in no federal estate tax being payable after allowing for the applicable credit amount. If a fractional share formula is used, the numerator will tend to be zero for a taxable estate not in excess of $5,000,000 in 2011-2012.

amount[135] and/or a percentage of the estate,[136] potentially forgoing a portion of the applicable exclusion amount. One finds such recommendations in terms of the 2010 Act.[137] Nonetheless, the forgone applicable exclusion amount may not be lost forever so long as the DSUEA remains available, making the unused applicable exclusion amount available to the surviving spouse. Although less flexible than other approaches discussed below, it is simpler and more predictable in remarriage situations, for example, where the decedent desires more assurances as to where assets will pass and how much will pass. To add more flexibility to the arrangement, a revocable trust rather than a Will might be employed, with the trustee authorized to make amendments to reflect additional changes in the law or other circumstances. Conversely, minimum funding amounts, also expressed as an absolute amount, may also be expressed in regards to funding the nonmarital share. At a minimum, attorneys should discuss with clients the concept of "ceilings" and "floors" in regards to both marital and nonmarital gifts.

(ii) *Contingent QTIP Election*. A second approach is to place more discretion in the personal representative or trustee in making a *Clayton*[138] contingent QTIP election. This is a type of partial QTIP election, but with a difference. Rather than dividing a single trust into two subtrusts for the QTIP and nonmarital shares, respectively, the portion of the estate for which the QTIP is elected passes to a marital trust, but the non-QTIP portion passes to a nonmarital trust in which the terms and beneficiaries are different from the terms and beneficiaries of the marital trust. This approach requires no formula clause; it relies on the personal representative or trustee's QTIP election, but the result resembles a traditional marital trust/nonmarital trust division.[139] If the client wishes both the QTIP and non-QTIP shares to be held for the benefit of the surviving spouse in a manner resembling a single marital trust, the planner could use a traditional partial QTIP provision with marital and nonmarital subtrusts, instead of a *Clayton* contingent QTIP.[140] This approach would be less flexible with respect to the nonmarital portion, but it could be more generous with respect to the surviving spouse, which is often a couple's planning objective.[141] If the surviving spouse is the trustee, the

135. *See, e.g.*, Jones, *supra* note 125 (sample language for an absolute dollar cap on a bequest for 2004-2005, 2006-2008, 2009, 2010, and 2011).

136. *See, e.g.*, Lawrence P. Keller & Anthony T. Lee, *Wills and Estate Plans Require New Flexibility to Reflect Tax Changes and Uncertain Future*, 74 N.Y. St. B.J. 19, 21 (Dec. 2002) (sample language imposing both an absolute dollar cap and a percentage of the estate limitation).

137. *See e.g.*, Shenkman & Akers, *supra* note 128, at 118-119 (sample Will formula clauses with caps and language acknowledging possible decreases in the $5,000,000 applicable exclusion amount).

138. 976 F.2d 1486 (5th Cir. 1992). *See* Treas. Reg. §§20.2056(b)-7(d)-3 & 20.2056(b)-7(h), Example 6 (as amended in 1998) (adopting the result in *Clayton*).

139. *See, e.g.*, Sebastian V. Grassi, Jr., *Drafting Flexibility into Estate Planning Documents After the 2001 Tax Act (with Sample Clauses)*, 17, No. 2 Prac. Tax Law. 7, 12-15 (Winter 2003) (sample contingent QTIP language).

140. *Id.* at 15-16 (sample language).

141. *See* Blattmachr et al., *supra* note 126, at 86 (discussing leaving all of the estate to a QTIP marital trust and Rev. Proc. 2001-38 concerns).

result of this approach is essentially no different from that of the next approach discussed (disclaimer), even though the mechanism to accomplish the "split" is very different.

(iii) *Disclaimer Will or Marital Trust with Disclaimer Clause.* Another approach is to place all of the discretion in the surviving spouse with variations on a disclaimer theme. A common suggestion is a "disclaimer Will" in which all of the estate passes to the surviving spouse outright or to a marital trust for the benefit of the surviving spouse, but the surviving spouse can disclaim all, or some portion, of the bequest such that it passes to the nonmarital trust or outright to nonmarital beneficiaries.[142] This flexibility avoids the creation of a bypass trust at the outset (one of the goals of the DSUEA), but permits its creation if changes in the tax law or the married couple's overall situation dictates otherwise. This might not work well in remarriage situations or otherwise strained relationships, because to work effectively it may require that the surviving spouse direct assets to a trust for the benefit of beneficiaries that he or she may not prefer.

This objection can be reduced by making the surviving spouse a beneficiary of the nonmarital trust in addition to the other beneficiaries. This trust must be designated to receive the disclaimed assets, without direction by the surviving spouse, in the Will if the disclaimer is to qualify as an effective disclaimer under §2518. However, even if the surviving spouse is a beneficiary of the trust to which the disclaimed assets will flow, the terms of the trust may be less generous (and the benefits of the assets may need to be shared with other beneficiaries) than those of the marital trust. Property held in any trust is certainly less desirable to the recipient than outright ownership of the assets.

It also suffers from the general drawbacks of disclaimers, many of which could be avoided with proper diligence in the administration of the estate and/or drafting responses: (a) they must be exercised within the 9-month window under IRC §2518(b)(2) (in comparison, a partial QTIP can be exercised within 15 months of death, considering extensions of time to file the estate tax return); (b) if the surviving spouse dies during the disclaimer period, statutes such as UPC §2-1105(b) in tandem with UPC §2-1102(4) would permit the personal representative to exercise a disclaimer. However, such authority may not exist in all cases. Moreover, the personal representative may be unable, as a matter of fiduciary duty, to divert property otherwise passing to the surviving spouse's estate;[143] (c) the

142. Grassi, *supra* note 139, at 17-18 (sample language); *see also* JEFFREY A. SCHOENBLUM, PAGE ON THE LAW OF WILLS, vol. 7 (Forms), ch. 28F (2010) (several examples of disclaimer clauses); Sebastian V. Grassi, Jr., *Drafting the Marital Deduction Disclaimer Trust After the 2001 Tax Act (with Sample Clauses and Trust Form)* (Part 1), 16 NO. 3 PRAC. TAX LAW. 29 (Spring 2002); Sebastian V. Grassi, Jr., *Drafting the Marital Deduction Disclaimer Trust After the 2001 Tax Act (with Sample Clauses and Trust Form)* (Part 2), 16 NO. 4 PRAC. TAX LAW. 7 (Summer 2002) (the Grassi articles are a very comprehensive treatment of this topic, with extensive sample language and forms). Form N in the Forms Supplement is a sample disclaimer Will.

143. *See generally* WILLIAM M. MCGOVERN ET AL., WILLS, TRUSTS AND ESTATES 91-93 (4th ed. 2010).

surviving spouse may be deemed to have accepted the property or a benefit of the property, foreclosing a disclaimer; and (d) if the family trust is the receptacle for the disclaimed property (rather than a separate disclaimer trust or subtrust created solely for this purpose), the regulations at Treas. Reg. §25.2518-2(e)(5), Examples 4-7, would forbid the surviving spouse's possession of certain powers over the family trust, such as a special power of appointment. Consequently, if it is desired that the surviving spouse have such special powers over some of the assets in the trust, one drafting response is to set aside such disclaimed property in the family trust as a subtrust over which the surviving spouse does not have such proscribed powers.[144]

(iv) *Enhancing Spousal Access to the Bypass Trust.* With the disclaimer Will in particular, in light of the uncertainty produced by EGTRRA, some planners recommended that the surviving spouse's interests in the nonmarital trust be enhanced by providing for distributions of income, invasions of principal, and so forth. This in part was intended to encourage the surviving spouse to disclaim assets to fund the nonmarital trust.[145] It also reflects that the bulk of a modest estate may rest in the nonmarital trust, and the surviving spouse might need access to those funds for his or her support. With the $5,000,000 inflation-adjusted applicable exclusion amount, these modifications may prove to be important to smaller estates.

c. Planning for Repeal of the Federal Estate Tax. If the federal estate tax were repealed completely, instruments that incorporate tax definitions and were structured in light of now irrelevant tax concepts would need to be interpreted. Many of the structures would probably no longer be needed, and the focus would shift to unwinding them. Others, such as marital formula clauses, could still be operative in that environment, but if applied in the new environment without modifications, could produce unexpected results.[146] In responding to the EGTRRA uncertainty, some planners recommended drafting using various alternatives, with provisions predicated on the existing law or, in the alternative, total and permanent repeal of the wealth transfer taxes.[147] Other planners believed that such efforts were largely a waste of clients' money, would probably turn out to be rendered inappropriate by future changes in the law, and may do some harm if the clauses are not well considered. New Wills or

144. *See* Casner & Pennell, *supra* note 77, at §§13.1.4.1 & 13.1.4.2 (discussing advantages and disadvantages of disclaimers).

145. *See, e.g.*, Keller & Lee, *supra* note 136, at 20.

146. As discussed above, formula clauses could assign all of the estate to the nonmarital trust, leaving nothing in the marital trust.

147. *See, e.g.*, Keller & Lee, *supra* note 136 (a comprehensive article with sample language alternatives addressing the possible courses of the estate tax). *See also* Jerold I. Horn, Flexible Wills and Trusts for Uncertain Times (2003) (a comprehensive collection of clauses anticipating a dizzying number of alternatives concerning EGTRRA and possible repeal of the estate tax).

codicils can better handle changes when there is more clarity.[148] However, relying on a subsequent new Will or codicil could be dangerous, because many clients may not return for the revisions, even though planners will be sure to provide them with various "exit letters" warning them of the unstable status of the law. There is also the risk that some clients may become incompetent and unable to execute the new instruments.[149]

If the federal estate tax were to be permanently repealed, tax-driven, tax-defined terms and clauses would dictate the disposition of the decedent's assets, even when the estate tax no longer exists. It is difficult to predict how the various expressions of formula clauses would be interpreted in the absence of an estate tax. However, there are some points to consider.

First, it would seem that more attention would need to be given to state law restraints on the disposition of assets (such as the elective share) because much marital gifting may be encouraged by the wealth transfer taxation consequences. For example, many of the articles in the estate planning literature that advise dispensing with the marital share simply pass the assets to the family trust.

Second, as a very fundamental matter, the standard formula clause needs to address what happens if there is no federal estate tax and where or to whom the assets are to pass. The client needs to focus on the disposition of assets (to the surviving spouse, to the children, and so forth), and in what form (outright, in trust) if wealth transfer taxes are not a concern. This would seem to require a complete alternative plan of disposition.[150] A disclaimer arrangement can address these issues simply, but one sacrifices decedent control over the disposition of assets.

Third, if estate taxes are eliminated, there will be additional emphasis on language permitting the elimination of unnecessary trusts and other structures. Some planners would include that language in trust instruments now.[151] With respect to life insurance in particular, there might

148. *See, e.g.*, Virginia F. Coleman, *Planning in the Face of Uncertainty After EGTRRA*, Advanced Estate Planning Techniques, SG062 ALI-ABA 353, 358 (ALI-ABA Continuing Legal Education, Feb. 21-23, 2002) (drafting for an estate-tax-free world today is not desirable unless a client insists on it and is willing to pay for an almost certainly futile effort).

149. Statutes such as UPC §5-411(a)(7) would permit a conservator with court permission to "make, amend or revoke" the protected person's Will. Further, if the principal planning instrument is a revocable trust, the trustee may be authorized to amend the trust document in response to changes in the law.

150. *See, e.g.*, Jonathan G. Blattmachr & Lauren Y. Detzel, *Estate Planning Changes in the 2001 Tax Act—More Than You Can Count*, 95 J. TAX'N 74, 85 (2001) (sample language to be added to formula clause dictating the passing of all assets to the family trust if there is no federal estate tax in effect at the time of death); Keller & Lee, *supra* note 136, at 21 (sample language providing that if the estate tax is repealed, the marital share disappears and all assets pass to the family trust).

151. *See, e.g.*, Grassi, *supra* note 139, at 8-9 (sample language for termination of the trust by an independent trustee and modifying spendthrift clause). Mr. Grassi also discusses an alternative in which a trust protector would hold the power to terminate the trust and/or hold a special power of appointment to distribute all of the assets of the trust. *Id.* at 9-11; Coleman, *supra* note 148, at 363 (discussing "self-destruct" clauses in QPRTs, GRATs, and other trusts).

be greater emphasis on term insurance or permanent insurance that permits greater inter vivos access to the policy proceeds.[152]

Finally, even if the federal estate tax were repealed and assuming all of the above considerations were made, it should not be ignored that there remains the possibility that in some states a *state* estate tax will still exist, or be re-established.

d. Planning for the Return of pre-EGTRRA Law. If the 2010 Act sunsets on December 31, 2012, as scheduled, the result will be to restore the estate tax to the pre-EGTRRA status, which would reduce the applicable exclusion amount to $1,000,000 and increase the maximum tax rate to 55 percent. This strikes us as an unlikely resolution by Congress, but after observing the political gridlock in 2010, any prediction is nothing more than speculation. However, this result would do the least amount of harm to the standard formula clauses. Indeed, disclaimer Wills might be revised to return to the more traditional formula approaches.

e. Conclusion. We cannot predict the future except to speculate that this continuing uncertainty will probably produce some overdrafting and perhaps unnecessary planning fees, some unintended consequences stemming from attempts to draft all-events alternative responses, and some unexpected actions by Congress. After reading all of this, we hope you can better appreciate the frustration of planners in these continuing uncertain times.

EXERCISE 16-1

PLANNING IN AN UNCERTAIN ENVIRONMENT

Edward C. Smith (age 62) and Rachel R. Jones (age 59) are married (neither was previously married), and they have two adult children, James and Jennifer. Edward and Rachel's health is good, and their combined net worth is $6,000,000 (consisting of $3,000,000 in 401(k) plan balances, with the balance composed of their personal residence, a rental property, and stocks and securities). Edward and Rachel plan to retire when Edward reaches age 66. Assume that their state of residence does not impose an estate tax.

In terms of the applicable exclusion amount and related matters, what marital deduction planning measures, if any, would you recommend?

152. *See, e.g.*, Stephan R. Leimberg & Albert E. Gibbons, *Life Insurance Decision-Making After September 11th and EGTRRA*, 29 Est. Plan. 36, 41 (2002) (discussing a so-called "Spousal Support ILIT," an irrevocable life insurance trust that permits distributions of insurance policy loans or withdrawals to the insured's loved ones during the insured's lifetime).

C. Reference Materials

Treatises

- John A. Bogdanski, Federal Tax Valuation ch. 4 (1996 & Supp. 2010) (*Discounts and Premiums*).
- A. James Casner & John N. Pennell, Estate Planning (6th ed. 1995 & Supp. 2009-2010) (a comprehensive three-volume treatise including a substantial wealth transfer taxation component).
- John R. Price & Samuel A. Donaldson, Price on Contemporary Estate Planning §2.14.1 (2011) (valuation discount opportunities); §§2.24-2.42.9 (drafting, planning for GSTT).
- Martin M. Shenkman & Stephen R. Akers, Estate Planning After the Tax Relief and Job Creation Act of 2010 (2011).
- Richard B. Stephens et al., Federal Estate and Gift Taxation: Including the Generation-Skipping Transfer Tax (8th ed. 2002 & Supp. 2011).
- Harold Weinstock & Martin Neumann, Planning an Estate, §2 (4th ed. 2002 & Supp. 2010) (overview of tax principles).
- Internal Revenue Service, Introduction to Estate and Gift Taxes, Publication 950 (rev. Dec., 2009), Cat. No. 14447X; available at http://www.irs.gov/pub/irs-pdf/p950.pdf (last visited May 3, 2011).

Articles

Planning Under the 2010 Act

- Marc S. Bekerman, *Credit Shelter Trusts and Portability — Does One Exclude the Other?*, 25 Prob. & Prop. 10 (May/June 2011).
- Jonathan G. Blattmachr et al., *Estate Planning After the 2010 Tax Relief Act: Big Changes, But Still No Certainty*, 114 J. Tax'n 68 (Feb. 2011).
- Alan S. Gassman & Christopher J. Denicolo, *The Role of Credit Shelter Trusts Under the New Estate Tax Law*, 38 Est. Plan. 10 (June 2011).
- Marvin D. Hills, *Subsequent Remarriage Complicates Exclusion Amount Portability*, 38 Est. Plan. 3 (May 2011).
- Melvin A. Warshaw, *Life Insurance Planning After the 2010 Tax Act*, 150 Tr. & Est. 48 (Apr. 2011).

Planning Under EGTRRA

- Steve R. Akers, *Estate Planning Under the 2001 Act — Planning and Drafting in an Uncertain Environment*, Planning Techniques for Large Estates, SH022 ALI-ABA 903 (ALI-ABA Continuing Legal Education, Nov. 18-22, 2002).

- Jonathan G. Blattmachr & Michael L. Graham, *Thinking About the Impossible for 2010—No Estate Tax and Carryover Basis*, 21 PROB. & PROP. 12 (May/June 2007).
- Virginia F. Coleman, *Planning in the Face of Uncertainty After EGTRRA*, ALI-ABA EST. PLAN. COURSE MATERIALS J. 23 (Aug. 2002).
- Philip A. Di Giorgio & Louis W. Pierro, *Postmortem Planning Allows Fine-Turning of a Client's Estate Plan*, 34 EST. PLAN 31 (2007).
- Sebastian V. Grassi, Jr., *Drafting the Marital Deduction Disclaimer Trust After the 2001 Tax Act (with Sample Clauses and Trust Form)* (Part 1), 16 No. 3 PRAC. TAX LAW. 29 (Spring 2002); (Part 2), 16 No. 4 PRAC. TAX LAW. 7 (Summer 2002).
- Sebastian V. Grassi, Jr., *Drafting Flexibility into Estate Planning Documents After the 2001 Tax Act (with Sample Clauses)*, 17 No. 2 PRAC. TAX LAW. 7 (Winter 2003).
- Jerold I. Horn, *Estate Planning and Drafting for the Economic Growth and Tax Relief Reconciliation Act of 2001 ("EGTRRA") (with Forms)*, ALI-ABA EST. PLAN. COURSE MATERIALS J. 33 (Dec. 2001).
- Jerold I. Horn, *The Chief Uncertainty in Estate Planning*, 21 No. 3 PRAC. TAX LAW. 57 (Spring 2007).
- Paula M. Jones, *Planning for the 10-Year Phase Out of Estate Tax (with Form)*, 17 No. 2 PRAC. TAX LAW. 57 (Winter 2003).
- Timothy B. Lewis, *How the Economic Growth & Tax Relief Act of 2001 Affects Basic Estate Planning Strategy—Tax & Non-Tax Considerations*, 15 UTAH B.J. 21 (Mar. 2002).
- Eric A. Manterfield, *Marital Planning While the Rules Are Changing*, 40 INST. ON EST PLAN. ¶700 (2006).
- Sergio Pareja, *Estate Tax Repeal Under EGTRRA: A Proposal for Simplification*, 38 REAL PROP. PROB. & TR. J. 73 (2003).
- John J. Scroggin, *Estate Planning to Cope with the Current Legislative Uncertainty*, 34 EST. PLAN. 10 (2007).
- Barbara A. Sloan, *Disclaimer Planning Revitalized Under EGTRRA*, Advanced Estate Planning Techniques, SG062 ALI-ABA 369 (ALI-ABA Continuing Legal Education, Feb. 21-23, 2002).

CHAPTER 17

Probate and an Estate Tax Return

A. The Estate Administration Process

Overseeing the preparation of the estate tax return is one of the significant responsibilities of the executor or personal representative of a taxable estate. Accordingly, this chapter first summarizes the general scheme of most estate administrations.[1]

1. Who Is the Client?

In almost all cases, with the principal exceptions being attorney personal representatives or professional trust department personal representatives, the personal representative will engage an attorney to advise him or her on the administration of the estate. The estate usually indemnifies the personal representative for the expenses of administration, including attorney fees, so it is the estate that will bear the cost.[2] It is important to clarify whether the attorney represents the estate, the personal representative, the beneficiaries, or some combination of those parties. This issue should be addressed in the engagement letter between the

1. For an overview of probate procedure *see* Jesse Dukeminier et al., Wills, Trusts, and Estates 38-49 (8th ed. 2009). For a more detailed discussion of administration, see Joel C. Dobris et al., Estates and Trusts ch. 13 (3d ed. 2007).
2. *See, e.g.*, UPC §§3-720 & 3-808.

personal representative and the attorney, and the other parties should be informed that the attorney does not represent them.[3]

Generally, the attorney is considered to represent only the personal representative.[4] Most attorneys will not also represent the estate or the beneficiaries because of inherent conflicts. In dealing with distributions, for example, it is common for the personal representative to insist on receiving a receipt for a distribution and a waiver of claims from the beneficiary. If a beneficiary refuses, the interests of the personal representative and the beneficiaries are immediately in conflict. A personal representative who is also a beneficiary may have conflicts with respect to tax elections or other administration decisions in which he or she may have a direct personal benefit. In that regard, the Will or other instrument should provide direction.[5] If the Will is contested by any current or potential beneficiaries such that the personal representative would be removed and lose his or her fee, the conflict becomes very immediate. Further, to represent the beneficiaries as a group would become unworkable for an attorney if the beneficiaries had conflicting interests among themselves.

If the personal representative is also a beneficiary in a contested matter, these lines become blurred. The fees of the attorney representing the personal representative may still be an expense of the estate, even though the reduction or elimination of contested amounts payable to other beneficiaries would redound to the benefit of the personal representative as a fellow beneficiary. However, if the attorney is asked to render services that will directly benefit the personal representative in his or her capacity as a beneficiary or creditor (e.g., in a separate claim for past home care services), the attorney fees should not properly be an expense of the estate. A well-crafted engagement letter should be used to avoid these problems at the outset. It should make clear to the personal representative/beneficiary and other beneficiaries that the attorney is only representing the personal representative in his or her capacity as personal representative, not as a beneficiary.[6]

2. Is Administration Necessary?

a. Intestate Cases. Reportedly, most Americans die intestate.[7] However, this does not necessarily require probate insofar as the decedent may not

3. ABA MODEL RULE OF PROFESSIONAL CONDUCT R. 4.3 arguably requires the lawyer representing the personal representative to dispel notions by the unrepresented parties that he or she is acting in a disinterested capacity.

4. *See* Malcolm A. Moore, *Conflicting Interests in Postmortem Planning*, 9 INST. ON EST. PLAN. ¶¶ 1900, 1921 (1977); JOHN R. PRICE & SAMUEL A. DONALDSON, PRICE ON CONTEMPORARY ESTATE PLANNING §1.6 (2011).

5. Moore, *supra* note 4, at ¶1920.

6. *See* ABA MODEL RULE 1.7, Conflict of Interest (comment 12 — "lawyer may not represent multiple parties to a negotiation whose interests are fundamentally antagonistic to each other").

7. According to one commentator, 72.3 percent of decedents with estates valued at $0-$99,999 were intestate. Higher rates of testacy were found with increasing wealth, with only 49.8 percent of those with estates in the $100,000-$199,999 range being intestate. For decedents in the $200,000-$1,000,000 wealth range, only 15.4 percent were intestate. *See* Lawrence W. Waggoner, *Marital Property Rights in Transition*, 59 MO. L. REV. 21, 29-30 (Winter 1994).

own significant assets beyond personal effects and some modest financial assets. The financial assets often pass by operation of law due to joint ownership or payable-on-death (POD) designations. Most personal effects don't have documents of title, and ownership passes easily to family members or to third parties at estate sales or through other dispositions. Even if the ownership of financial assets or an automobile does not allow the transfer of title by operation of law, some states permit the collection of personal property, including financial accounts, by affidavit.[8] Ownership of real estate that does not pass by operation of law will usually, however, require estate administration.[9]

b. Testate Cases. The Wills of some decedents are not probated for many of the same reasons noted above: primarily because the assets of the estate pass by operation of law due to other arrangements, so there is little call for estate administration. In particular, some decedents may actively avoid estate administration through the use of a revocable trust. As discussed in Chapter 15, it is standard practice that a pourover Will accompany a revocable trust. Probate of such a Will nevertheless may be necessary if not all assets were titled in the revocable trust at the decedent's death. Some practitioners probate the Will in any event in an attempt to secure the benefits of creditor bar statutes, discussed below. Even if a Will is not ultimately offered for probate, state law may require that the Will nevertheless be deposited with the appropriate court for safekeeping, sometimes referred to as "lodging" the Will.[10]

c. Estate Tax Returns. The federal estate tax (discussed in Chapter 16) may still apply to an estate not otherwise requiring administration. For example, a person owning only financial accounts could designate POD or transfer-on-death (TOD) beneficiaries, thus avoiding probate, but those asset transfers would nevertheless be subject to the estate tax. The Internal Revenue Code anticipates a filing obligation by the recipients of the decedent's property even if a personal representative or executor is not formally appointed.[11]

8. *See, e.g.*, UPC §3-1201; Cal. Prob. Code §§13100 & 13101 (West 1991 & Supp. 2011) (simple affidavit procedure for estates in which the value of real and personal property does not exceed $100,000); 755 Ill. Comp. Stat. Ann. 5/25-1 (West 2007) (affidavit procedure resembling UPC provisions); Mass. Ann. Laws. ch. 190B §3-1201 (LexisNexis Supp. 2011) (simple affidavit procedure for estates of personal property not exceeding $15,000 excluding motor vehicles); N.Y. Surr. Ct. Proc. §1301 (McKinney 1995 & Supp. 2011) (simplified provisions for estates with assets of $30,000 value or less and consisting only of personal property); Tex. Prob. Code Ann. §137 (Vernon 2003 & Supp. 2010) (affidavit filed with court in simplified procedure if the value of the estate, excluding exempt and homestead property, does not exceed $50,000).

9. *But see* Cal. Prob. Code §13200 (West 1991 & Supp. 2011) (permitting affidavit procedure for real property of small value).

10. *See, e.g.*, UPC §2-516; Fla. Stat. Ann. §732.901 (West 2010); 755 Ill. Comp. Stat. Ann. 5/6-1 (West 2007 & Supp. 2010); Mass. Ann. Laws. ch. 190B §2-516 (LexisNexis Supp. 2011); Tex. Prob. Code Ann. §75 (Vernon 2003).

11. The term "executor" for federal estate tax purposes includes any person in actual or constructive possession of any property of the decedent. *See* Treas. Reg. §20.2203-1 (1958).

d. Income Tax Returns. Federal and state income taxes must be considered for even a modest estate. The taxable year of the decedent ends on the date of death. If the decedent earned enough during the calendar year period prior to death to require the filing of an income tax return, it must be filed. If a spouse survives the decedent and the estate consents to filing a joint return with the survivor that includes the short year of the decedent, a separate return for the decedent can be avoided.[12] After the decedent's death, individual income tax returns no longer apply, but a fiduciary income tax return, federal Form 1041, may be required to report income earned during the administration of the estate.[13] If the probate estate exists for only an instant due to the passing of assets by operation of law, a Form 1041 return may not be required. For more complex estates requiring administration, filing of an income tax return may be required, even if an estate tax return, federal Form 706, is not required.

3. Postmortem Activities Preceding the Appointment of a Personal Representative

Probate administration generally does not commence until the personal representative is appointed, which occurs, at the earliest, when the Will has been offered for probate with the appropriate authority. Under the Uniform Probate Code (UPC), for example, an informal probate may not be opened until at least 120 hours have elapsed since the decedent's death.[14] However, there are some measures that must be taken immediately after death, such as funeral arrangements and securing the personal residence. To address this gap, the UPC and other state laws provide that the powers of the personal representative relate back in time if the acts are beneficial to the estate and further permit the personal representative to ratify the acts of others on behalf of the estate.[15]

4. Selecting a Form of Administration

There is much variation among the states in the types of estate administration. The "traditional" probate that has earned notoriety from probate avoidance literature is referred to as "formal" probate under the UPC structure, or "probate in solemn form" under other nomenclature. The other, simpler probate form is known under the UPC structure as

12. *See* IRC §6013(a)(3).
13. An estate may elect a fiscal year for income tax purposes. *See* IRC §441(b)(1).
14. *See* UPC §3-302.
15. *See* UPC §3-701; Cal. Prob. Code §8400 (West 1991 & Supp. 2011) (named executor may pay funeral expenses and take necessary measures for maintenance and preservation of the estate prior to appointment); Fla. Stat. Ann. §733.601 (West 2010) (powers of personal representative relate back in time to authorize acts that are made before appointment and are beneficial to the estate); 755 Ill. Comp. Stat. Ann. 5/6-14 (West 2007) (prior to issuance of letters executor has power to carry out any gifts of the decedent's body, burial, payment of any funeral expenses, and any other expenses for preservation of the estate); Mass. Ann. Laws ch. 190B §3-701 (LexisNexis Supp. 2011) (patterned after UPC provision); N.Y. Surr. Ct. Proc. §903 (McKinney 1994) (temporary administrator); Tex. Prob. Code Ann. §108 (Vernon 2003) (emergency application for payment of funeral and burial and personal property storage expenses).

"informal" probate, or "probate in common form" under other statutes. Like the UPC, many states offer both an informal and formal procedure.[16]

a. Commencing Informal Probate. The UPC approach is probably the purest form of informal probate. Under the UPC it is possible to open and close an estate without ever seeing a judge or even receiving a pro forma order signed by a judge, although one may request judicial "supervision" of portions of the administration. Under UPC §3-301, the application for informal probate is directed to the "Registrar," who is often a clerk of the probate court. The applicant must be an "interested person" as defined in UPC §1-201(23).[17] Assuming that the original Will has not been previously deposited with the court, it is submitted prior to or with the application for informal probate. If the Registrar is satisfied with the application, he or she will issue a written statement of informal probate, sometimes within days. The application for informal probate is usually accompanied by a request for the informal appointment of a personal representative. The personal representative may be approved at the same time, and "letters" or "letters testamentary" (or "letters of authority" in some states), certified by the court, will be issued. The letters offer written proof to third parties, such as financial institutions and purchasers of estate assets, that the personal representative is acting with authority, so the personal representative will typically request multiple copies that can be retained by the third parties. Exhibit 17.1 is an example of letters issued for an informal probate in a state generally following a UPC format (using the facts from Case Study 17-1). The UPC then requires that written notice of the opening of informal probate be given to heirs and devisees within 30 days.[18]

b. Commencing Formal Probate. Formal probate is a judicial proceeding with the attendant formalities of notice and hearing. Under the UPC the document requesting the opening of an estate is referred to as a "petition for formal probate" and requests a judicial order after notice and hearing.[19] Notice of the time and place of the hearing is sent to various interested persons, including the surviving spouse, children, other heirs and devisees, and any executor named in the Will.[20] In practice, in some jurisdictions the hearing may be a "nonappearance" hearing if there are no objections presented to the court during the notice period. The court may order probate if the petition is unopposed.[21] If there are objections, questions about the validity or construction of the Will, and so forth, the

16. *See, e.g.*, Cal. Prob. Code §10500 (West 1991) (estate administration without court supervision); Cal. Prob. Code §§8003, 8110, 8120 & 8124 (West 1991 & Supp. 2011) (formal notice); Fla. Stat. Ann. §733.212 (West 2010) (informal notice); Fla. Stat. Ann. §733.2123 (West 2005 & Supp. 2007) (formal notice). *Compare* N.Y. Surr. Ct. Proc. §1403 (McKinney 1995 & Supp. 2011) (service of process required).

17. An "interested person" includes heirs, devisees, children, spouses, creditors, and beneficiaries.

18. *See* UPC §3-306. An interested party can file a demand for notice with the probate court at any time after the death of the decedent. *See* UPC §3-204.

19. *See* UPC §3-402.

20. *See* UPC §3-403.

21. *See* UPC §3-405.

EXHIBIT 17.1 SAMPLE LETTERS TESTAMENTARY

District Court of MyCounty County, MyState 1234 Judicial Lane, MyCity, MyState 80023	
IN THE MATTER OF THE ESTATE OF ALICE GOODWIN SMITH **Deceased**	**COURT USE ONLY**
	Case Number: Division Courtroom

LETTERS [■] TESTAMENTARY [ ] OF ADMINISTRATION

ELISABETH BARNES SMITH was appointed or qualified by this Court or its Registrar on January 15, Current Year as:

■ Personal Representative.

☐ Successor Personal Representative.

These Letters are proof of the Personal Representative's authority to act pursuant to [State] law, except for the following restrictions, if any:

Date ______________________ Probate Registrar/ (Deputy) Clerk of Court

CERTIFICATION

Certified to be a true copy of the original in my custody and to be in full force and effect as of: ____________________.

Date ______________________ Probate Registrar/ (Deputy) Clerk of Court

proceedings may become protracted. A petition for the appointment of the personal representative is also filed with the court. After notice to interested persons, the court will determine who is entitled to appointment.[22] Letters may or may not be issued at that time, depending on local practice.[23]

22. *See* UPC §3-414.

23. An estate may be "informally" opened and "formally" closed, and vice versa, depending on the circumstances of the administration. For example, an estate may have opened informally, but as a result of disputes between the personal representative and others during the administration, the personal representative may decide to close the estate formally. He or she may want to do this to involve the court in a formal judicial review of the administration, giving all parties their day in court to object to the personal representative's conduct, with the objective of seeking a final, judicially sanctioned discharge order from the court. The hope is that this will preclude, or at least reduce, the likelihood of later claims being asserted by interested parties against the personal representative. It is our experience that this tactic almost invariably brings finality and closure to the proceeding.

Probate statutes, in conjunction with the Will, typically permit the personal representative to claim a fee for services rendered to the estate. The personal representative may decide not to claim the fee, particularly if the personal representative is the sole or principal beneficiary and receipt of the fee would produce needless taxable income. The IRS has issued guidance in this area.

Rev. Rul. 66-167
1966-1 C.B. 20

Statutory fees or commissions are not includible in the gross income of the executor of an estate, where he effectively waives his right to receive such fees or commissions within a reasonable time after commencing to serve as the executor and all his other actions with respect to the estate are consistent with an intention to render gratuitous service. The act of waiving said fees or commissions under these conditions will likewise effect no gift thereof.

. . . In the instant case, the taxpayer served as the sole executor of his deceased wife's estate pursuant to the terms of a will under which he and his adult son were each given a half interest in the net proceeds thereof. The laws of the state in which the will was executed and probated impose no limitation on the use of either principal or income for the payment of compensation to an executor and do not purport to deal with whether a failure to withdraw any particular fee or commission may properly be considered as a waiver thereof.

The taxpayer's administration of his wife's estate continued for a period of approximately three full years during which time he filed two annual accountings as well as the usual final accounting with the probate court, all of which reported the collection and disposition of a substantial amount of estate assets.

At some point within a reasonable time after first entering upon the performance of his duties as executor, the taxpayer decided to make no charge for serving in such capacity, and each of the aforesaid accountings accordingly omitted any claim for statutory commissions and was so filed with the intention to waive the same. The taxpayer-executor likewise took no other action which was inconsistent with a fixed and continuing intention to serve on a gratuitous basis.

The specific questions presented are whether the amounts which the taxpayer-executor could have received as fees or commissions are includible in his gross income for Federal income tax purposes and whether his waiver of the right to receive these amounts results in a gift for Federal gift tax purposes.

. . . The crucial test of whether the executor of an estate or any other fiduciary in a similar situation may waive his right to receive statutory commissions without thereby incurring any income or gift tax liability is whether the waiver involved will at least primarily constitute evidence of an intent to render a gratuitous service. If the timing, purpose, and effect of the waiver make it serve any other important objective, it may then be proper to conclude that the fiduciary has thereby enjoyed a realization of income by means of controlling the disposition thereof, and at the same time, has also effected a taxable gift by means of any resulting transfer to a third party of his contingent beneficial interest in a part of the assets under his fiduciary control. . . .

The requisite intention to serve on a gratuitous basis will ordinarily be deemed to have been adequately manifested if the executor or administrator of an estate supplies one or more of the decedent's principal legatees or devisees, or of those principally entitled to distribution of decedent's intestate estate, within six months after his initial appointment as such fiduciary, with a formal waiver of any right to compensation for his services. Such an intention to serve on a gratuitous basis may also be adequately manifested through an implied waiver, if the fiduciary fails to claim fees or commissions at the time of filing the usual accountings and if all the other attendant facts and circumstances are consistent with a fixed and continuing intention to serve gratuitously. If the executor or administrator of an estate claims his statutory fees or commissions as a deduction on one or more of the estate, inheritance, or income tax returns which are filed on behalf of the estate, such action will ordinarily be considered inconsistent with any fixed or definite intention to serve on a gratuitous basis. No such claim was made in the instant case.

Accordingly, the amounts which the present taxpayer-executor would have otherwise become entitled to receive as fees or commissions are not includible in his gross income for Federal income tax purposes, and are not gifts for Federal gift tax purposes. . . .

---

5. An Overview of Administration

Once a personal representative is appointed, the personal representative in his or her fiduciary role carries out the administration, so the focus is on the personal representative's activities. The activities, whether in an informal or formal probate, are largely the same. In an administration (either informal or formal) that is a "supervised administration" under a provision resembling UPC §§3-501 to 3-505, there will be interludes for required judicial hearings. In other administrations, even formal probate proceedings in some jurisdictions, the administration may proceed from petition to closing without the necessity for court appearances or judicial intervention at all. There is a lot of detail to administration. The following is an extremely brief overview.[24]

24. The personal representative will often perform a number of other tasks of a practical nature, such as making burial arrangements, locating the Will, inventorying the safe deposit box, canceling magazine and other subscriptions, redirecting mail delivery, and so forth. *See generally* THEODORE E. HUGHES & DAVID KLEIN, THE EXECUTOR'S HANDBOOK: A STEP-BY-STEP GUIDE TO SETTLING AN ESTATE FOR PERSONAL REPRESENTATIVES, ADMINISTRATORS, AND BENEFICIARIES (2d ed. 2001).

a. Estate Bank Accounts and Federal Tax Identification Number. The personal representative opens one or more bank accounts with checking privileges in the name of the estate and obtains a federal tax identification number for the estate. The personal representative generally files a form notifying the IRS of his/her/its appointment.[25]

b. Inventory. The personal representative inventories the assets and liabilities of the estate. UPC §3-706, for example, requires that the personal representative complete the inventory within three months after his or her appointment. The inventory requires a fair market value for each item as of the decedent's date of death, and the personal representative will often employ appraisers for assets that are not easily valued or are of significant value. This is an important part of filing the federal or state estate tax returns for the estate, inasmuch as date-of-death valuation is reported on the return unless the IRC §2032 alternate valuation is elected (which, of course, may require additional appraisals as of the alternate valuation date). Most probate rules require some form of inventory, but the degree of formality may vary.[26] An example of an inventory prepared for an informal probate in a state generally following a UPC format follows as Exhibit 17.2 (again, using the facts from Case Study 17-1; note that the nonprobate assets and postmortem expenses are excluded).

c. Asset Sales. The personal representative will weigh a number of factors in deciding how to dispose of the estate assets. Assets that are the subject of specific bequests will generally be distributed in kind. Assets that would be cumbersome to divide in kind among several beneficiaries may be sold. The liquidity needs of the estate (for expenses, taxes, claims, etc.) may dictate the sale of certain assets. Note, however, that the expenses associated with the sale of assets may only be deductible for federal estate tax purposes if the estate lacks the liquidity to pay its expenses, including taxes. Nevertheless, the personal representative might conclude that certain assets should be sold immediately to preserve their value during administration. These decisions are often made by the personal representative after consultation and comment by the beneficiaries and approval by the probate court.

25. *See generally* A. JAMES CASNER & JEFFREY N. PENNELL, ESTATE PLANNING §2.7.5 (6th ed. 1995 & Supp. 2009-2010).

26. *See, e.g.*, CAL. PROB. CODE §8800 (West 1991 & Supp. 2011) (inventory and appraisal generally filed four months after letters are issued); FLA. STAT. ANN. §733.604 (West 2010) (personal representative shall file inventory along with fair market value of listed property); 755 ILL. COMP. STAT. ANN. 5/14-1 (West 2007) (personal representative shall file inventory within 60 days of issuance of letters); MASS. ANN. LAWS. ch. 190B §3-706 (LexisNexis Supp. 2011) (inventory shall be made within three months of appointment of personal representative); N.Y. SURR. CT. PROC. §725 (McKinney 1994) (court to promulgate rules as to valuation of estate); and TEX. PROB. CODE ANN. §250 (Vernon 2003) (personal representative shall make an inventory including the fair market value of each item within 90 days of qualification). An inventory will often contain detailed, confidential information. Consequently, the UPC §3-706 inventory procedure permits mailing to interested persons in lieu of a court filing.

EXHIBIT 17.2 SAMPLE ESTATE INVENTORY

<table>
<tr><td>District Court of MyCounty County, MyState
1234 Judicial Lane, MyCity, MyState 80023</td><td rowspan="2">

COURT USE ONLY</td></tr>
<tr><td>IN THE MATTER OF THE ESTATE OF

ALICE GOODWIN SMITH

Deceased</td></tr>
<tr><td>Attorney or Party Without Attorney (Name and Address):

Robert M. Phillips, Esq.
1234 Main Street
MyCity, MyState 80000

Phone Number: (303) 555-1212 E-mail:
FAX Number: (303) 555-1213 Atty. Reg. #: 12345</td><td>Case Number:

11 PR 005

Division Courtroom</td></tr>
<tr><td colspan="2">INVENTORY</td></tr>
<tr><td colspan="2">Within three months after appointment, a Personal Representative shall prepare an Inventory of property owned by the Decedent that is subject to disposition by Will or intestate succession. The Inventory must list the property with reasonable detail, indicate the Decedent's interest in the property, and include the fair market value as of the Decedent's date of death. The type and amount of any liens and encumbrances on the property must also be listed. If additional property is discovered after the initial inventory has been completed, a supplemental inventory listing the newly discovered property shall be completed.

If additional space is needed, separate sheets may be used. The Inventory shall be sent to interested persons who request it or it may be filed with the Court.

Being sworn, I verify that the attached schedules contain a complete and accurate inventory of the real and personal property of this estate to the best of my knowledge, information and belief.

____
Signature of Personal Representative</td></tr>
<tr><td colspan="2">Subscribed and sworn to before me on ________________.

My commission expires ______________________.

____
Notary Public/(Deputy) Clerk of Court</td></tr>
</table>

SUMMARY

Schedule A	Real Estate		$ 1,385,000.00
Schedule B	Stocks and Bonds		4,440,700.00
Schedule C	Mortgages and Notes	None	
	Cash	170,327.24	
	Total Mortgages, Notes, and Cash		170,327.24
Schedule D	Insurance, Annuities, Pension & Profit Sharing Plans		3,620.00
Schedule E	(Conservatorship only) Property Held in Joint Tenancy		
Schedule F	Miscellaneous Property		11,575.00
Total Gross Value			$ 6,011,222.24
Encumbrances on Inventoried Assets			(6,800.00)
Total Net Value			$ 6,004,422.24

Schedule A Real Estate (State Name in which Title is Held)	Value
1. Lots 1 & 2, Rockrim Addition, MyCity, MyCounty, MyState (address 1236 Rockrim Circle, MyCity, MyState 80000), 100% titled in Alice Goodwin Smith	$ 1,200,000
Value of Item 1 is per actual sale of the property on February 28, Current Year.	
2. Lot 3, Rockrim Addition, MyCity, MyCounty, MyState (address 1238 Rockrim Circle, MyCity MyState 80000), a 50% undivided interest held by Alice Goodwin Smith, out of a 100% interest, titled as equal tenants in common, between Alice Goodwin Smith and Anna Katherine Simpson	185,000
Value of Item 2 is per a written appraisal dated February 1, Current Year prepared by Blake Associates, Ltd., 5345 Orison Street, MyCity, MyState 80000.	
Total Schedule A $	1,385,000

Schedule B Stocks and Bonds (State Name in which Title is Held)	Value
1. 75,736 shares of Vanguard Wellesley Income Fund (Admiral Class CUSIP# 921938205) titled in Alice Goodwin Smith	$4,014,000
2. 3,000 shares of Merck common stock (CUSIP# 589331107) titled in Alice Goodwin Smith	97,500
3. 1,000 shares of IBM common stock (CUSIP# 459200101) titled in Alice Goodwin Smith	84,000
4. 4,000 shares of Procter & Gamble common stock (CUSIP# 742718109) titled in Alice Goodwin Smith	234,000
5. Forty (40) United States Treasury Series EE Savings Bonds, titled in Alice Goodwin Smith	11,200
Total Schedule B $	4,440,700

continued on next page

Schedule C Mortgages, Notes and Cash (State Name in which Title Is Held)	**Value**
Mortgages and Notes	**$ None**
Cash	
1. Big Bank Certificate of Deposit, #345921, titled in Alice Goodwin Smith	$ 30,039.45
2. Big Bank Certificate of Deposit, #543654, titled in Alice Goodwin Smith	15,019.72
3. Last Bank Certificate of Deposit, #97A342, titled in Alice Goodwin Smith	80,122.73
4. Big Bank Savings Account, #345921, titled in Alice Goodwin Smith	30,019.72
5. Big Bank Checking Account, #123943, titled in Alice Goodwin Smith	15,000.00
6. Cash on hand in purse of Alice Goodwin Smith	125.62
[The addresses of the banks have been omitted to simplify the schedule.]	
Cash	$ 170,327.24
Total Schedule C	$ 170,327.24

Schedule D Insurance, Annuities, Pension and Profit Sharing Plans	**Value**
(Decedent's estate should include only those items payable to the estate.)	
1. Automobile insurance policy P-1 death benefit payable to the Estate of Alice Goodwin Smith	$1,000
2. Automobile insurance policy ambulance and funeral expense settlement payable to the Estate of Alice Goodwin Smith	2,620
[Inasmuch as these were claims against her daughter's automobile policy and not against a policy owned by the decedent, some attorneys might report this in Schedule F below.]	
Total Schedule D	**$ 3,620**

Schedule E (Conservatorship only) Property Held in Joint Tenancy	**Value**
Total Schedule E	**$**

Schedule F Miscellaneous Property (If Titled, State Name in which Title Is Held)	**Value**
1. 1998 Toyota Camry, VIN# JMB1932456786, titled in Alice Goodwin Smith	$ 7,500
Value is per N.A.D.A. Official Used Car Guide price.	

2.	Household furnishings, clothing, jewelry, and personal effects Value established of $3,200 for items by sale at a February 14, Current Year estate sale. Value established of $875 for items retained, per a written appraisal, dated February 1, Current Year, prepared by Jack Stock, licensed auctioneer, 1897 Main Street, HisCity, MyState 80001	4,075
	Total Schedule F	$ 11,575

Encumbrances on Inventoried Assets Schedule and Item Number	Description	Amount
1.	Schedule A, Item 1, Prior Year unpaid real property taxes	$ 5,000
2.	Schedule A, Item 2, Prior Year unpaid real property taxes	1,800
	[Under the probate statute of MyState, the encumbrances reported on the estate inventory are limited to obligations that are liens or encumbrances secured by the inventoried property. Real estate mortgages and purchase money automobile loans are accordingly included. General claims against the estate are not included. Real property taxes are included because the law of MyState treats them as a lien against the property as of January 1 of the following year, which in this situation is the year of death.]	
	Total Encumbrances	$ 6,800

d. Notice to Creditors. Most probate rules require a general notice to creditors, usually in a newspaper of general circulation.[27] UPC §3-801, for example, requires the publication of such a notice once a week for three consecutive weeks. The UPC notice provides that claims must be presented within four months after the date of the first publication of the notice or be forever barred. Reflecting due process concerns, such general notice may not bar the claims of known creditors.[28] Accordingly, UPC §3-801(b) permits[29] written notice to creditors requesting presentation of a claim within four months after the published notice or 60 days after the mailing or delivery of the notice, whichever is later, or the

27. *See, e.g.*, CAL. PROB. CODE §9051 (West 1991 & Supp. 2011) (notice given within four months of issuance of letters); FLA. STAT. ANN. §733.2121 (West 2010) (notice to creditors shall be published promptly and publication shall be once a week for two consecutive weeks); 755 ILL. COMP. STAT. ANN. 5/18-3 (West 2007) (personal representative must publish notice once each week for three successive weeks); TEX. PROB. CODE ANN. §294 (Vernon 2003) (personal representative shall publish notice in a newspaper within one month after receiving letters of administration); *but see* N.Y. SURR. CT. PROC. §1802 (McKinney 1996) (no notice to creditors required).

28. *See* Tulsa Professional Collection Services v. Pope, 485 U.S. 478 (1988).

29. Some of the state provisions previously cited also require notice to actual creditors as a supplement to the published notice. *See, e.g.*, CAL. PROB. CODE §9050 (West 1991 & Supp. 2011) (known or reasonably ascertained creditors given notice); 755 ILL. COMP. STAT. ANN. 5/18-3 (West 2007) (personal representative must mail or deliver notice to creditors of the estate).

claim will be barred. If the personal representative neglects to publish the general notice or send written notices, the estate may still be able to rely on statutes of limitation that are generally longer than the four-month bar but nevertheless may close as soon as one year after the decedent's death.[30] An example of a published notice to creditors prepared for an informal probate in a state generally following a UPC format follows as Exhibit 17.3, which is based on the facts of Case Study 17-1.

e. Payment of Claims and Taxes. Once the periods have run for the presentation of creditor claims, the personal representative will act on the claims by either allowing or rejecting them. The federal estate tax return is due nine months after the decedent's date of death and, barring extensions or deferred payment arrangements,[31] any tax must be paid at that time.[32] The personal representative will also need to ensure that the decedent's personal income taxes on pre-death income are timely paid, as well as preparing and filing any required fiduciary income tax returns and paying those taxes.

f. Distributions. If the estate's assets do not greatly exceed the reasonably anticipated claims and expenses of the estate (a surviving spouse's potential elective share is a claim that will be a consideration), the personal representative may choose not to risk interim distributions to the beneficiaries, but will instead wait until the claims period has passed and all valid claims and taxes have been paid. Some personal representatives will choose to wait longer and defer distributions until a final closing. Indeed, the personal representative may be personally liable for claims against the estate, including taxes, that are unpaid because the personal representative has distributed the assets and cannot recover them. The personal representative will usually request a written receipt from the distributees. Upon a final distribution, the receipt will usually request a full and final release of the estate and the personal representative for any liability in connection with the distributee's interest in the estate.[33]

The UPC also provides a number of rules governing the manner of distributions (distributions in kind, by partition, etc.). UPC §3-904, for

30. *See* UPC §3-803. *See generally* Sarajane Love, *Estate Creditors, the Constitution, and the Uniform Probate Code*, 30 U. Rich. L. Rev. 411 (1996); Mark Reutlinger, *State Action, Due Process, and the New Nonclaim Statutes: Can No Notice Be Good Notice If Some Notice Is Not?*, 24 Real Prop. Prob. & Tr. J. 433 (1990).

31. A six-month extension to file the return and pay the tax (but subject to interest on the unpaid tax) is routinely granted in most cases. *See* Treas. Reg. §20.6081-1, 65 Fed. Reg. 63025 (Oct. 20, 2000). Longer extensions are more involved. *See generally* Casner & Pennell, *supra* note 25, at §3.3.7.

32. In an estate subject to federal wealth transfer taxes, the personal representative may file other tax-related forms in addition to Form 706, including, in some cases, a request for prompt assessment of the tax. *See generally* Casner & Pennell, *supra* note 25, at §2.7.5. Some personal representatives do not file such requests; instead they rely on the closing letter issued by the IRS, which may be forthcoming in about one year after the return is filed in uncontested cases. For an extended discussion of the effect of a closing letter, see Casner & Pennell, *supra*, at §2.7.5 n.34.

33. *See generally* Robert Whitman, *Sorting Out Receipts and Releases*, 33 No. 2 ACTEC J. 142 (Fall 2007).

EXHIBIT 17.3 SAMPLE NOTICE TO CREDITORS

<table>
<tr><td>District Court of MyCounty County, MyState
1234 Judicial Lane, MyCity, MyState 80023</td><td rowspan="2">

COURT USE ONLY</td></tr>
<tr><td>IN THE MATTER OF THE ESTATE OF
ALICE GOODWIN SMITH
Deceased</td></tr>
<tr><td>Attorney or Party Without Attorney (Name and Address):
Robert M. Phillips, Esq.
1234 Main Street
MyCity, MyState 80000
Phone Number: (303) 555-1212 E-mail:
FAX Number: (303) 555-1213 Atty. Reg. #: 12345</td><td>Case Number:
11 PR 005
Division Courtroom</td></tr>
<tr><td colspan="2">NOTICE TO CREDITORS BY PUBLICATION</td></tr>
</table>

NOTICE TO CREDITORS

Estate of ALICE GOODWIN SMITH, Deceased

Case Number 11 PR 005

All persons having claims against the above-named estate are required to present them to the personal representative or to

■ District Court of MyCounty, MyState

☐ Probate Court of the City and County of MyCity, MyState

on or before (date) ______________________, or the claims may be forever barred.

Elisabeth Barnes Smith
Personal Representative
7745 East Brown Circle
MyCity, MyState 80000

Publish only this portion of the form.

INSTRUCTIONS TO THE NEWSPAPER:

MYCOUNTY LEGAL TIMES Name of Newspaper	______________________ Signature of Attorney for/or Personal Representative Date
Publish the above Notice to Creditors once a week for three consecutive calendar weeks	ROBERT M PHILLIPS Type or Print name of Attorney for Personal Representative

NOTE: Unless one year or more has elapsed since the death of the decedent, a personal representative shall cause a notice to creditors to be published in some daily or weekly newspaper published in the county in which the estate is being administered, or if there is no such newspaper, then in some newspaper of general circulation in an adjoining county. A copy of this form and the Proof of Publication should be filed with the Clerk of the Court.

example, provides for interest on general pecuniary bequests beginning one year after the appointment of the personal representative, unless the Will states otherwise.

g. Closing. In a formal probate, the personal representative will petition for an order of complete settlement of the estate.[34] The order will include details as to distributions to beneficiaries. In an informal probate the personal representative may close an estate by merely filing a sworn statement complying with UPC §3-1003.

B. CASE STUDY 17-1

The Estate of Alice Goodwin Smith

A FEDERAL ESTATE TAX RETURN

The Will of Alice Goodwin Smith was presented in Chapter 2. Ms. Smith passed away on January 8, this year (Current Year), at the scene of an automobile accident. Her daughter, Rebecca Simpson Smith-Brown, was the driver of the automobile in which Ms. Smith was a passenger. Rebecca was critically injured and passed away on January 10, Current Year.

This case study involves the preparation of a Form 706 federal estate tax return for Ms. Smith. Assume that the State of MyState imposes no wealth transfer taxes. Assume that the alternate valuation date will not be elected. Assume that the Chapter 2 Will is controlling. Assume that MyState is a common law property state that has adopted the Uniform Probate Code. If your preparation of Form 706 involves the application of any particular Internal Revenue Code provision that is not obvious, or involves assumptions or other conclusions, describe those in a memorandum.

Decedent

Alice Goodwin Smith; born January 15, [age 88], in Bockman, Iowa. Died, January 8, Current Year, near MyCity, MyState. She was a U.S. citizen, and her Social Security number is 530-02-9456. She lived in MyState for the past 57 years at 1236 Rockrim Circle, MyCity, MyState 80000. She was a homemaker and hadn't worked outside the home. Her husband, Charles Gordon Smith, an inventor and entrepreneur, was born on July 12, [90 years ago], in Des Moines, Iowa, Social Security number 530-01-9854, and passed away on February 18, [10 years ago]. Neither Alice nor her husband filed any federal gift tax returns, and no estate tax

34. *See* UPC §3-1001.

return was filed for the husband's estate (this is a simplifying assumption—in light of the size of Ms. Smith's estate, it is likely that an estate tax return would have been required for Mr. Smith). A death certificate, No. MCY 656120 was issued for Ms. Smith by MyCounty, MyState.

Family

A son, John Aston Smith, was born on June 24, [age 60]. His Social Security number is 523-00-1234. He is divorced and has a son, Jared William Smith, born on October 23, [age 25]. Jared lives with his mother at 124 Yellow Lane, Evanston, Illinois 60611. John lives in MyState at 1234 Willow Height Road, MyCity, MyState 80000. John is "estranged from the rest of the family." A daughter, Elisabeth Barnes Smith, was born on January 15, [age 56]. She is unmarried and has no children. She resides at 7745 East Brown Circle, MyCity, MyState 80000. Her Social Security number is 523-04-7865, and her telephone number is (999) 555-5555.

Another daughter, Alice Thayer Jones, was born on August 28, [age 54]. She is married and lives at 1035 Glenmoor Drive, HerCity, MyState 80001. Her Social Security number is 523-04-9996. She has a daughter, Susan Barker Jones, who was born on June 5, [age 24] (Social Security Number 523-07-9712).

A fourth daughter, Rebecca Simpson Smith-Brown, was born on September 15, [age 52]. As noted above, she passed away due to injuries suffered in the automobile accident that also took her mother's life. She was survived by a husband, Rick Brown, a daughter, Jennifer Anna Smith-Brown (born June 25, [age 21]; Social Security number 523-08-9345), and a son, Scott Richard Smith-Brown (born January 2, [age 17]; Social Security number 523-09-1116).

Ms. Smith is also survived by a Labrador retriever, Jacob, age five.

Assets

<u>A1</u> Personal residence at 1236 Rockrim Circle, MyCity, MyState 80000, more particularly described as Lots 1 & 2, Rockrim Addition, City of MyCity, County of MyCounty, State of MyState. Purchased 57 years ago for $12,500, currently appraised at $1,300,000, free and clear of liens and encumbrances.

<u>A2</u> Vacant lot addressed as 1238 Rockrim Circle, MyCity, MyState 80000, more particularly described as Lot 3, Rockrim Addition, City of MyCity, County of MyCounty, State of MyState. It was jointly purchased for $3,000 57 years ago with Ms. Smith's sister, Anna Katherine Simpson (1290 Tanglewood Lane, MyCity, MyState 80000) as tenants in common. Similar lots sell for approximately $500,000.

<u>A3</u> Life insurance policy on Ms. Smith's life with a face amount of $10,000, issued on June 2, [55 years ago], by the Everlasting Reliance Insurance Company, 1214 Dodge Avenue, Englewood Cliffs, New Jersey 07102, policy number 182-7853421. Elisabeth Barnes Smith is the sole beneficiary.

A4 Her 1981 Honda Accord LX was involved in an earlier accident and was scrapped. Ms. Smith recently purchased a used 1998 four-door Toyota Camry for $7,500, Vehicle Identification Number JMB1932456786.

A5 75,736 shares of the Vanguard Wellesley® Income Fund (Admiral Class), 3,000 shares of Merck common stock, 1,000 shares of IBM common stock, and 4,000 shares of Procter & Gamble common stock.

A6 $30,000 in savings account #345921 at Big Bank (123 Broad Street, MyCity, MyState 80000).

A7 $15,000 in checking account #123943 at Big Bank (that is her balance per her checkbook; the balance per the bank is $350 higher due to outstanding checks that have not yet cleared).

A8 A $30,000 certificate of deposit #346876 at Big Bank, and a $15,000 certificate of deposit #543654 at Big Bank.

A9 A $80,000 certificate of deposit at Last Bank, 2367 Stone Road, MyCity, MyState 80000.

A10 Forty (40) $100 face value Series EE Savings Bonds ($50 purchase price), all issued on July 1, [27 years ago], which have a current maturity value of $11,200.

A11 $75,000 certificate of deposit, #983420, at Second Bank, 9835 Rock Road, MyCity, MyState 80000, titled jointly in Ms. Smith and Alice Thayer Jones. Ms. Smith provided 100 percent of the funds represented by the certificate of deposit.

A12 $125.62 in Ms. Smith's purse.

A13 Household furnishings, clothing, jewelry, and personal effects worth $4,500 (tentative estimate).

A14 $825 monthly Social Security benefit (she already received an $825 check for December on January 3).

Debts

D1 Unpaid real property taxes on personal residence for the prior year, $5,000.

D2 $100 monthly withdrawal for casualty insurance (State Farm Insurance) on the personal residence and liability insurance on her automobile.

D3 One-half of the unpaid real property taxes on the vacant lot for the prior year, $1,800.

D4 Public Service Company of MyState—gas and electricity, $75.

D5 MyCity water and sewer, $25.

D6 Reliable Disposal—garbage, $15.

D7 International Communications—local phone and long distance charges, $30.

D8 Visa charge card #4692419245893 issued by Big Bank, zero balance.

D9 AAA Emergency Response, 3487 Neck Road, MyCity, MyState 80000 (for services rendered at the scene and transport to the hospital emergency room), $120.

D10 Karf Funeral Home, 2387 Homewood Lane, MyCity, MyState 80000 (cremation so no headstone or burial plot), $2,500.

[Note: Although this is not an exercise in estate administration, the nature of the subsequent events described in the additional information below demonstrates many of the typical administration measures and concerns that one would encounter in an estate of this size.]

Additional Information

1. Fee paid to Janet Brotzenheimer, CPA (33 Oak Drive, MyCity, MyState 80000); Form 1040 for prior year—$800; final Form 1040 for January 1-8, Current Year—$100; Form 1041 (December 31 year-end)—$1,200; Form 706—$3,000.

2. An accident investigation disclosed that Rebecca was not at fault. An automobile traveling in the wrong lane forced them off the road and the driver fled the scene. Assume that under MyState law, there is no tort claim that can be maintained by Ms. Smith's estate because her death was almost instantaneous (however, her estate could have a claim for funeral expenses). However, Rebecca's automobile policy paid a standard $1,000 death benefit (coverage P-1 under MyState insurance law) to Ms. Smith's estate, and the insurer also paid $2,620 to the estate (reflecting the ambulance and funeral services) to settle any estate claims. MyState is a "no-fault" automobile insurance state.

3. Wrongful death claims by Rebecca's immediate family and Ms. Smith's surviving children might be successful under MyState law under Rebecca's automobile coverage.

4. On March 2, Current Year, Elisabeth Barnes Smith delivered to the attorney for the estate a written renunciation of her right to a personal representative's fee (under MyState law, it would have been 3 percent of the gross estate value).

5. Fee of $625 paid to Carol A. Blum, Esq. (4600 Blue Moon Avenue, MyCity, MyState 80000) to evaluate legal options in connection with the automobile accident.

6. The case number for the probate case is 02 PR 005. Letters testamentary issued on January 15, Current Year.

7. The estate received no disclaimers.

8. Assume the following January 8, Current Year, stock prices. (These are not factually exact; however, use the amounts in the Form 706. Indeed, January 8 can fall on a weekend, so the security markets could be closed. *See* Treas. Reg. §20.2031-2(b)(1) for weighted average valuation rules based on trading days occurring both before and after the valuation date. The Wall Street Journal and other financial publications report this information on the following day. In practice one would usually request a report from a stock broker if there is a large portfolio, but one can find Internet sources of historical numbers. Yahoo Finance, for example, provides detailed historical stock quotes.)

Stock	High	Low	Close	CUSIP#
VWIAX	-	-	53.00	921938205
MRK	33	32	33.12	589331107
IBM	85	83	84.95	459200101
PG	58	59	58.64	742718109

9. Assume that for the 1998 Toyota Camry, the N.A.D.A. Official Used Car Guide price is $7,500 for a car in its condition.

10. The personal representative received the bank balances, with accrued interest, as of January 8.

Big Bank savings account	#345921	30,019.72
Big Bank checking account	#123943	15,350.00
Big Bank C.D.	#346876	30,039.45
Big Bank C.D.	#543654	15,019.72
Last Bank C.D.	#97A342	80,122.73
Second Bank C.D.	#983420	75,090.41

All of the banks are willing to convert the certificates of deposit to savings accounts without penalty.

11. Assume that the value of the U.S. Savings Bonds as of death was $11,200. In practice, one can access an online value calculator at http://www.publicdebt.treas.gov/sav/savcalc.htm.

12. The personal representative received a Form 712 Life Insurance Statement from Everlasting Reliance Insurance Company. The Form 712 line 15 face amount of the policy was $10,000, the line 21 accumulated dividends amount was $1,250.98, and the line 22 postmortem dividends amount was $2.76, producing a January 31, Current Year, one-sum proceeds (line 24) amount of $11,253.74.

13. Jack Stock, licensed auctioneer specializing in farm and ranch auctions, estate sales, equipment sales, and automobiles ("The Best Price Is Our Only Goal"), 1897 Main Street, HisCity, MyState 80001, produced an estate appraisal sheet, dated February 1, Current Year, for the household effects, furnishings, clothing, and appliances located in the personal residence, with a total value of $4,295. Mr. Stock charged the estate $150 for his appraisal services.

14. The estate paid $2,500 for valuations by Blake Associates, Ltd., 5345 Orison Street, MyCity, MyState 80000. The written appraisals, dated February 1, Current Year, valued the house at 1236 Rockrim Circle at $1,300,000, and valued the undivided one-half interest in the adjacent lot at $185,000.

15. John Aston Smith asserted a claim against the estate based on an alleged agreement with his mother concerning her care by him. John and his two sisters (the widowed brother-in-law refused to participate) settled the matter by the payment of $840 to John for lawn care and snow removal work, and $50,000 as a devisee (Alice and Elisabeth's residuary shares were reduced by that amount).

16. The devisees have agreed that Alice Thayer Jones is entitled to keep 100 percent of the $75,090.41 certificate of deposit that was jointly titled with the decedent at Second Bank.

17. Janet Brotzenheimer has advised the estate to claim Internal Revenue Code section 642(g) expenditures on Form 706 rather than on Form 1041.

18. The legal fees for estate administration to Tark Clark, Esq. (2450 Capstone Drive, Suite 101, MyCity, MyState 80000) were $6,000.

19. The personal residence sold for $1,200,000 on February 28, Current Year. The realtor, Janet Elkins (1623 Hill Avenue, MyCity, MyState, 80000), accepts lower commissions for estate sales, so the commission plus closing costs totaled $50,000, producing net proceeds to the estate of $1,150,000.

20. On February 14, Current Year, Alice and Elisabeth held an estate sale at the house. Most of the property was sold for $3,200, and that amount was split among the residuary devisees in their respective percentages of the residuary estate. Alice, Elisabeth, Jennifer Smith-Brown, and Scott Smith-Brown retained for themselves, divided in their respective percentages of the residuary estate, dishes and other items that Jack Stock had appraised at $875. MyState Hauling, Inc. took the rest of the unsold items to the local landfill. The hauling charge was $95. This division of the personal property deviated from Ms. Smith's dispositive scheme in her Will, which dictated that grandchildren should not receive any of the property. However, Alice and Elisabeth considered their approach to be a fairer way to deal with their niece and nephew, and as young adults Jennifer and Scott had a deep interest in the memento items retained from the estate. Ignore any gift tax implications of this arrangement, particularly because the aunts' annual gift exclusion would apply.

21. Ms. Smith did not rent or otherwise have access to a safe deposit box at the time of her death.

22. Ms. Smith's estate does not contain any IRC §2044 property from a prior gift or estate.

Other Administration Expenses

Probate filing fees, certified letters, certified Will (MyCounty County Clerk of Court), $117.

Legal advertising in MyCounty Daily, $25.

Death certificates (MyCounty Department of Health), $80.

Recording costs (vacant lot) and transfer fee (Toyota) (MyCounty County Clerk), $18.

Telephone, photocopies, cleaning supplies, advertising, signs, coffee and donuts (for estate sale), postage, gasoline, $812.

Cleaning service (Spotless Cleaning, P.O. Box 54, MyCity, MyState 80000), $425.

Plumber (Jack's Plumbing, 567 Bluff, MyCity, MyState 80000), $225.

State Farm Insurance (casualty insurance from date of death until sale), $214.

MyCity (water and sewer from date of death until sale), $38.

Public Service Company of MyState (gas and electric from date of death until sale), $200.

C. Reference Materials

Treatises

- John R. Price & Samuel A. Donaldson, Price on Contemporary Estate Planning §4.26.9 (2011) (unsupervised administration of estate); §4.26.1 (attorney serving as personal representative)
- Richard B. Stephens et al., Federal Estate and Gift Taxation: Including the Generation-Skipping Transfer Tax (8th ed. 2002 & Supp. 2011).

Articles

Intestate Administration

- Amy K. Rosenberg, *The Common Law Spouse in Colorado Estate Administration*, 35 Colo. Law. 85 (Sept. 2006).
- Lawrence W. Waggoner, *Marital Property Rights in Transition*, 59 Mo. L. Rev. 21, 29-30 (1994) (offering statistics on degree of testacy at various wealth levels).

Notice to Creditors in Probate

- Elaine H. Gagliardi, *Remembering the Creditor at Death: Aligning Probate and Nonprobate Transfers*, 41 Real Prop. Prob. & Tr. J. 819 (2007).
- Sarajane Love, *Estate Creditors, the Constitution, and the Uniform Probate Code*, 30 U. Rich. L. Rev. 411 (1996).
- Mark Reutlinger, *State Action, Due Process, and the New Nonclaim Statutes: Can No Notice Be Good Notice if Some Notice Is Not?*, 24 Real Prop. Prob. & Tr. J. 433 (1990).

Conflicts of Interest in Estate Administration (See also "Client Conflicts" in Ch. 1 reference materials.)

- Jonathan G. Blattmachr, *The Tax Effects of Equitable Adjustments: An Internal Revenue Code Odyssey*, 18 Inst. on Est. Plan. ¶¶ 1400, 1406.2 (1984).
- Joseph W. de Furia, Jr., *A Matter of Ethics Ignored: The Attorney Draftsman as Testamentary Fiduciary*, 36 U. Kan. L. Rev. 275 (1988).

- Malcolm A. Moore, *Conflicting Interests in Postmortem Planning*, 9 INST. ON EST. PLAN. ¶1900 (1977).
- Henry M. Ordower, *Trusting Our Partners: An Essay on Resetting the Estate Planning Defaults for an Adult World*, 31 REAL PROP. PROB. & TR. J. 313 (1996) (family and ethical considerations in estate planning for spouses).
- John R. Price, *Professional Responsibility in Estate Planning: Progress or Paralysis?*, 21 INST. ON EST. PLAN. ¶1800 (1987).
- Mark Reutlinger, Note, *Trusts: Consequences of Attorney's Good Faith Representation of Adverse Parties in Trust Administration —* Potter v. Moran, 55 CAL. L. REV. 948 (1967).
- Suzanne L. Shier, *Avoiding Attorney Liability When Representing a Fiduciary*, 34 EST. PLAN. 19 (2007).

Administration Expenses

- Jarald David August, *Final* Hubert *Regulations Fix Boundaries for Administrative Expenses*, 27 EST. PLAN. 195 (2000) (analysis of *Hubert* and final IRS regulations).
- Jonathan G. Blattmachr & Diana S.C. Zeydel, *Prop. Regs. on the Deduction for Administration Expenses and Claims*, 34 EST. PLAN. 3 (2007).

Settlements of Estate Disputes

- Donald Tescher & Jordan Kingsberg, *Tax Consequences of Settlements of Estate and Trust Disputes*, 33 EST. PLAN. 29 (2006).
- Donald Tescher & Jordan Kingsberg, *Settlements of Estate and Trust Disputes Must Consider the Tax Impact*, 33 EST. PLAN. 32 (2006).

Estate Tax Audits

- Ronald D. Aucutt, *Handling Estate Tax Disputes with the IRS*, 23 EST. PLAN. 457 (1996).
- Richard A. Carpenter, *Obtaining the Best Results in an IRS Estate Tax Audit*, 26 EST. PLAN. 302 (1999).
- C. Kirk Clark, *Basics: Preparing for the Federal Estate Tax Audit*, 17 VT. B.J. & L. DIG. 16 (Dec. 1991).
- Charles F. Newlin & Cynthia D. Glenn, *The Estate Tax Audit: How to Prepare and Succeed*, 19 EST. PLAN. 37 (1992).

Other

- Rev. Proc. 66-49, §2.05, 1966-1 C.B. 1257 ("actual selling price of an item within a reasonable time . . . after the valuation date may be the best evidence of its fair market value").
- Treas. Reg. §20.2053-3(d)(2) (as amended 1979) ("Expenses for selling property of the estate are deductible if the sale is necessary in order to pay the decedent's debts, expenses of administration, or taxes, to preserve the estate, or to effect distribution.").

Index

D